Java EE 7 Developer Handbook

Develop professional applications in Java EE 7 with this essential reference guide

Peter A. Pilgrim

BIRMINGHAM - MUMBAI

Java EE 7 Developer Handbook

Copyright © 2013 Packt Publishing

All rights reserved. No part of this book may be reproduced, stored in a retrieval system, or transmitted in any form or by any means, without the prior written permission of the publisher, except in the case of brief quotations embedded in critical articles or reviews.

Every effort has been made in the preparation of this book to ensure the accuracy of the information presented. However, the information contained in this book is sold without warranty, either express or implied. Neither the author, nor Packt Publishing, and its dealers and distributors will be held liable for any damages caused or alleged to be caused directly or indirectly by this book.

Packt Publishing has endeavored to provide trademark information about all of the companies and products mentioned in this book by the appropriate use of capitals. However, Packt Publishing cannot guarantee the accuracy of this information.

First published: September 2013

Production Reference: 1180913

Published by Packt Publishing Ltd.
Livery Place
35 Livery Street
Birmingham B3 2PB, UK.

ISBN 9781849687942

www.packtpub.com

Cover Image by Suresh Mogre (suresh.mogre.99@gmail.com)

Credits

Author
Peter A. Pilgrim

Reviewers
Antonio Gomes Rodrigues
Manjeet Singh Sawhney

Acquisition Editor
Kevin Colaco

Lead Technical Editor
Ritika Dewani
Joel Noronha

Technical Editors
Gauri Dasgupta
Kapil Hemnani
Monica John
Sonali Verenkar

Project Coordinator
Gloria Amanna
Kranti Berde

Proofreaders
Chrystal Ding
Paul Hindle
Mario Cecere

Indexers
Hemangini Bari
Mariammal Chettiyar
Rekha Nair
Monica Ajmera Mehta

Production Coordinator
Adonia Jones

Cover Work
Adonia Jones

About the Author

Peter A. Pilgrim is the 91st Oracle Java Champion, an independent contractor, a professional software developer and designer. Peter is an honors degree graduate of London South Bank University in 1990. He had already secured a Master's degree course for September 1991, but then instead elected to live and work in Germany for a few years in order to beat off the then, economic recession. He spent productive years at a joint-venture company developing spectroscopic scientific software in Fortran 77, C, Solaris, and X Windows.

After four years abroad Peter returned to London and continued his career in the industry with more C, C++, and UNIX development. He then leapt at a chance to get into investment banking with Deutsche Bank in 1998. It was at Deutsche Bank a week after joining them that Peter discovered Java was the next best thing since sliced bread, when a colleague dropped out of a programming Java training course. As the substitute person, Peter realized this peculiar Java language and platform was the future and the answer. Peter applied his studies to his day job and learnt Java applets, then Java Swing and switched over to the server side with Java Servlets with web applications involving the Struts framework.

In 2004, Peter created the JAVAWUG user group in London for the burgeoning development community who were interested in web development on the Java EE. What started as the Struts Networking Users Group in London quickly expanded to lot of other areas. The JAVAWUG ran for six years until 2010. He built a reputation for travelling to Java technology conferences in the US and Europe and being heavily involved in the wider community. He spoke at several developer conferences including QCon London, ACCU, Devoxx, Devoxx UK, and JavaOne. In 2007, Peter was elected to the Sun Microsystems' Java Champions program.

Today, Peter A. Pilgrim is a well-known specialist in Java Enterprise Edition (Java EE) technology, focused on the server-side and the implementation of electronic commerce. Peter has built professional Java EE applications for Blue-chip companies and top-tier investment and retail banks including Lloyds Banking Group, Barclays, UBS, Credit Suisse, Royal Bank of Scotland, and LBi. He is also a fan of Agile practices and Test Driven Development. Peter, currently, lives in South London with his long-term partner Terry, who is a Scottish Diva, business communication coach, and a singer—her voice is phenomenal.

Peter writes a blog at `http://www.xenonique.co.uk/blog/` and is on Twitter as `peter_pilgrim`.

Acknowledgment

I want to send out sincere grateful thanks to all of the reviewers of the book, who pointed out my many egregious errors. Their dedication to the task helped produce this high quality text that you are reading stand out. It is indeed a privilege to have these smart people who will prevent you going out into the public technical literary crowd with egg on your face, due to bad copy and mistaken content. I say thank you to my external reviewers, Antonio Gomes Rodrigues and Manjeet Singh Sawhney.

I want to thank members of the Packt Publishing team including Abhishek Kori, Kevin Colaco, Neha Mallik, Joel Noronha, Gloria Amanna, Ritika Dewani, Kranti Berde, and Kapil Hemnani. All of these folks worked hard to get this text into your hands. Finally, a special thank you goes to Dhwani Devater, who was the acquisition editor that approached me with the book concept and with whom I could not turn down such a challenging project. This book became my personal agenda known as "the project".

During the Devoxx UK 2013 conference, I discussed several ideas about Java EE 7 and beyond with David Blewin of Red Hat. I also met Aslak Knutsen from the Arquillian development team also from Red Hat. I want to thank those of you out in the wider community who saw the earlier presentations about Java EE 7; your feedback helped to derive the best quality for this book. I express gratitude to those followers and interested parties on the social networks of Twitter, Linked-In, Facebook, and Google+, who had kind words to say about writing a technical book.

I also want to say a big thank you to Markus Eisele for accepting my invitation to write the foreword for this, my first book. Markus is an excellent enterprise guy who happens to be an Oracle ACE Director and works for Msg in Germany. During 2013, I had a couple of tough months at times and Markus was there in spirit for me valiantly and graciously.

I thank members of the extended Pilgrim family, Mum and Dad and my sister for their support.

I wrote this book on a happenstance inquiry from Packt Publishing to help educate software developers, designers, and interested architects in Enterprise Java development. I gladly accepted the commission to write. I sieged this great opportunity. The book become the goal, the goal become "the project". I knew my life would change drastically from the regular software developer to a technical educator. It did whilst still holding down professional Java contracting gigs. I could not afford to let anyone down. The project became the mission, which was to give developers quality information, demonstrating good practice, and providing fair explanations around the concepts. I wanted to provide clear guidance in this fascinating area of technology. I am sure you have heard the saying about putting back good into the community. Well, this is true for me, too. Yet I wanted to give more than a return gift. I hoped to engage the worldwide Java community with a product, a concise and worthy Java EE 7 book. This is my first technical book.

The project was approximately 15 months in the making to get an initial schedule of promises to the real context of programming, testing and writing content. Emotionally and technically it was tough; I lived the rivers deep and mountains high.

Finally, I thank my wonderful Scottish lady, the love of my life, my dear partner, Terry for putting up with me and pushing me on, especially in the early phases of the project, saying several times in broad Glaswegian Patter, "Haud yer wheesht an' get oan wae it!". Thank you, I have done it.

About the Reviewers

Antonio Gomes Rodrigues earned his Masters degree at the University of Paris VII in France. Since then he has worked in various companies Java EE technologies in with the roles of developer, technical leader, technical manager of offshore projects, and performance expert.

He currently works on performance problems in Java EE applications.

> I would like to thank my wife Aurélie for her support.

Manjeet Singh Sawhney currently works for a well-known UK insurance company in Bromley (UK) as a Data Architect. Previously, he worked for global organisations in various roles, including development, technical solutions consulting, and data management consulting. Even though Manjeet has worked across a range of programming languages, his core language is Java. During his postgraduate studies, he also worked as a Student Tutor for one of the top 100 universities in the world where he was teaching Java to undergraduate students and marked exams and project assignments. Manjeet acquired his professional experience by working on several mission-critical projects serving clients in the Financial Services, Telecommunications, Manufacturing, Retail, and Public Sector.

> I am very thankful to my parents, my wife Jaspal, and my son Kohinoor for their encouragement and patience as reviewing this book took some of my evenings and weekends from the family.

www.PacktPub.com

Support files, eBooks, discount offers and more

You might want to visit www.PacktPub.com for support files and downloads related to your book.

Did you know that Packt offers eBook versions of every book published, with PDF and ePub files available? You can upgrade to the eBook version at www.PacktPub.com and as a print book customer, you are entitled to a discount on the eBook copy. Get in touch with us at service@packtpub.com for more details.

At www.PacktPub.com, you can also read a collection of free technical articles, sign up for a range of free newsletters and receive exclusive discounts and offers on Packt books and eBooks.

http://PacktLib.PacktPub.com

Do you need instant solutions to your IT questions? PacktLib is Packt's online digital book library. Here, you can access, read and search across Packt's entire library of books.

Why Subscribe?
- Fully searchable across every book published by Packt
- Copy and paste, print and bookmark content
- On demand and accessible via web browser

Free Access for Packt account holders

If you have an account with Packt at www.PacktPub.com, you can use this to access PacktLib today and view nine entirely free books. Simply use your login credentials for immediate access.

Instant Updates on New Packt Books

Get notified! Find out when new books are published by following @PacktEnterprise on Twitter, or the *Packt Enterprise* Facebook page.

To my lady Terry: Love conquers everything,

And lest we forget: Grandma Cecilia Prescod: "Them can skin them face now."

Table of Contents

Preface	**1**
Chapter 1: Java EE 7 HTML5 Productivity	**9**
Java EE 7	**9**
Enhanced HTML5 support	**10**
Java EE 7 architecture	**12**
Standard platform components and APIs	12
New productivity themes	13
Refinements	14
Java EE Platform	**15**
Java EE Profiles	18
Web Profile	18
Enterprise Profile	19
A working example	**21**
Entities	22
Business logic	25
The service endpoints	27
A WebSocket endpoint	28
A RESTful endpoint	31
The Entity Control Boundary pattern	36
Summary	**38**
Chapter 2: Context and Dependency Injection	**39**
Software engineering definitions	**39**
The Context and Dependency Injection service	**41**
Beans and bean types	42
Basic injection	45
Field injection	45
Setter injection	46
Constructor injection	46

Qualifiers	47
Built-in qualifiers	49
The CDI classpath scanning	49
Factory production	50
Generating new instances every time	52
Bean names and presentation views	53
Bean scopes	55
CDI initialization and destruction	56
The @PostConstruct annotation	57
The @PreDestroy annotation	57
Programmatic Lookup of the CDI Beans	58
Configuring a CDI application	59
Standalone CDI application	**60**
Building the standalone project with Gradle	**63**
Using the DeltaSpike CDI container tests	**64**
Injecting arbitrary objects using Producers	**69**
Advanced CDI	**72**
The lifecycle component example	72
Alternatives	74
The Arquillian test framework	**76**
A new kind of Java EE testing framework	76
Setting up of Arquillian	77
The disposable methods	79
CDI and crosscutting concerns	**82**
Interceptors	82
Decorators	87
Observers and events	90
Stereotypes	93
Summary	**93**
Chapter 3: Enterprise Java Beans	**95**
EJB protocols	**96**
Criticism of EJB	96
Simplification of EJB	97
Features of EJB components	**97**
Session beans	**99**
Stateless session beans	99
Concurrency and stateless session EJBs	102
Stateful session beans	103
Singleton session beans	111

The lifecycle of session EJBs	**115**
Lifecycle of stateless EJBs	115
Lifecycle of stateful session beans	116
Lifecycle of singleton session beans	118
Business interfaces	**120**
Local access	120
Remote access	120
Access summary	121
No interface views	121
EJB references	**122**
Asynchronous invocations	**123**
The relationship between EJB and CDI containers	**124**
Lightweight scope of EJBs	**125**
Summary	**126**
Chapter 4: Essential Java Persistence API 3.2	**129**
Entities	**130**
Defining Entity bean	130
An entity bean example	131
A Plain Old Java Object	131
A simple entity bean	133
Expanded entity bean definition	135
Annotating entity beans	139
Annotating entities with the instance variables	139
Annotating entities with property accessors	140
Comparing annotating styles	142
Running a simple entity bean test	**143**
The Gradle build file for the entity bean test	143
A stateful session bean	144
An entity bean integration test	146
A persistence context XML configuration	148
Arquillian configuration for the embedded GlassFish server	150
Running an integration test	152
The lifecycle of an entity bean	**153**
The new entity state	153
The managed entity state	153
The detached entity state	153
The removed entity state	154
EntityManager	**154**
Persistence context	154
The EntityManager methods	154
Transactional support	160
Application managed transactions	160

[iii]

Retrieving an EntityManager by injection	162
Retrieving an EntityManager by factory	162
Retrieving an EntityManager by the JNDI lookup	164
Moving further along with entity beans	**165**
Controlling the mapping of entities to the database table	165
Expanding the @Table annotation	165
Mapping the primary keys	167
The single primary key	168
Composite primary keys	169
Using the @IdClass annotation	169
Using the @Embeddable annotation	171
Using the @EmbeddedId annotation	173
JPQL	**175**
The dynamic queries	176
The named queries	177
The query parameters	178
The positional query arguments	179
The entity bean relationships	**180**
Mapping with the @OneToOne annotation	180
Mapping with the @OneToMany annotation	182
Mapping with the @ManyToOne annotation	183
Mapping with the @ManyToMany annotation	184
Configuration of persistence and the entity beans	**186**
The structure of the persistence unit configuration	186
The object-relational mapping files	187
Standard property configurations for the persistence units	189
Summary	**190**
Chapter 5: Object-Relational Mapping with JPA	**191**
Adding finesse to entity beans	**191**
Field binding	192
Binding eagerly	192
Binding lazily	192
The trade-off between eager and lazy	193
Cascades onto dependent entities	196
Cascade operations	196
Removal of orphans in relationships	197
Generated values and primary keys	198
Table auto increment	200
Sequence auto increment	202
Identity auto increment	203
Entity relationships revisited	**204**
One-to-one mapping	204
Persisting one-to-one unidirectional entities	208

Bidirectional one-to-one-entities	208
Persisting one-to-one bidirectional entities	209
Composite foreign keys in a one-to-one relationship	209

One-to-many mapping — 211
One-to-many relationship with a join column	213
Bidirectional one-to-many relationship	214
One-to-many using an explicit join table	216

Many-to-one mapping — 217
Many-to-one relationship with a join column	218
Bidirectional many-to-one relationship	220

Many-to-many mapping — 220
Bidirectional many-to-many relationship	221
Unidirectional many-to-many relationship	224

Mapping entity inheritance hierarchy — 225

Hierarchy in a single database table — 226
An example user story	227
Benefits and drawbacks of the single table strategy	230

Common base table hierarchy — 231
An example user story	231
Benefits and drawbacks of joined Inheritance	234

Table-per-class hierarchy — 235
An example user story	235
Benefits and drawbacks of table-per-class hierarchy	237

Extended entities — 238
Mapped super-classes — 238

Troubleshooting entity persistence — 240

Fetch performance — 241
Prefer lazily binding for maximum performance	241

Entity Relationship — 241
Prefer orphan removal	243
Excessive queries	243

Object corruption — 244

Summary — 244

Chapter 6: Java Servlets and Asynchronous Request-Response — 247

What are Java Servlets? — 248

Web containers — 248

The lifecycle of Java Servlets — 250
Loading Servlets	250
The Java Servlet initialization	251
The Java Servlet destruction	252

The Servlet request and response — 252
HTTP Servlets — 254
The deployment model — 255

Getting started with Java Servlets — 258
A simple Servlet — 258
The URL path mapping — 260
The Gradle build project — 262
The containerless Java web application — 263
Request and response — 268
The request parameters — 268
Headers — 269
The request attributes — 269
The session attributes — 271
The Servlet context attributes — 271
Redirecting the response — 272
The web deployment descriptor — 273
Mapping Java Servlets — 274
Configuring a session timeout — 276
Configuring MIME types — 277
Configuring the welcome page — 278
Configuring the error-handler pages — 278
Annotations and the web deployment descriptor — 279
The Servlet filters — 280
The Servlet filter annotation attributes — 281
The Servlet filter XML configuration — 282
The Servlet context listener — 283
Pluggable Servlet fragments — 286
Ordering multiple web fragments — 287
Asynchronous Java Servlets — 289
The asynchronous input and output — 289
A synchronous reader example — 290
An asynchronous reader example — 291
An asynchronous writer — 298
Alignment to the containers — 305
Aligning Servlets to the CDI container — 305
Miscellaneous features — 306
Mapping the URL patterns — 307
Rules for the URL path mapping — 307
Single thread model — 308
Summary — 308

Chapter 7: Java API for HTML5 WebSocket — 309
The rise of WebSockets — 310
Early web technology — 310

Enter HTML5 and WebSockets	311
WebSocket Java definitions	312
The WebSocket protocol	313
Server-side Java WebSockets	**314**
@ServerEndpoint	315
@OnMessage	316
Invoking Java WebSocket	316
Running WebSocket examples	319
Java WebSocket API	**319**
Native formats communication	319
Annotated WebSockets on the server side	320
Lifecycle WebSocket endpoint annotations	320
WebSocket sessions	321
A Java WebSocket chat server	**324**
The server side	325
The web client	331
Asynchronous operations	334
Client-side Java WebSockets	**335**
@ClientEndpoint	336
Annotated client example	336
Remote endpoints	339
Programmatic Java WebSocket	**340**
Encoders and decoders	**341**
Summary	**344**
Chapter 8: RESTful Services JAX-RS 2.0	**345**
Representational State Transfer	**345**
JAX-RS 2.0 features	347
Architectural style	**348**
REST style for collections of entities	349
REST style for single entities	350
Servlet mapping	**351**
Mapping JAX-RS resources	354
Test-Driven Development with JAX-RS	354
JAX-RS server-side endpoints	**357**
Defining JAX-RS resources	359
Testing JAX-RS resources	365
Path URI variables	368
JAX-RS annotations for extracting field and bean properties	370
Extracting query parameters	370
Extracting matrix parameters	371
Using default values	372
Extracting form parameters	373

| Field and bean properties | 374 |

JAX-RS subresources — 375
- Resolution by a subresource location — 375
- Resolution by a subresource method — 376

Generating a JAX-RS generic response — 377
- Response builder — 377
- Response status — 380
- Generic entities — 383
- Return types — 384
- Hypermedia linking — 385

JAX-RS client API — 389
- Synchronous invocation — 389
- Asynchronous invocation — 393

Asynchronous JAX-RS server side endpoints — 396

JAX-RS providers — 399

Filters — 399
- JAX-RS filters — 399
  - Server-side filters — 399
  - Client-side filters — 401
- JAX-RS interceptors — 405
- Binding filter and interceptors — 409
  - Dynamic binding — 411

Summary — 412

Chapter 9: Java Message Service 2.0 — 413

What is JMS? — 414
- Messaging systems — 416
  - Point-to-point messaging — 416
  - Publish-subscribe messaging — 418

JMS definitions — 420
- JMS classic API — 420
- JMS simplified API — 421
- JMS message types — 421

A quick JMS 2.0 example — 421

Establishing a JMS connection — 425
- Connecting to a JMS provider — 425
- Connection factories — 425
  - Default connection factory — 426
- Message destinations — 427
- JMSContext — 427
  - Retrieving a JMSContext — 432

Sending JMS messages	**433**
Upgrading message producers from JMS 1.1	433
Sending messages synchronously	434
Sending messages asynchronously	434
JMS message headers	435
Setting message properties	436
Setting a message delivery delay	436
Receiving JMS messages	**437**
Upgrade from JMS 1.1	437
Receiving messages synchronously	438
Receiving messages asynchronously	439
Non-shared subscriptions	440
Shared subscriptions	441
Durable topic consumers	441
Starting and stopping connections	443
Redelivery of messages	443
Other JMS-defined properties	444
Message-driven Beans (MDBs)	**444**
Activation configuration property	449
Message selectors	450
JMS exception handling	**451**
Upgrading JMS 1.1 code	**452**
Establish a JMS 1.1 connection	452
JMS and dependency injection	**455**
Injecting CDI beans	455
Injection of JMSContext resources	456
Injecting EJB beans	457
Definition of JMS resources in Java EE	457
Summary	**458**
Chapter 10: Bean Validation	**461**
Introduction to Bean Validation	**462**
New features in 1.1	462
A quick example	463
Constraint declarations	**466**
Elements of a constraint	466
List of built-in constraints	467
Hibernate Validator built-in constraints	469
Constraint violations	470
Applying constraint definitions	**471**
Custom validators	472

Groups of constraints	475
Class-level constraints	475
Partial validation	478
Constraint inheritance	**480**
Ordering groups of constraints	**481**
Method-level constraints	**483**
Method validation rules	486
Integration with Java EE	**486**
Default access to validator and validator factory	487
JAX-RS 2.0 integration	487
Summary	**488**
Chapter 11: Advanced Topics in Persistence	**491**
Persistence of map collections	**491**
The MapKey relationship	491
The MapKey join column relationship	495
Calling stored procedures	**498**
Stored procedure query	499
MySQL remote server example	500
Dynamic result set retrieval	501
Retrieving outbound parameter values	503
Stored procedure query annotations	505
Understanding the criteria API	**508**
Criteria queries	508
CriteriaUpdate	512
CriteriaDelete	513
Entity graphs	**515**
Worked example of a fetch plan	518
Miscellaneous features	**526**
Custom JPQL functions	526
Down-casting entities	527
Synchronization of persistence contexts	528
Entity listeners with CDI	528
Native query constructor mapping	530
Summary	**531**
Appendix A: Java EE 7 Platform	**533**
Platform containers	**533**
Global JNDI naming	534
Packaging	534
Bean XML configuration location	537
Persistence XML configuration location	537

Upgrading to Java EE 7 from J2EE versions	**538**
Legacy application programming interfaces	539
GlassFish 4 reference implementation	**540**
Installing basic GlassFish	541
Configuring MySQL database access	542
Configuring command line	543
Default resources	545
Appendix B: Java EE 7 Persistence	**547**
Persistence unit	**547**
XML schema documents for Java EE 7	549
Properties	549
XML representation of object-relational mapping	550
JPA miscellaneous features	**551**
Converters	551
Native constructor results	552
Transactions and concurrency	**553**
Entity managers	554
Transactions, entity managers, and session EJBs	554
Stateful session beans	556
Concurrency access locks	557
Optimistic locking	557
Pessimistic locking	558
Appendix C: Java EE 7 Transactions	**559**
Transactions	**559**
Java Transaction API	560
Two-phase commit transactions	560
Heuristic failures	561
Local transactions	562
Distributed transactions	562
Transaction services	**562**
Container-Managed Transactions (CMT)	562
Bean-Managed Transactions (BMT)	564
Isolation levels	565
JNDI lookup	569
Appendix D: Java EE 7 Assorted Topics	**571**
Concurrency utilities	**571**
Environment reference	572
Application container context	573
Contextual tasks	573

JSON-P	**576**
Streaming	577
Parsing JSON with Streaming API	578
Generating JSON with Streaming API	579
Object model	580
Parsing JSON with the object model	580
Generating JSON with the object model	582
Recommended reading	**583**
Index	**585**

Preface

Jack Dempsey said, "A champion is somebody who gets up, when he can't".

This is a book about the Java EE 7 platform and the goal is to guide the software developers, designers, and interested architects. The book is aimed at the technical delivery and will be of service to those who are curious about Java EE. The intention of this book is to be a reference guide to programmers who are already building enterprise applications at a novice level and feel that this is the time to improve their knowledge. The book is also relevant to experienced Java developers, who need to stay up-to-date with the seventh edition of the Java EE platform.

My aim is to take you on this stupendous journey so that eventually you will have mastery, satisfaction, and a grand element of purpose around the Java EE 7 platform. After reading this book, you will be able to start building the next generation Java application for your enterprise with all the flair and confidence of a programmer with experienced technical know-how. Mastery is the inner urge to get better at doing stuff that you have a passion for and this book will show you how much you can achieve. Your passion for Java EE 7 will drive your satisfaction.

Your journey will start with an introduction to the Java EE 7 platform, which provides an overview of the initiative, mission, and the description of the umbrella specification and the individual specifications. There you will find, brief explanations of the highlights of the new APIs and several updated ones. In the first chapter, we will see a sample application from the beginning. From then onwards, the book delves straight into the Context and Dependency Injection, which is one of the most important APIs in Java. After that, the book moves onto Enterprise Java Beans and discussion of the server-side endpoints. Along the way, the book introduces Gradle as a build tool and Arquillian, which is an integration-testing framework. Your journey continues with Java Persistence and follows on with chapters dedicated to JMS, Java Servlets, RESTful services, and WebSocket.

Preface

This is a reference book. The contents around Java EE 7 are not by any means exhaustive. This book only serves as a start and now, it is up to you to venture forth. Good luck!

What this book covers

Chapter 1, *Java EE 7 HTML5 Productivity*, introduces the developer to the new features of the Java EE 7 platform. The reader is presented with a cursory view of WebSocket and JAX-RS 2.0.

Chapter 2, *Context and Dependency Injection*, is a study in the managed beans that have contextual scope. The chapter delves into qualifiers, providers, and Interceptors.

Chapter 3, *Enterprise Java Beans*, is an overview of the oldest endpoint in Enterprise Java. After reading this chapter, the reader will be comfortable with the session beans, asynchronous methods, and poolable instances.

Chapter 4, *Essential Java Persistence API 3.2*, is the first of a double that dives into JPA from the top to the bottom. Developers will understand entities, tables, and the primary key fields and properties.

Chapter 5, *Object-Relational Mapping with JPA*, follows on from the previous chapter and engages the reader into mapping objects with JPA. We cover all of the cardinal relationships including one-to-one and one-to-many.

Chapter 6, *Java Servlets and Asynchronous Request-Response*, takes a break from the persistence modeling to focus on Java Servlets and writing Servlet filters and context listener. The reader will learn about the asynchronous input and output with Java Servlets.

Chapter 7, *Java API for HTML5WebSocket*, tackles the WebSocket technology from the perspective of Java. The developer will learn how to build new applications using this important API from both server and client.

Chapter 8, *RESTful Services JAX-RS 2.0*, is a deep dive into the Java RESTful service standard in its second edition. The reader will learn about the client-side JAX-RS API as well as new server-side features.

Chapter 9, *Java Message Service 2.0*, is a tour around the latest JMS API on the Java EE 7 platform. JMS is all about asynchronous message processing.

Chapter 10, *Bean Validation*, is a thorough engineering introduction into the wonderful world of constraint validation around POJOs. You will learn how to write your own custom constraint checks, and to group and order sets of validation constraints.

Chapter 11, Advanced Topics in Persistence, is a final dedicated chapter to persistence and it covers recent corner cases that have been recently fixed. The reader will learn how to invoke stored procedures and create fetch plans among other techniques.

Appendix A, Java EE 7 Platform, is a reference around the platform container configuration. This appendix has a material about XML configuration, the JNDI name space and packaging. It also has handy section on installing GlassFish 4.0, manually.

Appendix B, Java EE 7 Persistence, covers the configuration of JPA and most importantly the persistence unit. It has a useful table of all the JPA 2.1 properties. This appendix delves into miscellaneous parts of the specification including stateless session EJB, transactions, and concurrency.

Appendix C, Java EE 7 Transactions, is dedicated completely to Java EE transactions. The reader will find a useful overview of ACID principles, and local and distributed transaction. There is an excellent coverage of the heuristic failures and illustrations of the main transaction and consistency issues.

Appendix D, Java EE 7 Assorted Topics, is divided into two sections, namely: Concurrency Utilities API and JSON-Processing API. These are two new brand editions to the Java EE 7 specification. The reader will find these sections to be very handy references.

Online Chapter, Moving Java EE.next to the Cloud, is an explorative chapter from the heart that discusses the potential repercussions for the Java EE platform migrating to the cloud-computing environment.

You can download the online chapter from `http://www.packtpub.com/sites/default/files/downloads/7942EN_Chapter_12_Moving_Java_EE_next_to_the_cloud.pdf`.

What you need for this book

You will only need the Java SDK, an IDE, or a text editor, and the patience to learn. Technically, you can work with IntelliJ, Eclipse, or NetBeans to compile the source from the book. All of the source code examples in the book were created with the Gradle build tool, which is an open source software. They were created and executed against the Java EE 7 reference implementation: GlassFish Open Source Server Version 4.0.1.

Who this book is for

This book is for experienced Java developers. This book is not for dummies. The book is practically busting out of its seams, because there is so much information about all of the Java EE 7 technologies; therefore, we have included only the relevant stuff. *Java EE 7 Developer Handbook* covers the most crucial types of endpoints for new enterprise. This book will help many of you that have had prior experience with the platform. Whilst this book will not provide all the best practice and design patterns for Java EE 7, it does teach you the basics and the insider knowledge that will help you hunt for that information further afield.

Given there are more than 32 individual specifications involved in the umbrella Java EE 7, unfortunately, we could not fit every single topic inside this book. So that means coverage around **Java Server Faces**, **Java EE Connector Architecture**, and the new **Batch API** fell outside the remit of this volume. Something had to give, sadly, to ensure that we did include the most common denominator technologies that an engineer will face. We do give full attention to brand new Java EE 7 APIs, such as **Java WebSocket**, **Concurrency Utilities**, and **JSON Processing API**.

If you are unlucky (or lucky) like us, one day you arrive at your workplace, and suddenly you are told or requested to learn a new technology in a jig time. You already have a realization about time, which is a precious commodity and we should not waste it. This is why we focused on using up-to-date technology and build practices that we think are turning the world over.

Test Driven Development (**TDD**) has almost baked itself into the stone in the engineering world. Who professionally nowadays can proclaim within any organization that we do not test our software? This book reflects some of the best practices, by illustrating the testing codes. This book is not, however, a full treatise in testing, rather we show how Java EE 7 is more amenable than ever to write tests, if TDD is the way you want to practice your development.

Gradle is the next-generation build system of choice for us. It is rapidly being adopted and has won over some of the world's leading engineering teams in open source and behind closed doors. Gradle is adopted by Google's Android, Oracle's Open JavaFX project, and I can claim personally that a certain department in London at the Barclays Retail bank uses it daily. Gradle can work with Maven and Apache Ivy repositories.

Java EE 7 is the stopgap specification, we think, between the traditional client-server model and embracing the cloud platform. So the question is, when do we want to learn it? You will be rewarded, however, if you make the grade.

Conventions

In this book, you will find a number of styles of text that distinguish between different kinds of information. Here are some examples of these styles, and an explanation of their meaning.

Code words in text, database table names, folder names, filenames, file extensions, pathnames, dummy URLs, user input, and Twitter handles are shown as follows: "We placed `ProjectWebSocketServerEndpoint` and `ProjectRESTServerEndpoint` in the control subpackage, because these POJOs are manipulating the entities on behalf of the client side."

A block of code is set as follows:

```java
package je7hb.intro.xentracker.entity;

import org.hibernate.validator.constraints.NotEmpty;
import javax.persistence.*;
import javax.validation.constraints.Size;
import java.util.*;

@Entity
public class Project {
  @Id @GeneratedValue(strategy = GenerationType.AUTO)
  @Column(name = "PROJECT_ID") private Integer id;

  @NotEmpty @Size(max = 64)
  private String name;

  @OneToMany(cascade = CascadeType.ALL, mappedBy = "project",
    fetch = FetchType.EAGER)
  private List<Task> tasks = new ArrayList<>();

  public Project() {/* Required for JPA */}
  public Project(String name) {this.name = name;}

  public Integer getId() {return id;}
  public void setId(Integer id) {this.id = id;}
  public String getName() {return name;}
  public void setName(String name) {this.name = name;}

  public List<Task> getTasks() {return tasks;}
  public void setTasks(List<Task> tasks) {this.tasks = tasks;}
```

```java
    public boolean addTask(Task task) {
      if (!tasks.contains(task)) {
        Project oldProject = task.getProject();
        if (oldProject != null) {
          removeTask(task);
        }
        tasks.add(task);
        return true;
      } else {return false;}
    }

    public boolean removeTask(Task task) {
      if (tasks.contains(task)) {
        tasks.remove(task);
        task.setProject(null);
        return true;
      } else {return false;}
    }

    // hashCode(), equals(), toString() omitted
}
```

When we wish to draw your attention to a particular part of a code block, the relevant lines or items are set in bold:

```java
package je7hb.basic.arquillian;
import javax.decorator.Decorator;
import javax.decorator.Delegate;
import javax.inject.Inject;

@Decorator
@Premium
public class CreditProcessorDecorator implements CreditProcessor {

  @Inject SanctionService sanctionService;
  @Inject @Delegate @Premium CreditProcessor processor;

  @Override
  public void check(String account) {
    sanctionService.sanction(account, "EURGBP");
    processor.check(account);
  }
}
```

Any command-line input or output is written as follows:

```
gradle clean
gradle eclipse
gradle idea
Gradle run
gradle build
gradle build
```

New terms and **important words** are shown in bold. Words that you see on the screen, in menus or dialog boxes for example, appear in the text like this: "**Ramping up on Java concurrency**".

> Warnings or important notes appear in a box like this.

> Tips and tricks appear like this.

Reader feedback

Feedback from our readers is always welcome. Let us know what you think about this book—what you liked or may have disliked. Reader feedback is important for us to develop titles that you really get the most out of.

To send us general feedback, simply send an e-mail to `feedback@packtpub.com`, and mention the book title via the subject of your message.

If there is a topic that you have expertise in and you are interested in either writing or contributing to a book, see our author guide on `www.packtpub.com/authors`.

Customer support

Now that you are the proud owner of a Packt book, we have a number of things to help you to get the most from your purchase.

Downloading the example code

You can download the example code files for all Packt books you have purchased from your account at http://www.packtpub.com. If you purchased this book elsewhere, you can visit http://www.packtpub.com/support and register to have the files e-mailed directly to you. Alternatively, you can download the code from the author's GitHub account at https://github.com/peterpilgrim.

Errata

Although we have taken every care to ensure the accuracy of our content, mistakes do happen. If you find a mistake in one of our books—maybe a mistake in the text or the code—we would be grateful if you would report this to us. By doing so, you can save other readers from frustration and help us improve subsequent versions of this book. If you find any errata, please report them by visiting http://www.packtpub.com/submit-errata, selecting your book, clicking on the **errata submission form** link, and entering the details of your errata. Once your errata are verified, your submission will be accepted and the errata will be uploaded on our website, or added to any list of existing errata, under the Errata section of that title. Any existing errata can be viewed by selecting your title from http://www.packtpub.com/support.

Piracy

Piracy of copyright material on the Internet is an ongoing problem across all media. At Packt, we take the protection of our copyright and licenses very seriously. If you come across any illegal copies of our works, in any form, on the Internet, please provide us with the location address or website name immediately so that we can pursue a remedy.

Please contact us at copyright@packtpub.com with a link to the suspected pirated material.

We appreciate your help in protecting our authors, and our ability to bring you valuable content.

Questions

You can contact us at questions@packtpub.com if you are having a problem with any aspect of the book, and we will do our best to address it.

Java EE 7 HTML5 Productivity

Nile Rodgers, Le Freak said, "We called it DHM or Deep Hidden Meaning. Our golden rule was that all our songs had to have this ingredient: understanding the song's DNA."

This is a handbook about Java EE 7. According to the *Collins English Dictionary*, a handbook is a reference book listing brief facts on a subject or place or directions for maintenance or repair, as of a car. In this book, we will definitely not be repairing automobiles, but instead we will point the way forward on how the developers, designers, and architects, practicing or just interested enthusiasts, can make viable use of Java on the standard Enterprise Platform.

Java EE 7

The Java EE 7 standard defines the following extremely important architectural interfaces:

- EJB Container
- Web Container
- Context and Dependency Injection with type safety and events
- Java Servlet Specification and Configuration
- Optional application deployment descriptors
- Servlet and CDI extension points
- Support for web services RESTful and SOAP
- Better support for messaging systems
- Cache management on the enterprise

Enhanced HTML5 support

Java EE 7 is about features that offer the developers enhanced HTML5 support. **HTML** stands for **HyperText Markup Language** and is designed as a structure for presenting and structuring content for the **World Wide Web (WWW)**. *Sir Tim Berners-Lee* invented HTML and the first web browser in 1990. At the time of writing, the fifth revision of HTML is expected to be announced as an official standard by the end of 2014. HTML5 improves support for latest multimedia. The fruits of its labor have been deliberated upon since the **Web Hypertext Applications Technology Group (WHATWG)** (http://whatwg.org/html) meetings from 2004. HTML5 is an official standard of the **World-Wide Web Consortium (W3C)** (http://www.w3c.org/TR/html5), which is built on the joint venture work of the WHATWG and the W3C.

HTML5 now embraces new media types, which are one of the great highlights of it, namely video, audio, and canvas. The canvas is a special type of drawable apparatus in the web browser, where the web client developers can manipulate dynamic content with the JavaScript programs.

There is a series of new tag elements to give a better structure to HTML5 documents. New web applications are encouraged to write or generate HTML5 content with `article`, `section`, `header`, `footer`, `figure`, `figcaption`, `hgroup`, `nav`, `summary`, and `detail`, `time`, or `aside` tags. This is just a small sample of the new semantic and document structure of HTML5 tags. There are several tag elements, such as `center`, which are deprecated, because these features are better expressed with **Cascading Style Sheets (CSS)** rather than markup.

HTML5 is also an aggregation term that stands for the set of emerging multimedia technologies that are supported by the markup language. Browser support CSS 3 is regularly expected for HTML5 compatibility. Moreover, our industry is presently undergoing a mobile web application revolution on smartphones and, especially, tablet computing devices. HTML5 not surprisingly also adds the geolocation support, including the location tracking in the browser. It also covers offline session and local storage for web applications that run on mobile devices, such as smartphones or tablets. These applications can save state when the connection to the Internet is lost.

Some of the modern HTML5 supporting browsers actually have the 3D graphics support through a working standard called **WebGL**, which impacts the amount of data that is streamed from the server to the client. 3D graphics and high-resolution media generally entails a larger server-side push of data compared to lesser media websites. There is a sliding scale of capability with the current versions of Firefox, Safari, Chrome, and Opera browsers. The outlier is typically Microsoft's web browsers Internet Explorer 9 and 10. For those of you who want 3D effects without the reliance of WebGL you should take a look at the CSS 3 3D transformations.

Finally, JavaScript is a single thread in the execution in a web browser. There is no way to spawn multiple threads in modern standard W3C conforming web clients. HTML5 also embraces two fundamental groundbreaking changes: Web Works and WebSocket. Web Works is a JavaScript compatible API that allows web clients to run long-running code that does not block the browser. WebSocket is a new way for a browser and server to exchange an asynchronous communication without having to constantly send the metadata information. WebSocket is an extension of the TCP/IP Socket protocol specifically for HTTP communications.

Java EE 7 architecture

Let us start by understanding the non-cloud Java EE model architecture. This is revision material, if you already know the platform. For a beginner, reading this section is frankly essential.

Standard platform components and APIs

Java EE architecture can be thought of as four separate containers. The first one is called the **EJB** container for lifecycle management of **Enterprise Java Beans** and the second container is the web container for lifecycle management of Java Servlets and managed beans. The third container is called the **Application Client** container, which manages the lifecycle of the client-side components. Finally, the fourth container is reserved for Java Applets and their lifecycle.

The Java EE containers are runtime environments that hold Java applications deployed in the **Java Archive** (**JAR**) files. You can think of a JAR file as a bundle, but more accurately it is a special annotated ZIP file with a manifest. The JAR files are simply an assembly of compiled Java classes.

A fully conformant Java EE product, such as Glassfish or JBoss Application Server has both containers. As you can see from the following diagram, there are lots of API that these products have to implement in order to be certified as a standard product. The most difficult of these APIs have to do transactional, resource pool connection, and enterprise Java Beans.

Each of these standard API is a specification in its own right, and relevant information can be queried, downloaded, and examined from the Java Community Process website (`http://jcp.org`). Each specification has a unique number, which identifies the **Java Specification Request** (**JSR**) for the API. Indeed, the JSR for the Java EE 7 Platform Edition, is an assembly of many specifications, and has an official number 342.

The platform specification, such as the one that this book is written about, Java EE, then, is an ensemble of the JSRs into a higher-level specification. The platform specifications offer guarantees of interoperability, security, and serviceability of the individual JSR. In other words, not just any JSR can be automatically included in the platform specification. Each JSR fits the remit of the Enterprise Platform.

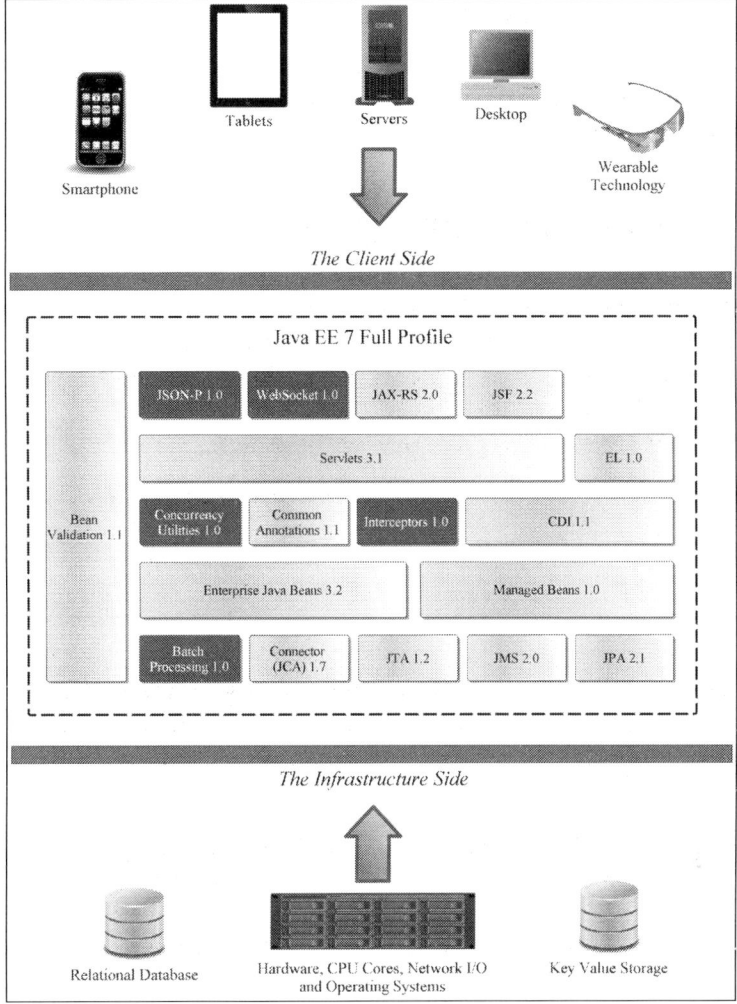

New productivity themes

The Developer productivity is a key theme for Java EE 7. There are four brand new specifications added to Java EE 7: Batch, Concurrency Utilities, WebSocket, and JSON-P.

Batch Processing API is introduced into Java EE 7 to reduce the dependency on the third-party framework. Batch processing is a field of information technology that predates Java by several decades and has its origins in the mainframe systems. Sadly, this topic of interest is out of the scope of this book.

Concurrency Utilities solves a long-standing issue with enterprise Java: how to spawn Java Thread processes without knowledge and control of the application server. The new Concurrency Utilities enhances the developers productivity with the managed thread pool and executor resources.

Java API for WebSocket specification allows Java enterprise applications to communicate with the new HTML5 WebSocket protocol.

Finally, JSON-P is a new specification that standardizes reading and writing the JSON content for the platform. The additional JSON library further reduces the reliance on the third-party libraries.

Refinements

Java EE 7 takes advantage of the **New Input Output (NIO)** in the Java SE edition to allow Java Servlets 3.1 to handle an asynchronous communication.

Java EE 7 extends the **Java Persistence API (JPA 2.1)** abilities for the developers. They can now invoke the stored procedures, execute bulk criteria updates and deletes, and control exactly which entities are eagerly or lazily fetched from the database within reason.

Expression Language (EL) 3.0 is not truly a new specification, but it is a broken-out specification from Servlets, JavaServer Pages, and JavaServer Faces. The developers can access the expression evaluator and invoke the processing custom expressions on, say, their own custom tag libraries or server-side business logic.

Perhaps, the most important change in Java EE 7 is the strengthening of **Context and Dependency Injection (CDI)** in order to improve type safety and the easier development of the CDI extensions. CDI, **Interceptors**, and **Common Annotations improve** type safe, dependency injection, and observing of the lifecycle events inside the CDI container. These three specifications together ensure that the extensions that address the crosscutting concerns can be written, and can be applied to any component. The developers can now write portable CDI extensions to extend the platform in a standard way.

Java EE 7 continues the theme that was started in the earlier editions of the platform, improving the ease-of-development and allowing the developers to write **Plain Old Java Objects (POJO)**.

As if to prove a point, the new **Java Transaction API (JTA)** introduces a new annotation `@javax.transaction.Transactional`, which allows any CDI or managed bean to take advantage of the enterprise transactions.

Java for RESTful Services (JAX-RS) has three crucial enhancements, the addition of the client-side API to invoke a REST endpoint, an asynchronous I/O support for the client and server endpoints, and hypermedia linking.

Bean Validation is a constraint validation solution for the domain and value object. It now supports the method-level validation, and also has better integration with the rest of the Java EE Platform.

Java Connector API (JCA) is improved for the **Enterprise Integration Architecture (EIA)** customers in terms of asynchronous execution, processing, and resources; enhancements in JCA affect the intersystem messaging in Message-Driven Beans in an especially powerful way. Sadly, JCA, JSF, and EL are topics, which are out-of-scope of this book.

Java EE Platform

The platform, then, is a balance between the three forces, namely the community of the enterprise Java developers, the product providers, and of course the enterprise that must uphold the business models.

The community requires standardization in order that they can easily embrace technology without the fear of vendor lock-in. They also want to be satisfied with a sound investment in the software development for years to come.

The vendors have an interest in selling their products, services, and support to the community of users for years to come. They also want to have a platform that lowers the barriers to compete against other vendors. It is helpful for them that there is a standard to aim for, a testable certification to achieve, in which they can brand their servers.

The specification for the Full Profile edition of Java EE 7 has the following APIs:

Name	Version	Description	JSR	Web Profile
Batch Process	1.0	Batch Processing (NEW)	352	
Bean Validation	1.1	Bean Validation framework	349	Y
Common Annotations	1.1	Common Annotations for the Java EE platform	250	Y
CDI	1.1	Contexts and Dependency Injection for Java EE	346	Y

Name	Version	Description	JSR	Web Profile
Concurrency Utilities	1.0	Concurrency Utilities for the Java EE platform (NEW)	236	
DI	1.0	Dependency Injection for Java	330	Y
EL	3.0	Unified Expression Language for configuration of web components and context dependency injection	341	Y
EJB	3.2	Enterprise Java Beans, entity beans and EJB QL	345	Y (EJB Lite)
Interceptors	1.2	Interceptor technology (NEW)	318	Y
JACC	1.4	Java Authorization Contract for Containers	115	
JASPIC	1.1 M/B	Java Authentication Service Provider Interface for Containers	196	
JavaMail	1.4	Java Mail API	919	
JAXB	2.2	Java API for XML Binding	222	
JAXP	1.4	Java API for XML Parsing	206	
JAX-RS	2.0	Java API for RESTful Services	339	Y
JAX-WS	1.3	Java API for XML –based Web Services including SOAP and WSDL	224	
JCA	1.7	Java EE Connector Architecture	322	
JMS	2.0	Java Message Service	343	
JPA	2.1	Java Persistence API	338	Y
JSF	2.2	Java Server Faces	344	Y
JSON-P	1.0	JavaScript Serialization Object Notation Protocol	353	Y
JSP	2.3	Java Server Pages	245	Y
Debugging support	1.0	Debugging Support for Other Languages such as Java Server Pages	45	Y
JSTL	1.2	Java Standard Template Library	245	Y
JTA	1.2	Java Transaction API	907	Y
Managed Beans	1.0	Managed Beans 1.1	342	Y
Servlet	3.1	Java Servlet	340	Y

Name	Version	Description	JSR	Web Profile
Web Services	1.3	Web services	224	
Web Services Metadata	2.1	Web services metadata	181	
WebSocket	1.0	Java API for WebSocket (NEW)	356	Y

There is also a subset of the Java EE 7 product, known as the **Web Profile** that only handles the web specific Java enterprise APIs. Examples of this sort of product are open source Apache Tomcat from the Apache Software Foundation, Caucho's proprietary Resin, and the ever popular open source embeddable Jetty Server. The Java EE 7 web container products have a much smaller subset of JSRs to implement.

You might have noticed that some of the Java EE APIs were supported already in some web containers, which existed before the profiles were standard in Java EE 6 (December 10, 2009).

Java Persistence, which maps entity beans, or persistence capable objects, to a relational database, is one of the most crucial and important application interfaces. JPA is a tremendous success for the portable object-relation mapping applications that works across the databases and application servers. Your code can move from one vendor's database connection to another. There is always a slight caveat emptor: there is no such thing as 100 percent portability. But without the standard framework, your developers would have to work an awful lot harder than tweaking a few database tables and configuring a different JDBC connection resource.

Portability and the future of the Java SE and EE platforms will be very important for moving your applications to the diverse, but unstandardized, cloud-computing environment. Although cloud computing was dropped from Java EE 7 late in the establishment of the specification, adopting Java EE 7 will help in the mid-term future when there is an official Java enterprise edition for the cloud. It is rather likely that in those modern utility computing environments, prospective business subscribers will welcome the ability to move from one cloud **PaaS** (**Platform as a Service**) vendor to another for a technical and/or business reason.

Standards, then, are very important to Java. It means that we can all move along in a positive direction with less fear of the unknown and that, ladies and gentlemen, is good for everybody. The API that your application code depends on is critical to its software lifecycle. Let's move on to the profiles.

Java EE Profiles

The formal definition of a profile is a specialization of a Java Platform Edition that includes zero or more **Java Community Process (JCP)** specifications (that are not part of the Platform Edition Specification). Java Enterprise Platform Edition defines two profiles, the **Full Profile** and the Web Profile product.

Java EE Web Profile, to give it its full official name, is the first profile defined by the standards committee, the JCP. The Web Profile defines a small subset of the Java EE components for delivering the web content. It specifically targets the Java web developers who are responsible for delivering the Java web applications.

The Web Profile offers a degree of completeness with its set of APIs. A business developer can write modern web applications that only access, execute, and perform against Web Profile. Most web applications require state-management and transactional demands. Even though a lot of Java Web Applications, written today rely less on direct calls to the Java Servlet API, in most cases they still tend to use a Java Web Framework.

Web Profile

The Web Profile has the following feature set of APIs:

- **Java Servlet API 3.1**: This framework provides handling for an HTTP request and response synchronously and now asynchronously
- **Enterprise Java Bean Lite 3.2**: This is a less demanding model of service endpoints, where the business logic of the application lives
- **Context and Dependency Injection 1.1**: This is a framework for the application that transfers the lifecycle and management of the connected objects to the container
- **Java Server Faces 2.2**: This is a component-based web user interface framework
- **Java Transaction API 1.2**: This is a framework for two-phase commit transactions
- **Java Persistence 2.1**: This is a framework for persisting POJO to a database
- **Web Socket 1.0**: This is a new specification for Java to engage the HTML5 WebSocket clients and servers

- **Bean Validation 1.1**: This is an upgraded framework to constrain the fields, properties, and methods of the value objects in an application
- **JAX-RS 2.0**: This is an upgraded framework for the Java Enterprise applications to handle the RESTful communications
- **JSON-P 1.0**: This is a brand new framework for the Java application read-and-write **JavaScript Schema Object Notation (JSON)** documents

With these small set of requirements, it is not surprising that the Java EE implementation providers find the Web Profile easier to implement.

> **Which Web Frameworks and Java EE 7**
>
> Usually the biggest question for the Java Enterprise developers in the past has been, what web framework to use? At the time of writing, JSF 2.2 is the only framework that is compatible. The purveyors of the other frameworks, such as Apache Wicket, WebWork, or even Spring MVC must update their services, especially to support the new asynchronous abilities in Java Servlets 3.1 and JAX-RS 2.0.
>
>
>
> The way we build web applications in 2013 is also changing, and the author expects some new innovations here in this space. Some applications are going straight to the RESTful applications by passing the older Front Controller and MVC architecture of traditional web frameworks from Java EE 6 or before. In those web applications, the interface is simply a barrage of the AJAX call-and-response calls from the client side, predominantly a single application communicating with a server-side backend.

Enterprise Profile

The Enterprise Full Profile is the complete set of API that matches the Platform Edition specification, which compliant providers must fulfill, in order to be certified as Java EE 7 compliant.

It's worth looking at each component of the platform and spending some time getting acquainted with them. There are an awful lot of individual specifications here and my advice is to use the Web Profile as a guide to getting into the Java EE 7 experience.

The following table is a guide to the key Enterprise services:

Name	Description
JTA	A standard API for demarcating the transactions in either the application or container.
EJB	Enterprise Java Beans are the transactional service endpoints that represent the interface to business logic for a client. They can be stateless, stateful, or singleton instances.
Managed Beans	Managed beans are endpoints with a contextual scope and they are type safe entities. Managed beans are managed by the Context and Dependency Injection container.
JDBC	JDBC is often quoted (wrongly) as Java Database Connectivity, a standard API for connecting to a relational database system. This component is part of the Standard Platform Edition.
JPA	Java Persistence API is the standard framework for the object-relational mapping of the Java objects to a database. JPA provides management of persistence through a persistence context. It allows the application developers to store data as the Java domain object rather than the relational tables. JPA is also available in the Java SE environments.
JMS	Java Message Service is a standard API for receiving and sending messages in a reliable transport, mostly asynchronously. JMS is based on the point-to-point messages and also publish-subscribe messaging. JMS is the basis for the Enterprise application integration in Java.
JNDI	Java Naming and Directory Interface is a standard API for looking up the location of the resources by name. It is a directory service used by the application components and the containers.
JAX-RS	Java API for RESTful services, a framework for processing the HTTP **Representation State Transfer** (**REST**) style requests and responses.
JAX-WS	Java API for the XML-based web services, a framework in Java to process the SOAP, WSDL documents in the distributed systems.
JavaMail	JavaMail is a standard API that allows the Enterprise Java application to send and receive e-mail. It has support for both the MIME and plain text e-mail.

Let's dispense with the theory and look at some of the Java EE 7 code.

A working example

In this section, we shall examine Java EE 7 from a sample project management application. The name of the application is `XenTracker`. It is a web application with EJB, the RESTful web services, and Persistence.

The development version of the `XenTracker` application, which has minimal styling and user interface enhancement, is shown in the following screenshot:

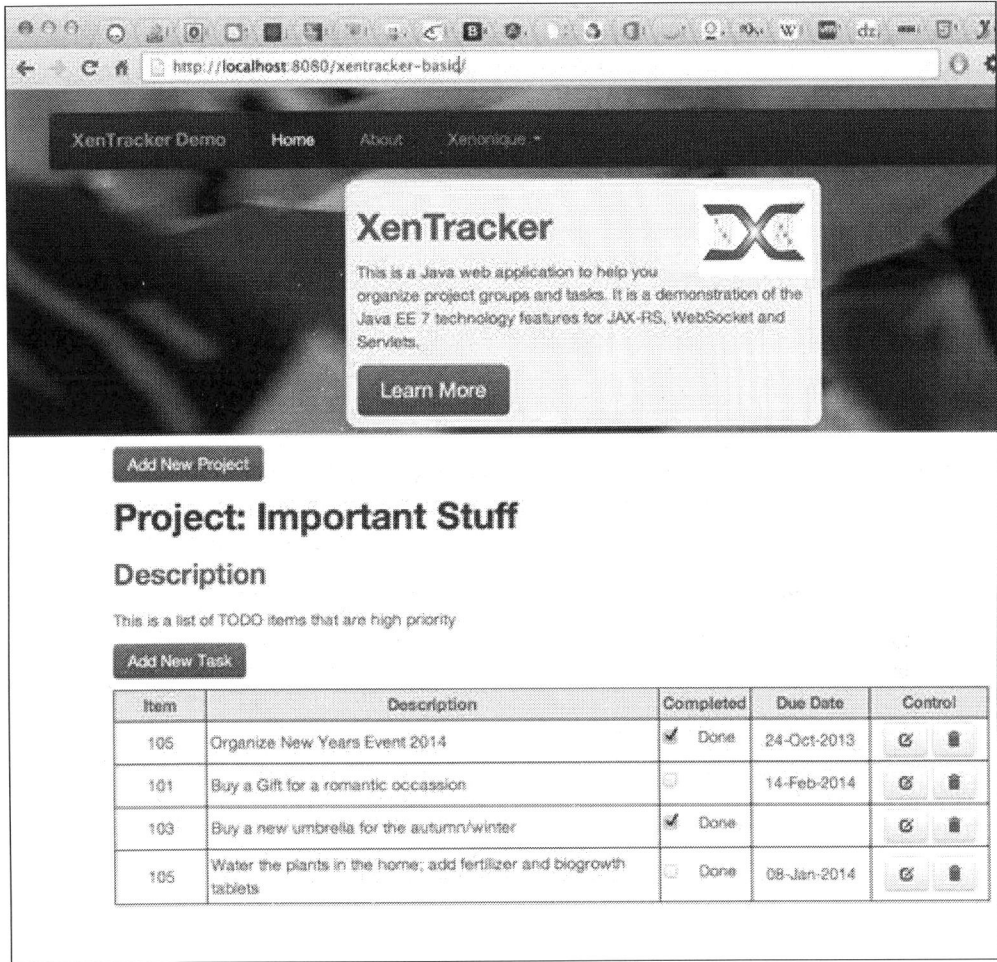

Entities

Our web application manages a couple of entities (also known as persistence capable objects), named `Project` and `Task`. The entities are mapped to the database table using the JPA annotations. We start with the entities in our Java EE 7 application, because it helps model the business requirements, and the domain of our boundaries. A project has zero or more task entries.

The definition for the `Project` entity is as follows:

```
package je7hb.intro.xentracker.entity;

import org.hibernate.validator.constraints.NotEmpty;
import javax.persistence.*;
import javax.validation.constraints.Size;
import java.util.*;

@Entity
public class Project {
  @Id @GeneratedValue(strategy = GenerationType.AUTO)
  @Column(name = "PROJECT_ID") private Integer id;

  @NotEmpty @Size(max = 64)
  private String name;

  @OneToMany(cascade = CascadeType.ALL, mappedBy = "project",
    fetch = FetchType.EAGER)
  private List<Task> tasks = new ArrayList<>();

  public Project() {/* Required for JPA */}
  public Project(String name) {this.name = name;}

  public Integer getId() {return id;}
  public void setId(Integer id) {this.id = id;}
  public String getName() {return name;}
  public void setName(String name) {this.name = name;}

  public List<Task> getTasks() {return tasks;}
  public void setTasks(List<Task> tasks) {this.tasks = tasks;}

  public boolean addTask(Task task) {
```

```
      if (!tasks.contains(task)) {
        Project oldProject = task.getProject();
        if (oldProject != null) {
          removeTask(task);
          }
        tasks.add(task);
        return true;
        } else {return false;}
      }

    public boolean removeTask(Task task) {
      if (tasks.contains(task)) {
        tasks.remove(task);
        task.setProject(null);
        return true;
        } else {return false;}
      }

    // hashCode(), equals(), toString() omitted
    }
```

> You can download the example code files for all Packt books you have purchased from your account at http://www.packtpub.com. If you purchased this book elsewhere, you can visit http://www.packtpub.com/support and register to have the files e-mailed directly to you. Alternatively, you can download the code from the author's GitHub account at https://github.com/peterpilgrim.

We observe that the class Project is declared with several annotations. @Entity marks this type as a JPA entity object and it has a default mapping to a database table called PROJECT. The @Id annotation designates the id field as a primary key. The @Column annotation overrides the default object-relational mapping and changes the table column name to PROJECT_ID instead of ID. The @GeneratedValue annotation informs JPA to automatically generate the primary key value for the project from the database connection provider.

The @NotNull annotation and @Size are from Bean Validation and Hibernate Validator frameworks respectively. They provide constraint checking at the source on the Project entity bean and they validate that the project's name field is not null and that the length of the field must be less than or equal to 64 characters. Incidentally, the Java EE 7 application servers will automatically invoke Bean Validation when this entity is inserted into, or updated to, the database.

Lastly, the `@OneToMany` annotation declares that the `Project` entity has a one-to-many relationship with another entity `Task`. *Chapter 5, Object-Relational Mapping with JPA*, is dedicated fully to the entity relationships, the database cardinalities, and the fetch types.

The definition for the `Task` entity is as follows:

```java
package je7hb.intro.xentracker.entity;

import org.hibernate.validator.constraints.NotEmpty;
import javax.persistence.*;
import javax.validation.constraints.*;
import java.util.Date;

@Entity
public class Task {
  @Id @GeneratedValue(strategy = GenerationType.AUTO)
  @Column(name = "TASK_ID") private Integer id;

  @NotEmpty @Size(max = 256)
  private String name;

  @Temporal(TemporalType.DATE)
  @Column(name = "TARGET_NAME") @Future
  private Date targetDate;

  private boolean completed;

  @ManyToOne(cascade = CascadeType.ALL)
  @JoinColumn(name = "PROJECT_ID")
  private Project project;

  public Task() {/* Required by JPA */}
  public Task(String name, Date targetDate, boolean completed) {
    this.name = name;
    this.targetDate = targetDate;
    this.completed = completed;
  }

  // getters and setters omitted()
  public Project getProject() {return project;}
  public void setProject(Project project) {
    this.project = project;
  }

  // hashCode(), equals(), toString() omitted
}
```

The entity `Task` represents a task in the business domain. The `Task` entity has a primary key too, mapped by the `@Id` annotation, which is also automatically generated on a database insertion. We also override the database column name to `TASK_ID`.

We declare Bean Validation constraints on the `Task` entities name field in exactly the same way as we do on `Project`, except a task has a longer length of string.

The `targetDate` is the due date for the task, which is optional, meaning that its value can be null. We use Bean Validation's `@Future` to constrain the target date to any date in the future. Finally, JPA requires us to explicitly define the temporal type whenever we map `java.util.Date`. In this case, we map `targetDate` to only SQL date types with the `@TemporalType` annotation.

A `Task` entity has a reverse mapping back to `Project`. In other words, a task is aware of the project that it belongs to; we call this a bi-directional relationship. We declare the `project` field with the annotation `@ManyToOne`.

Business logic

In order to be operational, we write business logic for our web application `XenTracker`. We require methods to create, update, and delete `Projects` and for `Tasks`. We also want to retrieve the list of projects and tasks for each project.

We shall use the session EJB for this purpose, because we want the lifecycle of business logic to be available as soon as our application is deployed to a Java EE 7 application server product or web container. EJBs support the transactions by default, they can be pooled by the server, their methods can be declared as asynchronous, and they are normally participants in monitoring with **Java Management Extensions (JMX)**. EJBs are discussed in detail in *Chapter 3, Enterprise Java Beans*.

First, we add some named queries to one of the entity beans. A named query is a way of storing a persistence query with the domain object. JPA only allows named queries to be declared with the entities.

Let us modify the `Project` entity as follows:

```
@NamedQueries({
  @NamedQuery(name = "Project.findAllProjects",
    query = "select p from Project p order by p.name"),
      @NamedQuery(name = "Project.findProjectById",
        query = "select p from Project p where p.id = :id"),
          @NamedQuery(name = "Project.findTaskById",
            query = "select t from Task t where t.id = :id"),})
@Entity
public class Project {/* ... */}
```

The annotation `@NameQueries` declares a set of `@NamedQuery` annotations attached to the `Project` entity bean. Each named query must have a distinct name and a **Java Persistence Query Language (JPQL)** statement. JPQL can have named parameters, which are denoted with the prefix of a colon character (`:id`).

In order to define a stateless session EJB, all we need to do is annotate a concrete class with the type `@javax.ejb.Stateless`. Our `ProjectTaskService` stateless session EJB is as follows:

```java
package je7hb.intro.xentracker.boundary;
import je7hb.intro.xentracker.entity.*;
import javax.ejb.*;
import javax.persistence.*;
import java.util.List;

@Stateless
public class ProjectTaskService {
  @PersistenceContext(unitName = "XenTracker")
  private EntityManager entityManager;

  public void saveProject(Project project) {
    entityManager.persist(project);
  }

  public void updateProject(Project project ) {
    Project projectToBeUpdated = entityManager.merge(project);
    entityManager.persist(projectToBeUpdated);
  }

  public void removeProject(Project project) {
    Project projectToBeRemoved = entityManager.merge(project);
    entityManager.remove(projectToBeRemoved);
  }

  public List<Project> findAllProjects() {
    Query query =
      entityManager.createNamedQuery("Project.findAllProjects");
    return query.getResultList();
  }

  public List<Project> findProjectById(Integer id) {
    Query query =
      entityManager.createNamedQuery("Project.findProjectById")
        .setParameter("id", id );
```

```
    return query.getResultList();
  }

  public List<Task> findTaskById(Integer id) {
    Query query =
      entityManager.createNamedQuery("Project.findTaskById")
        .setParameter("id", id );
    return query.getResultList();
    }
  }
```

Our session EJB depends upon persistence objects, so we inject an `EntityManager` object into it with the special annotation `@PersistenceContext`. The entity manager operation represents a resource connection to the database.

The methods `saveProject()`, `updateProject()`, and `removeProject()` respectively create, update, and delete the `project` entities from the database. The entity manager operations are covered in *Chapter 4, Essential Java Persistence API 3.2*. Because of the `CascadeType.ALL` definitions on the actual entities themselves, the dependent detail entity `Task` is looked after with the changes on the `Project` entity. You will learn about the cascade operations in *Chapter 5, Object-Relational Mapping with JPA*. So do we retrieve data back from the database?

The methods `findAllProjects()`, `findProjectById()`, and `findTaskById()` are so-called finder operations, the R in the acronym **CRUD (Create Retrieve Update Delete)**. Each of the methods accesses a particular named query, which we attach to the `Project` entity. The `findTaskById()` method, for example, gets the JPQL command named `Project.findTaskById` as a query instance. Notice that we can invoke the methods on that instance by chaining, so that the local variable is in fact unnecessary, and just serves as an education artifact.

The `ProjectTaskService` session has all of the operations to allow users to add, edit, and remove projects, and also to add, update, and remove tasks to and from projects. So now that we have our business logic, we can go forward and add a controller endpoint for web clients.

The service endpoints

Let's dive straight into the Java EE 7 pool and show off a Java-based WebSocket endpoint for our `XenTrack` application. We shall create a straightforward server-side endpoint that accepts a text message, which simply is the `project` ID, and returns the results as a JSON.

A WebSocket endpoint

The definition of the class `ProjectWebSocketServerEndpoint` is as follows:

```java
package je7hb.intro.xentracker.control;
import je7hb.intro.xentracker.boundary.ProjectTaskService;
import je7hb.intro.xentracker.entity.*;

import javax.ejb.*;
import javax.inject.Inject;
import javax.json.Json;
import javax.json.stream.*;
import javax.websocket.*;
import javax.websocket.server.ServerEndpoint;
import java.io.StringWriter;
import java.text.SimpleDateFormat;
import java.util.*;

@ServerEndpoint("/sockets")
@Stateless
public class ProjectWebSocketServerEndpoint {
  static SimpleDateFormat FMT = new SimpleDateFormat
    ("dd-MMM-yyyy");
  @Inject ProjectTaskService service;

  @OnMessage
  public String retrieveProjectAndTasks(String message) {
    int projectId = Integer.parseInt(message.trim());
    List<Project> projects = service.findProjectById(projectId);
    StringWriter swriter = new StringWriter();

    JsonGeneratorFactory factory = Json.createGeneratorFactory
      (new HashMap<String,
        Object>(){{put(JsonGenerator.PRETTY_PRINTING, true);}});
    JsonGenerator generator = factory.createGenerator(swriter);

    generator.writeStartArray();
    for (Project project: projects) {
      generator.writeStartObject()
        .write("id", project.getId())
        .write("name", project.getName())
        .writeStartArray("tasks");
```

```
      for (Task task: project.getTasks()) {
        generator.writeStartObject()
          .write("id", task.getId())
          .write("name", task.getName())
          .write("targetDate", task.getTargetDate() == null ? "" :
             FMT.format(task.getTargetDate()))
          .write("completed", task.isCompleted())
          .writeEnd();
        }
      generator.writeEnd().writeEnd();
      }
    generator.writeEnd().close();

    return swriter.toString();
    }
}
```

Although the `ProjectWebSocketServerEndpoint` class looks complicated, it is actually easy to write. We declare POJO with the `@ServerEndpoint` annotation, which annotates it as a Java WebSocket endpoint, and it becomes available as a server. The WebSocket clients can interact with this endpoint, by sending text data to a web context defined URL. For example, on my test this is `http://localhost:8080/xentracket/sockets`. The `@ServerEndpoint` annotation accepts a URL pattern value.

In Java EE 7 we must also declare `ProjectWebSocketServerEndpoint` as a stateless EJB with `@Stateless` in order to inject the `ProjectTasksService` EJB as a dependency. (This is a consequence of Java for WebSocket 1.0 specification.) Note that we can use `@javax.annotation.Inject` from CDI.

The unit test `ProjectRESTServerEndpointTest` running in the IDE is as shown in the following screenshot:

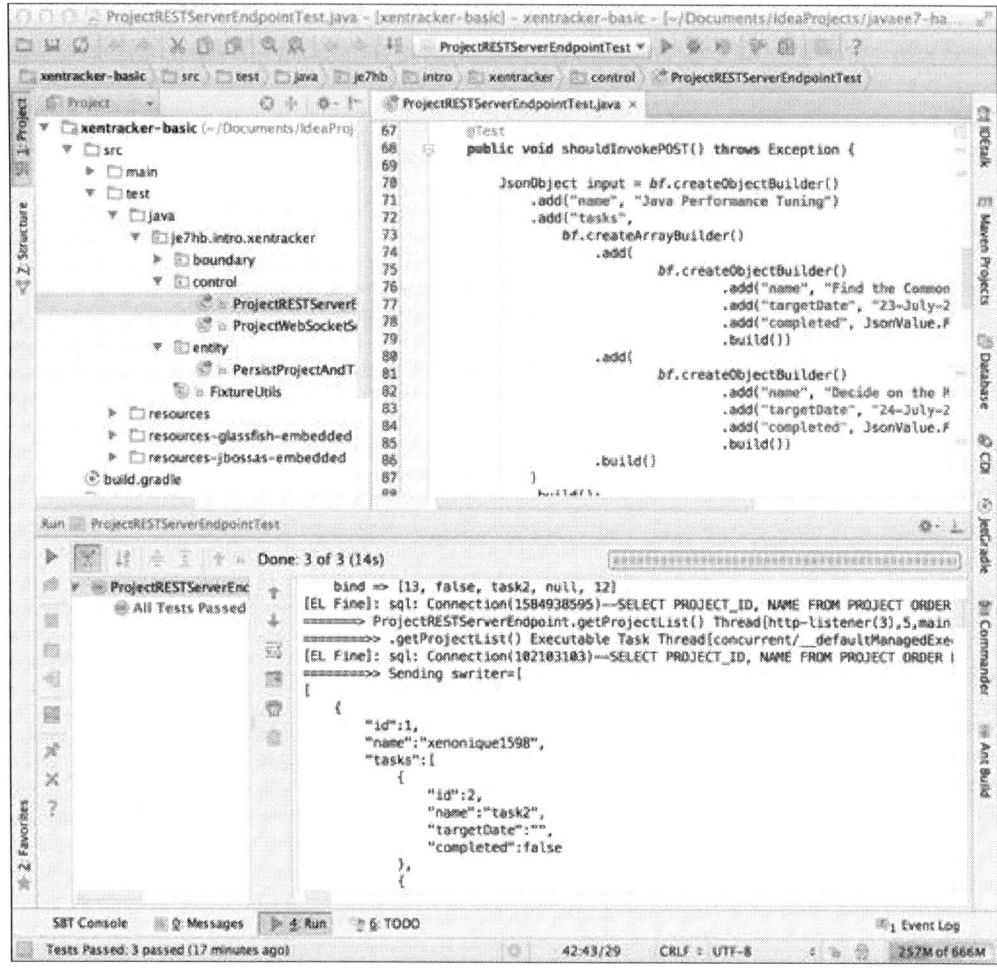

Next, we annotate the method `retrieveProjectAndTasks()` with the WebSocket annotation `@OnMessage`, which declares this method as the reception point for the incoming requests. There can be only one message per class per web application deployment.

Our method `retrieveProjectAndTasks()` accepts a text message, which we parse into a `project` ID integer. We then invoke the `ProjectTasksService` session to retrieve a list collection of the `Project` entities. Afterwards, we immediately turn that list into a JSON array output string using a `StringWriter` as a text buffer, and two new classes from the JSON-P streaming API namely: `JsonGeneratorFactory` and `JsonGenerator`.

We instantiate a `JsonGeneratorFactory` class with the literal Java `HashMap` trick to set up JSON output that is prettily printed. With the factory, we can write the JSON output using the fluent API `JsonGenerator`. The method call `writeStartArray()` starts the output stream for a JSON array. The method call `writeStartObject()` starts the output stream for a JSON object. We just call the generator's `write(String, X)` to send the JSON name and value pair. When we finish writing the JSON object and array, we must call `writeEnd()` to properly close `JsonValue`.

Finally, once we finish writing the JSON output, we call the generator's `close()` method. The target `java.io.StringWriter` now contains the JSON text value. The Java EE 7 WebSocket provider takes the return value and sends that data, the JSON array, to the other WebSocket peer. We shall quickly look at a JAX-RS example.

A RESTful endpoint

JAX-RS 2.0 is the RESTful standard framework for Java EE 7. We shall use JAX-RS to create the beginnings of a web application with a POJO that serves as a RESTful resource. In the interest of space in this book, we only consider the HTTP GET and POST methods. The GET method accepts a `project` ID and returns a JSON object that represents a project. The POST method accepts a JSON object and creates a new Project with or without dependent Task instances. The new Project instance returns as JSON.

The POJO class `ProjectRESTServerEndpoint` with a definition of a RESTful endpoint in the class called is as follows:

```
package je7hb.intro.xentracker.control;
import je7hb.intro.xentracker.boundary.ProjectTaskService;
import je7hb.intro.xentracker.entity.*;

import javax.ejb.Stateless;
import javax.inject.Inject;
import javax.json.*;
import javax.json.stream.*;
import javax.ws.rs.*;
```

```java
import java.io.StringWriter;
import java.text.SimpleDateFormat;
import java.util.*;
import static javax.ws.rs.core.MediaType.*;

@Path("/projects")
@Stateless
public class ProjectRESTServerEndpoint {
  static SimpleDateFormat FMT = new SimpleDateFormat
    ("dd-MMM-yyyy");
  static JsonGeneratorFactory jsonGeneratorFactory =
    Json.createGeneratorFactory();

  @Inject ProjectTaskService service;

  @GET @Path("/item")
  @Produces(APPLICATION_JSON)
  public String retrieveProject
    (@PathParam("id") @DefaultValue("0") int projectId ) {
    List<Project> projects = service.findProjectById(projectId);
    StringWriter swriter = new StringWriter();
    JsonGenerator generator =
      jsonGeneratorFactory.createGenerator(swriter);
    generateProjectsAsJson(generator, projects).close();
    return swriter.toString();
    }
  /* ... */
}
```

The `ProjectRESTServerEndpoint` is also a stateless session EJB and there really is no penalty in modern Java EE 7 products for how heavy a session EJB is. In fact, they are extremely lean; an application server for Java EE 7 can easily handle 10000 beans or more without issues. In the not too distant future, when we have Java EE standard for the cloud environment, the Java EE application server products will handle millions of EJBs and CDI managed beans.

We annotate the `ProjectRESTServerEndpoint` type with the JAX-RS annotation `@Path`, which notifies the JAX-RS provider that a POJO is an endpoint at the URL context path of `/projects`. For the JAX-RS projects, normally we also define an application path root, and it stands in front of the individual endpoints. For instance, on my test server the full URL context is `http://localhost:8080/xentracker/rest/projects/item`.

You have already seen the injection of the EJB `ProjectTaskService`, but we now see the `@GET` annotation from JAX-RS on the method `retrieveProject()`, which designates the endpoint for the HTTP `GET` requests from the client.

The `@PathParam` annotation identifies a parameter in the URL; it actually extracts a key parameter in the URL pattern. In this case, the parameter is called `id` in the input URL. For example, `http://localhost:8080/xentracker/rest/projects/item/1234` maps to the JAX-RS URL pattern `/projects/item/{id}`. Meanwhile, the `@DefaultValue` annotation defines a default `String` value, just in case the client did not specify the parameter, which avoids an error inside the server.

We refactor out the JSON generator code from before and simply call a static method in order to generate the correct output. Finally, the `@Produces` annotation informs the JAX-RS provider that his RESTful resource endpoint produces JSON.

Let's examine one RESTful endpoint for the HTTP `POST` request, where we want to insert a new project into the database. The definition method `createProject()` is as follows:

```
@POST @Path("/item")
@Consumes(APPLICATION_JSON)
@Produces(APPLICATION_JSON)
public String createProject(JsonObject projectObject)
throws Exception {
  Project project = new Project(projectObject.getString("name"));
  JsonArray tasksArray = projectObject.getJsonArray("tasks");
  if (tasksArray ! = null) {
    for (int j = 0; j<tasksArray.size(); ++j) {
      JsonObject taskObject = tasksArray.getJsonObject(j);
      Task task = new Task(taskObject.getString("name"),
        (taskObject.containsKey("targetDate") ?
        FMT.parse(taskObject.getString("targetDate")): null),
         taskObject.getBoolean("completed"));
      project.addTask(task);
      }
    }

  service.saveProject(project);
  StringWriter swriter = new StringWriter();
  JsonGenerator generator =
    jsonGeneratorFactory.createGenerator(swriter);
  writeProjectAsJson(generator, project).close();
  return swriter.toString();
  }
```

Java EE 7 HTML5 Productivity

The method is annotated with `@POST` from JAX-RS. It consumes and produces JSON, so we annotate it with `@Consumes` and `@Produces`. JAX-RS knows about JSON-P in the Java EE 7 edition, so our method directly accepts a `JsonObject` instance. In other words, we get the conversion from a `String` to a `JsonObject` object for free!

Unfortunately, we must retrieve individually the name, value, and array pairs from the JSON input, and create our domain objects. There is no substitute for work. Given `JsonObject`, we build a new `Project` instance, and optionally the associated `Task` objects. `JsonObject` has a number of convenient calls such as `getString()`, `getNumber()`, and `getBoolean()`. Unfortunately, we must convert the formatted target date string and we must deal with the optional JSON tasks array, because it can be null. It is possible to check if the value exists in the `JsonObject` object by calling `containsKey()`, since a `JsonObject` is a type of `java.util.Map`.

Once we have the `Project` instance, we save it to the database using the `ProjectTaskService` boundary service. Afterwards, we use the refactored JSON generator method to write the `Project` instance to the client.

To complete our brief tour of JAX-RS, we shall add another HTTP `GET` method to our RESTful endpoint. This time, however, we will make it asynchronous in operation. The home page of our web application `XenTracker` always executes an AJAX request; whenever it loads in the browser, it queries all of the projects in the database. Let's say 1000 web users are simultaneously accessing the application in a couple of minutes and each user has say an average of 10 projects with an average of 25 tasks between them, how would we scale this query?

With a stateless session EJB such as `ProjectRESTServerEndpoint`, we can use the new Concurrency Utilities API in Java EE 7 to achieve an asynchronous output. Let us apply it to the method `getProjectList()` now as follows:

```
/* ... */
import javax.ws.rs.container.AsyncResponse;
import javax.ws.rs.container.Suspended;

/* ... */
public class ProjectRESTServerEndpoint {
  /* ... */
  @Resource(name = "concurrent/LongRunningTasksExecutor")
  ManagedExecutorService executor;

  @GET
  @Path("/list")
  @Produces(MediaType.APPLICATION_JSON)
```

```java
public void getProjectList
   (@Suspended final AsyncResponse asyncResponse) {
  executor.submit(new Runnable() {
    @Override
    public void run() {
      List<Project> projects = service.findAllProjects();
      StringWriter swriter = new StringWriter();
      JsonGenerator generator = jsonGeneratorFactory
      .createGenerator(swriter);
      generateProjectsAsJson(generator, projects)
      .close();
      Response response =
        Response.ok(swriter.toString()).build();
      asyncResponse.resume(response);
    }
  });
}
}
```

In JAX RS 2.0 we must also add a special class as a method parameter. `AsyncResponse` is the object context for an asynchronous response. The `AsyncResponse` object has all of the server-side information to enable the JAX-RS API to send data back to the client from another Java thread from the executor thread pool. Typically, the application retrieves a Concurrent Utility Task (new in Java EE 7, see *Appendix D, Java EE 7 Assorted Topics*), which is the responding thread, and for long-running operations it is not associated with the main JAX-RS request processing thread. The parameter `asyncResource` is also annotated with `@Suspended` in order to suspend the output of the response, because we want to halt the response until the application invokes the long-running task. Inside the task, given an `AsyncResponse object`, we call the `resume` method with the JAX-RS response to send back to the client. Note that in this example, because we are using an inner class `Runnable`, we must set the method parameter's modifier to `final`.

We take advantage of the Concurrency Utilities API; in particular, we inject a `ManagedExecutorService` into the EJB with the `@Resource` annotation. The `@Resource` annotation is from Common Annotation API such as, `@Inject`, but it injects the database connection, connectors, and now managed concurrency services. The method `getProjectList()` is exactly one statement long. It creates a `Runnable` task, an anonymous inner class, and then submits it to the executor pool running inside the Java EE 7 application server. At some point after the submission, the task is invoked, and it delivers a response to the RESTful client on a separate thread.

> **Ramping up on Java concurrency**
>
>  The best book of multiple threads programming in Java with JVM at the time of writing is *Java Concurrency in Practice* by *Brian Goetz*, Oracle's Java language architect. The author strongly recommends this book to learn how to use the Java concurrency features such as synchronization primitives, executors as in Java EE 7, atomic wrappers, futures, and scheduled services.

The `Runnable` task instantiates a `java.ws.rs.core.Response` object instance in order to build a generic entity, which is the list of projects generated as JSON. Our most important responsibility is to cause the output to be sent back to the client by resuming an asynchronous response context; we invoke the method `AsyncResponse.resume()` with the generic response.

This is the end of the worked example tour of some new features of Java EE 7. The full application can be found with this book's source code. There are two variations of the `XenTracker` application: an initial edition, and a completely refined and finessed business example.

The Entity Control Boundary pattern

This worked example is based on a recent Java EE design pattern called the **Entity Control Boundary (ECB)** design pattern. It identifies a component part of a system from key perspectives: the entity, the control, and the boundary.

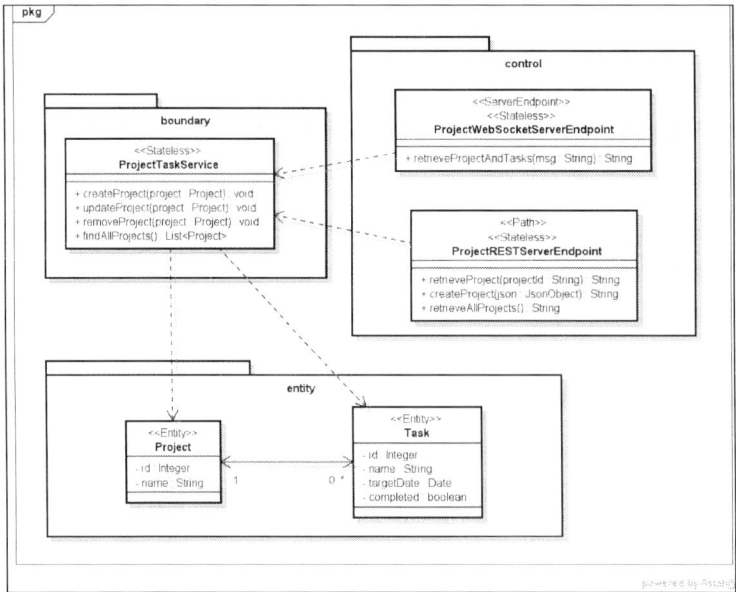

The boundary layer of the component represents the separation of the business and presentation code. In our worked example, we placed the `ProjectTaskService` EJB in the boundary subpackage, because effectively it is the business façade of the application.

The control layer of the component manages the flow of data to the internal data inside the component. We placed `ProjectWebSocketServerEndpoint` and `ProjectRESTServerEndpoint` in the control subpackage because these POJOs are manipulating the entities on behalf of the client side. Of course, it is a matter of debate and decent architectural sense whether business logic is placed either on the boundary or on the control layers in the application's architecture.

Finally, the entity layer of the component is reserved for the application's domain objects. We placed the entity beans `Project` and `Task` in the entity subpackage, because they are rich domain objects managed by JPA.

Summary

Java EE 7 is a step towards moving the Enterprise platform to a cloud-computing platform. Until we get to the next standard, Java EE 7 offers HTML5 productivity, and it delivers new features such as WebSocket, asynchronous communications over Servlets, RESTful endpoints, and Concurrent Utilities.

We covered in the first chapter the new features in Java EE 7 by first explaining the HTML5 movement. HTML5, we learned, is more than just a markup language, it also embraces semantics, a much improved document structure, APIs for mobile-device awareness, 3D graphics, support for the Canvas drawing, offline storage, styling content through CSS3, and exciting new APIs such as WebSocket and Web Worker.

By now we understand the overall architecture of the Java EE 7 platform. The platform sits between the infrastructure of the hardware including the operating system, network, filing systems, and the JVM-and the thousands of web clients and other business-to-business consumers. All of these are boundaries and are considered endpoints. There are two different profiles available in Java EE 7 standard: the Full and Web Profiles. The Web Profile is a reduced set of JSRs.

We took the time to examine a worked example of Java EE 7 new features with a web application called `XenTracker`. We saw highlights such as WebSocket and an asynchronous JAX-RS output.

In the subsequent chapters, we will introduce **Gradle** as a build system. The book's source code relies entirely on Gradle. We will learn how to write the integration tests with Java EE 7 application by using an open source framework called **Arquillian**. We use some Arquillian to clearly demonstrate the features of Java EE 7 and also rely on the embedded application server container, the reference implementation GlassFish 4 open source application server.

The next chapter gets us further in understanding the DHM of Java EE 7, by rolling the ball with CDI.

2
Context and Dependency Injection

Ray Charles said, "I am not a blues singer. I am not a jazz singer. I am not a country singer. But I am a singer who can sing the blues, who can sing jazz, who can sing country."

This chapter covers the important and essential framework that is the soul of Java EE 7. It is called Context and Dependency Injection. The API first made its appearance, officially, in Java EE 6, and now in Java EE 7 is the paramount framework for binding dependent managed beans together.

Before we get started, it may be helpful for us to revise some software engineering definitions.

Software engineering definitions

- **What is a context, or rather what do we mean by a context?**: In software engineering, a context is a separation of a concern around a set of components, objects, functions, and variables that have a determined lifecycle around the scope. The context exists for the overall lifetime of an application and it can be repeated. In CDI, the context is the meta-information that surrounds a POJO: the lifecycle, the scope, the dependencies to other objects, and the interactions.

- **What is a domain?**: The domain is the purpose of the software application and describes the business sector, market, or principal reason that requires the software. The software architects and designers are overheard in corridors at work and conferences discussing the business domain. After all, the software serves some purpose and thus the domain describes the reason for its existence, whether it is an airline reservation system, an electronic commerce application, or the front office trading system at an investment bank. The domain reflects the requirements for software and it is not the same as context, because a domain is an architectural characteristic.

- **What is a Java interface?**: A Java interface is a programming language feature that permits unrelated object types to share behaviors (methods), and thus provides a means of communication whilst allowing those objects to maintain the separation of domain.

- **What is encapsulation?**: Encapsulation is a programming language feature of Java and other object-oriented languages that permits the bundling of data with the operation that behaves on that data. Java supports encapsulation through the class `keyword`.

- **What is polymorphism?**: Polymorphism is the ability to create a variable, function, or type that has more than one form. Polymorphism is exhibited in Java with object types that share a common hierarchy sharing methods of the same name.

- **What is method overloading?**: Method overloading in the Java programming language is the ability to create multiple behaviors (methods) with the same name, where the parameter types differ.

- **What is a dependency?**: A dependency is an association between two different object types, where the primary type requires a reference to another secondary object type. A dependency serves as an interaction between the source and target types.

- **What is a dependency injection?**: A dependency injection is the function of an external lifecycle manager to establish the association between the primary and secondary object types and automatically introduce the dependency before the methods are invoked on the primary object. Usually, this dependency injection means retrieving the object instance from a special factory instance, rather than instantiating the objects directly. The external lifecycle manager can be an application framework, part of a computing platform, or even a feature of the programming language. In a Java framework, APIs such as Java EE and Context Dependency Injection, SEAM, Guice, and Spring Framework provide dependency injection.

Now that we have those definitions in our forebrains, let us move on to CDI properly.

The Context and Dependency Injection service

CDI stands for **Context and Dependency Injection**. It was originally standardized as JSR-299. The Hibernate object relation mapper inventor and Ceylon lead developer, *Gavin King* submitted the proposal called *Web Beans* to the Enterprise-expert group in 2006. The name of the JSR was changed in 2009 from Web Beans to CDI for the Java EE platform. The JSR-299 specification for CDI was aligned with the specification JSR-330, dependency injection for Java, which was jointly developed by Guice creator *"Crazy" Bob Lee* and Spring Framework creator, *Rod Johnson*.

CDI is upgraded to version 1.1 for Java EE 7 standard and the JSR is 346.

CDI was inspired and influenced by other existing dependency injection frameworks including SEAM, Guice, and Spring Framework. CDI features stronger typing than SEAM, and relies on lesser external XML configuration than Spring Framework.

The original purpose of CDI was to unify the managed bean component model in Java Server Faces with the then EJB component model. However, CDI now far exceeds the original remit in Java EE 7 as the universal component model for the Enterprise.

The first responsibility of CDI is the context. CDI provides the lifecycle management of the stateful components to well-defined, but extensible lifecycle context.

The second responsibility of CDI is dependency injection. CDI provides the ability to inject dependencies (components) into an application in a typesafe way, which includes the configurability to decide which component implementation is injected at the deployment stage.

- CDI is a framework available in both the client and server.
- CDI decouples the client from the server and thus supports loose coupling. This means the target implementation can vary without affecting the client.
- CDI is all about automatic lifecycle management with collaborating components. CDI provides the components with contextual information. The strong typing of the CDI model means that the errors are caught at compilation rather than encountering a `ClassCastException` at the execution time.
- The stateful components can have their dependency injected safely and can interact with other services by simple calling methods.
- CDI also has a lifecycle event model. Interested objects can register themselves to listen to the event notifications.
- CDI has the ability to decorate the injected components and the ability to associate the interceptors with the components in a typesafe fashion.

The following diagram illustrates the built-in contextual scopes inside the CDI container:

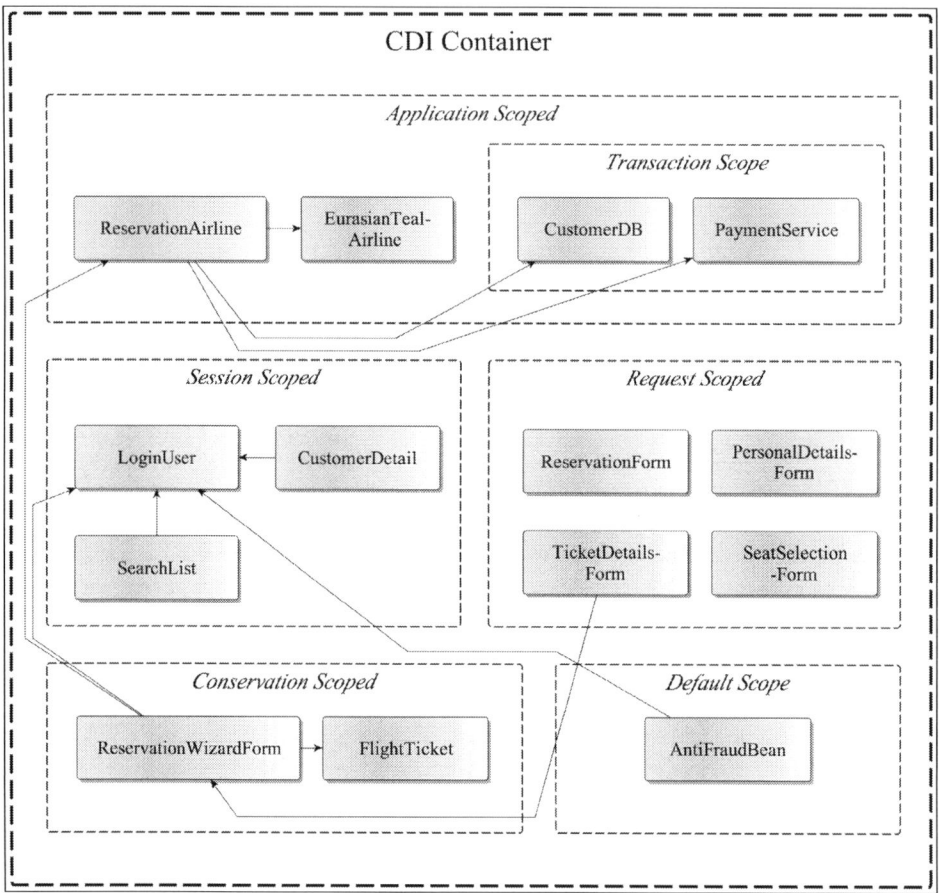

Beans and bean types

A bean in CDI is a source of the contextual objects that define the application state with or without a logic. Almost any Java object can be treated as a CDI bean.

Beans are instantiated by the CDI container and their lifecycle is determined by the stateful context that they belong to. In other words, all CDI beans have a stateful context.

CDI 1.1 chiefly describes the environment around the Java EE environment, although the implementation such as JBoss Weld can execute in the Java SE standalone application.

Inside a Java EE environment there are components known as managed beans. A CDI bean is one that is managed by the CDI container, whereas the EJB container manages EJB, and the Servlet container manages a Java Servlet. In Java EE 7, the CDI container is different from the other two containers, EJB and Servlet, in terms of managing the stateful component beans by the contextual instances.

Formally, a CDI bean has the following attributes:

- One or more bean type that is not empty
- Associated with at least one qualifier
- Has a determined and well-defined CDI scope
- Has a set of interceptor bindings
- Has a bean implementation
- Optionally can have an **expression language** (EL) bean name

In the CDI specification, the bean type refers to the managed object inside the container. The visibility of the bean type is defined from its *scope* and also lifecycle. It is worth remarking that almost all the Java types can be CDI bean types.

The Java types that can be CDI bean types are as follows:

- A bean type may be a Java interface, a concrete class, or an abstract class, and it may be declared final or have final methods.
- A bean type may be a generic type with the type parameters and variables.
- A bean type may be an array type.
- A bean type may be a primitive Java type, which means that the corresponding wrapper types will be used and instantiated. The wrapper types are defined in the package `java.lang`.
- A bean type may be raw type, which is a Java Collection type that is parameterized as compilation type (Pre Java SE 5).

Given the preceding rules most non-Java EE plain old objects can be automatically treated as CDI bean types and no special declarations are required. The CDI container behind the scenes will proxy the bean instances and it uses the Java Reflection API with the byte-code manipulation. Therefore, there are certain circumstances where the container cannot create a certain bean type.

Context and Dependency Injection

The exceptions to the rules are as follows:

- The bean type does not have a public default no-argument constructor
- The bean type is an inner class that is declared not static
- The bean type is not a concrete class
- The bean type is annotated with `@Decorator`
- The bean type is a class that declares a final or has a final method
- The bean type is annotated with the EJB component defining annotation or declared as an EJB class in the deployment XML configuration `ejb-jar.xml`
- The bean type is an array or a primitive type

Let us summarize some of these definitions into a handy reference as follows:

Term	Definition
Bean type	The bean type is the type hierarchy that the bean provides, which of course, is the interface or class, and ancestor types. The CDI injection container always uses the type as the primary identifier for determining whether a bean will provide an instance.
Qualifier	A qualifier is a way to distinguish between multiple beans that implement a desired bean type. Qualifiers are the type safe annotations and allow a client to choose between multiple bean-type implementations.
Scope	CDI beans all have a well-defined scope, which determines the lifecycle and the visibility of the instances. The CDI scopes are fully extensible and the standard provides built-in scopes, which includes the request, session, application, and conversation scope. The beans can also be dependent and inherit the scope of their injection scope.
EL name	A bean may define an EL name. The facility is provided for non-type safe access. EL names tend to be used by the Java Server Faces views. They can only be used by external and extension frameworks, which are built on top of Java EE standard.
Interceptors	A CDI interceptor is a feature that allows the developers to implement crosscutting concerns, such as security or logging as a bean's methods are invoked. Interceptors are a step up from the classic decorator design pattern.
Implementation	All CDI beans by definition provide an implementation of the types that define them. Implementations are typically in a class.

Basic injection

The key principle of dependency injection, from the definition, is that only the beans instantiated by the CDI container are managed. The CDI container is the external lifecycle provider and the way you behave with it is to respect the cardinal rule, "Don't call us, we'll call you.", *The Hollywood Agency principle*.

Before CDI, in Java EE 5 specification there was already injection from the EJB container objects `@EJB`, `@PersistenceContext`, `@PersistenceUnit`, and `@Resource`. Unfortunately only components known to the application server could be injected in such a scheme. CDI is a general-purpose dependency injection framework and it is type safe.

Let us assume we are able to run inside a CDI container, and we are building an airline reservation application. We will define a couple of types defined by their contract, such as an airline and a payment service.

Some Java interface declarations for a software domain-flight reservation system are as follows:

```
interface CreditService {
  void check();
  }

interface Airline {
  void reserve();
  }
```

The context for these bean types `CreditService` and `Airline` implies a user story about making an airline reservation. For now, we will assume that the lifetime of the bean typed live for the duration of the application.

Field injection

For our first example, let us create an airline reservation system as a simple CDI bean.

```
public class ReservationService {
  @Inject Airline airline;
  }
```

This class `ReservationService` uses a CDI managed bean and it does not yet do anything special. We do, however, declare a dependency on an `Airline` instance though. The annotation `@javax.inject.Inject` declares that the field `airline` will be associated with the default `Airline` type object. We call this field *injection*. Let us proceed a bit further.

Setter injection

```
public class ReservationService {
  @Inject
  public void setAirline(Airline airline) {
    /* Do something here */
  }
}
```

We can attach the `@Inject` annotation to a setter method too.

What happens if we are in a situation where another colleague has developed the code already and there was a method to initialize the object already there. CDI can also help us in this situation. Look at the following declaration for a `ReservationService` class:

```
public class ReservationService {
  @Inject
  public void startVTTYConnection
    (Airline airline, PaymentService ps) {
    /* ... */
  }
}
```

CDI copes with the initialization methods seamlessly. In fact, CDI allows a web bean to have multiple injection and initialization points.

Constructor injection

CDI can also inject the dependencies into the constructors. It is all quite type safe as follows:

```
public class ReservationService {
  @Inject
  public ReservationService(Airline airline, PaymentService ps) {
    /* ... */
  }
}
```

Wherever a constructor is declared with the `@Inject` annotation, the CDI container injects any dependent instances that it finds in the contextual scope of the target bean type. The CDI container also injects any necessary field instances in the bean type by the time the constructor is called that are appropriate to the field's contextual instance. We will talk more about scope later in this chapter.

>  For constructor injection, a CDI bean type can only have one constructor with the injection points.

If the bean does not declare a constructor with a `@Inject` annotation, the CDI container will call the no-arguments constructor. The default is called only if there are no other constructors defined.

The CDI injection is type safe and exceedingly appropriate for simple POJOs.

Qualifiers

Qualifiers allow CDI to differentiate by beans with the same type. A qualifier configures a specific bean type to be injected into the target object.

Qualifiers are defined with the Java interface annotations. They are defined as `@Target({METHOD, FIELD, PARAMETER, and TYPE})` and `@Retention(RUNTIME)`. There are standard qualifiers in CDI, but you may also define your custom qualifier for your own projects.

Let us define two more example qualifiers.

```
@Qualifier
@Retention(RUNTIME)
@Target({METHOD, FIELD, PARAMETER, TYPE})
public @interface ShortTermCredit { }
```

This is for a credit service provider to annotate the short-term applications.

```
@Qualifier
@Retention(RUNTIME)
@Target({METHOD, FIELD, PARAMETER, TYPE})
public @interface LongTermCredit { }
```

And this one is for the long-term applications.

Using the knowledge we now have, we can simply write a CDI implementation for a short-term provider.

```
interface CreditProvider {
  double computeAPR(double criteria, double base);
}

@ShortTerm
```

Context and Dependency Injection

```
class HighStreetCreditProvider implements CreditProvider {
  double computeAPR(double criteria, double base) {
    return 24.753;
  }
}
```

The class `HighStreetCreditProvider` can be injected into a target, if the injection point specifies the `@ShortTermCredit` annotation.

```
class CreditService {
  @Inject @ShortTerm CreditProvider shortTermProvider;
  @Inject @LongTerm  CreditProvider longTermProvider;

  public void processCredit() {/* ... */}
  /* ... */
}
```

Qualifiers also work with the CDI productions. The following is a long-term credit provider that provides more reasonable annual percentage age albeit for a much longer term:

```
class GuiltsCreditProvider implements CreditProvider {
  double computeAPR( double criteria, double base ) {
    return 1.41457;
  }

  int months() {return 66;}

  @Produces
  @LongTerm
  public CreditProvider createCreditProvider() {
    return new GuiltsCreditProvider();
  }
}
```

Built-in qualifiers

Here is a table of the built-in qualifiers in Context and Dependency Injection.

Qualifier Name	Description
`@javax.enterprise.inject.Any`	This is the qualifier given to every bean instantiated and managed by the CDI container. It is also the qualifier supplied to the injection points. The only exception is where declaration is with the `@New` qualifier.
`@javax.enterprise.inject.Default`	If a bean does not explicitly declare a qualifier other than `@Named`, the bean has the qualifier `@Default`.
`@javax.enterprise.inject.Named`	This qualifier gives a CDI bean a name, which allows the JSF view or other presentation toolkit to refer it. Note that this access is not strongly typed at the compilation time.
`@javax.enterprise.inject.New`	The qualifier `@New` annotation causes a new instance to be created by the CDI container instead of using the contextual instance. In CDI 1.1, the use of `@New` is deprecated.

The CDI classpath scanning

How does CDI know exactly what classes to find in a JAR module? CDI scans the modules in an Enterprise application. In Java EE 6, the CDI container scans the Java archive files and searches for a `beans.xml` XML-deployment descriptor. For a simple JAR or an EJB module, it expects to find `META-INF/beans.xml`. In a WAR file, this file should be in the location `WEB-INF/beans.xml`. The `beans.xml` file is not meant for declaring the CDI beans, unlike Spring Framework.

The `beans.xml` file can be empty and its presence serves to trigger the CDI container to scan the archive. In Java EE 7 and in particular CDI 1.1, the presence of `beans.xml` is mandatory. Specifying a bean discovery mode in the XML file can control scanning.

```
<beans xmlns = "http://xmlns.jcp.org/xml/ns/javaee"
  xmlns:xsi = "http://www.w3.org/2001/XMLSchema-instance"
  xsi:schemaLocation = "http://xmlns.jcp.org/xml/ns/javaee
  http://xmlns.jcp.org/xml/ns/javaee/beans_1_1.xsd"
  version = "1.1" bean-discovery-mode = "all">
</beans>
```

The attribute `bean-discovery-mode` can have the following values: none, annotated, and all. The default value is annotated, which informs the CDI constructor to scan for all the annotated beans and dependencies; all means consider every object as a possible bean type, and none means do not scan this archive for the CDI bean types.

The `beans.xml` file determines Alternatives, Interceptors, and Decorators, about which we will learn later.

Factory production

How does CDI handle the situation, where your dependency instance does not have an arguments constructor? Sometimes we want to allow the application control to how and when to instantiate a bean type

CDI deals with factory creation with a feature called producers, which unsurprisingly involves the `@Produces` annotation. The fully qualified package annotation is called `@javax.enterprise.inject.Produces`, which informs the CDI container to create an instance of a bean type using the recipient method instead of instantiating the dependency by invoking its no-argument constructor.

Let's look at an example of a factory class as follows:

```
class EurasianTealAirline implements Airline {
  /* ... */
}

public class AirlineProducer {
  @Produces @Premium
  public Airline connectAirline() {
    return new EurasianAirline();
  }
}
```

The class `AirlineProducer` acts as a factory for the `Airline` components, which actually are the `EurasianAirline` types, and notice, it is also a premium business connection.

Traditionally, a factory is used to demarcate different type a of bean types in order to delay until runtime the type of object created because the calling code does not know the exact type of dependency. Usually, an enumerated value is passed to the factory in code or during external configuration. With CDI, we use special custom annotation for this.

It is instructional to see the qualifier annotation for the `@Premium` as follows:

```
import static java.lang.annotation.ElementType.FIELD;
import static java.lang.annotation.ElementType.METHOD;
import static java.lang.annotation.ElementType.PARAMETER;
import static java.lang.annotation.ElementType.TYPE;
import static java.lang.annotation.RetentionPolicy.RUNTIME;

import java.lang.annotation.Retention;
import java.lang.annotation.Target;

import javax.inject.Qualifier;

@Qualifier
@Retention(RUNTIME)
@Target({TYPE, METHOD, FIELD, PARAMETER})
public @interface Premium
```

We define a custom annotation with a runtime retention policy, which can be declared on the class, at a method call, before a type field, and in the method argument positions.

Given these definitions, we can use CDI to inject a specific dependency in a bean and/or service that we are using. If we have a Java-standalone application, a web frontend specifically for customers that only fly with the premium airline services, we would write something like the following:

```
public class FrontEndPremiumUI extends WebFrontController {
  @Inject @Premium private Airline luxuryService;

  public void handleForm
     (HttpRequest request, HttpResponse response, FormModel form) {
     luxuryService.reserve()

     /* ... */

     renderView(request, response);
  }

  /* ... */
}
```

Context and Dependency Injection

The key line of this user interface code is as the following:

```
@Inject @Premium private Airline luxuryService;
```

The line instructs the CDI container to inject a dependency of the `Airline` bean type that is specifically qualified as a `@Premium` into the bean `FrontEndPremiumUI`. The CDI container searches for a matching bean type and finds the factory `AirlineProducer`. It then invokes the method `connectAirline()`, which returns an instance of `EurasianTealAirline`.

There is an alternative to define a producer using the initialization method to construct an accessible field. The `producer` field is the value that will be injected into the targets.

```
public class AirlineProducerAlternative {
  @Produces @Premium Airline airline;

  @Inject
  public void initialize(SpecialContext ctx) {
    airline = new EurasianTealAirline(ctx);
  }
}
```

Inside the class `AirlineProducerAlternative`, we inform the CDI container that the field `airline` is initialized by the factory. In our application, we call the method `initialize()` in order to create a `EurasianTealAirline` component with a component `SpecialContext` that is also injected in.

The CDI container manages the lifecycle of the beans and adds contextual information to it. This means that the instances will be shared by other threads and components managed by the same CDI container.

We do not have to create and use qualifier for simple POJOs that have no discriminating bean types. The CDI container has a default qualifier for bean types. The annotation is called `@javax.enterprise.inject.Default`.

Generating new instances every time

Sometimes injecting a shared instance from the CDI container is not the behavior that your target bean requires. There are sometimes security issues, concurrency behaviors, and other object safety reasons where a new instance is required.

A new instance can be forced from CDI by using the @New annotation in a producer.

```
public class AirlineProducer {
  @Produces
  public Airline connectAirline(@New Airline airline) {
    return new EurasianAirline(airline);
  }
}
```

This @New annotation is very much like the prototype scope behavior as seen in Spring Framework.

Bean names and presentation views

There is another way to distinguish the CDI beans and that is to optionally give a bean a name. The main reason you would want to do this is to permit a bean to be referenced from the presentation view framework such as JSF. (A full chapter on JSF is out of scope for this book.)

To make a bean accessible through EL, use the @Named built-in qualifier.

```
@Inject @Named("longTermProvider") @LongTermCredit
CreditProvider guiltsProvider;
```

If you do not provide the name of the bean, then the @Named qualifier allows you to access the bean by using the name, with the first letter in lowercase. The following two injection points are equivalent in terms of referencing the same CDI bean by name.

```
class Donkey {  }

class DonkeyRider {
  @Inject @Named donkey donkey1;
  @Inject @Named('donkey') donkey2;
}
```

Both field variables donkey1 and donkey2 will reference the same CDI bean, provided that the CDI bean is not annotated with @New, of course.

To access the long-term credit bean through JSF, we would write something like the following inside a JSF **Facelet** view:

```
<div id = "promoArea">
  <h1>Amazing Credit Offer!</h2>
  <p>Only available to 30<sup>th</sup> September 2014</p>
  <h:form>
```

Context and Dependency Injection

```
      <h:inputText value = "#{applyForm.quote}"
        title = "quotation value"/>
      <h:inputText value = "#{applyForm.term}"
        title = "length of text"/>
      <h:commandButton value = "Apply Now!"
        id = "offerSubmitButton"
          action = "#{longTermProvider.applyForCredit}"/>
    </h:form>
</div>
```

This extraction of complicated JSF Facelet illustrates how a named CDI bean type is accessed in the `<h:commandButton>` tag. A customer clicking on the button invokes the method `applyForCredit()` on the CDI bean type.

Let's move onwards to the built-in CDI scopes. Illustration of the airline reservation system with several bean types' associated scopes is shown in the following screenshot:

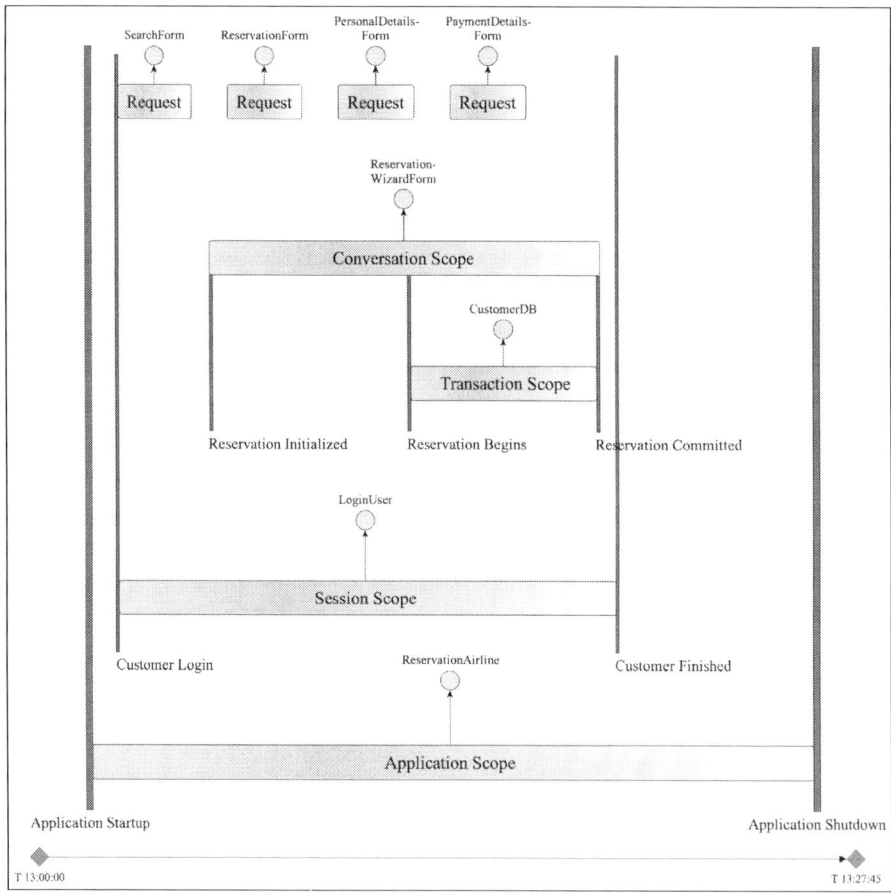

Bean scopes

In the CDI container there are five predefined scopes, and all of them apart from `@Dependent` are associated with a bean to provide contextual information. The scopes have different lifetimes and thus different durations.

Scope	Annotation	Duration
Request	`@RequestScoped`	The beans declared against the request scope live only in existence for the lifetime of HTTP Servlet Request, invocation of remote EJB, a delivery of message to a Message Driven Bean, or a web service endpoint. After the request has been serviced, the bean is destroyed.
Session	`@SessionScoped`	The beans declared against the session scope live for the lifetime of HTTP session, which is a user's interaction with a web application across multiple HTTP requests. The session scoped beans are only destroyed when the same HTTP session associated with them is destroyed.
Application	`@ApplicationScoped`	The beans declared against the application scope live for the lifetime of all users' interactions with a web application. In other words, the beans live as long as the web application executes in the managed web container and therefore, the CDI container. Only when the application is destroyed (or undeployed) are the associated application scope beans destroyed.

Scope	Annotation	Duration
Dependent	@Dependent	The beans declared against the dependent scope are never shared between the injection points. The injection of a dependent bean lives as long as the lifecycle of the target object to which they are bound. In other words, the CDI container does not manage the dependent beans.
Conversation	@ConversationScoped	The beans declared against the conversation scope are shared across multiple requests in the same HTTP session as long as they associate with the active conversation state. Once the beans fall out of the active connection state (workflow) they are primed for destruction by the CDI container.

For the historical record, the first three scopes are defined by JSR-299 CDI and the JSF API. The last two scopes are only defined by JSR-299.

Advanced Java EE developers can also extend and implement the custom scopes. In order to do so, new scope must declare with the @javax.inject.Scope annotation or @javax.enterprise.context.NormalScope meta-annotation. Beginners in CDI should stay clear of the extensions until they have gained suitable experience.

It is recommended that the developers use @javax.inject.Inject annotation as much as possible, especially for EJB references, over @javax.ejb.EJB. Try it!

CDI initialization and destruction

The applications can register the post-construction and pre-destruction callbacks on the CDI bean types.

The @PostConstruct annotation

When the CDI bean is created, it is associated with a scope. It is possible to register a lifecycle callback method that the CDI framework should call after dependency injection, but also before the class is put into the service.

First, in the managed bean or in any of its superclasses, you define a callback method, which performs the custom initialization. Second, annotate the method with the `@javax.annotation.PostConstruct` annotation.

```
class DVLA {
  static String generateKey() {/* ... */}
  static void clearAndReset(String key) {/* ... */}
}

class VehicleRegistration {
  private String dvlaKey;
  private String registration;

  @PostConstruct
  public void resetValues() {
    registration = "";
    dvlaKey = DVLA.generateKey("SWANSEA")
  }
}
```

The CDI container will call the `resetValues()` method in this bean type `VehicleRegistration` after all the injections have occurred; therefore, the bean has been fully wired after all the other initializers have been invoked. Sometimes an application wants to apply a look-up dependency to a third-party library as a late binding, and associating the component in the constructor is not appropriate.

The @PreDestroy annotation

When the CDI bean is created, it is associated with a scope. It is possible to register a lifecycle callback method that the CDI framework should call after dependency injection, but before the class is put into the service.

First, in the managed bean or in any of its superclasses, you define a callback method, which performs the custom initialization. Second, annotate the method with the `@javax.annotation.PreDestroy` annotation.

```
class DVLA {/* ... */}

class VehicleRegistration {
```

```
    private String dvlaKey;
    private String registration;
..
  @PreDestroy
  public void releaseCache() {
    DVLA.clearAndReset(registration);
  }
}
```

The CDI framework will invoke the `@PreDestroy` method before the bean type goes out of the contextual scope.

Programmatic Lookup of the CDI Beans

Although the CDI container follows the *Hollywood Agency Principle*, there is a way to retrieve a bean instance directly. The developers can programmatically ask for an instance of the bean type, to deal with special cases.

```
public class DVLARegistrationCentre {
  @Inject Instance<DVLA> dvla;
  public DVLA getDVLA() {
    return dvla.get();
  }
}
```

The `@javax.enterprise.inject.Instance` annotation allows the application to dynamically obtain the instances of the beans with a specified combination of qualifiers.

The class `DVLARegistrationCenter` has a method to retrieve the `DVLA` instance and the instance that is returned is decided by the designation. The `get()` method of the instance produces a contextual instance of the bean.

Qualifiers can be specified at the injection point with annotations.

```
@Target({METHOD, FIELD, PARAMETER, TYPE})
public @interface Police { }

@Target({METHOD, FIELD, PARAMETER, TYPE})
public @interface Secure { }

public class DVLARegistrationCentre {
  @Inject @Police @Secure Instance<DVLA> dvla;
  public DVLA getDVLA() {
    return dvla.get();
  }
}
```

In this case, we obtain a different Driver Vehicle Licensing Authority type specific to the UK civil government service and hopefully it is secure.

Advanced readers will notice that this looks extremely similar to the Spring Framework retrieval of the Spring bean from that dependency injection framework. The difference here is that the lookup is provided by the annotations, and therefore is strong typed, not by the name of the bean.

What types of special cases could there be?

- Instance lookup is useful if the qualifiers can vary dynamically at runtime
- We want to iterate over all the beans of a certain type
- We want to provide a fallback method, where there is no bean that satisfies the type and the set of qualifiers

The following is an example to iterate all the beans in the CDI container of a specified type:

```
class DVLA {
  public void init() {/*...*/}
  /* ... */
}

@Inject
void initRegistries(@Any Instance<DVLA> registries) {
  for (DVLA registry: registries) {
    registry.init();
  }
}
```

We use the `@Any` qualifier to override the `@Default` annotation in order to remove the restriction of the bean type suitable for injection. Remember, the `@Any` qualifier says that you are declaring an injection point, where you do care about contextual information of the CDI bean.

Configuring a CDI application

It is very easy to configure a CDI application. All you need to do is provide a file called `beans.xml`, which must be found on the classpath. The file can be completely empty. For web applications, the standard dictates that the `beans.xml` file must live in the `WEB-INF` directory. For the EJB modules or the JAR files must live in the `META-INF` directory.

Standalone CDI application

We have had enough theory. Let us now visit a sample application. This example will use the Java EE reference implementation project for CDI, which is called **Weld**. The Weld project is available on Red Hat JBoss website at `http://seamframework.org/Weld`.

In this example, we are using CDI 1.1, which is sufficient for the example. The project uses Gradle, the build system written in the Groovy programming language. Because we use Gradle in the book's source code, we present in this chapter only a very small guide to this build tool, which is gaining popularity among the leading developers.

The `build.gradle` file is as follows:

```
apply plugin: 'java'
apply plugin: 'maven'
apply plugin: 'eclipse'
apply plugin: 'idea'

// Define equivalent Maven GAV coordinates.
group = 'com.javaeehandbook.book1'
archivesBaseName = 'ch02-cdi-standalone'
version = '1.0'

repositories {
  mavenCentral()
}

dependencies {
  compile 'org.jboss.weld.se:weld-se-core:1.1.9.Final'
  compile 'org.slf4j:slf4j-simple:1.6.1'
  testCompile 'junit:junit:4.11'
}

task wrapper(type: Wrapper) {
  gradleVersion = '1.7'
}

// Override Gradle defaults - a force an exploded JAR view
sourceSets {
  main {
    output.resourcesDir = 'build/classes/main'
    output.classesDir = 'build/classes/main'
  }
```

```
  test {
    output.resourcesDir = 'build/classes/test'
    output.classesDir = 'build/classes/test'
  }
}

task(run, dependsOn: 'classes', type: JavaExec) {
  main = 'je7hb.standalone.HelloWorld'
  classpath = sourceSets.main.runtimeClasspath
  args 'Mary', 'Peter', 'Jane'
}
```

The source code sample in project is organized in a directory structure exactly the same as an Apache Maven 3 project. The source code lives under the folder paths `src/main/java` and `src/main/resources`, and the test code lives under `src/test/java` and `src/test/resources`. These folder paths are relative to the root of the project.

The entire code to the main program that we execute in the standalone Weld container is as follows:

```
package je7hb.standalone;

import org.jboss.weld.environment.se.Weld;
import org.jboss.weld.environment.se.WeldContainer;
import org.jboss.weld.environment.se.bindings.Parameters;
import org.jboss.weld.environment.se.events.*;

import javax.enterprise.event.Observes;
import javax.inject.Singleton;
import java.util.List;

@Singleton
public class HelloWorld {
  public void initialMe(@Observes ContainerInitialized event,
    @Parameters List<String> parameters) {
    System.out.println("Initialization from CDI");
    for (int j = 0; j<parameters.size(); ++j) {
      String param = parameters.get(j);
      System.out.printf("parameters[%d] = %s\n", j, param);
    }
    System.out.println("Complete.");
  }
```

Context and Dependency Injection

```java
    public void greet(String[] names) {
      System.out.print("Hello ");
      for (int j = 0; j<names.length; ++j) {
        System.out.printf("%s%s",(j > 0 ? (j == names.length-1 ?
          " and " : ", ") : ""), names[j]);
      }
      System.out.println();
    }

    public static void main(String[] args) {
      Weld weld = new Weld();
      WeldContainer container = weld.initialize();

      HelloWorld helloBean = container.instance()
        .select(HelloWorld.class).get();
      helloBean.greet(args);

      weld.shutdown();
    }
  }
```

Here are some remarks about the `HelloWorld` example. The Java EE 7 does not define a standard standalone API for CDI yet, so we have to import in the classes directly from the reference implementation Weld SE.

In the main program, we programmatically bootstrap the CDI container. Once the `WeldContainer` is initialized, we can obtain the bean instances quite easily. The `HelloWorld` instance is a `@Singleton` object and is retrieved from the container. The code is exhibit type safety and there is no casting required to get the object instance. Once we have the instance, we invoke the methods on it just like any another object.

Finally, in order to complete this example, we need an empty `beans.xml` file. This file is stored under the folder path `src/main/resources/META-INF`.

Building the standalone project with Gradle

In order to build the project, you need Gradle installed on your system workstation. You can download the latest distribution from the Gradle official website: `http://www.gradle.org/downloads`

In order to build the example, just execute the following command line:

`gradle build`

If you need a loadable project for Eclipse, execute the following command line:

`gradle eclipse`

If you need a loadable project for JetBrains' IDEA, execute the following command instead:

`gradle idea`

Any of the preceding Gradle commands will generate the project files that will import the files into your favorite **Integrated Developer Environment** (**IDE**). Once you have the project in the IDE, running the `HelloWorld` program with the arguments `Jane, Peter, Mary`, produces the output:

```
Initialization from CDI framework
Complete.
Hello Jane, Peter and Mary

Process finished with exit code 0
```

You can also execute the example from the command line, with the Gradle custom command from the script.

`Gradle run`

To build a project with Gradle, one executes the following command:

`gradle build`

To reset the project to clean state, one executes the following command:

`gradle clean`

Of course Gradle is a fully featured build environment with scores of additional tasks and commands. I recommend you visit the Gradle website (http://gradle.org) to learn more about Gradle. Packt Publishing also has a recent book: *Gradle Effective Implementation Guide* by *Hubert Klein Ikkink*. You will also find out about the build environment and tools in the appendices at the end of this book.

Using the DeltaSpike CDI container tests

Let us take a different tack. Although there is no standard API for using CDI outside of a Java EE environment such as standalone Java SE, there is a project called DeltaSpike. This is an open source project that defines a wrapper API around two common CDI implementations JBoss Weld and Apache Open Web Beans. The URL is http://deltaspike.apache.org/.

Let us modify the Gradle build script to add dependencies for the Weld container as follows:

```
// Define equivalent Maven GAV coordinates.
group = 'com.javaeehandbook.book1'
archivesBaseName = 'ch02-cdi-standalone'
version = '1.0'
ext.deltaspikeVersion = '0.3-incubating'

dependencies {
  compile 'org.jboss.weld.se:weld-se-core:1.1.9.Final'
  compile 'org.slf4j:slf4j-simple:1.6.1'
  compile "org.apache.deltaspike.cdictrl:deltaspike-cdictrl-api:
    ${deltaspikeVersion}"
  compile "org.apache.deltaspike.cdictrl:deltaspike-cdictrl-weld:
    ${deltaspikeVersion}"

  testCompile 'junit:junit:4.11'
}
```

This is almost the same definition as before, except for the dynamic property deltaspikeVersion, which allows the version number of the dependency to be configured to be changed. Incidentally, you can switch to the other DeltaSpike implementation, Apache Open Web Beans, by changing the dependency to:

```
dependencies {
  compile 'org.apache.openwebbeans:openwebbeans-impl:1.1.6'
  compile 'org.apache.openwebbeans:openwebbeans-ee:1.1.6'
  compile "org.apache.deltaspike.cdictrl:
    deltaspike-cdictrl-api: ${deltaspikeVersion}"
```

```
    compile "org.apache.deltaspike.cdictrl:
      deltaspike-cdictrl-owb: ${deltaspikeVersion}"
    /* ... */
    }
```

Let us create a couple of qualifier annotations. We create one to represent a premium and expensive service, and a second to represent a budget service.

```
// Economy.java
@Qualifier
@Retention(RUNTIME)
@Target({TYPE, METHOD, FIELD, PARAMETER})
public @interface Economy { }

// Premium.java
@Qualifier
@Retention(RUNTIME)
@Target({TYPE, METHOD, FIELD, PARAMETER})
public @interface Premium { }
```

The preceding annotation must exist in separate Java class files. Next, we will create a traveler service for airlines. The service is not at all useful, but it will demonstrate the testing, the qualifiers, and the dependency injection. It will simply allow us to retrieve a random flight given an airline code.

```
public interface TravelService {
  FlightSet findRandomByAirline(String airline);
}
```

The simplified definition of the budget travel service, unsurprisingly, called BudgetTravelServiceImpl is as follows:

```
@Economy
public class BudgetTravelServiceImpl implements TravelService {
  @Override
  public FlightSet findRandomByAirline(String airline) {
    Airline airlineBudget = new Airline("CHP","Cheap Budget");
    return new FlightSet(Arrays.asList(new AirlineRoute(
      "LGW", "DUB", parseDate("20131110-12:30:00 GMT"),
        parseDate("20131110-14:00:00 GMT"),
          airlineBudget, 69.0), new AirlineRoute("LHW", "PAR",
            parseDate("20131110-16:45:00 -0500 GMT"),
              parseDate("20131110-20:00:00 -0700 +0100"),
                airlineBudget, 79.0)));
  }
}
```

Context and Dependency Injection

We can also define an expensive service called `TravelFunkServiceImpl` as follows:

```
@Premium
public class TravelFunkServiceImpl implements TravelService {
  @Override
  public FlightSet findRandomByAirline(String airline) {
    Airline airlineBrit = new Airline("BRS","British Stars");
    return new FlightSet(Arrays.asList(new AirlineRoute(
      "NYC", "SFO", parseDate("20131110-16:45:00 -0500"),
        parseDate("20131110-20:00:00 -0700"),
          airlineBrit, 250.0)));
  }
}
```

So now, we write an elegant and a simple unit test with the `DeltaSpike` library to verify the CDI container (either JBoss Weld or Apache Open Web Beans) injects the correct travel service according to the qualifier annotation.

```
package je7hb.travelfunk;
import je7hb.standalone.*;
import org.junit.Test;
import javax.inject.Inject;
import static org.junit.Assert.assertNotNull;

public class TravelServiceTest extends AbstractCdiContainerTest {
  @Inject @Premium TravelService premiumTravelService;
  @Inject @Economy TravelService economyTravelService;

  @Test
  public void shouldInjectPremiumService() {
    System.out.printf("premiumTravelService=%s\n",
      premiumTravelService);
    assertNotNull(premiumTravelService);
    FlightSet flight =
      premiumTravelService.findRandomByAirline("BRS");
    assertNotNull( flight );
  }

  @Test
  public void shouldInjectEconomyService() {
    System.out.printf("economy=%s\n", economyTravelService);
    assertNotNull(economyTravelService);
    FlightSet flight =
      economyTravelService.findRandomByAirline("BRS");
    assertNotNull(flight);
  }
}
```

The distilled magic of the `DeltaSpike` library lies within the `AbstractCdiContainerTest` implementation, which is part of this book's source code project. For JUnit testing, we need to make sure that we have a brand new CDI container for the invocation of the test methods. There is a restriction for the CDI container, in that they do not play very well in parallel executions from the same Java `ClassLoader`; therefore, before each test method is invoked, we first have to make sure that the container is initialized appropriately and also the conversation context is cleared. The following source code is targeted for JUnit; you will need to modify it accordingly for another testing framework such as TestNG.

First, the CDI container is created with the static method of `CdiContainerLoader`, which will retrieve a JBoss Weld or Apache Open Web Beans. The container is instantiated in the static helper method `startUpContainer()`, because we want only to initialize the test container when the test class is loaded, and before test methods are invoked on it. Once we have the `CdiContainer` type, we boot up, and then start all of the conversational contexts in it.

```java
import org.apache.deltaspike.cdise.api.*;
import org.junit.*;
import javax.enterprise.context.RequestScoped;
import javax.enterprise.context.spi.CreationalContext;
import javax.enterprise.inject.spi.*;

public abstract class AbstractCdiContainerTest {
  protected static CdiContainer cdiContainer;

  @Before
  public final void setUp() throws Exception {
    cdiContainer.getContextControl()
    .stopContext(RequestScoped.class);
    cdiContainer.getContextControl()
    .startContext(RequestScoped.class);

    BeanManager beanManager = cdiContainer.getBeanManager();
    CreationalContext creationalContext =
      beanManager.createCreationalContext(null);

    AnnotatedType annotatedType =
      beanManager.createAnnotatedType(this.getClass());
    InjectionTarget injectionTarget =
      beanManager.createInjectionTarget(annotatedType);
    injectionTarget.inject(this, creationalContext);
  }
```

Context and Dependency Injection

```
    @After
    public final void tearDown() throws Exception {
      if (cdiContainer != null) {
        cdiContainer.getContextControl()
        .stopContext(RequestScoped.class);
        cdiContainer.getContextControl()
        .startContext(RequestScoped.class);
      }
    }

    @BeforeClass
    public final synchronized static void startUpContainer()
    throws Exception {
      cdiContainer = CdiContainerLoader.getCdiContainer();
      cdiContainer.boot();
      cdiContainer.getContextControl().startContexts();
    }

    @AfterClass
    public final synchronized static void shutdownContainer()
    throws Exception {
      if (cdiContainer != null) {
        cdiContainer.shutdown();
        cdiContainer = null;
      }
    }
}
```

After JUnit invokes the test methods of the class, we ask the CDI container to shut down. This procedure is illustrated in the method `shutdownContainer()`.

The other two methods, `setUp()` and `tearDown()`, are designed to start and stop conversational context before and after a test method is invoked. In the `setUp()` method, we make sure that the qualifier annotations are injected into the test class instance before the test method is invoked. In the previous unit test, the CDI container will look up the travel service `TravelService` and find the correct type of service according to qualifier, for example, `@Premium` or `@Economy`.

Typically, to simulate the request arriving from a web service client, the request scope context should be restarted for each test. Therefore, in the `tearDown()` method, we explicitly stop and restart the request conversational scope context.

To complete the example, here is the utility class, `Util`, which contains a static method to parse the formatted date, time, and time zone.

```
import java.text.SimpleDateFormat;
import java.util.Date;

public final class Utils {
  private final static SimpleDateFormat FORMATTER =
    new SimpleDateFormat("yyyyMMdd-hh:mm:ss Z");
  public final static Date parseDate(String s) {
    try {
      Date date = FORMATTER.parse(s);
      return date;
    }
    catch (Exception e) {
      throw new RuntimeException
        ("unable parse date time from string ["+s+"]",e);
    }
  }

  private Utils() { }
}
```

Now that we understand the CDI qualifiers, let's move forward.

Injecting arbitrary objects using Producers

What happens if we want to inject an object or type at runtime, dynamically? CDI allows us to do this with the concept of productions. Producer methods are the way to inject arbitrary objects into the container, which are not registered as beans through the annotations. Typically, this is the way to get dynamic behavior.

Let us suppose we have a payment system for checking credit worthiness with some financial service legal entity. It is a very simple credit model-you only need an account number - and we can define a contract for this service as a Java interface.

```
public interface CreditProcessor {
  public void check(String account);
}
```

Context and Dependency Injection

We will reuse the annotations from the standalone travel service example, `@Premium` and `@Economy`. We are given the business requirement for the economy as a high volume and high turnover, and the model leverages lots of promotional workers who act on behalf of the businesses to find and locate customers. There are a lot of dynamics and so it can be modeled as a production using the following `HouseholdCredit` class:

```
public class HouseholdCredit {
  private static AtomicInteger counter = new AtomicInteger(1000);

  @Produces
  @Economy
  public CreditProcessor createCreditProcessor() {
    return new StreetCreditProcessor
      ("promoter"+counter.getAndIncrement());
  }

  public static class StreetCreditProcessor
  implements CreditProcessor {
    private final String workerId;

    public StreetCreditProcessor(String workerId) {
      this.workerId = workerId;
    }

    @Override
    public void check(String account) {/*...*/}

    @Override
    public String toString() {
      return "StreetCreditProcessor{" +
        "workerId='" + workerId + '\'' +
        '}';
    }
  }
}
```

The key annotation is `@javax.enterprise.inject.Produces`, which informs the CDI container that the application is responsible for creating a particular bean type. The `@Produces` annotation designates a POJO application bean as producer of a CDI managed beans.

> Do not confuse CDI's `@Produces` with another Java EE 7 annotation `@javax.ws.rs.Produces`, which is part of JAX-RS. See *Chapter 8, RESTful Services JAX-RS 2.0*.

The class `HouseholdCredit` declares to CDI that it can generate a `CreditProcessor` with the qualifier `@Economy`. It does this by instantiating a static inner class called `StreetCreditProcessor`, but also notice that this type is not annotated explicitly. The CDI container will locate this particular bean type and create it by instantiating a `Household` object for the lifetime of the container, and then invoking the production method, when required by the injection point. The conversation context of the supplied bean is decided at the injection point, as you can see in the following unit test:

```java
package je7hb.standalone;

import je7hb.travelfunk.AbstractCdiContainerTest;
import org.junit.Test;
import javax.inject.Inject;
import static org.junit.Assert.*;

public class CreditProcessorTest extends AbstractCdiContainerTest {
  private @Inject @Economy CreditProcessor agent;

  @Test
  public void shouldInjectStreetCredit() {
    assertNotNull(agent);
    agent.check("12354678");
    System.out.printf("agent=%s\n", agent );
  }
}
```

It is instructive to examine the following output from the program with the CDI container test debugging switched on.

The output from the program is as follows:

```
AbstractCdiContainerTest#startUpContainer() cdiContainer=null
29 [main] INFO org.jboss.weld.Version - WELD-000900 1.1.9 (Final)
117 [main] INFO org.jboss.weld.Bootstrap - WELD-000101 ...
Initialization from CDI
Complete.
AbstractCdiContainerTest#setUp() containerRefCount=1,
  cdiContainer=org.apache.deltaspike.cdise.weld.
WeldContainerControl@49b35574
agent = StreetCreditProcessor{workerId = 'promoter1000'}
AbstractCdiContainerTest#tearDown() containerRefCount = 1,
  cdiContainer = org.apache.deltaspike.cdise.weld.
WeldContainerControl@49b35574
AbstractCdiContainerTest#shutdownContainer() cdiContainer =
  org.apache.deltaspike.cdise.weld.WeldContainerControl@49b35574

Process finished with exit code 0
```

Advanced CDI

In this section, we will advance the context and dependency injection to listening and acting on the lifecycle events, and choose between alternative implementations through configuration.

The lifecycle component example

In the section, *CDI initialization and destruction*, we discussed the lifecycle methods for the CDI managed beans. Let us look at a unit test example that demonstrates the concepts. We will build the other side of the `CreditProcessor` example, which is the premium rate version.

```java
package je7hb.standalone;
import javax.annotation.PostConstruct;
import javax.annotation.PreDestroy;

@Premium
public class PremiumCreditProcessor implements CreditProcessor {
  @Override
  public void check(String account) {
    if (!account.trim().startsWith("1234")) {
      throw new RuntimeException("account:["+account+"] is not
        valid!");
    }
  }

  @PostConstruct
  public void acquireResource() {
    System.out.println( this.getClass()
      .getSimpleName()+"#acquireResource()");
  }

  @PreDestroy
  public void releaseResource() {
    System.out.println( this.getClass()
      .getSimpleName()+"#releaseResource()");
  }
}
```

The class `PremiumCreditProcessor` is a CDI managed bean, which is associated with the `@Premium` qualifier. It has two lifecycle methods `acquireResource()` and `releaseResource()`.

The CDI container invokes `@PostConstruct` annotated methods after the bean type has been constructed. By the time the `@PostConstruct` method is called the CDI container has already initialized any instance field properties in the bean type and the super classes, which are managed by the CDI container. This lifecycle method is designed for all managed beans to initialize the additional resources, such as lazy-loadable and/or expensive resources, which need to be allocated.

The CDI container on managed beans invokes the `@PreDestroy` method, when the context with which they are associated is about to be destroyed. This lifecycle method is designed for the CDI managed beans to release any resources and/or de-allocate expensive resources, for example, freeing up data handles or memory.

Let us look at the following unit test:

```
package je7hb.standalone;
import je7hb.travelfunk.AbstractCdiContainerTest;
import org.junit.Test;
import javax.enterprise.context.RequestScoped;
import javax.inject.Inject;

import static org.junit.Assert.assertNotNull;

public class ExpensiveCreditProcessorTest extends
AbstractCdiContainerTest {
  @Inject @Premium @RequestScoped
  private CreditProcessor agent;

  @Test
  public void shouldInjectExpensiveCredit() {
    assertNotNull(agent);
    agent.check("12345678");
    System.out.printf("agent=%s\n", agent);
  }
}
```

For the first time, in this unit test, we are making use of a specific scope, the request-scope, which is designed for the web servlet containers. Essentially, the request-scope is a collection of short-lived managed objects in a map collection. The request scope only exists for the duration of a single incoming HTTP web request that reaches the application server. As soon as the web request is consumed and a response is sent back to the client by a Java Servlet or something else, the objects in the Request scope should be garbage collected because the CDI container (and the web container) will destroy it.

Context and Dependency Injection

The trick to the unit test lies within super class, the AbstractCdiContainerTest, specifically the tearDown() method where the Request scope is stopped and then restarted order to ensure the current instance is destroyed. Obviously, running in Weld Standalone SE and not inside an application server makes this code interesting.

Let us now turn our attention to getting configuration of beans when we want to deliver a special type of instance to a client, when we have a choice of alternatives.

Alternatives

CDI supports the concepts of alternatives, for situations where you have more than one implementation of an interface or plain object class. For example, you could have more than one type of food processor, which may be supplied by third parties and might be outside of our control. Your application may have a requirement that dictates only a certain processor that can be active at any time in the program.

Let us illustrate alternatives with an interface called FoodProcessor, which simply communicates the product's brand to the caller.

```
// FoodProcessor.java
public interface FoodProcessor {
    public String sayBrand();
}
```

Now let us define the implementations of our suppliers with just two classes like so:

```
// NouveauFoodProcessor.java
public class NouveauFoodProcessor implements FoodProcessor {
    @Override public String sayBrand() {
        return "Nouveau";
    }
}

// XenoniqueFoodProcessor.java
import javax.enterprise.inject.Alternative;

@Alternative
public class XenoniqueFoodProcessor implements FoodProcessor {
    @Override public String sayBrand() {
        return "Xenonique";
    }
}
```

In one of those brands of food processor, XenoniqueFoodProcessor, we designate at least one to be an alternative with the @Alternative annotation. There must be one implementation that is the default, which in this case is the class called NouveauFoodProcessor. How does the CDI container know which instance to plug into the application?

By default, if there is no configuration, then the CDI container will inject the NouveauFoodProcessor in to the type that requires it. If we want to specify the alternative, then we need to configure that in an XML configuration file, which is the bean container file META-INF/beans.xml the content looks like as follows:

```xml
<?xml version="1.0" encoding="UTF-8"?>
<beans xmlns="http://java.sun.com/xml/ns/javaee"
       xmlns:xsi="http://www.w3.org/2001/XMLSchema-instance"
       xsi:schemaLocation="http://java.sun.com/xml/ns/javaee
                  http://java.sun.com/xml/ns/javaee/beans_1_1.xsd">
   <alternatives>
     <class>je7hb.standalone.alternatives
       .XenoniqueFoodProcessor</class>
   </alternatives>
</beans>
```

The alternative class is specified in the absolute XPath of /beans/alternative/class. The text of this element is the fully qualified name of the concrete class.

Alternatives can be useful for injecting a separate test service. Perhaps it could be a mock object or a prototype implementation that another developer team in the investment bank will fulfill at some later stage in the grand development phase.

So let us provide, now, a customary unit test to prove this fact:

```java
import javax.inject.Inject;
public class AlternativesFoodProcessorTest
extends AbstractCdiContainerTest {
    private @Inject FoodProcessor foodProcessor;

    @Test
    public void shouldInjectAlternative() {
        assertNotNull(foodProcessor);
        assertEquals("Xenonique",
          foodProcessor.sayBrand());
    }
}
```

The unit test is based on our DeltaSpike standalone abstract container. We simply instantiate the FoodProcessor type and verify that the instance is, indeed, a XenoniqueFoodProcessor, which of course it is.

Perhaps, you will have noticed that even though the DeltaSpike container is a step up from the standalone JBoss Weld SE examples; in fact it gives more portability to another CDI Container, namely Apache Open Web Beans; however it is still not enough for wide portability.

There are many more Java EE 6 products and, since the formal release, Java EE 7 products on the market that are fully certified and standardized implementations of the specification, and some are pending reaching that condition. Although DeltaSpike is a great solution, it does not cover all of them. We need something that is a testing framework, makes use of the CDI scope exactly the same as inside an application server and fully reproduces the conversational scope. This framework is called Arquillian and now we will study the essentials in the next section.

The Arquillian test framework

Arquillian is a new approach for writing Java EE testing. In the past developers and engineers have been used to writing mock objects and unit tests that run outside of the application container for sheer productivity, efficiency, and speed.

A new kind of Java EE testing framework

Arquillian is a framework that merges the functional and integration testing. It takes control of the lifecycle of the application server container so that it can provide a test execution in an easier manner to developers.

- Arquillian manages the lifecycle of the target container, which can be a CDI or EE container.
- It bundles the test case, dependencies, and resources into a much smaller distribution than usual, which it calls the **ShrinkWrap** archives.
- Arquillian deploys the said ShrinkWrap archives to the runtime target container, and then proceeds to enrich the test case with dependency injection and other runtime declarative resources.
- The unit test cases are executed inside the target container. The results of the unit tests are made available to the test runner.
- After executing the test cases, Arquillian shuts down the target container; meanwhile, the unit test results are available for reporting.

Arquillian bundles up the unit test and dependencies into clever assemblies of class and deploys them to a CDI or Java EE container, and thus developers know that their code actually runs well inside the product, instead of guessing at the accuracy of mock implementation.

You can get more information about Arquillian from the the JBoss website `http://www.jboss.org/arquillian.html`. Most of the time, you probably do not want to manually download the Arquillian framework, instead you will probably integrate into a Maven build or for this written book, add it as the build dependencies for Gradle.

Setting up of Arquillian

Arquillian works with popular testing frameworks JUnit and TestNG out-of-the-box, and it also integrates into IDE such as IntelliJ IDEA, NetBeans, and Eclipse.

In this section, we will set up an Arquillian with the Gradle build tool. The following is the new `build.gradle` file with new dependencies on Gradle:

```
apply plugin: 'java'
apply plugin: 'maven'
apply plugin: 'eclipse'
apply plugin: 'idea'

group = 'com.javaeehandbook.book1'
archivesBaseName = 'ch02-cdi-arquillian'
version = '1.0'

repositories {
  mavenCentral()
  maven {
    url 'http://repository.jboss.org/nexus/content/groups/public''
  }
}

dependencies {
  compile 'org.jboss.spec:jboss-javaee-6.0:1.0.0.Final'
  compile 'org.jboss.arquillian:arquillian-bom:1.0.3.Final'

  testCompile 'org.jboss.weld.se:weld-se-core:1.1.9.Final'
  testCompile 'org.slf4j:slf4j-simple:1.6.4'
  testCompile 'org.jboss.arquillian.container:
    arquillian-weld-ee-embedded-1.1:1.0.0.CR3'
```

```
    testCompile 'org.jboss.arquillian.junit:
      arquillian-junit-container:1.0.2.Final'
    testCompile 'junit:junit:4.11'
  }

  task wrapper(type: Wrapper) {
    gradleVersion = '1.7'
  }

  // Override Gradle defaults - a force an exploded JAR view
  sourceSets {
    main {
      output.resourcesDir = 'build/classes/main'
      output.classesDir = 'build/classes/main'
    }
    test {
      output.resourcesDir = 'build/classes/test'
      output.classesDir = 'build/classes/test'
    }
  }
```

The URL http://repository.jboss.org/nexus/content/groups/public is introduced as a second repository, in order to retrieve the correct dependencies from the JBoss Red Hat servers. Apart from this change and the extra dependencies, it looks very much the same.

Arquillian has two parts: core and the embedded container adaptors. There is core of the framework, the support classes, and one runner from JUnit or TestNG; and then there is the adaptor. In order to run successfully, at least one embedded container must be specified. In the unit test, here we are using the Weld Java EE embedded container, namely arquillian-weld-ee-embedded-1.1. However, you are free to choose another container adaptor, of which there are several, such as the JBoss application or the GlassFish servers.

> Arquillian even allows developers to test their execution against multiple containers, but only one can be selected for the runtime. The way to do test across many application servers is through configuring the Maven profiles or the Gradle setting properties. This is an advanced topic and details can be found online at http://gradle.org/docs/current/userguide/working_with_files.html.s

The disposable methods

Let us revisit the classes that we created with the `@Produces` annotation. Remember the annotation `@Produces` informs the CDI container to instantiate a bean type dynamically through an application client factory. Having created a bean type, we should consider end of life of factory bean types. What if the bean was expensive to create or if the bean had held on to the resource handle? How could we safely release such a resource to the operating system via the JVM, naturally? This is the purpose of the `@Dispose` annotation.

When a contextual bean goes out of scope, it is destroyed. To destroy a bean, the CDI container calls any `@PreDestroy` callbacks for the bean and destroys any `@Dependent` objects before disposing of the object.

An application can perform custom cleanup of the created objects by using a dispose method. Marking the parameter with the annotation `@javax.enterprise.inject.Disposes` designates it as a disposal method.

The revised code for the class `HouseholdCredit` is as follows:

```java
public class HouseholdCredit {
  private static AtomicInteger counter = new AtomicInteger(1000);

  @Produces
  @Economy
  public CreditProcessor createCreditProcessor() {
    CreditProcessor proc = new StreetCreditProcessor
      ("promoter"+counter.getAndIncrement());
    System.out.printf("#createCreditProcessor() "+ "creates proc =
      %s\n", proc);
    return proc;
  }

  public void releaseCreditProcessor
    (@Disposes @Economy CreditProcessor proc) {
    System.out.printf("#releaseCreditProcessor() "+
      "dispose proc = %s\n", proc);
  }

  public static class StreetCreditProcessor
  implements CreditProcessor {
    private final String workerId;
    public StreetCreditProcessor(String workerId) {
      this.workerId = workerId;
    }
    /*... same as before ... */
  }
}
```

Context and Dependency Injection

Note that the disposal method accepts the same qualifier annotation as the production factory method. This is important; the CDI container should complain at runtime if the qualifiers and the conversational scope, if any, between the production and disposal methods do not match.

The modified unit test with the Arquillian framework to verify the operation of the `HouseholdCredit` bean is as follows:

```java
package je7hb.basic.arquillian;
import org.jboss.arquillian.container.test.api.Deployment;
import org.jboss.arquillian.junit.Arquillian;
import org.jboss.shrinkwrap.api.ShrinkWrap;
import org.jboss.shrinkwrap.api.asset.EmptyAsset;
import org.jboss.shrinkwrap.api.spec.JavaArchive;
import org.junit.Test;
import org.junit.runner.RunWith;
import javax.inject.Inject;
import static org.junit.Assert.assertNotNull;

@RunWith(Arquillian.class)
public class EconomyCreditProcessorTest {
  @Deployment
  public static JavaArchive createDeployment() {
    JavaArchive jar = ShrinkWrap.create(JavaArchive.class)
      .addClasses(Economy.class, Premium.class,
        CreditProcessor.class, HouseholdCredit.class,
          PremiumCreditProcessor.class)
      .addAsManifestResource(EmptyAsset.INSTANCE, "beans.xml");
    System.out.println(jar.toString(true));
    return jar;
  }

  private @Inject @Economy CreditProcessor processor;

  @Test
  public void should_create_greeting() {
    System.out.printf("processor = %s\n", processor);
    assertNotNull(processor);
    processor.check("1234");
  }
}
```

An Arquillian JUnit test case requires three important items: the `@RunWith` annotation with the `Arquillian` class reference, the deployment static method, which is annotated, and at least one method annotated with the `@Test` method.

The deployment method is annotated with `@Deployment`, which is part of the Arquillian testing framework, and is responsible for creating, the ShrinkWrap bundle. The `ShrinkWrap` API is very similar to the static builder factory. The object is instantiated and then properties are set on the builder through the add method. The classes to be deployed are explicitly added, and adding a blank CDI bean configuration file follows it. (Java Packages can also be specifically deployed.)

The output of running this unit test is as follows:

```
3d3e541b-c6b9-4e58-918d-febae05ead20.jar:
/je7hb/
/je7hb/basic/
/je7hb/basic/arquillian/
/je7hb/basic/arquillian/HouseholdCredit.class
/je7hb/basic/arquillian/PremiumCreditProcessor.class
/je7hb/basic/arquillian/
  HouseholdCredit$StreetCreditProcessor.class
/je7hb/basic/arquillian/Economy.class
/je7hb/basic/arquillian/CreditProcessor.class
/je7hb/basic/arquillian/Premium.class
/META-INF/
/META-INF/beans.xml
21 [main] INFO org.jboss.weld.Version - WELD-000900 1.1.9 (Final)
Household#createCreditProcessor() creates proc =
  StreetCreditProcessor{workerId='promoter1000'}
processor = StreetCreditProcessor{workerId = 'promoter1000'}
check for account [1234]
Household#releaseCreditProcessor() dispose proc =
  StreetCreditProcessor{workerId='promoter1000'}
```

The `println()` statement in the deployment static method is actually dumping the contents of the ShrinkWrap bundle. It can be useful to see this debuggable output in some certain situations, but for normal development work it will be annoying for other staff. So, I recommend that you don't forget to remove that debug line.

From the preceding screen output, we can see the Arquillian framework bundles up the classes into a bundle, performs the dependency execution, and executes the test. Most importantly, it handles the lifecycle of the container beans.

Moreover, because the test works in Weld, in the CDI container as it truly runs, there is really good confidence to assume that it work, as expected in the GlassFish and JBoss application server. After all, this is exactly all about the standards and portability of the code.

Let us move to the penultimate area of CDI for this overly long tutorial. How can the CDI container manage crosscutting concerns for managed beans?

CDI and crosscutting concerns

CDI helps us with writing type safe and portable crosscutting concerns, where a technical component spans across different areas of application. If these concerns were implemented as a traditional code they would be scattered across the entire application through duplicated code, moreover entangled with the core business logic.

Interceptors

CDI supports two ways of extending the functionality of the bean managed by the container, namely: Interceptors and Decorators.

Interceptors are the way to add crosscutting concerns to several managed beans. A classic example of a crosscutting concern is logging, because it is a feature that is a part of multiple domains. Practically any software system may require the logging ability. The issue is how to specify this in a clean way, which does not interfere with the application business logic of the class; it should not break encapsulation and provide flexibility.

An Interceptor is a bean declared with the `@javax.interceptor.Interceptor` annotation. The method Interceptor should have call `@javax.interceptor.AroundInvoke` that takes the `javax.interceptor.InvocationContext` as a parameter.

Let us look at an example of this Interceptor, but first we need an additional user defined annotation as follows:

```
package je7hb.basic.arquillian;
import javax.interceptor.InterceptorBinding;
import java.lang.annotation.Inherited;
import java.lang.annotation.Retention;
import java.lang.annotation.Target;

import static java.lang.annotation.ElementType.METHOD;
```

```
import static java.lang.annotation.ElementType.TYPE;
import static java.lang.annotation.RetentionPolicy.RUNTIME;

@Inherited
@Target({TYPE, METHOD})
@Retention(RUNTIME)
@InterceptorBinding
public @interface TransactionalBound { }
```

We define `@TransactionalBound` custom annotation, which is a type of `@InterceptorBinding`. This annotation declares that wherever we declare a class or method with this annotation, we denote a join-point, which is a specific location in our code, to inject a CDI Interceptor.

Let us now define the custom Interceptor for our annotation now as follows:

```
package je7hb.basic.arquillian;
import javax.interceptor.AroundInvoke;
import javax.interceptor.Interceptor;
import javax.interceptor.InvocationContext;

@Interceptor
@TransactionalBound
public class TransactionalBoundInterceptor {
  @AroundInvoke
  public Object handleTransaction(InvocationContext ctx)
  throws Exception {
    System.out.println("#handleTransaction *before* "+
      "invocation");
    Object value =  ctx.proceed();
    System.out.println("#handleTransaction *after* "+
      "invocation");
    return value;
  }
}
```

The class `TransactionalBoundInterceptor` is declared as an Interceptor, bindable with the `@Interceptor` annotation; it has a `@AroundInvoke` method. The `handleTransaction` method accepts an invocation context object, and simply does nothing special, it executes the invocation context's target method. The point is that the interception method can manage the transaction in a real application, it can deal with exceptional conditions or in this case log to the console.

Context and Dependency Injection

All we need now is the managed bean and it is as follows:

```
package je7hb.basic.arquillian;
import javax.annotation.*;
import javax.enterprise.inject.Default;

@Default
public class TransactionalCreditProcessor
implements CreditProcessor {
  @Override
  @TransactionalBound
  public void check(String account) {
    if (!account.trim().startsWith("1234")) {
      throw new RuntimeException
        ("account:["+account+"] is not valid!");
    }
    System.out.printf("Inside Transactional Account [%s]"
      + "is Okay\n", account);
  }

  @PostConstruct
  public void acquireResource() {
    System.out.println( this.getClass()
      .getSimpleName()+"#acquireResource()");
  }

  @PreDestroy
  public void releaseResource() {
    System.out.println( this.getClass()
      .getSimpleName()+"#releaseResource()" );
  }
}
```

The `TransactionalCreditProcessor` class is another type of the credit processor that makes use of transaction. We apply our custom annotation `@TransactionalBound` to the `check()` method in order to add transaction behavior injected around the invocation of the method. The `check()` method is the target join-point of the `@TransactionalBound` annotation. Any such join-points are the target of the invocation context in the `TransactionalInterceptor`.

Finally, this bean is declared as `@Default`, which is the default qualifier. In order to enable the Interceptors, we need to add a CDI beans configuration file as follows:

```xml
<?xml version = "1.0"?>
<beans
  xmlns = "http://java.sun.com/xml/ns/javaee"
  xmlns:xsi = "http://www.w3.org/2001/XMLSchema-instance"
  xsi:schemaLocation = "
    http://java.sun.com/xml/ns/javaee
      http://java.sun.com/xml/ns/javaee/beans_1_1.xsd">
  <interceptors>
    <class>je7hb.basic.arquillian
    .TransactionalBoundInterceptor</class>
  </interceptors>
</beans>
```

The `beans.xml` file simply declares the Interceptors for the application. We can have more than one Interceptor, but you always have to declare it.

Let us finish up the example with the unit test based on the Arquillian framework as follows:

```java
package je7hb.basic.arquillian;
/* ... as before ... */

@RunWith(Arquillian.class)
public class TransactionalCreditProcessorTest {
  @Deployment
  public static JavaArchive createDeployment() {
    JavaArchive jar = ShrinkWrap.create(JavaArchive.class)
    .addClasses(Economy.class, Premium.class,
      CreditProcessor.class, Transactional.class,
        TransactionalCreditProcessor.class,
          TransactionalInterceptor.class)
    .addAsManifestResource(
      "je7hb/basic/arquillian/interceptors/beans.xml",
        ArchivePaths.create("beans.xml"));
    return jar;
  }

  private @Inject CreditProcessor processor;

  @Test
```

Context and Dependency Injection

```
    public void shouldProcessTransactionalCredit() {
      System.out.printf("processor = %s\n", processor );
      assertNotNull(processor);
      processor.check("1234");
    }
}
```

The ShrinkWrap bundle requires the location path of the custom `beans.xml` file, which configures the transactional interpreter. The rest of the cost is largely the same as before and you already understand it, so let us go straight to the output.

```
b73cfb6f-ad2f-4165-b1cf-f8fffad507eb.jar:
/je7hb/
/je7hb/basic/
/je7hb/basic/arquillian/
/je7hb/basic/arquillian/TransactionalInterceptor.class
/je7hb/basic/arquillian/TransactionalCreditProcessor.class
/je7hb/basic/arquillian/Transactional.class
/je7hb/basic/arquillian/Economy.class
/je7hb/basic/arquillian/CreditProcessor.class
/je7hb/basic/arquillian/Premium.class
/META-INF/
/META-INF/beans.xml
23 [main] INFO org.jboss.weld.Version - WELD-000900 1.1.9 (Final)
TransactionalCreditProcessor
   $Proxy$_$$_WeldSubclass#acquireResource()
processor = je7hb.basic.arquillian.TransactionalCreditProcessor
   $Proxy$_$$_WeldSubclass@73a1dd83
TransactionalInterceptor#handleTransaction *before* invocation
Inside Transactional Account [1234] is Okay
TransactionalInterceptor#handleTransaction *after* invocation
TransactionalCreditProcessor
   $Proxy$_$$_WeldSubclass#releaseResource()

Process finished with exit code 0
```

From examining the output of this unit test, we can see that the transactional Interceptor is fired as on the call to the `CreditProcessor.check()` method, which is actually the dynamic proxy subclass of `TransactionCreditProcessor`, which has had the Interceptor logic interwoven into it.

Also, we can also say that CDI still manages the lifecycle of the bean in the correct fashion, the so-called expensive resource is acquired and released in the right order.

Decorators

Another way to extend the bean functionality is to create a Decorator for a managed bean. An Interceptor allows the bean behavior to modify through a crosscutting concern. A Decorator only allows a bean's contractual interface to be modified. In CDI, Decorators are created dynamically. A Decorator only decorates the interfaces that it implements.

A CDI Decorator is a Java class that is annotated with the `@Decorator` annotation and it is also configured as a registered Decorator in the configuration file `beans.xml`. A CDI Decorator bean class must also have a delegate injection join-point, which is declared with the `@Delegate` annotation. Both `@Decorator` and `@Delegate` are found in the Java package `javax.decorator`.

Let us look at Decorator for a credit-processing example. Suppose we had a unique requirement for only premier-care customers, who require a call to the sanctioning service before the business can supply any credit. Let us hypothesize that the sanctioning service is a placeholder for legal regulations in the financial services. First we need to define the service as follows:

```java
package je7hb.basic.arquillian;

public class SanctionService {
  public void sanction( String account, String ccyPair ) {
    System.out.printf("SanctionService#sanction
       (" +"account = %s, other = %s )\n", account, ccyPair);
  }
}
```

`SanctionService` is very simple, because it prints the arguments to the console. We will move on to the CDI Decorator bean.

```java
package je7hb.basic.arquillian;
import javax.decorator.Decorator;
import javax.decorator.Delegate;
import javax.inject.Inject;

@Decorator
@Premium
public class CreditProcessorDecorator implements CreditProcessor {

  @Inject SanctionService sanctionService;
  @Inject @Delegate @Premium CreditProcessor processor;
```

```
    @Override
    public void check(String account) {
      sanctionService.sanction(account, "EURGBP");
      processor.check(account);
    }
}
```

First we annotate the class with @Decorator, but also notice we are denoting this type with the @Premium annotation, which if you remember is a custom qualifier for our tests.

The field processor is denoted as an injection point with the @Delegate annotation, and again it matches the type of credit processor we want to inject in this bean, which is for premier-care customers.

Incidentally, the delegate injection point may be stationed in front of a field, a constructor parameter, or an initializer method parameter of the Decorator class.

SanctionService is injected into this bean and in the check() method, we actually call the method sanction() with the account code and the currency pair, foreign exchange standard to represent monetary transfer from Euros to British Pounds before we invoke the check() method of credit processor.

We need to add the beans.xml file configuration in order to declare the Decorator to CDI.

During initialization, the CDI Container injects the SanctionService in to the bean type CreditProcessorDecorator. When we call the check() method with this bean type, our decorator invokes the sanction() method with the account code and the foreign exchange currency pair EURGBP. If the real time sanction() method returns normally then the decorator invokes the check() method of the delegate credit processor.

Decorators must be declared inside the beans.xml file configuration in order to be active in the application:

```
<?xml version = "1.0"?>
<beans
  xmlns = "http://java.sun.com/xml/ns/javaee"
  xmlns:xsi = "http://www.w3.org/2001/XMLSchema-instance"
  xsi:schemaLocation = "
    http://java.sun.com/xml/ns/javaee
      http://java.sun.com/xml/ns/javaee/beans_1_1.xsd">
  <decorators>
  <class>je7hb.basic.arquillian
    .CreditProcessorDecorator</class>
  </decorators>
</beans>
```

We can have more than one Decorator and we an have multiple Decorators and Interceptors in the configuration file.

Our test case is as follows:

```java
package je7hb.basic.arquillian;
/* ...as before... */

@RunWith(Arquillian.class)
public class CreditProcessorDecoratorTest {
  @Deployment
  public static JavaArchive createDeployment() {
    JavaArchive jar = ShrinkWrap.create(JavaArchive.class)
    .addClasses(Economy.class, Premium.class,
      CreditProcessor.class, CreditProcessorDecorator.class,
        PremiumCreditProcessor.class, SanctionService.class)
    .addAsManifestResource
      ("je7hb/basic/arquillian/decorators/beans.xml",
        ArchivePaths.create("beans.xml"));
    System.out.println(jar.toString(true));
    return jar;
  }

  @Inject @Premium CreditProcessor processor;

  @Test
  public void shouldProcessTransactionalCredit() {
    System.out.printf("processor = %s\n", processor);
    assertNotNull(processor);
    processor.check("1234");
  }
}
```

In the unit test, we only have to define the injection point that is required. It is a credit processor that is qualified as premium. CDI will take care of the rest, the exact type of bean to be injected, and in this case the decorated bean `CreditProcessorDecorator`, the lifecycle management of the beans, and other dependencies.

The output of running this unit case is as follows:

```
93327296-d137-45a2-ad11-fec5fa7d7b2a.jar:
/je7hb/
/je7hb/basic/
/je7hb/basic/arquillian/
/je7hb/basic/arquillian/SanctionService.class
```

```
/je7hb/basic/arquillian/CreditProcessorDecorator.class
/je7hb/basic/arquillian/PremiumCreditProcessor.class
/je7hb/basic/arquillian/Economy.class
/je7hb/basic/arquillian/CreditProcessor.class
/je7hb/basic/arquillian/Premium.class
/META-INF/
/META-INF/beans.xml
22 [main] INFO org.jboss.weld.Version - WELD-000900 1.1.9 (Final)
PremiumCreditProcessor$Proxy$_$$_WeldSubclass#acquireResource()
processor = je7hb.basic.arquillian.PremiumCreditProcessor
  $Proxy$_$$_WeldSubclass@9a68065
Inside the CreditProcessorDecorator#check()
SanctionService#sanction(account = 1234, other = EURGBP)
Account [1234] is Okay
End of the CreditProcessorDecorator#check()
PremiumCreditProcessor$Proxy$_$$_WeldSubclass#releaseResource()

Process finished with exit code 0
```

As you can clearly see, the embedded Weld container creates a proxy of the premium credit processor bean. The CDI container also instantiates the bean `CreditProcessorDecorator` and injects the dependencies. Eventually, the bean's `check()` method is called, and we can see the sanction service being called first, before the delegate proxy bean is called.

Observers and events

CDI allows decoupling of the consumer and a target dependency through the custom application events. The CDI event is a type safe replacement for the **Observer Design Pattern (ODP)**. It works through the type safe annotations and generics to completely decouple the subject of action (event producers) from the observers (event consumers). The CDI events and observers can be fine-tuned through the qualifiers in this model.

Applications create a POJO event class to serve as the payload. An event that represents when a create application has been approved is as follows:

```
package je7hb.standalone.events;
public class ApplicationApproved {
  private final String message;

  public ApplicationApproved(String message) {
    this.message = message;
  }
  public String getMessage() {return message;}
}
```

Next, we need an event producer. Let us create one with field with the type `javax.enterprise.event.Event` in order to fire events to interested parties. This is the class `ApprovalNotifier` as follows:

```java
package je7hb.standalone.events;
import javax.enterprise.event.Event;
import javax.inject.Inject;

public class ApprovalNotifier {
  @Inject Event<ApplicationApproved> eventSource;

  public void fireEvents(String msg) {
    eventSource.fire(new ApplicationApproved(msg));
  }
}
```

The CDI container injects an instance of the parameterized type `Event<ApplicationApproved>`. In order to notify observers for this type of event, we simply invoke the `fire()` method.

Third and lastly, we need an observer. With the CDI events, we can write a simple POJO to receive notifications. The class `CreditApprovalPostProcess` is as follows:

```java
package je7hb.standalone.events;
import javax.enterprise.event.Observes;
import javax.inject.Inject;

public class CreditApprovalPostProcess {
  @Inject ExternalServices externalServices;

  public void postApproval
    (@Observes ApplicationApproved application) {
    externalServices.process(application);
  }
}
```

The purpose of this class is to listen to credit approvals and communicate them to the external service. We add the annotation `@javax.enterprise.event.Observes` to the event type. CDI does not require us to register with an event source. The container takes care of all of the details and the wiring of consumer to producer. It really is rather simple.

The type-safe manner, indeed, comes into its own when we apply the CDI qualifiers with events and observers. Let's take the example further. Suppose we want a separate notification for premium customers who take long-term credit.

Context and Dependency Injection

First, we modify the `ApprovalNotifier` POJO, add another event source, which is qualified as `@LongTerm`. An abridged version of this class is as follows:

```
public class ApprovalNotifier {
  /* ... */
  @Inject @LongTerm
  Event<ApplicationApproved> longTermEventSource;

  public void fireLongTermEvents( String msg ) {
    longTermEventSource.fire(new ApplicationApproved(msg));
  }
}
```

Adding the `@LongTerm` qualifier to the event source strongly associates the event source with only those observers. We only add an extra method to the POJO class `CreditApprovalPostProcess` as follows:

```
public class CreditApprovalPostProcess {
  @Inject ExternalServices externalServices;

  /* ... */
  public void postLongTermApproval
    (@LongTerm @Observes ApplicationApproved app) {
    externalServices.process(app);
  }
}
```

The method postLongTermApproval() takes a type with the qualifier @LongTerm, and the CDI container only invokes this method with bean type associated with the qualifier. Interestingly enough, the original postApproval() in the event consumer is equivalent to the qualifier of @Any. In other words, both of these declarations are the same:

```
void postApproval( @Observes ApplicationApproved app )
void postApproval( @Observes @Any ApplicationApproved app )
```

And this implies the event sources definitions too:

```
@Inject ExternalServices externalServices;
@Inject @Any ExternalServices externalServices;
```

Stereotypes

Stereotypes are a way of combining a single CDI scope and other annotations in a useful group. The CDI stereotypes are themselves annotations, which are declared with the annotation `@javax.enterprise.inject.Stereotype`.

The CDI stereotypes can be thought of as macros for the annotations and thus can reduce the verbosity of several qualifiers and scoped annotations. A stereotype for a premium credit check and long-term interest customer is as follows:

```
@Stereotype
@Retention(RUNTIME) @Target(TYPE)
@Secure @Premium @LongTerm @Transactional
public @interface HighValue {}
```

This CDI stereotype `HighValue` custom annotation binds together three other qualifiers and a transactional scope. In this way, we are modeling some common purpose. If the stereotype does not declare a scope, it is assumed to be `@Default`. A stereotype may also bind other CDI stereotypes.

Summary

In this chapter, we looked at CDI, the standard API for managed beans with conversational scope in Java EE 7.

- **Context**: The ability to bind lifecycle and interactions to stateful components together in a semantic encapsulated boundary, which is type safe and extensible
- **Dependency Injection**: The ability to inject a dependent component into an object in a type safe manner and includes the capability to decide on the implementation of those dependent components at runtime

We saw that CDI is a very elegant solution and straightforward method for dependency injection. CDI managed beans can practically be a plain old Java object (POJO). Most of the time, CDI managed beans are concrete classes, which may or may not implement one or more Java interfaces, or extend a single abstract class. A CDI bean may be declared `final` or have `final` methods, and they can be generic parameterized types. CDI supports application factories that produce managed bean types. If required, an application can also use a disposal factory in order to clean up resources. CDI support producer methods that allow the application to overcome limitations in the container. The application can supply a custom factory that creates bean types for the container. CDI also support disposal methods, which may be associated with the same factory class.

CDI managed beans can be differentiated by qualifiers, which are custom Java annotations. It is also possible to programmatically look up a bean by type and qualifier. Moreover, most applications will make use of the `@Inject` annotation for dependency injection.

The CDI container supports five default scopes for managed beans, namely `@RequestScoped`, `@SessionScoped`, `@ApplicationScoped`, `@ConversationScoped`, and `@Dependent`. It is possible to define further custom scopes. The CDI beans are automatically associated with associated contextual scope, which defines their lifecycle. In other words, CDI managed beans live their lives in a well-defined scope. However, if the bean is declared `@Dependent` scope then the lifecycle is managed by the JVM.

At the end of an HTTP session any associated CDI managed beans with `@SessionScoped` are destroyed, and then they can be garbage collected by the JVM.

At the end of an HTTP request any associated CDI managed beans with `@RequestScoped` are destroyed, and then they can be garbage collected by the JVM.

We learnt how to develop a standalone CDI application for Java SE using JBoss. We wrote some basic unit tests with Gradle as the build tool. Next, we moved on to the open source project DeltaSpike, which is an open source framework for a standalone CDI container with semi-portable code, and we developed test cases around more features of CDI. We increased our learning about writing abstract test case to handle the startup and shutdown of the CDI container. We saw there were limitations with such tools, and we understood them.

Finally, we moved to the Arquillian framework, which was an integration unit test framework that assembled tight bundles and deployed them to an embedded application server seamlessly. We also saw how to extend our Gradle build, and wrote more involved unit tests to see the lifecycle operations, namely post construction and pre-destruction, and how to extend CDI managed beans with Decorators and Interceptors.

In the next chapter, we will move to the EJB container, which has a different behavior to CDI and where EJBs do not have contextual scope generally.

3
Enterprise Java Beans

The Reverend, *Jesse Jackson* said, "I am not a perfect servant. I am a public servant. In 1999, **Enterprise Java Beans (EJBs)** first appeared in the J2EE 1.0 specification. There were these heavyweight EJB components that ran inside an EJB container. EJBs were the original **endpoints** of the Java enterprise platform. The basic idea was that a client application would remotely make calls to a remote EJB endpoint in order to do some unit of work. The architecture was decidedly pre-cloud computing and client server. J2EE EJBs were either stateless or stateful; they could also be entity beans; and finally there was a concept of endpoints designed for sending and receiving data inside message-oriented systems, which are called **Message Driven Beans** (**MDBs**). MDBs were also part of the J2EE ecosystem. MDBs are covered in *Chapter 9, Java Message Service 2.0*.

In *Chapter 2, Context and Dependency Injection* we talked about Context and Dependency Injection and managed beans that are tied to a contextual scope. The CDI container managed CDI beans. EJBs are managed by an EJB container, and unlike CDI managed beans there is no contextual scope associated with them at all. EJBs have their own lifecycle that is tied to the deployment of the application inside the server. EJB, CDI, and the JPA specifications rely heavily on annotations for strong type checking with the Java compiler.

EJB are endpoints for an invocation call from an EJB client. The communication between the EJB client and server takes place on a defined protocol; it can be local calls between components running inside the same **Java Virtual Machine** (**JVM**), or it can be distributed remote calls across to another JVM over the network.

EJB protocols

The local protocol is equivalent to calling a function on the JVM call frame stack. So it is just like invoking a function and therefore it is the fastest.

The network protocol is called **RMI-IIOP** and originally it was designed for distributed communication between Java EJB applications and other non-Java systems. **IIOP** stands for **Internet Inter-ORB Protocol**, which is a protocol that delivers **Common Object Request Broker Architecture** (**CORBA**)to the Java platform. IIOP is a much older technology sanctioned for distributed communication of software that supports cross platform systems. **RMI** stands for **Remote Method Invocation**, and this is the standard Java technology to send messages, serializable Java objects from one JVM to another, across a network. Therefore the term RMI-IIOP stands for RMI over IIOP.

Criticism of EJB

CORBA is a much earlier communication and object data specification created by the **Object Management Group** (**OMG**) in the late 1990's, which was originally designed to allow software components written in different languages and running on different platforms to work together. Actually, CORBA was superseded in the twenty first century by the popularity of **Service Oriented Architecture** (**SOA**). The idea of using XML Web Services and invocation remote service function by sending and receiving data using SOAP and other protocols.

The point of this preamble is the EJB ,which in the beginning of the twenty first century was based on some fairly old standards. There are not many businesses that develop with CORBA nowadays, because of the poor implementations of the standard which could be incompatible yet were deemed certifiable; the standard process was mired in politics and different ulterior business motives. By the time CORBA and OMG organizations got their act together, the world had moved on to **Representational State Transfer** (**REST**) systems and orchestration through Web Services.

Business users of the earlier J2EE specification found that RMI-IIOP, historically, was painfully slow and there was a performance penalty; this was because the early EJB specifications only allowed RMI-IIOP. In J2EE 1.2 release, the idea of local interface was created to address this penalty. A local interface is close in performance to a method call. Behind the scenes a call to EJB is happening through a proxy.

With all this legacy technology, no wonder developers and architects were put off EJB for building agile enterprise applications. Eventually the expert group did realize there were issues with J2EE.

Simplification of EJB

The breakthrough for Enterprise Java Beans came in EJB 3.0 (JSR-220), which was a radical departure from the J2EE specification and was delivered in Java EE 5. The EJB specification was simplified substantially; the focus was on the idea of *ease-of-development*, which was achieved through the heavy reliance on annotations. The use of annotations brought much sought after affordance to the programming of Java EE applications. The influence of the movement and worldwide interest in Ruby on Rails was also felt through the idea of convention over configuration that practiced a less verbose code, and lesser dependence on XML configuration files.

Gavin King, the creator of Hibernate, was a firm believer in the EJB 3.0 specification. Many features of Hibernate found their way into the EJB *entity bean* specification as the Java Persistence API. Entity beans and JPA are covered in a subsequent chapter.

> You only learn one thing about EJBs in Java EE 7: that they are lightweight POJO, which can come and go. Stateless EJBs are the simplest endpoints that you can reach in Java EE. Stateful EJBs have a higher price because of the their implicit connection with the client.

Features of EJB components

There are three types of EJB:

Bean Type	Description
Session	Executes a useful activity of work for client; it can also be a web service endpoint. The term session implies that there is a hidden handle that is the reference between a client and the server endpoint.
Message	An asynchronous endpoint that consumes, reads a message object from a message queue, and performs some unit of work.
Entity	Represents an entity from a database or other persistence store, especially in the older J2EE specifications. Entity EJB are not endpoints for client invocations, and have been usurped by Java Persistence API.

This chapter covers the session EJB. The other bean types have chapters specifically dedicated to them.

EJB have a list of standard features:

EJB feature	Description
Remote invocation	EJB component declared as remote beans can be called over a network connection using the RMI-IIOP.
Local invocation	EJB component declared as a local bean can only be called by reference in the same JVM.
Web service invocation	EJB component declared as web service can be called using web service invocation.
Transactions	EJB components can participate in transactions that are managed by the application server, the EJB container, or they can create their own transaction context and manage the transaction themselves.
Asynchronous method invocation	The EJB container and the application server will invoke the EJB component endpoint on a particular thread. The writer does not have to concern themselves with multiple thread programming.
Deployment	EJB components are deployed and managed by an EJB container, which manages their lifecycle. Unfortunately EJB components do not have contextual scope in the way CDI managed beans do.
Dependency Injection	Other components and resources can be injected to an EJB component.
Security	EJB component may have role based Java EE security applied at the invocation call site or on the entire type itself.
Naming Directory	EJB component may be given a specific name from JNDI in order to allow EJB clients to look it up by reference name.
Job Scheduling	An EJB component endpoint method may be declared as a scheduled call, a method that is executed in the background by the EJC container at least once in the future or more than once periodically.

Session beans

A session EJB is a component that encapsulates specific behavior to process the business logic of an application. Session EJBs have no concept of persistence.

There are three types of session bean available in the EJB specification. They are **stateless**, **stateful**, and **singleton** beans.

Stateless session beans

A stateless session bean is an EJB component that does not maintain state information between client invocations. If you need conversational state and contextual awareness you look to CDI.

Stateless session beans, then, are reserved by design to serve EJB clients that have no requirement to have a conversation. The client just wants to invoke a function on the endpoint and do some useful work on the server, and then carry on with the rest of instructional life.

In EJB 3.x denoting a stateless enterprise bean is very easy. You simply use the @javax.ejb.Stateless annotation on the class. The class can be a **Plain Old Java Object (POJO)**. Let us simply define one now:

> Some people believe that stateless session EJB should have been really called Poolable Beans, because these types of EJB are usually allocated from a resource inside the application server.

To declare a stateless session EJB, you add the annotation @Stateless to the class. Here is an example of a customer service EJB:

```
package je7hb.basic.ejb;
import javax.ejb.Stateless;
import java.util.*;

@Stateless
public class SupportHelpDesk {

    private List<String> agents = Arrays.asList(
        "Agnes","Brian","Harry","Sally","Tom","Pamela",
        "Mark","Wendy","Marcia","Graeme","Pravztik",
        "Hadeep", "Florence", "Robert", "Zoe", "Frank");
```

```
        public String getNextAgentName() {
            return agents.get((int)( Math.random() *
                agents.size() ));
        }
    }
```

It does not get easier than this. Annotate the POJO with the stateless annotation on the type. When this EJB is deployed in the application server, it will be assigned an allocation pool size, which can be configured by the system administrator; the Java EE product vendor determines the actual connection pool size. The application server instantiates `SupportHelpDesk` as a stateless session EJB, and most implementations will wrap a hidden proxy object around the instance. This proxy delegate has opaque container methods and it has a delegation method that invokes one public method `getNextAgentName()`, which in turn returns a random name of agent.

Let us look at the Gradle build file for this project:

```
// Same Plug-in imports as before
group = 'com.javaeehandbook.book1'
archivesBaseName = 'ch03-ejb'
version = '1.0'

repositories {
    mavenLocal()
    mavenCentral()
    maven {
        url 'https://maven.java.net/
            content/groups/promoted'
    }
    maven {
        url 'http://repository.jboss.org/
            nexus/content/groups/public'
    }
}

dependencies {
    compile 'org.glassfish.main.extras:\
        glassfish-embedded-all:4.0.1-b01'
    compile 'javax:javaee-api:7.0'

    testCompile 'junit:junit:4.11'
    testCompile 'org.jboss.arquillian.junit:\
        arquillian-junit-container:1.0.3.Final'
    testCompile 'org.jboss.arquillian.container:\
        arquillian-glassfish-embedded-3.1:1.0.0.Final-SNAPSHOT'
}
// Typical Gradle Project - Same as before
```

Only the dependency management is important as shown in the preceding build file. We are using the Arquillian test framework again, and we explicitly add a dependency on a real application server, GlassFish.

Let's move on to the unit test, which is an Arquillian integration test:

```
package je7hb.basic.ejb;
/* Other imports omitted */
import javax.ejb.EJB;
import static org.junit.Assert.assertNotNull;

@RunWith(Arquillian.class)
public class SupportHelpDeskTest {
    @Deployment
    public static JavaArchive createDeployment() {
        JavaArchive jar = ShrinkWrap.create(JavaArchive.class)
                .addClasses(SupportHelpDesk.class)
                .addAsManifestResource(
                        EmptyAsset.INSTANCE,
                        ArchivePaths.create("beans.xml"));
        return jar;
    }

    @EJB SupportHelpDesk desk;

    @Test
    public void shouldRetrieveDifferentAgents() {
        System.out.printf("Support help desk = %s\n", desk );
        for ( int j=0; j<5; ++j ) {
            String agent  = desk.getNextAgentName();
            System.out.printf("The next agent = %s\n",agent);
            assertNotNull(agent);
        }
    }
}
```

In order to reference the stateless EJB inside the same JVM, and in the same EJB container, we explicitly obtain a reference to the bean using the @EJB. This is similar to the CDI injection, but not quite the same; this injection of a local reference takes place without contextual scope, and the EJB container provides it whenever the EJB bean is created.

The test method `shouldRetrieveDifferentAgents()` in this unit test executes a simple for-do loop that invokes the EJB service method. The test result prints random agent names to its users. Here is the abbreviated output of the test for study:

```
  INFO: Created virtual server server
Aug 27, 2013 3:53:40 PM org.apache.catalina.realm.JAASRealm
  setContainer
INFO: Setting JAAS app name glassfish-web
Aug 27, 2013 3:53:40 PM com.sun.enterprise.web.WebContainer
  loadSystemDefaultWebModules
...
INFO: Loading application [test] at [/test]
Aug 27, 2013 3:53:41 PM org.glassfish.deployment.admin.
  DeployCommand execute
INFO: test was successfully deployed in 2,658 milliseconds.
Support help desk = je7hb.basic.ejb.SupportHelpDesk@790ffd6
The next agent = Sally
The next agent = Graeme
The next agent = Pravztik
The next agent = Pamela
The next agent = Florence
PlainTextActionReporterSUCCESS
No monitoring data to report.
...
Aug 27, 2013 3:53:41 PM com.sun.enterprise.v3.server.AppServerStartup
  stop
INFO: Shutdown procedure finished
Process finished with exit code 0
```

We will cover referencing of session EJB by clients and the lifecycle later on. Let us move onto the second type of session EJB, the stateful ones.

Concurrency and stateless session EJBs

We have seen how to create a stateless session EJB. The developer may be tempted to think these beans can easily handle concurrency. However, act with extreme caution. An EJB property field will share state Java threads that are passing the component, whereas local variables that are declared inside the method are shared only by the thread context. There are no guarantees on concurrency for a stateless session EJB. This is important to understand, especially when EJBs are instantiated from a fixed size pool of EJBs inside an application server.

A stateful session bean has a lifecycle. The EJB container has the responsibility to allocate a bean to a particular client. By marking a bean as stateless, we humbly declare this bean can be associated with any EJB client. In the end, the code inside method may alter fields of the bean, but we cannot guarantee that the values of those fields will remain the same in the next invocation of the same bean and possibly on a different Java thread.

If you are thinking about concurrency and Java EE then read ahead to *Appendix D, Java EE 7 Assorted Topics*.

Stateful session beans

A stateful session bean is a session EJB that keeps track of handle to the client caller. In other words, a session EJB maintains state that preserves for each request from a user. Unlike a stateless session bean, a stateful session bean is not shared. The state is only removed once the client terminates. It cannot be reclaimed. The state only remains for the duration of the client-service communication.

One way to think of this idea is that the user has a conversation with the stateful session EJB until it ends or the handle is explicitly released.

We will use an e-commerce shopping cart to demonstrate stateful session EJB. Let us introduce the concept of business interfaces, but first we need an entity to pass between the client and EJB session bean, which we call a customer. Here is a customer POJO shown in the following section:

```java
package je7hb.basic.ejb;
import java.io.Serializable;

public final class Customer implements Serializable {
    private final String firstName;
    private final String lastName;

    public Customer(String firstName, String lastName) {
        this.firstName = firstName;
        this.lastName = lastName;
    }

    public String getFirstName() { return firstName;}
    public String getLastName() { return lastName;}

    @Override
```

```
    public String toString() {
        return "Customer{" +
          "firstName='" + firstName + '\'' +
          ", lastName='" + lastName + '\'' +
        '}';
    }

    // equals() and hashCode() methods omitted
}
```

The `Customer` value object is serializable in order to support remoting, marshalling, and unmarshalling using RMI-IIOP especially across different JVMs. Marshalling is the process of serializing a Java object to an output stream to create data that obeys a predefined protocol. Unmarshalling is the process of reading information from an input stream with data in the predefined protocol and recreating an active Java object.

There were two types of interfaces for session EJBs: local and remote interfaces. Local interfaces are great for speed, reduced latency, and co-location of server. Remote interfaces are great for network distributions call across two different JVMs.

In Java EE 7, business interfaces can use annotations: `@javax.ejb.Remote`, which is reserved for session EJB that require a remote call interface, and `@java.ejb.Local`, which is reserved for session EJB that requires local references.

Let us look at these interfaces, starting with the remote business interface:

```
package je7hb.basic.ejb;
import javax.ejb.Remote;
import java.util.List;

@Remote
public interface ShoppingCart {
    void initialize(Customer customer);
    void addOrderItem(OrderItem item);
    void removeOrderItem(OrderItem item);
    List<OrderItem> getOrderItems();
    void release();
}
```

Now, let us look at the local business interface:

```
package je7hb.basic.ejb;
import javax.ejb.Local;
import java.util.List;

@Local
public interface ShoppingCartLocal {
    void initialize(Customer customer);
    void addOrderItem(OrderItem item);
    void removeOrderItem(OrderItem item);
    List<OrderItem> getOrderItems();
    void release();
}
```

Both interfaces are fairly straightforward. For this purpose, notice that the contracts are the same for both the remote and local business interface. Note the naming convention for these interfaces, the remote is simply named as a typical class name, say ShoppingCart, whereas the local interface has the suffix Local appended to the class name, say ShoppingCartLocal.

Now let us create the bean implementation of both interfaces in one class:

```
package je7hb.basic.ejb;

import javax.ejb.Remove;
import javax.ejb.Stateful;
import java.util.ArrayList;
import java.util.List;

@Stateful
public class ShoppingCartBean
  implements ShoppingCart, ShoppingCartLocal {
    private List<OrderItem> orderItems =
      new ArrayList<OrderItem>();
    private Customer customer = null;
    private boolean initialized = false;

    @Override
    public void initialize(Customer customer)  {
        System.out.printf(
          "SCB#initialize() called%s\n", this );
        this.customer = customer;
        initialised = true;
    }
```

```java
        protected void check() {
            if ( !initialised )  {
                throw new RuntimeException(
                        "This shopping cart is not initialised");
            }
        }

        @Override
        public void addOrderItem(OrderItem item) {
          System.out.printf("SCB#addOrderItem() called%s\n", is );
            check();
            orderItems.add( item );
        }

        @Override
        public void removeOrderItem(OrderItem item) {
          System.out.printf("removeOrderItem() called%s\n", this);
          check();
          orderItems.remove( item );
        }

        @Override
        public List<OrderItem> getOrderItems() {
            check();
            return orderItems;
        }

        @Remove
        public void release() {
            System.out.printf("SCB#release() called%s\n", this );
            orderItems.clear();
            customer = null;
        }
    }
```

The `ShoppingCartBean` bean is annotated with `@javax.ejb.Stateful`, which denotes it as a stateful session bean. It also extends both business interfaces, namely: `ShoppingCart` and `ShoppingCartLocal`.

There is an `initialize()` method, which is the entry point for starting a shopping cart with empty content. It is the method that would be called from a native client, an EJB client or other way into this session bean. The method accepts a customer object, and stores it in the EJB.

The `check()` method performs a sanity check and verifies that the stateful EJB was associated with a customer.

The `addOrderItem()` and `removeOrderItem()` methods append an order item or remove an order from the collection of order items, respectively.

The method `getOrderItems()` returns the list collection of order items to the caller.

Finally, the method `release()` clears the list collection of order items, sets the internal customer of the stateful EJB to null. This method is also annotated with @ `javax.ejb.Remove` that also makes sure the customer resource is released. If the EJB container detects that the stateful EJB is not being used anymore after a reasonable time period, say the user goes off to lunch without completing the task, the associated HTTP Session, if any, expires.

There is another way to write `ShoppingCartBean` that helps to simplify the POJO:

```
@Stateful
@Remote({ShoppingCartLocal.class}
@Local({ShoppingCartLocal.class}
public class ShoppingCartBean {  /* ... */ }
```

The `@Remote` and `@Local` annotations both accept class parameters for situations where the bean does not implement its business interfaces.

For completeness, let us see the definitions of the `OrderItem` class:

```
package je7hb.basic.ejb;
import java.io.Serializable;

public final class OrderItem implements Serializable {
    private final int quantity;
    private final Product product;

    public OrderItem(int quantity, Product product) {
        this.quantity = quantity;
        this.product = product;
    }

    public int getQuantity() { return quantity; }
    public Product getProduct() { return product; }
 // equals(), hashCode() and toString() ommitted
}
```

And also the `Product` class:

```
package je7hb.basic.ejb;
import java.io.Serializable;
import java.math.BigDecimal;

public final class Product implements Serializable {
    private final int id;
    private final String name,description;
    private final BigDecimal price;

    public Product(int id, String name,
            String description, BigDecimal price ) {
        this.id = id;
        this.name = name;
        this.description = description;
        this.price = price;
    }

    public int getId() {return id; }
    public String getName() { return name; }
    public String getDescription() {
        return description; }
    public BigDecimal getPrice() {
        return new BigDecimal(price.doubleValue());
    }

    // equals(), hashCode() and toString() ommitted
}
```

As usual, let us see all of this code in action with another Arquillian integration test. Here is the code:

```
package je7hb.basic.ejb;
// imports omitted
@RunWith(Arquillian.class)
public class ShoppingCartBeanTest {
    @Deployment
    public static JavaArchive createDeployment() {
        /* ... */
        return jar;
    }
```

```java
        Product p1 = new Product(
                1000, "IWG", "Iron Widget Grayson",
                new BigDecimal("4.99" ));
        Product p2 = new Product(
                1002, "MSB", "Miller Steel Bolt",
                new BigDecimal("8.99" ));
        Product p3 = new Product(
                1004, "ASCC", "Alphason Carbonite",
                new BigDecimal("15.99" ));
    Customer customer = new Customer("Fred","Other");

    @EJB ShoppingCartLocal cart;
    void dumpCart( List<OrderItem> items ) { /* ... */ }

    @Test
    public void shouldAddItemsToCart() {
        System.out.printf("cart = %s\n", cart);
        assertNotNull(cart);

        cart.initialize(customer);

        System.out.printf("Initial state of the cart\n");
        dumpCart( cart.getOrderItems());

        OrderItem item1 = new OrderItem( 4, p1 );
        cart.addOrderItem( item1 );
        assertEquals( 1, cart.getOrderItems().size() );

        System.out.printf("After adding one item\n");
        dumpCart( cart.getOrderItems());

        OrderItem item2 = new OrderItem( 7, p2 );
        cart.addOrderItem( item2 );
        assertEquals(2, cart.getOrderItems().size());

        System.out.printf("After adding two items");
        dumpCart( cart.getOrderItems());

        OrderItem item3 = new OrderItem( 10, p3 );
        cart.addOrderItem( item3 );
        assertEquals(3, cart.getOrderItems().size());

        System.out.printf("After adding three items\n");
        dumpCart( cart.getOrderItems());
        cart.release();
    }
}
```

Enterprise Java Beans

The EJB Container injects the `ShoppingCart` session stateful bean into the test, or rather the Arquillian performs this task. Simply declaring the annotation `@EJB` in the client causes the EJB Container to inject a reference to the dependency.

The test defines a set of products and a customer as properties, and in the test method `shouldAddItemsToCart()` we exercise the stateful bean. First, we reset the shopping cart bean with a customer by calling the method `initialize()`, and proceed to add order items to the cart. We assert on each addition the correct size of the order item collection.

Finally, to simulate the finishing of the cart by the user, we call the bean's `release()` method. In a true application, this method would be precipitated in a checkout or reset-cart-empty-status function.

There is a method `dumpCart()`, which iterates over the order items and calculates the total price of the content, whilst at the same time printing the contents to the standard output.

We could have been more pedantic in the unit test and verified the sum total of the cart for each addition of an order item. This is left as an exercise to the order; more relevant would be to rewrite the test so far into proper behaviorally driven design tests.

Here is a screenshot of the test:

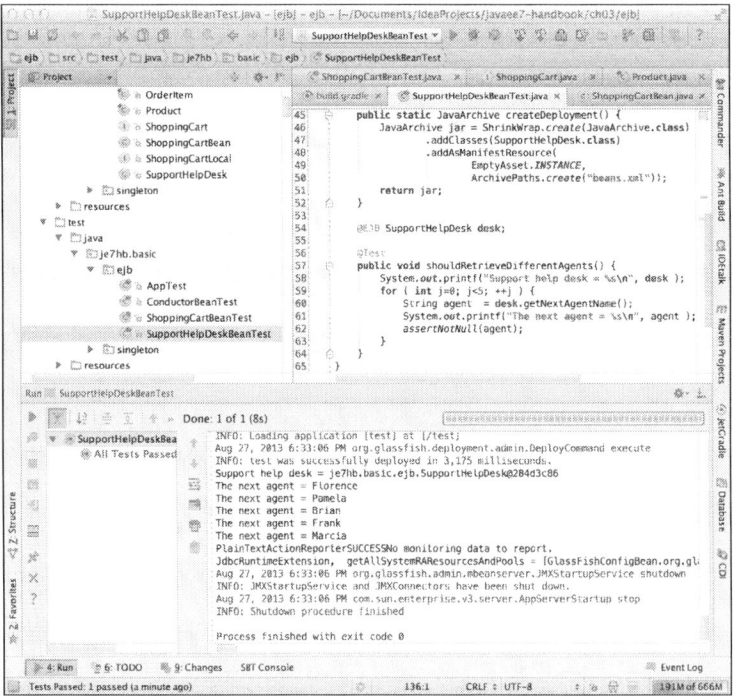

Singleton session beans

Java EE 6 introduced the notion of Singleton session beans into the specification. A singleton is an object that is only instantiated once per application. A purpose of a singleton usually is a global reference point that connects other dependencies. A singleton bean exists for the entire lifetime of the application. As the EJB container, which presumably lives inside a Java EE product, starts the application, singleton session beans are also started. The clients that concurrently access the instance share a singleton bean. When the EJB container removes the application, singleton enterprise bean instances are released.

A singleton session bean instance exists for the entire lifecycle of the enterprise application and there is only one instance per application. They are useful for start-up business logic. If there is a particular connection resource that needs to be shared by other enterprise java beans in the application, and usually those resources need to be the first items that exist in an application, singleton bean instances are designed for these requirements.

An EJB singleton session bean is declared with the annotation `@javax.ejb.Singleton` on a concrete class. The singleton may extend business interfaces or extend a super class.

Let us declare a business interface for a singleton EJB session bean. Suppose we have a business requirement for a conductor component that orchestrates the work of other components in an application. We can write a remote interface for our EJB like this:

```
package je7hb.basic.ejb;
import javax.ejb.Remote;

@Remote
public interface Conductor {
    public void orchestrate( String data );
}
```

The `Conductor` interface defines the remote access contract for our EJB. We already know how to write the local business interface, so we do not repeat this code here. Here is the session EJB singleton class, `ConductorBean`:

```
package je7hb.basic.ejb;
import javax.annotation.*;
import javax.ejb.Singleton;
import java.util.Properties;

@Singleton
```

```java
public class ConductorBean implements Conductor {
    private final Properties properties = new Properties();

    @Override
    public void orchestrate(String data) {
       System.out.printf("ConductorBean#orchestrate( %s ) %s\n",
            data, this );
    }

    @PostConstruct
    public void appStartUp() {
        properties.putAll(System.getProperties());
        System.out.printf("ConductorBean#init() %s\n" +
               "java.version=%s\n", this,
               properties.get("java.version") );
    }

    @PreDestroy
    public void appShutDown() {
        System.out.printf("ConductorBean#shutdown() %s\n", this );
        properties.clear();
    }
}
```

We annotate `ConductorBean` with `@Singleton` and notice that we also added lifecycle hook methods so that we can find out exactly when this EJB component is initialized by the EJB container and also when it is about to be destroyed.

The singleton bean simply stores a `properties` object, which is initialized with the system properties in the `appStartUp()` method and cleared inside the `appShutDown()` method.

Here is another Arquillian integration test that demonstrates how our EJB component works:

```java
package je7hb.basic.ejb;

// imports omitted
import javax.ejb.EJB;
import static org.junit.Assert.assertEquals;

@RunWith(Arquillian.class)
public class ConductorBeanTest {
```

```
    @Deployment
    public static JavaArchive createDeployment() {
        JavaArchive jar = ShrinkWrap.create(JavaArchive.class)
            /* ... */;
        return jar;
    }

    @EJB Conductor conductor1;
    @EJB Conductor conductor2;
    @EJB Conductor conductor3;

    @Test
    public void shouldInjectSingletonEJB() {
        System.out.printf("conductor1 = %s\n", conductor1 );
        conductor1.orchestrate("conductor1");
        System.out.printf("conductor2 = %s\n", conductor2 );
        conductor1.orchestrate("conductor2");
        System.out.printf("conductor3 = %s\n", conductor3 );
        conductor1.orchestrate("conductor3");
        assertEquals( conductor2, conductor1 );
        assertEquals( conductor2, conductor3 );
        assertEquals( conductor1, conductor3 );
    }
}
```

There are three separate references to the ConductorBean in the unit test. Because they are references to a singleton session EJB component, all of the instances should be exactly the same object, a single instance in the EJB component. The is purpose of the unit test is to validate this assertion. We expect the value of the object reference conductor1 to be equal to conductor2, which in turn is equal to conductor3, otherwise we do not have a singleton instance, but a serious problem!

Enterprise Java Beans

This test does pass with flying colors, let's look at its screenshot:

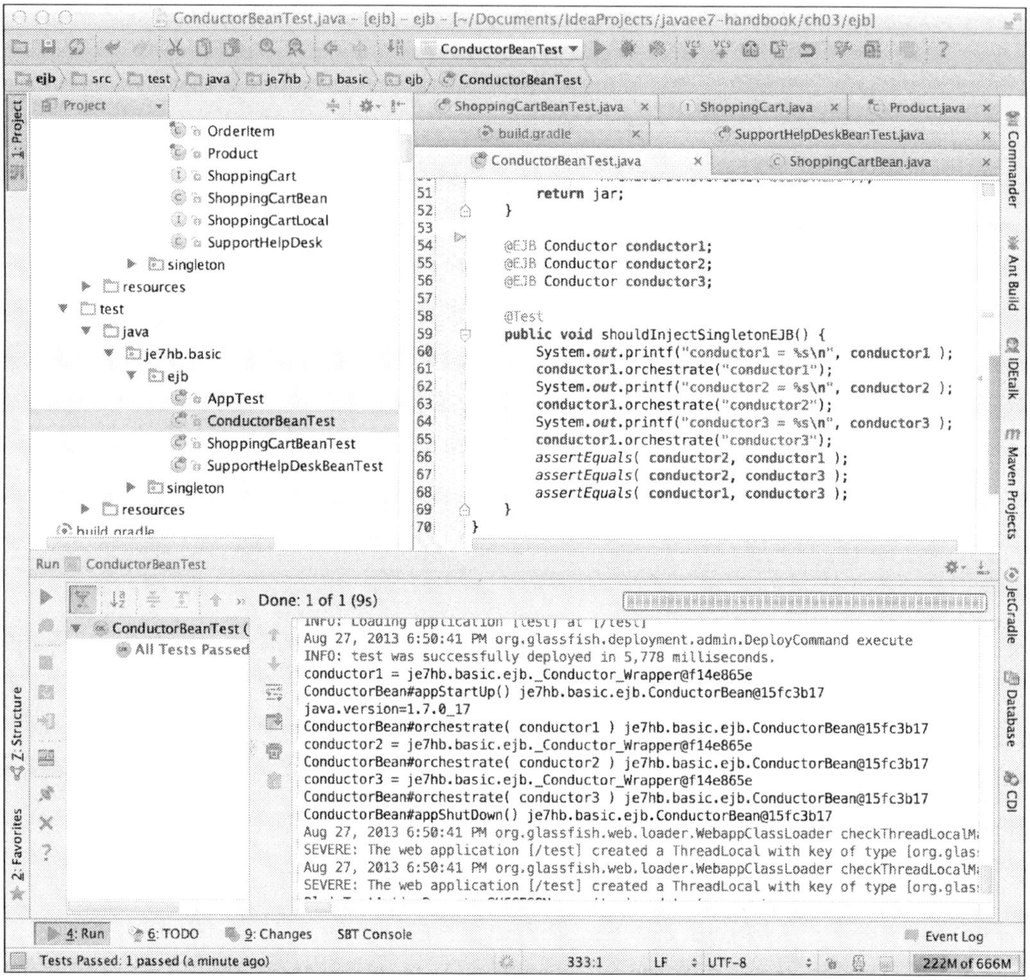

The output clearly illustrates that the singleton instance is just that one single instance shared by EJB client references. It also shows the container calling the initialization and the predestruction methods.

The lifecycle of session EJBs

The EJB container is responsible for instantiating session EJB and removing them when the application starts and eventually is destroyed.

Lifecycle of stateless EJBs

The lifecycle for a stateless session EJB is fairly straightforward. We really can think of them as poolable beans, that is, components that are instantiated by the EJB container from collection of EJB instances. A system administrator can configure the size of the preallocation of each type of EJB in an application.

>  This is completely an anathema to the current cloud provider configuration. Read more at cloud providers, auto scaling, and roles in *Online Chapter, Moving Java EE.next to the Cloud*.

A stateless session EJB has two states. The first state is the non-existence and therefore there is no possible action on the bean. The EJB container has the responsibility to instantiate the EJB at startup time, and if the EJB container supports dynamic allocation of resources, it instantiates the stateless session bean when a request must be served.

In order to initialize the component, the container will invoke the `newInstance()` method of the class to create an object bean instance, thereby invoking the default constructor. The container will then inject dependencies into the bean if there are any such dependencies, and afterwards it will call the methods that have been annotated with `@PostConstruct`.

Once these action have been completed, the stateless session bean is ready for the application, and can serve the incoming requests.

Deallocation of the stateless session bean occurs during the application shutdown, and the EJB container is responsible for management of the procedure of destruction. If there are methods that have been annotated with `@PreDestroy` then those methods are invoked. Afterwards, the EJB container releases the EJB to the internal resource pool, and it may also simply discard the object instance, after some cleaning up, to the garbage collector.

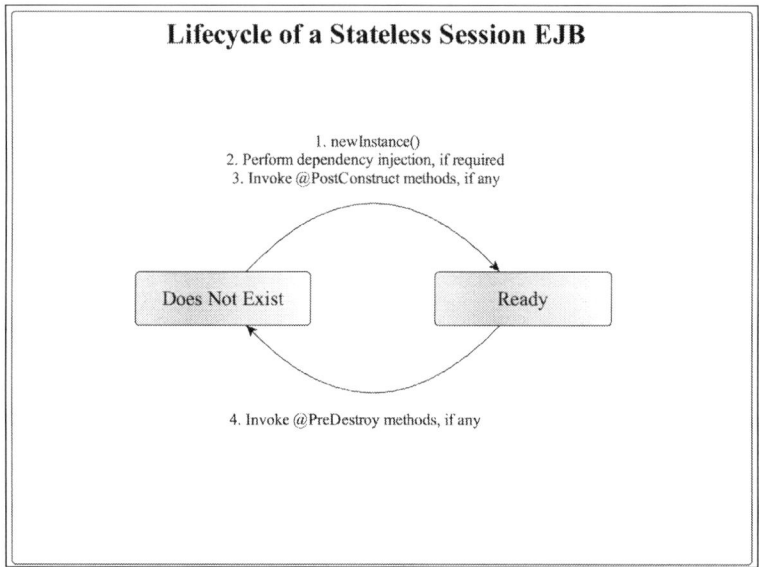

Lifecycle of stateful session beans

A stateful session bean has a slightly different lifecycle to the stateless bean, because it has to preserve state potentially between different requests from the associated EJB client. The EJB container manages the lifecycle of these poolable beans in different way in order to conserve resources. A stateful session bean has three possible states.

A stateful session bean starts in the non-existence state; the EJB container will bring it to life by following the same procedure as the stateless session bean. The container will call the `newInstance()` method to create an object instance, perform the dependency injection of field properties, if required, and it will invoke the methods that are annotated with `@PostConstruct`, if any are defined. Finally, the container will call the `ejbCreate()` method for backwards compatibility with the earlier J2EE specifications, should such a method be defined.

Because the state must be preserved and also the ratio between users of the system usually far exceeds the poolable supply of stateful beans, the EJB container is designed to swap out state and save the information associated with the bean. The bean may have to be deallocated by the Java EE product in order to give another urgent part of the system more resources. So the EJB container can passivate a stateful session bean; in this the bean writer has a chance to save important states of the bean into persistent storage, for example, a relation database or key-value store. The EJB container will call methods annotated with @PrePassivate:

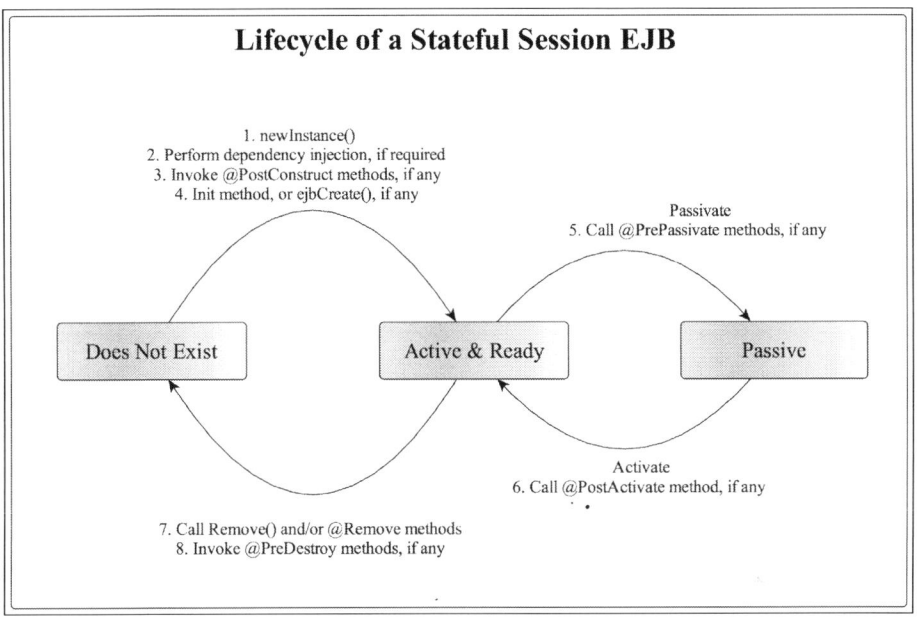

In order to regenerate the state of the stateful session bean, the EJB container will allow the bean to activate and restore its private state before the bean is functionally ready. The EJB container will call any methods on the bean that are annotated with @PostActivate. During activation (or reactivation) of the bean, the EJB container will not have to perform dependency injection on the bean. Activation will usually occur if there is an incoming request or method invocation from the EJB client and the bean has already been passivated.

One can think of the activation-passivation procedure, perhaps, with the notion of the real user starting a shopping cart experience but leaving the cart and website open whilst going off for lunch with a colleague. They will expect to come back to their computers, log back on, continue with the same web application, and then expect to see a responsive website with the contents of the cart still preserved as before the meal.

Taking the earlier example of `ShoppingCartBean`, using the stateful session bean, we could preserve the shopping cart of the user when ever the EJB container wanted to save the state, passivate the bean. We could save the customer and the shopping cart together using an annotated `@PrePassivate` method, and perhaps we could use the Java Persistence API and an injected persistence context. In the `@PostActivate()` method, the customer and the shopping cart could be restored by reading the data from the same persistence storage.

Lifecycle of singleton session beans

The lifetime of a singleton session bean is almost the same as that of a stateless session bean. There are only two states: the non-existent state and the ready state.

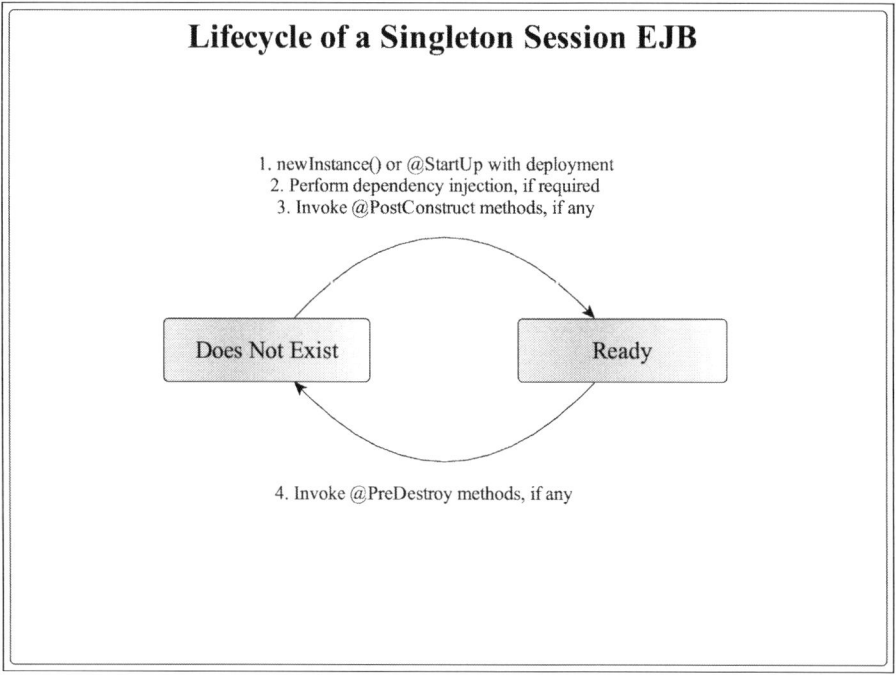

The first state is the non-existence and therefore there is no possible action on the bean. In order to transit to the ready state, the EJB container instantiates the bean, performs dependency injection, and call any methods annotated with `@PostConstruct`.

Singleton session beans can also be annotated `@javax.ejb.StartUp`, which signals to the EJB container and application server to initiate the object instance as soon as the application is deployed successfully.

The singleton bean instance is only destroyed before the application is undeployed and as the application is halted. If there are methods annotated with `@PreDestroy` on the instance, then those methods will be called in order to give the application a chance to release important resources and save status to the database.

Of course during an application server crash, there can hardly be a chance that `@PreDestroy` will be called, although some application server Java EE providers might offer some extra solution to help with these types of situations.

You might be wondering that if you have more than one singleton bean instance, and they have dependencies between themselves, how to configure the order of initialization? The answer is to use annotation called `@javax.ejb.DependsOn`.

Let us see an example in code of two singleton bean instances with startup and dependency annotations:

```java
@Startup
@Singleton
public class ConductorBean implements Conductor {
    private Properties properties;
    @PostConstruct
    void appStartUp() {
        // initialize properties ...
    }
    // ...
}

@Startup
@Singleton
@DependsOn("ConductorBean")
public class FacilitatorBean implements Facilitator {
    @EJB private Conductor conductor;
    private WorkState state;
    @PostConstruct
    void init() {
        // initialize work state ...
    }
    // ...
}
```

The `FacilitatorBean` and the `ConductorBean` are singleton bean instances, which are initialized as soon as the application that they contained is deployed to the application server. The `FacilitatorBean` is a singleton instance that depends on the existence of `ConductorBean` being the first constructed. It uses the conductor, an EJB client reference, in order to initialize its own state `WorkState`.

Business interfaces

We will now examine the two types of business interface access in more detail.

Local access

As we have seen already, every session bean must have a business interface that enables a client to invoke methods on it. Session beans can have no Java interface and the EJB container will generate one dynamically as a hidden proxy.

The `@javax.ejb.Local` annotation denotes the local business interface. It is the default if the session bean does not specify an interface. A local business interface can only be invoked if the EJB component runs on the same JVM. If your architecture is different then you should favor creating a remote business interface instead of adding to the local one.

A local business interface is certainly comparable to a direct invocation call and depending on the Java EE product and its implementation it will translate to dynamic invocation across a proxy to the singleton bean instance. It will certainly be faster than the equivalent network call. Therefore, the arguments and results of the local access are passed by reference. There is no marshaling or serialization of the arguments or return types to be expected here.

Local access is location dependent for obvious reasons.

Remote access

The remote business interface is purely for a remote invocation from one JVM to another JVM, therefore these calls travel across the network, even if they are co-located on the same physical server.

In order to enable remote access, the session bean requires an annotation called `@javax.ejb.Remote` declared on the implementing class or the Java interface.

Remote access is more expansive than local access because the parameters, the arguments, and return type must be marshaled and serialized, if only for byte-order encoding. The arguments and the return type are passed by value.

Remote access is location independent.

Access summary

Here is a table summarizing the two types of business interface:

Local	Remote
Location dependent	Location independent
Object are passed by value	Objects are passed by reference
Object serialization is not required	Objects must be serializable
Almost direct coupling between the target and client components	Proxy and loose coupling between the target and client components
Invocations are cheap – 2 step JVM dispatch calls	Invocations are expensive across the network
No network error costs	Adds the extra cost of supporting remote access to handle communication error

No interface views

The annotation `@javax.ejb.LocalBean` is designed for session beans that do not expose a business interface to clients. By default any session bean that does not declare an implementing interface representing a local or remote view is taken by the specification as a *no-interface* view. EJB specification allows local business interfaces to be optional. This means the developer does not have to define a local interface.

Here is an example of a no-interface stateless session EJB:

```
package je7hb.basic.ejb;
import je7hb.basic.ejb.examples.*;
import javax.ejb.*;
import javax.inject.Inject;

@Stateless
@LocalBean
public class PostTradeProcessor {

    @EJB DataRepository dataRepository;
    @EJB EnrichmentManager enrichmentManager;
    @Inject MatchingEngine matchingEngine;

    public void preProcess( Product product ) { /* ... */ }
    public void process( Product product ) { /* ... */ }
    public void postProcess( Product product ) { /* ... */ }
}
```

In this class `PostTradeProcessor` there is no business interface defined as a local view. The annotation `@LocalBean` informs the EJB container that the business interface locally is derived from all of the public methods called inside the EJB. In the example, the methods `preProcess()`, `process()`, and `postProcess()` are exposed as the client view.

As you witnessed in the previous example, `PostTradeProcessor` actually relies on dependency injection of references through the annotations `@Inject` and `@EJB`.

EJB references

The EJB container is able to inject references of session beans into an application. It turns out that the CDI container can achieve the same effect. Most of the time, developers can rely on `@Inject` from CDI to add a dependency, since this annotation is designed to work with managed beans, and the fact is an EJB is a type of managed beans.

> First inject EJB references with `@javax.inject.Inject` to ensure your application's longevity and if that fails to work because of, say, a circular reference or strange behavior, revert to `@javax.ejb.EJB`.

CDI managed beans may be injected into an EJB. However, there are restrictions on the scope. A stateless session or singleton EJB normally is injectable into a CDI bean, because the lifetime of EJB generally exceeds the CDI managed bean.

There is one other tried and tested way to get a reference to an EJB, and that is to use the JNDI. But going down this track leads you to dependency lookup and far away from dependency injection.

This is the JNDI way:

```
public void someWorkMustBeDone() {
    PostTradeProcessor processor = null;
    try {
        Context context = (Context)
            new InitialContext();
        processor = (PostTradeProcessor)
            context.lookup(
                "java:comp/PostTradeProcessor");
```

```
        } catch (NamingException e) {
            throw new RuntimeException(e);
        }

        hangTen(processor); // ...
    }
```

This code is only useful in tight corners of development.

Asynchronous invocations

EJB methods may be marked as annotation @javax.ejb.Asynchronous to inform the EJB container that they invoke tasks separate to the container invocation Java thread. An asynchronous method returns a void element or it is Future<V>, where V is the value type that is being returned.

Here is an example of a session bean using asynchronous invocation:

```
@Singleton
public class AsyncWebpageDownloader {
    @Asynchronous
    @Lock(LockType.READ)
    public Future<String> fetchWebPage(String url)
    throws IOException {
        String data = createReport(url);
        return new AsyncResult<String>(data);
    }

    private String createReport(String url) throws IOException {
        URLConnection http = new URL("url")
                .openConnection();
        InputStream in = http.getInputStream();
        ByteArrayOutputStream baos = new ByteArrayOutputStream();
        baos.write( (url+":\n").getBytes());
        try {
            byte[] buf = new byte[8192];
            int len;
            while ((len = in.read(buf)) > 0) {
                baos.write(buf, 0, len);
                nap();
            }
            baos.close();
```

```
        } finally {
            in.close();
        }

        return baos.toString();
    }

    private void nap() {
        try {
            Thread.sleep(200);
        } catch (InterruptedException ignored) {
        }
    }
}
```

The EJB `AsyncWebpageDownloader` has a single method called `fetchWebPage()` that is annotated with `@Asynchronous`. We also add a concurrency hint to the container with an annotation `@javax.ejb.Lock`, to configure this call point with a reader's lock. The method accepts a URL and downloads a web page from the internet into memory. In order to simulate a long running operation, we add some time delays to the file download inside the I/O loop. At the end of the process, the downloaded content is returned to the caller as `Future<String>` instance. The result is stored in a special type `javax.ejb.AsyncResult`.

The relationship between EJB and CDI containers

In Java EE 7, EJB container has this sole responsibility and it is worth remarking that the EJB container is not the same as the CDI container. Although in some internal implementations of the Java EE 7 standard there may be subtle differences between each bean type. Indeed, in the JSR-342 specification document, there is no mention at all of CDI. It is theoretically possible to rewrite all types of EJBs as CDI managed beans. In future Java EE platform editions, the relationship between the EJB and CDI container should be more clearly defined.

Lightweight scope of EJBs

EJB in Java EE 7 are lightweight. In fact the discussion and debate about heavyweight versus lightweight misses the point. Every software system that we now employ in our application will be almost certainly managed by a container. Whether that container is a CPU on a chip or a Java EE application server really is neither here nor there. What matters to most technicians and definitely to business is the ability for the components to be on scale on demand. Does the container infrastructure simplify the architecture? Does the container infrastructure overlap or conflict with another type of containerization? Think about it this way. How many layers of ingredients are you going to put on that pizza base? You and I would just like to enjoy a nice tasting pizza at the end of the day. It is this ability to mix and match that serves EJB in Java EE 7.

Lastly, to emphasize the point, observe the demand for poolable session EJB in application servers over time from 2002 to 2013:

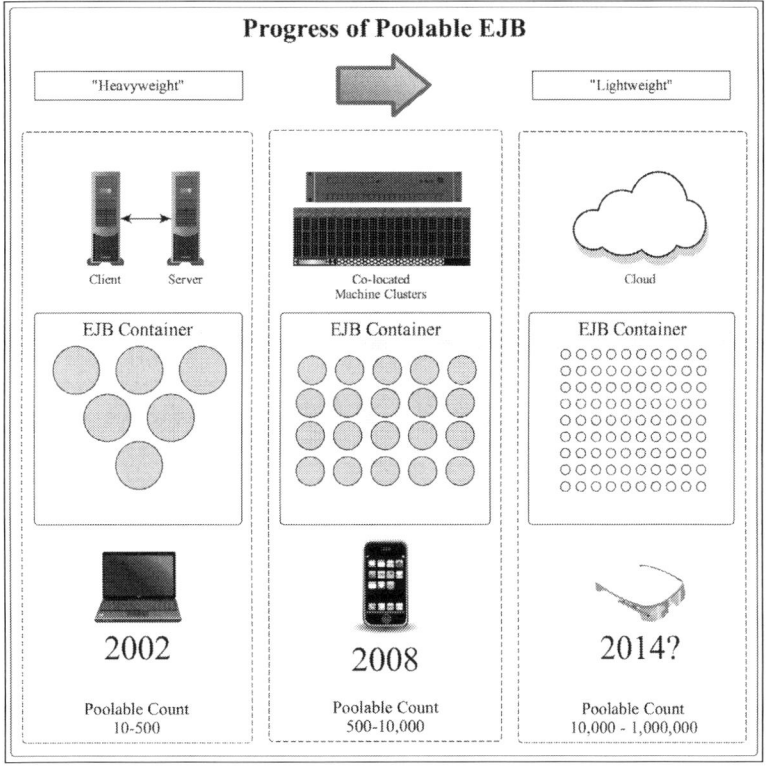

Application servers in the cloud computing environment will be expected to pool over one million EJB instances and auto scale all of them. Now if that is not considered lightweight, I really do not know what is.

Enterprise Java Beans

An EJB can serve as JAX-RS 2.0 endpoint (*See Chapter 8, RESTful Services JAX-RS 2.0*):

```
@Path("/projects")
@Stateless
public class ProjectRESTServerEndpoint { /* ... */ }
```

An EJB can be WebSocket server-side endpoint (*See Chapter 7, Java API for HTML5WebSocket*):

```
@ServerEndpoint("/sockets")

@Stateless

public class ProjectWebSocketEndpoint { /* ... */ }
```

An EJB can even be Java Servlet (*See Chapter 6, Java Servlets and Asynchronous Request-Response*):

```
@WebServlet("/browse")

@Stateless

public class ProjectBrowse extends HttpServlet { /* ... */ }
```

Nonetheless, I strongly recommend that you continue to separate your concerns, your view from model-control logic. Please do not follow the previous example as good practice.

Summary

In this chapter on EJB session bean instance, we have seen how POJOs can easily be annotated to be either stateful, stateless, or singleton EJB components. A session EJB is essentially the Java component at the other end of the telephone line; they are the end points that perform some useful action of work.

A session bean, is simply the foundation layer to writing business server objects inside a Java EE application server. Session beans are called by EJB client applications. An EJB can be the client of another EJB. EJB are endpoints of invocation. An EJB container manages all EJBs.

There are two ways an EJB client can fundamentally invoke a method in a session bean. The implementation bean may define a remote business interface and annotate it with `@javax.ejb.Remote`; and/or it may also define a local business interface and annotate it `@javax.ejb.Local`.

The EJB container determines the lifecycles of the three types of session beans. Stateful session beans are the only type that supports activation and passivation. Java EE is about adding metadata to a simple Java class and then letting the container manage its lifecycle.

In the next two chapters, *Chapter 4, Essential Java Persistence API 3.2* and *Chapter 5, Object-Relational Mapping with JPA* we will go head-first into Java Persistence. The ability to save user content into a database or backing store using object-relational mapping techniques is a crucially important feature.

4
Essential Java Persistence API 3.2

Alice Walker said, "In search of my mother's garden, I found my own."

In the last chapter, we introduced the session beans, which are the business service endpoints for your Java EE application. In this chapter, we are changing over to persistence, in what used to be called entity EJBs in the older J2EE specifications, but are now simply called **Persistence Capable Objects (PCO)**.

The **Java Persistence API (JPA)**, JSR 338, Version 3.2 is the specification that mandates how persistence can be applied to the objects in the Java EE product. One solution is storing data and a standard. Other solutions do exist, which also handle the problem of accessing and reading data into different types of long-term storage products. JPA 3.2 adds advanced features, such as ability to work with stored procedures, mapped entities, and fetch plans. You can read about these features in *Chapter 11, Advanced Topics in Persistence*.

Entities and the Java Persistence API first appeared in Java EE 5 as EJB 3.0 open source frameworks, such as Red Hat's Hibernate and Spring Framework, and proprietary solutions such as Oracle's TopLink also heavily influenced them.

The Java Persistence API is the standard object relation mapping API for both Java SE and Java EE. It means that you can use JPA inside the container and outside of it in a standalone program. JPA is based on POJO that are denoted, annotated, or configured in XML, to be persisted somewhere. In other words, JPA does not care or dictate exactly where your data is stored, it simply helps to map data from the Java objects to the underlying data storage and vice versa. The data store can be a relation database for maximum effectiveness, and it can also be a document database with limited functionality. The only limits are the type of **Object/Relational Mapping (ORM)** implementation and the complexity of the data model.

Essential Java Persistence API 3.2

JPA is a specification and there are several implementations, which include, unsurprisingly, Hibernate, Apache OpenJPA, and also EclipseLink. The EclipseLink is a product that serves as the reference implementation of JPA, which was denoted to Eclipse Foundation by Oracle, and in a previous life, EclipseLink was offered under a different guise as TopLink Essentials. OpenJPA is an open source alternative for the JPA implementation.

As this is supposed to be a reference handbook, we will only see the essential cookbook features of JPA. It is not a substitute for the JPA official specification, which is quite extensive. Nor does it compete with other writings, articles, and tomes that are purely aimed at Java Persistence and data storage. Rather, this chapter is the foundation description, it will get you started writing the entity classes for your next business Java EE application. *Chapter 5, Object-Relational Mapping with JPA*, advances this knowledge into more intermediate-level problems of persistence.

Entities

An entity is a persistence capable object. For the Java platform and in the language of Java, it is a plain and simply object instance that has been specially marked (or in the vernacular of the older object relational mapper product, enhanced) in a way that means that it can be persisted to long-term storage, which, for most of us souls, is a relational database.

An entity for the cloud-enabled Java EE products can also be persisted to a cloud database with usually some tighter restrictions on what you can do with those types of objects.

JPA entities are mapped to the database tables or views. Going forward with this chapter, we are going to consider only relational databases.

Defining Entity bean

What is an entity bean? The answer is almost any class can be declared as an entity bean.

- An entity bean is an object that has been annotated with `@javax.persistence.Entity`
- An entity bean must have a public accessible no-arguments constructor
- An entity bean cannot be declared `final` and nor can any methods or instance methods inside of it be declared `final`

- An entity bean must be a top-level class, it cannot be an inner class for example
- An entity bean cannot be a Java `interface` nor can it be a Java `enum`
- An entity bean can be a concrete class or an abstract class, because entity beans support object-oriented inheritance and polymorphism through associations and types

Persistence of entity beans is extended to special cases: if an entity bean inherits from a non-entity bean and also if a non-entity bean inherits from an entity bean, only the persistent entity beans parts will be guaranteed to be stored.

For entity beans that need to be transferred over a network, for example in a remote connection, we recommend that the entity bean implement the `javax.io.Serializable` marker interface. In fact, we strongly recommend this for all of your entity beans, in order to allow them to be detached from and reattached to the persistence context session. We will discuss more on this notion of attachment to persistence contexts in later sections.

There is one more way to denote an object as an entity bean, which is not by using the `@Entity` annotation, but by declaring it inside an XML configuration file.

Therefore, the process to make an ordinary Java class be persisted to long-term storage is to add metadata to the class, which can be applied through the annotations or an XML configuration file. It is the sole responsibility of the JPA provider to perform the correct database operations in order to save the entity to storage (and load it back again of course).

An entity bean example

Let's review an example of a JPA entity bean, in which we will see two versions of this class is as follows:

A Plain Old Java Object

The following class is a data object, a POJO, which represents a record of a particular genre of fictional books that have been popular for over 100 years. Some books from this particular genre about spying, intergovernmental agencies, and other forms of esoteric investigations, have been turned into motion-picture and television productions. The class `SpyThriller`, which contains an identity number, the writer of the book, the year it was published, and of course the title, is as follows:

```
package je7hb.basic.jpa;

public class SpyThriller {
```

```java
    private long id;
    private String writer;
    private int year;
    private String title;

    public SpyThriller() {}

    public SpyThriller(String writer, int year, String title) {
       this.writer = writer;
       this.year = year;
       this.title = title;
       }

    public long getId() {return id;}
    public void setId(long id) {this.id = id;}

    public String getWriter() {return writer;}
    public void setWriter(String writer) {this.writer = writer;}

    public int getYear() {return year;}
    public void setYear(int year) {this.year = year;}

    public String getTitle() {return title;}
    public void setTitle(String title) {this.title = title;}

    // toString() method omitted
    }
```

So far there is nothing special to see here in the SpyThriller bean. These are the usual pair methods for fulfilling the constraints of a valid JavaBean object that has properties. It is important to note that we can access each property of this Java bean through the getter and setter methods.

Note that we have the constructor that can populate all of the fields of the bean, except for the identity property, which is called id. We will see in this section, why this was written this way.

Let us now transform this bean into a JPA entity bean with some annotations. The second version of our bean is as follows:

A simple entity bean

The `SpyThriller` bean with some annotations that transforms it into a working entity bean is as follows:

```
package je7hb.basic.jpa;
import javax.persistence.*;

@Entity
public class SpyThriller {
  @Id
  @GeneratedValue(strategy = GenerationType.AUTO)
  private long id;
  private String writer;
  private int year;
  private String title;

  public SpyThriller() {}

  // Full constructor omitted

  public long getId() {return id;}
  public void setId(long id) {this.id = id;}

  public String getWriter() {return writer;}
  public void setWriter(String writer) {this.writer = writer;}

  public int getYear() {return year;}
  public void setYear(int year) {this.year = year;}

  public String getTitle() {return title;}
  public void setTitle(String title) {this.title = title;}

  // toString() method omitted
}
```

First, we applied the annotation `@javax.entity.Entity` to the class itself, which denotes that the bean is a persistent capable object suitable for enhancement.

Second, we also make sure that this POJO is serializable and it can be detached from the persistent session by extending the `java.io.Serializable` marker interface. This means that the `SpyThriller` entity bean can also be sent across a network, for example, using a session bean with a remote business interface.

Essential Java Persistence API 3.2

Third, we applied the `id` property with two new annotations: `@javax.entity.Id` and `@javax.entity.GeneratedValue`.

The annotation `@Id` denotes a Java property to be the primary key of the entity bean. In particular, every entity must have a primary key. The primary key of the entity is the unique identifier for the bean inside the database.

The annotation `@GeneratedValue` denotes the entity has a unique value that is generated by the database. There are different strategies for creating the database unique identifier, and in the preceding example, `strategy=AUTO` means that we are relying on the database to explicitly generate this identifier for our `SpyThriller` bean.

So, when we first insert a `SpyThriller` bean into the database, the identifier `id` will be automatically generated for us by the underlying database, and the bean's `id` property will be populated with this value by the JPA provider. This is the reason why the identifier `id` was not specified as part of the bean's constructor arguments.

In `SpyThriller`, all of the properties, the fields of the bean, are by default persistent capable, and they will be stored inside the database. What happens if we do not want this persistence for a particular field? We can apply to the field an annotation `@javax.entity.Transient`. Another version of our entity bean so far is as follows:

```
@Entity
public class SpyThriller extends java.io.Serializable {
  @Id
  @GeneratedValue(strategy = GenerationType.AUTO)
  private long id;
  private String writer;
  private int year;
  private String title;

  @Transient
  private String secretCode;

  public SpyThriller() {}
  // Same code as before
}
```

In the preceding code fragment, the field `secretCode` is not persistent capable, and it will never be stored inside the database because it is annotated with `@Transient`.

Let us summarize the annotations so far as follows:

Annotation	Description
@Entity	Specifies the bean as persistence capable
@Id	Specifies the primary key of the entity bean
@GeneratedValue	Specifies the value of the property generated using a strategy in the underlying database or custom implementation
@Transient	Specifies the property is not being persisted inside the database

Expanded entity bean definition

The JPA specification is designed to allow programming by convention-over-configuration in order to ease software development. This means there are reasonable defaults; it follows the principle of least astonishment.

There are more annotations that the last example code hid from the naked eye. Let us look at an expanded definition of entity bean as follows:

```
import javax.persistence.*;

@Entity(name = "SpyThriller")
@Table(name = "SPY_THRILLER_BOOK")
public class SpyThriller extends Serializable {
  @Id
  @GeneratedValue(strategy = GenerationType.AUTO)
  @Column(name = "BOOK_ID", table = "THRILLER_BOOK",
    unique = true, nullable = false,
    insertable = true, updatable = true)
  private long id;
  @Basic(fetch = FetchType.EAGER)
  @Column(name = "AUTHORS", nullable = false)
  private String writer;
  @Column(name = "BOOK_YEAR", nullable = false)
  private int year;
  @Column(name = "TITLE", nullable = false)
  private String title;

  public SpyThriller() {}
}
```

The @Table annotation

The `@javax.entity.Table` annotation specifies the target name of the database table, and applying the annotation to the code allows us to override the default. Every entity bean typically represents a single row in a database table, and each database table has a set of table columns. In order for the JPA provider to map the entity to the database, it needs to know the database table name. If the `@Table` annotation is not provided, then the name of the entity bean is used. Because the database systems support only certain character cases, be it only uppercase, lowercase, or mixed case, with or without some underscore characters, there has to be a way out for the software developer to explicitly override the sensible convention on their chosen system.

In most cases, the database table name will default to the uppercase of the entity bean's class name with underscores in between the camel case. For example, `SpyThriller` is mapped to `SPY_THRILLER`. If you need a specific datable table name then use the `@Table` annotation.

The @Entity annotation

For the purpose of the **Java Persistence Query Language (JPQL)**, `@javax.entity.Entity` allows the entity query name to be overridden. Please note that the query name is not necessarily the same as the target database name. The annotation `@Table` sets the database table name. `@Entity` specifies that the Java class is persistence capable under a JPA provider, and is suitable for enhancement and mapping to a database.

The @Basic annotation

The `@javax.entity.Basic` annotation defines the simple enhancement possible in JPA. It maps a field or persistent property to a database column. It maps the Java primitive types, the primitive wrapper types, the serializable types, the user-defined serializable types, and certain standard class types from SDK and certain array types. See the following table for the full list.

The main use of `@Basic` defines how the JPA provider actually retrieves dependent columns and links to the associated records from the database. There are two forms of access: LAZY and EAGER.

```
publicenumFetchType {LAZY, EAGER};
@Target({METHOD, FIELD}) @Retention(RUNTIME)
```

The EAGER strategy informs the JPA provider that the data must be readily fetched. In other words, it should be fetched eagerly. The LAZY strategy informs the JPA provider that it permits it to fetch the data, only when the property or field is about to be accessed. The default mode is EAGER.

A list of valid mappings for `@Basic` field/properties is shown in the following table:

Class and types	Remarks
Java primitive types	`boolean`, `byte`, `char`, `short`, `int`, `long`, `float`, `double`
Java wrapper types	`java.lang.Boolean`, `java.lang.Byte`, `java.lang.Character`, `java.lang.Short`, `java.lang.Integer`, `java.lang.Long`, `java.lang.Float`, `java.lang.Double`
Serializable type	Standard Java serialized types and user-defined types implementing the `java.io.Serializable` marker interface
Enums	Standard Java enumerations
String	The standard `java.lang.String` implementation
Math	`java.math.BigInteger` and `java.math.BigDecimal`
Database JDBC temporal types	`java.sql.Date`, `java.sql.Time`, and `java.lang.DateTime`
Array primitives	`byte[]` and `char[]`
Wrapper Primitives	`java.lang.Byte[]` and `java.lang.Character[]`

The JPA specification, as you can see yourself, allows most types to be mapped by default to the database. The extra wrapper array primitives and array primitives are quite useful for the **binary object** (**BLOB**) mapping.

The @Column annotation

As each entity bean maps to a single database table row, there is another annotation that corresponds to `@Table`. The annotation `@javax.entity.Column` specifies how a field or persistent property maps to a database table column.

The `@Column` annotation allows the configuration of the database table name, whether it can be a null column, whether a new record with that column can be inserted, and/or whether an existing record with that particular column can be updated.

Most of the time developers will just want to override the column name, and see if the column can contain the NULL values or not.

In the preceding example code there are two examples where we override the configuration. We override the field `year` to the target database column name `BOOK_YEAR` because in the Apache Derby database, year is a reserved keyword! Also, we override the `writer` field to map explicitly the target database column name AUTHORS.

A table of the `@javax.entity.Column` annotation arguments is as follows:

Name	Type	Description	Default Value
name	String	The name of the column.	The name of the field or property
unique	Boolean	Defines if this column is unique in the database table.	false
nullable	Boolean	Defines if this column accepts the NULL values.	false
insertable	Boolean	Defines whether this column is included in the SQL INSERT command generated by the JPA provider.	true
updatable	Boolean	Defines whether this column is included in the SQL UPDATE commands that are generated by the JPA provider.	true
columnDefinition	Boolean	Defines SQL fragment that is used when generating the database description language for the column, for example, CLOB NOT NULL.	Generated SQL from the JPA provider, which creates the database table column
table	String	Defines the database table that contains the column. This argument is used to override the primary table from the entity.	Column is in the primary table of the entity bean
length	int	The column length. This argument is only applicable for a String value column.	255
precision	int	The precision for a decimal type column. This is typically for real number database columns.	0
scale	int	The scale for a decimal column. This is typically configured only for real number database columns.	0

All the `@Column` annotation arguments are optional, but at least one argument must be defined for sensible operation.

Annotating entity beans

As a developer, you can annotate the field variables of an entity bean in order to inform the JPA provider how to enhance the object-relation mapping to the target database table. You have seen how this works previously, but there is a second way to annotate entity beans. Alternatively, you can also annotate the getter and setter methods on entity beans.

The decision to annotate on the field variables or the getter properties is down to personal preference. After all is considered, you in the role as the bean provider make this decision. Let us look at the case of the getter and setter annotations.

Annotating entities with the instance variables

Here is an entity bean class for a train system, `Train`, which is a very simple data object. It has three field variables standing for the source and target locations, and a time that is formatted as a long primitive with the pattern: `yyyyMMdd`.

```
package je7hb.basic.jpa;
import javax.persistence.*;
import java.io.Serializable;

@Entity
public class Train implements Serializable {
  @Id
  @GeneratedValue(strategy = GenerationType.AUTO)
  private long id;

  @Column(name = "FROM_LOC", nullable = false)
  private String from;

  @Column(name = "TO_LOC", nullable = false)
  private String to;

  /** Pattern format yyyyMMdd */
  @Column(name = "TRAIN_DATE")
  private int trainDate;

  public Train() {this(null,null,0);}
```

```
    public Train(String from, String to, int trainDate) {
      this.from = from;
      this.to = to;
      this.trainDate = trainDate;
    }

    public long getId() {return id;}
    public void setId(long id) {this.id = id;}

    public String getFrom() {return from;}
    public void setFrom(String fromLoc) {
      this.from = fromLoc;
    }

    public String getTo() {return to;}
    public void setTo(String toLoc) {this.to = toLoc;}

    public int getTrainDate() {return trainDate;}
    public void setTrainDate(int trainDate) {
      this.trainDate = trainDate;
    }
    // toString() method omitted
  }
```

The `Train` entity class is annotated on the field variables: `id`, `from`, `to`, and `trainDate`. We have used the `@Column` annotation to explicitly specify the target database column names, because the field variables named are mostly reserved keywords in the underlying database.

Annotating entities with property accessors

The same entity class annotated on the getter and setter methods is as follows:

```
    package je7hb.basic.jpa;

    import javax.persistence.*;
    import java.io.Serializable;

    @Entity
    public class Train implements Serializable {
      private long id;
      private String from;
      private String to;
      private int trainDate;
```

```java
    public Train2() {this(null,null,0);}

    public Train(String from, String to, int trainDate) {
      this.from = from;
      this.to = to;
      this.trainDate = trainDate;
      }

    @Id
    @GeneratedValue(strategy = GenerationType.AUTO)
    public long getId() {return id;}
    public void setId(long id) {this.id = id;}

    @Column(name = "FROM_LOC", nullable = false)
    public String getFrom() {return from;}
    public void setFrom(String fromLoc) {
      this.from = fromLoc;
      }

    @Column(name = "TO_LOC", nullable = false)
    public String getTo() {return to;}
    public void setTo(String toLoc) {this.to = toLoc;}

    /** Pattern format yyyyMMdd */
    @Column(name = "TRAIN_DATE")
    public int getTrainDate() {return trainDate;}
    public void setTrainDate(int trainDate) {
      this.trainDate = trainDate;
      }

    // toString() method omitted
    }
```

Moving the annotations to the getter and setter methods has one advantage in that it allows the LAZY instantiation of the property. Let us suppose the Train entity had an expensive or large-dependent entity bean that implied significant performance cost, then annotating the getter and setter properties may be useful.

Developer, the bean provider, must ensure that there is no public access to the fields of the instance variables. In particular, the clients of entity bean and related entity beans must always call the getter methods in to access an entity's properties.

Essential Java Persistence API 3.2

For entity beans that are standalone, the decision to annotate the field variables versus the accessor methods can be trivial. When entity bean is part of the object hierarchy, then choosing one style or the other is very important. If you choose the field instance for the root class of the hierarchy, you are advised to follow it for all the subentity bean classes. Do not mix the two styles.

Comparing annotating styles

A table of cost and benefits of annotating the instance variables versus the property accessor methods is as follows:

	Benefits	Costs
Instance Variable	• Fastest performance, avoids the overhead of the method calls • The JPA provider persistence manager has direct access in order to read and write from and to the DB • Less lines of code	• Not possible to achieve the LAZY initialization • Can be expensive for the property objects that really require the LAZY initialization
Property Accessor	• The LAZY initialization of the property • Creation of the values on demand • Provides a simple way to add an extra behavior during the initialization	• Performance loss with extra method calls • Impact on properties, if entity bean is involved in a query • More lines of code

There are two styles to annotate JPA and entity beans. Injecting into the bean getter and setter methods, obviously, provides a way of intercepting the incoming argument, and also computing a result or triggering some other action. On the other hand, we recommend that entities should be kept relatively simple, and serious business logic should go into either Bean Validation or service endpoints.

Choose one style of annotating entity beans at the beginning of your software development team's project and stay with it for the duration. Remember not to mix the annotation styles in the entity bean hierarchies, especially.

Running a simple entity bean test

In this section, we will run a simple entity bean test with the Arquillian framework.

The Gradle build file for the entity bean test

We are using the setup of Gradle, Arquillian test framework, Apache Derby, and embedded Glassfish server. The project's Gradle build file `build.gradle` is as follows:

```
apply plugin: 'java'
apply plugin: 'maven'
apply plugin: 'eclipse'
apply plugin: 'idea'

// Define equivalent Maven GAV coordinates.
group = 'com.javaeehandbook.book1'
archivesBaseName = 'ch04-jpa-simple'
version = '1.0'

repositories {
  mavenLocal()
  mavenCentral()
  maven {
    url 'https://maven.java.net/content/groups/
    promoted'
  }
  maven {
    url 'http://repository.jboss.org/nexus/content/
      groups/public'
  }
}

dependencies {
  compile 'javax:javaee-api:7.0'
  runtime 'javax:javaee-api:7.0'

  testCompile 'junit:junit:4.11'
  testCompile 'org.jboss.arquillian.junit:
  arquillian-junit-container:1.0.3.Final'
  testCompile 'org.jboss.arquillian.container:
  arquillian-glassfish-embedded-3.1:1.0.0.CR4'
```

```
    runtime 'org.glassfish.main.extras:
      glassfish-embedded-all:4.0.1-b01'
    }

  task wrapper(type: Wrapper) {
    gradleVersion = '1.6'
    }

  // Override Gradle defaults - a force an exploded JAR view
  sourceSets {
    main {
      output.resourcesDir = 'build/classes/main'
      output.classesDir = 'build/classes/main'
      }
    test {
      resources {
        srcDir 'src/test/resources'
        }
      resources {
        srcDir 'src/test/resources-glassfish-embedded'
        }

      output.resourcesDir = 'build/classes/test'
      output.classesDir = 'build/classes/test'
      }
    }
```

We included a couple of extra dependencies in order to run the unit tests, which are the GlassFish embedded container and the Java EE 7 API. We also have two separate resource folders under the test tree `src/test/resources` and `src/test/resources-glassfish-embedded`. The reason why we have done this will become apparent.

A stateful session bean

First, we will define a session bean to act as a mediator to the database as follows:

```
packageje7hb.basic.jpa;

import javax.ejb.Stateful;
import javax.persistence.EntityManager;
import javax.persistence.PersistenceContext;
import javax.persistence.PersistenceContextType;
import javax.persistence.Query;
import java.util.List;
```

```
@Stateful
public class SpyThrillerBookBean {
  @PersistenceContext(unitName = "testDatabase",
    type = PersistenceContextType.EXTENDED)
  private EntityManager entityManager;

  public void addBook(SpyThriller movie) throws Exception {
    entityManager.persist(movie);
  }

  public void deleteBook(SpyThriller movie) throws Exception {
    entityManager.remove(movie);
  }

  public List<SpyThriller> getBooks() throws Exception {
    Query query = entityManager.createQuery
      ("SELECT m from SpyThriller as m");
    return query.getResultList();
  }
}
```

The code shows a session EJB named SpyThrillerBookBean of the stateful type, which we have already seen in *Chapter 3, Enterprise Java Beans*. The stateful session bean requires a javax.persistence.PersistenceContext object that is injected into the service by the EJB container. The SpyThrillerBookBean acts as the central processor for the SpyThriller entity beans.

PersistenceContext is annotated with an extended conversation scope, which allows the transaction context to live through multiple method requests. This is useful to support work flow in a web application. We also have to explicitly name the persistence unit, with which the persistence context used in this stateful EJB is associated. In this case, the persistent context refers to a unit named testDatabase.

It is entirely possible to have multiple persistence contexts injected into a session bean.

There are methods on the stateful bean to add a book, addBook(), remove a book, deleteBook(), and retrieve a list of the books from the database, getBook().

In the listing method getBook(), we make use of the JPA query facility from the entity manager. We create a query object that uses the **Java Persistence API Query Language (JPQL)**, which looks like native SQL, but it is different.

Essential Java Persistence API 3.2

JPQL is the query language for EJB and is designed to support portable entity bean with retrieving data, updating data, and insertion of new data, and JPQL also supports bulk update and delete operations. In the example code, we are using JPQL with a static String statement. There are other ways to define the JPQL statements with the annotations, and we will come to them in a later section of this chapter.

An entity bean integration test

Let us now examine the unit test for this stateful EJB with the entity bean with Arquillian.

```
packageje7hb.basic.jpa;
// other imports omitted
import javax.ejb.EJB;
import java.util.List;
import static org.junit.Assert.*;

@RunWith(Arquillian.class)
public class SpyThrillerBookBeanTest {
  @Deployment
  public static JavaArchive createDeployment() {
    JavaArchive jar = ShrinkWrap.create(JavaArchive.class)
    .addPackage(SpyThrillerBookBean.class.getPackage())
    .addAsResource("test-persistence.xml",
      "META-INF/persistence.xml")
    .addAsManifestResource(EmptyAsset.INSTANCE, "beans.xml");
    return jar;
  }

  @EJBSpyThrillerBookBeanbookService;

  @Test
  public void shouldPersistEntities() throws Exception {
    assertEquals(0, bookService.getBooks().size());
bookService.addBook(new SpyThriller
  ("The Spy Who Came in from the Cold", 1963,
    "John Le Carre" ));
  bookService.addBook(new SpyThriller
    ("Casino Royale", 1953, "Ian Fleming"));
  bookService.addBook(new SpyThriller
    ("The Hunt for Red October ", 1984, "Tom Clancy"));
  bookService.addBook(new SpyThriller
    ("Bravo Two Zero", 1993, "Andy McNab"));
```

```
    bookService.addBook(new SpyThriller
      ("On Her Majesty's Secret Service", 1963, "Ian Fleming"));

    List<SpyThriller> list = bookService.getBooks();
    assertEquals( 5, list.size());

    for (SpyThriller movie : list) {
      System.out.printf("movie = %s\n", movie);
      bookService.deleteBook(movie);
      }

    assertEquals(0, bookService.getBooks().size());
    }
}
```

The first difference between this test class, `SpyThrillerBookBeanTest`, and the previous integration tests is the method named `addPackage()`, which is part of the `ShrinkWrap` builder. `AddPackage()` registers all of the classes in the supplied Java package for deployment.

The second difference is that we supplied an additional XML configuration for deployment, which is named `test-persistence.xml` in the source code. In the build tree, the file becomes the persistence context configuration `META-INF/persistence.xml`. We will see this XML configuration in a bit.

The EJB container injects a reference to the stateful bean `SpyThrillerBookBean` for the purpose of testing. We could also use `@javax.inject.Inject` for future proofing.

In the actual test method, we invoke all the service methods of the stateful bean. First, we assert that the database table should be empty; there should be no `SpyThriller` entities in it. Next, we insert a number of entities. We assert again the number of entities that should be stored in the database. After that, we retrieve a list collection of the entities, we iterate over this list in order to delete individual entities. Finally, we assert the database is empty, and if all things are right and good, then the test should pass. However, we need to set up and configure the persistence context.

A persistence context XML configuration

Let us look at the persistence context file for the unit test as follows:

```xml
<persistence version = "2.1"
  xmlns = "http://xmlns.jcp.org/xml/ns/persistence"
    xmlns:xsi = "http://www.w3.org/2001/XMLSchema-instance"
      xsi:schemaLocation =
        "http://xmlns.jcp.org/xml/ns/persistence
          http://java.sun.com/xml/ns/persistence
            /persistence_2_1.xsd">

<persistence-unit name = "testDatabase" transaction-type = "JTA">
<provider>
org.eclipse.persistence.jpa.PersistenceProvider
</provider>
<jta-data-source>jdbc/arquillian</jta-data-source>
<properties>
<property name = "eclipselink.ddl-generation"
  value = "drop-and-create-tables"/>
<property name = "eclipselink.ddl-generation.output-mode"
  value = "both"/>
<property name = "eclipselink.logging.level.sql"
  value = "FINE"/>
<property name = "eclipselink.logging.parameters"
  value = "true"/>
<property name = "eclipselink.create-ddl-jdbc-file-name"
  value = "createDDL.jdbc"/>
</properties>
</persistence-unit>
</persistence>
```

The persistence configuration defines one `persistence-unit` XML element and that is the session context, if you will, mapping `EntityManager` to the database. It is possible to have more than one `persistence-unit` inside the persistence configuration file.

There are two transaction types of persistence units: `JTA` and `RESOURCE_LOCAL`.

The `JTA` variety is the type that can only run inside a Java EE application server; **JTA** stands for **Java Transaction API**. These persistence unit types have transactional support by default. The application server, via the EJB and JPA container, will provide a JTA data source to the entity manager.

The `RESOURCE_LOCAL` variety is for standalone Java SE applications, and therefore allows JPA to be used outside of a Java EE application server. It is also possible to specify a non-JTA data source inside a Java EE application. In this case, using `RESOURCE_LOCAL` in such an application means the data source is not going to be a JTA data source, and therefore will not have transactions.

When we declare a persistence unit with a JTA data source, then we also need to specify the name of the data source, which in this configuration is named `jdbc/arquillian`.

A table of the EclipseLink configuration properties is as follows:

Property	Description
`eclipselink.ddl-generation`	Specifies how EclipseLink can automatically generate the table and database for a persistence unit. The values can be either `create-table` or `drop-and-create-tables`.
`eclipselink.ddl-generation.output-mode`	Specifies how Eclipse can execute the DDL schema. The valid values can be set to either `sql-script`, `database`, or both.
`eclipselink.logging.level.sql`	Specifies the JDK logging level for EclipseLink. The valid values are `OFF`, `SEVERE`, `WARNING`, `INFO`, `CONFIG`, `FINE`, `FINER`, `FINEST`, `ALL`.
`eclipselink.logging.parameters`	Specifies if the SQL parameters should be logged or not. This is useful for debugging the native SQL the JPA provider generates.
`eclipselink.create-ddl-jdbc-file-name`	Specifies the name of the DDL created tables and schema script that is generated when the output-mode is set to both or `sql-script`.
`eclipselink.drop-ddl-jdbc-file-name`	Specifies the name of the DDL drop tables and schema script that is generated when the output-mode is set to both or `sql-script`.
`eclipselink.jdbc.driver`	Specifies the JDBC database driver class name for the Java SE deployment.
`eclipselink.jdbc.url`	Specifies the JDBC database URL class name for the Java SE deployment.

Essential Java Persistence API 3.2

Property	Description
`eclipselink.jdbc.user`	Specifies the JDBC database login username for the Java SE deployment.
`eclipselink.jdbc.password`	Specifies the JDBC database login password for the Java SE deployment.

Since JPA 2.0, these EclipseLink JDBC configuration properties have been superseded by standard additional properties for the JPA providers.

Appendix B, Java EE 7 Persistence, has a full description of the standard JPA properties.

Arquillian configuration for the embedded GlassFish server

We configure specific properties for the JPA provider in order to allow it to connect to the database. In this case, we are using the embedded GlassFish server. We need to tell Arquillian how to set up the data source. We set this up in another configuration file named `src/test/resources/arquillian.xml`.

```xml
<?xml version = "1.0" encoding = "UTF-8"?>
<arquillian xmlns = "http://jboss.org/schema/arquillian"
   xmlns:xsi = "http://www.w3.org/2001/XMLSchema-instance"
     xsi:schemaLocation = "http://jboss.org/schema/arquillian
       http://jboss.org/schema/arquillian/arquillian_1_0.xsd">
<container qualifier = "glassfish-embedded" default = "true">
<configuration>
<property name = "resourcesXml">
src/test/resources-glassfish-embedded/
glassfish-resources.xml
</property>
</configuration>
</container>
</arquillian>
```

Since our example is using Apache Derby, we tell Arquillian where to find the additional setup of the GlassFish resources.

I know it looks a little complicated, this indirection, but it is useful when switching between different application servers in order to make a separate integration test.

Suppose next week, Monday, there was suddenly a requirement to make a test with the JBoss application server, then we would simply make a change, and add in extra configurations in a new folder, presumably named `src/test/resources-jboss-as-embedded`. (Of course we would modify `SourceSet` accordingly in the `build.gradle` file and make sure we create the profile configuration, in order to anticipate every new application server request that arrives in the product backlog, going forward.)

The GlassFish resource configuration file, `src/test/resources-glassfish-embedded/glassfish-resources.xml`, is as follows:

```
<?xml version = "1.0" encoding = "UTF-8"?>
<!DOCTYPE resources PUBLIC"-//GlassFish.org//
   DTD GlassFish Application Server 3.1 Resource Definitions//EN"
     "http://glassfish.org/dtds/glassfish-resources_1_5.dtd">
<resources>
<jdbc-resource pool-name = "ArquillianEmbeddedDerbyPool"
   jndi-name = "jdbc/arquillian"/>
<jdbc-connection-pool name = "ArquillianEmbeddedDerbyPool"
   res-type = "javax.sql.DataSource" datasource-classname =
     "org.apache.derby.jdbc.EmbeddedDataSource"
        is-isolation-level-guaranteed = "false">
<property name = "databaseName" value = "build/databases/derby"/>
<property name = "createDatabase" value = "create"/>
</jdbc-connection-pool>
</resources>
```

The XML schema for this file is specific to the GlassFish application server. It configures a JDBC connection pool, and thus the JTA enabled data source. Notice how the Derby database is stored in the build folder, and is compatible with the Gradle build infrastructure `build/databases/derby`.

Finally, we throw in a log configuration file so that developers can see the console output. The file, which is specific only to the GlassFish application server, and is named `src/test/resources-glassfish-embedded/glassfish-resources.xml` is as follows:

```
handlers = java.util.logging.ConsoleHandler
java.util.logging.ConsoleHandler.formatter =
   java.util.logging.SimpleFormatter
java.util.logging.SimpleFormatter.format = %4$s: %5$s%n
java.util.logging.ConsoleHandler.level = FINEST
```

As we can see, GlassFish makes use of the standard JDK logging facility.

Essential Java Persistence API 3.2

Running an integration test

The output running the Arquillian integration unit test is as follows:

```
JUnitStarter -ideVersion5 je7hb.basic.jpa.SpyThrillerBookBeanTest
sql: --SELECT BOOK_ID, TITLE, AUTHORS, BOOK_YEAR FROM SPY_THRILLER
sql: --UPDATE SEQUENCE SET SEQ_COUNT = SEQ_COUNT + ? WHERE
  SEQ_NAME = ?
    bind => [50, SEQ_GEN]
sql: --SELECT SEQ_COUNT FROM SEQUENCE WHERE SEQ_NAME = ?
  bind => [SEQ_GEN]
sql: --INSERT INTO SPY_THRILLER
  (BOOK_ID, TITLE, AUTHORS, BOOK_YEAR) VALUES (?, ?, ?, ?)
bind => [1, John Le Carre, The Spy Who Came in from the Cold,
  1963]
movie = SpyThriller{id = 1, writer =
  'The Spy Who Came in from the Cold', title = 'John Le Carre',
    year = 1963, secretCode = '823056538'}
movie = SpyThriller{id = 2, writer = 'Casino Royale', title =
  'Ian Fleming', year = 1953, secretCode = '416058911'}
sql: --DELETE FROM SPY_THRILLER WHERE (BOOK_ID = ?)
bind => [2]
movie = SpyThriller{id = 3, writer =
  'The Hunt for Red October ', title = 'Tom Clancy', year =
    1984, secretCode = '825011405'}
movie = SpyThriller{id = 4, writer = 'Bravo Two Zero',
  title = 'Andy McNab', year = 1993, secretCode = '831259338'}
movie = SpyThriller{id = 5, writer =
  'On Her Majesty's Secret Service', title = 'Ian Fleming',
    year = 1963, secretCode = '56561882'}

INFO: HV000001: Hibernate Validator 5.0.0.Final

PlainTextActionReporterSUCCESSDescription:
  add-resources AdminCommandnull
JDBC connection pool ArquillianEmbeddedDerbyPool created
  successfully.
JDBC resource jdbc/arquillian created successfully.

--Connected: jdbc:derby:build/databases/derby
  User: APP
  Database: Apache Derby  Version: 10.9.1.0 - (1344872)
  Driver: Apache Derby Embedded JDBC Driver Version: 10.9.1.0 -
    (1344872)
Aug 03, 2013 11:42:36 AM com.sun.enterprise.v3.server.AppServerStartup
stop

INFO: Shutdown procedure finished
Process finished with exit code 0
```

The lifecycle of an entity bean

Entities are managed by the instances of `javax.entity.EntityManager` in the Java application. Entities have a lifecycle of four states: new, managed, detached, and removed.

The new entity state

An entity bean is in the new state when it is instantiated with the Java new operator, or serialized from the object stream. In the new state, entity bean is not associated with any `EntityManager` instance whatsoever. An alternative way to specify this is to say that the entity bean has no persistence context, and therefore, no persistence identity.

The managed entity state

An entity bean is in the managed state when it is associated with an `EntityManager` instance and that instance is still valid in terms of the JVM. A managed entity bean has a definite persistence context and identity.

The detached entity state

An entity bean is in the detached state when it is no longer associated with an `EntityManager`. A detached entity can be found if the entity bean is serialized into an object stream so that it is transferred across the network from one JVM to another. A detached entity can be found if its associated `EntityManager` goes out of scope.

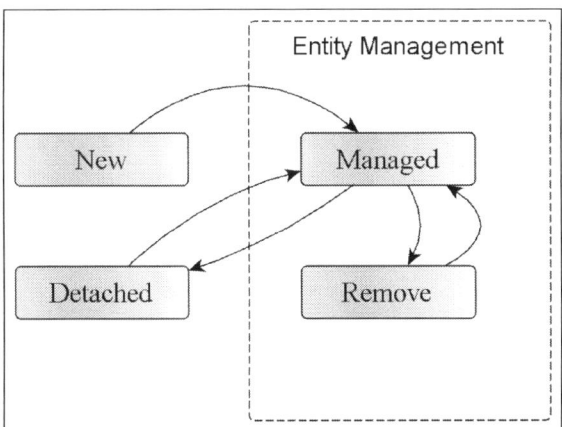

Fig: Diagram of entity Lifecycle states

A detached entity bean can be reattached with `EntityManager` during a merge operation, as we will see later in the discussion around management.

The removed entity state

An entity bean is in the removed state when it has been flagged for removal from the database. The entity bean is deleted from the database, and the mapped row is deleted from the table row when the enclosing transaction successfully commits.

EntityManager

`EntityManager` in the JPA provider maintains a cache of the entity instances. It is solely responsible for mapping the Java entity bean to and from the database, using the JPA provider solution.

Persistence context

Persistence context is associated with an entity manager. Its job is to allow the entity manager to reference entity beans that are created, updated, retrieved, and deleted. It also has another job, and that is to merge entity beans that are detached with the current instance from the underlying database.

The EntityManager methods

`EntityManager` has several methods to handle persistence of entity beans. The entity manager in JPA is always associated with one single persistence context. Inside the persistence context, there are zero or more entity bean instances, which must be unique in terms of storage to a database.

Developers program against the `EntityManager` API in order to create and remove the persistent entity instances, to find entities by their primary key, and to query over entities.

A simplified view of the `EntityManager` interface is as follows:

```
packagejavax.persistence;
import java.util.Map;
import javax.persistence.metamodel.Metamodel;
import javax.persistence.criteria.*;

public interface EntityManager {
  void persist(Object entity);
  <T> T merge(T entity);
  void refresh(Object entity);
  void remove(Object entity);
```

```java
void clear();
void detach(Object entity);
boolean contains(Object entity);

void flush();
void setFlushMode(FlushModeType flushMode);
FlushModeType getFlushMode();

<T> T find(Class<T> entityClass, Object primaryKey);
<T> T find(Class<T> entityClass, Object primaryKey,
  Map<String, Object> properties);
<T>T find(Class<T> entityClass, Object primaryKey,
  LockModeType lockMode);
<T> T find(Class<T> entityClass, Object primaryKey,
  LockModeType lockMode, Map<String, Object> properties);
<T> T getReference(Class<T> entityClass, Object primaryKey);

void lock(Object entity, LockModeType lockMode);
void lock(Object entity, LockModeType lockMode,
Map<String, Object> properties);

void refresh(Object entity, Map<String, Object> properties);
void refresh(Object entity, LockModeTypelockMode);
void refresh(Object entity, LockModeType lockMode,
  Map<String, Object> properties);

LockModeType getLockMode(Object entity);

void setProperty(String propertyName, Object value);

Map<String, Object>getProperties();

Query createQuery(String qlString);
Query createNamedQuery(String name);

<T> TypedQuery<T>createQuery(CriteriaQuery<T>criteriaQuery);
<T> TypedQuery<T>createQuery(String qlString,
  Class<T>resultClass);
<T> TypedQuery<T>createNamedQuery(String name,
  Class<T> resultClass);

Query createNativeQuery(String sqlString);
Query createNativeQuery(String sqlString, Class resultClass);
```

```
Query createNativeQuery(String sqlString,
  String resultSetMapping);

voidjoinTransaction();
void close();
boolean isOpen();

EntityTransactiongetTransaction();
EntityManagerFactory getEntityManagerFactory();

CriteriaBuildergetCriteriaBuilder();
Metamodel getMetamodel();
}
```

When you first look at this interface, you are probably thinking that this is a lot to take in. The truth is, you only need to know a dozen method calls, and the rest of the API will sink in as you start to make advanced applications, because you will start to ask more questions about how to write stuff to solve a business problem.

Persisting new instances

The `EntityManager.persist()` method is the most important, it calls the JPA provider to manage the current entity bean. If the current entity is unmanaged, it becomes managed. The entity P is saved into the database, or before a transaction commit, or as a result of the flush operation.

Given the entity bean P, the semantics of the save or insert operation are as follows:

- If the entity bean P is managed, then the state is unchanged; it will still be managed. If those relationships are configured to cascade (`cascade=PERSIST` or `cascade=ALL`), then the persist operation will cause other beans relevant and referenced by the input bean to become managed by the persistence context.

- If the entity bean P is removed, then the bean becomes managed again.

- If the entity bean P is detached, then the bean can throw an `EntityExistsException` exception. The result appears because the client has not called merge on the current entity instance in a cache, or it can be that the cache is stale and out of the date, or similarly the entity already has a row with the primary or foreign key constraint violation.

The reader should particularly note that the method named `EntityManager.persist()` will not guarantee the immediate execution of an SQL INSERT instruction. The JPA provider and its persistence manager implementation decide exactly when saving to the database is carried out. Hence the reasoning behind waiting until just before the enclosing transaction commits, or flushing the persistence context cache directly through the call.

It is possible to find out if a particular entity bean is managed or not with the method `EntityManager.contains()`.

Removing the existing instances

The `EntityManager.remove()` method is a signal to the persistence entity manager to evict the entity bean from its cache, and also to eventually delete the entity from the underlying database. The removal occurs immediately, before the transaction commits, or as a result of the flush operation.

Given an entity bean P, the removal operation semantics are as follows:

- If the entity P is a new instance, then it is ignored by the remove operation. However, if P has references to other entities that are managed by the entity manager, and if those relationships are set to cascade (`cascade=REMOVE` or `cascade=ALL`), then those dependent elements are also set to be removed.

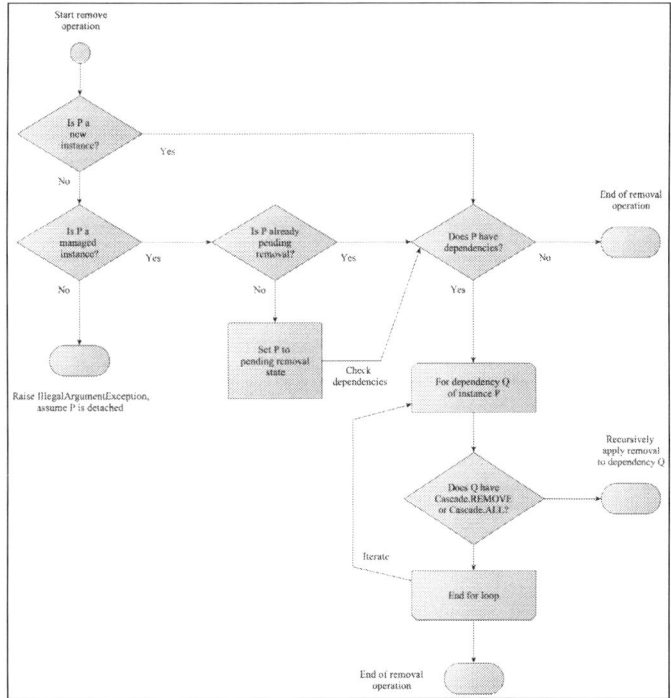

- If the entity `P` is a managed instance, then it is switched to the remove state, a signal for the eventual deletion from the persistence storage. If `P` has references to other entities that are managed by the entity manager, and if those relationships are set to cascade (`cascade=REMOVE` or `cascade=ALL`), then those dependent elements are set as pending removal.
- If the entity `P` is detached from a persistence context, then the JPA provider will raise an `IllegalArgumentException` exception.
- If the entity `P` is already set for removal, then nothing happens, the behavior is a no-operation (no-op). The dependencies of `P`, if any, are considered for removal.

Refreshing the entity bean instances

The `EntityManager.refresh()` method causes an entity bean to be refreshed from the database. For a managed entity bean, calling this method causes data to be overridden from the table columns in the current database. The refresh operation can also cascade to other instances, if those instances are annotated with `cascade=REFRESH` or `cascade=ALL`.

If the entity bean is in the new, detached, or removed states, then the JPA provider will raise an `IllegalArgumentException` exception.

Detaching the entity bean instances

The entity bean is detached if and when the instance is disassociated from its corresponding persistence unit. Detachment can occur, if the entity bean is part of transaction, which is rolled back. The reference to the entity bean will no longer valid. Application call themselves invoking `EntityTransaction.rollback()`. The application can detach entity from the persistent unit by calling `EntityManager.detach()`. Finally, an entity becomes detached if it is serialized over the network from the server to the client, or simply removed from the entity manager `EntityManager.remove()`.

Once the entity bean becomes detached, it will not track persistence context and the entity manager. Nor will there be any additional proxy operations applied to it. This means when accessing the detached bean with a dependent field or properties that reference other entities-especially if they are designated as `LAZY`-those references may be out-of-date or may even be null, that is they are simply not accessible. Rephrased in another way, the JPA provider is not able to lazily bind fields or accessor properties that were not bound before the entity detachment.

In this situation, if you want to reassociate a detached entity bean with a persistence context, then you must call the method `EntityManager.merge()`. The merge operation propagates the state of the detached entities into the persistent entities managed by the entity manager. It is important to note that the changes in the detached entity are not propagated immediately to the persistent storage. The changes are reflected in the entity instance in memory. The changes are saved to the database by calling `EntityManager.persist()` separately.

Given the entity bean P, the semantics of the merge operation are as follows:

- If P is a detached bean, the state of P is copied onto a pre-existing managed instance P'.
- If P is a new instance, the state of P is copied onto a new managed instance P'.
- If P is a removed instance, the JPA provider will raise an `IllegalArgumentException` exception.
- If P is a managed instance, JPA will ignore the merge operation. However, it will cascade the merge operation to any dependent entity beans, if they are annotated with `cascade=MERGE` or `cascade=ALL`.

The JPA provider does not merge the fields that have been marked `Eager.LAZY`, especially those fields that have not been fetched at the time of the call.

> Merging between the JPA provider implementations is certainly not guaranteed in the specification. If you truly want such a feature, then it might be best to look at marshaling the entity bean into the XML configuration or the JSON dump.

We will deal with several of the other important methods on the `EntityManager` interface in *Chapter 5, Object-Relational Mapping with JPA*.

Flushing the pending instances to the database

`EntityManager.flush()` causes the JPA provider and persistence context to attempt to save the current changing instances to the database. This call is useful for long transactions and when you would like to ensure that some SQL operations actually hit the database store. However, until the transaction commits (or rolls back), if the underlying database follows the **ACID** (**Atomicity, Consistency, Isolation, and Durability**) standards, then no other database sessions will be able to see the updated changes to the affected database tables and rows.

Essential Java Persistence API 3.2

The standard does not mandate what and when the entity beans should be flushed to the database. Calling `EntityManager.flush()` is a hint to the JPA provider to initiate writing the SQL INSERT and SQL UPDATE statements to the database driver as soon as possible. It is certainly not an immediate call to action.

Transactional support

For the Java EE applications that execute inside a Java EE 7 application server product, the container provides transactions. This is known as container manager entity management. The instance of `EntityManager` and the associated persistence context is available to all the application components that either inject it or programmatically look it up and use the manager. The entity manager is associated with a single JTA transaction for the lifetime of the service request.

As we have already seen in the stateful bean example, `SpyThrillerBean`, we can rely on an upstream component to demarcate the boundaries of a transaction. The upstream component may be Servlet, another session bean, or even a web service, or a RESTful service endpoint.

Application managed transactions

It is useful to know how JPA transactions work in a standalone Java SE application. Custom transaction management is also useful in certain Java EE applications, where there is a business requirement to roll your own transaction.

The application is responsible for creating and destroying an `EntityManager` and associated persistence context. In order to create a new entity manager, the application retrieves a reference to the factory class of the JPA provider in a portable fashion. An application can inject `javax.persistence.EntityManagerFactory` into the component.

```
@PesistentUnit EntityManagerFactory emf;
EntityManager em;

public void createEntityManager() {
  em = emf.createEntityManager();
}
```

Once we have a new entity manager in the bean, then we need an instance of the Java Transaction API user transaction instance. We can inject the instance of `javax.transaction.UserTransaction` in the application component, then we associate it to the entity manager in the business logic method.

An example source code fragment, which shows how to begin and end a user-defined transaction, using an injected JTA instance is as follows:

```
@PesistentUnit EntityManagerFactory emf;
EntityManager em;

@Resource UserTransaction utx;

public void createEntityManager() {
  em = emf.createEntityManager();
}

public void performSomeWork() {
  em = emf.createEntityManager();
  try {
    utx.begin(); // Start TX

    em.persist(payrollEntity);
    em.merge(customerEntity);
    em.remove(trackingEntity);

    utx.commit(); // End TX
  } catch (Exception e) {
    utx.rollbaback(); // End TX
  }
}
```

Because `UserTransaction` is a system wide component in that it is supplied by the application server, we inject it as a dependency using `@javax.annotation.Resource`.

The definition of `UserTransaction` for reference is as follows:

```
package javax.transaction;

public interface UserTransaction {
  void begin() throws NotSupportedException, SystemException;
  void commit() throws RollbackException,
    HeuristicMixedException, HeuristicRollbackException,
      SecurityException, IllegalStateException,
        SystemException;
  void rollback() throws IllegalStateException,
    SecurityException, SystemException;
  void setRollbackOnly() throws IllegalStateException,
    SystemException;
  int getStatus() throws SystemException;
  void setTransactionTimeout(int i) throws SystemException;
}
```

You can find out more about transactions in *Appendix C, Java EE 7 Transactions*.

Retrieving an EntityManager by injection

We have already seen how a stateful session bean can obtain an EntityManager. We used the EJB container injection mechanism to do this as follows:

```
@Stateless
public class DepositAccountManager {
  @PersistenceContext("retail-north-west")
  private EntityManager em;

  /* ... */
  public void switchDepositToSaving( Sting acc) {
    Account account = em.createQuery
      ("select d from Account d "+ "where d.account = :account");
    .setParameter("account", acc)
    .getResultList().get(0)
    account .setAccountType(AccountType.SAVING)
    em.persist(account);
    }
}
```

Here we have a fictional stateless session bean DepositAccountManager with a transaction local persistence context injected into it. The method switchDepositToSaving() executes a JPQL query that retrieves one record from the database. We switch record to a saving account, and then save the record back to the store.

Notice how we are able to parameterize the account by supplying it as an argument to the query, and also the syntax for the tokenized arguments in the dynamic JPQL string.

Retrieving an EntityManager by factory

It is also possible to retrieve an EntityManager from EntityManagerFactory inside an application that runs inside an application server. Here is a new version of the spy thriller book stateful session bean that illustrates the technique of using a persistence unit factory in order to acquire the entity manager. The session bean named SpyThrillerBookWithFactoryCreationBean is as follows:

```
packageje7hb.basic.jpa;
import javax.annotation.*;
import javax.ejb.*;
import javax.persistence.*;
import java.util.List;
```

```java
@Stateful
public class SpyThrillerBookWithFactoryCreationBean {
  @PersistenceUnit(unitName = "testDatabase")
  privateEntityManagerFactory factory;
  private EntityManager em;

  @PostConstruct
  public void init() {
    em = factory.createEntityManager();
  }

  @PreDestroy
  @Remove
  public void destroy() {
    em.close();
  }

  public void addBook(SpyThriller movie) throws Exception {
    em.persist(movie);
    em.flush();
  }

  public void deleteBook(SpyThriller movie)
  throws Exception {
    em.remove(movie);
    em.flush();
  }

  public List<SpyThriller> getBooks() throws Exception {
    Query query = em.createQuery
      ("SELECT m from SpyThriller as m");
    return query.getResultList();
  }
}
```

The annotation `@javax.persistence.PersistenceUnit` injects a reference to the persistence unit in the session bean.

We also add the lifecycle handle methods with annotations `@PostConstruct`, `@PreDestroy`, and `@Remove` to respectively create the entity manager, and close it after the user has finished with the bean.

Essential Java Persistence API 3.2

In the preceding code, we compensated for the lack of a way to programmatically instantiate an `EntityManager` with an explicit extended transaction persistence context. Hence, we have extra calls to `Entity.flush()`, immediately after the save and delete operations.

Retrieving an EntityManager by the JNDI lookup

The final way of obtaining an `EntityManager` is programmatic. We can acquire an entity manager instance by using the JNDI lookup.

An example of using the JNDI lookup in a session bean, which is a rewrite of `SpyThrillerBook` from earlier, is as follows:

```java
package je7hb.basic.jpa;
import javax.annotation.Resource;
import javax.ejb.*;
import javax.persistence.*;
import java.util.List;

@Stateful
@PersistenceContext(unitName = "testDatabase",
  name = "myLookupName",
    type = PersistenceContextType.EXTENDED)
public class SpyThrillerBookWithJNIDILookupBean {

  @Resource private SessionContext ctx;

  public EntityManager getEntityManager() {
    return (EntityManager)ctx.lookup("myLookupName");
  }
  public void addBook(SpyThriller movie) throws Exception {
    getEntityManager().persist(movie);
  }

  public void deleteBook(SpyThriller movie)
  throws Exception {
    getEntityManager().remove(movie);
  }

  public List<SpyThriller> getBooks() throws Exception {
    Query query = getEntityManager().createQuery
      ("SELECT m from SpyThriller as m");
    return query.getResultList();
  }
}
```

We apply the `@PersistenceContext` annotation of the type of the session bean; here the class is named `SpyThrillerBookWithJNIDILookupBean`. This annotation takes three arguments: the name of the persistence unit, `testDatabase`, the JNDI name that is exported, `myLookupBean`, and the persistent unit type, `EXTENDED`.

We also inject the `javax.ejb.SessionContext` object into the bean from the EJB container. It is this object that provides a method to look up the persistence unit. The entity manager is programmatically found by the exported JNDI name in the `@PersistenceContext` annotation.

Moving further along with entity beans

Java Persistence API is quite a specification in that it provides seamless persistence in an easy way, and is also configurable. Writing an object-relational mapping framework is not for the faint-hearted, and takes a lot of time and supreme amount of energy to get the correct operation, let alone standardize how different solutions can work together.

We shall delve deeper into building the metadata for the entity beans in order to get the best out of JPA for our professional project requirements, starting with the mapping of entities to the database table.

Controlling the mapping of entities to the database table

We learnt that by simply applying the `@Entity` annotation to a POJO, we could turn it into a persistence capable object, an entity bean. We also learnt earlier in this chapter that we control how the fields and the property accessors can be mapped explicitly to a database column.

Through the use of metadata, most of the time using the annotation, we build a picture of the fields for the benefit of the object-relation mapping. The JPA provider takes this information and works on our behalf to transparently manage the persistence entities.

Expanding the @Table annotation

The `@javax.persistence.Table` annotation specifies more control in how an entity bean is mapped to the underlying database. It allows developers to define the best database table that an entity is mapped to.

A table of the `@Table` parameters is as follows:

Name	Type	Description	Default Value
Name	String	Specifies the name of the target database table.	Derived by the JPA provider from the entity bean class name
Catalog	String	Specifies the database catalog for the target table.	The default database catalog
Schema	String	Specifies the database schema for the target table.	The default database schema for the application
uniqueConstraints	UniqueConstraint[]	Specifies additional SQL constraints to be applied on the SQL CREATE of the table. These are only applied if the table generation is enabled.	No additional constraints
Indexes	Index[]	Specifies additional indexes for the table. These are only applied if table generation is enabled.	No additional indexes

An example of all of the table specific annotations used to add metadata for a fictional `Payroll` entity bean, which is compatible with the JPA 2.1 specification, is as follows:

```
@Entity
@Table(name = "PAYROLL_EZ", schema = "HUMAN_RESOURCES",
   catalog = "EUROPE", uniqueConstraints = @Unique
     (columnNames = "PAYROLL_PRINT_SER"), indexes = {
       @Index(name = "index1", columnNames = {
         "firstName", "lastName"}))
public class Payroll implements java.io.Serializable {
  /*...*/

  @Id
  long payrollId;
  String firstName;
  String lastName;
  @Column(name = "PAYROLL_PRINT_SER")
  String payrollSerial;
  /*...*/
}
```

The entity `Payroll` is mapped to the target database table named `PAYROLL_EZ`, the schema `HUMAN_RESOURCES`, and the catalog `EUROPE`.

We create a unique constraint for this table; we do not want to payroll the print rolls to have the same *ID* for two or more different employees or state members! We create a specific database index for this payroll database table such that searching for staff with their first and last names will perform faster than normal. (Ideally, in our fictional organization, no two employees will ever have the same first and last name, no matter how it grows in future years.)

Mapping the primary keys

All entity beans must have a primary key to ensure that they can be persisted to the database. An entity is a lightweight persistence capable domain object, and the primary key is the reference to locating the row in the database table of the underlying database.

JPA is not designed for entities that do not have any representation of a primary key. For such functional requirements then, you probably have to think about a specific document database solution outside of the Java EE 7 standard.

The single primary key

We have seen how to map an entity to a database with one column representing the primary key.

Recap of the entity named `ContactConsumer1`, with a single field named `contactId`, representing the single primary key column `CONTACT_ID`, in the database table `CONTACT_CONSUMER_1` is as follows:

```
package je7hb.basic2.jpa;
import javax.persistence.*;
import java.io.Serializable;

@Entity
public class ContactConsumer1 implements Serializable {
  @Id
  private long contactId;

  @Column(name = "FIRST_NAME", nullable = false)
  private String firstname;

  @Column(name = "LAST_NAME", nullable = false)
  private String lastname;

  public long getContactId() {return contactId;}
  public void setContactId(long contactId) {
    this.contactId = contactId;
  }

  public String getFirstname() {return firstname;}
  public void setFirstname(String firstname) {
    this.firstname = firstname;
  }

  public String getLastname() {return lastname;}
  public void setLastname(String lastname) {
    this.lastname = lastname;
  }

  // toString() method and constructors omitted
}
```

This is the simplest way of mapping an entity with a single primary key.

Composite primary keys

JPA can also be an entity map with more than one primary key to multiple database columns. There are two ways to create composite primary keys with JPA.

Using the @IdClass annotation

The first way maps a POJO with a separate class that contains a set of primitive fields, and the getter and setter methods. The annotation `@javax.persistence.IdClass` specifies a composite primary key class on the target entity.

A class designated as a separate identity composite key must follow these rules:

- An IdClass, a composite key class, must have the following features:
    - It must implement the marker interface `java.io.serializable`
    - It must be public with a no-arguments default constructor
    - It must have valid `hashCode()` and `equals()` methods
- The fields in the composite key class must correspond with exactly the same as the fields or property accessor in the entity
- The matching entity bean can be found with an instance of the composite key class (`@IdClass`) by calling `EntityManager.find()`

The consumer rewritten to support a composite primary key class is as follows:

```
@Entity
@IdClass(Contact2PK.class)
public class ContactConsumer2 implements Serializable {
  @Id
  private long contactId;

  @Id
  @Column(name = "FIRST_NAME", nullable = false)
  private String firstname;

  @Id
  @Column(name = "LAST_NAME", nullable = false)
  private String lastname;

  // Constructors omitted

  public long getContactId() {return contactId;}
```

```java
    public void setContactId(long contactId) {
      this.contactId = contactId;
    }

    public String getFirstname() {return firstname;}
    public void setFirstname(String firstname) {
      this.firstname = firstname;
    }

    public String getLastname() {return lastname;}
    public void setLastname(String lastname) {
      this.lastname = lastname;
    }

    // toString() method omitted
}
```

In the class `ContactConsumer1`, there are three fields that constitute the composite primary key: `contactId`, `firstname`, and `lastname`. Entity uses the field annotations with `@Id`. The class is annotated `@IdClass`, which takes the single argument, the reference to the composite key class.

The composite key `classContact2PK` is as follows:

```java
package je7hb.basic2.jpa;
import java.io.Serializable;

public class Contact2PK implements Serializable {
   private long contactId;
   private String firstname;
   private String lastname;

   public long getContactId() {return contactId;}
   public void setContactId(long contactId) {
      this.contactId = contactId;
   }

   public String getFirstname() {return firstname;}
   public void setFirstname(String firstname) {
      this.firstname = firstname;
   }

   public String getLastname() {return lastname;}
   public void setLastname(String lastname) {
```

```
    this.lastname = lastname;
  }

// hashCode(), equals() method omitted
// toString() method omitted
}
```

Notice how, in the composite key class, the names and types of the fields as well as the property accessor match the same in the entity bean.

The `hashCode()` and `equals()` methods are omitted in the example, but they can be generated by any of the popular IDEs.

How are composite primary key classes used? The answer is that we can use the `EntityManager.find()` method, which takes two arguments: the class of the entity that will be returned, and an instance of the composite key class.

An extract of a unit test method that illustrates the use case is as follows:

```
@PersistenctContext EntityManager em;

public void shouldRetrieveByCompositeKey() {
  ContactConsumer2 consumer =
    new ContactConsumer2(100, "Annabel", "Smith")
  em.persist(consumer)

  ContactConsumer2 consumerCopy = em.find
    (ContactConsumer2.class, new Contact2PK
      (consumer.getContactId(), consumer.getFirstname(),
        consumer.getLastname()));
  assertEquals(consumer, consumerCopy)
}
```

We create an entity bean, then we save it to the database using the entity manager. We search for the entity using a composite primary key instance. Finally, we check if the two entities are the same.

Using the @Embeddable annotation

This second way of creating the composite primary keys relies on the embedded object instances into the entity bean. In this way, the fields and properties are delegated to the separate primary key object class. In order to delegate the primary key to a delegate class instance, use the annotation `@javax.persistence.Embeddable`.

A class that is designated as embeddable must follow these rules:

- The embeddable entity beans are annotated with @Embeddable instead of @Entity
- The embeddable entities must implement the marker interface java.io.Serializable
- It must have valid hashCode() and equals() methods
- The embeddable classes are special entities that only exist as part of another entity
- An embeddable class may have the single value attributes or collection of the values, each of which must be following the general rules of the JPA specification
- An embeddable entity can also contain other embeddable classes to represent their state
- An embeddable entity may contain the relationships to other entities, including other embeddable entities

The contact primary key record is transformed into an embeddable entity as follows:

```java
@Embeddable
public class Contact3PK implements Serializable {
   private long contactId;
   @Column(name = "FIRSTNAME")
   private String firstname;
   @Column(name = "LASTNAME")
   private String lastname;

   public long getContactId() {return contactId;}
   public void setContactId(long contactId) {
     this.contactId = contactId;
     }

   public String getFirstname() {return firstname;}
   public void setFirstname(String firstname) {
     this.firstname = firstname;
     }

   public String getLastname() {return lastname;}
   public void setLastname(String lastname) {
     this.lastname = lastname;
     }
```

```
public Contact3PK() {
  this(0,null,null);
  }

public Contact3PK(long contactId, String firstname,
  String lastname) {
  this.contactId = contactId;
  this.firstname = firstname;
  this.lastname = lastname;
  }

// A copy constructor
public Contact3PK(Contact3PK ref) {
  this.contactId = ref.contactId;
  this.firstname = ref.firstname;
  this.lastname = ref.lastname;
  }

// equals() and hashCode() methods omitted
// toString() method omitted
}
```

We first annotate the `Contact3PK` class with `@Embeddable`, which denotes to the JPA provider that this class is embeddable, a composite primary key instance.

It has exactly the same primary key columns as fields: `contactId`, `firstname`, and `lastname`. We have also placed the `@Column` metadata into the class now. We do not have to place the `@Id` annotations on this type, because we made the class embeddable, and therefore this information is now implied.

Finally, embeddable must have correct and valid `hashCode()` and `equals()` methods in order for persistence to function successfully.

To conclude, we added a copy constructor to this composite key class, to make it easier for other developers to create copies of this entity in a test and production development work.

Using the @EmbeddedId annotation

In order to make use of the embeddable class in an entity, the enclosing entity simply declares a reference field or the accessor property of the embeddable class, and annotates it with `@javax.persistence.EmbeddedId`.

The contact consumer class is refactored to make use of the embeddable entity instance as follows:

```
packageje7hb.basic2.jpa;
import javax.persistence.*;
import java.io.Serializable;

@Entity
public class ContactConsumer3 implements Serializable {
  @EmbeddedId
  private Contact3PK contact;
  private String location;

  public ContactConsumer3() {
    this( new Contact3PK(), null);
  }

  public ContactConsumer3(Contact3PK contact, String location) {
    this.contact = contact;
    this.location = location;
  }

  public Contact3PK getContact() {return contact;}
  public void setContact(Contact3PK contact) {
    this.contact = contact;
  }

  public String getLocation() {return location;}
  public void setLocation(String location) {
    this.location = location;
  }

  // equals() and hashCode() methods omitted
  // toString() method omitted
}
```

The entity bean, `ContactConsumer3`, no longer defines separate primary key metadata. Instead, it delegates to `Contact3PK`, the embeddable entity with the annotation `@EmbeddedId`. Every annotation of `@EmbeddedId` must reference a class that is marked up with `@Embeddable` (or the corresponding ORM XML syntax).

We also threw in the additional field location to demonstrate that the entity bean can also still define additional columns of its own.

An extract of a unit test to demonstrate the principle of the embeddable entity objects is as follows:

```
@PersistenctContext EntityManager em;

public void shouldRetrieveByEmbeddableKey() {
  ContactConsumer consumer = new ContactConsumer3
    (new Contact3PK(200, "Benjamin", "Ferguson"), "Glasgow"));
  em.persist(consumer)

  ContactConsumer3 consumerCopy = em.find(ContactConsumer3.class,
    new Contact3PK(consumer.getContact()));
  assertEquals(consumer, consumerCopy)
}
```

We construct the embeddable `Contact3PK` entity bean before we construct the entity bean `ContactConsumer3`. We save it to the database using the entity manager. Next, we retrieve the same entity that was just saved with a new copy of the composite key object. This is exactly where a copy constructor is useful.

JPQL

The JPA standard specification has a description of JPQL, which allows developers to write queries for entities and their persistent state. JPQL is designed to be portable from one JPA provider to another. These JPQL are guaranteed to work regardless of the underlying database.

As with many technologies, especially when the Java EE platform is moving to the cloud, some features of JPQL are achievable and others are not. This might sound like a contradiction in terms, but it is very important when your business is deciding whether to invest in the cloud computing vendor. One of the most important facets of information technology is storing large and exceptionally huge quantities in multiple stores. The next part is deciding how to access and then analyze it for the results.

So JPQL is a large specification in itself, and this chapter only gives the essentials of how to get started. For JPQL, see the JPA specification for the query language syntax. JPQL is very similar to the native SQL language by design.

There are two forms of the JPQL queries, namely dynamic and named.

The dynamic queries

A dynamic query JPQL is a query that is generated from `java.lang.String`. We have already seen this example earlier in the chapter.

A dynamic JPQL example from the earlier discussion on composite keys is as follows:

```
@PersistenceContext entityManager;

public List<ContactConsumer1> findContactConsumers(long id)
throws Exception {
  Query query = entityManager.createQuery
    ("SELECT c from "+ ContactConsumer1.class.getSimpleName()+
     " as c where c.contactId = :contactId");
  query.setParameter("contactId", id);
  return query.getResultList();
}
```

We create `javax.persistence.Query` from the entity manager with the JPQL syntax. To achieve better portability, we take the simple class name of the entity. The String also defines a JPQL WHERE clause to filter out the record with the matching contact ID, and return the list collection as a result to the caller.

JPQL for this business method looks like the following code:

```
SELECT c FROM ContactConsumer1 as c
WHERE c.contactId = :contactId
```

We can refer to the entity name by its class name, `ContactConsumer1`. If there is an ambiguity, we could use the fully qualified class name with the package name too.

The parameters in JPQL are prefixed with a colon (:) character as we can see with the token, `:contactId`. This is an example of a named parameter.

If there are no matching records in the database, we get an empty; otherwise, the caller will get one entity. We assume the contact record is unique in the database table.

The named queries

In the JPA programming, the named JPQL queries are annotated on the entity bean itself. This is called creating static queries on an entity bean. We define static queries using the annotation `@javax.persistence.NamedQuery` on the entity bean concerned. Most of the time you define more than one named static query on an entity, and therefore you use `@javax.persistence.NamedQueries`, which takes one argument: an array of the `NamedQuery` annotations.

It is best to illustrate this with an example code. The context is that we have a requirement to create the entity bean for running a Java user group for our location and territory, and we need to define some portable queries to find the members quickly, concisely, and efficiently.

We can use a single `NamedQueries` annotation with an array of the `NameQuery` annotations for this purpose. Here is the simplified code to a `JUGMember` entity bean. We have removed the cruft methods to make it easier to understand.

```java
@Entity
@NamedQueries( {
  @NamedQuery(name = "JUGMember-findAllMembers",
     query = "select object(m) from JUGMember m"),
       @NamedQuery(name = "JUGMember-findByFirstAndLastName",
          query = "select object(m) from JUGMember m " +
             "where m.firstname = :firstname and " +
                "m.lastname = :lastname"),
                @NamedQuery(name = "JUGMember-findByLanguage",
                   query = "select object(m) from JUGMember m "+
                      "where m.language = :language")})
public class JUGMember implements Serializable {
  @Id
  @GeneratedValue(strategy = GenerationType.AUTO)
  private long memberId;
  private String firstname;
  private String lastname;
  private String language;
  private String country;
  private int experience;

  // The usual JPA cruft methods omitted
}
```

Here we have a JUGMember entity bean with three static named queries: JUGMember-findAllMembers, JUGMember-findByFirstAndLastName, and JUGMember-findByLanguage.

Inside the @NamedQuery annotations, an entity may declare as many JPQL statements as required. There is one important restriction: the names must be unique across the entire persistence unit, hence the long names, in our opinion, will be pragmatic and descriptive.

The query parameters

The named queries are great and would be useless if we could not use them in a program. In order to use a defined static query, we only require the entity manager. The entity manager has a special method named createNamedQuery that allows the session bean to reference a static named query defined in the persistence unit.

The restriction is that the code injecting EntityManager must be defined with the actual entity beans so that the queries can be located inside the persistence context.

A sample extract of a stateful session bean that illustrates how to access the named queries is as follows:

```
@Stateful
public class JUGMemberServiceBean {
  @PersistenceContext(unitName = "testDatabase",
    type = PersistenceContextType.EXTENDED)
  private EntityManager entityManager;
  // save() and delete() omitted

  public List<JUGMember> findAllMembers() {
    return entityManager.createNamedQuery
      ("JUGMember-findAllMembers")
    .getResultList();
  }

  public List<JUGMember> findByFirstAndLastName
    (String firstname, String lastname) {
    return entityManager.createNamedQuery
      ("JUGMember-findByFirstAndLastName")
    .setParameter("firstname", firstname)
    .setParameter("lastname",lastname)
    .getResultList();
  }
```

```
public List<JUGMember> findByLanguage(String language) {
  return entityManager.createNamedQuery
    ("JUGMember-findByLanguage")
  .setParameter("language", language)
  .getResultList();
  }
}
```

The so-called finder methods of the session bean each reference the static query by name. For instance, the method `findByLanguage()` invokes the entity manager to create the static query named JUG-findByLanguage, which creates a query instance. Next, it sets the named parameter language to the method's only argument. It then executes the query with an invocation of `getResultList()`.

The positional query arguments

JPQL also supports the positional arguments, which are probably very familiar to those of you who invested in Java before the turn of the century, in particular JDBC 1.0 had these too.

The positional arguments are identified by the (?) question mark followed by an index number. Let's look at the entity bean JUGMember class again with one additional name query with the positional argument:

```
@Entity
@NamedQueries( {
  /* ... as before ... */, @NamedQuery
    (name = "JUGMember-findByExperience",
      query = "select object(m) from JUGMember m "+
        "where m.experience = ?1")
  })
public class JUGMember implements Serializable {
  /* ... as before ... */,
  }
```

There is an additional name query named JUG-findByExperience that uses a positional argument ?1. This query allows us to search each JUG member for the number of years of professional IT experience. The positional arguments start with the index of 1 just like in JDBC.

The corresponding implementation method in the session bean for the additional named query is as follows:

```
@Stateful
public class JUGMemberServiceBean {
  /* ... as before ... */,
  public List<JUGMember> findByExperience(int experience) {
    return entityManager.createNamedQuery
      ("JUGMember-findByExperience")
    .setParameter(1, experience)
    .getResultList();
    }
}
```

The only difference in this code and the previous is in the `Query.setParameter` call, which takes an integer parameter indicating the position in the JPQL statement.

The entity bean relationships

To close out this chapter, this section discusses the entity bean relationships. The entity beans are allowed to link to other entities through a single value or collection references. The relationships can be bidirectional or unidirectional.

We will cover the more advanced examples of the entity relationship, including the differences between unidirectional and bidirectional, in the next chapter.

Mapping with the @OneToOne annotation

The `@javax.persistence.OneToOne` relationship is a direct association between one entity bean and another. The relationship can be expressed at either one or both entities. If each of the entities can refer to the other, then the relationship is bidirectional, otherwise, it is a unidirectional relationship.

By default all the relationships in the Java programming language are unidirectional. In order to establish bidirectional annotations, metadata must also apply to the other entity in order to create an inverse relationship.

In the relational databases, the inverse relationship always exists, and can be inferred through the relational data model.

A simple example of the use of the `@OneToOne` annotation with entities is as follows:

```
@Entity
public class Address implements java.io.Serializable {
  @Id
  @Column("ADDRESS_ID")
  private int addressId;
  /* ... */
}

@Entity
public class Employee implements java.io.Serializable {
  @Id
  @Column(name = "EMP_ID")
  private int employeeId;

  @OneToOne
  @JoinColumn(name = "EMPLOYEE_ADDRESS_FK",
    referencedColumnName = "ADDRESS_ID")
  private Address address;
  /* ... */
}
```

Here we have two entities, `Employee` and `Address`, and we defined a unidirectional association, a one-to-one relationship, between an `Employee` instance and an `Address` instance expressed in the Java programming language. `Employee` has a reference to `Address`, but the `Address` instance has no information about the `Employee` instance.

In order to define an entity relationship more succinctly, we introduce a new annotation `@javax.persistence.JoinColumn`. This annotation specifies the target database column for joining an entity association to another, or it specifies the persistence collection.

In the resultant employee database table `EMPLOYEE`, there is a foreign key column named `EMPLOYEE_ADDRESS_FK` that contains the values from the database table column `ADDRESS.ADDRESS_ID`.

Mapping with the @OneToMany annotation

The `@javax.persistence.OneToMany` annotation expresses an entity that can be related to multiple instances of another entity type. The `@OneToMany` relationship is added to a `java.util.Collection` field variable.

In a unidirectional relationship, the target entity of the one-to-many relationship does not maintain a single value reference back to the source entity.

In a bidirectional relationship, the target entity of the one-to-many relationship does maintain a single value reference pointing back to the source entity.

Let us look at an example of a `@OneToMany` entity relationship. The following code defines a project entity that owns a collection of the task entities:

```
@Entity
public class Project implements java.io.Serializable {
  /* ... */

  @OneToMany
  private Collection<Task> tasks;

  public Collection<Task> getTasks() {return tasks;}

  public void setTasks(Collection<Task> tasks) {
    this.tasks = tasks;
  }
  /* ... */
}

@Entity
public class Task implements java.io.Serializable {
  @Id @Column(name = "TASK_ID")
  private int id;

  private int length;
  private String title;
  private Description;
  /* ... */
}
```

The preceding code shows that the entity `Project` references a collection of the entity `Task`. There is no inverse relationship, because the entity `Task` does not reference the entity `Project`. The entity `Project` is the owner of the one-to-many relationship.

The ORM provider, following the rules of the JPA specification, applies the mapping so that the entity `Project` is mapped to the target database table named `PROJECT`. The entity `Task` is mapped to the database table named `TASK`. The provider maps the association to a join table named `PROJECT_TASK`, which has two foreign key columns: a foreign key that maps to the unique rows in the table `PROJECT` and the other foreign key column that maps to the unique rows in the table `TASK`. The foreign key columns are the same type as the reference source and target entities, respectively.

Mapping with the @ManyToOne annotation

The `@javax.persistence.ManyToOne` annotation expresses the entity relationship of multiple instances of entities being associated to one entity. This relationship is the polar opposite of the `@OneToMany` relationship.

In a unidirectional relationship, the target entity of a many-to-one relationship does not have a collection of references pointing back to the source entities.

In a bidirectional relationship, the target entity of a many-to-one relationship does maintain a collection of references pointing back to the source entities.

Let us look at an example of a `@ManyToOne` entity relationship. The following code defines the relationship where multiple employee entities share a security clearance entity instance.

```
@Entity
public class Employee implements java.io.Serializable {
  /* ... */

  @ManyToOne
  private Clearance clearance;

  public Clearance getClearance() {return clearance;}
  public void setClearance(Clearance clearance) {
    this.clearance = clearance;
    }
  }

@Entity
public class Clearance implements java.io.Serializable {
  @Id private int securityId;
  private String securityLevel;
  /* ... */
  }
```

Here we have two entities `Employee` and `Clearance`, and we defined a unidirectional many-to-one association between multiple `Employee` instances and a `Clearance` instance expressed in the Java programming language. Zero or more `Employee` instances defines a reference to a shared `Clearance` instance, but the `Clearance` instance has no information about any of the `Employee` instances.

Under the rules of the JPA specification, the entity `Employee` is mapped to the target database table named EMPLOYEE. The entity `Clearance` is mapped to a table named CLEARANCE. The table EMPLOYEE contains a foreign key column to the table CLEARANCE. The JPA provider will create a foreign column named CLEARANCE_SECURITY_ID, because SECURITY_ID is the mapped primary key column of the target entity, which in this case is the entity `Clearance`. The foreign key column is the same type as the primary key column in the target entity.

Mapping with the @ManyToMany annotation

The `@javax.persistence.ManyToMany` annotation expresses the entity relationship of multiple instances of entities being associated to multiple instances of the other entity type. The annotation `@ManyToMany` is placed on a `java.util.Collection` field value or the property accessor of the source entity bean.

In a unidirectional relationship, the target entities of a many-to-many relationship do not have a collection of references pointing back to the source entities.

In a bidirectional relationship, the target entities of a many-to-many relationship do maintain a collection of references pointing back to the source entities.

The many-to-many relationships can be split into two relationships usually, the one-to-many and many-to-one relationship between the two entities. This procedure typically applies to the logical and physical data modeling in the database, and also at the conceptual level.

Here is an example of the many-to-many relationship that associates many products to the invoices. A product can be a part of an invoice; many products go to make one invoice. An invoice usually has products that a customer has ordered; an invoice has many products.

```
@Entity
public class Product implements java.io.Serializable {
  @Id
  @Column("PROD_ID")
  private int id;
  @Column("PROD_NAME")
```

```
    private String name;
    @ManyToMany
    private Collection<Invoice> invoices;
    public Collection<Invoice> getInvoices() {
      return invoices;
      }
    public void setInvoices(Collection<Invoice> invoices) {
      this.invoices = invoices;
      }
  /* ... */
  }

@Entity
public class Invoice implements java.io.Serializable {
  @Id
  @Column("INV_ID")
  private int id;
  @Column("INV_NAME")
  @Temporal(Temporal.DATE)
  private Date name;
  @ManyToMany(mappedBy = "invoices")
  private Collection<Product> product;
  public Collection<Product> getProducts() {
    return product;
    }
  public void setProducts(Collection<Product> product) {
    this.product = product;
    }
  /* ... */
  }
```

This code represents a bidirectional many-to-many relationship. We have two entities, Product and Invoice. The entity Product references a collection of entities type Invoice. The entity Invoice references a collection of entities Product.

Each entity defines an annotation of the collection. The many-to-many annotation of the products inside the Invoice entity uses the mappedBy argument to establish the owner of the relationship. The owner of the relationship is Product. By specifying the mappedBy attribute, we allow the mapping information to be shared in both directions for the relationship.

Given this example, the JPA provider maps the source entity Product to the database table named PRODUCT. It maps the target entity Invoice to the database table named INVOICE. It creates a join table with the conjugation named PRODUCT_INVOICE. It will have two foreign key columns.

The JPA provider will create a foreign column in the join table named INVOICE_PROD_ID, because PROD_ID is the mapped primary key column of the target entity, which in this case is the entity INVOICE. The foreign key column is the same type as the primary key column in the target entity.

The JPA provider will create a foreign column in the join table named PRODUCT_INV_ID, because INV_ID is the mapped primary key column of the target entity, which in this case is the entity named PRODUCT. The foreign key column is the same type as the primary key column in the target entity.

It is possible to create a unidirectional many-to-many relationship too, but in this case we need to explicitly define a join table.

Configuration of persistence and the entity beans

In order to use JPA in a Java application, the entity beans require configuration for the data source and the persistence context. The persistence context is a file named persistence.xml, and it is found in the META-INF/ folder of Java Archive.

The structure of the persistence unit configuration

A persistence configuration XML file defines a collection of the persistence units. There must be at least one persistence unit in the file for it to be useful. A persistence unit represents a persistence context in the application, and it has a name. The name is used in an application to link EntityManager with the persistence unit. The linkage is defined with the @PersistenceContext annotation.

A persistence unit has two types of transactions: JTA and RESOURCE_LOCAL.

```
<persistence version = "1.0"
  xmlns = "http://java.sun.com/xml/ns/persistence"
    xmlns:xsi = "http://www.w3.org/2001/XMLSchema-instance"
      xsi:schemaLocation = "http://java.sun.com/xml/ns/persistence
        http://java.sun.com/xml/ns/persistence/
          persistence_1_0.xsd">

  <persistence-unit name = "{NAME}"
    transaction-type = "{TX-TYPE}">
  <provider>{PersistenceProvider}</provider>
```

```xml
    <!-- By default your mappings defined in orm.xml -->
    <!-- file, which is discovered automatically. -->
    <mapping-file>META-INF/my-mappings.xml</mapping-file>
    ...
    <jar-file>my-additional-jar.jar</jar-file>
    ...
    <!-- Enables auto discovery of persistent classes, -->
    <!-- otherwise they must be listed using <class>-->
    <exclude-unlisted-classes>false</exclude-unlisted-classes>

    <properties>
    ...
    </properties>
    </persistence-unit>
</persistence>
```

The transaction type `JTA` is normally configured inside a Java EE application, because the data source is usually configured with a transaction manager inside the product provider, such as the GlassFish or WebLogic servers.

It is possible to use the default JPA provider, provided by the Java EE product provider, or to supply your own provider implementation. Configuration for the JPA provider is in the `<provider>` XML element.

Inside the `persistence.xml` file again, a persistence unit can include an additional JAR file to load, in order to provide extra support to the application at deployment. The `<jar-file>` XML element declares the persistence entity beans. The persistence unit can rely on auto discovery of the entity beans or it can explicitly declare the classes that will be loaded by the `<class/>` XML element.

The `<exclude-unlisted-classes/>` stanza is specific for the Java EE environments only. It is a Boolean value that determines if the JPA provider scans for the annotated entity beans in the top level of the persistence unit. If this is not the case, then set this value to `false` in order to allow the JPA provider to find the annotated entity bean not in the top level. The `<exclude-unlisted-classes/>` XML element is helpful in certain situations for the embeddable, mapped super-classes, and converter classes.

The object-relational mapping files

There is an alternative way to specify the object-relational mapping, using a mapping file, which is particularly interesting if you do not have access to the source of the persist entities for a business reason. To specify a mapping file, use the `<mapping-file>` XML element. The object-relation mapping file contains the mapping information for the classes listed in it.

Here is a portable JPA 2.0 object-relational mapping file of the earlier `SpyThriller` entity bean. This file is named `sample-orm.xml` in the source code.

```xml
<?xml version = "1.0" encoding = "UTF-8"?>
<entity-mappings version = "2.0"
  xmlns = "http://java.sun.com/xml/ns/persistence/orm"
    xmlns:xsi = "http://www.w3.org/2001/XMLSchema-instance"
      xsi:schemaLocation =
        "http://java.sun.com/xml/ns/persistence/orm_2_0.xsd">
<description>Mapping persistent entity in XML.</description>
<entity name = "SpyThriller" class = "SpyThriller"
  access = "FIELD">
<table name = "SPY_THRILLER_BOOK"/>
<attributes>
<id name = "id">
<generated-value strategy = "AUTO"/>
<column name = "BOOK_ID" nullable = "false"
  unique = "true" insertable = "true" updatable = "true"
    table = "THRILLER_BOOK"/>
</id>
<basic name = "writer">
<column name = "AUTHORS" nullable = "false"/>
</basic>
<basic name = "year">
<column name = "BOOK_YEAR" nullable = "false"/>
</basic>
<basic name = "title">
<column name = "TITLE" nullable = "false"/>
</basic>
<transient name = "secretCode"/>
</attributes>
</entity>
</entity-mappings>
```

The ORM mapping file is largely similar to the annotation version, although in my opinion a little verbose compared to the annotated source code. Most software development will, I think, tend to prefer the annotations. On the other hand, the XML mapping file is a standard option that permits migration and upgrade. There is a route for pre-JPA solutions and older J2EE classes to enter the modern age of persistence.

An object-relational file mapping may be specified in the META-INF/ directory of the root of the persistence unit, or the META-INF/ directory of any JAR file referenced by the persistence unit. It will then be loaded by the JPA provider at deployment.

Standard property configurations for the persistence units

In JPA 2.1, there are additional properties that can be used to configure the database connection. In most cases inside the Java EE application, the database connection is configured inside the Java EE product, and provided as a data source to the application.

For the benefit of writing the standalone Java SE applications and unit tests, perhaps to support other forms of integration tests, you can supply additional properties in a persistence unit configuration.

Property	Description
javax.persistence.transactionType	Specifies the JPA PersistenceUnitTransactionType enumeration property JTA or RESOURCE_LOCAL
javax.persistence.jtaDataSource	Specifies the transactional JPA javax.sql.DataSource
javax.persistence.nonJtaDataSource	Specifies the non-transaction JPA javax.sql.DataSource
javax.persistence.jdbc.driver	Specifies the JDBC driver class name for the Java SE deployments (since JPA 2.0)
javax.persistence.url	Specifies the JDBC driver URL for the Java SE deployments (since JPA 2.0)
javax.persistence.user	Specifies the JDBC database username for the Java SE deployments (since JPA 2.0)
javax.persistence.password	Specifies the JDBC database password for the Java SE deployments (since JPA 2.0)

Summary

The Java Persistence API is a large endeavor to learn and represent lots of lasting evidence of a breakthrough of thought and achievement by the Java community. Standardizing how a Java application can seamlessly save and retrieve the objects to and from a relational database is no mean feat. Consequently, JPA is extremely powerful for both the Java SE and Java EE engineers.

We touched on the fundamentals of JPA in this chapter. We saw how a simple POJO can be transformed into a persistence capable object, an entity bean, with some annotations. We learnt how to save an entity to the database, how to remove it from the database, and how to retrieve all the instances.

We added the `@Entity`, `@Id`, `@GeneratedValue`, `@Column`, and `@Table` annotations to an example bean.

You now understand how to write an integration unit test with Gradle, the Arquillian framework, embedded GlassFish, and the EclipseLink JPA provider.

We discussed the lifecycle of the entity manager, and the four different states of an entity bean. We touched on the transactional support. We saw how to create the composite primary keys in the entity beans with either `@IdClass` or the embeddable class styles. We built some queries using JPQL. We advanced our understanding of JPA by retrieving the entities using the composite key records.

Closing out the chapter, we made a short detour to the entity relationships and the four fundamental multiplicities: `@OneToOne`, `@OneToMany`, `@ManyToOne`, and `@ManyToMany`.

Finally, we looked at the configuration of the persistence unit, and that was just the start. In the next chapter, we will extend our knowledge on the entity relationships in depth.

5
Object-Relational Mapping with JPA

Michael McDonald, five-time Grammy award winner, singer said, "I realized early on that I wouldn't sing for very long if I kept trying to sound like James Brown!". In the previous chapter, we covered the fundamentals of entity beans, the Plain Old Java Objects (POJOs) that are enhanced through metadata so that they can be persisted to a relational database or other long-term storage.

The Java Persistence API is a very involved specification and supports the flexibility and features of relational databases and the mapping of Java objects to database tables and columns. In this chapter, we venture much deeper in the JPA specification so that we further configure how JPA persistence provider maps persistence objects—entities—to a database.

We shall start by adding some finesse to entity beans.

Adding finesse to entity beans

As our first port of call, let us revisit how to configure field mappings and property accessors in the entity beans.

Field binding

There are two forms of binding in JPA: lazy and eager. The binding is controlled by the enumeration `javax.persistence.FetchType`. Binding determines when the persistence provider loads state into an entity. The process of loading state from the database is called **fetching**. In order to preserve performance, for simple entities the JPA provider will load state eagerly (`FetchType.EAGER`), especially for simple primitive type fields. This also applies to state load for fields implicitly annotated as `@Basic`. For collections of objects, the JPA provider will load the state lazily (`FetchType.LAZY`) in order to avoid the possibly of loading a deeply nested object graph, which inevitably would kill your application's performance.

Software engineers generally make a decision on the part of the entity object graph that is set to EAGER or LAZY. It depends on the query, and naïve consideration can lead to the infamous N+1 query problem. Later in this chapter, we cover the issues around excessive queries. Java EE 7 and JPA 2.1 introduce the idea fetch plan that can help balance the performance of queries. See *Chapter 11, Advanced Topics in Persistence*.

Binding eagerly

In JPA 2.1, the value of `FetchType.EAGER` is the `fetch` attribute default for many annotations including `@Basic`, `@ManyToOne` and `@OneToOne`. The EAGER value is a specification requirement on the JPA provider to eagerly fetch data relevant to the field or property accessor of the entity.

For direct reference the default value in the specification helps the persistence provider, the JPA vendor, write viable implementation that performs as expected. The idea is borrowed from the principle of least astonishment.

Binding lazily

The enumeration value `FetchType.LAZY` is the default value for the `fetch` attribute in most of the JPA annotations: `@ElementCollection`, `@ManyToMany`, and `@OneToMany`.

When an entity can load multiple dependent entities, the default value in specification does help persistence providers to treat collections as lazily loaded entities.

You should always treat the `FetchType.LAZY` value as a hint to the JPA provider to do the right thing. There is no guarantee that it will obey the advice, and the provider is allowed to analyze the persistence context and only then decide to honor the hint if it is possible, and of course, makes sense.

Let us suppose we have a smart implementation of the JPA specification and we have two entities, the master and the detail. The master is associated with the detail in a one-to-many relationship. By default this would be lazy fetch. What if our smart JPA provider recognizes at runtime that a set of master entities only ever has one detail? In other words, a smart JPA provider may choose to eagerly load the master and detail in one operation because of some internal secret-sauce optimization algorithm.

The trade-off between eager and lazy

Here is some code to illustrate the trade-off between the eager and lazy loading definitions.

The entity `Customer` has a name and address and a set of invoices. For the purposes of the discussion we do not see the source code for the `Address` and `Invoice` entities.

The code now follows:

```
@Entity
public class Customer implements java.io.Serializable {
  @Id
  @Column(name="CUST_ID")
  private int id;

  @OneToOne
  @JoinColumn(name="CUSTOMER_ADDRESS_REF",
    referencedColumnName="ADDRESS_ID")
  private Address address;
  /* ... */

  @OneToMany
  private List<Invoice> invoices;

  public List<Invoice> getInvoices() { return invoices; }
  public void setInvoices( List<Invoice> invoices ) {
    this.invoices = invoices; }
}
```

The `Customer` entity has a one-to-one relationship with an `Address` entity, which is another way of saying every customer has an address. The `Customer` entity has a list collection of Invoice entities, which represents a one-to-many relationship. A single customer may have ten, a thousand and one, or zero invoices.

Object-Relational Mapping with JPA

Without any further annotations, when a JPA provider loads the state of the `Customer` entity from the database, it will also load the `Address` entity eagerly, because there is a direct reference to the other entity. The JPA Provider will also eagerly load the state for `Customer` for properties that are primitive and basic JDBC database types.

For the collection properties, when a JPA provider loads the state of the `Customer`, it will lazily load the associated `Invoice` entities from the database. This is the default behavior to achieve common-sense performance. The JPA provider will only load states for the dependent records in the customer record if the method `getInvoices()` is invoked in an external call.

It is probably not efficient to load a customer with a huge collection of invoices and such a penalty of time and loading may not make sense for all applications, because retrieving entire setS of records may be unnecessary if the end client is only interested in a few. Specifying the attribute `FetchType.LAZY` infers the loading of state is on-demand.

The EAGER strategy is a requirement on the persistence provider runtime that data be eagerly fetched. The LAZY strategy is a hint (not a requirement) to the persistence provider runtime that data should be loaded lazily when it is first accessed.

Let's revisit the example code and reverse the fetch style for both properties in the customer entity:

```
@Entity
public class Customer implements java.io.Serializable {
  @Id
  @Column(name="CUST_ID")
  private int id;

  @OneToOne(fetch=FetchType.LAZY)
  @JoinColumn(name="CUSTOMER_ADDRESS_REF",
    referencedColumnName="ADDRESS_ID")
  private Address address;
  /* ... */

  @OneToMany(fetch=FetchType.EAGER)
  private List<Invoice> invoices;
```

```
    public Address getAddress();
    public void setAddress(Address address) {
      this.address = address;   }

    public List<Invoice> getInvoices() { return invoices; }
    public void setInvoices( List<Invoice> invoices ) {
      this.invoices = invoices; }
  }
```

Here in this version of Customer entity, the Address entity is loaded on demand, at the behest of the persistence provider. The full list of invoices associated with the Customer record is loaded eagerly whenever the JPA Provider decides to load the master entity. The invoices are already loaded for this version of the customer by the time getInvoices() method is called.

> Many engineers tackle the issue of dependency and responsibility by splitting the association into an idiom called master and detail. The master usually is the owner of the detail. If the master record does not exists and the child detail does exist, then it makes no semantic sense. A child detail record with no parent master is considered orphaned or a free record. There are some synonyms of the master-detail, namely: parent-child, master, and slave.

If we intend to have a customer entity that is instantiated, persisted, and then detached from the persistence context, then a detached customer entity will have a full set of customer invoices to hand, but will not have ready access to the address entity. Potentially, having the full invoices could be architecturally useful for an application that sends data back to a remote client, like a web client. In this circumstance, there is a clear advantage in pre-binding some associations like we have done with the invoices.

Overriding the invoices' collection association to be eagerly loaded (FetchType. EAGER) could have a consequence: what if the Invoice entity actually contains other associations? If the invoice entity also contains more unseen entities that are eagerly bound and therefore fetched from the database, our little application could see possible performance degradation, because the persistence context is loading unnecessary entities.

Deciding if and when to override the default fetching strategy for entities is a delicate matter of application design. As software designers and architects, we certainly have to think rather carefully about how to improve the efficiency of the JPA applications and we have to avoid creating JPA cascades, a snow storm of load states between eagerly loaded entities, which appear to be out-of-control.

Cascades onto dependent entities

JPA allows related entities to cascade life-cycle operations across references. We have seen to override the fetching of load state for entities. Fetching, however, is nothing to do with lifecycle management. JPA allows the developer to control how a dependent entity is saved or updated, merged, deleted, refreshed, and detached to and from the database with the parent [master] entity. The cascade behavior can be precisely controlled by configuring the **cascade** attribute on the entity relationship annotations: `@OneToOne`, `@OneToMany`, `@ManyToOne`, and `@ManyToMany`.

Cascade operations

The enumeration `javax.persistence.CascadeType` defines the different level of cascade operations. Here is the source code for it:

```
public enum CascadeType {
  ALL,
  PERSIST,
  MERGE,
  REMOVE,
  REFRESH,
  DETACH
}
```

To define all cascade operations for the customer entity we should also propagate on the address record. Then we configure the `@OneToOne` annotation as follows:

```
@Entity
public class Customer implements java.io.Serializable {
   /* ... */

   @OneToOne(cascade=CascadeType.ALL)
   @JoinColumn(name="CUSTOMER_ADDRESS_REF",
     referencedColumnName="ADDRESS_ID")
   private Address address;
   /* ... */
}
```

Let's understand the meaning of the cascade operation:

Given a `Customer` entity, when the `EntityManager` is called with `persist()` with this object, this operation will also be invoked on the `Address` object referenced by the field.

The cascade repeats for other `EntityManager` operations: `remove()`, `merge()`, `refresh()`, and `detach()`, because the address is annotated with `CascadeType.ALL`.

The follow table describes the cascade operation enumerations in detail.

Operation	Description
ALL	This equivalent to the following `cascade={PERSIST, MERGE, REMOVE, REFRESH, DETACH}`
PERSIST	Specifies that the entity manager saves or updates the dependent entity to the database when the master entity is also persisted.
MERGE	Specifies that the entity manager merges the dependent entity with the existing copy in the database when the master entity is also merged.
REMOVE	Specifies that the entity manager removes the dependent entity from the database when the master entity is also removed.
REFRESH	Specifies that the entity manager refreshes the dependent entity from the database when the master entity is also refreshed.
DETACH	Specifies that the entity manager detaches the dependent entity when the master entity is also detached. (Since JPA 2.1)

The cascade annotation attribute provides the engineer a flexible way to configure the lifecycle of dependent entities. The control provided can save the developer's time and avoid engineers having to write boilerplate code themselves that cascades database operations.

Removal of orphans in relationships

JPA allows the engineers to configure the behavior of orphans in a one-to-one or many-to-one relationship. An orphan is an entity instance that is already set pending to be removed because it was removed from the relationship (the collection), or because it was replaced by a new entity (in the collection). The issue, here, is that when we remove an entity from a collection, we have a dependent detail entity that is no longer referenced by the master. This is reflected inside the target database with a record that is no longer being used. Hence the database row becomes orphaned.

For example, if we have a customer record already persisted to the database with our address. If we replace the reference in the `Customer` entity with a null pointer, what do we want to have happened in the database? Clearly we want to remove the `ADDRESS` row from the database table record.

Likewise, as we continue the example, if one of the Invoice entities is removed from the list collection of invoices in the `Customer` entity, then the `Invoice` is no longer referenced from the master `Customer` record. We possibly have an `INVOICE` row in the database table that is orphaned and no longer used by the application.

JPA allows the orphans to be removed only on `@OneToOne` and `@OneToMany` relationships. This attribute is called `orphanRemoval` and it expects a Boolean value, which by default is set to `false`.

Here is an example of the use of orphan removal applied only to the invoices in the customer entity:

```
@Entity
public class Customer implements java.io.Serializable {
  /* ... */
  @OneToMany(orphanRemoval=true)
  private List<Invoice> invoices;
  public List<Invoice> getInvoices() { return invoices; }
  public void setInvoices( List<Invoice> invoices ) {
    this.invoices = invoices; }
}
```

We apply the orphan removal operation in the `Invoice` dependent entity in the `Customer` entity code example. JPA provider will act should one or more of the `Customer` instances be removed from the collection of `Invoice` objects. The orphan removal operations take place when the `EntityManager` flushes the persistence context with the master `Customer` entity; it will then automatically remove the orphaned invoice records from the database table.

Finally, the removal of orphans is entirely separate to the `Cascade.REMOVE` operations. It happens independently of the cascade operations, if set.

Let us now look at the last method of finessing entity beans under JPA—how to configure automatic generation of primary key values for entities.

Generated values and primary keys

Many relational databases support the automatic generation of primary keys, which can be extremely useful when inserting new records into a database table. However, the database vendors traditionally provide non-portable ways to achieve auto incrementing integers. Some databases support the creation of **database sequence** types, some databases have a master incremental table value or view, and some databases have some completely novel schemes to generate unique identifiers.

The JPA specification allows the Java developer to use a strategy into order to create primary keys automatically. The key to defining strategy is in the annotation, which we have already seen, called `@javax.persistence.GeneratedValue`. This annotation only supports simple primary keys. The strategy attribution has the following definition:

```
public enum GenerationType {TABLE, SEQUENCE, IDENTITY, AUTO };
```

The enumeration `@javax.persistence.GeneratedType` has four values and they are described in the following table:

Value	Description
TABLE	Specifies that the persistence provider generates primary keys for the entity from the supplied database table, which is defined by the additional generator attribute.
SEQUENCE	Specifies that the persistence provider generates primary keys for the entity from the supplied database sequence, which is defined by the additional generator attribute.
	WARNING: Sequence strategy is not portable across database vendors.
IDENTITY	Specifies that the persistence provider generates primary keys for the entity from the special database identity column, which is defined by the additional generator attribute.
	WARNING: Identity strategy is not portable across database vendors.
AUTO	Specifies that the persistence provider picks a strategy for the entity that is appropriate to the database vendor in order to generate primary keys. The AUTO strategy may expect a particular sequence, table, or identity or it may generate one of them.
	This is the most portable of the strategies.

Table auto increment

The `GeneratedType.TABLE` enumeration is the most portable of the settings. A database table is created or updated by the persistence provider with two columns. The first column is the sequence name that requires the increment and the second column is the current value.

Let us modify the earlier customer entity to use a table identity for its customer ID:

```
@Entity
public class Customer implements java.io.Serializable {
  @Id
    @GeneratedValue(value=GeneratedType.TABLE,
       generator="CUSTOMER_SEQ")
  @Column(name="CUST_ID")
  private int id;

  /* ... */
}
```

The Customer entity now uses the auto increment through a database table strategy and it declares a sequence name called CUSTOMER_SEQ. The persistence context may create a table called SEQUENCE_TABLE with the columns SEQUENCE_NAME and SEQUENCE_VALUE.

Here is what this table will look like:

SEQUENCE_NAME	SEQUENCE_VALUE
CUSTOMER_SEQ	146273
INVOICE_SEQ	23941580
EMPLOYEE_SEQ	2081

There is a row for each sequence in the table, and every time the persistence provider requires a primary key for a new entity, it will read the current value and then increment value and store it back into the SEQUENCE_TABLE. The new current value, which was just incremented, is the one supplied to the entity as a new primary key.

The database table is most likely shared with other entities in the same persistence context, and therefore the database schema.

The TABLE strategy is portable across different database vendors, because it is simply a regular database table generated by the persistence provider, and gives the engineer control of how sequences are created for the application. The table and how the table is incremented can be configured with, say, pre-allocation, which might be important for data population insertion performance. Pre-allocation is very useful in situations when there are lots of insertions are happening.

There are issues with the TABLE strategy, namely to do with concurrency access. If the database table is shared between two or more JVMs in a clustered environment without some synchronization of access to the underlying database table, an application could cause inconsistency issues and of course failure to insert records with the others.

JPA also provides a special annotation called @javax.persistence.TableGenerator, which can further configure generation of primary keys from the table strategy. This annotation requires a reference name, the sequence name, which is provided by the @GeneratedValue annotation. Using the @TableGenerator annotation, a developer can set the initial value, the pre-allocation size, optionally the database table, catalogue, or schema, and also set the column name of the entity primary key.

Here is a revised example of the customer entity that now uses the @TableGenerator annotation:

```
@Entity
public class Customer implements java.io.Serializable {
    @Id
    @GeneratedValue(strategy=GeneratedType.TABLE,
        generator="CustomerSeq")
    @TableGenerator(
        name="CustomerSeq",
        catalog="APP_KEYS",
        table="APP_IDS_TABLE",
        pkColumnName="SEQ_KEY",
        valueColumnName="SEQ_VALUE",
        pkColumnValue="CUSTOMER_ID",
        initialValue=1000000,
        allocationSize=25)
    private int id;

    /* ... */
}
```

Object-Relational Mapping with JPA

This example specifies that the primary key id of the entity `Customer` is generated with the table strategy. The name of the sequence generator is called `CustomerSeq`, and we specify an explicit database schema called `APP_KEYS`, which is an optional attribute. The actual database table is called `APP_IDS_TABLE` with the primary column name called `SEQ_KEY` and the value column name called `SEQ_VALUE`. The database column name for the primary key of the entity is called `CUSTOMER_ID`; hence we do not require an additional `@Column` annotation just to override the column name. The `@TableGenerator` specifies an initial value of 100000 and we have a pre-allocation size of 25 (the default value is 50).

Overall, the `@TableGenerator` annotation allows developers to have more control of the auto-generation of primary keys for this strategy, rather than just declaring an identity with the `@GeneratedValue`.

Sequence auto increment

The `GeneratedType.SEQUENCE` enumeration specifies that the primary key of the entity is populated according to a database sequence. Database sequences are only implemented by database vendors such as Oracle, DB2, Postgres and Apache Derby. Therefore using `SEQUENCE` strategy is an implementation concern, if you choose this strategy for an application.

The JPA provides an additional annotation `@javax.persistence.SequenceGenerator` that can give more precise control of how the sequence is generated. The annotation allows the allocation size to be defined, as well as the name of the sequence itself.

Let us modify the earlier customer entity to use a sequence identity for its customer ID:

```
@Entity
public class Customer implements java.io.Serializable {
  @Id
    @GeneratedValue(value=GeneratedType.TABLE,
        generator="CUSTOMER_SEQ")
@SequenceGenerator(name="CUSTOMER_SEQ",
        sequenceName="CUSTOMER_SEQ",
        initialValue=3000000, allocationSize=50 )
    @Column(name="CUST_ID")
    private int id;

  /* ... */
}
```

The `Customer` entity now uses the auto increment through sequence strategy and it declares a sequence name called CUSTOMER_SEQ. The persistence context may create a database vendor specific sequence object called CUSTOMER SEQUENCE and with only one integral column, say NEXT_VAL.

The sequence object will have an INCREMENT size value, and starting value, and allocation size value. Some database providers that support sequence objects allow them to cycle around, although this feature is not supported by the current JPA 2.1 specification.

Every time the persistence provider requires a new value for the entity, it will create the sequence object for the next value. The database will take off automatically incrementing the value itself.

Although the sequence strategy is least portable, it has the benefit of being the best able to support concurrency across JVMs; and sequence objects are efficient in pre-allocation of primary key identities.

Identity auto increment

The `GeneratedType.IDENTITY` enumeration specifies that the primary key of the entity is populated according to a database specific identity column. Database identity columns are only implemented by some database vendors such as MySQL, SQL Server, Sybase, and Apache Derby.

An identity column is a column that stores numbers that increment by one with each insertion. Identity columns are sometimes called auto-increment columns.

Let us modify the earlier customer entity to use an identity column for its customer ID:

```
@Entity
public class Customer implements java.io.Serializable {
  @Id
   @GeneratedValue(value=GeneratedType.IDENTITY,
      generator="CUSTOMER_SEQ")
  @Column(name="CUST_ID")
  private int id;

  /* ... */
}
```

It is very easy to create an identity with the annotation `@GeneratedValue`. JPA provides no other special annotation for identity columns.

There are drawbacks for identity columns. The first concern is the fact that the next primary key is only available after the record has been inserted into the database. The second concern is that it is not possible to have a pre-allocation of primary key identities, and it could be a performance problem when and if your application produces proportionally more insertions than reads on certain entity beans.

Entity relationships revisited

In the previous chapter, we saw that an entity can be associated with another through a relationship, which can be one-to-one, one-to-many, many-to-one, or many-to-many. Relationships under JPA are polymorphic, which means you can take advantage of object oriented inheritance, if required.

JPA requires for all relationship mapping that there is one side that is identified as the target and therefore the opposite side is the owner. The primary key of the target entity is always referenced in the mapping of entity relationships.

In Java and JPA, entity relationships are by default unidirectional, which means that it is straightforward to traverse from the master-the owning entity-to the detail-the target entity. The Java developer must explicitly supply the inverse direction in order to facilitate bidirectional entity relationships.

Relationships are defined by association of primary keys in database tables (and views) to foreign keys in other tables (and views) inside a relational database. In the owning database table, the master, there is a database column containing the foreign keys of the target database table, the detail, which defines the primary keys. Associations are defined by the possibility to traverse to individual rows of the target database table from the source database table using the foreign key to primary mapping.

The source and target entity in the relationship model how the engineer can navigate from one entity to the other.

One-to-one mapping

The one-to-one mapping relationship maps one entity directly to another entity. The annotation is `@javax.persistence.OneToOne`.

The property or accessor method may be further annotated with the `@javax.persistence.JoinColumn` to further identify the target database column that contains the primary key in the target entity.

Let us look at the full attributes of the `@OneToOne` annotation:

Attribute	Type	Description	Default Value
targetEntity	String	The attribute represents the entity class that is the target of the relationship. For 99% of cases, you will not have to specify this relationship explicitly, since the persistence provider should be able to find the relationship.	Implied by the declaration point on the field or property accessor
cascade	String	This attribute specifies how and when the lifecycle of the dependent entity is included in any cascade operations (`CascadeType.ALL`, `CascadeType.PERSIST` etc.)	No operations are cascaded
fetch	String	This attribute specifies how the dependent entity is retrieved in a relationship. The valid values are `FetchType.EAGER` and `FetchType.LAZY`.	FetchType.EAGER
optional	Boolean	This attribute specifies if the relationship can be null or not. The default value is `true`; and by setting this to `false` a non-null relationship must exist between the entities.	true
mappedBy	String	This attribute specifies the field or accessible property accessor for the source owning entity for bidirectional relationships.	None
orphanRemoval	Boolean	This attribute specifies how removal operation takes place when the target entity is removed from the source owning entity. If the value is set to `true`, then the deletion of the target from the source entity will be cascaded to the target itself.	false

We already saw some examples of one-to-one mapping in the previous chapter.

Object-Relational Mapping with JPA

Let us examine in detail the relationship between the employee and the address:

```
@Entity
public class Employee implements java.io.Serializable {
    /*...*/

    @OneToOne(cascade = CascadeType.ALL)
    @JoinColumn(name="EMPLOYEE_ADDRESS_FK",
            referencedColumnName="ADDRESS_ID")
    private Address address;

    public Address getAddress() { return address; }
    public void setAddress(Address address) {
        this.address = address; }

    /*...*/
}
```

We have established a one-to-one unidirectional relationship between the `Employee` entity and the `Address` entity. The owner of the relationship is `Employee` and this determines the navigability.

Here, we configure the relationship with the `@JoinColumn` annotation in order to customize the database column name `EMPLOYEE_ADDRESS_FK` and also to specify the reference database column name in the target entity `ADDRESS_ID`.

Here is a table that describes the attributes for `@JoinColumn` annotation.

Attribute	Type	Description	Default Value
name	String	This attribute specifies the name of the foreign key that associates to the target entity. The foreign key is in the table of the source, the owner entity.	Implied by the declaration point on the field or property accessor
referencedColumn-Name	String	This attribute specifies the name of the primary key in the target entity. The reference column is in the table of the target entity.	The same name as the target database column

[206]

Attribute	Type	Description	Default Value
unique	Boolean	This attribute specifies whether the column is unique. It is also a short cut for the @UniqueConstraint annotation for a single field.	false
nullable	Boolean	This attribute specifies if the foreign key column is nullable or not.	true
insertable	Boolean	This attribute specifies if this foreign key is included in SQL INSERT operations by the persistence provider.	true
updatable	Boolean	This attribute specifies if this foreign key is included in SQL UPDATE operations by the persistence provider.	true
columnDefinition	String	Defines an additional SQL fragment that is used in the DDL generated by the persistence provider.	None
table	String	Specifies the name of the table that contains the column.	Implied by the containing entity
foreignKey	ForeignKey	Specifies the foreign constraint for the join column.	Default constraints generated by the persistence provider

Persisting one-to-one unidirectional entities

It is easy to save one-to-one related entities using JPA. All you need are the entity beans themselves and then use a method to create the dependency, and thus the association.

Here is an example that creates and saves both `Employee` and `Address`:

```
@PersistenceContext EntityManager em;

public void create() {
  Employee employee = new Employee();
  Address address = new Address();
  employee.setAddress(address);
  em.persist(employee);
}
```

This will work because we have chosen `CascadeType.ALL` and thus saving the `Employee` entity, cascades the operation from the owning entity to the dependent entity, which is the `Address`.

We have chosen to allow nullable references in the relationship, and therefore we can adopt a method that removes the address from the employee record, shown as follows:

```
@PersistenceContext EntityManager em;
public void clearAddress( int empId ) {
  Employee employee = em.find(Employee.class, id );
  employee.setAddress( null );
  em.persist(employee);
}
```

Now, let us move on to the bidirectional relationship.

Bidirectional one-to-one-entities

Now let us make this one-to-one relationship between an employee and an address bidirectional. In order to achieve this, we still have to inform JPA which one of these entities is the owner of the relationship. In this case, we still want the employee entity to be owner of the address.

Here is the code to achieve a bidirectional relationship:

```
@Entity
public class Address implements java.io.Serializable {
    /*...*/
```

```
    @OneToOne(mappedBy="address")
    private Employee employee

    public Employee getEmployee() { return employee; }
    public void setEmployee(Employee employee) {
        this.employee = employee; }
    /*...*/
}
```

In the `Address` entity, we add a brand new field employee and annotate it with `@OneToOne`. Here, we supplied the inverse property `mappedBy="address"` in order to complete the inverse relationship.

Persisting one-to-one bidirectional entities

In Java code, persisting the bidirectional entities must always be built from both sides of the relationship. Entities in Java behave like any other Java object that has a relationship. As a developer, you are required to configure both sides of the relationship in memory.

Here is a code that creates the `Employee` and `Address` records for a bidirectional association:

```
@PersistenceContext EntityManager em;
public void create() {
  Employee employee = new Employee();
  Address address = new Address();
  employee.setAddress(address);
  em.persist( employee );
}
```

Failure to configure both sides of the relationship in bidirectional mappings can result in peculiar data management errors.

Let's move on to mapping composite foreign keys.

Composite foreign keys in a one-to-one relationship

JPA can map entities with composite keys into one-to-one relationships. For this task, we need to annotate the field or property accessor with `@javax.persistence.JoinColumns`, which accepts an array of `@JoinColumn` declarations.

Object-Relational Mapping with JPA

Here is an example of a record, a shipping record, with a set of properties:

```
@Entity
public class Shipping implements Serializable{
  private long id;
  private String delivery;
  private String carrier;
  private String costCenter;
  /*...*/
}
```

Let's suppose we are only interested in the one-to-one relationship between the `Invoice` and the `Shipping` entities, except we only want to associate across `id` and `costCenter`.

Here is some example code, which demonstrates what we can achieve with a composite key:

```
@Entity
public class Invoice implements java.io.Serializable {
  /*...*/
  @ManyToOne
  @JoinColumns({
      @JoinColumn(name="SHIPPING_ID",
        referencedColumnName="ID"),
        @JoinColumn(name="COST_CENTER_REF",
        referencedColumnName="COST_CENTER") })
  private Shipping shipping;

  public Shipping getShipping() { return shipping; }
  public void setShipping( Shipping shipping) {
    this.shipping = shipping; }

}
```

The code in the `Invoice` class creates a one-to-one relationship, which may be a `null` reference, meaning an invoice can have no shipping record at all.

JPA maps the entity `Invoice` into the database table called `INVOICE` and with the additional database columns, which are the foreign key for referencing the shipping entity, namely `SHIPPING_ID` and `COST_CENTER`.

One-to-many mapping

The one-to-many mapping relationship maps one entity directly to multiple entities. The annotation is `@javax.persistence.OneToMany`. The source entity is owner of a collection of target entities.

The inverse relationship of a one-to-many is a many-to-one. By contrast to either to one-to-many or many-to-one relationships, the inverse of many-to-many relationship is itself.

Let us look at the full attributes of the `@OneToMany` annotation:

Attribute	Type	Description	Default Value
targetEntity	String	This optional attribute represents the entity class that is the target of the relationship. If the property is used as a raw type then the attribute must be specified.	The parameterized type of the collection when defined using Java generics
cascade	String	This attribute specifies how and when the lifecycle of the dependent entity is included in any cascade operations (`CascadeType.ALL`, `CascadeType.PERSIST` etc.)	No operations are cascaded
fetch	String	This attribute specifies how the dependent entity is retrieved in a relationship. The valid values are `FetchType.EAGER` and `FetchType.LAZY`.	`FetchType.LAZY`
mappedBy	String	This attribute specifies the field or accessible property accessor for the source owning entity for bidirectional relationships.	None
orphanRemoval	Boolean	This attribute specifies how a removal operation takes place when the target entity is removed from the source owning entity. If the value is set to `true`, then the deletion of the target from the source entity will be cascaded to the target itself.	`false`

Object-Relational Mapping with JPA

Let's see an example of a one-to-many in action. Employee records can have multiple telephone numbers for work, home, fax, mobile, and so on. Here is a simple phone entity bean.

```
@Entity
public class Phone implements java.io.Serializable {
  @Id @Column(name="PHONE_ID")
  private int id;
  private String type;    // home,work,main,fax
  private String interCode; // international prefix
  private String areaCode;
  private String localCode;
}
```

The `Phone` entity has a primary id, a phone type, and international, area, and local dialing codes. We assume that the application has an automatic parser for deciphering a full telephone number into its constituent dialing code parts.

Here is the `Employee` modified to accept a list collection of telephone entities:

```
@Entity
public class Employee implements java.io.Serializable {
    @Id @Column(name="EMP_ID")
 private long id;
    /*...*/

    @OneToMany(cascade = CascadeType.ALL)
    private List<Phone> phones;

    public List<Phone> getPhones() { return phones; }
    public void setPhones(List<Phone> phone) {
        this.phones = phones; }
}
```

In this example, the JPA provider creates a join table linking the `Employee` to `Phone` entities, which by default is `EMPLOYEE_PHONE`. The table has two database columns: the first is the primary key of the `Employee` entity, which is called `Employee_EMP_ID`, and the second is the foreign key of the `Phone` entity, which is called `Phone_PHONE_ID`.

Let us see this in tabular form, as shown next:.

The table EMPLOYEE:

EMP_ID	EMP_TYPE	FIRST_NAME	LAST_NAME
32368	Perm	Vernon	Reid
40201	Contractor	Paul	Gilbert

The table PHONE

PHONE_ID	TYPE	INTER_CODE	AREA_CODE	LOCAL_CODE
1002	Work	+44	207	5459923
1004	Work Fax	+44	207	5451234
1006	Home	+1	812	1237884

The table EMPLOYEE_PHONE

Employee_EMP_ID	Phone_PHONE_ID
32668	1002
32368	1004
40201	1008

Of course, we assume that the underlying database allows lower and upper case names for its entities.

One-to-many relationship with a join column

A `@OneToMany` can be defined with either a join table, or foreign key in the target object's table referencing the source object table's primary key. If we choose the second option, with the foreign key in the target entity then to uphold the relationship, we need to add a `@JoinColumn` annotation to the list collection field or property accessor.

Let's add a join column to the employee entity:

```
@Entity
public class Employee implements java.io.Serializable {
  /*...*/

  @OneToMany(cascade = CascadeType.ALL)
  @JoinColumn(name="EMP_FK_ID",
    referencedColumnName="EMP_ID")
  private List<Phone> phones;
}
```

Here the join column is actually created as part of the dependent entity Phone. In other words, the extra column is a foreign key in the target entity, which the entity directly has no responsibility to take care of and there is no equivalent in Java!

Consequently, a unidirectional one-to-many mapping is only officially supported in JPA 2.0 or better. Such a standard conforming persistence provider creates a database table PHONE with an additional foreign key column EMPLOYEE_FK_ID. The join table is unnecessary in this relationship type.

The table PHONE looks like the following:

PHONE_ID	TYPE	INTER_CODE	AREA_CODE	LOCAL_CODE	EMP_FK_ID
1002	Work	+44	207	5459923	32368
1004	Work Fax	+44	207	5451234	32368
1006	Home	+1	812	1237884	40201

The solution to the update problem for an unknown foreign key, which has existed since JPA 1.0, is to make the one-to-many relationship bidirectional, or use an explicit join table with an explicit foreign constraint that always enforces a one-to-many relationship in the database.

Let's look at the bidirectional form first.

Bidirectional one-to-many relationship

The target entity requires a many-to-one mapping.

The Phone entity takes a new property, the employee, and references to the owning entity.

```
@Entity
public class Phone implements java.io.Serializable {
    /* ... as before ... */
    @ManyToOne
    @JoinColumn(name="EMP_ID_FK")
    private Employee employee;
}
```

Now the `Phone` entity knows about the database column as a foreign key. We can certainly access the employee in Java programming.

In order to be bidirectional the owning entity must be configured with an inverse mapping. It needs to know what the field is or the property accessor that provides the inverse reference back to the source entity.

For the `Employee` entity, we provide this information with the `mappedBy` attribute.

```
@Entity
public class Employee implements java.io.Serializable {
    /*... */

    @OneToMany(cascade=CascadeType.ALL, mappedBy="employee")
    private List<Phone> phones;

    /*...*/
}
```

The `@OneToMany` signifies that the list collection of `Phone` entities is managed and owned by the Employee and there is an inverse relationship through the method call chain `Employee.getPhones().get(N).getEmployee()`, where N is some primitive integer type.

Therefore to add a new `Phone` and to remove a `Phone` entity record, we can have methods in the `Employee` entity like the following:

```
@Entity
public class Employee implements java.io.Serializable {
  /*...*/
  public boolean addPhone( Phone phone) {
    if ( ! phones.contains( phone) ) {
      Employee oldEmployee = old.getEmployee();
      if ( oldEmployee != null ) {
      removePhone( oldEmployee )
    }
  phones.add( phone );
    return true;
    }
  else { return false; }
  }

  public boolean removePhone( Phone phone ) {
    if ( phones.contains( phone) ) {
      phones.remove(phone);
```

[215]

```
        phone.setEmployee(null);
        return true;
      }
    else { return false; }
    }
  }
```

It is very important to ensure that in the Java application both references link to each other.

The `removePhone()` safely demonstrates how to delete the `Phone` entity from the employee entity and sets the reference to null; there is a check that the record is part of the collection beforehand.

The `addPhone()` adds a new phone entity to the employee's list collection provided it is not already contained. We sanity check the method by removing the `Phone` entity from the old `Employee` record, if any, and check if it was managed beforehand by reusing the `removePhone()` method. The new phone entity is added to the employee's current list collection, and the inverse relationship is also set in the phone entity.

One-to-many using an explicit join table

JPA allows developers to explicitly define a join table with the candidate keys from the respective database tables. The `@javax.persistence.JoinTable` annotation configures join table for all of the types of relationship: `@OneToOne`, `@OneToMany`, `@ManyToOne`, and `@ManyToMany`. The `@JoinTable` annotation specifies the owning side of the relationship in Java. It requires an array of join columns and for inverse relationship an array of inverse join columns.

In the following code,, we have our two entities `Employee` and `Phone`. The `Employee` entity-side is annotated explicitly as a join table:

```
@Entity
public class Employee implements java.io.Serializable {
  /*...*/

  @OneToMany(cascade = CascadeType.ALL)
  @JoinTable(name="EMP_PHONE_LINK",
    joinColumns=
      @JoinColumn( name="EMP_FK",
        referencedColumnName="EMP_ID"),
    inverseJoinColumns=
        @JoinColumn( name="PHONE_FK",
```

```
                referencedColumnName="PHONE_ID",
                unique=true )
    )
    private List<Phone> phones;
}
```

The phone list collection field is annotated with @JoinTable, with a single join column and a single inverse join column. Of course, we could have additional columns in a combination of primary and foreign keys for advanced situations.

With the code above, the JPA provider creates a database join table called EMP_PHONE_LINK with two foreign columns, namely EMP_FK and PHONE_FK. Excuse the badly named database column, but I think it illustrates the point—the reference column names points back to the constituent entities and therefore database tables: EMP_ID and PHONE_ID.

In order to enforce the constraint of the one-to-many relationship, we set the unique attribute, which is on the @JoinColumn, to true on the inverse part of the relationship.

If you choose not to specify a table explicitly, then the default join table name of the join table is a concatenation of the owning entity and the dependent names, delimited with an underscore.

This concludes the section on one-to-many relationship in JPA. We will now move on to the inverse mapping.

Many-to-one mapping

The many-to-one mapping relationship associates a collection of multiple entities directly to one single entity. The annotation is @javax.persistence.ManyToOne. The source entities collectively share ownership of a single entity.

The inverse relationship of a many-to-one is a one-to-many. In comparison to a many-to-many relationship, remember that inverse of a many-to-many relationship is itself.

Let us look at the full attributes of the `@ManyToOne` annotation:

Attribute	Type	Description	Default Value
targetEntity	String	This optional attribute represents the entity class that is the target of the relationship. If the property is used as a raw type then the attribute must be specified.	The parameterized type of the collection when defined using Java generics
cascade	String	This attribute specifies how and when the lifecycle of the dependent entity is included in any cascade operations (CascadeType.ALL, CascadeType.PERSIST etc.)	No operations are cascaded
fetch	String	This attribute specifies how the dependent entity is retrieved in a relationship. The valid values are FetchType.EAGER and FetchType.LAZY.	FetchType.EAGER
optional	Boolean	This attribute specifies if the relationship can be null or not. The default value is true; and by setting this to false then a non-null relationship must exist between the entities.	true

Many-to-one relationship with a join column

Let us take two different entities for this example: many projects have an association to a particular project type, or expressed in the reverse: for a given type there can be zero or more projects.

Here is the `ProjectType` entity:

```
@Entity
public class ProjectType implements java.io.Serializable {
    @Id private int id;
```

```
    private String name;
    private String description;
    /* ... */
}
```

Here is the `Project` entity, which is the owner of the relationship:

```
@Entity
public class Project implements java.io.Serializable {
    @Id private int id;
    private String name;
    private String description;

    @ManyToOne(cascade=CascadeType.ALL)
    @JoinColumn(name="PROJ_TYPE_FK")
    private ProjectType type;

    public ProjectType getType() { return type; }
    public void setType(ProjectType type) {
        this.type = type; }
    /* ... */
}
```

In the above class `Project`, the `@JoinColumn` annotation configures the additional database column with a name `PROJ_TYPE_FK`. By default, the persistence provider will concatenate the entity name with the foreign key name delimited with an underscore character (the database table column `PROJECT_TYPE_ID`).

Most applications will use `@ManyToOne` with the `@JoinColumn` in order to configure an alternative database column name.

The relationship between the `Project` and `ProjectType` is unidirectional in the example and here are the possible states of the database tables:

`PROJECT_TYPE` (table):

ID	Name	Description
579	FXTRADING	FX Trading
404	MARKETING	Trading Sales and Marketing

PROJECT (table):

ID	Name	Description	PROJ_TYPE_FK
1	FXDAILYREP	FX daily trading report	579
2	ONBOARD	New customer onboarding project	404
3	FXFIXINCOME	FX Fix Income Upgrade	579

Bidirectional many-to-one relationship

The bidirectional many-to-one relationship is the exact mirror on the one-to-many relationship. The only difference is that the entity is ultimately the owner of the relationship in terms of a Java programming. See the section *One-to-many mapping*.

Be careful with cascade operations in a many-to-one mapping, especially in circumstances where the single entity is used like a database enumeration type. Removing an entire collection of project records could delete the project type too. You probably want to manage the cascade types with a set of defined operations.

Many-to-many mapping

The many-to-many mapping relationship associates a collection of multiple entities to another collection of multiple entities. In the Java Persistence, this annotation is called `@javax.persistence.ManyToMany`. The Java developer must define which side of the relationship is the owner regardless of whether the true association is unidirectional or bidirectional. In database terms, all many-to-many associations are by definition bidirectional.

The inverse relationship of a many-to-many is a many-to-many, which is different to the associations of one-to-many and many-to-one.

All `@ManyToMany` associations require a `@JoinTable` as this is the practical way to represent this relationship in a relational database.

Let us look at the full attributes of the `@ManyToMany` annotation:

Attribute	Type	Description	Default value
targetEntity	String	This optional attribute represents the entity class that is the target of the relationship. If the property is used as a raw type then the attribute must be specified.	The parameterized type of the collection when defined using Java generics
cascade	String	This attribute specifies how and when the lifecycle of the dependent entity is included in any cascade operations (CascadeType.ALL, CascadeType.PERSIST etc.)	No operations are cascaded
fetch	String	This attribute specifies how the dependent entity is retrieved in a relationship. The valid values are FetchType.EAGER and FetchType.LAZY.	FetchType.LAZY
mappedBy	String	This attribute specifies the field or accessible property accessor for the source owning entity for bidirectional relationships.	None

Bidirectional many-to-many relationship

In the example code, we extend the `Project` entities with a many-to-many association of `Employee` entities. That is, multiple projects have zero or one employee and zero or one project have multiple employees.

Object-Relational Mapping with JPA

Here is the revised class for `Project`:

```
@Entity
public class Project implements java.io.Serializable {
    @Id private int id;
    /*...*/

    @ManyToMany(cascade={CascadeType.PERSIST,
        CascadeType.MERGE,CascadeType.DETACH)}
    @JoinTable(name="PROJECT_EMPLOYEE",
        joinColumns={ @JoinColumn(name="PROJ_ID_FK",
            referencedColumnName="ID" ) },
        inverseJoinColumns={
            @JoinColumn(name="EMPL_ID_FK",
            referencedColumnName="EMP_ID" ) }
    private List<Employee> employees;

    public List<Employee> getEmployees() { return employees; }
    public void setEmployees(List<Employee> employees) {
        this.employees = employees; }

    /* ... */
}
```

Because this class `Project` declared the list of employees with a join table, it is the owner of the relationship. The database table is explicitly defined as `PROJECT_EMPLOYEE`; the join columns are appropriately named as `PROJ_ID_FK` and `EMP_ID_FK`, which are foreign keys to their respective tables.

Project configures a limited set of cascade operations from the `Project` to the `Employee`. By default, the case operations do not take place, but we allow general persistence, merging, and detaching of entities.

Let us tie the other side of the relationship into the `Employee` entity.

```
@Entity
public class Employee implements java.io.Serializable {
    /*...*/

    @ManyToMany(mappedBy="employees")
    private List<Project> projects;

    public List<Project> getProjects() { return projects; }
    public void setProjects(List<Project> projects) {
        this.projects = projects; }
}
```

An employee has a set of projects or not, and we complete the definition of bidirectional relationship by declaring projects are owned by the Employee entity. We do this with the mappedBy attribute. It is important to define the mappedBy attribute in order to prevent duplicate join table being added to the database.

The JPA provider assumes that there are actually two separate relationships: a one-to-many and many-to-one, when the mappedBy attribute is not used. This could actually be the requirement for your business application, but it might be better to annotate the entities as properly separate @OneToMany and @ManyToOne with defined @JoinTable to avoid confusion.

Here are the sample database tables for the previous code:

PROJECT (table)

ID	Name	Description
1	FXDAILYREP	FX daily trading report
2	ONBOARD	New customer onboarding project
3	FXFIXINCOME	FX Fix Income Upgrade

EMPLOYEE (table)

EMP_ID	FIRST_NAME	LAST_NAME
32368	Vernon	Reid
40201	Paul	Gilbert
50203	Jennifer	Batten
60205	Joe	Satriani

PROJECT_EMPLOYEE

EMP_ID_FK	PROJ_ID_FK
32368	3
40201	2
50203	1
50203	3
40201	2
60205	3

Unidirectional many-to-many relationship

Mapping a unidirectional many-to-many relationship is fairly straightforward. The association has to be declared on the owner side with a `@ManyToMany`. The target association has no direct relationship to the owner: no `@ManyToMany` is required.

Let's take another example with the project entity. Every project has zero or more milestones, and some milestones are shared between projects.

Here is the `Project` code with a new field, a list collection of `Milestone` entities:

```
@Entity
public class Project implements java.io.Serializable {
    @Id private int id;
    /*...*/

    @ManyToMany(cascade=CascadeType.ALL, fetch=LAZY )
    @JoinTable(name="PROJECT_HAS_MILESTONE",
        joinColumns={ @JoinColumn(name="PROJ_ID_FK",
            referencedColumnName="ID" ) },
        inverseJoinColumns={
            @JoinColumn(name="MILESTONE_ID_FK",
                referencedColumnName="ID" ) }
    private List<Milestone> milestones;

    public List<Milestone> getMilestones() { return milestones; }
    public void setMilestones(List<Milestones> milestones) {
        this.milestones = milestones; }

    /* ... */
}
```

We use a join table as always for many-to-many association. The `@JoinTable` annotation declares the table name as PROJECT_HAS_MILESTONE, and the join columns at PROJ_ID_FK and MILESTONE_ID_FK respectively. So this code is semantically the same as the previous bidirectional example between projects and types.

Here is the code for the Milestone entity bean:

```
@Entity
public class Milestone implements java.io.Serializable {
    @Id private int id;
    @Column(nullable=false)
    private String name;
    private float tolerance;
    @Column(nullable=false)
```

```
    private String requirements;
    @Temporal(TIMESTAMP) private Date startDate;
    @Temporal(TIMESTAMP) private Date finishDate;
    /* ... */
}
```

In a unidirectional `@ManyToMany` association we do not declare the target side of the relationship and therefore there is no need for the annotation in the Milestone object.

As with all bidirectional relationships, Java Persistence requires the developer to connect object instances with each other. There is no secret sauce in the current JPA 2.1 specification that automates these connections.

Finally, we switch the cascade operation on the owner side of the many-to-many relationship back to `CascadeType.ALL`. So persistence will perform operations such as `CascadeType.PERSIST` and `CascadeType.REMOVE` on the dependent Milestone records, if the master `Project` entity is affected. As with all performance questions, always take measurements before and after, multiple times within a micro-benchmark—don't guess! Use the measurements to reason about the bottlenecks before modifying application code.

This concludes the entire section on entity relationship mapping.

Mapping entity inheritance hierarchy

Relational database management systems are programs that enable, extract, modify, and store information data in the relational model. The relational model is a structure of storage, which is a two dimensional table of rows and columns and is based on the relationship between a set of items in a table column for one entity and another of set of table columns, such that they form a intersection set. Consequently, the database of fixed entities is flat and monomorphic. However it is a structure that is easy to understand and allows businesses to view their data as tabular information.

On the other hand, Java, as an Object-Oriented Programming language, supports inheritance. Apart from encapsulation, inheritance is an essential concept of Java, the mother programming language, and many other alternative JVM programming languages. Unfortunately supporting object inheritance is something that relational databases were not designed to do. Before standardization with JPA, many independent projects such as Hibernate and TopLink supported different strategies that mapped object class hierarchies to database tables.

Object-Relational Mapping with JPA

The JPA specification defines three inheritance mechanisms, which are defined as follows:

```
package javax.persistence;

public enum InheritanceType {
    SINGLE_TABLE, TABLE_PER_CLASS, JOINED }
```

The mechanism is brought into play by taking one of the previous enumerations `InheritanceType` and applying it with annotation `@javax.persistence.Inheritance`.

The default strategy for JPA is the **Single Table**, while the **Table per Class** is an optional feature for the persistence provider to provide; in other words, not all JPA vendors may support the strategy.

Hierarchy in a single database table

Single table inheritance `SINGLE_TABLE` is the easiest strategy to understand. A single database table stores all the object instances in the entire inheritance strategy. The table has database columns for every attribute for every class in the hierarchy. The way the extraction, modification, and storage works is through a special designated column, which is called a **discriminator column**.

As usual, we take a sample user story to work through as an example.

A business requires a marketing entity that takes a campaign name, a concept of promoting the campaign, a set of one or more products involved, and it is has to maintain versions. Different departments inside the business will be writing and modifying the campaign and it is a user requirement that different versions of the campaign are maintained for senior executives to be able to review and sign off different marketing promotions.

The formal approach to this marketing is called solution, information value, and access, and is normally written as the *Four Ps* renamed and reworked to provide a customer orientation focus: Product, Promotion, Price, and Place of distribution.

An example user story

Here is a first stab at implementing this marketing entity using the single database table strategy:

```
@Entity
@Table(name="MARKETING_HIERARCHY")
@Inheritance(strategy=InheritanceType.SINGLE_TABLE)
@DiscriminatorColumn(name="MARKET")
@NamedQueries({
    @NamedQuery(name="Marketing.findAll",
                query="SELECT m FROM Marketing m"),
    @NamedQuery(name="Marketing.findByCampaign",
                query="SELECT m FROM Marketing m WHERE m.campaign = :campaign"),
})
public class Marketing implements java.io.Serializable {

    @Id @GeneratedValue
    private int id;
    @Column(unique=true)
    private String campaign;
    private String promotion;
    private BigBecimal budget;

    @OneToMany(cascade=Cascade.ALL)
    @JoinColumn(name="PRODUCT_ID", referencedColumnName="ID")
    private List<Product> products;

    @Version
    private int version;

    public Marketing() { }
    /* ... */
}
```

The `@javax.persistence.Table` annotation is optional, we use `@Table` in the `Marketing` entity to explicitly configure the database table, namely `MARKETING_HIERARCHY`. The `@Inheritance` is declared at the root entity of the hierarchy.

There are a couple of new annotations in the above. The discriminator column is declared with the `@javax.persistence.DiscriminatorColumn` and it specifies the name of the column that acts as the differentiator between the object types.

The `@javax.persistence.Version` annotation is a new one that we have not yet covered before. It specifies the version field or property accessor of the entity that serves as its optimistic lock value. There can only be one `@Version` property for a class, and configuring here in the root entity of the hierarchy means the subclass entities do not have to declare it.

The `@NameQuery` annotations define JPQL queries for the root entity. The `Marketing.findAll` retrieves all Marketing entities including subclass entities. The `Marketing.findByCampaign` retrieves a `Marketing` entity or subclass by its campaign name. Note that the campaign property is set as a unique database table column. The named queries are polymorphic.

Finally, we have a one-to-many association between `Marketing` and a list column of `Product` entities. For the purposes of this direction, let us assume that it is unidirectional.

With the root entity defined, we can define sub class entities. The business is happy with the first cut and now they come with a request for more marketing types, which are namely agency and direct. Moreover, the business wants the technology department to focus on giving the place of distribution more impetus.

The agency type is one where the business contracts a digital media agency to handle marketing of products online. The direct type is one where the business takes care of the marketing straight to the customer internally, perhaps through a letter, paper, and/or telephone campaigns.

Here is the agency marketing entity:

```
@Entity
@DiscriminatorValue("AGENCY")
@NamedQueries({
    @NamedQuery(name="AgencyMarketing.findAll",
                query="SELECT m FROM AgencyMarketing m"),
    @NamedQuery(name="AgencyMarketing.findByCampaign",
                query="SELECT m FROM AgencyMarketing m WHERE c.campaign = :campaign"),
})

public class AgencyMarketing extends Marketing {
    private String agency;
    private BigDecimal agencyBudget;

    public AgencyMarketing() { }
    /* ... */
}
```

Here is the direct marketing entity:

```
@Entity
@DiscriminatorValue("DIRECT")
@NamedQueries({
    @NamedQuery(name="DirectMarketing.findAll",
                query="SELECT m FROM DirectMarketing m"),
    @NamedQuery(name="DirectMarketing.findByCampaign",
                query="SELECT m FROM DirectMarketing m WHERE
m.campaign = :campaign"),
})
public class DirectMarketing extends Marketing {
    private String customerOrientation;

    @OneToMany(cascade=Cascade.ALL)
    @JoinColumn(name="DEPT_ID", referencedColumnName="ID")
    private List<Department> departments;

    public DirectMarketing() { }
    /* ... */
}
```

For both entities `AgencyMarketing` and `DirectMarketing`, notice we make use of the annotation `@javax.persistence.DiscrimatorValue`. The discriminator value specifies the value of the discriminator column for entities of the given type. `DirectMarketing` entities have the discriminator value `DIRECT` and the `AgencyMarketing` entities have the value `AGENCY`.

It was not supplied, but by default the `Marketing` entities will have a JPA vendor supplied value. So maybe we should apply `@DiscriminatorValue(name="MARKET")` to those root entities.

The named queries for each of these sub entities operate differently: they are constrained to the entity type and sub classes thereof. For example, `AgencyMarketing.findAll` retrieves all the entities that are a type of `AgencyMarketing` and respectively `DirectMarketing.findAll` retrieves all the entities that are a type of `DirectMarketing`.

There is only one database table for this strategy, so let's see some example data. Because of electronic page constraints, I have split the table into left and right-hand side views; the left most column is the primary key.

Here is the single table `MARKETING_HIERARCHY` (left):

ID	M'_TYPE	CAMPAIGN	PROMOTION	BUDGET	VERSION
1	MARKET	Food Plaza	Supermarkets	23500750	64
2	AGENCY	Green	Sustainable	1000000	12
3	DIRECT	National	Railways	9500300	7
4	AGENCY	Metro	Bank	1500000	10

`MARKETING_HIERARCHY` (right):

ID	AGENCY	AGENCY_BUDGET	CUSTOMER_ORIENTATION
1	NULL	NULL	NULL
2	Top	500000	NULL
3	NULL	NULL	Television Adverts
4	Star	250000	NULL

Notice how the table is filled with `NULL` values in the database columns, the representations of field and property accessors that are not mapped by the entity class.

Benefits and drawbacks of the single table strategy

The single table strategy has the benefit of fastest performance, because it is efficient to retrieve and store the data. There is one place to go. There are no database table joins to apply when the JPA provider performs the object-relational mapping. The provider only requires a discriminator `WHERE` clause that lists the object type identities.

So if the number of entity types is low and also the object hierarchy is fairly flat, then the efficiency of queries is fast. The persistence provider probably has to write a lot of `UNION` SQL clauses in order to retrieve all the data for an entity class and its sub types. It is the multitude of union queries that will most likely affect performance with this strategy given a wide or deep object hierarchy.

If the object hierarchy is generally stable from change and is mostly fixed, or even sealed, then the single table strategy is a great option to choose. The obvious drawbacks are when your object hierarchy is changing a lot or when a new entity has to be added. This could impact the database administration and the existing rows in the table, which will have to be refactored in order to include more extra columns. You also have to think carefully about removing any database columns that then become unnecessary in the long run.

The other drawback is about object entity size. If and when the object has too many properties and fields to store, for example an extensive XML document record for a particular domain such as **Financial Product Mark-up XML Language (FPML)** that has the potential for more than 256 different properties, then the single strategy table is not, perhaps, an optimal solution. The limit is the number of database columns that can be stored in a table and all database servers impose different restrictions; therefore, having entities with abnormally large numbers of properties reduces your portability.

Your mileage will also vary if there are specific database columns in the entire entity hierarchy that cannot be set to NULL. The single table strategy may not be appropriate for such a circumstance.

Common base table hierarchy

The joined or multiple table inheritance is another strategy for persistence in JPA. It is also called a logical inheritance solution for the reasons that properties that are part off entities are mapped almost into the same database table. The InheritanceType.JOINED is object-relational mapping strategy in which fields that are specific to an entity subclass are mapped to a separate table from the fields that are common to the parent class, and a join is performed to instantiate the subclass.

An example user story

Let's rework the previous user story about business marketing into the joined/multiple inheritance strategy. Here is the code for the Marketing entity:

```
@Entity
@Table(name="MARKETING")
@Inheritance(strategy=InheritanceType.JOINED)
@DiscriminatorColumn(name="MARKETING_TYPE")
@DiscriminatorValue("M")
@NamedQueries({
    @NamedQuery(name="Marketing.findAll",
                query="SELECT o FROM Marketing m"),
    @NamedQuery(name="Marketing.findByCampaign",
                query="SELECT o FROM Marketing m WHERE "+
                    "c.campaign = :campaign"),
})
```

Object-Relational Mapping with JPA

```java
public class Marketing implements java.io.Serializable {

    @Id @GeneratedValue
    private int id;

    @Column(unique=true)
    private String campaign;
    private String promotion;
    private BigBecimal budget;

    @OneToMany(cascade=Cascade.ALL)
    @JoinColumn(name="PRODUCT_ID", referencedColumnName="ID")
    private List<Product> products;

    @Version
    private int version;

    public Marketing() { }
    /* ... */
}
```

The only difference is the new value for the `@Inheritance` annotation, which is `InheritanceType.JOINED`. The root database table of the entity changes from `MARKETING_HIERARCHY` to `MARKETING` in order to reflect that the table stores only this exact entity class. The name queries are also the same as in the single database table strategy. There is also a `@DiscrimininatorValue` annotation applied to this class to differentiate `Marketing` instances from the other types in the hierarchy.

Here is the code for the sub entity class `AgencyMarketing`:

```java
@Entity
@Table(name="AGENCY_MARKETING")
@DiscriminatorValue("A")
@NamedQueries({
    @NamedQuery(name="AgencyMarketing.findAll",
                query="SELECT m FROM AgencyMarketing m"),
    @NamedQuery(name="AgencyMarketing.findByCampaign",
                query="SELECT m FROM AgencyMarketing m "+
                      "WHERE m.campaign = :campaign"),
})
public class AgencyMarketing extends Marketing {
    private String agency;
    private BigDecimal agencyBudget;

    public AgencyMarketing() { }
    /* ... */
}
```

And here is the code for the sub entity class `DirectMarketing`:

```
@Entity
@Table(name="DIRECT_MARKETING")
@DiscriminatorValue("D")
@NamedQueries({
    @NamedQuery(name="DirectMarketing.findAll",
                query="SELECT m FROM DirectMarketing m"),
    @NamedQuery(name="DirectMarketing.findByCampaign",
                query="SELECT m FROM DirectMarketing m "+
                    "WHERE m.campaign = :campaign"),
})
public class DirectMarketing extends Marketing {
    private String customerOrientation;

    @OneToMany(cascade=Cascade.ALL)
    @JoinColumn(name="DEPT_ID", referencedColumnName="ID")
    private List<Department> departments;

    public DirectMarketing() { }
    /* ... */
}
```

In the joined/multiple-inheritance strategy, both sub entities have separate database tables assigned: `AGENCY_MARKETING` and `DIRECT_MARKETING`, respectively. The name queries are unchanged. The discriminator values have been abbreviated, but semantically they remain unchanged.

It is helpful to look at tabular output of sample database table in order to reason about the persistence strategy.

Table `MARKETING`:

ID	M'_TYPE	CAMPAIGN	PROMOTION	BUDGET	VERSION
1	M	Food Plaza	Supermarkets	23500750	64
2	A	Green	Sustainable	1000000	12
3	D	National	Railways	9500300	7
4	A	Metro	Bank	1500000	10

Table `AGENCY_MARKETING`:

ID	AGENCY	AGENCY_BUDGET
2	Top	500000
4	Star	250000

Table `DIRECT_MARKETING`:

ID	CUSTOMER_ORIENTATION
3	Television Adverts

The entity with primary key ID=1 is a `Marketing` instance. Entities with ID matching 2 and 4 are `AgentMarketing` instances and finally the entity with ID matching 3 is a `DirectMarketing` instance. Examine the discriminator column, which is abbreviated to M'_TYPE in the above table MARKETING.

Benefits and drawbacks of joined Inheritance

The largest benefit of the joined strategy is that the data is spread over the separate tables that mirror the object class instance. This ensures great comprehensibility when only certain properties and attributes are selected, and they are restricted to a specific entity type.

Another benefit of this strategy is that certain database columns can be constrained to non-NULL, because each table manages a particular entity field or property accessor.

Introducing a new type in the hierarchy is relatively straightforward. Only the properties declared in the entity class are mapped to a new database table, therefore there is no interference in the super entity classes and other sibling entity classes.

Also, changing around the fields and the property classes in the declared entity class does not interfere with the super entity classes and other siblings. There is great benefit from the joined strategy in the field of prototyping a system for a business.

The obvious drawback with the joined table strategy is the combination of separate JOIN SQL clauses, which the persistence provider has to apply to in order to retrieve the combined object instance. The higher up in the entity class hierarchy, the more ancestral the target type, the more the join clauses are required across the known database tables. The discriminator column in each entity can alleviate these symptoms when the persistence provider, internally, implements a lazy-loading design.

In general, the poorest performance will be those queries that require root entities, because they will retrieve all the types in all of the multiple tables.

There is also the issue of software engineering practice, or rather agile development, where it is common nowadays to refactor member instance and property accessor on the fly. Developers can pull-up or push-down instance members to ancestors or subclasses with the delicate touch and selection of menu-bar actions in an IDE. With entities backed by a real database, this may be problematic for less Greenfield environments; a data migration plan may be necessary for hierarchical changes aimed at postproduction environments.

Table-per-class hierarchy

The table-per-class inheritance is the final strategy for persistence in JPA, which is an optional part of specification for the persistence provider. In order to keep your application, you may choose to avoid this strategy. The InheritanceType.TABLE_PER_CLASS is object-relational mapping strategy in which only the outermost concrete entity classes in an object hierarchy are mapped to a separate and dedicated database table. There are no shared database tables, and there are no shared columns. However, there are one or more primary key columns in each of the dedicated tables; the primary key structure is shared around the database tables.

An example user story

Let's rework the previous user story about business marketing into the table-per-class inheritance strategy. In this example, we now make the root entity an abstract class, so that there can be never any Java instances of this direct type.

Here is the code for the Marketing entity:

```
@Entity
@Inheritance(strategy=InheritanceType.TABLE_PER_CLASS)
@NamedQueries({
    @NamedQuery(name="Marketing.findAll",
                query="SELECT o FROM Marketing m"),
    @NamedQuery(name="Marketing.findByCampaign",
                query="SELECT o FROM Marketing m WHERE c.campaign = :campaign"),
})
public abstract class Marketing implements java.io.Serializable {
    @Id @GeneratedValue
    private int id;
```

```
        @Column(unique=true)
        /* As before in the single table strategy... */

    public Marketing() { }
    /* ... */
}
```

In the previous code, we apply the strategy `InheritanceType.TABLE_PER_CLASS` to the entity. We no longer require the discriminator column and so that annotation has been removed.

Even though there can be no entity instance of the abstract type `Marketing`, we can still keep and write named queries that reference it.

Here is the code for the sub entity class `AgencyMarketing`:

```
@Entity
@Table(name="AGENCY_MARKETING")
@NamedQueries({
    @NamedQuery(name="AgencyMarketing.findAll",
                query="SELECT m FROM AgencyMarketing m"),
    @NamedQuery(name="AgencyMarketing.findByCampaign",
                query="SELECT m FROM AgencyMarketing m WHERE
m.campaign = :campaign"),
})
public class AgencyMarketing extends Marketing {
    private String agency;
    private BigDecimal agencyBudget;

    public AgencyMarketing() { }
    /* ... */
}
```

Here is the code for the sub entity class `DirectMarketing`:

```
@Entity
@Table(name="DIRECT_MARKETING")
@NamedQueries({
    @NamedQuery(name="DirectMarketing.findAll",
                query="SELECT m FROM DirectMarketing m"),
    @NamedQuery(name="DirectMarketing.findByCampaign",
                query="SELECT m FROM DirectMarketing m WHERE
m.campaign = :campaign"),
})
```

```
public class DirectMarketing extends Marketing {
    private String customerOrientation;

    @OneToMany(cascade=Cascade.ALL)
    @JoinColumn(name="DEPT_ID", referencedColumnName="ID")
    private List<Department> departments;

    public DirectMarketing() { }
    /* ... */
}
```

It is not necessary to have a discriminator column or value for both `AgencyMarketing` and `DirectMarketing` entities when using the table-per-class strategy.

It is instructive to look at the result database table.

Table `AGENCY_MARKETING`:

ID	CAMPAIGN	PROMOTION	BUDGET	VERSION	AGENCY	AGENCY_BUDGET
2	Green	Sustainable	1000000	12	Top	500000
4	Metro	Bank	1500000	10	Star	250000

Table `DIRECT_MARKETING`:

ID	CAMPAIGN	PROMOTION	BUDGET	VERSION	CUST'_ORIENTATION
3	National	Railways	9500300	7	Television Adverts

As you can see only concrete entity classes are mapped to the database using `TABLE_PER_CLASS`.

Benefits and drawbacks of table-per-class hierarchy

The largest benefit of the table-per-concrete class strategy is shared with the joined strategy. When a new branch entity subclass is added to the application then only one other new corresponding database table is required, which of course is great for designing prototype and introducing hierarchy changes at the beginning of a software application.

Introducing a new field or property accessor in a super class (or for that matter removing one) means the change must percolate through the subclasses in that affected node in the hierarchy. It means modifying the database tables for all the affected subclass entities.

If there is a need to have database columns that are non-`NULL`, then the strategy allows for non-nullable columns.

There is also a performance impact for the table-per-concrete class strategy. The persistence provider has to generate `UNION` SQL select statement to retrieve an entity and its sub-type in combination. On the other hand, if only a single entity type is mostly required, then this strategy can be efficient, because only a query that retrieves one database table is required. Because of the generation of `UNION` SQL statement, this strategy also shares the drawback with the joined strategy, if mostly ancestor entities are queried and modified.

Table-per-class inheritance may not be appropriate if the entity queries are supposed to be ordered or joined in a query. The JPA persistence provider will first order any queries by class then by other user defined ordering.

Having seen the JPA handle entity inheritance in this section, we shall look at the situation where the mappings can be shared across super classes.

Extended entities

JPA supports the ability to map entities that share a super class. The object's inheritance is not mapped, but the mapping of the superclass is shared and therefore reused. This is in contrast to the entity inheritance modeling in the previous section.

Mapped super-classes

A mapped **superclass** is a non-entity class that contains metadata information: a class that has persistence annotations, which is quite similar to the table-per-class inheritance, but has no support or ability to be queried, stored, and modified into the database. A mapped superclass is not an entity and therefore has no equivalent database table (or view) applied.

The entity subclasses of the mapped superclass contain the necessary persistence capable information in order to map the object instance into a database table.

The annotation `@javax.persistence.MappedSuperclass` declares an object class an extended persistence capable object, but it is not an entity. A mapped super class can declare persistent fields and accessor properties. It is non-entity and therefore cannot be part of queries, JPQL, or other entity relationships.

Here is an example of the `Marketing` class as a mapped superclass:

```
@MappedSuperclass
public abstract class Marketing implements java.io.Serializable {
    @Id @GeneratedValue
    private int id;

    private BigBecimal budget;
    /* As before in the single table strategy... */

    public Marketing() { }
    /* ... */
}
```

This version of `Marketing` is not an entity and therefore cannot be queried. Hence there are named queries applied to this class; they have been removed.

Here is the `AgencyMarketing` entity using the mapped superclass:

```
@Entity
@Table(name="AGENCY_MARKETING")
@NamedQueries({
    @NamedQuery(name="AgencyMarketing.findAll",
                query="SELECT m FROM AgencyMarketing m"),
    @NamedQuery(name="AgencyMarketing.findByCampaign",
                query="SELECT m FROM AgencyMarketing m WHERE m.campaign = :campaign"),
})
public class AgencyMarketing extends Marketing {
    private String agency;
    private BigDecimal agencyBudget;

    public AgencyMarketing() { }
    /* ... */
}
```

The entity `AgencyMarketing` is mapped to a single database table AGENCY_MARKETING. It has all of the columns defined in the `Marketing` superclass and its own class. This entity can have named queries, which only retrieve the instances of the `AgencyMarketing`, since this class is not taking part in entity inheritance strategy.

The `@MappedSuperclass` is very useful for applications that share a set of common persistence fields across entities. Developers can provide persistent properties across a whole domain, for example an auditing mapped superclass is easily written.

JPA provides another annotation `@javax.persistence.AttributeOverride`. This is useful to override the mapping in a super class. It requires the name of the field or the property accessor and then the configuration for the new database column.

Here is an example of its use in the `DirectMarketing` entity:

```
@Entity
@Table(name="DIRECT_MARKETING")
@AttributeOverride(name="budget",
    column=@Column(name="FIELD_BUDGET"))
@NamedQueries({
    @NamedQuery(name="DirectMarketing.findAll",
                query="SELECT m FROM DirectMarketing m"),
    @NamedQuery(name="DirectMarketing.findByCampaign",
                query="SELECT m FROM DirectMarketing m WHERE m.campaign = :campaign"),
})
public class DirectMarketing extends Marketing {
    private String customerOrientation;
    /* ... */

    public DirectMarketing() { }
    /* ... */
}
```

The application of `@AttributeOverride` to `DirectMarketing` entity overrides the budget field of the `Marketing` mapped super class into the database column name called `FIELD_BUDGET` for the database table `DIRECT_MARKETING`.

Troubleshooting entity persistence

It is very thorough and clean specification that allows the skilled developer to write persistence code as Java object with meta data. The meta data allows the JPA provider to store data into a relational database. The technical content of JPA specification is of such a high level that cloud computing providers are already attempting to adapt it to their specialist environments, which have included key-value No-SQL database, albeit with limitations.

Nevertheless, if your development is targeted at relational databases then JPA can help your application evolve at fast agile pace without having to handcode native SQL statements.

Fetch performance

In the earlier part of the chapter, we introduced the topic of fetching and accessing information from database tables into entity object instances. A huge factor that influences the performance of JPA application is the object model: how an entity is associated with an other dependent entity. The more dependent entities there are in a master entity, the more work the persistence provider must do. The object model and how these entities are mapped to the database tables influence the persistence provider.

It is useful to remember that `FetchType.LAZY` is the default for `@OneToMany` and `@ManyToMany` associations; `FetchType.EAGER` is the default for `@OneToOne` and `@ManyToOne` association.

For certain situations, provided you always follow the golden rule: measure before and rule, then you override the `FetchType.EAGER` for the one-to-one and many-to-one associations. If you switch to lazily binding dependent object, be prepared to factor in detachment from the entity manager and reattachment.

Prefer lazily binding for maximum performance

If you are sending a master entity with a lazily bounded dependent entity across a JVM boundary across the network, and if the client suddenly expects to access the dependency, then there will be a problem on the client side application. One way to get out of this fix to have an aggregated view, a so-called projection view object.

Finally, binding affects query performance. The way the persistence provider eventually optimizes query could vary between lazily and eagerly bounded dependent entities.

Entity Relationship

The entity relationship and object-relational mapping can be problematic. Choosing the correct `java.util.Collection` interface obviously early in the development goes a long way to good design. Some persistence providers extend the JPA specification by allowing ordered collections. On the other hand, for true application portability across a number of database vendors it may be best to take control of this in your application. An ordered collection can be achieved with an artificial positioning field and it can, of course, be completed with a JPQL query with a particular ORDER BY clause. There are also a couple of further annotations to look for in the JPA specification that can be applied to entity relationships: they are called `@javax.persistence.OrderBy` and `@javax.persistence.OrderColumn`.

Object-Relational Mapping with JPA

Here is an example of `@OrderColumn` in use with our employee entity, once again, on one-to-many association with phone records:

```
@Entity
public class Employee implements java.io.Serializable {
    /*...*/

    @OneToMany(cascade = CascadeType.ALL)
    @OrderColumn(name="PHONE_ORDER")
    private List<Phone> phones;

    public List<Phone> getPhones() { return phones; }
    public void setPhones(List<Phone> phone) {
        this.phones = phones; }
}
```

The `@OrderColumn` may only be specified on a one-to-many or a many-to-many association. This annotation specifies that the persistence provider order the list collection of Phone entities using the field or property accessor called PHONE_ORDER, which must exist on the Phone entity.

The `@OrderBy` annotation specifies the ordering of a collection of dependent entities when the persistence provider retrieves those entities. Thus `@OrderBy` has subtly different behavior from the `@OrderColumn`; the latter implies a modification of the database schema.

Let's rework the employee entity with the `@OrderBy` annotation:

```
@Entity
public class Employee implements java.io.Serializable {
    /*...*/

    @OneToMany(cascade = CascadeType.ALL)
    @OrderBy("interCode ASC, areaCode ASC")
    private List<Phone> phones;
    /*...*/
}
```

In the previous code, the collection of Phone entities are ordered by the international code and then by area code; both orders are ascending. It is possible to reverse the order, make the ordering descend with DESC. If no order is supplied, then the default is ASC. As you can see, you delimit separate different orders by using a comma as a delimiter.

In terms of efficiency, when you have full administrative control of the database, then use `@OrderColumn`, because the order is then persistent inside the database. If you have no control because the database is owned by a different division, team, or even is a third-party, then you may prefer to use `@OrderBy`.

Prefer orphan removal

In JPA 2.0 and better you are advised to think about the `orphanRemoval` attribute in the entity relationship. This flag handles the situation when you remove an entity from a collection of entities, for example in `@OneToMany` association. In JPA 1.0, the developer had to invoke `EntityManager.remove()`. In JPA 2.0, the entity itself will handle removal automatically with `orphanRemoval=true` even if the cascade operation `CascadeType.REMOVE` is omitted.

Excessive queries

It is quite easy to get into trouble with one-to-many relationships with queries on the master object. Object-relational mapping providers have denoted this issue as the `N+1` problem (or more accurately `M(1+[N of R(M)])`).

Suppose we have `Project` and `Task` entities in a one-to-many relationship. We have M projects and each project entity stores N project tasks and if we also say the binding is `FetchType.EAGER`, then for every `Project` query the persistence provider has to make N additional queries to retrieve the `Task` information.

The problem exacerbates itself in search listing. Display a list of projects to the user with their tasks. It is retrieving the list of projects and dependent task entities that causes excessive queries.

From the point-of-view of the persistence provider, the simplest native SQL queries would look exactly like the following:

```
-- One operation to retrieve
SELECT * FROM PROJECT

-- For each row from EMPLOYEE then execute
SELECT * FROM TASK WHERE PROJECT_ID = ?
```

The solution is to use a technique called **Joined Fetching**, which results in both Project and Tasks data being retrieved in a single query.

```
SELECT p FROM Project p JOIN FETCH p.tasks
```

Object corruption

JPA specification supports bidirectional relationships and the persistence providers do a fantastic job to allow these entity associations to be mapped to a database. A Java developer has to ensure that the application updates both sides of the relationship. If the entity is added to one side of the relationship, the inverse relationship must be also taken care of, otherwise object corruption will take place at some stage during persistence.

Summary

In this chapter, we have seen how to improve the efficiency of entity beans in relationships. You are now in a position to add finesse to our your JPA code. We can bind entity object eagerly as well as lazily and learned about the trade-off in the fetching strategy.

There was a section on auto-generation of primary key columns and now we can use different strategies for `@GeneratedValue`. These include table, sequence, and identity generators.

We cover the JPA cascade operations and how they allow us to propagate important lifecycle events to dependent entities. We saw how these cascade events can be fairly useful to update and manage dependent entities.

We revisited entity relationships and covered them in depth for both unidirectional and bidirectional associations. We explored in full the four relationships: `@OneToOne`, `@OneToMany`, `@ManyToOne`, *and* `@ManyToMany`.

We delved into entity inheritance and three strategies that JPA supports. We examined in depth the `InheritanceType.SINGLE_TABLE`, `InheritanceType.JOINED` and `InheritanceType.TABLE_PER_CLASS`; and discussed the advantages and disadvantages of all of them. Finally, we covered mapped super classes, where a common ancestor non-persistence capable class can be shared by many entities. To close off, we looked at some of the common performance issues that can occur when developing with JPA, especially with queries.

This chapter and the previous one in beginning Java Persistence should now empower you, the humble Java EE developer, to write persistence services for enterprise session bean, those endpoints that are the starting block for any compliant enterprise application. All you now have to do is starting coding. The book and this chapter have full source code available with working examples of all the entity associations, entity inheritance, and fetch strategies for reference.

Chapter 11, *Advanced Topics in Persistence*, covers more advanced topics and new features in JPA 2.1, which discusses queries and EJB QL, Criteria queries, and object relational mapping using `java.util.Map` collections and persistence with database stored procedures.

For the next chapter, we move away from persistence and delve into Java Servlet programming with a slant to asynchronous input and output. Servlets are the foundation for web application in Java EE, and asynchronous I/O allows the servers and endpoints to scale.

6

Java Servlets and Asynchronous Request-Response

Oprah Winfrey said, "I'm black, I don't feel burdened by it, and I don't think it's a huge responsibility. It's part of who I am. It does not define me."

Java Servlet is perhaps one of the oldest application programming interfaces for running Java on a web application server. It is the conceptual mirror of the original Java Applet, the sandbox environment that allowed byte codes to be run in a JVM, embedded into a web browser. Java Servlet is a remote endpoint for an HTTP communication also, in a sort of sandbox environment, but now we call it a web container.

From Java Servlets, in the late 1990's, there came a flurry of technologies to do with the World Wide Web and the exponential growth of the Internet, which saw the ushering of the contemporary digital age in fast communication. Java Servlets expanded and were supported by **Java Server Pages (JSP)**, **Java Server Page Tag Libraries (JSTL)**, and then **Java Server Faces (JSF)**.

Java Servlets are the foundation of understanding how Java works in a web environment using the Java EE 7 specification and the Standard. Although the humble Servlet is not the only way to generate dynamic web content for today's digital media, social networking, and cloud computing requirements for a scalable and sustainable business, it is so well known by the Enterprise Java professionals, it is worth your while getting to know how it operates.

In this chapter, we will cover only the essential features of the traditional Java Servlet model. There are lots of tutorials, online descriptions, and, of course, books that describe how Java Servlets handle the requests and responses in a synchronous fashion. The aim of the chapter is to review the new features of Java Servlet 3.1 including the improvements in the API to handle asynchronous input and output. But first, let us understand exactly what Java Servlets are. Why do we need them and how do we use them?

What are Java Servlets?

A Java Servlet is a web component managed container. Java Servlets are based on the Java technology, they generate dynamic content, and hence the container that manages them is capable of delivering dynamic content to the web client. Because Java Servlets are built, most of the time, in the Java language, they are executed in a **Java Virtual Machine (JVM)**, and the container that manages them controls their entire lifecycle and is responsible for starting and stopping them. Servlets interact with the world through a protocol called **request-response**.

A web client sends a request to the container that dispatches the request to a specific Java Servlet, which in turn processes the request, and then generates a response. The web client receives the response of the Servlet and can take further action accordingly.

Web containers

In the business, we normally call these containers web containers, because they not only manage the dynamic content components, such as Java Servlets, but also JSP and JSF, and deliver static content, such as HTML, images, and other MIME content.

Web containers communicate with the outside world, the web client with the HTTP and HTTPS protocols. These specifications are the foundation of the World Wide Web, and allow the Java components to communicate over the Internet's hypermedia platform. The standard and certified web containers for Java all implement HTTP/1.1, which are the HTTP protocols, governed by the **Request For Comments (RFC)** standards, namely RFC 2619 (June 1999), which defines the standard.

The Java Servlets specification talks about the container as a Servlet container. For the most part, this is an artifact of history of the Enterprise platform; Servlets were one of the earliest Java Enterprise Editions standards to be delivered along with Enterprise Java beans. For all intents and purposes, the Servlet containers are practically web containers in the open source and business worlds. There was a time in the beginning, in the first implementations of Enterprise Java, where only Servlets existed. There was no JSP or JSF, and hence the name, Servlet container, stuck around and continues to this day.

A web container can be a separate entity of a web server, as Apache Tomcat is separate to the Apache HTTP Server. A web container can also be part of a full application server, such as the GlassFish server. A web browser client communicates with the web applications inside a web container using the Java Servlet API, which is the standard library for the HTTP communications.

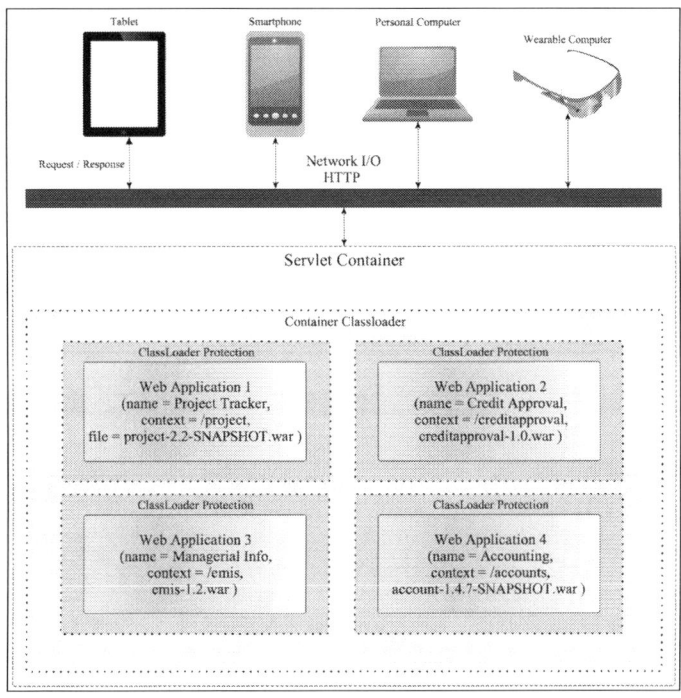

The Servlet container (or web container) manages the lifecycle of the web applications, which are deployed to it (or undeployed from it). Each web application is separated from the other, because they are associated with their own `ClassLoader`, so effectively no instances of the class context are visible to any of the parallel contexts. All web applications in the container will share the boot classpath and the web container's common `ClassLoader`. Each web application has a combination of Java Servlet, filter, context listeners, and dynamic content, JSP or JSF. Many traditional business applications employed a web framework in order to add the robust application architecture, and to avoid dealing with the low-level Java Servlet API.

The lifecycle of Java Servlets

Java Servlets are governed by a web container (a Servlet container). The specification describes a full lifecycle of events for a Servlet. In particular, web container is responsible for loading and instantiating Servlets. The container then dispatches the requests to Servlets. Finally, when web container shuts down, it will give a chance to Servlets to close down appropriately. This is the basic model of operation.

Web container has one other important responsibility. It can host different web applications all at the same time in order to share the web server or the application server. The container must protect the web applications from interfering with each other. Therefore, Java Servlets in one web application are limited from deliberately and directly invoking, through a Java invocation, another Servlet in another web application, shared inside the same web container. It is an early form of multi-tenancy in the Java EE specification.

The package name for Servlets is called `javax.servlet`, and for the HTTP Servlets it is `javax.servlet.http`.

Java Servlets are defined by interface, namely `javax.servlet.Servlet`, which defines the methods that all Servlets must implement.

Loading Servlets

Java Servlets are loaded when a web application is started. The Standard defines the loading time as a choice between when the web container starts or is delayed until the container determines the Servlet is needed to service a request. In other words, it is a choice for the web container implementers to make. Developer does not have any say in exactly how a Java Servlet is loaded.

For a standalone container such as Tomcat, it makes perfect sense to load the web application with its Java Servlets as soon as possible.

For a cloud computing provider, now or in the future, it may only make sense to lazily load the web application and only deliver those system resources as the circumstance-permitting may be.

Chapter 6

The Java Servlet initialization

The web container initiates Servlet before it can start servicing the requests from the HTTP clients. After loading a Java Servlet, the container makes a call to the `init()` method. The initialization call allows a Java Servlet to acquire generic resources from other Enterprise components such as Java data persistence providers, transaction services, and other resources. The initialization call only happens once per Servlet, and the `init()` method must complete successfully in order for Servlet to participate in further requests.

Web container also supplies the `init()` method with a `javax.servlet.ServletConfig` object. In this way, a system specific configuration can be passed to Servlet at the initialization time. Servlet can read the initialization parameters as the name and value parameters, and act upon them. A collection of the initialization parameters could be the details to connect to a database, for example the hostname, port, user credentials, and database schema name.

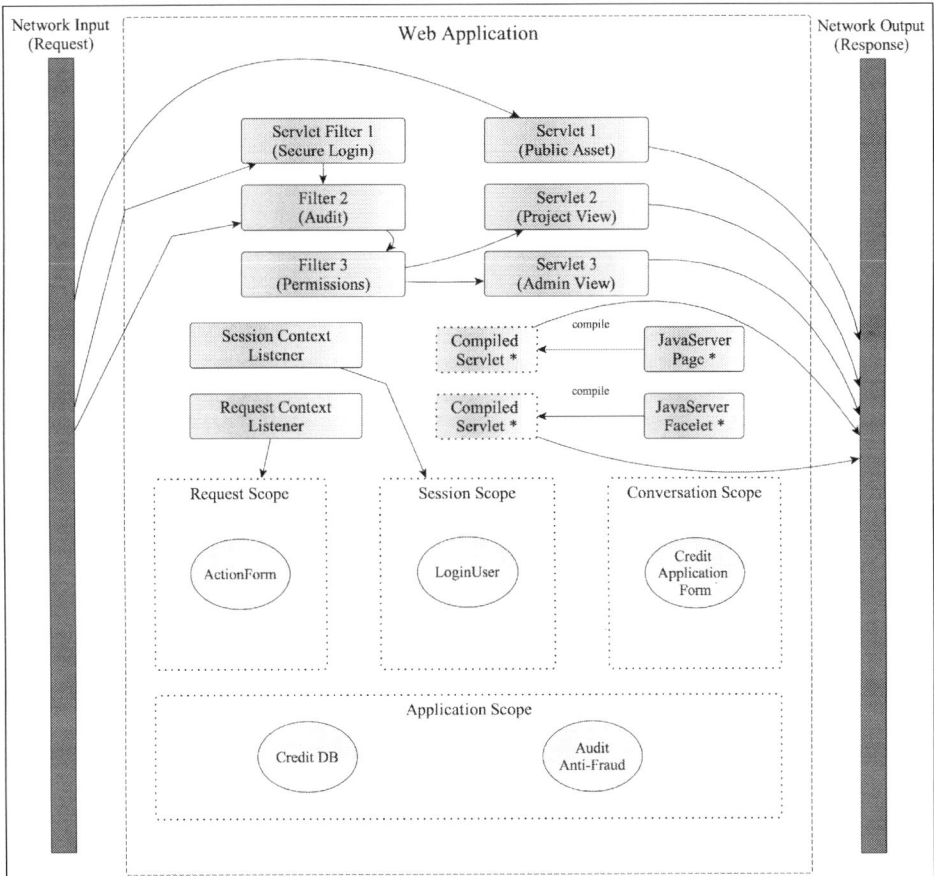

The Java Servlet destruction

Web container gives a chance for a Servlet to know when it is being released from service. This is the time for a Java Servlet to release any expensive resources, connections, and other handlers, and perform clean up, as needed. The container calls the `destroy()` method on Servlet.

The Servlet request and response

Web container dispatches the incoming requests to a particular web application, which it configures by the URL routing information. Once the container identifies the application, it dispatches the request to a Servlet. The container invokes the `service()` method on Servlet with the following two arguments: `javax.servlet.ServletRequest` and `javax.servlet.Response`.

`ServletRequest` contains all the information about the incoming request. In particular, it has the details of the Servlet request parameters, name and value pairs, the MIME content and length, if any, and the remote host and port of the web client.

`ServletResponse` contains all the information for Servlet to generate the response. The response assists Servlet in sending back a suitable response. `ServletResponse` has `java.io.OutputStream`, in which a Servlet can write a dynamic response. It can also set the MIME type and length of the response with the appropriate character encoding.

It is important to understand that the Servlet model was abstracted at the very beginning to allow Servlets to serve inputs other than the HTTP requests.

Most of the time, as a developer, you would see the `javax.servlet.HttpServletRequest` and `javax.servlet.HttpServletResponse` objects, as it is far easier to write Servlets that inherit from the abstract base class `javax.servlet.HttpServlet`.

The following table summarizes the `javax.servlet.Servlet` calls:

Method Name	Return Type	Description
init(ServletConfig config)	void	Web container invokes this method to allow a Servlet to know that it has been loaded and is about to be put into service.
		The Servlet instance can throw an `UnavailableException` or `ServletException` exception to denote when the initialization has failed. If this happens, then the web container does not put the Servlet instance into service.
getServletConfig()	ServletConfig	Returns the `ServletConfig` object, which contains the initialization and startup parameters for this Servlet. Developers do not normally override this method.
getServletInfo()	String	Returns the Servlet information as plain text only: the author, version, and production details.
service(ServletRequest request, ServletResponse response)	void	It is called by web container in order to allow Servlet to process a request and send a response.
		Servlet may throw an `UnavailableException` or `ServletException` exception for an incoming request. If `ServletException` is thrown, web container takes an action, and cleans up the request.
		During processing, Servlet may throw a `java.io.IOException` exception, if an input or output exception occurs.
destroy()	void	Web container calls this method just before Servlet is taken out of service.
		Web container does not call the destroy method, if the Servlet instance fails to be initialized.

A Servlet can throw two types of exceptions, namely `javax.servlet.UnavailableException` and `javax.servlet.ServletException`.

`ServletException` defines a general class of exception thrown by all the Servlet types. There is really no difference between it and the standard checked exception. It can record an error message and an optional root cause.

`UnavailableException` is a subclass of `ServletException` and the unavailable exception signifies that Servlet cannot be initialized or it can immediately service the incoming request. The `UnavailableException` class has a method `isPermanent()` that the framework can query to find out, if Servlet is permanently or temporarily disabled.

For the permanent situation, web container removes the Servlet instance from the in-active-service collection. For the temporary situation, web container will remove Servlet from service for N number of seconds, which can be established from a call to `getUnavailableSeconds()`. The only difference between permanent and temporary is the call to the `UnavailableException` constructor.

HTTP Servlets

The abstract base class `javax.servlet.http.HttpServlet` is a subclass of `javax.servlet.GenericServlet`, and implements the `Servlet` and `ServletConfig` interfaces. As mentioned before, it is far easier to write Java Servlets that extend this abstract class, because it has facilities to support the HTTP protocol.

The `HttpServlet` class takes care of decoding the HTTP method, by delegating to the following methods:

HTTP METHOD	Method	Description
GET	doGet	This Servlet method is reserved for the HTTP GET requests, which retrieve information that is determined by the request URI.
POST	doPost	This method is reserved for the POST requests, which deliver to Servlet the content to store and/or update related to the request URI. The Post requests are usually blocks of data, form submissions, and extending a database with extra information.
PUT	doPut	This method is reserved for the PUT requests, which are similar to the POST request, but insert a brand new entity related to the request URI. The equivalent request would insert a new row into a database table.

HTTP METHOD	Method	Description
DELETE	`doDelete`	This method is reserved for the DELETE requests, which are actions to remove information, the entity related to the request URI.
HEAD	`doHead`	This method is reserved for the HEAD requests, which are actions to return only the HTTP header information related to the request URI. Web container does not return a message body to the client in this protocol.
OPTIONS	`doOptions`	This method is reserved for the OPTIONS requests, which are details about the request-response choices available for a particular URI.
TRACE	`doTrace`	This method is reserved for the TRACE requests, which are actions to send back only a reflection of the incoming message related to the web request. Servlet should perform no irreversible and critical business processing with the application data in this protocol. A trace allows a web client the product of what has been received at the Servlet end.

Developers who subclass the `HttpServlet` class rarely have to override the `service()` method, because this Servlet adds additional methods that map the HTTP request into one of the preceding methods.

The deployment model

Servlets are deployed to a web container using a specialized form of **Java Archive (JAR)**, it is called a **Web Archive (WAR)**, otherwise known as a WAR file. The WAR file is a deployment of a single web application that is deployed by a web container. The WAR file contains dynamic elements, such as Java classes organized in packages. It can also contain JSP, tag libraries, third-party libraries, and also static content.

The structure of a WAR is standard in Java EE and is based on a special directory or folder name that is reserved for the metadata content called `/WEB-INF`. This is similar to `/META-INF` in JAR in that the directory is hidden from view; the web container does not serve any content underneath the directory. Any other folder or files other than these two are servable by the web container.

Folder or File	Description
`/`	The root directory of the web archive and also the web application
`/WEB-INF`	The root directory for the web application metadata that is hidden from view
`/WEB-INF/web.xml`	The web application deployment descriptor file (optional in the Java EE 7 application server and the web profile conformant container)
`/WEB-INF/classes`	A subdirectory reserved for the compiled Java classes in an exploded view
`/WEB-INF/lib`	A subdirectory reserved for the third-party libraries distributed with the web application
`/WEB-INF/tld`	A subdirectory specially reserved for the tag library definitions (circa J2EE 1.4)
`/WEB-INF/tags`	A subdirectory specially reserved for the tag library definitions

Under the root folder, developers can organize the structure of the web application however feels right. A sample web application with some content, which is organized in a meaningful and modern way is as follows:

```
/index.jsp
/pages/header.jsp
/pages/footer.jsp
/content/
/content/application.jsp
/content/app/sales/
/content/app/marketing/
/content/app/humanresources/
/images/icon.png
/javascript/jquery.js
/javascript/modernizer.js
/styles/
```

```
/styles/main.css
/styles/desktop/ie9.css
/styles/tablet/ios.css
/styles/tablet/android.css
/styles/mobile/
/WEB-INF/web.xml
/WEB-INF/classes/
/WEB-INF/lib/
/WEB-INF/tags/
```

The root of the JAR file is the root directory for the web application. Web containers deploy a WAR file to a web context usually by the base name of the filename, which usually derives the default name of the web application. For example, given a WAR file named `seaside.war`, the default web context will be named `seaside`. To reach the PNG file from a locally installed web container, we might have a URL reference, such as `http://localhost:8080/seaside/images/icon.png`.

To summarize the point for the WAR file, the compiled Java classes (or from any other alternative JVM programming language) are dumped in the `/WEB-INF/classes` directory. The `/WEB-INF/lib` directory is where all the third-party or internal JAR libraries are copied to.

The web deployment file `web.xml`, which is covered later, configures Java Servlets, the Servlet filters, and listeners for your application. It is always found in the `/WEB-INF` subdirectory. Finally, your web application, if it makes use of the JSP, JSF technology, may require the tag libraries and/or define its own custom set of tag libraries and fragments for rendering the definitions of extra tag libraries. lives in the folder `/WEB-INF/tags`.

Finally, your application can place static resources and dynamic pages in structure that makes sense to your organization and, of course, to your architecture.

A WAR file is a Zip file of all of the entire web applications with metadata. Deployment to web container is usually performed through a build system, such as Apache Ant, Maven, or Gradle. Some web containers provide specialist tools to deploy the WAR files, which can be standalone plugin programs for IDE, or be operated through the administration web pages inside an application server.

Getting started with Java Servlets

There is a reason why we have not examined a web deployment context file up until now. With Java Servlet 3.1, you do not have to define a context file, because developers can choose to write Servlets using the annotations, and web container can work out how to build the metadata for the Servlet at the deployment time.

A simple Servlet

It is time to examine a sample Java Servlet and we will introduce the annotations. The code for `SimpleServlet` is as follows:

```
package je7hb.servlets.simple;

import javax.servlet.ServletException;
import javax.servlet.annotation.WebServlet;
import javax.servlet.http.HttpServlet;
import javax.servlet.http.HttpServletRequest;
import javax.servlet.http.HttpServletResponse;
import java.io.IOException;
import java.io.PrintWriter;
import java.util.Date;

@WebServlet("/simple")
public class SimpleServlet extends HttpServlet {

  @Override
  protected void doGet(HttpServletRequest req,
    HttpServletResponse resp)
  throws ServletException, IOException {
    resp.setContentType("text/plain");
    PrintWriter pwriter = resp.getWriter();
    pwriter.printf("This is the class `%s'\n"+
      "The date time is %s\n", this.getClass().getName(),
        new Date());
  }
}
```

The preceding code is perhaps the easiest Servlet that you can develop and deploy to an application server or web container.

The `SimpleServlet` subclasses the abstract base class `HttpServlet`, and chooses to override the `doGet()` method, which handles the HTTP GET protocol request. The Servlet class is also annotated with `@javax.servlet.annotation.WebServlet`. This is one of many new annotations since Servlet 3.0 and the Java EE 7 specifications.

The `doGet()` method takes two parameters, namely `HttpServletRequest` and `HttpServletResponse`. With the response object, Servlets sets the content type of the response to text/plain. This should only be set once per response for a given request. The method retrieves a `PrintWriter` instance for the response. The `getWriter()` method is one of the many convenient methods in `HttpServletReponse`. Servlet generates the output of the Servlet's full class name, and the current data and time.

By the way the `HttpServletResponse` interface also has a `getOutputStream()` method that returns `java.io.OutputStream`. This is useful for streaming the output applications. Let me warn you to decide on using either `OutputStream` or `Writer`. Once the output has been pushed to the HTTP response then the Servlet framework prevents the application from changing the content type mid-flow.

Annotating a class with `@WebServlet`, unfortunately, is not a free-for-all. A Java class annotated with `@WebServlet` must be a subclass of `HttpServlet`. The annotation serves to purely define a Servlet component in a web application. In particular, a Servlet can have a unique name and can respond to a set of URL patterns. In the `SimpleServlet` code, we are declaring Servlet with the name as `simple`.

In order to access this Servlet on a web container, for example, we would specify a URL like the following URL:

```
http://<host>[:<port>]/<web-app>/simple
```

Where `host` is the hostname of the server, `port` is the port number, and `web-app` specifies the name of the web application.

A table of the attribute definitions for the `@WebServlet` annotation is as follows:

Attribute	Type	Description	Default Value
name	String	Defines the name of Servlet.	Empty
value	String []	Defines the URL patterns of Servlet.	None
urlPatterns	String []	Defines the URL patterns of Servlet.	
loadOnStartup	Int	Specifies the load-on-startup order of Servlet.	-1
initParams	WebInitParam []	The initial parameters of Servlet.	None
asyncSupported	Boolean	Specifies if Servlet supports asynchronous operations and processing or not.	false
		See also the `ServletRequest.startAsync()` methods.	
displayName	String	The display name of Servlet	Empty string
description	String	The description for a Servlet	Empty string
smallIcon	String	Specifies a path to a small icon	None
largeIcon	String	Specifies a path to a large icon	None

The URL path mapping

According to the preceding information, we could have annotated Servlet with specific URL patterns and given it internally, a different name. Some additional usages of the `@WebServlet` annotations with the same Servlet are as follows:

```
@WebServlet(urlPatterns = {"/simple"}, name = "simple")
public class SimpleServlet extends HttpServlet {/*... */}
// For example, http://localhost:8080/mywebapp/simple
```

This annotation declares the exact same Servlet configuration as the previous example code. `SimpleServlet` will be invoked by web container with any URL pattern matching /simple. The URL patterns are exact and therefore, the preceding pattern does not match the URL /simple/1, which presumably would be useless in a RESTful application. If you want to match anything after the forward slash (/) then you must use something like the following code:

```
@WebServlet(urlPatterns = {"/simple/*"}, name = "simple")
public class SimpleServlet extends HttpServlet {/*... */}
// For example, http://localhost:8080/mywebapp/simple/1
// For example, http://localhost:8080/mywebapp/simple/glasgow
```

What if we wanted to configure Servlet to respond to certain names? We can achieve this requirement with two URL patterns like the following:

```
@WebServlet(urlPatterns = {"/sarah","/paul"}, name = "simple")
public class SimpleServlet extends HttpServlet {/*... */}
// For example, http://localhost:8080/mywebapp/sarah
// or http://localhost:8080/mywebapp/paul
```

Web container only invokes `SimpleServlet` when the incoming URL request matches the pattern. The forward slash characters (/) at the beginning of the patterns are significant. They serve to demarcate the URL paths.

See the *Miscellaneous features* section of this chapter, for further information on the URL patterns.

Now we have a Java Servlet, so what do we need to install it onto a web container? The answer is that we have to assemble it as a compiled Java class into a WAR file, a web application archive. So let's use Gradle to do it, and we are going to deploy it onto a GlassFish application server, but in this chapter, we make use of building a so-called container-less web application. This is just a fancy name for running an embedded web container or application server from the standard entry into a Java application, the JVM invokes `main(String args[])`.

The Gradle build project

The Gradle build for the `SimpleServlet` example is as follows:

```
apply plugin: 'java'
apply plugin: 'war'
apply plugin: 'maven'
apply plugin: 'eclipse'
apply plugin: 'idea'

group = 'com.javaeehandbook.book1'
archivesBaseName = 'ch06-servlets-basic'
version = '1.0'

repositories {
  mavenCentral()
  maven {
    url 'https://maven.java.net/content/groups/promoted'
  }
  maven {
    url 'http://repository.jboss.org/nexus/content/groups/public'
  }
}

dependencies {
  providedCompile 'org.glassfish.main.extras:
    glassfish-embedded-all: 4.0.1-b01'
  compile 'org.glassfish.main.extras:
    glassfish-embedded-all: 4.0.1-b01'
  compile 'javax: javaee-api: 7.0'

  testCompile 'junit: junit: 4.11'
}

war {
  // webXml = file("src/main/webapp/WEB-INF/web.xml")
}

// Override Gradle defaults - a force an exploded JAR view
sourceSets {
  main {
    output.resourcesDir = 'build/classes/main'
    output.classesDir   = 'build/classes/main'
  }
```

```
  test {
    output.resourcesDir = 'build/classes/test'
    output.classesDir   = 'build/classes/test'
    }
  }

  task(run, dependsOn: 'classes', type: JavaExec) {
    description = 'Runs the main application'
    main =
      'je7hb.common.webcontainer.embedded.glassfish.EmbeddedRunner'
    classpath = sourceSets.main.runtimeClasspath
    args 'Mary', 'Peter', 'Jane'
    standardInput = System.in
  }
```

In the build file, the most crucial dependency is `glassfish-embedded-all`; it has to be the very first dependency, otherwise the execution of the embedded runner fails with a `ValidationException` exception. The exception happens because the GlassFish application serve, uses the Hibernate Validator as the default Bean Validation component. Luckily, Gradle does pay attention to the order of the dependencies, because the embedded runner works from the command line and also from an IDE.

The build file adds some additional repositories, the Maven GlassFish Promoted and the JBoss Public sites.

Because we have a Servlet in the application, Gradle applies the War plugin, which generates a WAR file for ourselves in the folder `build/libs`. The extra configuration of the project dependencies named as `providedCompile` ensures that the embedded glassfish dependency is not included into the WAR file.

Finally, in the Gradle task named `run`, that is a type of the Java execution task, we override the standard input to `System.in`, because we want the embedded runner, which we will see shortly, to respond to the console input.

Let us move on to the GlassFish embedded runner.

The containerless Java web application

In order to go and demonstrate the container-less application, the following example uses the GlassFish embedded API, at the time of writing. Since GlassFish is the reference implementation to Java EE 7, we should see how to invoke it, start the server, stop the server, and most importantly deploy a web application to the server.

Java Servlets and Asynchronous Request-Response

It is possible to go container-less with other servers, such as Apache Tomcat, Jetty, and Caucho Resin. The book does not cover those approaches, however, and there is sure to documentation online that explains how to configure those containers for Java EE 7 and Servlets 3.1.

GlassFish has well documented embedded document online since Version 3.1.2 and this is the information we have used in the code. Fortunately, the API is still compatible with GlassFish 4.0.1 at the time of writing, which means we can use it.

The code for `EmbeddedRunner` is as follows:

```java
package je7hb.common.webcontainer.embedded.glassfish;

import org.glassfish.embeddable.*;
import java.io.File;
import java.util.Scanner;
import java.util.concurrent.atomic.AtomicBoolean;

public class EmbeddedRunner {
  private int port;
  private AtomicBoolean initialized = new AtomicBoolean();
  private GlassFish glassfish;

  public EmbeddedRunner(int port) {
    this.port = port;
  }

  public EmbeddedRunner init() throws Exception{
    if (initialized.get()) {
      throw new RuntimeException
        ("runner was already initialized");
    }

    BootstrapProperties bootstrapProperties =
      new BootstrapProperties();
    GlassFishRuntime glassfishRuntime =
      GlassFishRuntime.bootstrap(bootstrapProperties);

    GlassFishProperties glassfishProperties =
      new GlassFishProperties();
    glassfishProperties.setPort("http-listener", port);
    glassfish =
      glassfishRuntime.newGlassFish(glassfishProperties);
    initialized.set(true);
```

```java
      return this;
    }

  private void check() {
    if (!initialized.get()) {
      throw new RuntimeException("runner was not initialised");
      }
    }

  public EmbeddedRunner start() throws Exception {
    check();
    glassfish.start();
    return this;
    }

  public EmbeddedRunner stop() throws Exception {
    check();
    glassfish.stop();
    return this;
    }

  public EmbeddedRunner deployWithRename
    (String war, String newContext ) throws Exception {
    Deployer deployer = glassfish.getDeployer();
    deployer.deploy(new File(war), "--name="+newContext,
      "--contextroot = "+newContext, "--force=true");
    return this;
    }

  public static void main(String args[]) throws Exception {
    EmbeddedRunner runner =
      new EmbeddedRunner(8080).init().start();
    runner.deployWithRename
      ("build/libs/ch06-servlets-basic-1.0.war", "mywebapp");
    Thread.sleep(1000);
    System.out.printf
      ("**** Press the ENTER key to stop "+"the server ****");
    Scanner sc = new Scanner(System.in);
    while(!sc.nextLine().equals(""));
    runner.stop();
    }
}
```

As you can see in the program, `EmbeddedRunner` looks like a barrel and stock Java application. In the `main()` program, we instantiate the object with a port number 8080, initialize the runner, and start the server. The program then proceeds to deploy a WAR file from the build, it delays for one second, and then waits for the user to type ENTER. As soon as the user does it, the program stops the server, and exits normally.

The GlassFish server is launched by initializing an instance with two types of properties, namely `bootstrap` and `standard`. These properties help developers to configure special GlassFish-only features. The `bootstrap` properties can be used to configure an installation root, if the server or launch space already has a version of GlassFish installed. For this example, we do not use this feature. The standard properties can configure the instance root, the configuration file locally of a particular domain area, and also services and port numbers.

In `EmbeddedRunner`, we configure only the HTTP listener for the embedded server, which is passed into the `init()` method as 8080. Having created a `GlassfishRuntime` instance, the runner invokes a new Glassfish object instance, which represents the application server.

The methods `start()` and `stop()`, start and stop the application server respectively.

The `deployWithRename()` method is a convenient method that deploys the simple Servlet WAR file to the server, and it does a unique rename of the web context from the clumsy `ch06-servlets-basic-1.0`, which by default is the base name of the WAR file without the suffix. In this case, the web application context is renamed `mywebapp`.

Now that we have a Java Servlet, a Gradle build file, and an embedded runner application, we can invoke it, and run the program. Here is how, with the following Gradle commands:

```
$ Gradle clean
$ Gradle war
$ Gradle run
```

Enter in your favorite web browser URL `http://localhost:8080/mywebapp/simple`. The output on the page should be something like the following:

```
This is the class `je7hb.servlets.simple.SimpleServlet'
The date time is Sat Feb 02 16:45:52 GMT 2013
```

To complete this section, here is a different version of the same Servlet, but this time we configure the initialization parameters through the annotations. This Servlet is called `SimpleServletWithInitParams`.

```java
package je7hb.servlets.simple;
import javax.servlet.annotation.WebInitParam;
import javax.servlet.annotation.WebServlet;
// Additional imports from before are omitted

@WebServlet(name = "servletWithInitParams", urlPatterns =
  {"/initparams"}, initParams =
    {@WebInitParam(name = "source", value = "East Croydon"),
      @WebInitParam(name = "target", value = "London Bridge"),
        @WebInitParam(name = "time", value = "11:57:00")})
public class SimpleServletWithInitParams extends HttpServlet {
  @Override
  protected void doGet(HttpServletRequest req,
    HttpServletResponse resp)
  throws ServletException, IOException {
    resp.setContentType("text/plain");
    PrintWriter pwriter = resp.getWriter();
    pwriter.printf("This is the class `%s'\nThe date "+
      "time is %s\n", this.getClass().getName(), new Date());
    for ( String name: Collections.list
      (this.getServletConfig().getInitParameterNames())) {
      pwriter.printf("init parameter: %s = %s\n", name,
        getServletConfig().getInitParameter(name));
    }
  }
}
```

The extra bit of code in this example retrieves `java.util.Enumeration` of the Servlet initialization parameters. In the Servlet method, we call the utility static `list()` method of `java.util.Collections` to turn the `Enumeration` into `java.util.Iterator<String>`. (This is an artifact from Java's history when the Servlet API, which was created in 1999, existed long before the release of Java SE 5, generic types, and annotations in 2005!) We then iterate through the parameters and dump their values to the Servlet's response, the output buffer, using the `PrintWriter` instance.

When running the embedded runner, if you invoke this Servlet with the quasi URL `http://localhost:8080/mywebapp/initparams`, you should see the output like the following:

```
This is the class
  `je7hb.servlets.simple.SimpleServletWithInitParams'
The date time is Mon Feb 04 20:04:58 GMT 2013
init parameter: time = 11:57:00
init parameter: source = East Croydon
init parameter: target = London Bridge
```

The `@WebInitParam` annotation accepts three attributes: `name`, `value`, and `description`. The `name` attribute specifies the Servlet's initialization parameter name, `value` is the associated value, and `description` is self-explanatory.

Congratulations, this is your first Java Servlet! Best of all, you did not have to specify a web XML deployment context, better known as a `web.xml` file.

Request and response

For Servlets to be useful, we need to read the HTTP request, and then generate a response. HTTP Servlets provide two types of instances: `HttpServletRequest` and `HttpServletResponse`.

The request parameters

The Servlet framework decodes the HTTP protocol parameters sent by the client into a specific map of key and values. The methods on `HttpServletRequest` to access these parameters are `getParameter()`, `getParameterNames()`, and `getParameterMap()`. The `getParameter()` method returns the first value in an array of the query string data values. This is because the HTTP standard allows an HTTP request to be formed with multiple parameter associations.

To retrieve a CGI query data in a URI, such as `/fooAction?name=Mary&bus=249`, we can write a code like the following:

```
HttpServletRequest request = ...
String name = request.getParameter("name");
int busNumber = Integer.parseInt(request.getParameter("bus"));
```

The Servlet framework does not allow setting of the parameters.

Headers

Every HTTP request usually has header information, which describes the client-side information relevant to the user: the invocation method, date and time, the acceptable content types, cache-control, the user agent, zero or more cookies, an optional authorization, and a whole lot more. The Servlet framework exposes through the `HttpServletRequest` interface with the methods: `getHeader()`, `getHeaders()`, and `getHeaderName()`.

Let's inspect a Servlet that demonstrates reading all the HTTP header information as follows:

```
@WebServlet(name = "reportHeader", urlPatterns =
  {"/reportHeaders"},
public class ReportHeaders extends HttpServlet {
  @Override
  protected void doGet(HttpServletRequest req,
    HttpServletResponse resp)
  throws ServletException, IOException {
    resp.setContentType("text/plain");
    PrintWriter pwriter = resp.getWriter();
    pwriter.printf("Header information:\n");
    for (String name: Collections.list
      (req.getHeaderNames())) {
      pwriter.printf("%s = %s\n", name,req.getHeader(name));
      }
    }
}
```

The `ReportHeader` servlet iterates through all of the headers with `getHeaders()`, which returns `Enumeration<String>`, and then we use the Java Collection framework to manipulate this type into `List<String>`. For each key in the collection, we dump the header to the Servlet's response writer.

The request attributes

The request attributes are objects that are associated with the HTTP request, hence they are scoped. The request attributes only live for the lifetime of processing a request through the Servlet framework. The attributes are removed after the response has been sent back to the client. If you remember from *Chapter 2*, *Context and Dependency Injection*, this request scope is the reason why there is a `@RequestScoped` annotation for the bean types.

The request attributes are available on `HttpServletRequest` with the methods `getAttribute()`, `getAttributeNames()`, and `setAttribute()`. The attributes are useful for passing the attributes from one Servlet instance. The Servlet framework provides a `RequestDispatcher` instance to forward a request on to another or include the content from another Servlet.

The following is an example of a Servlet that geolocates a city to a dealer. This use case is a car manufacturer's business:

```java
@WebServlet(name = "carProduct", urlPatterns = {"/carProduct"},
public class CarProduct extends HttpServlet {

  @Override
  protected void doGet(HttpServletRequest req,
    HttpServletResponse resp)
  throws ServletException, IOException {
    String city = req.getParameter("city")
    req.setAttribute("dealerId", findNearestDealerFromCity(city));
    RequestDispatcher rd = req.getDispatcher("/viewDealer")
    rd.forward(req,resp);
    }
}
```

The `CarProduct` Servlet sets a request scope attribute `dealerId` with the value obtained from the CGI query parameter `city`. There is a method `findNearestDealerFromCity()`, we assume, that handles the geolocation search for us. The `doGet()` method obtains a `RequestDispatcher` instance from `HttpServletRequest`, and forwards it to the next Servlet named `viewDealer`.

Let's review the code for the `ViewDealer` Servlet as follows:

```java
@WebServlet(name = "viewDealer", urlPatterns = {"/viewDealer"},
public class ViewDealer extends HttpServlet {

  @Override
  protected void doGet(HttpServletRequest req,
    HttpServletResponse resp)
  throws ServletException, IOException {
    String dealerId = (String)req.getAttribute("dealerId");
    /* ... */
    generateContent(req, resp, dealerId);
    }
}
```

The subsequent Servlet is able to retrieve the request scope attribute `dealerId`, and generate the content around this information.

The session attributes

The Servlet framework provides a means to track the requests that emanate from the same device that is operated by a user. Because of the stateless nature of HTTP, the framework associates similar request from the same client and user in either an HTTP cookie or through URL rewriting. For Servlet containers that support HTTPS protocol connections, the Servlet framework will use standard SSL handshake with encrypted key exchange.

A Servlet session has a lifecycle, which is unique to an HTTP client device, and it is a means for data to survive multiple requests to the Servlet container. A session is a scope and a collection name and value attributes. The Servlet sessions can optionally time out with expiration, and if the session does expire, then the servlet container will remove the information.

The session attributes are available in the `HttpSession` instance with the methods `getAttribute()`, `setAttribute()`, and `getAttributeNames()`. The `HttpSession` instance acquired from the `HttpServletRequest` object is like the following code:

```
HttpServletRequest request = ...
HttpSession session = request.getSession();
CustomerData custData = (CustomerData)
session.getAttribute("customerData");
session.setAttribute("checkoutInfo", "PRIVILEGED");
```

As with the request scope attribute, we have to cast to a `String` on the `getAttribute()` method, because this call returns an `Object`. The session scope is closely aligned with the CDI `@SessionScoped` annotation.

The Servlet context attributes

Every Java Servlet has an association to `ServletContext`, which is shared between all Servlets in the web application. The specification declares a rule: there is one context per web application per JVM. `ServletContext` is an ideal place to share a cache of read-only values that are used for the entire lifecycle of the application.

In the JSF, JSP, and CDI specifications, `ServletContext` is known as the application scope. The CDI `@ApplicationScoped` corresponds with this unique instance. The key methods for the `ServletContext` interfaces are `getAttribute()`, `setAttribute()`, and `getAttributeNames()`.

Here is a small illustration of the application-wide Servlet loading static data, which is supposed to be read-only. `ServletContextDemo` is as follows:

```java
@WebServlet(name = "servletContextDemo",
  urlPatterns = {"/servletContextDemo"},
public class ServletContextDemo extends HttpServlet {
  @Override
  public void init(ServletConfig config) {
    config.getServletContext()
    .setAttribute("dataValues",
      Arrays.asList(1,2,3,5,8,13,21,34,55,89));
  }

  @Override
  protected void doGet(HttpServletRequest req,
    HttpServletResponse resp)
  throws ServletException, IOException {
    resp.setContentType("text/plain");
    PrintWriter pwriter = resp.getWriter();
    List<Integer> series =
      (List<Integer>)getServletContext()
    .getAttribute("dataValues");
    pwriter.printf("series=%s\n", series);
  }
}
```

During initialization of `ServletContextDemo`, we store the Fibonacci series as an integer collection inside `ServletContext`, which we can access from the `ServletConfig` instance. When the user invokes HTTP GET on this Servlet, we retrieve the data series from `ServletContext`, and send its contents as the response. Inside the `doGet()` method, we access `ServletContext` from `HttpServletRequest`.

Redirecting the response

There are occasions in a web application where the response must be redirected to another location. The Servlet framework sends an HTTP URL redirection to the client (web browser) with a URL that informs where to get the content. We can write the Servlet code to do that as follows:

```java
HttpServletResponse httpServletResponse =
  httpServletResponse.sendRedirect
    (httpServletResponse.encodeRedirectURL
      (httpServletRequest.getContextPath()+
        "/carProduct"));
```

This code extraction redirects the client to the earlier `CarProduct` Servlet. Because URL redirects can go to any site on the Internet, for example, `http://www.bbc.co.uk/news`, we must add the web application context path to the URI. After issuing a redirect, the `HttpServletResponse` instance will be in an undefined state. It is a good practice to encode the URL path with the convenience call `encodeRedirectURL()`.

Many developers apply the technique of `POST-REDIRECT-GET`. This design pattern effectively avoids returning a rendered web page directly for an incoming request and instead instructs the web browser to load a different the page with a follow up HTTP GET request.. This is an advanced technique out-of-scope for discussion in this book.

The web deployment descriptor

The web deployment descriptor XML file is the traditional method for Java web developers to configure Servlets, filters, and listeners in a Java EE application. The file must be named `web.xml`, and the specification mandates that it will be found in the WAR file under the folder `WEB-INF/`.

The web deployment descriptor describes the Servlet classes, filters, and listeners, the environment and resources, and other configurations of a web application. Putting the information all together, inform the web container how to serve the content from the incoming web requests.

The simplest possible deployment descriptor for Servlet 3.1 and beyond looks just like the following code:

```xml
<?xml version = "1.0" encoding = "ISO-8859-1"?>
<web-app xmlns = "http://java.sun.com/xml/ns/javaee"
  xmlns:xsi = "http://www.w3.org/2001/XMLSchema-instance"
    xsi:schemaLocation = "http://java.sun.com/xml/ns/javaee
      http://java.sun.com/xml/ns/javaee/web-app_3_1.xsd"
        version = "3.1">
</web-app>
```

XML has a well-defined schema definition that can be found on Oracle's public website at `http://java.sun.com/xml/ns/javaee/web-app_3_1.xsd`. The root XML element must be `<web-app>`.

Mapping Java Servlets

An expanded deployment descriptor maps the annotated Servlets from earlier, `SimpleServlet` and `SimpleServletWithInitParams`, into the equivalent XML file as follows:

```xml
<?xml version = "1.0" encoding = "UTF-8"?>
<web-app xmlns = "http://java.sun.com/xml/ns/javaee"
   xmlns:xsi = "http://www.w3.org/2001/XMLSchema-instance"
      xsi:schemaLocation = "http://java.sun.com/xml/ns/javaee
         http://java.sun.com/xml/ns/javaee/web-app_3_1.xsd"
            version = "3.1">
<display-name>A Simple Application</display-name>
  <servlet>
    <servlet-name>simple</servlet-name>
      <servlet-class>
         je7hb.servlets.simple.SimpleServlet
      </servlet-class>
    <load-on-startup>1</load-on-startup>
  </servlet>

  <servlet-mapping>
    <servlet-name>simple</servlet-name>
      <url-pattern>/simple</url-pattern>
  </servlet-mapping>

  <servlet>
    <servlet-name>initparams</servlet-name>
      <servlet-class>
         je7hb.servlets.simple.SimpleServletWithInitParams
      </servlet-class>
      <init-param>
        <param-name>source</param-name>
        <param-value>Liverpool Central</param-value>
      </init-param>
      <init-param>
        <param-name>target</param-name>
        <param-value>London Euston</param-value>
      </init-param>
      <init-param>
        <param-name>time</param-name>
        <param-value>17:45:00</param-value>
      </init-param>
        <load-on-startup>2</load-on-startup>
  </servlet>
```

```
    <servlet-mapping>
      <servlet-name>initparams</servlet-name>
      <url-pattern>/initparams</url-pattern>
    </servlet-mapping>
</web-app>
```

The first thing to notice is the greater verbosity of the XML configuration compared to the annotations on the Servlet classes. On the other hand, auto-completion XML is an essential feature of all of the best IDEs nowadays. The root element of this XML document is `<web-app>`. According to the Servlet specification, the subelements can be arranged in an arbitrary order. Hence, for better readability, we arranged the grouping of the `<servlet>` element next to the corresponding mapping element `<servlet-mapping>`.

The `<servlet>` element defines a Java Servlet with the name and the fully qualified class name. The tag allows multiple instances of the Servlet class to be used, but mapped by different class names. The name for each Servlet is unique across the deployment descriptor. The `<servlet>` element can also optionally accept the initialization parameters.

The `<servlet-mapping>` elements configure how the web container maps a Servlet or associates it with an incoming web request. It takes Servlet and at least one URL pattern.

The `<load-on-startup>` element allows developers to configure the initialization order for Servlets. The configuration is an integer value starting from zero; the lower the number, the higher the priority. It comes in useful when your application has a Servlet that must be started before an other Servlet. A reasonable situation is initializing a database connection, reading data from static files, or setting up a cache of application-wide constant values.

Two servlets mapping can share a Servlet class. An example of a Servlet for a retail superstore business model that has two operational divisions, namely home and garden, and food store market, is as follows:

```
<servlet>
  <servlet-name>homegarden</servlet-name>
    <servlet-class>superstore.ProductListing</servlet-class>
    <init-param>
      <param-name>operations</param-name>
      <param-value>home_and_garden</param-value>
    </init-param>
</servlet>

<servlet>
```

```xml
    <servlet-name>foodstore</servlet-name>
      <servlet-class>superstore.ProductListing</servlet-class>
      <init-param>
        <param-name>operations</param-name>
        <param-value>food_store</param-value>
      </init-param>
</servlet>

<servlet-mapping>
   <servlet-name>homegarden</servlet-name>
     <url-pattern>/garden/*</url-pattern>
</servlet-mapping>

<servlet-mapping>
   <servlet-name>foodstore</servlet-name>
     <url-pattern>/food/*</url-pattern>
</servlet-mapping>
```

The `ProductListing` Servlet is shared between two URL patterns, because the Servlet class is given two different names `homegarden` and `foodstore`. The Servlet names are then mapped to separate URL patterns.

A URL pattern can begin with the wildcard character (*), in which case it is really an extension, or it is placed at the end of the string after a forward slash character (/).

Suppose there is a fictional website named `www.hype7.co.uk` and assume there is an appropriate URL rewriting going on behind the scene, then the food items are accessible through an example, such as `http://www.hype7.co.uk/food/fish/seabass/recipe/101`. The same processing takes for the gardening section of the e-commerce store: `http://www.hype7.co.uk/garden/sheds/wooden/list`.

Execution of the code inside Servlet can distinguish between the operations by inspecting the Servlet initialization parameters. You have already seen how to do this.

Configuring a session timeout

Web container provides a `javax.servlet.http.HttpSession` object instance for each unique web client that connects to the web application. `HttpSession` is designed for saving and retrieving the content that survives from the Servlet request. The session can be approximated to the user's session, it does not maintain the conversational state, however.

The configurator can control how long `HttpSession` will stay alive for a web client through `web.xml`.

The developer can configure how long HttpSession will stay alive for an idle web client through `web.xml`. Inside the deployment descriptor, the `<session-config>` element is a child `<web-app>` element, we can set the value of the idle time of 10 minutes as follows:

```
<session-config>
   <session-timeout>30</session-timeout>
</session-config>
```

`<session-config>` is a subelement of the `web-app` root element. The `<session-timeout>` element specifies the time in minutes.

Configuring MIME types

In order to support **Multipurpose Internet Mail Extensions** (**MIME**) types in the web application, developers can specify the types and their association file suffixes. Web container uses a mapping of suffixes to MIME type when it is asked to serve the static content. The mapping is defined by the `<mime-mapping>` element, which has two subelements, namely `<extension>` and `<mime-type>`, in order respectively.

An example of these MIME settings is as follows:

```
<mime-mapping>
   <extension>csv</extension>
      <mime-type>application/csv</mime-type>
</mime-mapping>
<mime-mapping>
   <extension>pdf</extension>
      <mime-type>application/pdf</mime-type>
</mime-mapping>
```

The `<mime-mapping>` element is a direct child of the `<web-app>` root document element.

Given a fictional two URLs that represent a static resource URL, if the preceding MIME mapping is applied in the web application, then `http://localhost:8080/mywebapp/datasheet/whitepaper.csv` and `http://localhost:8080/mywebapp/datasheet/whitepaper.pdf` serve as the comma-separated value and the PDF files respectively.

Dynamic resources such as a Servlet, JSP, or JSF must set their respective content type by calling the `ServletResponse.setContentType()` method with the standard MIME type string accordingly.

Configuring the welcome page

A web application can configure its own welcome page, which serves as the default, when the URL is just referenced by the directory. By default, the welcome page is `index.jsp` and then `index.html`. The welcome pages are useful when the web request is referencing just the path and not a resource. They specify the files that the containers are searching in the path directory in order to serve the client. The element `<welcome-file-list>` is a child of `<web-app>`, and configures these settings.

An example of the configuration in the web deployment descriptor is as follows:

```
<welcome-file-list>
  <welcome-file>index.xhtml</welcome-file>
  <welcome-file>index.jsp</welcome-file>
  <welcome-file>index.html</welcome-file>
</welcome-file-list>
```

Web container will search for `index.jsp`; if it is there on the path, the container serves it. Otherwise, the container looks for the next file on the list, and it then attempts to find the static resource `index.html` in order to serve that.

Configuring the error-handler pages

The container can only configure to serve error pages if a Java Servlet generates an error code in order to signify an abnormal request. The web deployment descriptor allows developers to direct HTTP errors to a specific page, which is useful for providing an application error page.

The `<error-page>` element configures error handling for a specific HTTP error code, such as 404, the resource does not exist, or 500, the resource is forbidden from access. This element is a child of the `<web-app>` element and it has two children. The `<error-code>` tag specifies the HTTP error code and the `<location>` tag specifies a resource to serve as the error-handling page, which can be a dynamic resource.

An example of the error-handling XML is as follows:

```
<error-page>
  <error-code>404</error-code>
  <location>/errors/404.html</location>
</error-page>
```

In the previous example, the XML maps the HTTP Error 404 to the specific error page as a static HTML file.

In order to send an error in a Servlet, you can invoke the method `sendError()` on the `HttpServletResponse` object as the following code demonstrates:

```
resp.sendError(HttpServletResponse.SC_NOT_FOUND);
```

`SC_NOT_FOUND` is a static constant, which is final and a primitive integer with the value of 404.

Annotations and the web deployment descriptor

Annotations and the web deployment descriptor can be freely mixed. Developer has control of whether the configuration in `WEB-INF/web.xml` overrides the annotations. Web container will ignore Servlet 3.0 and better annotations on any defined classes, if the `<web-app/>` element is supplied with an attribute `metadata-complete`, and is set to `true`.

A web container with a deployment descriptor is as follows:

```
<?xml version = "1.0" encoding = "ISO-8859-1"?>
<web-app xmlns = "http://java.sun.com/xml/ns/javaee"
  xmlns:xsi = "http://www.w3.org/2001/XMLSchema-instance"
    xsi:schemaLocation = "http://java.sun.com/xml/ns/javaee
       http://java.sun.com/xml/ns/javaee/web-app_3_0.xsd"
         version = "3.0" metadata-complete = "true">
<!-- . . . -->
</web-app>
```

Applying `metadata-complete = "true"` causes the Servlet container to ignore the annotations on any Java Servlets, filters, and listeners. Setting `metadata-complete` to `true`, effectively says that the web deployment descriptor is the configuration, and replicates the behavior of the Servlet web container before Version 3.0.

The order of priority for a web container is to load and process the annotations, if they are present. Web container will search for the annotations in two locations: compiled classes under the folder `/WEB-INF/classes` and also the libraries in JARs under `/WEB-INF/lib`. It will apply the configuration to create internal metadata. Only afterwards will web container examine `/WEB-INF/web.xml` for the metadata configuration. The reason for this behavior is that there may not be any web deployment descriptor available, as you have already seen in the first Servlet example.

The Servlet filters

The Servlet filters are components that can intercept an incoming request and outgoing response before it gets to a Java Servlet. The filters can be chained together through the configuration of the web deployment descriptor or through the annotations. Filters do not normally generate the content, rather they are designed to transform, modify, or adapt a request around a resource. The filters can be used for logging, security, and performance monitoring.

A Servlet filter implements the `javax.servlet.Filter` interface. A Servlet filter implements the `doFilter()` method, which takes three arguments: `ServletRequest`, `ServletResponse`, and `javax.servlet.FilterChain`.

`FilterChain` is a simple interface with one method `doFilter()`, which is the way to transfer the control to the next filter in the chain.

Let's review, together, a working example as follows:

```java
package je7hb.servlets.simple;
import javax.servlet.*;
import javax.servlet.annotation.WebFilter;
import javax.servlet.annotation.WebInitParam;
import javax.servlet.http.*;
import java.io.IOException;
import java.util.Date;

@WebFilter(filterName = "MySimpleFilterLogger", urlPatterns =
  {"/*"}, initParams = {@WebInitParam(name = "fruit",
    value = "Pear"),})
public class SimpleLoggingFilter implements Filter {
  private FilterConfig filterConfig;

  public void init(FilterConfig filterConfig) {
    System.out.printf("init() on %s\n"+
      "Metadata filter name=%s\n", getClass().getSimpleName(),
        filterConfig.getFilterName());
    this.filterConfig = filterConfig;
  }

  public void doFilter(ServletRequest request,
    ServletResponse response, FilterChain filterChain)
    throws IOException, ServletException {
    System.out.printf("doFilter() on %s at %s\n",
      this.getClass().getSimpleName(), new Date());
```

```
      System.out.printf("init parameter on 'fruit' is %s\n",
        filterConfig.getInitParameter("fruit"));
      filterChain.doFilter(request, response);
    }

    public void destroy() {
      System.out.printf("destroy() on %s\n",
        getClass().getSimpleName());
    }
  }
```

This filter `SimpleLoggingFilter` is annotated by the name `MySimpleFilterLogger` with the URL patterns (/*) such that it intercepts all the requests. The class dumps the output to the console output. A filter has initialization and destruction methods, which web container invokes as the web application starts up or shuts down accordingly.

Inside the `doFilter()` method, executing the `filterChain.doFilter()` method is the critical part, because that call passes the control back to web container, and then it causes the execution of the next filter in line or the actual resource.

The Servlet filter annotation attributes

A table of the `@WebFilter` attributes is as follows:

Attribute	Type	Description	Default Value
filterName	String	Defines the name of the filter.	Empty
Value	String []	Defines the URL patterns of the filter.	None
urlPatterns	String []	Defines the URL patterns of the filter.	None
initParams	WebInitParam []	The initial parameters of the filter.	None
servletNames	String []	Specifies names of Servlets to which the web container applies the filter.	None
dispatcherTypes	DispatcherTypes []	Specifies the dispatcher types that the filter applies. A filter can intercept requests to {FORWARD, INCLUDE, REQUEST, ASYNC, ERROR} dispatchers.	REQUEST

Attribute	Type	Description	Default Value
`displayName`	String	The display name of the filter.	None
`description`	String	The description for a filter.	Empty string
`smallIcon`	String	Specifies a path to a small icon.	None
`largeIcon`	String	Specifies a path to a large icon.	None

The Servlet filter XML configuration

If you prefer not to declare the annotations, then the filter must be declared in a deployment descriptor, the `web.xml` file. An XML fragment that configures the filter is as follows:

```xml
<filter>
  <filter-name>MySimpleFilterLogger</filter-name>
    <filter-class>
       je7hb.servlets.simple.SimpleLoggingFilter
    </filter-class>
    <init-param>
      <param-name>fruit</param-name>
      <param-value>strawberry</param-value>
    </init-param>
</filter>

<filter-mapping>
   <filter-name>MySimpleFilterLogger</filter-name>
   <url-pattern>/*</url-pattern>
</filter-mapping>
```

`<filter>` and `<filter-mapping>` are direct subelements of the `<web-app>` element, and they are visually similar to the Servlet mappings.

The `<filter>` element declares the filter name, fully qualified class name, and optionally the initialization parameters. The `<filter-mapping>` element associates a filter name with a set of the URL patterns.

To implement a security servlet filter, the logic of the `doFilter()` method would change to only execute the next filter on completion of a check.

The following code is an example of securing a resource with a Servlet filter:

```
public void doFilter(ServletRequest req, ServletResponse res,
  FilterChain filterChain)
throws IOException, ServletException {
  HttpServletRequest req2 = (HttpServletRequest)req;
  HttpServletResponse res2 = (HttpServletResponse)res;
  if (req2.getUserPrincipal().getName() .equals("admin")) {
    filterChain.doFilter(req, res);
    }
  else {
    res2.sendError(HttpServletResponse.SC_UNAUTHORIZED);
    }
}
```

The previous filter code allows the requests to propagate to the next filter or resource, only if the incoming request has the JavaEE user principal authorization. If the request is unauthorized, the filter sends the client to the error page, if defined. Notice how we recast the Servlet and response objects to `HttpServletRequest` and `HttpServletResponse`.

Obviously the Java EE web container will need to have security principals and realms defined externally to the web application in order for this filter to work.

The Servlet context listener

The Servlet context listener are classes that allow a web application to listen to the lifecycle events. In the world of Java Servlets, there are four types of contexts, namely page, request, session, and application. Each of these contexts represents lifetimes of the objects, when they got associated with those contexts. The page context is found in JSP, while the remaining ones are available to Java Servlets.

The following table lists the context and the scope with the available events associated with the appropriate listener:

Context	Event Description	Java Interface
Application	The Servlet context starts when the first request is pushed to the web application	`javax.servlet` `ServletContextListener`
	The Servlet context stops just before the web application shuts down	
	The Servlet context attribute is added	`javax.servlet` `ServletContextAttributeListener`
	The Servlet context attribute is removed	
	The Servlet context attribute is replaced	
Session	Session creation	`javax.servlet.http` `HttpSessionListener`
	Session invalidation	
	Session destruction	
	The Session attribute added	`javax.servlet.http` `HttpSessionAttributeListener`
	The Session attribute removed	
	The Session attribute replaced	
	Session is activated or passivized	`javax.servle.http` `HttpSessionActivationListener`
	An object has been bound to or unbound from the session	`javax.servlet.http` `HttpSessionBindingListener`
Request	The Servlet request creation	`javax.servlet` `ServletRequestListener`
	The Servlet request destruction	
	The Servlet attribute added	`javax.servlet` `ServletRequestAttributeListener`
	The Servlet attribute removed	
	The Servlet attribute replaced	
Asynchronous Events	A timeout occurred, termination or completion of an asynchronous event	`javax.servlet` `AsyncListener`

The listener interfaces are found in `javax.servlet` and `javax.servlet.http` respectively. Concrete implementation of these listener interfaces can be annotated with `@javax.servlet.annotation.WebListener`, and then web container picks up the metadata.

An example of the Servlet session context listener for a web application is as follows:

```java
@WebListener
public class AppServletContextListener implements
  ServletContextListener {
  @Override
  public void contextInitialized(ServletContextEvent sce) {
    System.out.printf("contextInitialized() on %s\n"+
      "source = %s\n", getClass().getSimpleName(),
        sce.getSource());
  }

  @Override
  public void contextDestroyed(ServletContextEvent sce) {
    System.out.printf("contextDestroyed() on %s \n"+
      "source = %s\n", getClass().getSimpleName(),
        sce.getSource());
  }
}
```

If you choose not to annotate the listener classes, then the web container requires you to write the metadata information in `WEB-INF/web.xml`.

```xml
<web-app>
  <display-name>ExampleApplication</display-name>
  <listener>
    <listener-class>
      je7hb.servlets.simple.AppServletContextListener
    </listenerclass>
  </listener>
<!-- ... -->
</web-app>
```

The XML element `<listener>` specifies a context listener and it takes a child element `<listener-class>`, which specifies the fully qualified class name.

The Servlet specification says that the order of the listener declarations in which they appear in the web deployment descriptor file determines initialization order during start up of the application. In other words, the first context listener in the registration means the first to the initialized. Web container will sort the listeners into types first, for example it will collect all the Servlet context listeners, and then instantiate them. Web container will invoke the listeners in the order of their registration.

On the shutdown of the web application, the Servlet context, the listeners are invoked, and the shutdown occurs in reverse order of their registration.

There is a problem, therefore, with only annotated event listeners, in that there is no current specification way to order them through the `@WebListener` annotation. The only way to order the registration of the event listener is through the deployment descriptor.

Pluggable Servlet fragments

Web container allows the web applications to contain both the annotations and metadata in the XML files named **web fragments**. If there is no web deployment descriptor file `web.xml` or the `meta-complete` attribute is set to `false`, then web container is obliged to search the plain old JAR files placed in the `WEB-INF/lib` directory for the pluggable Servlet annotations. The container is also obliged to search the JAR special named files named web fragments in the folder `META-INF/`, which match `web-fragment.xml`. The contents of `web.xml` and `web-fragment.xml` are almost the same.

Web fragments are descriptors that introduce pluggability into the Servlet specification. It can be seen as a weak form of modularity without enforcement of the class boundaries. Fragments allow different JAR files from other projects, which maybe separate, to be brought together, and assemble into a WAR file, and hence a web application.

Let's suppose we have a fictional example of an integrated library implemented as web fragment. We have an ACME electronic commerce, and the web development team in the organization packaged a library as a two event listener, namely an HTTP session listener and a Servlet context listener. They have also given us a Servlet filter to handle user security.

A possible `web-fragment.xml` file for this situation is as follows:

```xml
<web-fragment>
  <listener>
    <listener-class>
      acme.LoginUserServletContextListener
    </listener-class>
  </listener>
  <listener>
    <listener-class>
      acme.LoginUserSessionContextListener
    </listener-class>
  </listener>
```

```xml
<filter>
  <filter-name>userSecurityFilter</filter-name>
  <filter-class>acme.UserSecurityFilter</filter-class>
</filter>

<filter-mapping>
  <filter-name>userSecurityFilter</filter-name>
  <url-pattern>/*</url-pattern>
</filter-mapping>
<web-fragment>
```

This file could be part of an `acme-user-security.jar` file and placed in the `WEB-INF/lib` directory.

Ordering multiple web fragments

You may be wondering what can happen if I have more than one web fragment inside an application. How do we go about establishing an order of registration?

There are two ways to achieve the ordering in the modular web fragments. In the deployment descriptor file `web.xml`, we can use a special XML element named `<absolute-ordering>`. In any web fragment file `web-fragment.xml`, we can use another XML element named `<ordering>`.

Let's see an example:

```xml
<web-app>
  ...
  <absolute-ordering>
    <name>Fragment1</name>
    <others/>
    <name>Fragment2</name>
  <absolute-ordering>
</web-app>
```

The XML element `<absolute-ordering>` lists other web fragments by the name from the subelement `<name>` and the order is the first listed, the first initialized. Note the special `<others>` XML element in there, which is a placeholder for all other web fragments that may or may not exist in the web application. The reading of this ordering, then, is `Fragment1`, any other web fragments, and then `Fragment2`.

Web fragments can also contain ordering themselves. An example of this ordering named `Fragment3` is as follows:

```
<web-fragment>
  <name>Fragment3</name>
  ...
  <ordering>
    <before>
      <others/>
    </before>
    <after>
      <name>SalesFragement</name>
      <name>Fragment2</name>
    </after>
  </ordering>
</web-fragment>
```

First of all, a web fragment can have given a name. The child of the root element named `<name>` specifies the name of the preceding web fragment.

In a web fragment, the XML element `<ordering>` defines the order. A web fragment can specify the registration to appear before or after other fragments, as you saw in the previous example. There, `Fragment3` is initialized before other fragments, and also after particular fragments `SalesFragment` and `Fragment2` have been successfully initialized. So we see that these orderings are metadata and declarative instructions for the Servlet 3.0 or better container to observe in a web application.

It is instructive to inspect the reverse of this ordering as follows:

```
<web-fragment>
  <name>Fragment4</name>
  ...
  <ordering>
    <before>
      <name>SalesFragement</name>
      <name>Fragment3</name>
    </before>
    <after>
      <others/>
    </after>
  </ordering>
</web-fragment>
```

In the previous example, `Fragment4` is initialized after all other web fragments, but before `SalesFragment` and the previous `Fragment3`.

Ordering cannot be achieved currently with the annotations at least with the Java Servlet 3.1 specification, so they must be applied with the XML configuration files. However, as we have seen before, these XML deployment descriptors, and the fragment files can be more or less empty save the ordering, and still the annotations on the Java classes will work.

Of course, the Servlet web container will disable scanning for and processing the annotations when the attribute `metadata-complete` is set to `true` in either `<web-fragment>` or a `<webapp>` root XML element.

Asynchronous Java Servlets

The advancement of the web technology since 2005 has been about attaining asynchronous communications. The first breakthrough with these techniques came through the AJAX frameworks, which exploited a little used client-side API in the Internet Explorer web browser and then the subsequent web browsers to send a request asynchronously to a server, and then wait for a response in a non-blocking fashion. The key AJAX was the evolution of JavaScript as an accepted programming language in the browser and non-blocking input and output.

The technology then moved to COMET, which is a neo-logistic term (coined by *Alex Russell*) for a collection of techniques for streaming data from the server to the multiple clients without these clients then requesting data. Finally, we have HTML 5 WebSockets as an up and coming standard.

Java API for WebSockets is covered in *Chapter 7, Java API for HTML5WebSocket*, of this book. Both the AJAX and COMET terms are a play on words; both are common household cleaning agents in USA and perhaps in Europe. As a side note in history, it was possible to have asynchronous communications since the very first Java Applets, as they could create and open TCP/IP sockets for long periods of time, provided the web page remained opened in the browser.

This section reviews the asynchronous requests and responses with Java Servlets.

The asynchronous input and output

In the earliest days of the Java SDK, all the inputs and outputs were synchronous; by this term, we mean the inputs and outputs were blocking. A Java thread would block on data push to the output or a data read, if the resource was not available. So the Java SDK engineers fixed this issue with a new API named **New Input and Output** (**NIO**), in the Java SDK 1.4. The non-blocking input and output operations are the basis of building the scalable server-side applications.

NIO is a non-blocking API based on Channels, Buffers, and Selectors. Since Java SE 7, in 2012, Java NIO has been upgraded to NIO2, which supports the portable file system operations such as symbolic links, polling directory and the file notifications, and the file attribute information.

Non-blocking I/O is only available for Java Servlets and filters, and only for asynchronous requests. In order to process a web request in an asynchronous fashion, another thread will be activated to process the request, and generate the response. The idea is not to block the dispatching threads that the container actually uses itself.

A synchronous reader example

It is instructive to review the code for blocking I/O in order to obtain an appreciation of the asynchronous operations. Suppose our task was to write a Servlet that would process large volumes of data. We are instructed to write a Servlet component that analyses volumes of text and the web client will push data as an HTTP POST request. This data could arrive from an AJAX style HTTP POST form request, which is a typical modern web application that performs user-friendly file upload, and provide a visual update to the user.

A first cut at this code in a class named `DataBlockingIOServlet` is as follows:

```
@WebServlet(urlPatterns = {"/reader/*"}
public class DataBlockingIOServlet extends HttpServlet {
  protected void doPost(HttpServletRequest request,
    HttpServletResponse response)
  throws IOException, ServletException {
    ServletInputStream input = request.getInputStream();
    byte[] buffer = new byte[2048];
    int len = -1;
    while (( len = input.read(buffer)) ! = -1) {
      String data = new String(buffer, 0, len);
      System.out.printf("data=[%s]\n", data);
    }
  }
}
```

The essential method `doPost()` obtains `ServletInputStream` from the Servlet request instance. We use traditional Java I/O methods from `package java.io` to read data from the stream into a buffer of 2048 bytes in size. We simply dump the input data into the standard console.

This code is fine from the standpoint of a single web client using the server. Our problems will arise from scalability when lots of web clients start to access `DataBlockingIOServlet`. When the file sizes exceed our 2048 buffer, or when they exceed the internal buffers of web container, or when they exceed the size of the network operating system, we will find the JVM blocks on `ServletInputStream`. If the web client starts sending data to Servlet, and then for some strange reason pauses for a long time, then Servlet and the associated container thread will be blocked. The point is, any sort of blocking on a web container thread (or the application server thread) is bad. It is bad for other resources also, including other web applications that also share the facilities of the container. For these reasons alone, blocking the inputs and outputs puts severe restrictions on the ability of a container to scale and meet the demands of multiple consumers.

The blocking of input and output will also occur on `ServletOutputStream`, although we have not shown it in the code example. For instance, if we wrote a similar Servlet to the stream investment data to a consuming web client.

An asynchronous reader example

Clearly the solution is to use the non-blocking input and output. Servlet 3.1 provides a way out and allows the web container to transfer responsibility to Servlet developer to just read and write data to and from consumer, but still enforce the control of the Servlet container threads.

The Servlet 3.1 specification adds event listeners `javax.servlet.ReadListener` and `javax.servlet.WriteListener`.

The interface declaration for `ReadListener` is as follows:

```
public interface ReadListener extends java.util.EventListener {
  public void onDataAvailable();
  public void onAllDataRead();
  public void onError(Throwable t);
}
```

`ReadListener` is an event listener, which is invoked by web container on notification of an available asynchronous input. The methods on this class are invoked when the HTTP request data is guaranteed to be readable without non-blocking.

Java Servlets and Asynchronous Request-Response

After an asynchronous context has been obtained and started, then a `ReadListener` implementation is registered with a call to `ServletInputStream.setReadListener()`.

Method	Descriptor
onDataAvailable	Provided an instance of `ReadListener` is registered with `ServletInputStream`, this method is only invoked by the container the first time, when it is possible to read data. Subsequently, the container will invoke this method, if and only if the `ServletInputStream.isReady()` method has been called and has returned `false`. This method is one to retrieve data from the stream and then for the implementation to process it.
onAllDataRead	The container invokes this method when all of the data has been read from the input. In reality, this means the web client has closed the connection after sending all of the data.
onError	The container invokes this method when something has gone wrong and there is a plausible error. Here, the implementation can take action on the error. The exception is passed to the method.

There are two other methods in `ServletInputStream`, which can be of use. These were added in Servlet 3.1. The `isReady()` method returns a `boolean`, and it specifies when data can be read from the stream without blocking. The `isFinished()` method also returns a `boolean`, and it specifies when all data for this particular request has been read.

With this information, we can write an asynchronous Servlet. The implementation code is as follows:

```
package je7hb.servlets.simple;
import javax.servlet.*;
import javax.servlet.annotation.WebServlet;
import javax.servlet.http.*;
import java.io.IOException;

@WebServlet(name = "AsyncReaderServlet",
  urlPatterns = {"/reader"}, asyncSupported = true)
public class AsyncReaderServlet extends HttpServlet {
  @Override
  public void init(ServletConfig config)
  throws ServletException {
```

Chapter 6

```java
    super.init(config);
    System.out.printf("init() called on %s\n",
      getClass().getSimpleName());
  }

  public void doGet(HttpServletRequest request,
    HttpServletResponse response)
  throws IOException, ServletException {
    System.out.printf("doGet() called on %s\n",
      getClass().getSimpleName());
    processRequest(request);
  }

  public void doPost(HttpServletRequest request,
    HttpServletResponse response)
  throws IOException, ServletException {
    System.out.printf("doPost() called on %s\n",
      getClass().getSimpleName());
    processRequest(request);
  }

  private void processRequest(HttpServletRequest request)
  throws IOException {
    System.out.printf("processRequest() called %s" +
      " on thread [%s]\n", getClass().getSimpleName(),
        Thread.currentThread().getName());
    AsyncContext context = request.startAsync();
    ServletInputStream input = request.getInputStream();
    input.setReadListener(new AsyncReadListener(input, context));
  }

  private class AsyncReadListener implements ReadListener {
    private ServletInputStream input;
    private AsyncContext context;

    private AsyncReadListener(ServletInputStream input,
      AsyncContext context) {
    this.input = input;
    this.context = context;
    }

    @Override
    public void onDataAvailable() {
      try {
```

```java
        StringBuilder sb = new StringBuilder();
        int len = -1;
        byte buffer[] = new byte[2048];
        while (input.isReady() && (len = input.read(buffer))
          != -1) {
          String data = new String(buffer, 0, len);
          System.out.printf("thread [%s] data: %s\n",
            Thread.currentThread().getName(), data);
        }
      } catch (IOException ex) {
        ex.printStackTrace(System.err);
      }
    }

    @Override
    public void onAllDataRead() {
      System.out.printf("thread [%s] onAllDataRead()\n",
        Thread.currentThread().getName());
      context.complete();
    }

    @Override
    public void onError(Throwable t) {
      System.out.printf("thread [%s] Error occurred=%s\n",
        Thread.currentThread().getName(), t.getMessage());
      context.complete();
    }
  }
}
```

In order to be recognized by web container as an asynchronous Servlet, it must be annotated with `@WebServlet` and the `asyncSupport` attribute set to `true`.

Although this example Servlet `AsyncReaderServlet` is long, there is really nothing to it. The most important method is the refactored method `processRequest()`, which starts the asynchronous communication. The `processRequest()` method is shared between the `doGet()` and `doPost()` methods. Inside the method, Servlet retrieves the `javax.servlet.AsyncContext` instance from the `HttpServletRequest` instance and starts the process. The `AsyncContext` class represents the execution context for an asynchronous operation. The method, then, retrieves `ServletInputStream`, and then creates an inner class, an event listener, `AsyncReadListener`, and registers it with the stream.

`AsyncReadListener` is the event listener that reads data asynchronously from the web client. Inside the method `onDataAvailable()`, the event listener only dumps data to the standard output. In a business application, you will store data or act on it. The inner class also prints out the current thread by the name for analysis.

If there is an error in processing, then the container will invoke the `onError()` method. It is important to close the asynchronous context, and this is exactly what this method does.

Similarly, once all the data has been read, the container will invoke the `onAllDataRead()` method, and the asynchronous context is also closed with a call to `complete()`. In both of these callbacks, the application can take action.

In order to test this asynchronous Servlet, we need a test client. Since we can execute a container-less embedded GlassFish server application, we can write a modified and refactored example.

The code for this new test client is as follows:

```
package je7hb.common.webcontainer.embedded.glassfish;

import java.io.BufferedWriter;
import java.io.OutputStreamWriter;
import java.net.HttpURLConnection;
import java.net.URL;
import java.util.Scanner;
import java.util.StringTokenizer;

public class EmbeddedAsyncReaderRunner extends
  AbstractEmbeddedRunner {
  private static final String LOREM_IPSUM =
    "Lorem ipsum dolor sit amet, consectetur adipisicing " +
      "elit, sed do eiusmod tempor incididunt ut labore et " +
        "dolore magna aliqua. Ut enim ad minim veniam, quis " +
          /* ... */ est laborum.";

  public EmbeddedAsyncReaderRunner(int port) {
    super(port);
  }

  public static void main(String args[]) throws Exception {
    EmbeddedAsyncReaderRunner runner = (EmbeddedAsyncReaderRunner)
    new EmbeddedAsyncReaderRunner(8080).init().start();
    runner.deployWithRename
      ("build/libs/ch06-servlets-basic-1.0.war", "mywebapp");
```

```java
      Thread.sleep(1000);
      String path = String.format
        ("http://localhost:%d/%s/%s", 8080, "mywebapp", "reader");

      URL url = new URL(path);
      System.out.printf
        ("Client connecting to server on path %s\n", path);
      HttpURLConnection conn =
        (HttpURLConnection) url.openConnection();
      conn.setChunkedStreamingMode(2);
      conn.setDoOutput(true);
      conn.connect();
      try (BufferedWriter output = new BufferedWriter
        (new OutputStreamWriter(conn.getOutputStream()))) {
        System.out.println("Sending data ...");
        output.write("Beginning Text");
        output.flush();
        System.out.println("Sleeping ...");
        Thread.sleep(3000);
        System.out.println("Sending more data ...");
        StringTokenizer stk =
          new StringTokenizer(LOREM_IPSUM," \t,.");
        while ( stk.hasMoreTokens()) {
          output.write( stk.nextToken());
          output.flush();
          Thread.sleep(200);
          }
        System.out.println("Finishing client");
        output.write("Ending Text");
        output.flush();
        output.close();
        }
      System.out.println("Check standard console ");
      Thread.sleep(1000);
      System.out.println("Disconnecting and shutdown");
      conn.disconnect();
      runner.stop();

       System.exit(0);
      }
  }
```

Chapter 6

The `EmbeddedAsyncReaderRunner` class is a main application and starts an embedded GlassFish server instance; it deploys the WAR file as a web application as we saw earlier in the chapter.

Instead of waiting for a console input to terminate the application, the program creates a URL connection to the asynchronous Java Servlet, and then invokes an HTTP POST request to it. The text of the Lorem Ipsum is fed one word at a time to Java Servlet using the HTTP URL connection. The words are pushed at the rate of one every 200 milliseconds. Notice how the client flushes the buffer to ensure the data is sent over the network.

After all of the words of the text are fed in, the connection is disconnected, and the embedded runner is halted. We have to call `System.exit` in order to halt the Java threads in the container-less application.

The output of the application-and it is instructive to review the thread names-is as follows:

```
INFO: Loading application [mywebapp] at [/mywebapp]
Feb 11, 2013 11:24:40 AM org.glassfish.deployment.admin.DeployCommand execute
INFO: mywebapp was successfully deployed in 2,452 milliseconds.
Client connecting to server on path http://localhost:8080/mywebapp/reader
Sending data ...
Sleeping ...
init() called on AsyncReaderServlet
doPost() called on AsyncReaderServlet
processRequest() called AsyncReaderServlet on thread
   [http-listener(2)]
thread [http-listener(2)] data: Beginning Text
Sending more data ...
thread [http-listener(4)] data: Lorem
thread [http-listener(3)] data: ipsum
thread [http-listener(1)] data: dolor
thread [http-listener(5)] data: sit
thread [http-listener(2)] data: amet
thread [http-listener(4)] data: consectetur

thread [http-listener(5)] data: laborum
Finishing client
Check standard console
```

```
thread [http-listener(2)] data: Ending Text
thread [glassfish-web-async-thread-1] onAllDataRead()
Disconnecting and shutdown
Feb 11, 2013 11:24:59 AM
  org.glassfish.admin.mbeanserver.JMXStartupService shutdown
FileMonitoring shutdown
INFO: JMXStartupService and JMXConnectors have been shut down.
contextDestroyed() on AppServletContextListener
```

The threads' names `http-listener(1)` to `http-listener(5)` demonstrate that the GlassFish server allocates a thread pool to serve each HTTP push from the test client. Clearly, flushing the output buffer in the test buffer causes data to be sent across the network and then the asynchronous servlet, and its `AysncReadListener` retrieves the data from the web client. This is seen by the output of one word of the Lorem Ipsum text to the console at a time. Once the stream has finished, the test application closes the HTTP URL connection, which causes the Servlet container to invoke the `onAllDataRead()` method; notice how the thread is named `glassfish-web-async-thread-1`.

The actual Java thread will be different with another application server or web container. It is therefore recommended not to rely on specific server semantics.

An asynchronous writer

The Servlet 3.1 specification adds the event listeners for the production of asynchronous output `javax.servlet.WriteListener`.

The interface declaration for `WriteListener` is as follows:

```
package javax.servlet;
public interface WriteListener extends java.util.EventListener {
  public void onWritePossible();
  public void onError(final Throwable t);
}
```

After an asynchronous context has been obtained and started, then a `WriteListener` implementation is registered with a call to the instance method `ServletOutputStream.setWriteListener()`.

Method	Descriptor
`onWritePossible`	Provided an instance of `WriteListener` is registered with `ServletOutputStream`, this method will be invoked by the container the first time, when it is possible to write data. Subsequently, the container will invoke this method if and only if the `ServletOutputStream.isReady()` method has been called and has returned `false`. This method is one to write data that pushes data down the stream to the client.
`onError`	The container invokes this method when something has gone wrong and there is a plausible error. Here, the implementation can take action on the error. The exception is passed to the method.

To illustrate the asynchronous output, we can write a Servlet that streams the Lorem Ipsum text to a web client. The code for the Servlet `AsyncWriterServlet` is as follows:

```
package je7hb.servlets.simple;
import javax.servlet.*;
import javax.servlet.annotation.WebServlet;
import javax.servlet.http.*;
import java.io.IOException;
import java.io.PrintStream;
import java.util.StringTokenizer;

@WebServlet(name = "AsyncWriterServlet",
  urlPatterns = {"/writer"}, asyncSupported = true)
public class AsyncWriterServlet extends HttpServlet {

  private static final String LOREM_IPSUM =
    "Lorem ipsum dolor sit amet, consectetur adipisicing " +
      "elit, sed do eiusmod tempor incididunt ut labore et " +
        "dolore magna aliqua. Ut enim ad minim veniam, quis " +
          "nostrud exercitation ullamco laboris nisi ut " +
            "aliquip ex ea commodo consequat. Duis aute irure " +
              "dolor in reprehenderit in voluptate velit esse " +
                "cillum dolore eu fugiat nulla pariatur. " +
                  Excepteur " + "sint occaecat cupidatat non
                    proident, sunt in " + "culpa qui officia
                      deserunt mollit anim id " + "est laborum.";
```

```java
@Override
public void init(ServletConfig config) throws ServletException {
  super.init(config);
  System.out.printf("init() called on %s\n",
    getClass().getSimpleName());
}

public void doGet(HttpServletRequest request,
  HttpServletResponse response)
throws IOException, ServletException {
  System.out.printf("doGet() called on %s\n",
    getClass().getSimpleName());
  processResponse(request, response);
}

public void doPost(HttpServletRequest request,
  HttpServletResponse response)
throws IOException, ServletException {
  System.out.printf("doPost() called on %s\n",
    getClass().getSimpleName());
  processResponse(request, response);
}

private void processResponse(HttpServletRequest request,
  HttpServletResponse response)
throws IOException {
  System.out.printf("processRequest() called %s" +
    " on thread [%s]\n", getClass().getSimpleName(),
      Thread.currentThread().getName());
  AsyncContext context = request.startAsync();
  ServletOutputStream output = response.getOutputStream();
  output.setWriteListener
    (new AsyncWriteListener( output, context));
}
/*... inner class ... */
}
```

This `AsyncWriterServlet` Servlet is the opposite of the reader Servlet, in that it creates `WriterListener` as an event listener. This servlet is annotated with `@WebServlet`, and it has an attribute `asyncSupported` set to `true`. The refactored method `processRequest()` is the key, in that it creates an asynchronous context. The context is started, and `AsyncWriterListener` is created and registered on `ServletOutputStream`.

`AsyncWriterServlet` utilizes an inner class `AsyncWriteListener` in order to push data asynchronously to the client endpoint. The listing for this class-and note that it is a type of `WriteListener`-is as follows:

```
private class AsyncWriteListener implements WriteListener {
  private ServletOutputStream output;
  private AsyncContext context;

  private static final String LOREM_IPSUM =
    "Lorem ipsum dolor sit amet, consectetur adipisicing " +
      "elit, sed do eiusmod tempor incididunt ut labore et " +
        /* ... */ est laborum.";

  private AsyncWriteListener(ServletOutputStream output,
    AsyncContext context) {
    this.output = output;
    this.context = context;
    System.out.printf("thread [%s] AsyncWriteListener()\n ",
      Thread.currentThread().getName());
  }

  @Override
  public void onWritePossible() {
    System.out.printf("thread [%s] onWritePossible() " +
      "Sending data ...\n", Thread.currentThread().getName());
    StringTokenizer stk =
      new StringTokenizer(LOREM_IPSUM," \t,.");
    PrintStream ps = new PrintStream(output);
    try {
      while (output.isReady() && stk.hasMoreTokens()) {
        if (stk.hasMoreTokens()) {
          ps.println(stk.nextToken());
          ps.flush();
          Thread.sleep(200);
        }
      }
      ps.println("End of server *push*");
      ps.flush();
      ps.close();
      System.out.printf("thread [%s] Finished sending ...\n",
        Thread.currentThread().getName());
    }
    catch (Exception e) {
      e.printStackTrace(System.err);
    }
```

```
        finally {context.complete();}
    }

    @Override
    public void onError(Throwable t) {
      System.out.printf("thread [%s] Error occurred=%s\n",
        Thread.currentThread().getName(), t.getMessage());
      context.complete();
    }
  }
}
```

In order to generate an asynchronous response, web container invokes the `WriterListener` instance with calls to the `onWritePossible()` method. It is likely the method call is invoked on a separate worker thread. The difference between `WriterListener` and `ReaderListener` is that the whole thread is responsible for pushing the entire data set asynchronously. `AsyncWriteListener` sends the data as a word of the Lorem Ipsum at time every 200 milliseconds and flushes the output buffer in order to push the data across the network.

The Servlet container only ever invokes the `onError()` method if something goes wrong with the server push. The disadvantage of `WriteListener` seems to be that the entire Java thread is held onto by the whole dataset, because we have to push it fully to the web client. Perhaps it is best to save the pointers on how much of the dataset is written in an instance variable in a business application.

Let's look at the test application that will invoke this Servlet. It is another embedded GlassFish runner application. However, this program will wait for the streamed responses from `AsyncWriterServlet`.

The code in its entirety is as follows:

```
package je7hb.common.webcontainer.embedded.glassfish;
import java.io.*;
import java.net.HttpURLConnection;
import java.net.URL;

public class EmbeddedAsyncWriterRunner extends
  AbstractEmbeddedRunner {
  public EmbeddedAsyncWriterRunner(int port) {
    super(port);
  }

  public static void main(String args[]) throws Exception {
    EmbeddedAsyncWriterRunner runner =
      (EmbeddedAsyncWriterRunner)
```

```
      new EmbeddedAsyncWriterRunner(8080).init().start();
      runner.deployWithRename
        ("build/libs/ch06-servlets-basic-1.0.war", "mywebapp");
      Thread.sleep(1000);
      String path = String.format
        ("http://localhost:%d/%s/%s", 8080, "mywebapp", "writer");
      URL url = new URL(path);
      System.out.printf
        ("Client connecting to server on path %s\n", path);
      HttpURLConnection conn = (HttpURLConnection)
      url.openConnection();
      conn.setChunkedStreamingMode(2);
      conn.setDoInput(true);
      conn.setDoOutput(true);
      conn.connect();
      try (BufferedReader input = new BufferedReader
        (new InputStreamReader(conn.getInputStream()))) {
        System.out.println("Client receiving data ...");
        int len = -1;
        char buffer[] = new char[2048];
        while ((len = input.read(buffer)) != -1 ) {
          String data = new String(buffer,0,len).trim();
          System.out.printf
            ("--> client received data: %s\n", data);
        }
        System.out.println
          ("Client finished with receiving data ...");
      }
      System.out.println("Check standard console ");
      Thread.sleep(3000);
      System.out.println("Client disconnecting and shutdown");
      conn.disconnect();
      runner.stop();

      System.exit(0);
    }
}
```

`EmbeddedAsyncWriterRunner` is another container-less application that executes an embedded GlassFish server, and deploys a WAR file to it. The program makes an HTTP URL connection to the deployed Servlet and sends a request to it. The program waits on the connection for Servlet to respond. It dumps each successful read of the input stream, which is a word from the Lorem Ipsum text, to the standard output. After the input stream is closed, because `AsysncWriteServlet` closes the connection, the application will shut down the embedded runner, and then terminate itself.

The output of executing this program is as follows:

```
INFO: mywebapp was successfully deployed in 2,587 milliseconds.
Client connecting to server on path
   http://localhost:8080/mywebapp/writer
init() called on AsyncWriterServlet
doPost() called on AsyncWriterServlet
processRequest() called AsyncWriterServlet on thread
   [http-listener(2)]
thread [http-listener(2)] AsyncWriteListener()
thread [http-listener(2)] onWritePossible() Sending data ...
Client receiving data ...
--> client received data: Lorem
--> client received data: ipsum
--> client received data: dolor
--> client received data: sit
--> client received data: amet
--> client received data: consectetur

--> client received data: laborum
--> client received data: End of server *push*
thread [http-listener(2)] Finished sending ...
Client finished with receiving data ...
Check standard console
Client disconnecting and shutdown
Feb 11, 2013 9:08:36 PM
   org.glassfish.admin.mbeanserver.JMXStartupService shutdown
FileMonitoring shutdown
INFO: JMXStartupService and JMXConnectors have been shut down.
contextDestroyed() on AppServletContextListener

INFO: Shutdown procedure finished
```

In the GlassFish server implementation, a Java thread `http-listener(2)` is used to push the data entirely to the web client. However, because the application uses the standard API, this will be hidden from developers. The Servlet container providers are free to develop implementations that will execute from the thread pool services that give the best performance.

Alignment to the containers

The Servlet specification is one of the oldest in the Java EE platform. Over a period of time, it has been updated to allow Servlets to integrate with newer parts of the platform, such as CDI, EJB, JAX-RS, and WebSocket.

Aligning Servlets to the CDI container

The Java Servlet 3.1 specification mentions that the resources can be injected into a Servlet. If the web container provider has support for CDI, then the CDI container can inject the contextual objects into a web application using the `@javax.inject.Inject` annotation.

CDI is available on web containers and the application servers that implement the Java EE 7 Web Profile and Full Profile. The CDI components can just be injected into Servlet on those environments.

An example of the CDI services injected into Servlet is as follows:

```java
@WebServlet(urlPatterns = {"/randomword"})
public class CDIServlet extends HttpServlet {
  @Inject private RandomWordService service;

  @Override
  protected void doGet(HttpServletRequest req,
    HttpServletResponse resp)
  throws ServletException, IOException {
    resp.setContentType("text/plain");
    PrintWriter pwriter = resp.getWriter();
    pwriter.printf("This is the class `%s'\n" +
      "The date time is %s\n" + "random word = %d\n",
        getClass().getName(), new Date(), service.getNextWord());
  }
}
```

Since Servlet 3.1 is part of Java EE 7, there is no need to bootstrap the CDI container as a separate service. The CDI container is available in conforming web containers as can be seen in the preceding example, `CDIServlet`, which injects a `RandomWordService.Alignment` Servlet to the EJB container.

References to stateful and stateless EJB can also be injected into Servlets and filters, if they meet either conformance with the Web Profile or Full Profile. The annotation `@javax.ejb.EJB` can be used in a Java Servlet component to reference an external EJB.

```java
@WebServlet(urlPatterns = {"/cart/*"})
public class ShoppingCartServlet extends HttpServlet {
  @EJB private ShoppingCartServiceBean cartBean;

  @Override
  protected void doGet(HttpServletRequest req,
    HttpServletResponse resp)
  throws ServletException, IOException {
    processRequest( req, res );
    }
//
}
```

In this example code for `ShoppingCartServlet`, the Servlet container on behalf of the EJB container injects an EJB reference into Servlet during the initialization phase. The internal logic of the application server processes the injection point with the correct representation, which is either a local or remote EJB proxy instance. The result is transparent to developer.

If the web application is running in the same JVM as the EJB implementation, then in order to use such EJB references in a Servlet, the web application must have references to the home and local interfaces in an accompanying JAR file, which is deployed in the `WEB-INF/lib` directory. These interfaces are usually Java interfaces, and not normally the implementations themselves.

If the web application uses an EJB that is remote, it does not run inside the same JVM, then a JAR file with the necessary home and remote interfaces must be prepared. This JAR file is also placed in the `WEB-INF/lib` directory of the web application.

Miscellaneous features

This section covers useful features of the Java Servlet specification.

Mapping the URL patterns

The URL pattern determines how the web container maps a HTTP Request to a Servlet resource. A URL pattern can map to a specific Servlet, an extension mapping, or be treated as the default processor.

Given an URL pattern as a string, then the following logic applies:

- If the URL pattern begins with a forward slash character (/) and ends with (/*) character, then this sequence is valid for the path mapping. We saw some examples of the URL patterns in `SimpleServlet`, earlier in this chapter.
- For web container to interpret an URL path as an extension mapping, the pattern must be stringed with the prefix (*.). Some examples of extension mapping are `*.jsp`, `*.jsf`, and `*.facelet`.
- A URL pattern containing only the forward slash (/) character indicates to web container the associated or referenced Servlet is the default Servlet of the web application. The default Servlet can be either denoted by annotation or specified in the web deployment descriptor.

If none of the preceding logic applies, then the URL pattern is used for exact matches only.

Rules for the URL path mapping

Web container maps the incoming request to a particular Servlet using rules according to the specification. The algorithm stop-at-the-first successful true condition implies that the search and mapping exercise is complete, and no further action is required.

The rules are as follows:

1. Web container will attempt to find an exact match of the path of the request to the Servlet's path. A successful match selects the Servlet.
2. Web container will recursively try to match the path of the Servlet using the longest path first, by stepping down the path tree a directory at a time, using the path separator (/). The longest match determines the Servlet selected.
3. If the last segment in the URL path contains an extension (for example, `.jsp`), web container will attempt to match a Servlet that handles the requests for the extension. An extension is defined as part of the last segment after the last full stop (.) character.
4. If neither of the previous rules works in selecting an appropriate Servlet, web container will attempt to serve the content that is appropriate for the resource requested. If the web application defines a default Servlet, then it is selected and used.

Single thread model

`javax.servlet.SingleThreadModel` is a Java interface instructed to the Servlet container to only allow a single web request to invoke on a Java Servlet. This interface is now deprecated in Servlet 3.1. Originally, this feature was designed in the specification to contain the thread management on a single resource. Nowadays, `SingleThreadModel` is a bottleneck and a severe throttle for the scalable web applications, especially now that we have the asynchronous input and output in Java Servlets 3.1.

Summary

Java Servlet is a fundamental specification of the Java EE platform, it is the basis of the web applications and support. We have seen that Servlets can provide the synchronous input and output to the web clients over HTTP. Servlets have different scopes: request, session, and servlet context.

In this chapter, we learnt about how Servlets are initialized and destroyed, how they can retrieve the initialization parameters. Servlets are configurable through the annotations and there is no need to write a single web deployment descriptor `WEB-INF/web.xml` in order to deploy a web application.

The web applications are deployed to a web container using a WAR file. The Servlet 3.1 specification allows a web application to be built from web fragments. If the JAR files are distributed in a WAR file and the correct information is set in the deployment descriptor, then those JAR files will be searched for the annotated Servlet, filter, and listener classes.

The Java Servlet 3.1 specification introduces the asynchronous input and output for the first time. Java Servlet and filter can be written to take advantage of the NIO of the Java platform. Asynchronous I/O is one way to build scalable web components on the server.

Finally, CDI and EJB references can be injected into the Servlet web components. In the next chapter, we will explore Java WebSocket API, a brand new edition to the Enterprise platform. We have seen that Java Servlet can handle asynchronous communications, but HTML5 WebSocket is the exciting challenge, and it is ideally suited for scalable end-to-end messaging.

7
Java API for HTML5WebSocket

Jon Bon Jovi, singer and songwriter said, "Don't get too comfortable with who you are at any given time—you may miss the opportunity to become who you want to be."

This chapter is about Java HTML5**WebSocket** in the Java EE 7 edition, which is Java's standard application programming interface to the exciting new communication feature in the HTML5 specification. The HTML5 specification defines a WebSocket as a communication channel that operates over the World Wide Web in a *full-duplex* mode: it affords HTML and web applications, for the very first time, a standard for building real-time and event-driven architectures. This definition can be confusing terminology for a beginner. Fortunately, the new WebSocket features in Java EE are an improvement and a higher abstraction over general networking.

An **endpoint** is an application or program that sits on one end of a communication. Obviously, we need two endpoints in order to communicate any data. An endpoint can receive data or it can send data to and across the network.

The term **full duplex** means that communication can be started from either end-point. Both endpoints can send and receive data simultaneously: it is bi-directional.

The term **half-duplex** describes the other side of the coin, where only one endpoint can send data and the other receives it. The endpoint is the producer and the other end-point is the consumer. These terms are derived etymologically from the telephony industry and earlier forms of computer networking.

The HTML5WebSocket has the following affordances:

- A much smaller payload of header data in comparison to standard HTTP requests-response
- Bi-directional communication stream using just one connection
- A lower latency stream in comparison to HTTP request-response

There is already a wide set of applications using WebSockets even before the W3C standard committee has fully resolved and reached version 1.0 release.

The rise of WebSockets

The WebSocket standard is overseen by the **Web Hypertext Application Technology Working Group (WHATWG)** and is the culmination of many earlier attempts to provide asynchronous HTTP communication in a scalable.
(See `http://www.whatwg.org/`).

Early web technology

The core of the web is the underlying protocol for communication, the **Hypertext Transfer Protocol (HTTP)**. A web client submits an HTTP request to a remote server over the Internet, and then waits for the server to respond. The user experiences this behavior as a delay for the web page to load, however briefly. The **User Experience** (UX) can attempt to design a work-around as much as possible, but eventually if the latency and the network is long enough then this sequence of events become interminable.

The earliest technologies attempted to avoid delay in the HTTP request and response. They provided more immediate responses to the web client by building on HTTP technologies using plug-ins and proprietary features inside web browsers. As options, they were clever, but non standard and non portable.

The first technique may surprise some people. Since 1995, Java has been executable in the web browser; the Java Applet permitted access to the richer networking API of the JVM platform and it also provided multithread programming

The second technique was through a discovery of the XML HTTP Request library, which Microsoft implemented in the Internet Explorer web browser. Web engineers found out **Asynchronous JavaScript and XML Request and Response (AJAX)**.Other web browser providers such as Mozilla Firefox, Opera, and Apple Safari quickly copied the AJAX API. The AJAX phenomenon took off with websites such as Google Maps and Google Mail that provided a partial page request and demonstrate partial page response rendering.

Let's step back a little bit. HTTP 1.0 permits a client to open a connection to a web server. The client would send a request with HTTP headers, the server would respond in due course with a content response, a MIME type, and then the content. Afterwards, the connection would be severed. There is a large eyesore problem with such a protocol: it does not scale upwards. The server has to acquire and release a relatively expensive resource, an HTTP connection, which is essentially a TCP/IP socket as far as the operating system is concerned. A program that continuously opens and closes socket will perform worse than one that maintains one open socket for the conversation. In HTTP 1.1, there is an opportunity to hold on to a socket connection with the special request header: Keep-Alive. Unfortunately this is not an answer either, because holding onto a socket means that it is not shared by another web client, and thus this solution also fails to scale to big data users with a single JVM. Nevertheless this is ultimately the secret behind the technique known as **Long Polling**.

The Long Polling technique is a favorite technique of COMET or Push servers. COMET and AJAX are plays on words for common household cleaning products found in USA and Europe. In COMET, the web client makes a request to the web server. The web server sends a response but never actually closes the connection; it tricks the browser into holding onto the connection, and every so often the client initiates a request to the server. These infrequent requests effectively poll the connection and the web server can push data to the client. As long as the connection is not broken then the illusion is held and to the user it looks like the server is pushing data to the client.

There are more exotic techniques, which use the existing HTTP / 1.1 communication standards, and many projects have found success in the open with them. Unfortunately they all suffer the ignominy of sending the HTTP request headers with every request. The older techniques may mean the latency is just not low enough for a very high interactive online game or a business that need very fast speed real-time data.

Enter HTML5 and WebSockets

HTML5 is a set of standards and working group defined by the WHATWG. One of the standards is called WebSockets. The purpose of the WebSockets is to define a standard that permits web clients and server to initiate a persistent connection that will allow asynchronous requests and responses. Both sides of the communication channel can send data to the other end of the channel.

WebSockets are an example of peer-to-peer communications. A P2P network is one where any endpoint can act as a *client* or a *server* for other connections on the network.

WebSocket Java definitions

The following are the definitions of WebSocket Java.

- The **WebSocket Endpoint** is the component that enables the peers to send data and receive data to and from the connection. In JSR 356 the Java Web Socket endpoint is the component that represents one side of the sequence of interactions between connected peers. A Web Socket endpoint has two states: connected or disconnected.

- The **WebSocket Connection** is a completed route of communication between peers that have agreed beforehand on a protocol handshake. The connection is maintained as a network between two WebSocket endpoints until one of them is closed or forcefully severed by the application or web browser runtime.

- A **WebSocket Peer** represents an application that is participating in communications over a WebSocket endpoint.

- A **WebSocket Session**, in the WebSocket parlance, is the representative set of data communications, over time, shared by two peers across two separate endpoints. A session is the conduit for identifying the sequence of these communications across two peers.

- A **Server WebSocket Endpoint** is a peer that accepts initiation requests from clients-remote endpoints-to connect to its WebSocket. The implementation will provide a WebSocket or create one when there is a connection request. The server aids in the handshake protocol and activates a session between the client and the server endpoints, establishing a connection. The server endpoint does not initiate other connections or act as a client.

- A **Client WebSocket Endpoint** is the peer that creates a WebSocket (or retrieves a pooled WebSocket from the implementation) and invokes a connection request on a remote endpoint in order to start a WebSocket session. When the remote endpoint accepts the connection request then the client is bound into the WebSocket session. The client does not accept connections from other remote endpoints or act as a server.

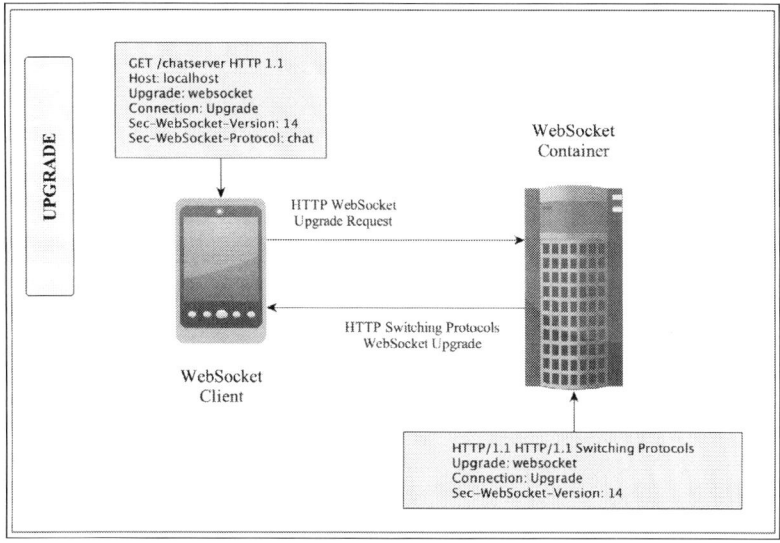

The WebSocket protocol

The client and server must negotiate a handshake in order to establish a WebSocket connection. A client initiates an HTTP Request to the server first of all, then server and client upgrade from the HTTP protocol to the WebSocket protocol.

After the completion of a successful handshake, the client and server can send messages at any time. The messages that appear in the connection channel follow the WebSocket protocol.

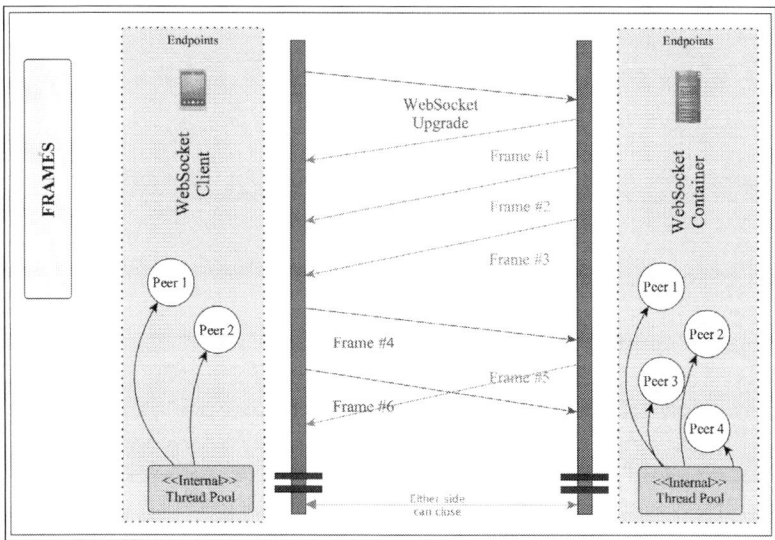

Server-side Java WebSockets

In Java EE 7, the Java package `javax.websocket` is the root for WebSockets. There is one package underneath this one for server endpoints: `javax.websocket.server`.

The server-side endpoint in Java represents one end of the peers. Java applications with WebSocket endpoints are created through programming directly against the library. Otherwise, the endpoints are determined by annotations in the JSR 356 specification.

The annotation `javax.websocket.server.ServerEndpoint` is applied to classes that execute an endpoint on the server. The annotation requires a URL pattern fragment similar to the Servlet 3.1 annotation `@javax.servlet.WebServlet`, which determines how the implementation provider routes an incoming WebSockets request to the endpoint.

We can annotate a POJO so that it will be registered as a server-side WebSocket endpoint, but how can we receive messages from the client? The answer is annotation: `@javax.websocket.OnMessage`. This annotation declares a particular method to receive messages that arrive on the WebSocket connection.

Let's take a look at a simple echo server example:

```java
package je7hb.websocket.basic;
import javax.websocket.OnMessage;
import javax.websocket.server.ServerEndpoint;

@ServerEndpoint("/echo")
public class EchoWebSocketServer {

  @OnMessage
  public String doListen(String message) {
    return "Echo: Got your message (" + message +
      "). Thanks";
  }
}
```

This is, perhaps, the simplest Java WebSocket server that one can write. The `@ServerEndpoint` annotation declares the class `EchoWebSocketServer` as a server-side endpoint in that it is capable of receiving connection requests from clients. The URL pattern `"/echo"` declares how the WebSocket implementation routes the request to the endpoint.

The method `doListen()` is annotated with `@OnMessage` and declares to the implementation what method to invoke when a message has been received on the connection. Note that the return type of the method `doListen()` is `String`. It is possible to return a message to the client directly, which is of course exactly the function of the method.

@ServerEndpoint

Let's look at the annotations in detail; here is the table of attributes for the annotations for `@javax.websocket.server.ServerEndpoint`:

Attribute	Type	Description	Default Value
value	String	Defines the URI or URI template where the endpoint will be deployed. The URI must begin with a character """/". Trailing """/" characters are ignored.	None
subProtocols	String []	Defines an ordered array of WebSocket protocols that this endpoint supports.	None
decoders	Decoder[]	Specifies an ordered array of encoder classes this endpoint will use.	None
decoders	Encoder[]	Specifies an ordered array of encoder classes that the endpoint will use.	None
configurator	Class<? Extends ServerEndPoint-Configurator>	Defines a custom configurator that the developer would like to use to configure a logical endpoint instance.	ServerEndpoint-Configuration.class

@OnMessage

Here is the table of attributes for the `@javax.websocket.OnMessage`:

Attribute	Type	Description	Default Value
`maxMessageSize`	`long`	Specifies the maximum size in bytes for the incoming message.	None

There is only one attribute allowed. The `maxMessageType` attribute sets the maximum size of the message following the successful completion of the initial handshake.

Invoking Java WebSocket

We can define a Java WebSocket endpoint on the server side. There would be no point in defining the WebSocket unless there was a way of calling it. We only require a simple HTML5 and JavaScript web page to do this. WebSockets are supported by most of the modern web browsers: Mozilla Firefox, Google Chrome, Apple Safari, and Microsoft Internet Explorer.

The page that invokes the `EchoWebSocketServer` looks like the following:

```
<!DOCTYPE html>
<head>
<meta charset="utf-8"/>
<title>Echo Server Side WebSocket Test</title>
<script language="javascript" type="text/javascript">
  var wsUri = "ws://localhost:8080/mywebapp/echo";
  var output;

  function init() {
    output = document.getElementById("output");
    testWebSocket();
  }

  function testWebSocket() {
    websocket = new WebSocket(wsUri);
    websocket.onopen = function (evt) {
      onOpen(evt)
    };
```

```
    websocket.onclose = function (evt) {
      onClose(evt)
    };
    websocket.onmessage = function (evt) {
      onMessage(evt)
    };
    websocket.onerror = function (evt) {
      onError(evt)
    };
}

function onOpen(evt) {
  writeToScreen("CONNECTED");
  doSend("HTML5 Java WebSockets Rocks!");
}

function onClose(evt) {
  writeToScreen("DISCONNECTED");
}

function onMessage(evt) {
  writeToScreen('<span style="color: blue;">RESPONSE:'
    + evt.data + '</span>');
  websocket.close();
}

function onError(evt) {
  writeToScreen('<span style="color: red;">ERROR:</span>'
    + evt.data);
}

function doSend(message) {
  writeToScreen("SENT: " + message);
  websocket.send(message);
}

function writeToScreen(message) {
  var pre = document.createElement("p");
  pre.style.wordWrap = "break-word";
  pre.innerHTML = message;
  output.appendChild(pre);
}
```

```
    window.addEventListener("load", init, false);
</script>
<head>
<body>
<h2>WebSocket Test</h2>
<div id="output"></div>
</body>
</html>
```

This is mostly an adaption of the code that exists on the HTML5 community website: `http://websocket.org/`. It is about as simple as it can get for a *Hello World* example for WebSockets.

The page is mostly JavaScript. There is one `h2` header and a `div` layer element with an `id` of "output". An event handler `init()` is registered on the page, as soon as it is loaded with the browser. The first action of the function `init()` finds the `output` div layer in the Document Object Model. The second invokes the `testWebSocket()` function.

The function `testWebSocket()` creates a `WebSocket` and then registers callback functions on it on various events. On the JavaScript side, one listens for when the web sockets are opened or closed, or when a message is received, and if there is an error on the channel.

The function `onOpen()` is a callback function in JavaScript, which is invoked when the WebSocket successfully makes a connection to the remote endpoint, which is in our case the `EchoWebSocketServer`. The function sends a message down the channel to the server by calling the helper function `doSend()`.

Upon reception of the message on the WebSocket, the JavaScript function `onMessage()` is invoked. This function appends a new text element with the message to the output div layer by calling the helper function `writeToScreen()`.

Running WebSocket examples

The code that deploys the WebSocket is exactly the same as the `EmbeddedRunner` in the Servlet chapter. The only difference is the name of the WAR file. We use an embedded GlassFish server instance and deploy a WAR file to it with the WebSockets endpoint. The open source project **Tyrus** (on Java .Net https://java.net/projects/tyrus) is the reference implementation of the Java WebSockets specification inside the GlassFish project. Tyrus is responsible for creating WebSocket endpoints by scanning the WAR file for the appropriate `@ServerEndpoint` annotations. Once it finds them, the implementation validates the class and then generates configuration around each endpoint, which intercepts the URI template, and then activates the WebSocket for service.

Java WebSocket API

The WebSocket API expresses a view of the HTML5 standard for WebSocket, which defines the model inside a web browser and the protocol for communication. In terms of the Java API, a WebSocket endpoint is a Java object that represents a terminated socket connection between two peers. If two different Java applications have a Web Socket connection, then each one will have an instance of a Java WebSocket.

There are two ways to create a Java WebSocket. The easiest way is to develop endpoints using the Java annotations. The less travelled road is to develop endpoints against the WebSocket API programmatically. The developer writes classes and implements the classes required by the WebSocket API. The second way means the developer writes behavior for a WebSocket to produce and consume messages, publish itself as a configured endpoint, and write code to register itself for client connections and/or connect to remote endpoints.

Native formats communication

The HTML5 standard for WebSocket defines three native formats for communication: text, binary, and pong.

The native format Text is the `java.lang.String` in Java and for JavaScript programming language corresponds to the type `String`. So we have a one-to-one association.

Binary format is `java.nio.ByteBuffer` in Java and the type `ArrayBuffer` in JavaScript. (Some web browsers may also permit the DOM type Blob in JavaScript; since the standard is not completely ratified, you would be very wise to check your integration!)

The Pong format is also `java.nio.ByteBuffer` in Java and the type `ArrayBuffer` in JavaScript. The Ping and Pong format is a special format for checking the connectivity between two WebSockets. In the networking parlance, these types of messages are often called *heartbeats*. In the current WebSocket standard, please note there is no defined API to send either a Ping or Pong message using JavaScript.

Let's continue with the annotated WebSocket endpoints.

Annotated WebSockets on the server side

Developers have access to the lifecycle of the WebSocket through annotations, which unsurprisingly are very similar to the JavaScript implementation. The annotations are `@javax.websocket.OnMessage`, which you have already seen `@javax.websocket.OnOpen`, `@javax.websocket.OnClose`, and `@javax.websocket.OnError`. These annotations, apart from `@OnMessage`, do not accept any attributes. All of the annotations are only applied to instance methods in a Java class.

Lifecycle WebSocket endpoint annotations

Here is a table of these annotations:

Lifecycle Annotation	Description
`@OnOpen`	This annotation decorates a Java method that wishes to be called when a new WebSocket session is open.
`@OnMessage`	This annotation decorates a Java method to receive incoming WebSocket messages. Each WebSocket endpoint may only have one message handling method for each of the native WebSocket message formats: text, binary, and pong.
`@OnClose`	This annotation decorates a Java method that wishes to be called when an existing WebSocket session is closed.
`@OnError`	This annotation decorates a Java method that wishes to be called when an existing WebSocket session has an error. The application method can thus handle the error and perform further tasks.

This method-level annotation can be used to make a Java method receive incoming WebSocket messages. Each WebSocket endpoint may only have one message handling method for each of the native WebSocket message formats: text, binary, and pong.

WebSocket sessions

The Java WebSocket API defines a session object that represents a conversation between two peers. The `javax.websocket.Session` is an interface, which defines a number of methods that a developer may invoke to get extra information about the connection, session data, the lifecycle, and also perform the close action on the connection. Moreover, the `Session` object is the way to associate the conversation with the peer into a semantic context in terms of a business application.

Each WebSocket session has a unique session ID, which is associated with one and only one session instance. An implementation may choose to implement a WebSocket connection pool and therefore an instance may be appropriately reused. In such cases, the specification stipulates that a reused session instance must have a new unique session ID.

The session instance in a distributed Java EE container can also be passivated on managed server node instance and therefore migrated to another node. Implementations of the Java WebSocket API are permitted to migrate the WebSocket session instances from one node to another for the purposes of load balancing and failover. The only rule is that the provider must preserve the WebSocket session of any connected peers seamlessly and transparently. This is particularly interesting from the point of view of a cloud-computing platform. This, probably, will be a common question for application architects. How do WebSocket connections, nodes, and servers scale? The simplest answer, perhaps, is to choose a provider that reliably has the non-functional requirements that your business needs.

Methods annotated with lifecycle events `@OnOpen`, `@OnClose`, `@OnMessage`, and `@OnError` annotation are permitted to accept a `javax.websocket.Session` object as an argument. The implementation will inject the session instance into the method call.

Methods annotated with `@OnMessage` annotation additionally can also declare a `@javax.websocket.PathParam` argument in order to accept WebSocket connection arguments.

Here is a table for the methods of `javax.websocket.Session`:

Method	Return Type	Description
`getContainer()`	`WebSocketContainer`	Gets the container of which this session is a part.
`addMessageHandler( MessageHandler handler)`	`void`	Registers a handler to receive incoming messages in the session conversation (text, binary or pong).

Method	Return Type	Description
`getMessageHandlers()`	`Set<MessageHandler>`	Retrieves an immutable copy of the set of `MessageHandler` associated with the session.
`removeMessageHandler( MessageHandler handler )`	`void`	Removes the supplied `MessageHandler` from the set of handlers associated with this session. If the message handler is in use then invoking this call may block the caller.
`getProtocolVersion()`	`String`	Gets the version of the WebSocket protocol currently being used.
`getNegotiated-Subprotocol()`	`String`	Gets the sub protocol agreed after the WebSocket handshake for this conversation.
`getNegotiated-Extensions()`	`List<Extension>`	Retrieves a list of extensions that have been agreed for use in the session conversation.
`isSecure()`	`boolean`	Returns a Boolean flag about the underlying socket connection. If a secure transport is being used (https) then this method returns `true`.
`isOpen()`	`Boolean`	Returns a Boolean flag, if the socket connection is open or closed.
`getMaxIdleTime()`	`Long`	Specifies the number of milliseconds allowed before the container closes a WebSocket channel.
`setMaxIdleTime( long millisecond)`	`void`	Sets the number of milliseconds before the conversation is ended, because of inactivity, which means no data is sent or received over a period of time.

Method	Return Type	Description
setMaxBinaryMessage-BufferSize(int length)	void	Sets the maximum length of incoming binary messages.
getMaxBinaryMessage-BufferSize()	int	Gets the maximum length of incoming binary messages.
setMaxTextMessage-BufferSize(int length)	void	Sets the maximum length of incoming text messages.
getMaxTextMessage-BufferSize()	int	Gets the maximum length of incoming text messages.
getAsyncRemote()	RemoteEndpoint.Async	Returns a reference to a RemoteEndpoint object, which represents the peer of the conversation that is able to send messages asynchronously to the peer.
getBasicRemote()	RemoteEndpoint.Basic	Returns a reference to a RemoteEndpoint object, which represents the peer of the conversation that is able to send messages synchronously to the peer.
getId()	String	Gets the unique identifier for this session instance.
close()	void	Closes the current conversation with a normal status code and no reason text.
close(CloseReason reason)	void	Closes the current conversation with a specific reason for ending the session.
getRequestURI()	URI	Retrieves the URI under which this session was opened including the full query string.
getRequestParameter-Map()	Map<String, <List<String>>	Retrieves a map collection of the request parameters associated with the request and also the underlying session.

Method	Return Type	Description
getQueryString()	String	Returns the query string associated with the request for this session at opening time.
getPathParameters()	Map<String, String>	Retrieves a map collection of the path parameters and values associated with the request for this session at opening time.
getUserProperties()	Map<String, Object>	Retrieves a map collection of user-defined properties. This map is valid when the connection is open and therefore any information is at risk as soon as the connection session is closed.
getUserPrincipal()	Principal	Gets the authenticated user for this WebSocket session object or null if there is no authenticated user.
getOpenSessions()	Set<Session>	Returns a copy of the set collection of all the open WebSocket sessions that represent connections to the same endpoint, to which this session represents a connection.

Although there are lots of methods in javax.websocket.Session, the most important methods are: getId(); getRemoteBasic() and getRemoteAsync(); isOpen(), close(), and getRequestParameterMap().

Now let us see a more capable server-side WebSocket application.

A Java WebSocket chat server

In this section, we will examine the code for a chat server, a rudimentary version that demonstrates the features of Java WebSocket. The chat server allows users with WebSocket enabled web browser to chat online. This chat server has only one room, which is a severe restriction for a business application. On the other hand, there is no form of authentication, and anyone with a browser can join in the chat room. The example also features context and dependency injection.

The server side

Perhaps, the easiest way to start the code review is to look at the endpoint. So we will look at this now:

```java
package je7hb.websocket.basic;

import javax.annotation.*;
import javax.enterprise.context.ApplicationScoped;
import javax.inject.Inject;
import javax.websocket.*;
import javax.websocket.server.ServerEndpoint;

import static je7hb.websocket.basic.ChatUtils.*;

@ServerEndpoint("/chat")
public class ChatServerEndPoint {
  @Inject @ApplicationScoped
  private ChatRoom chatRoom;

  @PostConstruct
  public void acquire() {
    System.out.printf("%s.acquire() called in thread: [%s]\n",
      getClass().getSimpleName(),
      Thread.currentThread().getName());
  }

  @PreDestroy
  public void release() {
    System.out.printf("%s.release() called\n",
      getClass().getSimpleName());
  }

  @OnOpen
  public void open(Session session) {
   System.out.printf("%s.open() called session=%s\n",
      getClass().getSimpleName(), session );
  }

  @OnClose
  public void close(Session session) {
    System.out.printf("%s.close() called  
      session=%s\n", getClass().getSimpleName(), session);
  }
```

```java
    @OnMessage
    public void receiveMessage(
  String message, Session session ) {
      System.out.printf("%s.receiveMessage() called
        with message=`%s', session %s, thread [%s]\n",
        getClass().getSimpleName(), message, session,
        Thread.currentThread().getName() );

      String tokens[] = message.split(DELIMITER);
      String command  = tokens[0];
      String username = ( tokens.length > 1 ? tokens[1] : "" );
      String text     = ( tokens.length > 2 ? tokens[2] : "" );

      ChatUser user = new ChatUser(session,username);
      if ( LOGIN_REQUEST.equals(command)) {
        chatRoom.addChatUser(user);
      }
      else if ( LOGOUT_REQUEST.equals(command)) {
        chatRoom.removeChatUser(user);
      }
      else if ( SEND_MSG_REQUEST.equals(command)) {
        chatRoom.broadcastMessage(username,text);
      }
      else {
        encodeErrorReply(session,username,
          String.format("unknown command: %s", command));
      }
    }
  }
```

This class `ChatServerEndpoint` is annotated as a WebSocket server endpoint and any requests with the URL fragment `"/chat"` are directed to it.

Notice, there is CDI application scoped bean `ChatRoom` injected into the endpoint. In this way, we are able to converse with users of the chat room feature. Although not really necessary for the function, we also add the CDI lifecycle events to the endpoint.

Next, we have specific life cycle methods `open()`, `close()`, and `receiveMessage()` that are annotated with `@OnOpen`, `@OnClose` and `@OnMessage` to respond to WebSocket connection events. In these methods we dump to the standard console the name of the current thread and session object solely for the purpose of debugging.

The method `receiveMessage()` does the real work of deciphering the incoming message from the chat client application, which is implemented in HTML5 and JavaScript. The method creates a `ChatUser` object and executes an action in the `ChatRoom` application scoped bean. Otherwise it will send a reply text as an error message back to the chat client.

Let us look at the other classes in the application, starting with the `ChatUser` class:

```
package je7hb.websocket.basic;
import javax.websocket.Session;

public class ChatUser {
  private final Session session;
  private final String username;

  public ChatUser(Session session, String username) {
    this.session = session;
    this.username = username;
  }

  public Session getSession() { return session; }
  public String getUsername() { return username; }

  @Override
  public String toString() {
    return "ChatUser{" +
        "session=" + session +
        ", username='" + username + '\'' +
        '}';
  }
}
```

The class `ChatUser` is an immutable Java object, which associates the chat username with a WebSocket session instance. The methods `hashCode()` and `equals()` methods are omitted, but are included in the source code for the book.

We will move on the handy utility class for the chat server, which is the class `ChatUtils`:

```
package je7hb.websocket.basic;
import javax.websocket.*;
import java.io.IOException;

public class ChatUtils {
  public final static String SYSTEM_USER   = "*SYSTEM*";
  public final static String DELIMITER     = ":::";
  public final static String LOGIN_REQUEST  = "LOGIN";
  public final static String LOGOUT_REQUEST = "LOGOUT";
  public final static String SEND_MSG_REQUEST= "SENDMSG";
  public final static String MESSAGE_REPLY="MESSAGE_REPLY";
  public final static String ERROR_REPLY="ERROR_REPLY";

  private ChatUtils() { }

  public static void encodeMessageReply(
Session session, String username, String text ) {
     encodeCommonReply(session, MESSAGE_REPLY, username, text);
  }

  public static void encodeErrorReply(
Session session, String username, String text ) {
     encodeCommonReply(session, ERROR_REPLY, username, text);
  }

  public static void encodeCommonReply(Session session,
String token, String username, String text) {
     if ( session.isOpen()) {
       try {
        session.getBasicRemote().sendText(
token + DELIMITER + username + DELIMITER + text);
       } catch (IOException e) {
        e.printStackTrace();
       }
     }
  }
}
```

Chapter 7

The utility class has a generic method `encodeCommonReply()`, which generates an appropriate response, an encoded text string, and sends it to the remote endpoint. The method uses a DELIMITER string and a reply token with a supplied text message from the caller. In particular, note how the method retrieves the reference to the synchronous endpoint handler in order to send a message back to the peer. Of course, it would be easier to change this to the asynchronous version by invoking the alternative function `session.getBasicAsync()` instead. The method also checks if the WebSocket peers are active by calling `isOpen()` on the session instance; and hence avoid sending a text message to a dead connection.

There are two helper methods `encodeMessageReply()` and `encodeErrorReply()` that invoke the generic method. The `encodeMessageReply()` sends a normal text message to the connected peer of the session and the other method encodes an error reply text.

The constant strings are also copied to the JavaScript implementation of the client. Of course, we could have been pedantic and made all of them Java enumerations if we wanted to.

These methods are statically imported in the `ChatServerEndpoint` and the `ChatRoom` class, which will we now study:

```java
package je7hb.websocket.basic;
import javax.annotation.*;
import javax.annotation.PreDestroy;
import javax.enterprise.context.ApplicationScoped;
import java.util.*;
import java.util.concurrent.*;

import static je7hb.websocket.basic.ChatUtils.*;

@ApplicationScoped
public class ChatRoom {
  private ConcurrentMap<String,ChatUser> peers
      = new ConcurrentHashMap<>();

  @PostConstruct
  public void init() {
    System.out.printf(">>>> %s.init() called\n",
        getClass().getSimpleName());
  }
```

```java
  @PreDestroy
  public void destroy() {
    System.out.printf(">>>> %s.destroy() called\n",
        getClass().getSimpleName());
  }

  public void addChatUser( ChatUser user) {
    peers.putIfAbsent(user.getUsername(), user);
    broadcastMessage(SYSTEM_USER,
      String.format("user: %s has joined the chat room.",
      user.getUsername()));

    List<String> peerUsers = new ArrayList<>();
    for ( String peerUsername: peers.keySet()) {
      if ( !peerUsername.equals(user.getUsername())) {
        peerUsers.add(peerUsername);
      }
    }
    StringBuilder membersList = new StringBuilder();
    for ( int j=0; j<peerUsers.size(); ++j) {
      if ( j != 0 ) membersList.append(", ");
      membersList.append(peerUsers.get(j));
    }
    encodeMessageReply(user.getSession(), SYSTEM_USER,
      String.format("The chatroom has members: [%s]",
        membersList.toString()));
  }

  public void removeChatUser( ChatUser user ) {
    peers.remove(user.getUsername()) ;
    broadcastMessage(SYSTEM_USER,
        String.format("user: %s has left the chat room.",
            user.getUsername()));
  }

  public void broadcastMessage(
String targetUsername, String message )
  {
    for ( ChatUser peerUser: peers.values() ) {
      if ( peerUser.getSession().isOpen() ) {
        encodeMessageReply(
          peerUser.getSession(),
          targetUsername, message);
      }
    }
  }
}
```

The `ChatRoom` class makes use of a `ConcurrentMap` collection to associate username to `ChatUser` instances. Remember the `ChatUser` associates a username to a WebSocket session instance. The class itself is annotated as CDI application scope bean so that as soon as the web application is deployed and after the first web request, a `ChatRoom` instance will be created in the `ServletContext`.

We demonstrate that CDI injection does work with the bean by annotating lifecycle methods `init()` and `destroy()`.

The method `addChatUser()` registers a new peer connection to the map of chat user connections. The hardest thing for this method to process would be extremely easy in functional language or JDK 8 with Lambdas. We have to iterate through the peers and filter out the current peer, which is the new peer. With the result set, we send a message back to the new peer revealing how many people are in the chat room now.

The method `removeChatUser()` removes an existing peer connection from the map of chat user connections.

The brunt of the work is handled by the `broadcastMessage()`, which sends the supplied message to the connected peers. Again, we check that the session instance for each remote peer instance is alive before sending a text message down the connection.

The web client

The web client is based on single-page application, which means that it has no navigation to separate pages; all of the user interaction takes place on loading a single web page. There is a single JSP called `chat.jsp` that represents the web client, and it uses the popular JQuery Framework (http://jquery.org/) to help with the JavaScript manipulation of the HTML elements.

The full version of the web client contains the JavaScript calls that are derived from the WHATWG demonstration. Please refer to the book's source code for details.

The simplified HTML5 code for the file `chat.jsp` looks like the following:

```
<!DOCTYPE html>
<head>
<title>WebSocket Chat Server Example</title>
<link rel="stylesheet" media="all" href="styles/chat.css" />
<script src="scripts/jquery-1.9.1.js" ></script>
```

```javascript
<script language="javascript" type="text/javascript">
    var DELIMITER        = ":::"
    var LOGIN_REQUEST    = "LOGIN"
    var LOGOUT_REQUEST   = "LOGOUT"
    var SEND_MSG_REQUEST = "SENDMSG"
    var MESSAGE_REPLY    = "MESSAGE_REPLY";
    var ERROR_REPLY      = "ERROR_REPLY";
    var wsUri = "ws://localhost:8080/mywebapp/chat";
    var websocket;
    var outputDiv;
    var messagesDiv
    var username = "(none)"

    function init() {
      outputDiv = $("#output");
      messagesDiv = $("#messages");
      openWebSocket();
    }

    function openWebSocket() {
      websocket = new WebSocket(wsUri);
      /* ... */
}

    function onOpen(evt) { writeToScreen("CONNECTED");}
    function onClose(evt) { writeToScreen("DISCONNECTED");}
function onMessage(evt) { /* ... */ }
    function onError(evt) { /* ... */ }

    function sendMessage(message) {
      var msg = SEND_MSG_REQUEST +
        DELIMITER + username +
        DELIMITER + message
      protocolMessage("Sending Message: " + msg);
      websocket.send(msg);
    }

    function logout() { /* ... */ }
    function login() {
      var msg = LOGIN_REQUEST +
          DELIMITER + username
      protocolMessage("Sending Message: " + msg);
      websocket.send(msg);
    }
```

```
    function writeToScreen(message) {
        var pre = document.createElement("p");
        pre.style.wordWrap = "break-word";
        pre.innerHTML = message;

        outputDiv.append(pre)
        outputDiv.animate( {
          scrollTop: outputDiv[0].scrollHeight
        }, 1000 )
    }

    function protocolMessage(message) { /* ... */ }
    $(document).ready( function() { /* ... */ });
</script>
</head>
<body>
<h2>Java EE 7 WebSocket Chat Server Example</h2>
<div id="login">
  Username: <input type="text" id="username" /><br/>
<input type="button" value="Login" name="action" id="loginButton" />
<input type="button" value="Logout" name="action" id="logoutButton" />
</div>
<div id="control">
  Enter your message: <br/>
<input type="text" id="messageText" name="messageText" />
</div>
<div id="messages">
<b>PROTOCOL MESSAGES:</b><br/>
</div>
<div id="output"></div>
</body>
</html>
```

In this JSP page, we have four `div` layers: `login`, `control`, `messages` and `output`. A lot of the code looks similar to the previous example, the `EchoWebSocketServer`. There are differences, however. At the beginning of the page, we include a style sheet and the JQuery library.

The JQuery library invokes the method function `init()` when the page is loaded into the browser. The method saves the reference of two div layers into a couple of variables: `messagesDiv` and `outputDiv`. It then proceeds to invoke the `openWebSocket()` function.

The function `openWebSocket()` creates a brand new WebSocket in JavaScript, and registers a set of event handler methods.

The workhorse of the application is the `onMessage()` function, which breaks up the text string from the remote chat server application. The function calls the JavaScript `String.split()` function to tokenize the incoming text string. The function writes the text to the `messagesDiv` using the helper function `writeToScreen()`. The style of message is controlled by the reply code received from the server; the function expects a `MESSAGE_REPLY` or an `ERROR_REPLY`.

JQuery applications are wired initially through the `ready()` closure function.

The chat web application has an HTML text field and two buttons for the user to enter a username and then join the chat room and also to leave it. The page uses JQuery to bind the button press event to methods `login()` and `logout()`. These methods create the encoded text messages with the values from the elements on the page and then send a text message down the open WebSocket.

If the user joins the chat room successfully, we disable the username text field. If the user leaves the chat room, then we enable the username text field again. This logic prevents the user changing the login username inside the web application.

In order to participate in a chat room, the web application has another text field and a dedicated div layer messages for the broadcasts. The text field with the ID `messageText` is bound to a key press event handler, which is a JavaScript closure. Only when the key press is the return key (the key code 13), will a message from the user be sent to the chat server.

JQuery has nice animation features and particularly the functions `writeToScreen()` and `protocolMessage()` make use of the automatic scrolling to the end of the content for each of the respective div layers.

This completes the chat server description and example. The file for the cascading style sheet can be found in the book's accompanying source code bundle.

Asynchronous operations

There is a big problem with chat room examples, which we have seen. It does not scale completely for a large number of users. The issues are on the server side.

The broadcast part of the `ChatRoom` currently uses synchronous response. In order to truly scale, we should make use of the `javax.websocket.RemoteEndpoint.Async`. Implementing the logic for the `Async` interface and the `javax.websocket.SendHandler` provides better asynchronous behaviour.

There is also an issue of ordering of messages in asynchronous communications. Robbie Williams, the northern Englishman, pop singer summarizes this superbly with lyrics such as *"Before I arrive, I can see myself leaving"*. For a chat application, it is very important that any user's messages are broadcast to other users in order that they are sent.

Java has multiple threads and normally invoking separate unmanaged threads in a Java EE application is anti-pattern, because the application server (or web container) has no means of controlling such threads. A managed server is not responsible for threads that it did not directly create.

Client-side Java WebSockets

The Java WebSocket API also allows developers to write client endpoints. They can be easily defined with annotation and of course with more difficulty by programming against the configuration API.

The annotation `@javax.websock.ClientEndpoint` denotes a client specific WebSocket endpoint.

Here is the code for a sample client WebSocket:

```java
package je7hb.websocket.basic;
import javax.websocket.ClientEndpoint;
import javax.websocket.OnMessage;
import javax.websocket.Session;

@ClientEndpoint
public class ClientEchoEndpoint {

  @OnMessage
  public void messageReceived( Session session, String text ) {
    System.out.printf("Message server text: %s\n", text);
  }
}
```

The client `ClientEchoEndpoint` is defined as an annotated WebSocket endpoint. The implementation will register this class as a WebSocket event handler and when messages are sent to this connection the implementation will invoke the life-cycle event handler `messageReceived()`. The method `messageReceived()` is annotated with `@OnMessage`.

@ClientEndpoint

Let's look at the annotations in detail; here is the table of attributes for the annotation `@javax.websocket.ClientEndpoint`.

Attribute	Type	Description	Default Value
subProtocols	String []	Defines an ordered array of WebSocket protocols that this client supports.	None
decoders	Decoder[]	Specifies an ordered array of encoder classes this client will use.	None
decoders	Encoder[]	Specifies an ordered array of encoder classes that the client will use.	None
configurator	Class<? Extends ClientEndPoint-Configurator>	Defines a custom configurator that the developer would like to use to configure a logical client endpoint instance.	ClientEndpoint-Configurator.class

Annotated client example

A WebSocket client is useful for publish and subscribe clients, where the client makes a connection to the server and then changes its mode of operation to that of mostly reading data from the server endpoint. Real-time data can be information about products, inventory updates, any row change in a database, or any data that requires notification.

We will use a streaming service that wraps a single price as an example. We will create an annotated `@ClientEndpoint`.

```
@ClientEndpoint
public class ClientPriceReaderEndpoint {

  @OnOpen
  public void openRemoteConnection( Session session) {
    System.out.printf(
```

```
            "%s.openRemoteConnection( session = [%s], ",
            getClass().getSimpleName(), session);
    }

    @OnMessage
    public void messageReceived( Session session, String text ) {
        System.out.printf(">>>> RECEIVED text : %s\n", text);
    }

    @OnClose
    public void closeRemote(CloseReason reason, Session session) {
        System.out.printf(
            "%s.closeRemote() session = [%s], reason=%s",
            getClass().getSimpleName(), session, reason);
    }

}
```

We annotate this type ClientPriceReaderEndpoint as @ClientEndPoint, which means it is able to receive messages. This endpoint has similar life-cycle methods @OnMessage, for a message that is received and @OnOpen for when a remote connection is established. With @OnClose annotated method, in particular, note that you can find out why the connection was closed with the CloseReason parameter.

You may wonder what is the difference between a @ClientEndPoint and a @ServerEndPoint, especially since we have been told that HTML5 WebSocket is the peer-to-peer connections? A client-side connection is not made available to the URI space of the web server. In other words, this is a Java implementation design feature in that client-side WebSockets do not have URIs.

A client needs a WebSocket server endpoint to connect to, so let's examine a server-side one that continuously updates a single price:

```
package je7hb.websocket.basic;
import javax.enterprise.concurrent.*;
import javax.enterprise.context.ApplicationScoped;
import javax.websocket.*;
import javax.websocket.server.ServerEndpoint;
/* ... */

@ApplicationScoped
@ServerEndpoint("/streamingPrice")
```

```java
public class StreamingPriceWebSocketServer {
  @Resource(name = "concurrent/ScheduledTasksExecutor")
  ManagedScheduledExecutorService executorService;
private Object lock = new Object();
  private BigDecimal price = new BigDecimal("1000.0");
  private BigDecimal unitPrice = new BigDecimal("0.01");

  @OnOpen
  public void openRemoteConnection( final Session session) {
    executorService.scheduleAtFixedRate(new Runnable() {
      @Override
      public void run() {
        try {
          session.getBasicRemote()
            .sendText("PRICE = " + price);
          synchronized (lock) {
            if (Math.random() < 0.5) {
              price = price.subtract(unitPrice);
            } else {
              price = price.add(unitPrice);
            }
          }
        } catch (IOException e) {
          e.printStackTrace(System.err);
        }
      }
    }, 500, 500, MILLISECONDS);
  }
}
```

This type `StreamingPriceWebSocketServer` is a server-side endpoint, because it is annotated with `@ServerEndpoint` and it occupies the URI space of `/streamingPrice` after the web context path. For demonstration purposes only, we cheat here by taking advantage of the `@OnOpen` lifecycle to create a scheduled managed task. You can read about Managed Executors in *Appendix D, Java EE 7 Assorted Topics*. Essentially, the managed task, the anonymous inner class `Runnable` is executed every 500 milliseconds with an initial delay of 500 milliseconds.

The managed task has a reference to the incoming `Session` instance. It retrieves a `BasicRemote` in order to send update text messages about the price. We use a random generator to move the price up or down by a unit, which happens inside a synchronization block. The managed task sends the latest price update to the peer remote WebSocket. The task ends afterwards and the `ManagedScheduledExecutorService` will invoke a new task at the next period.

Advanced readers will know that there are a couple of issues with this demonstration code. What happens to the concurrent managed task when the peer WebSocket closes or the network is broken? How does this implementation scale with multiple peers?

 Whenever you acquire a resource, ensure that you release it. Whenever you spawn a managed task, also code the means to halt it gracefully. Failure to enforce this advice could be ruinous in the long-term running of your application.

In the book's source code, there is an embedded runner that demonstrates Java client-side WebSocket. A standalone application needs to tell the WebSocket framework that a client endpoint has a connection to a remote server. Here is how this is done:

```
WebSocketContainer container =
   ContainerProvider.getWebSocketContainer();
container.connectToServer(ClientPriceReaderEndpoint.class,
   new URI("ws://localhost:8080/mywebapp/streamingPrice"));
```

We retrieve a `javax.websocket.WebSocketContainer` from the **ContainerProvider**. The container is the application view of the Java WebSocket implementation. This service provider interface has a key method `connectToServer`, which registers an `Endpoint` with the container. The client endpoint is associated with the remote URI.

The book's source code also deploys an example JSP page. Point your browser to `http://localhost:8080/mywebapp/index.jsp` after launching the embedded runner.

Remote endpoints

Any Java WebSocket can send a message to the peer by taking a `Session` instance and retrieving a `RemoteEndpoint` reference.

```
RemoteEndpoint.Basic remote = session.getBasicRemote();
remote.sendText("This is it!");
```

This code is valid for client and server-side web sockets. The `RemoteEndpoint.Basic` is a representation of the peer. The `RemoteEndpoint.Async` is the interface for asynchronous communications. The developer cannot only send text messages, but they can also write binary messages and for the more advanced Ping and Pong messages.

Programmatic Java WebSocket

The Java WebSocket specification also defines a programmatic Java interface for connections. Without annotation, a POJO has to extend the abstract class `javax.websocket.Endpoint` and write the implementation methods: `onOpen()`, `onClose()` and `onError()`.

Here is an implementation of the echo WebSocket from earlier:

```java
public class EchoProgramServerEndpoint extends Endpoint {
  public void onOpen( final Session session,
          EndpointConfig config) {

    session.addMessageHandler(
      new MessageHandler.Whole<String>() {
      @Override
      public void onMessage(String message) {
        System.out.printf(
          "Received message=%s\n", message);
        try {
          session.getRemoteBasic()
            .sendText("ECHO "+message);
        }
        catch (Exception e) { }
      }
    });

  }

  public void onClose(Session session,
          CloseReason closeReason) {
    /* ... */
  }

  public void onError(Session session,
          Throwable throwable) {
    /* ... */
  }
}
```

In the `onOpen()` method inside the `EchoProgramServerEndpoint`, we register a `MessageHandler` in order to receive messages from remote peers. A `MessageHandler` has two sub interfaces: `Whole` or `Partial`. The `Whole` interface is designed for applications that want to consume entire messages as they arrive. The `Partial` interface is designed for applications that consume partial messages.

The anonymous message handler in `EchoProgramServerEndpoint` accepts a String text message from the remote peer. It then sends the echo message back to the peer with the captured `Session` instance from the `onOpen` method parameter.

Encoders and decoders

Java WebSocket has the capability to interpret message types beyond the standard `java.lang.String`. The way it works is through the registration of encoders and decoders on the endpoint.

Let's review our chat server application again. Instead of using hard corded String on the Java, for the actual commands we can elect to use Java enumerations. This is the replacement code:

```java
public enum ChatCommand {
  LOGIN("Login"), LOGOUT("Logout"), SEND("Send"),
  RECEIVE("Receive"), UPDATE("Update");

  private String text;

  ChatCommand( String text) { this.text = text; }

  public static ChatCommand convert( String str) {
    if ( str != null ) {
      for ( ChatCommand item: values() ) {
        if (item.text.equalsIgnoreCase(str)) {
          return item;
        }
      }
    }
    return null;
  }

  public String asText() { return text; }
}
```

The `ChatCommand` is a Java `enum` that accepts a text parameter that corresponds to the JavaScript/HTML5 front end. The method `convert()` attempts to parse a case insensitive string in a `ChatCommand`. The method `asText()` returns the text. We use both of these methods in the encoder and decoder types.

We now require a new server endpoint with the registration of encoders and decoders:

```
@ServerEndpoint(value="/chatserver",
    encoders = ChatCommandEncoder.class,
    decoders = ChatCommandDecoder.class)
public class ChatServerEndpoint {
  /* ... */
}
```

The new `ChatServerEndpoint` now informs the WebSocket container so that it accepts two types: `ChatCommandEncoder` and `ChatCommandDecoder`. What do these types actually look like? Actually they are sub interface implementations of the `javax.websocket.Encoder` and `javax.websocket.Decoder`. The sub interface `Encoder.Text` is used for String text representations. Here is the starting implementation for an encoder:

```
import javax.websocket.*;

public class ChatCommandEncoder
implements Encoder.Text<ChatCommand> {
  @Override
  public String encode(ChatCommand cmd) {
    return cmd.asText();
  }

  @Override
  public void init(EndpointConfig config) { }

  @Override
  public void destroy() { }
}
```

The `ChatCommandEncoder` is a generic sub type of `Encoder.Text` interface and the most important method is `encode()`, which simply encodes the Java enumeration as a text String. The function for the encoder is to translate the Java type to the WebSocket message type.

An encoder `init()` is called from the WebSocket container when the web application starts up. The `EndpointConfig` allows advanced developer to customize the encoder's behavior around the configuration. The container will also call the encoder's `destroy()` method when the web application gracefully shuts down.

Let's inspect the decoder implementation, which is relatively straightforward too:

```java
import javax.websocket.*;

public class ChatCommandDecoder
   implements Decoder.Text<ChatCommand> {
   @Override
   public ChatCommand decode(String s) throws DecodeException {
     ChatCommand value = ChatCommand.convert(s);
     if ( value == null)
       throw new DecodeException(s, "Cannot decode text");
     return value;
   }

   @Override
   public boolean willDecode(String s) {
     return ChatCommand.convert(s) != null;
   }

   @Override
   public void init(EndpointConfig config) { }

   @Override
   public void destroy() { }
}
```

The `ChatCommandDecoder` is a type of generic sub interface of `Decoder.Text`. The method `willDecode()` allows the Java WebSocket container to find out if String can be converted. Here we make use of the `ChatCommand.convert()` method from earlier. The `decode()` method performs the parsing of the input text. If the String cannot be converted, we throw a `DecodeException`, rather than just returning a null reference pointer. Finally, the `Decoder` types have the same life-cycle methods.

So far we have seen text message based encoders and decoders. There are other types available in Java WebSocket:

- The sub interfaces `Encoder.TextStream` and `Decoder.TextStream` are designed for sending and receiving Java objects to a character stream.
- The sub interfaces `Encoder.Binary` and `Decoder.Binary` are designed for serializing and de-serializing Java objects to and from binary messages.
- The sub interfaces `Encoder.BinaryStream` and `Decoder.BinaryStream` are designed for writing and reading Java objects to a binary stream.

Summary

We have seen that WebSocket can dramatically reduce unnecessary network traffic and save on latency, and we know that WebSocket can scale to higher in comparison to previous solutions such as long-polling AJAX requests and COMET.

The Java WebSocket API is a new powerful technical enabler for building scalable web applications, especially on the JVM. This new standard, delivered as part of the Java EE 7 platform, allows simple POJOs to be annotated as a server endpoint with `@ServerEndpoint`, or as a client endpoint with `@ClientEndpoint`.

The API has event handling in Java that mirrors the actual design in JavaScript. A WebSocket can fire an open, close, message received, and error event. These can be intercepted with annotations, namely `@OnOpen`, `@OnClose`, `@OnMessage`, and `@OnError`.

Java WebSocket endpoints can participate in **Context and Dependency Injection (CDI)** and EJB containers. A WebSocket conversation is sustained by recording the session instance in a dependency bean.

When we retrieve the remote endpoint WebSocket, we can write a synchronous message back to the client or we can elect to write an asynchronous message. The key to this important decision lies squarely in the developer, writing code to the sub interfaces `RemoteEndpoint.Basic` and `RemoteEndpoint.Async`.

We learned that the endpoints could have encoder and decoders to handle messages as Java objects. There is also a programmatic equivalent API that complements declarative WebSocket annotations.

In the next chapter, we will rummage around Java RESTful services, including the all-new powerful client-side API.

8
RESTful Services JAX-RS 2.0

Roy T. Fielding, Creator of REST Style Architecture said "When I say hypertext, I mean the simultaneous presentation of information and controls such that the information becomes the affordance through which the user (or automation) obtains choices and selects actions."

This chapter covers the Java API for RESTful services otherwise abbreviated to JAX-RS. It was the year, 2000, when *Roy Fielding* published his PhD thesis entitled **Representational State Transfer: an Architecture Style**. Since its publication over the past decade there has been a rapid growth of interest, applications, and implementations of REST style interfaces and application.

Representational State Transfer

Representational State Transfer (REST) is a style of information application architecture that aligns the distributed applications to the HTTP request and response protocols, in particular matching Hypermedia to the HTTP request methods and **Uniform Resource Identifiers** (**URI**).

Hypermedia is the term that describes the ability of a system to deliver self-referential content, where related contextual links point to downloadable or streamable digital media, such as photographs, movies, documents, and other data. Modern systems, especially web applications, demonstrate through display of text that a certain fragment of text is a link to the media.

Hypermedia is the logical extension of the term hypertext, which is a text that contains embedded references to other text. These embedded references are called links, and they immediately transfer the user to the other text when they are invoked. Hypermedia is a property of media, including hypertext, to immediately link other media and text.

In HTML, the anchor tag `<a>` accepts a `href` attribute, the so-called hyperlink parameter.

The World Wide Web is built on the HTTP standards, Versions 1.0 and 1.1, which define specific enumerations to retrieve data from a web resource. These operations, sometimes called Web Methods, are `GET`, `POST`, `PUT`, and `DELETE`. Representational State Transfer also reuses these operations to form semantic interface to a URI.

Representational State Transfer, then, is both a style and architecture for building network enabled distributed applications. It is governed by the following constraints:

- **Client/Server**: A REST application encourages the architectural robust principle of separation of concerns by dividing the solution into clients and servers. A standalone, therefore, cannot be a RESTful application. This constraint ensures the distributed nature of RESTful applications over the network.

- **Stateless:** A REST application exhibits stateless communication. Clients cannot and should not take advantage of any stored context information in the server and therefore the full data of each request must be sent to the server for processing.

- **Cache:** A REST application is able to declare which data is cacheable or not cacheable. This constraint allows the architect to set the performance level for the solution, in other words, a trade-off. Caching data to the web resource, allows the business to achieve a sense of latency, scalability, and availability. The counter point to improved performance through caching data is the issue of expiration of the cache at the correct time and sequence, when do we delete stale data? The cache constraint also permits successful implementation providers to develop optimal frameworks and servers.

- **Uniform Interface:** A REST application emphasizes and maintains a unique identifier for each component and there are a set of protocols for accessing data. The constraint allows general interaction to any REST component and therefore anyone or anything can manipulate a REST component to access data. The drawback is the Uniform Interface may be suboptimal in ease-of-use and cognitive load to directly provide a data structure and remote procedure function call.

- **Layered Style:** A REST application can be composed of functional processing layers in order to simplify complex flows of data between clients and servers. Layered style constraint permits modularization of function with the data and in itself is another sufficient example of separation of concerns. The layered style is an approach that benefits load-balancing servers, caching content, and scalability.
- **Code-on-Demand**: A REST application can optimally supply downloadable code on demand for the client to execute. The code could be the byte-codes from the JVM, such as a Java Applet, or JavaFX WebStart application, or it could be a JavaScript code with say JSON data. Downloadable code is definitely a clear security risk that means that the solution architect must assume responsibility of sandboxing Java classes, profiling data, and applying certificate signing in all instances. Therefore, code-on-demand, is a disadvantage in a public domain service, and this constraint in REST application is only seen inside the firewalls of corporations.

In terms of the Java platform, the Java EE standard covers REST applications through the specification JAX-RS and this chapter covers Version 2.0.

JAX-RS 2.0 features

For Java EE 7, the JAX-RS 2.0 specification has the following new features:

- Client-side API for invoking RESTful server-side remote endpoint
- Support for Hypermedia linkage
- Tighter integration with the Bean Validation framework (See *Chapter 10, Bean Validation*)
- Asynchronous API for both server and client-side invocations
- Container filters on the server side for processing incoming requests and outbound responses
- Client filter on the client side for processing outgoing request and incoming responses
- Reader and writer interceptors to handle specific content types

Architectural style

The REST style is simply a Uniform Resource Identifier and the application of the HTTP request methods, which invokes resources that generate a HTTP response. Although Fielding, himself, says that REST does not necessarily require the HTTP communication as a networker layer, and the style of architecture can be built on any other network protocol.

Let's look at those methods again with a fictional URL (http://fizzbuzz.com/)

Method	Description
POST	A REST style application creates or inserts an entity with the supplied data. The client can assume new data has been inserted into the underlying backend database and the server returns a new URI to reference the data.
PUT	A REST style application replaces the entity into the database with the supplied data.
GET	A REST style application retrieves the entity associated with the URI, and it can be a collection of URI representing entities or it can be the actual properties of the entity
DELETE	A REST style application deletes the entity associated with the URI from the backend database.

The user should note that PUT and DELETE are idempotent operations, meaning they can be repeated endlessly and the result is the same in steady state conditions.

The GET operation is a safe operation; it has no side effects to the server-side data.

REST style for collections of entities

Let's take a real example with the URL `http://fizzbuzz.com/resources/`, which represents the URI of a collection of resources. Resources could be anything, such as books, products, or cast iron widgets.

Method	Description
GET	Retrieves the collection entities by URI under the link `http://fizzbuzz.com/resources` and they may include other more data.
POST	Creates a new entity in the collection under the URI `http://fizzbuzz.com/resources`. The URI is automatically assigned and returned by this service call, which could be something like `http://fizzbuzz.com/resources/WKT54321`.
PUT	Replaces the entire collection of entities under the URI `http://fizzbuzz.com/resources`.
DELETE	Deletes the entire collection of entities under the URI `http://fizzbuzz.com/resources`.

As a reminder, a URI is a series of characters that identifies a particular resource on the World Wide Web. A URI, then, allows different clients to uniquely identify a resource on the web, or a representation. A URI is combination of a **Uniform Resource Name** (**URN**) and a **Uniform Resource Locator** (**URL**). You can think of a URN like a person's name, as way of naming an individual and a URL is similar to a person's home address, which is the way to go and visit them sometime.

In the modern world, non-technical people are accustomed to desktop web browsing as URL. However, the web URL is a special case of a generalized URI.

A diagram that illustrates HTML5 RESTful communication between a JAX RS 2.0 client and server, is as follows:

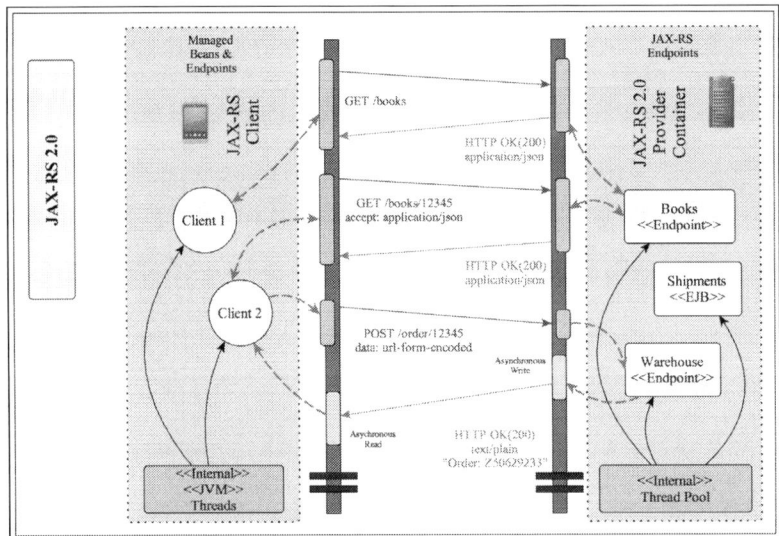

REST style for single entities

Assuming we have a URI reference to a single entity like `http://fizzbuzz.com/resources/WKT54321`.

Method	Description
GET	Retrieves the entity with reference to URI under the link `http://fizzbuzz.com/resources/WKT54321`.
POST	Creates a new sub entity under the URI `http://fizzbuzz.com/resources/WKT54321`. There is a subtle difference here, as this call does something else. It is not often used, except to create Master-Detail records. The URI of the subentity is automatically assigned and returned by this service call, which could be something like `http://fizzbuzz.com/resources/WKT54321/D1023`
PUT	Replaces the referenced entity's entire collection with the URI `http://fizzbuzz.com/resources/WKT54321`. If the entity does not exist then the service creates it.
DELETE	Deletes the entity under the URI references `http://fizzbuzz.com/resources/WKT54321`.

Now that we understand the REST style we can move on to the JAX-RS API properly.

>  **Consider carefully your REST hierarchy of resources**
>
> The key to build a REST application is to target the users of the application instead of blindly converting the business domain into an exposed middleware. Does the user need the whole detail of every object and responsibility in the application? On the other hand is the design not spreading enough information for the intended audience to do their work?

Servlet mapping

In order to enable JAX-RS in a Java EE application the developer must set up the configuration in the web deployment descriptor file. JAX-RS requires a specific servlet mapping to be enabled, which triggers the provider to search for annotated classes.

The standard API for JAX-RS lies in the Java package `javax.ws.rs` and in its subpackages. Interestingly, the Java API for REST style interfaces sits underneath the Java Web Services package `javax.ws`.

For your web applications, you must configure a Java servlet with just fully qualified name of the class `javax.ws.rs.core.Application`. The Servlet must be mapped to a root URL pattern in order to intercept REST style requests.

The following is an example code of such a configuration:

```xml
<?xml version="1.0" encoding="UTF-8"?>
<web-app xmlns="http://xmlns.jcp.org/xml/ns/javaee"
  xmlns:xsi="http://www.w3.org/2001/XMLSchema-instance"
  xsi:schemaLocation="http://xmlns.jcp.org/xml/ns/javaee
  http://xmlns.jcp.org/xml/ns/javaee/web-app_3_1.xsd"
  version="3.1"
  metadata-complete="false">
  <display-name>JavaEE Handbook 7 JAX RS Basic
   </display-name>
  <servlet>
    <servlet-name>javax.ws.rs.core.Application
    </servlet-name>
    <load-on-startup>1</load-on-startup>
  </servlet>
  <servlet-mapping>
    <servlet-name>javax.ws.rs.core.Application
    </servlet-name>
```

```
    <url-pattern>/rest/*</url-pattern>
  </servlet-mapping>
</web-app>
```

In the web deployment descriptor we just saw, only the servlet name is defined, `javax.ws.rs.core.Application`. Do not define the servlet class. The second step maps the URL pattern to the REST endpoint path. In this example, any URL that matches the simplified Glob pattern `/rest/*` is mapped. This is known as the application path.

A JAX-RS application is normally packaged up as a WAR file and deployed to a Java EE application server or a servlet container that conforms to the Web Profile. The application classes are stored in the `/WEB-INF/classes` and required libraries are found under `/WEB-INF/lib` folder. Therefore, JAX-RS applications share the consistency of configurations as servlet applications.

The JAX-RS specification does recommend, but does not enforce, that conformant providers follow the general principles of Servlet 3.0 plug-ability and discoverability of REST style endpoints. Discoverability is achieved in the recommendation through class scanning of the WAR file, and it is up to the provider to make this feature available.

An application can create a subclass of the `javax.ws.rs.core.Application` class. The Application class is a concrete class and looks like the following code:

```
public class Application {
  public Application() { /* ... */ }
  public java.util.Set<Class<?>> getClasses() {
    /* ... */ }
  public java.util.Set<Object> getSingletons() {
    /* ... */ }
  public java.util.Map<String,Object> getProperties() {
    /* ... */ }
}
```

Implementing a custom `Application` subclass is a special case of providing maximum control of RESTful services for your business application. The developer must provide a set collection of classes that represent JAX-RS end points. The engineer must supply a list of Singleton object, if any, and do something useful with the properties.

The default implementation of `javax.ws.rs.core.Application` and the methods `getClasses()` and `getSingletons()` return empty sets. The `getProperties()` method returns an empty map collection. By returning empty sets, the provider assumes that all relevant JAX-RS resource and provider classes that are scanned and found will be added to the JAX-RS application.

Majority of the time, I suspect, you, the developer will want to rely on annotations to specify the REST end points and there are Servlet Context listeners and Servlet Filters to configure application wide behavior, for example the startup sequence of a web application.

So how can we register our own custom `Application` subclass? The answer is just subclass the core class with your own class.

The following code explains what we just read:

```
package com.fizbuzz.services;

@javax.ws.rs.ApplicationPath("rest")
public class GreatApp extends javax.ws.rs.core.Application {
   // Do your custom thing here
}
```

In the custom `GreatApp` class, you can now configure logic for initialization. Note the use of `@ApplicationPath` annotation to configure the REST style URL. You still have to associate your custom `Application` subclass into the web deployment descriptor with a XML Servlet name definition.

> **Remember the Application Configuration**
>
> A very common error for first time JAX-RS developers is to forget that the web deployment descriptor really requires a servlet mapping to a `javax.ws.js.core.Application` type.

Now that we know how to initialize a JAX-RS application, let us dig deeper and look at the defining REST style endpoints.

Mapping JAX-RS resources

JAX-RS resources are configured through the resource path, which suffixes the application path. Here is the constitution of the URL.

```
http://<hostname>:<port>/<web_context>/<application_path>/<resource_path>
```

The `<hostname>` is the host name of the server. The `<port>` refers to the port number, which is optional and the default port is 80. The `<web_context>` is the Servlet context, which is the context for the deployed web application. The `<application_path>` is the configuration URI pattern as specified in the web deployment descriptor `@ApplicationPath` or the Servlet configuration of Application type. The `<resource_path>` is the resource path to REST style resource.

The final fragment `<resource_path>` defines the URL pattern that maps a REST style resource. The resource path is configured by annotation `javax.ws.rs.Path`.

Test-Driven Development with JAX-RS

Let us write a unit test to verify the simplest JAX-RS service. It follows a REST style resource around a list of books. There are only four books in this endpoint and the only thing the user/client can do at the start is to access the list of books by author and title. The client invokes the REST style endpoint, otherwise known as a resource with an HTTP `GET` request.

The following is the code for the class `RestfulBookService`:

```java
package je7hb.jaxrs.basic;
import javax.annotation.*;
import javax.ws.rs.*;
import java.util.*;

@Path("/books")
public class RestfulBookService {
  private List<Book> products = Arrays.asList(
    new Book("Sir Arthur Dolan Coyle",
      "Sherlock Holmes and the Hounds of the Baskervilles"),
    new Book("Dan Brown", "Da Vinci Code"),
    new Book("Charles Dickens", "Great Expectations"),
    new Book("Robert Louis Stevenson", "Treasure Island"));

  @GET
  @Produces("text/plain")
```

```java
    public String getList() {
      StringBuffer buf = new StringBuffer();
      for (Book b: products) {
        buf.append(b.title); buf.append('\n'); }
      return buf.toString();
    }

    @PostConstruct
    public void acquireResource() { /* ... */ }
    @PreDestroy
    public void releaseResource() { /* ... */ }

    static class Book {
      public final String author;
      public final String title;
      Book(String author, String title) {
        this.author = author;
        this.title = title;
      }
    }
}
```

The annotation @javax.ws.rs.Path declares the class as a REST style end-point for a resource. The @Path annotation is assigned to the class itself. The path argument defines the relative URL pattern for this resource, namely /books.

The method getList() is the interesting one. It is annotated with both @javax.ws.rs.GET and @javax.ws.rs.Produces.

The @GET is one of the six annotations that conform to the HTTP web request methods. It indicates that the method is associated with HTTP GET protocol request.

The @Produces annotation indicates the MIME content that this resource will generate. In this example, the MIME content is text/plain.

The other methods on the resource bring CDI into the picture. In the example, we are injecting post construction and pre destruction methods into the bean.

This is the only class that we require for a simple REST style application from the server side. With an invoking of the web resource with a HTTP GET Request like http://localhost:8080/mywebapp/rest/books we should get a plain text output with list of titles like the following:

```
Sherlock Holmes and the Hounds of the Baskervilles
Da Vinci Code
Great Expectations
Treasure Island
```

RESTful Services JAX-RS 2.0

So do we test this REST style interface then? We could use **Arquillian Framework** directly, but this means our tests have to be built specifically in a project and it complicates the build process. Arquillian uses another open source project in the JBoss repository called **ShrinkWrap**. The framework allows the construction of various types of virtual Java archives in a programmatic fashion. We use ShrinkWrap just to build a Web Archive, and the code is really quite straightforward, because we have already seen it in previous chapters.

Let's look at the unit test class `RestfulBookServiceTest` in the following code:

```
package je7hb.jaxrs.basic;
// import omitted

public class RestfulBookServiceTest {
  @Test
  public void shouldAssembleAndRetrieveBookList()
  throws Exception {
    WebArchive webArchive =
      ShrinkWrap.create(WebArchive.class, "test.war")
      .addClasses(RestfulBookService.class)
      .setWebXML(
        new File("src/main/webapp/WEB-INF/web.xml"))
      .addAsWebInfResource(
         EmptyAsset.INSTANCE, "beans.xml");
    File warFile = new File(webArchive.getName());
    new ZipExporterImpl(webArchive)
      .exportTo(warFile, true);
    SimpleEmbeddedRunner runner =
      SimpleEmbeddedRunner.launchDeployWarFile(
        warFile, "mywebapp", 8080);
    try {
      URL url = new URL(
        "http://localhost:8080/mywebapp/rest/books");
      InputStream inputStream = url.openStream();
      BufferedReader reader = new BufferedReader(
        new InputStreamReader(inputStream));
      List<String> lines = new ArrayList<>();
      String text = null;
      int count=0;
      while ( ( text = reader.readLine()) != null ) {
        lines.add(text);
        ++count;
        System.out.printf("**** OUTPUT **** 
           text[%d] = %s\n", count, text );
      }
```

```
        assertFalse( lines.isEmpty() );
        assertEquals("Sherlock Holmes and the Hounds
          of the Baskervilles", lines.get(0));
        assertEquals("Da Vinci Code", lines.get(1));
        assertEquals("Great Expectations", lines.get(2));
        assertEquals( "Treasure Island", lines.get(3) );
    }
    finally {
      runner.stop();
    }
  }
}
```

In the unit test method, `shouldAssembleAndRetrieveBookList()`, we first assemble a virtual web archive with an explicit name `test.war`. The WAR file contains the `RestfulBookService` services, the Web deployment descriptor file `web.xml` and an empty `beans.xml` file, which if you remember is only there to trigger the CDI container into life for this web application.

With the virtual web archive, we export the WAR as a physical file with the utility `ZipExporterImpl` class from ShinkWrap library, which creates the file `test.war` in the project root folder.

Next, we fire up the `SimpleEmbeddedRunner` utility that is part of the book's appendix. It deploys the web archive to an embedded GlassFish container. Essentially, this is the boilerplate to get to deliver a test result.

We, then, get to the heart of the test itself; we construct a URL to invoke the REST style endpoint, which is `http://localhost:8080/mywebapp/rest/books`. We read the output from the service endpoint with Java standard I/O line by line into a list collection of Strings. Once we have a list of collections, then we assert each line against the expected output from the rest style service.

Because we acquired an expensive resource, like an embedded Glassfish container, we are careful to release it, which is the reason, why we surround critical code with a try-finally block statement. When the execution comes to end of test method, we ensure the embedded GlassFish container is shut down.

JAX-RS server-side endpoints

We have looked at a simple `GET` request on a JAX-RS simple resource. In order to create a useful business application, we need the other web request methods, namely `POST`, `PUT`, and `DELETE`.

JAX-RS common server annotation

JAX-RS defines annotations for defining server side REST style endpoint, which are found in the Java package `javax.ws.rs`.

The following is a table of these annotations:

Annotation	Description
`@Path`	Defines the relative URI path for the REST style Java class and configures where it is installed and mapped.
`@GET`	Defines a method on the Java class REST style resource to accept HTTP GET requests.
`@POST`	Defines a method on the Java class REST style resource to accept HTTP POST requests.
`@PUT`	Defines a method on the Java class REST style resource to accept HTTP PUT requests.
`@DELETE`	Defines a method on the Java class REST style resource to accept HTTP DELETE requests.
`@HEAD`	Defines a method on the Java class REST style resource to accept HTTP HEAD requests.
`@TRACE`	Defines a method on the Java class REST style resource to accept HTTP TRACE requests.
`@PathParam`	Defines a URI fragment parameter that permits the developer to extract from the REST request into the resource class. URI path parameters are extracted from the request URI, and the parameter name must match information found in the URI path template variables specified in the `@Path` class-level annotation.
`@QueryParam`	Defines a (CGI-style) query parameter that permits the developer to extract from the REST request.
`@Consumes`	Specifies MIME media representations that the REST style consumes from the client. Typically, this is useful for a REST style uploading application, which only accepts a certain media type of document.
`@Produces`	Specifies the MIME media representation that the REST style endpoint produces for the client.
`@Provider`	Specifies extra resource information that is useful for extending the capabilities of the JAX-RS runtime with custom features for your application. This annotation can be seen as a sort of factory object or virtual constructor for building filters, interceptors, and dynamic features.

Obviously, a Java method can only accept one of the HTTP request annotations. It is illegal, for instance, to annotate a single method with @GET and @POST; and the JAX-RS provider will generate an error.

Defining JAX-RS resources

Let's look at a more realistic example of JAX-RS service endpoint. We will develop a REST style endpoint that can accept a registered set of users. The service allows a client to register a user with a log-in name, first and last name, and a secret code. Admittedly, this service is contrived, however this shows how to implement a JAX-RS service completely and we will see how to test it thoroughly. The following table shows the REST style URI for the service:

URI	Purpose
`<mywebapp>/rest/users`	Refers to list of registered users
`<mywebapp>/rest/users/pilgrimp`	Refers to a specific user
`<mywebapp>/rest/users/goslingj`	Refers to another specific user

Where `<mywebapp>` is the placeholder for URL `http://localhost/mywebapp/`

The following code shows our data value class, `User`:

```
package je7hb.jaxrs.basic;

public final class User implements Comparable<User> {
  private final String loginName, firstName, lastName,
    secretName;

  public User(String loginName, String firstName,
    String lastName, int secretCode) {
    this.loginName = loginName;
    this.firstName = firstName;
    this.lastName = lastName;
    this.secretCode = secretCode;
  }

  public String getLoginName() { return loginName; }
  public String getFirstName() { return firstName; }
  public String getLastName() { return lastName; }
  public int getSecretCode() { return secretCode; }
```

```java
  @Override
  public int compareTo(User ref) {
    return loginName.compareTo(ref.loginName);
  }

  // hashcode(), equals(), toString() methods omitted
}
```

For storage of the user, we will rely on Singleton EJB, which is called `UserRegistry`. The following code explains it:

```java
package je7hb.jaxrs.basic;
/* ... imports omitted */

@Singleton
@Startup
public class UserRegistry {
  private ConcurrentMap<String,User> registeredUsers
    = new ConcurrentHashMap<>();

  public void addUser( User user ) {
    registeredUsers.put( user.getLoginName(), user );
  }

  public void removeUser( User user ) {
    registeredUsers.remove(user.getLoginName());
  }

  public User findUser( String loginName ) {
    return registeredUsers.get(loginName);
  }

  public List<User> getUsers( ) {
    List<User> users =
      new ArrayList<>(registeredUsers.values());
    Collections.sort(users);
    return users;
  }

  @PostConstruct
  public void postConstruct() { /* ... */ }
  @PreDestroy
  public void preDestroy() {  /* ... */ }
}
```

As a reminder, this is a stateless session EJB, which is annotated with `@Startup`, because we want the bean instance to be immediately available as soon as the web application is deployed. We also annotate the class with `@Singleton` to ensure only the EJB instance is available for the entire application.

Now let's look at the following code of the REST style resource, which is implemented by the class called `RegisteredUserResource`:

```java
package je7hb.jaxrs.basic;
import javax.ejb.*;
import javax.ws.rs.*;

@Path("/users")
@Stateless
public class RegisteredUserResource {
  @EJB
  private UserRegistry userRegistry;

  @GET
  @Produces("text/csv")
  public String listUsers() {
    StringBuilder buf = new StringBuilder();
    for ( User user : userRegistry.getUsers()) {
      buf.append( user.getLoginName()
        +","+user.getFirstName()+",");
      buf.append( user.getLastName()
        +","+user.getSecretCode()+"\n");
    }
    return buf.toString();
  }

  @GET
  @Path("{id}")
  @Produces("text/csv")
  public String getUser( @PathParam("id") String loginName ) {
    User user = userRegistry.findUser(loginName);
    if ( user == null ) {
      return "";
    }
    StringBuilder buf = new StringBuilder();
    buf.append( user.getLoginName()
      +","+user.getFirstName()+",");
```

```java
      buf.append( user.getLastName()
        +","+user.getSecretCode()+"\n");
      return buf.toString();
    }

    @POST
    @Path("{id}")
    public void addUser( @PathParam("id") String loginName,
    @FormParam("firstName") String fname,
    @FormParam("lastName") String lname,
    @FormParam("secretCode") int code )
    {
      User user = new User(loginName,fname,lname,code);
      userRegistry.addUser(user);
    }

    @PUT
    @Path("{id}")
    public void amendUser( @PathParam("id") String loginName,
    @FormParam("firstName") String fname,
    @FormParam("lastName") String lname,
    @FormParam("secretCode") int code )
    {
      User user = userRegistry.findUser(loginName);
      if ( user == null ) {
        throw new UnknownUserException(
          "unknown login name: ["+loginName+"]");
        }
        else {
          User user2 = new User(
            user.getLoginName(), fname, lname, code );
          userRegistry.addUser(user2);
        }
    }

    @DELETE
    @Path("{id}")
    public void deleteUser(
    @PathParam("id") String loginName) {
      User user = userRegistry.findUser(loginName);
      if ( user == null ) {
        throw new UnknownUserException(
          "unknown login name: ["+loginName+"]");
      }
```

```
        else {
          userRegistry.removeUser(user);
        }
      }
    }
}
```

The class implements all of the four HTTP web request methods. It is surprising that the JAX-RS resource, `RegisteredUserResource`, itself is written as a Stateless session EJB. The reason for this is to do with the progression of the initial JAX-RS specification 1.0 predated the Context and Dependency Inject and EJB instance facilities and at the time of writing was not clear JAX-RS 2.0 will work. Nonetheless, the procedure is solid and it is the intention of the standard JavaEE 7 to support JAX-RS, CDI and EJB injection.

The class `RegisteredUserResource` injects the singleton EJB `UserRegistry` and therefore can make use of the store. The class is annotated with the relative REST style URI path/users.

The `listUsers()` method has `@Produces` annotation that is different, `text/csv` stands for comma-separated values, which is a file format supported by popular spreadsheet programs such Microsoft Excel and Libre Office. Hence, this method generates comma-delimited output for each user in the registry.

The method `getUser()` introduces us to URI path variables. Variables are denoted with the braces ({ }). The annotation `@PathParam("{id}")` adds a variable to the current path and permits a method to be extracted from the URL template. This is the way to process a REST style by identifier and the annotation is applied to the method argument. This method attempts to find the User record by log-in name. If it can retrieve the object `getUser()`, it returns a CSV representation otherwise the output is empty text. This method is important for testing the REST resource as we shall see later.

In order to add a new user to the registry, there is `@POST` annotation on the `addUser()` method. Here is a new annotation `@javax.ws.rs.FormParam`, which specifically retrieves HTTP form parameters from the incoming request. They correspond directly with HTML Form submissions. The `@FormParam` requires the name of the form request parameter and we apply them to the method arguments. The JAX-RS implementation injects the form parameters and the identifier variable during invocation of the method. The `addUser()` method simply constructs a new User record and adds it to the registry. There is no side effect and output response rendered for a POST. The JAX-RS implementation will respond with a HTTP Response Code 200 on successful execution of the method.

The method `amendUser()` is almost the same as the `addUser()`, because it uses the same parameters with `@PathParam` and `@FormParm` annotations. The difference is the amendment assuming that a User record already exists in the registry. It saves a new version of the User record into the registry. The amendment is associated with the `@PUT` annotation and associated HTTP PUT requests.

The method `deleteUser()` is the last method and this annotated with the `@Delete` annotation and associated HTTP DELETE requests. This method only requires the path parameter to identifier the specify user to delete.

>  **Prefer to specify the MIME type**
>
> You should seriously consider specifying the media type with `@Produces` for all methods of the REST resource, especially if you are passing multiple MIME types. If you write a custom resource method that can return more than one MIME content type with `ResponseBuilder`, then it is definitely helpful to the client to set media type.

You may be wondering about the custom exception `UnknownUserException`. If an arbitrary exception is raised during the JAX-RS request on the server side, then the client (or user) sees a HTTP Response 500 code (Forbidden). This is probably not the error you want users or developers to see.

The following is the code for the exception class:

```
package je7hb.jaxrs.basic;
import javax.ws.rs.WebApplicationException;
import javax.ws.rs.core.*;

public class UnknownUserException
extends WebApplicationException {
  public UnknownUserException(String message) {
    super( Response.status(
      Response.Status.NOT_FOUND).
    entity(message).type(
      MediaType.TEXT_PLAIN_TYPE).build());
  }
}
```

This custom exception extends the `WebApplicationException` exception. In the constructor, we make use of the JAX-RS Response builder object to generate a **HTTP 404 error (NOT_FOUND)**, add our message string as the entity and set the media type to text/plain MIME content. This is the key to building custom JAX-RS messages, and I hope you will not see many of these error message in your applications.

Testing JAX-RS resources

The obvious way to test a JAX-RS resource, in a clean, concise, and solid way, is to deploy the resource to a container and then have a test harness that invokes each of the endpoints. By running inside a container we can have a high degree of confidence that the final code will run in a production environment.

Let us now look at how to write a test for all of these processes. The following is the code for the unit test `RegisteredUserResourceTest`. Be warned, it is fairly big for now:

```
package je7hb.jaxrs.basic;
/* ... imports omitted */

public class RegisteredUserResourceTest {
  public static final String ROOT_RES_PATH =
    "http://localhost:8080/mywebapp/rest/users";
  public static final String USER_RES_PATH =
    ROOT_RES_PATH+"/pilgrimp";
  private static SimpleEmbeddedRunner runner;

  @BeforeClass
  public static void beforeAllTests() throws Exception {
    WebArchive webArchive =
      ShrinkWrap.create(WebArchive.class, "testusers.war")
    .addClasses(RegisteredUserResource.class,
    /* . . . */     }

  /* ... */

  @Test
  public void shouldAddOneUser() throws Exception {
    Map<String,String> params =
      new HashMap<String,String>() {
        {
        put("firstName",    "Peter");
        put("lastName",     "Pilgrim");
        put("secretCode",   "19802014");
        }
      };

      List<String> output = makePostRequest(
        new URL(USER_RES_PATH), params);
      assertTrue(output.isEmpty());
```

```
        List<String> lines = makeGetRequest(
          new URL(USER_RES_PATH) );
        assertFalse(lines.isEmpty());
        assertEquals("pilgrimp,Peter,Pilgrim,19802014",
          lines.get(0));
    }

   /* ... */
}
```

The class `RegisteredUserResourceTest` is fairly involved and more than that code is devoted to creating the environment for the test. Having said all of that, the test does work.

The first part of the call is the refactoring of the `ShrinkWrap` packaging and the embedded container launch to the JUnit methods `beforeAllTests()` and `afterAllTests()`. These are static methods so that they are only invoked when the class is loaded, just before the series unit test method is executed and after the test has run in the class.

The unit test makes use of a utility class `WebMethodUtils`, which has a series of static methods to make HTTP request method calls to a remote server. The utility class uses the JDK classes, `javax.net.URL`, `javax.net.HttpURLConnection` also standard I/O. (In order to save space, the `WebMethodUtils` class is not shown, but you can access it from the book's website.)

The first test, the method `shouldAddOneUser()`, creates a HTTP POST request of a user with form data. A literal hash map collection is created with name and value pairs to simulate form request data. A HTTP POST request is made to the JAX RS Resource with the form parameters. This is the responsibility of the static call to `makePostRequest()` with the URL `http://localhost:8080/mywebapp/rest/users/pilgrimp`. There should be no output and there is an assertion for empty text. Next, the unit test method makes a call to `makeGetRequest()` with the same URL. We should expect the output from the REST style to be comma delimited as `"pilgrim,Peter,Pilgrim,19802014"`, which of course the actual output matches to. In this way, we validate that information was stored by the JAX-RS service. The following code shows the validation:

```
@Test
public void shouldAmendOneUser() throws Exception {
  shouldAddOneUser();

  Map<String,String> params2 = new HashMap<String,String>(){
    {
      put("firstName",   "Pierre");
      put("lastName",    "Pilgrim");
      put("secretCode",  "87654321");
    }
  };

  List<String> output = makePutRequest(
    new URL(USER_RES_PATH), params2);
  assertTrue(output.isEmpty());
  List<String> lines = makeGetRequest(
    new URL(USER_RES_PATH) );
  assertFalse(lines.isEmpty());
  assertEquals("pilgrimp,Pierre,Pilgrim,87654321",
    lines.get(0));
}
```

The second test method `shouldAmendOneUser()` follows a similar principle and it executes HTTP POST to insert the record followed by a HTTP PUT and then a HTTP GET. The test validates the operation of the PUT method by editing the user record from the client side. In this case, the first name is changed to `Pierre` and the secret code to a different number. The GET request validates the data has been changed by the endpoint. The following code shows what we just read:

```
@Test
public void shouldDeleteOneUser() throws Exception {
  shouldAddOneUser();

  List<String> output = makeDeleteRequest(
    new URL(USER_RES_PATH));
  assertTrue(output.isEmpty());
  List<String> lines = makeGetRequest(
    new URL(USER_RES_PATH) );
  assertTrue(lines.isEmpty());
}
```

The third test method `shouldDeleteOneUser()` creates a HTTP POST method with a user and invokes the HTTP DELETE method. The GET request validates the data has been removed. The output text should be blank.

In the book's source code, you will see the fourth and final test method `shouldAddTwoUsers()` should verify that the JAX-RS Resource can maintain more than one User record. There, we create two different User records with HTTP POST web request. In this test method, we invoke the HTTP GET with the parent URL `http://localhost:8080/mywebapp/rest/users` and we validate the CSV output. The list of users is sorted by the login name, which you can see in the `UserRegistry` class, namely the `getUsers()` method.

Here is a little to the wise, the unit test, although it follows a **Behavioral-Driven Design** pattern, which is nice, is not the best way to achieve the result. We will see later how to achieve better testing with the JAX-RS Client API.

Path URI variables

As we have seen in the previous section, path variables are placeholders inside a URL template that represent a value that changes on the request. Path variables are denoted within brace characters for example, `"/users/{id}"`. A Path variable can be a simple name or it can be a regular expression.

The Path variable as a simple name is defined by combination of alphabetic and numerical characters. In fact, the path variable can be any character apart from spaces, backslash and special terminal characters. The URI variable must match the regular `"[^/]+?"`. For best practice, it is probably best to stick to the Java identifier syntax.

The following is an example of simple variable conventions:

```
@Path("/users/{username47}")
public class ACMEUserResource {
  @GET
  @Produces("text/xml")
  public String getUserList( ) {
    // username is null, so return a list collection
    /* ... */
  }

  @GET
  @Produces("text/xml")
  public String getUser (
    @PathParam("username47") String username ) {
    /* ... */
  }
}
```

Chapter 8

In the example class we just saw, ACMEUserResource is annotated with a path URI template with one variable, which is called username47. There are two methods, namely, getUser() and getUserList(). The getUser() method accepts a single argument, a named path parameter /users/{username47}. JAX-RS will invoke this method if there is a matching URL request such as /users/jamesdean. On the other hand, if the incoming URL request was just defined as /users then JAX-RS, instead, will choose the getUserList() method, because the method does not require a path parameter.

Path variable can also be defined with custom regular expressions to further restrict the characters that can be matched. The following is an example of the same JAX-RS resource, where we restrict the match to lowercase and uppercase alphanumeric and underscore characters.

```
@Path("/users/{username47: [a-zA-Z_] [a-zA-Z_0-9]*}")
public class ACMEUserResource { /* ... */ }
```

A @Path value can have leading or trailing slash character (/). Given the regular expression, the JAX-RS runtime parses the template for matching URI path elements. In this case, username47 accepts a path element that can start with an underscore character. A path name can start with a leading or trailing slash character.

It is possible to have a URI path template with more than one variable. Each variable name must be surrounded with braces. The following is an example of a widget REST style resource for a warehouse business.

```
@Path("/widgets/{range}/{manufacturer}/{productId}")
public class ACMEInventoryResource {
  @PathParam("range")
  private String range;
  @PathParam("manufacturer")
  private String manufacturer;
  @PathParam("productId")
  private String productId;

  /* ... */
}
```

This class ACMEInventoryResource accepts a resource with three variables and the JAX-RS provider will attempt to activate it on matching URL requests. The developer of this resource must take into account that perhaps one, two, or three of the parameters may or may not be selected.

JAX-RS annotations for extracting field and bean properties

JAX-RS has several annotations for extracting field and bean properties from in the incoming HTTP request. We have already seen some of them such as `@PathParam`, which extracts data from the URI template path and `@FormParam`, which extracts data from form request parameters.

JAX-RS has some additional annotations to extract further data from the HTTP request.

Annotation	Description
`@Context`	Injects JAX-RS context information into the class field and bean property of method parameter.
`@CookieParam`	Extracts data from cookies declared in the request header.
`@FormParam`	Extracts data from form request data in a POST and PUT request and where the content type is encoded with `application/x-www-form-urlencoded`.
`@HeaderParam`	Extracts the data value from a HTTP header parameter.
`@MatrixParam`	Extracts the data value from a URI matrix parameter.
`@PathParam`	Extracts the data value from a URI template parameter.r
`@QueryParam`	Extracts the data value from a URI query parameter, which is the same as the old fashion CGI query parameter.
`@DefaultValue`	Injects a default value into the class field and bean property of method parameter when the JAX-RS runtime cannot find an appropriate value.

Extracting query parameters

The annotation `@javax.ws.js.QueryParam` allows data values to be extracted from the query component of the incoming request URI, the web request.

Let us look at a JAX-RS resource that demonstrates the use of `@QueryParam`. The business case is a website that delivers job search for contractors and permanent staff. For this example, we show only the contract search for candidate. We allow contractors to search for jobs by minimum and maximum rate, the currency, and also allow the unit rate to be set. For example, contract can be set by hours per day, a daily rate, or sometimes a weekly rate.

The following is the code for the `JobSearchService` REST style resource:

```
@Path("/contracts")
public class JobSearchService {
  @GET
  public String getJobs(
    @QueryParam("ccy")      String ccy,
    @QueryParam("unitrate") String unitrate,
    @QueryParam("minrate")  int minrate,
    @QueryParam("maxprice") int maxrate)
  {
    /*...*/
  }
}
```

The resource is invoked by a URI template matching the `/contracts`. The JAX-RS runtime calls the method `getJobs()` with a HTTP GET request. In order to fulfill the request the URI must be supplied with all of the expected query parameters.

The following URIs match this resource.

```
/contracts?ccy=GBP&unitrate=PER_DAY&minrate=250&maxrate=750
/contracts?maxrate=470&minrate=325&ccy=GBP&unitrate=PER_DAY
/contracts?&unitrate=PER_HOUR&ccy=EUR&minrate=30&maxrate=90
```

It is an interesting note and a nice technique that query parameters can be combined with `@DefaultValue` annotations.

Extracting matrix parameters

Matrix parameters are a form of URI pattern that contains name and value pairs. The form of the URI is as follows `"/something;param1=value1;param2=value2"`. The URI pattern contains name and value pair separated with an equal character (`:`) and the pairs delimited by the semi-colon character (`;`).

The following is an example of JAX-RS resource that makes use of `@javax.ws.js.MatrixParam` annotation:

```
@Path("/admin")
public class ValuationService {
  @GET
  @Path("{customer}")
  public String getValue(
    @MatrixParam(«price») String price,
    @MatrixParam(«quantity») int quantity)
```

```
  {
    return String.format(
      "Customer [%s] want price [%s] at quantity: [%d]"
         customer, price, quantity );
  }
}
```

This class `ValuationService` responds to the URL pattern such as `/admin/janet_fripps`. The JAX-RS runtime provider will invoke this class given the matching URI and the method `getValue()`.

For the URI pattern `/admin/janet_fripps`, the method generates the following text:

```
Customer janet_fripps wants price null at quantity null.
```

For the URI pattern `/admin/janet_fripps;price=24.99`, the method generates the following text:

```
Customer janet_fripps wants price 24.99 at quantity null.
```

For the URI pattern `/admin/janet_fripps;price=24.99;quantity=12`, the method generates the following text:

```
Customer janet_fripps wants price 24.99 at quantity 12.
```

For the alternative URI pattern: `/admin/mark_webber;quantity=7;price=39.99`, the method generates the following text:

```
Customer mark_webber wants price 39.99 at quantity 7.
```

Using default values

JAX-RS permits default values to be defined for path variable on the class field and bean property or method argument. The `@javax.ws.rs.DefaultValue` annotation specifies a default value, if the metadata is not present in the request.

The following is an example of the annotation in action:

```
@Path("/aston/{year}/{model}/{engine}")
public class CarProductResource {
  @DefaultValue("2014") @PathParam("year")
    private String range;
  @DefaultValue("Solar") @PathParam("model")
    private String model;
  @DefaultValue("2155") @PathParam("engine")
    private int engineCc;

  /* ... */
}
```

This `CarProductResource` class is a fictional example resource for a British car manufacturer and it caters for the firm's idea of organizing their business of selling cars around the combination of year, model, and an engine size. Here, we have gone through the trouble of ensuring that all three parameters are always set to a value, even if one or more parameters are missing from the web request to the resource.

Extracting form parameters

JAX-RS extracts form parameters with the annotation `@javax.ws.rs.FormParam`. Form parameters are submitted from a web client and encoded by the browser in standard format. They are normally sent with a HTTP POST or PUT request.

We already have seen how to extract form parameters in the `UserRegistry` example earlier in this chapter. The following is this code again for perusal.

```
@Path("/users")
@Stateless
public class RegisteredUserResource {
  @POST @Path("{id}")
  @Consumes("application/x-www-form-urlencoded")
  public void addUser( @PathParam("id") String loginName,
    @FormParam("firstName") String fname,
    @FormParam("lastName") String lname,
    @FormParam("secretCode") int code )
    {
      User user = new User(loginName,fname,lname,code);
      userRegistry.addUser(user);
    }

  /* ... */
}
```

The `@Consumes` annotation on the resource method, directly stipulates how this method will behave, the MIME content, it will only be triggered by the JAX-RS runtime to act on HTML form requests.

There is an alternative way to access form parameters generically. In this case, we do need the `@Consumes` annotation and must use the JAX-RS specific `javax.ws.js.core.MultivaluedMap` collection. The multi-value map is a map collection of keys to a list of values. Each dictionary key can map to more than one value, which is an allowed feature of the HTTP specification.

Here is an alternative implementation of the `addUser()` method that demonstrates the generic form parameter logic:

```
@Path("/users")
@Stateless
public class RegisteredUserResource {
  /* ... */
  @POST
  @Path("{id}")
  @Consumes("application/x-www-form-urlencoded")
  public void addUser( @PathParam("id") String loginName,
    MultivaluedMap<String,String> formParams)
  {
    User user = new User(
      formParams.getFirst("firstName"),
      formParams.getFirst("lastName"),
      formParams.getFirst("secretCode"));
    userRegistry.addUser(user);
  }

  /* ... */
}
```

It is interesting to note, we call `getFirst()` to retrieve the value of the key from the multi-value map.

Field and bean properties

When the JAX-RS runtime instantiates a resource at runtime, it will also inject values into the fields of the resource and JavaBeans. It will inject values into method parameter before invocation of the matched resource method after URI path matching. The runtime will pay attention particularly to the following annotations: @CookieParam, @Context, @FormParam, @HeaderParam, @MatrixParam, @PathParam, @QueryParam.

The JAX-RS runtime perform injection at object creation time and therefore the annotations are checked for incompatible contextual scope, but the standard does not enforce the restriction, instead it recommends that the runtime warn the developer when the annotation is used in a problematic scope.

The following are the rules for the injection of parameter values:

- The runtime will apply conversion for an object type V for which `javax.ws.js.ext.ParamConverter` is available via registered `javax.ws.js.ext.ParamConverterProvider`.
- Injection applies automatically to primitive types.
- Types that have a constructor with a single String argument.
- Types that have a static method named `valueOf()` or `fromString()` with a single String argument and also return an instance of the type. If both methods are available, then for a non-enumerated type the runtime must choose `valueOf()`, otherwise for an enumerated type the runtime chooses `fromString()`.
- The type is a specific Java collection and a generic type `List<T>`, `Set<T>`, or `SortedSet<T>`.
- For any of these injection values, the developer can choose to annotate the injection point with a `@DefaultValue`.

JAX-RS subresources

The JAX resource can delegate to subresource and this feature allows developers, designers, and architects to build modular REST style applications with better separation of concerns, higher cohesion, and reduced coupling.

A JAX-RS subresource is a class method annotated with `@Path`, which indicates that the method is a subresource method or a subresource locator. Resource classes are able to partially process a request and provide another subresource, which processes the remainder of the request. In short, this is all about delegation.

JAX-RS permits subresource to be fulfilled by location, where another delegate class fulfills the URI template match.

Resolution by a subresource location

Take for example, a fashion store business that maintains a number of key accounts, the designer houses. The main entry point into the REST style interface could be separated out into constituent parts. The following code shows two JAX-RS resource classes `FashionStore` and `DesignerHouse`:

```
@Path("/")
public class FashionStore {
  @Path("/designers/{id}")
```

```
    public DesignerHouse getDesigner( @PathParam("id") int id )
    {
      DesignerHouse house = houseData.findById(id)
        return house;
    }
  }

  public class DesignerHouse {
    @GET
    public String getDetails() { /*...*/ }

    @Path("/principal")
    public String getPrincipal() { /*...*/ }
  }
```

The root URI pattern `@Path("/")` matches the class `FashionStore`, and therefore this master resource behaves like the root of the entire REST style interface. This class may well have other responsibilities in true business applications.

Given an incoming request for a listed designer HTTP GET request, the `FashionStore` delegates to a subresource through the method `getDesigner()`. The method is annotated with `@Path("/designers/{id}")` and it returns a subresource object `DesignerHouse`.

JAX-RS runtime provider will see the `DesignerHouse` object that was returned and then proceed to process the remaining parts of incoming URI with that object. In the specification, this is called Subresource Resolution by Location. JAX-RS then proceeds to process HTTP GET request and invokes the `getDetails()` method and after this call completes, the process is complete.

Resolution by a subresource method

The alternative subresource resolution strategy makes the code part of the parent resource. The JAX-RS resource processes the HTTP request directly. This is known as the Subresource Resolution by Direct Method.

Let's add one more method to our fashion store example that will clarify resolution by direct method. There is a requirement for certain staff to get cashier information in order to deal with specific customer requests such returns of garment, collection, alterations, and other usual requests. All such staff must work with an authorized cashier information stamp for these daily tasks and audit.

The following code shows the additional subresource method:

```
@Path("/")
public class FashionStore {
  @GET
  @Path("/staff/{domain}/{staffCode}")
  public String getCashierInfo(
    @PathParam("staffCode") String staffCode,
    @PathParam("domain") String domain ) {
      return cashierManagerService.findByCodeAndDomain(
        staffCode,domain)
  }
}
```

The HTTP GET request `/staff/2042/summerbys` will cause the JAX-RS runtime to activate the method `getCashierInfo()`.

> **Path resources and responses**
>
> Path URI and response are two sides of the same coin in the pure REST style. The REST style should ideally look like hypertext. Every addressable bit of information contains an address either explicitly through links and ID, or implicitly through the media type and its representation.

Generating a JAX-RS generic response

JAX-RS provides means to generate response generically. The abstract class `javax.ws.js.core.Response` is a contract object, which the developer uses to produce a generic response with metadata for the JAX-RS runtime provider. An application can extend this class directly or it can create an instance of Response object with the nested inner class `javax.ws.js.core.Response.ResponseBuilder`. Most applications tend to use the `ResponseBuilder`.

We have already seen an illustration of Response and ResponseBuilder in the custom `UnknownUserException` exception class. Go back and revisit the user registry example in *Defining JAX-RS Resources*, if you need to study.

Response builder

The `Response` class has several static methods that create and return a `ResponseBuilder` object.

To create an OK response, with HTTP Response code of 200, we can invoke the `ok()` method. We can also supply an entity of the response with the `entity()` method, which specifies the payload to send back to the client. We can set the MIME content of the entity too.

After configuring the `ResponseBuilder`, we then need to actually construct a response, which is sent to the client, by calling the `build()` method.

The following code shows a sample class that demonstrates some of the ways to build generic response outputs programmatically:

```java
package je7hb.jaxrs.basic;
import javax.ws.rs.core.MediaType;
import javax.ws.rs.core.Response;

public class SampleResponse {
  public Response generateSimpleOk() {
    return Response.ok().build();
  }

  public Response generateSimpleOkWithEntity() {
    return Response.ok().entity("This is message")
    .type(MediaType.TEXT_PLAIN_TYPE).build();
  }

  public Response generateSimpleOkWithEntityXml() {
    return Response.ok().entity("<msg>This is
      message</msg>")
    .type(MediaType.TEXT_XML_TYPE).build();
  }

  public Response generateSimpleOkWithGermanyLang() {
    return Response.ok()
    .language („de_de")
    .entity(„<msg>Einfaches boetschaft</msg>")
    .type(MediaType.TEXT_XML_TYPE).build();
  }

  public Response generateUnauthorisedError() {
    return Response.status(Response.Status.UNAUTHORIZED)
      .build();
  }
```

```
    public Response generateUnauthorisedWithEntityXml() {
      return Response.status(Response.Status.UNAUTHORIZED)
      .entity("<msg>Unauthorised</msg>")
      .type(MediaType.TEXT_XML_TYPE).build();
    }
}
```

In the `SampleResponse` class, we just saw, to avoid subtle literal string errors, note how we make use of the `javax.ws.rs.core.MediaType`. Static definitions of this class are used to set the MIME content as an argument to the response builder's `type()` method.

It is also possible to set the language and the character encoding of the response with methods `language()` and `encoding()`. Although not shown here, `ResponseBuilder` does have more additional methods in order to configure response headers, last modification date, expiration date and time, new cookies, and links for purpose of URI redirection.

`MediaType` class defines static constants, such as `APPLICATION_JSON_TYPE`, `TEXT_PLAIN_TYPE`, and `TEXT_HTMLTYPE`. The class also defines String equivalents of these, such as `APPLICATION_JSON` ("application/json"), `TEXT_PLAIN` ("text/plain"), and `TEXT_HTML` ("text/html").

This, then, is useful for setting the value `@Produces` and `@Consumes` in JAX-RS resource methods. For instance, we can write the code in the following way:

```
    @GET
    @Produces(MediaType.TEXT_PLAIN)
    public String getList() { /* ...*/
    return buf.toString();
}
```

Response status

The class `javax.ws.js.core.Response.Status` defines a set of enumeration values that correspond to the response code in the HTTP 1.1 communication standard. Refer to the following table:

Enumerated Constant	Code	Description
ACCEPTED	202	Request has been accepted, but the processing has not been completed.
BAD_GATEWAY	503	The server, while acting as a gateway or proxy, received an invalid response from the upstream server whilst attempting to fulfill the client's request (Since JAX-RS 2.0).
BAD_REQUEST	400	The server due to malformed syntax cannot understand the request. The client should not repeat the request.
CONFLICT	409	The request could not be completed due to a conflict with the current state of the resource. This is a useful state when two REST requests attempt to update the resource at the same time on a user defined transaction.
CREATED	201	The request was successful and the new resource was created.
FORBIDDEN	403	The server understood the request, but it is refusing to fulfill it. This response can be reported to the client to hint that the request is not secure without making it public why the request was denied.
GONE	410	The request resource is no longer available at the server and no forwarding address is known. Perhaps, REST style for deleting of the resource has already arrived in the inbox and the server knows somehow that resource has flag set: pending for deletion in the next 24 hours or so.
HTTP_VERSION_NOT_SUPPORTED	505	The server does not support, or refuses to support, the HTTP protocol that was used in the request message. (Since JAX-RS 2.0.)

Enumerated Constant	Code	Description
INTERNAL_SERVER_ERROR	500	The server encountered an expected condition, which prevented it from fulfilling the request. A useful case for this system might be JAX-RS that cannot connect to external dependent service, for example, credit brokerage or order warehouse system.
LENGTH_REQUIRED	411	The server refuses to accept the request without a defined Content-Length value in the HTTP headers. (Since JAX-RS 2.0.)
METHOD_NOT_ALLOWED	405	The method in the Request-URI is not allowed for the resource identified by the Request-URI (Since JAX-RS 2.0) — an example of this might be an immutable resource of secure, static, or reputable constant source of information.
MOVED_PERMANENTLY	301	The requested resource has been assigned a new permanent URI and any other references to this resource should use the new URI.
NO_CONTENT	204	The server fulfilled the request, but does not need to return an entity body.
NOT_ACCEPTABLE	406	The resource identified by the request is only capable of generating response entities, which have content characteristics that are not acceptable with the headers sent in the request.
NOT_FOUND	404	The server has not found anything matching the Request URI. (Since JAX-RS 2.0.)
NOT_IMPLEMENTED	501	The server does not support the functionality required to complete the request. (Since JAX-RS 2.0.)
NOT_MODIFIED	304	If the client performs a conditional GET request and access is allowed, but the document has not been modified, the server should return this error. It is very rare that a REST application will make a conditional GET request.
OK	200	The request was successful.

Enumerated Constant	Code	Description
PAYMENT_REQUIRED	402	The server blocked this request, because commercial payment is required (JAX-RS 2.0.)
PRECONDITION_FAILED	412	The precondition given in one or more of the request-header fields evaluated to be false when it was tested on the server. (Since JAX-RS 2.0.)
PROXY_AUTHENTICATION_REQUIRED	407	The client did not first authenticate itself with the proxy (JAX-RS 2.0.)
REQUEST_TIMEOUT	408	The client did not produce a request within the time that the server was prepared to wait. (JAX-RS 2.0.) — An easy example is a ticket reservation on an airplane.
REQUEST_URI_TOO_LONG	414	The server refuses to service request, because the Request-URI is longer than the server is willing to interpret (JAX-RS 2.0.)
REQUEST_RANGE_NOT_SATISFIABLE	416	The server refuses to process a request, if the value in the Range request-header exceeds the constraints of the selected resource (JAX-RS 2.0.)
SEE_OTHER	303	This is HTTP redirection that informs the client to make an alternative GET method on an alternative URI.
SERVICE_UNAVAILABLE	503	The server is currently unable to handle the request due to temporary overloading or maintenance of the server. The status implies that the temporary condition will be alleviated after some delay.
TEMPORARY_REDIRECT	307	The requested resource resides temporarily under a different URI.
UNAUTHORIZED	401	The requested resource requires user authorization.
UNSUPPORTED_MEDIA_TYPE	415	The server refuses to service the request, because the entity of the request is in a format not supported by the endpoint.

`ResponseBuilder` has several helpful functions to build a response. The `Response` object is supported in both server and client JAX-RS APIs. Users are encouraged to take advantage of the strong type safety by referencing static constants in Java class rather than loose literal strings.

Generic entities

Since Java has generics, how does JAX-RS take care of parameterized collection types? The answer is the runtime requires some help, because of **type erasure**.

In order to inform the runtime about a generic collection, there is a class, which developers can use, called `javax.ws.rs.core.GenericEntity`.

The following code shows a REST style planning resource that illustrates how to return a generic collection to the client.

```
@Plan("plans")
public PlanningResource {
  @Path("{id}")
  @GET
  @Produces(MediaType.APPLICATION_JSON)
  public Response getPlanList( @PathParam("id") String id ) {
    List<Plan> plans = findPlanCollectionById(id);
    Collections.sort( plans
      new AscendingDateOrderComparator() );
    GenericEntity entity =
      new GenericEntity<List<Plan>>(plans);
    return Response.ok(entity).build();
  }
}
```

The `PlanningResource` class has a resource method `getPlanList()`, which retrieves a list of business plans from a persistence store in the application. It sorts these `Plan` objects into ascending order and then wraps the list collections of plans in a `GenericEntity`. The method returns a response with the generic entity.

After the resource method returns the entity, the JAX-RS runtime will then take care of the rest of the response processing. The runtime applies a converter, if it was registered, to map each `Plan` entity object into the required media type `"application/json"` and the assembled response is sent over the wire to the client.

Return types

Resource methods are allowed to return `void`, `Response`, `GenericEntity`, or another Java type. These return types are mapped to the response sent to the client.

- A `void` results in an entity body with a (`NO_CONTENT`) 204 status code.
- A Response results in entity body mapped from the entity property inside. If the entity property is null then this generates a (`NO_CONTENT`) 204 status code. If the status property of the Response is not set, the runtime generates a (`OK`) 200 status code for the non-null entity code.
- A `GenericEntity` results in an entity body mapped from the Entity property. If the return value of the Entity property is not null then the runtime generates a 200 status code. A null value for the Entity properties causes the runtime to generate a 204 status code.
- For all other Java types, the runtime generates a status code if it is possible to map the result to a known `MessageBodyWriter` or default converter. If the runtime identifies this result, which is not-null, it returns a 200 status code otherwise it will generate a 204 status code. For an object instance that is an anonymous inner class, the JAX-RS runtime will, instead, use the superclass.

It is the responsibility of the developer to supply additional converters beyond the JAX-RS standard. They may do so through the `@Provider` annotation in order to register custom filters and entity interceptors.

Converting Entities to JSON

Java EE 7 provides the Java API for JSON Processing (JSON-P) to define a standard library to parse, generate, and query JSON. Out of the box this library does not supply readymade providers to JAX-RS. In the reference implementation under GlassFish, there does appear to be two classes called `JsonStructureBodyReader` and `JsonStructureBodyWriter`, which act as JAX-RS providers. If you are stuck for choice, alternatively, you can use GSON, which is a JSON library that many developers have had some success with. You will need to write a custom `ReadInterceptor` and `WriteInterceptor` implementation in order to integrate it into your application.

Hypermedia linking

Hypermedia linking is the ability for REST services to explicitly reference other endpoints in order to allow a client to navigate information. This capability is actually a constraint of fully REST application architecture and the term for it is **Hypermedia as the Engine of Application State (HATEOS)**. The design of HATEOS system implies that a REST client requires only basic knowledge to interact with an application. The best way to understand this is to think of hyperlinks in HTML. A web browser knows that an HTML anchor element is a navigation point to another HTTP resource. If a user clicks on an anchor, this is instruction to surf to the next web page. The engine of application state for a web browser is the uniform access rule to a spider web of Internet HTTP servers. No special protocols are required beyond the norm.

JAX-RS 2.0 supports Hypermedia by allowing a RESTful server endpoint to add special linkage information to the headers of a HTTP Response. The information in the HTTP header is separate to the actual content. So the response can be anything such as JSON or XML or byte stream and the developer can add linkage information to it.

The class `javax.ws.rs.core.Response.ResponseBuilder` has a couple of methods `link()` and `links()`. These methods create instances of `javax.ws.rs.core.Link`, which is the class that encapsulates hypermedia links. A `link()` accepts a URI that references the target resource and parameter. A parameter is a relative name for the navigation link called `rel` or it can be `code`.

`Link` relations are descriptive attributes that associated with hyperlink and define the semantic meaning of the relationship between the source and destination resources. `Link` relations are used in HTML5 as the common cascading style sheet. The following line of code shows the same:

```
<link href="stylesheets/bootstrap.css" rel="stylesheet" />
```

In REST and JAX-RS 2.0 the `rel` parameter is retained in a hypermedia link. The `Link` class adds a `title`, `type`, and optional of map of key-value parameters.

To understand better, let's adapt the book RESTful endpoint with hypermedia links. We will start with a refactored class as shown in the following code:

```
@Path("/hyperbooks")
public class RestfulBookServiceWithHypermedia {
   private List<HyperBook> products = Arrays.asList(
```

```java
    new HyperBook(101,"Sir Arthur Dolan Coyle",
      "Sherlock Holmes and the Hounds of the Baskervilles"),
    new HyperBook(102,"Dan Brown",
      "Da Vinci Code"),
    new HyperBook(103,"Charles Dickens",
        "Great Expectations"),
    new HyperBook(104,"Robert Louis Stevenson",
      "Treasure Island"));
  private final JsonBuilderFactory factory;

  public RestfulBookServiceWithHypermedia() {
    factory = Json.createBuilderFactory(null);
  }

  @GET
  @Path("{id}")
  @Produces({"application/json"})
  public Response getProduct(@PathParam("id")int id) {
    HyperBook product = null;
    for ( HyperBook book: products ) {
      if ( book.id == id ) {
        product = book; break;
      }
    }
    if ( product == null)
    throw new RuntimeException("book not found");
    return Response.ok(product.asJsonObject())
    .link("http://localhost:8080/order/"+
      id+"/warehouse", "stock")
    .build();
  }
  // ...
}
```

In this endpoint `RestfulBookServiceWithHypermedia`, we changed the URI from `/books` to `/hypermedia` for the type in order to avoid a conflict between resources. This class creates `JsonBuilderFactory` that we use later. We have given all the hypermedia books a new Java type `HyperBook` and they have a unique ID.

The method `getProduct()` maps to HTTP GET request and accepts a REST path parameter ID, which references the bookID. The code attempts to look up the product by the ID. If the product does exists, we convert the `Hyperbook` instance to a JSON representation with call to `asJsonObject()`. We use the JSON-P API from Java EE 7 (See *Appendix D, Java EE 7 Assorted Topics* for more details).

If it is not found in the list, then a `RuntimeException` exception is thrown. The key to the method is `link()` call that accepts an URI for the link header and a value for the `rel` parameter. The method generates a response header that looks like the following code:

```
header[Link] = <http://localhost:8080/order/101/warehouse>;
 rel="stock"
header[Date] = Sun, 18 Aug 2013 17:38:33 GMT
header[Content-Length] = 105
header[Content-Type] = application/json
```

The link relation is a navigation to a warehouse note on a particular order that has a `rel` name stock and the URI `http://localhost:8080/order/101/warehouse`. It is also possible to generate a collection of link headers for a given response. In order to achieve this aim, we need to invoke indirectly `Link.Builder` class.

Let's add one method to retrieve all the hypermedia books in our endpoint, the following code will explain how to do just that:

```
@GET
@Produces({"application/json"})
public Response getProductList() {
  JsonObjectBuilder builder =
    factory.createObjectBuilder();
  JsonArrayBuilder arrayBuilder =
    factory.createArrayBuilder();

  List<Link> links = new ArrayList<>();
  for ( HyperBook book: products ) {
    arrayBuilder.add( book.asJsonObject() );
    links.add(
      Link.fromPath("http://localhost:8080/order/" +
        book.id + "/warehouse")
      .rel("stock")
      .build());
  }
  builder.add("products", arrayBuilder.build());

  return Response.ok(builder.build())
  .links( links.toArray( new Link[]{}))
  build();
}
```

The method `getProducts()` maps also HTTP GET request, but without any parameter and returns a JSON array of all products, the hypermedia books. In order to create a collection of link relations, we use `ArrayList<Link>`.

For each hypermedia product, we iterate over all of them, we need a link relation builder. The static call `Link.fromPath()` instantiates a `Link.Builder` instance from a String. From there, we set `rel` parameter name using the `rel()` method and then obtain a `Link` instance by calling `build()`.

At the same time when we are creating link relations, we create a `JsonArray` object. We obtain the JSON representation of the `Hyperbook` instance and add it to the `JsonArray`. The final part of the puzzle is, while building the response, the conversion of the `ArrayList<List>` to the `Link[]` primitive array for the `links(Links...)` call.

The output for the HTTP Response headers looks something like this:

```
header[Link] =
 <http://localhost:8080/ordering/104/shipment>; rel="ship",
 <http://localhost:8080/ordering/103/shipment>; rel="ship",
 <http://localhost:8080/ordering/102/shipment>; rel="ship",
 <http://localhost:8080/ordering/101/shipment>; rel="ship"
header[Date] = Mon, 19 Aug 2013 08:26:01 GMT
header[Content-Length] = 314
header[Content-Type] = application/json
```

As you can observe the `Links` HTTP response is actually comma-delimited. The client-side JAX-RS 2.0 delivers this view resembles the following code extract:

```
@Test
public void shouldRetrieveHyperbooks() throws Exception {
  WebTarget target = ClientBuilder.newClient()
   .target(
     "http://localhost:8080/mywebapp/rest/hyperbooks");
  Response response = target.request().get();
  // ...
  Set<Link> links = response.getLinks();
  assertFalse(links.isEmpty());
  for (Link link: links) {
    System.out.printf(
      "link relation uri=%s, rel=%s \n",
        link.getUri(), link.getRel());
  }
  assertEquals(200, response.getStatus());
}
```

From the unit test method `shouldRetrieveHyperbooks()`, we are using the JAX-RS 2.0 client side API that we will discuss, very soon, in the section. The important point in the code is retrieval of `Link` in a `Set` collection from the response. The client side can conveniently parse that set of link relations in the instance, which is very useful. From there, we can get access to the URI, parameter `rel` name, the type, and other parameters.

The output should appear as the following:

```
link relation uri=http://localhost:8080/ordering/103/shipment,
   rel=ship
link relation uri=http://localhost:8080/ordering/102/shipment,
   rel=ship
```

This covers building a response. Let's now move to the client side.

JAX-RS client API

JAX-RS 2.0 introduces the client framework for the first time, which also supports callbacks and asynchronous request and response. The really nice feature of this API, improves on the writing invocations of the JAX-RS servers by hand. As you saw in the section called *Test-Driven Development with JAX-RS*, writing URL code and the I/O in standard Java can be, how can I say, laborious?

Synchronous invocation

The client API lies in the **javax.ws.js.client** package, which contains useful classes such as **AsyncInvoker**, **Client**, **ClientBuilder**, **Entity**, **SyncInvoker** and **WebTarget**.

The following table outlines the responsibilities of these classes.

Class	Description
AsyncInvoker	This is a Java interface that defines a uniform contract interface for asynchronous invocation.
Client	This is a Java interface that represents the contract of all clients, which are the main entry points to the client side API. The client defines a builder pattern for flexibility.
ClientBuilder	This is the abstract class for the Client API, which the developer configures in order to connect the request URI on the server side. The developer can optionally configure a client with SSL, security key store, and a hostname verifier.

Class	Description
ClientRequestContext	An interface that defines the contract for context data for the purpose of processing the client request.
ClientRequestFilter	An interface that defines the contract for a custom request filter. Implementations of this interface must be annotated with @javax.ws.rs.ext.Provider.
ClientResponseContext	An interface that defines the contract for context data for the purpose of processing the client response.
ClientResponseFilter	An interface that defines the contract for a custom response filter. Implementations of this interface must be annotated with @javax.ws.rs.ext.Provider.
Entity	A final class that encapsulates the message entity including the associate variant.
FactoryFinder	A final class for the JAX-RS time to find the implementation of the client framework.
Invocation	An interface that defines the contract for a client request invocation.
InvocationCallback	An interface that defines the contract callback that the client code implements to respond to events from processing the response.
ResponseProcessingException	An exception thrown if the JAX-RS runtime finds there is a problem in processing the response from the resource, which could be in an error in deserialization or failure to filter the entity.
SyncInvoker	The uniform interface to synchronous invocation.
WebTarget	Represents the resource target URI on the server side.

It is very straight forward to connect to resource URI using the JAX-RS Client API. The first class to examine is the `javax.ws.js.client.ClientBuilder`, which has a static method called `newBuilder()`. This method returns a `ClientBuilder` that the developer can configure independently with `javax.net.ssl.SSLContext` and also supply `java.security.KeyStore` for encryption. The overloaded methods on the client builder `keyStore()` and `SSLContext()` provide the configuration.

Chapter 8

If your application is not using security at the moment through SSL, then you can invoke the static method `newClient()` and obtain a `javax.ws.js.client.Client` instance. With this object, you can configure the target, the resource URI that will be called with the method `target()`, which returns a `javax.ws.js.client.WebTarget` instance.

With `WebTarget`, you configure additional path, query parameters, and matrix parameters. Invoking the method `request()` on the web target returns a `javax.ws.js.client.Invocation.Builder` instance.

Finally, as the developer, you get to invoke the request to the server, the remote resource URI with the call to `get()`, `put()`, `post()`, or `delete()`.

On the face of it, going through this chain of object classes, might appear to be confusing and complicated, but actually it is quite an elegant design and a clear definition of separation of concerns. By the way, the `Invocation.Builder` interface is an extension of the `javax.ws.js.client.SyncInvoker` interface.

Let us rewrite the first unit test client that we saw for the book list to use this new JAX-RS client side API. The following is the new class `RestfulBookServiceClientTest` in its entirety:

```
package je7hb.jaxrs.basic;
/* imports ommitted */

import javax.ws.rs.client.ClientBuilder;
import javax.ws.rs.client.WebTarget;
import javax.ws.rs.core.Response;

public class RestfulBookServiceClientTest {
  private static SimpleEmbeddedRunner runner;
  private static WebArchive webArchive;

  @BeforeClass
  public static void assembleDeployAndStartServer()
  throws Exception {
          /* See the book's source code  .. */
  }

  /* ... */

  @Test
```

```java
    public void shouldRetrieveBookList() {
      WebTarget target = 
        ClientBuilder.newClient()
      .target(
        "http://localhost:8080/mywebapp/rest/books");
      Response response = target.request().get();
      assertNotNull(response);
      String text = response.readEntity( String.class );
      String arr[] = text.split("\n");
      assertEquals("Sherlock Holmes and the Hounds of 
        the Baskervilles", arr[0] );
      assertEquals("Da Vinci Code", arr[1] );
      assertEquals("Great Expectations", arr[2]);
      assertEquals( "Treasure Island", arr[3] );
    }
  }
```

In this integration test `RestfulBookServiceClientTest`, we make use of `ShinkWrap` in order to create a virtual WAR file. We then launch an embedded GlassFish instance and deploy the WAR file to it. The new code is the `ClientBuilder` invocation, which creates a `Client` instance and then the `WebTarget` instance. The unit test invokes the request URI on the server and it retrieves a `javax.ws.js.coreResponse` object.

All we need to do with the response is retrieve the content and we do that by reading the entity as a String. Behind the scenes the method `readEntity()` opens `java.io.InputStream` and performs more or less the same code in the older unit test, except since the JAX-RS 2.0 does this, means that our code is much cleaner.

With the content as a Java String, we just split it to an array by the delimited new line characters and run the assertions to complete the test.

What happens if there is an issue with the server? The target resource at the URI fails to generate an OK response, HTTP Response Code 200. If there is an error the JAX-RS runtime will do its best to map the error code to an exception under the package `javax.ws.js.ext`. This package defines exceptions that correspond to the HTTP response error codes and the classes are named like `BadRequestException`, `ForbiddenException`, `InternalServerErrorException` and `ServiceUnavailableException` to name a few.

Asynchronous invocation

The client JAX-RS also has a means for generating an asynchronous request. Now this is potentially useful for building a type of non-blocking request and response architecture. The design of the JAX-RS API, again, makes this avenue remarkably simple.

Asynchronous client request can rely on a `java.util.concurrent.Future` or an `Invocation` callback method that the developer provides. Let's look at the Future option first.

The following is a new unit test `RestfulBookServiceAsyncClientTest`:

```
public class RestfulBookServiceAsyncClientTest {
  /* ... as before ... */

  @Test
  public void shouldRetrieveBookListAsynchronously()
  throws Exception {
    WebTarget target =
      ClientBuilder.newClient()
    .target(
      "http://localhost:8080/mywebapp/rest/books");
    Future<Response> future =
      target.request().async().get();

    Response response = future.get(3, TimeUnit.SECONDS );
    String text = response.readEntity(String.class);
    String arr[] = text.split("\n");
    assertEquals("Sherlock Holmes and the Hounds of
      the Baskervilles", arr[0]);
    assertEquals("Da Vinci Code", arr[1]);
    assertEquals("Great Expectations", arr[2]);
     assertEquals( "Treasure Island", arr[3]);
  }
}
```

The essential difference in the asynchronous version compared to the synchronous one is the addition of the `async()` method call after the `request()` method. This method call returns an instance of `javax.ws.js.client.AsyncInvoker`. The difference with this type is all of the overloaded method calls on it such as `get()`, `put()`, `post()`, and `delete()` return Future objects, which means the request to the remote server does not block the calling Java thread.

In order to retrieve the response from the server wrap in the Future object, we invoke the `get()` method and in the unit test example we supply a timeout value. Of course, this call will block the calling Java thread during that duration, and then there is the possibility of the value being ready or not. Still, the call duration is useful for situations where you require some execution time limit, and once the Future has been retrieved it becomes immutable, you cannot reuse it. Instead, you must make another invocation of the web service.

The JAX-RS Client API provides another way to find out the response of an asynchronous invocation. The programmer, in this case, creates and supplies a callback object of the type `InvocationCallback<Response>`.

The following is a further example in the asynchronous unit test class:

```java
public class RestfulBookServiceAsyncClientTest {
  /* ... as before ... */
  private static class MyCallback
  implements InvocationCallback<Response> {
    public CountDownLatch ready = new CountDownLatch(1);
    public volatile String text = "";
    public volatile Throwable failure = null;

    @Override
    public void completed(Response response) {
      text = response.readEntity( String.class );
      ready.countDown();
    }

    @Override
    public void failed(Throwable throwable) {
      failure = throwable;
      ready.countDown();
    }
  }
  @Test
  public void shouldRetrieveBookListAsyncWithCallback() {
    WebTarget target =
      ClientBuilder.newClient()
    .target(
      "http://localhost:8080/mywebapp/rest/books");

    MyCallback callback = new MyCallback();
    Future<Response> future =
      target.request().async().get(callback);
```

```
      try {
        callback.ready.await(3, TimeUnit.SECONDS);
        if ( callback.failure != null )
        callback.failure.printStackTrace(System.err);
        assertNull(callback.failure);
        String arr[] = callback.text.split("\n");
        assertEquals("Sherlock Holmes and the Hounds of "+
          "the Baskervilles", arr[0] );
        assertEquals("Da Vinci Code", arr[1] );
        assertEquals("Great Expectations", arr[2]);
        assertEquals( "Treasure Island", arr[3] );
      }
      catch (Exception e) {
        e.printStackTrace();
        throw new RuntimeException(e);
      }
    }
  }
}
```

The class `MyCallback` implements the `javax.ws.js.client.InvocationCallback` interface. We use a `java.util.concurrency.CountDownLatch` so that we can ensure that this class is actually invoked by the JAX-RS run time in either the success or failure capacity. JAX-RS invokes the `completed()` method if the data is fully available. On an error, JAX-RS invokes the `failed()` method. In either case, we count down the latch to zero and record the salient information for later. It is important to note, that the callback executes on a different thread to the unit test method, which is why we must be careful in our concurrency synchronization. It is so very easy to get multi-threading badly wrong in Java.

The method `shouldRetrieveBookListAsyncWithCallback()` is largely the same as before. Instead, we invoke the invocation builder with `get()` call and pass an instance of our callback `MyCallback` to it. Incidentally, this call returns a future object, however we are not using it in this unit test method.

We await the countdown latch to hit zero inside the unit test method. When it does, we know that the callback has been invoked. If the callback was invoked because of failure, we print the stack trace to the standard error channel. On normal execution in the unit test method thread, we can retrieve the text string and perform the assertions.

This example does illustrate that may be a developer should separate the business model logic of validating data from the infrastructure of JAX-RS request and response.

Asynchronous JAX-RS server side endpoints

JAX-RS 2.0 permits asynchronous generation of the output response in a manner that is similar to the Servlet 3.0 standard, in particular `javax.servlet.AsyncContext`. In order to achieve this in a REST style resource, somehow the JAX-RS must be informed that the resource method can be executed in another thread internally to the provider. The client does not need to know the exact details of where the method is invoked under the hood.

In order to inform the JAX-RS runtime, that a resource method generates asynchronous output, supply the annotation `@javax.ws.rs.container.Suspended` and also a new argument `@javax.ws.rs.container.AsyncResponse`. Yes, there is another JAX-RS sub-package called `javax.ws.rs.container` with classes and interfaces specifically for server-side containers.

In order to set a JAX-RS to fully asynchronous, the user must annotate the method with `@javax.ejb.Asynchronous`. Therefore, the JAX-RS resource has to be defined as a session EJB in Java EE 7, it can be either a stateless bean or a singleton.

The following is an example of another book REST style resource, but delivered as an asynchronous EJB:

```java
package je7hb.jaxrs.basic;
import javax.ejb.*;
import javax.ws.rs.*;
import javax.ws.rs.container.*;
import javax.ws.rs.core.*;
import java.util.*;

@Path(«/async/books»)
@Stateless
public class RestfulBookAsyncService {

  private List<Book> products = Arrays.asList(
    new Book("Miguel De Cervantes", "Don Quixote"),
    new Book("Daniel Defoe", "Robinson Crusoe"),
    new Book("Jonathan Swift", "Gulliver's Travels"),
    new Book("Mary Shelley", "Frankenstein"),
    new Book("Charlotte Bronte", "Jane Eyre"));
```

```
@GET
@Asynchronous
@Produces(MediaType.TEXT_PLAIN)
public void getList(
  @Suspended AsyncResponse asyncResponse) {
  final long SLEEP=500;
  final int N=10;
  try {
    for (int j=0; j<N; ++j ) {
      System.out.print(".");
      System.out.flush();
      Thread.sleep(SLEEP);
    }
  }
  catch (InterruptedException e) {
    e.printStackTrace();
  }
  System.out.println(".\n");
  StringBuffer buf = new StringBuffer();
  for (Book b: products) { buf.append(b.title);
  buf.append('\n'); }
  Response response =
  Response.ok(buf.toString()).build();
  asyncResponse.resume(response);
}

static class Book {
  public final String author;
  public final String title;

  Book(String author, String title) {
    this.author = author;
    this.title = title;
  }
}
}
```

Inside the `RestfulBookAsyncService` class, the `getList()` resource method is triggered on a HTTP GET request on the URI. We contrived in this method to delay the generation of the output with a thread sleep call, so that it is easy to study the output. As soon as the JAX-RS implementation detects the `@Suspended` invocation; it will pause the output of the response to client on `AsyncResponse`. It is the combination of the EJB `@Asynchronous` and `@Suspended AsyncResponse` that causes the fire-and-forget behavior on the server side.

After the deliberate delay, the `getList()` method builds the generic response and then passes it to the `AsyncResponse` instance with a call to `resume()`. This call signals to the runtime that the asynchronous response will be resumed.

If the method is not annotated with `@Asynchronous`, then the JAX-RS runtime executes in a synchronous fashion, but the `AsyncResponse` will be still suspended.

The output from the unit test produces the following result:

```
RestfulBookAsyncService#acquireResource()
RestfulBookAsyncService.getList() thread: [Thread[http-
listener(1),5,main]]
retrieve list asynchronously ..........

sending data back now on thread: [Thread[http-listener(1),5,main]]
**** response=org.glassfish.jersey.client.ScopedJaxrsResponse@3ae4568d
**** text=Don Quixote
Robinson Crusoe
Gulliver's Travels
Frankenstein
Jane Eyre
```

The extract sample of the output shows the invocation of the REST endpoint in the class `RestfulBookAsyncService`. In the working code, which you find in the source code and the website, we added `@PostConstruct` and `@PreDestroy` annotation methods. We also make use of the JAX-RS Client asynchronous API to invoke the resource in a unit test.

Let's move on to the filtering and interception of the resource and how the JAX-RS can do more advanced processing for your enterprise applications.

Why must I turn to EJB for full asynchronous operations?

At first glance, it does appear strange that for full asynchronous operation, a resource must be annotated as a session EJB (`@Stateless` or `@Singleton`) and the resource method requires a `@javax.ejb.Asynchronous`. Luckily, for us developers, Java EE containers treat EJB in a much smarter way than they did J2EE. A session EJB is no longer a monolithic behemoth of burden that it was once, modern Java EE servers are perfectly capable of creating thousands of EJB instances on the fly. There is no longer a need to even pool EJB instances as we once did! I do think, personally, that the EJB and CDI expert group missed a trick by not having an annotation for CDI `@javax.annotation.Asynchronous`.

If you prefer not use to EJB then you may want to investigate the Concurrency API. You can find out more about Java EE 7 *ManagedExecutorService* in *Appendix D, Java EE 7 Assorted Topics*.

JAX-RS providers

The JAX-RS 2.0 specification now standardizes extensions to the runtime that allow developers to write portable authentication, encoding and decoding, and logging without the vendor lock-in of proprietary code. JAX-RS provides an interceptor framework to handle advanced situations. The specification describes two styles of intercepted JAX-RS communication, namely, filtering and entity interceptors.

Filters are strikingly similar in concept to Java Servlet filters, especially in the way they can modify or process the incoming REST request and the response. Filters predominantly take care of HTTP Header information and they execute before and after request and response resource processing.

On the other hand, Entity Interceptors are designed for the manipulation of the payload data. They can be written to encrypt and decrypt the message body of a JAX-RS REST message. (If you have an Enterprise Messaging background, then the penny has already started to drop.)

Filters

JAX-RS filters are available on the client and the container APIs, the packages `javax.ws.js.client` and `javax.ws.js.container`.

JAX-RS filters

On the client side, there are two types of filter, namely the Java interface `ClientRequestFilter` and `ClientResponseFilter`. For each direction, there is a corresponding context interface `ClientRequestContext` and `ClientResponseContext`.

On the server side, there are two types of filter, namely the Java interface `ContainerRequestFilter` and `ContainerResponseFilter`. For each direction, there is a corresponding context interface `ContainerRequestContext` and `ContainerResponseContext`.

Let us look at the server side filter as a start.

Server-side filters

JAX-RS executes the `ContainerRequestFilter` filter before invoking the wrapped target resource. JAX-RS executes `ContainerResponseFilter` after invoking the wrapped target resource.

The category of `ContainerRequestFilter` is divided into two more filter styles. A filter can be pre-matching or post-matching. The default is the post-matching. Pre-matching filters are designed to modify request attributes and header attributes before the JAX-RS runtime perform path pattern matching on the URI resource.

In order to designate a `ContainerRequestFilter` is a pre-matching filter, the class must be annotated with `@javax.ws.js.container.PreMatching`.

If we wanted to copy the HTTP Header parameter User Agent and shadow it for a processing pipeline, we could write a filter in the following way:

```
package je7hb.jaxrs.basic;
import javax.ws.rs.container.ContainerRequestContext;
import javax.ws.rs.container.ContainerRequestFilter;
import javax.ws.rs.container.PreMatching;
import javax.ws.rs.ext.Provider;
import java.io.IOException;

@Provider
@PreMatching
public class AddExtraUserAgentFilter implements
  ContainerRequestFilter {
  @Override
  public void filter(ContainerRequestContext context)
  throws IOException {
    String userAgent =
      context.getHeaderString("User-Agent");
    if ( userAgent != null ) {
      context.getHeaders().putSingle(
        "X-User-Agent-Copy", userAgent );
    }
  }
}
```

The filter `AddExtraUserAgentFilter` is annotated as `@javax.ws.js.ext.Provider`. The class implements `ContainerRequestFilter` and the method `filter()`. We look up the header parameter by name from the supplied context. Since this agent usually is supplied by the client, we can make a copy of the parameter into a new header key and value pair called `X-User-Agent-Copy`.

If we wanted to, the flexibility of the JAX-RS API, allows us to change the `User-Agent` string. Since this filter is annotated with `@PreMatching` then the runtime will invoke this filter before proceeding with the URI path pattern matching phase and before the target resource is invoked.

Suppose we wanted to have a filter that automatically added an expiration time to the HTTP Response header for any JAX-RS Resource. We could write a container response filter like the following code:

```
package je7hb.jaxrs.basic;
import javax.ws.rs.container.*;
import javax.ws.rs.ext.Provider;
/* ... imports omitted */

@Provider
public class AutoExpirationDateFilter implements
ContainerResponseFilter{
  private static SimpleDateFormat formatter =
    new SimpleDateFormat("EEE, dd MMM yyyy HH:mm:ss Z");
  @Override
  public void filter(ContainerRequestContext reqCtx,
    ContainerResponseContext resCtx)
  throws IOException {
    if ( reqCtx.getMethod().equals("GET")) {
      Date oneHour = new Date(
        System.currentTimeMillis() + 60* 1000 );
      resCtx.getHeaders().add("Expires",
        formatter.format( oneHour));
    }
  }
}
```

In the class `AutoExpirationDateFilter` which implements the contract from `ContainerResponseFilter`, the `filter()` method accepts two context parameters and it is extremely useful to have access to both the request and response context objects.

We only add the expiration response header field for HTTP GET request, so in the method we can check this situation. With the response context, we add the expiration header with a properly formatted date and timestamp.

Client-side filters

Writing JAX-RS filters for the client side is a one step filter, because there is no URI path pattern matching occurring. The developer has a choice of two filter types, namely, `ClientRequestFilter` and `ClientResponseFilter`. The JAX-RS filter will invoke `ClientRequestFilter` just before the HTTP request is sent to the remote URI resource. Similarly, after the remote URI resource processes the data and sends back a response, then the JAX-RS runtime invokes `ClientResponseFilter` instance.

We shall now inspect the code for a useful bit of kit in our toolkit. What happens if we have problem with some production code involving JAX-RS? Would it not be nice to debug to a standard console (and perhaps later to a logging facility) the requests going from the client to the remote URI resource and reading the server response? It would be nice to have a master client that we can travel around the business and validate the communication is functioning correctly between the client and server.

So the following is the basis of a debuggable logger for JAX-RS client, albeit incomplete:

```java
package je7hb.jaxrs.basic;
import javax.ws.rs.client.*;
import javax.ws.rs.ext.Provider;
/* ... imports omitted */

@Provider
public class DebugClientLoggingFilter
implements ClientRequestFilter, ClientResponseFilter {

  @Override
  public void filter(ClientRequestContext reqCtx)
  throws IOException {
    System.out.printf("**** DEBUG CLIENT REQUEST ****\n");
    System.out.printf("uri: %s\n", reqCtx.getUri());
    if ( reqCtx.getEntity() != null ) {
      System.out.printf("entity: %s\n",
        reqCtx.getEntity().getClass().getName() + "@" +
          Integer.toHexString(
            System.identityHashCode( reqCtx.getEntity())));
    }
    System.out.printf("method: %s\n", reqCtx.getMethod());
    System.out.printf("mediaType: %s\n",
      reqCtx.getMediaType());
    System.out.printf("date: %s\n", reqCtx.getDate());
    System.out.printf("language: %s\n",
      reqCtx.getLanguage());
    for (String name: reqCtx.getHeaders().keySet()) {
      System.out.printf("header[%s] => %s\n",
        name, reqCtx.getHeaderString(name) );
    }
    for (String name: reqCtx.getCookies().keySet()) {
```

```
      System.out.printf("cookie[%s] => %s\n",
        name, reqCtx.getHeaderString(name) );
    }
    System.out.printf("**** END CLIENT REQUEST ****\n\n");
  }
  // ... incoming filter method }
```

This class `DebugClientLoggingFilter` implements both the client request and response filters. As you can see the two different context objects `ClientRequestContext` and `ClientResponseContext` provide a wealth of information.

From the client, we are able to find out the request URI, the entity, the method, media type, language, headers, and cookies. Similarly, from the server we can debug the status, status code, response length, the date, headers, and cookies.

Once the remote endpoint has serviced the request, we expect a response, which can also be filtered. The following is the other incoming implementation filter method:

```
@Override
public void filter(ClientRequestContext reqCtx,
  ClientResponseContext resCtx)
throws IOException {
  System.out.printf("**** DEBUG CLIENT RESPONSE ****\n");
  System.out.printf("status: %s\n", resCtx.getStatus());
  System.out.printf("status info: %s\n",
    resCtx.getStatusInfo());
  System.out.printf("length: %s\n", resCtx.getLength());
  System.out.printf("mediaType: %s\n",
    resCtx.getMediaType());
  System.out.printf("date: %s\n", resCtx.getDate());
  System.out.printf("language: %s\n", resCtx.getLanguage());
  for (String name: resCtx.getHeaders().keySet()) {
    System.out.printf("header[%s] => %s\n",
      name, resCtx.getHeaderString(name) );
  }
  for (String name: resCtx.getCookies().keySet()) {
    System.out.printf("cookie[%s] => %s\n",
      name, resCtx.getHeaderString(name) );
  }
  System.out.printf("**** END CLIENT RESPONSE ****\n\n");
}
```

We have access to the response header, content type, length, data, and also cookies. To find out more information, it is worth your while examining the API in detail for both `ClientRequestContext` and `ClientResponseContext`.

To configure the filter from the unit test, we set up the `ClientBuilder` in the following way:

```
@Test
public void shouldRetrieveBookList() throws Exception {
  WebTarget target = ClientBuilder.newClient()
    .register(new DebugClientLoggingFilter())
    .target(
      "http://localhost:8080/mywebapp/rest/async/books");
  Future<Response> future =
    target.request().async().get();
  /* ... */
}
```

`DebugClientLoggingFilter` is registered on the builder object.

The following is a screenshot of the unit test in action:

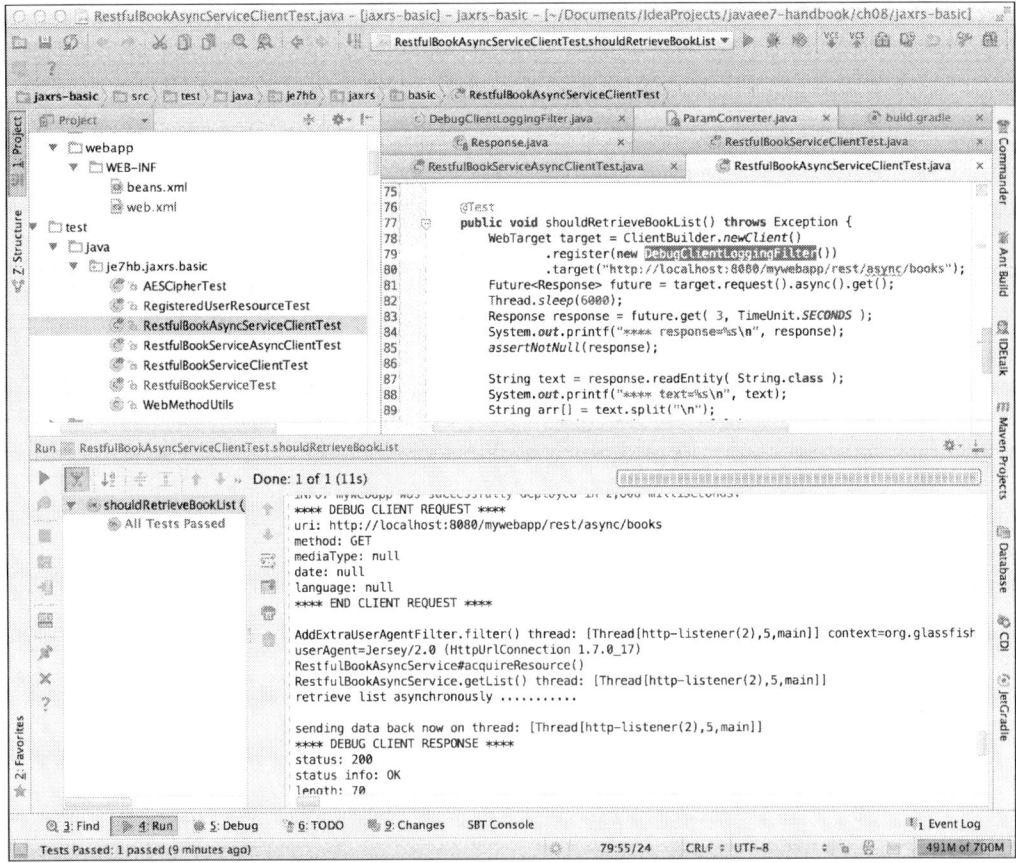

If you are going to unit test the server response in an application, why would you not choose the JAX-RS client side library? It is a no brainer.

We shall move on to entity interceptors.

JAX-RS interceptors

Inceptors handle message bodies, the actual payload of the request and response to the remote JAX-RS resource. Entity interceptors are executed in the call stack frame as their corresponding reader or writer, which means there are involved in the same Java thread.

There are two types of interceptors, namely, `javax.ws.rs.ext.ReaderInterceptor` and `javax.ws.rs.ext.WriterInterceptor`. The reader interceptor is designed to wrap around the execution of the `javax.ws.rs.ext.MessageBodyReader` types. The writer interceptor is designed to wrap around the execution of `javax.ws.rs.ext.MessageBodyWriter`.

Why would developers want to create an interceptor? One circumstance may be to provide encryption and destruction around a particular resource type of data. Another idea would be generate secure digital signatures for any type of output.

Here is an example of both `ReaderInterceptor` and `WriterInterceptor` that performs AES encryption and decryption:

```java
package je7hb.jaxrs.basic;
import javax.crypto.*;
import javax.ws.rs.WebApplicationException;
import javax.ws.rs.ext.*;
import java.io.*;

@Provider
public class AESCipherInterceptor
implements ReaderInterceptor, WriterInterceptor{
  private final AESCipher cipher;

  public AESCipherInterceptor() throws Exception {
    final byte[] salt =
      { 1,2,4,8,16,32,64,-64,-32,-16,-8,-4,-2,-1};
    final String password = «java1995»;
    cipher = new AESCipher(password, salt);
  }
```

```java
    @Override
    public Object aroundReadFrom(
      ReaderInterceptorContext context )
    throws IOException, WebApplicationException {
      InputStream old = context.getInputStream();
      context.setInputStream( new CipherInputStream(
        old, cipher.getDecryptCipher()));
      try {
        return context.proceed();
      }
      finally {
        context.setInputStream(old);
      }
    }

    @Override
    public void aroundWriteTo(
      WriterInterceptorContext context )
    throws IOException, WebApplicationException {
      OutputStream old = context.getOutputStream();
      context.setOutputStream( new CipherOutputStream(
        old, cipher.getEncryptCipher()));
      try {
        context.proceed();
        context.getHeaders().add("X-Encryption", "AES");
      }
      finally {
        context.setOutputStream(old);
      }
    }
  }
```

I should say immediately as a professional developer you never expose the security credentials to hacking in source code. The password and salt would be securely obtained by proper means through a secure channel.

In order to be truly secure in the communication, first, you could make the connection protocol SSL. Second, ensure the plain text of the password is never passed in the stream and share the password verbally, orally in a face-to-face meeting. Third, generate the salt using `javax.security.SecureRandom`. Share the salt in an out-of-band communication between the server and the client in an initial hand shaking mechanism.

The annotation `@Provider` is applied to the interceptor class `AESCipherInterceptor` and therefore JAX-RS server side runtime becomes aware of its existence.

The class `AESCipherInterceptor` uses a helper class `AESCipher` to delegate the business of configuration key generator, cipher streams and the business of configuring AES in secure Java. This leaves the two implementation methods `aroundReadFrom()` and `aroundWriteTo()` relatively free of clutter.

The style of programming for both of these methods follows that of **Aspect Oriented Programming (AOP)**. We temporarily replace the input or output stream, before invoking the target in the context. After the invoked method returns we restore the previous stream. We must surround the invocation with a `try-finally` block to ensure the restoration always happens regardless of the normal or abnormal termination of the target method.

We add an additional header to the response output in the `aroundWriteTo()` method.

The following is the code for the delegate class, `AESCipher`:

```
package je7hb.jaxrs.basic;
/* ... imports omitted */

public class AESCipher {
  private final KeyGenerator keyGen;
  private final Cipher encryptCipher, decryptChipher;

  public Cipher getEncryptCipher() { return encryptCipher;}
  public Cipher getDecryptCipher() { return decryptCipher;}

  public AESCipher( String passwordText, final byte[] salt )
  throws Exception {
    keyGen = KeyGenerator.getInstance("AES");
    final char[] password = passwordText.toCharArray();
    SecretKeyFactory factory =
      SecretKeyFactory.getInstance("PBKDF2WithHmacSHA1");
    KeySpec spec = new PBEKeySpec(
      password, salt, 65536, 128);
    SecretKey tmp = factory.generateSecret(spec);
    SecretKey aesKey = new SecretKeySpec(
      tmp.getEncoded(), "AES");

    encryptCipher = Cipher.getInstance(
      "AES/CBC/PKCS5Padding");
```

```java
    IvParameterSpec ivParameterSpec =
      new IvParameterSpec(aesKey.getEncoded());
    encryptCipher.init(Cipher.ENCRYPT_MODE,
      aesKey, ivParameterSpec);

    decryptCipher = Cipher.getInstance(
      "AES/CBC/PKCS5Padding");
    decryptCipher.init(Cipher.DECRYPT_MODE,
      aesKey, ivParameterSpec);
  }

  public byte[] encrypt( String plainText ) {
    ByteArrayOutputStream outputStream =
      new ByteArrayOutputStream();
    CipherOutputStream cipherOutputStream =
      new CipherOutputStream(outputStream,
        encryptCipher);
    try {
      cipherOutputStream.write(plainText.getBytes());
      cipherOutputStream.flush();
      cipherOutputStream.close();
      return outputStream.toByteArray();
    }
    catch (Exception e) {
      e.printStackTrace(System.err);
      return null;
    }
  }

  public String decrypt( byte[] cipherText ) {
    ByteArrayOutputStream output =
      new ByteArrayOutputStream();
    ByteArrayInputStream inputStream =
      new ByteArrayInputStream(cipherText);
    CipherInputStream cipherInputStream = null;
    try {
      cipherInputStream = new CipherInputStream(
        inputStream, decryptCipher);
      byte[] buf = new byte[1024];
      int bytesRead;
      while ((bytesRead =
        cipherInputStream.read(buf)) >= 0) {
        output.write(buf, 0, bytesRead);
      }
```

```
      cipherInputStream.close();
      return  new String(output.toByteArray());
    }
    catch (Exception e) {
      throw new RuntimeException(e);
    }
  }
}
```

The `AESCipher` utilizes the **Java Cryptography Extension (JCE)** API in order to security encrypt and decode an array of bytes to and from a String. The details of these API calls are out-of-scope for this book. Oracle has a good site to find out more information http://www.oracle.com/technetwork/java/javase/tech/index-jsp-136007.html. I recommend the following book *Beginning Java Security* by *David Hook*.

We shall move on to binding filter and interceptors and how a developer can control which JAX-RS resources are matched to these types.

Binding filter and interceptors

As it stands, the `AESCipherInterceptor` class from previous section has a global binding. This means it will be invoked for all JAX-RS Resources in the application! We most likely do *not* want to encryption and decryption for all of the REST style resources in our application.

A filter or entity interceptor can be associated with a resource class or method by declaring a new binding annotation in the spirit of the Context and Dependency Injection (CDI). Annotations for association are declared with the JAX-RS meta-annotation `@javax.ws.js.NameBinding`.

We can create a custom annotation for denoting resources that need secure encryption. The following code is a new annotation called `@Encrypt`:

```
@NameBinding
@Target({ ElementType.TYPE, ElementType.METHOD })
@Retention(value = RetentionPolicy.RUNTIME)
public @interface Encrypt { }
```

This is a runtime annotation and it can only be applied to class types or methods.

Now we can bind this annotation to the interceptor by applying to the class in the following way:

```
@Encrypt
@Provider
public class AESCipherInterceptor
implements ReaderInterceptor, WriterInterceptor {
  /* ... as before as */ }
```

To complete the puzzle, we only need to apply the custom annotation to methods in a REST style resource that we want to protect. Following is a particular class, called SensitiveResource, which demonstrates the principle:

```
@Path("/docs")
public class SensitiveResource {
  @Encrypt
  @GET
  @Path("{id}")
  @Produces("text/plain")
  public SensitiveDocument retrieve(
    @PathParam("id") String file )
  {
    /*...*/
  }

  @Encipher
  @POST
  @Path("{id}")
  @Consumes(MediaType.MULTIPART_FORM_DATA)
  public SensitiveDocument store(
    @PathParam("id") String file,
  @FormParam("file") InputStream inputStream )
  {
    /*...*/
  }
}
```

The method `retrieve()` in this REST style endpoint is annotated with `@Encrypt`. The JAX-RS provider will work out that this particular HTTP GET request on this resource is bound to the `AESCipherInterceptor`. The write interceptor will be invoked after the resource generates the response, which causes the response to be encrypting before the JAX runtime sends the result back to the client.

The resource method `store()` is triggered on HTTP POST request and also annotated with the `@Encrypt` method. This informs the runtime to bind an instance of the `AESCipherInterceptor` to the resource method. The read interceptor will be invoked first to decrypt the input stream before invoking the resource method, which results in the HTML Form encoded to be decrypted. Note that we must also annotate the resource method with `@Consume` tag, which stipulates the single HTML form parameter is a MIME multipart form upload.

Dynamic binding

There is still one other way to configure binding to a resource. Whereas the `@NameBinding` annotation means the configuration is a static means for a dynamic or runtime application of behavior that we cannot use this feature. Luckily, JAX-RS 2.0 provides an additional interface `javax.ws.js.container.DynamicInterface`.

The dynamic interface is designed for the registration of post-matching providers during a JAX-RS application initialization at the time of deployment. There is one single interface to implement called `configure()` and it takes two arguments, namely `javax.ws.js.container.ResourceInfo` and `javax.ws.js.core.FeatureContext`.

Let us write a new configuration feature class `AESCipherDynamicFeature`, which supports dynamic binding. Following is the new code snippet:

```
@Provider
public class AESCipherDynamicFeature
implements DynamicFeature
@Override
public void configure(ResourceInfo resourceInfo,
   FeatureContext config ) {
  if ( SensitiveResource.class.isAssignableFrom(
     resourceInfo.getResourceClass() &&
       resourceInfo.getResourceMethod()
     .isAnnotationPresent(
     GET.class)) {
    config.register(
       new AESCipherInterceptor() );
    }
  }
}
```

The class must be annotated with the `@Provider` in order to be successfully scanned by the JAX-RS runtime. Once the runtime discovers the new feature and it can see that the class is a type of `DynamicFeature` then the runtime invokes `configure()` method. We verify the resource that we want to protect is the target, and we also check the REST style resource method is the correct one to apply this interceptor. Is this resource method the HTTP GET request method? When these conditions are true, then we use the `FeatureContext` instance to configure and associate an instance of the interceptor with the resource.

Summary

The REST style API is improved in Version 2.0 for Java EE 7. In this chapter, we covered the essentials of Representational State Transfer, the architectural style of the application.

We saw how to write REST style endpoints for collections of entities and how that progresses to single entities. REST is about the design of URI patterns and templates. We learnt how to configure the servlet mapping for JAX-RS applications.

We built a sample JAX resource endpoint with the HTTP request protocols `GET`, `PUT`, `POST`, and `DELETE`. We applied the corresponding annotations: `@GET`, `@PUT`, `@POST`, and `@DELETE`. We mapped URL fragments to JAX-RS server side resources and subresources with the `@Path` annotation. We configure dynamic behavior through path variable and we are able to extract values from the URI template; and now we can also extract data using the various annotations, such as `@QueryParam`, and `@FormParam`.

JAX-RS sub-resources can be configured by location or directly in the same resource. We saw that architecting resources into sub-resources is preferred as best practice, because it separates concerns and leads to better modularity in the code base for the long term; therefore reducing the technical debt and high maintenance.

We explored the new Client API in JAX-RS 2.0 and witnessed how it can help unit test to RESTful endpoints. We understood how to write asynchronous input and output application to leverage another JAX-RS 2.0 feature.

JAX-RS resources have the option to generate custom response using the `ResponseBuilder` and `Response` classes. We revealed that JAX-RS `Provider` instances are the key to extending the runtime and the door to writing custom functionality through server or client side filter, or the entity interceptors.

The next chapter Java Message Service investigates Java EE 7's latest support for sending and receiving data through a messaging system.

9
Java Message Service 2.0

Federick D. Gregor, the first African-American to pilot and command a NASA Space Shuttle mission said, "When I arrived back at Aircraft Ops [Operations], in my little bin that I put my helmet in, there was a little message that said, "Call Don [Donald R.] Puddy".

The **Java Message Service (JMS)** API predates Java EE (or J2EE 1.2 released on December 12, 1999) and has only had one specification update since its inception. The JMS 2.0 specification is the long overdue update for Java EE 7. Java Message Service standardizes a common messaging layer for enterprise Java applications.

JMS is based on an interesting field of endeavor for business IT communication which is called **Message Oriented Middleware.** These enterprise message products allow different components distributed on different servers and a lot of time-distributed applications across separate companies to communicate with each other by sending messages from one system to another. The field of messaging permits enterprise architects to design systems that flow business data asynchronously out of one system into another.

The developer should be warned that JMS is a low-level Java library that permits these types of systems to be written. It is low-level because there is an entire abstraction of messaging above JMS, which is **Enterprise Information Architecture (EIA)**. EIA is concerned with architectural design patterns surrounding messaging systems, channels, and their respective components. It has abstractions and descriptions around routing, data transformation, aggregation, filtering, and channels.

[ If you are interested in EIA and higher level abstraction, please refer to Gregor Hophe and Bobby Woolf's classic book — *Enterprise Integration Patterns*.]

What is JMS?

Java Message Service is an API that applications can utilize to create, send, receive, and read messages mostly asynchronously and reliably over a messaging system in order to build systems that are loosely coupled.

Enterprises are heavily dependent on messaging systems for their daily operations. It does not matter whether they are a large Fortune 500 company or small medium businesses. Here is a very high-level example of an architecture that the majority of investment banking IT businesses typically have in their global operations. Let's say that we are a fictional institution called *Simple Bank PLC*, a private limited company in the United Kingdom. Simple Bank relies on a division of labor, sometimes called silos, to separate the work of the trading desks from the work back office: the front office makes the deals on the trades and the back office validates records and manages the post-processing of the deal after the trades have been agreed.

In this simplified bank architecture, technically, Simple Bank has two systems: one for the front office and the other for the back office. How do these systems communicate over the entire life cycle of software enterprise applications that are installed in a bank and still have a long-term view of maintainability? The answer is that this simple bank installed a proprietary messaging system to act as a conduit between the two system and this systems allows asynchronous, reliable, and robust communication.

Here is the story: a long time ago, Simple Bank invested in enterprise Java in order to integrate their many bespoke systems with the JV and future-proof their architecture and strengthen their software development lifecycle. The bank started to use the JMS API as part of Java EE to write its own internal processes and applications around the message system.

Like similar investment banks, Simple Bank has several different components. In the front office, there is Exposure and Limits, which is an enterprise component to perform credit checking on trades. It has a Portfolio Management component that allows traders, sales, and marketing staff to manage accounts directly and indirectly for counterparties and private investment customers. After the year 2012, because Simple Bank now operates and trades also in the United States of America and it is listed as a legal entity on the stock market in New York, Simple Bank is required to comply with the **Dodd-Frank** (Reform and Consumer Protection Act: `http://en.wikipedia.org/wiki/Dodd%E2%80%93Frank_Wall_Street_Reform_and_Consumer_Protection_Act`). There is a huge signification investment in a recent Regulatory Reporting component that takes care of sending XML data to the US regulatory government bodies.

Moving to the back office, there is a component for an Electronic Management Information System, which is supposedly a very crucial component for the bank's board. The top senior executives require this component to find out about the bank's key market data, the business of running a bank, and the overall balance sheet: day-to-day, week-to-week, and month-to-month. There is a Profit and Loss center component in the back office system which typically is part of the proprietary electronic trading system (which is not illustrated) that Simple Bank relies on to create end-of-day reports. In the global operation of most investment banks, which are now 24-hour trading, the act of computing real-time profit and loss and trading days are complicated by time zones, local business holidays, and big data. And this brings up Batch Operations, which are key essential tasks such as calculating the entire trade volume at the end of the day and computing expensive derivative risk operations and trade rate curves that are essential long running operations.

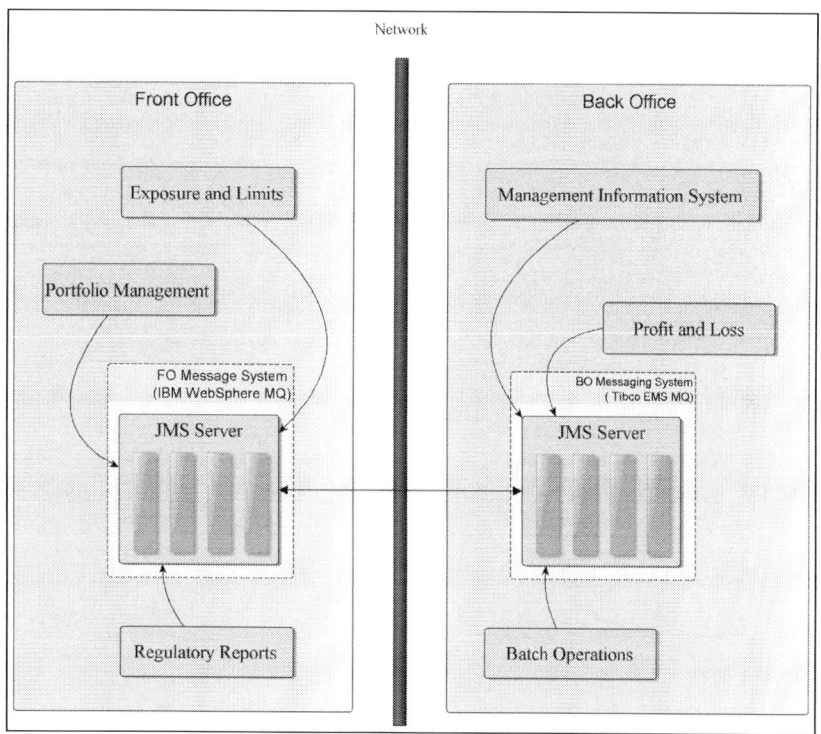

All of these enterprise components need a way to communicate with each other. The old fashion way was to make Remote Procedure Calls, which is very low-level and imperative way of communication and requires knowledge about networking. The modern way is to allow each component to send messages to each other over a guaranteed delivery system. XML is the message content type of choice for a lot of investment banks. Today, many of them use a popular variant that falls under the guise of **Financial Product Mark-up Language (FPML)** to another. In our Simple Bank example, there are two of them: one dedicated system by IBM WebSphere MQ installed in the front office and the other is a Tibco Enterprise Messaging System middleware in the back office. There is an internal network; also an intranet that bridges the two message systems.

Why are there two different vendor systems? To add more salt to the wound, let's just say that Simple Bank was a result of a recent merger and acquisition situation. Simple Bank is a long term IBM customer and was taken over by Bigger and Better Bank, which is a long time Tibco customer. This sort of enterprise asset inconsistency is not untypical in a technology-driven business operation. Messaging systems are tied up with requirements, profitable business reasons, and real-world application of technology. They are an interesting mixture.

Messaging systems

There are two types of messaging, namely **point-to-point (P2P)** and **publish-subscribe (Pub-Sub)**.

Point-to-point messaging

In point-to-point messaging, a producer sends a message over a queue channel and exactly one consumer receives it and processes it. A channel is a reliable conduit for a producer and consumer to communicate by messages. Once the message in the channel is delivered to the consumer, then it is no longer available in the channel.

In normal practice, production and consumption of messages takes place asynchronously. In other words, the producer does not have to block and wait whilst the message is being sent and the messaging system that delivers the message to the consumer is also not blocked on a Java thread. However, JMS 2.0 does allow you to synchronously publish messages. It is also possible within JMS 2.0 for a point-to-point consumer to receive messages both asynchronously and synchronously.

Point-to-point (P2P) model

Do not confuse this with another concept in distributed networking software that also shares the abbreviation (peer-to-peer) in message-oriented middleware. The P2P model is designed for messaging communication where there is one and only one component for each message.

The P2P model can be used in an e-commerce application that processes a customer order. A customer entry component sends an XML order to a warehouse system which will then process the order and update the business internal and external inventory. The warehouse system is responsible for reducing the stock count of products and therefore the e-commerce front end system at a later time shows a reduced stock frame.

Here is an illustration of a point-to-point model for a typical e-commerce application:

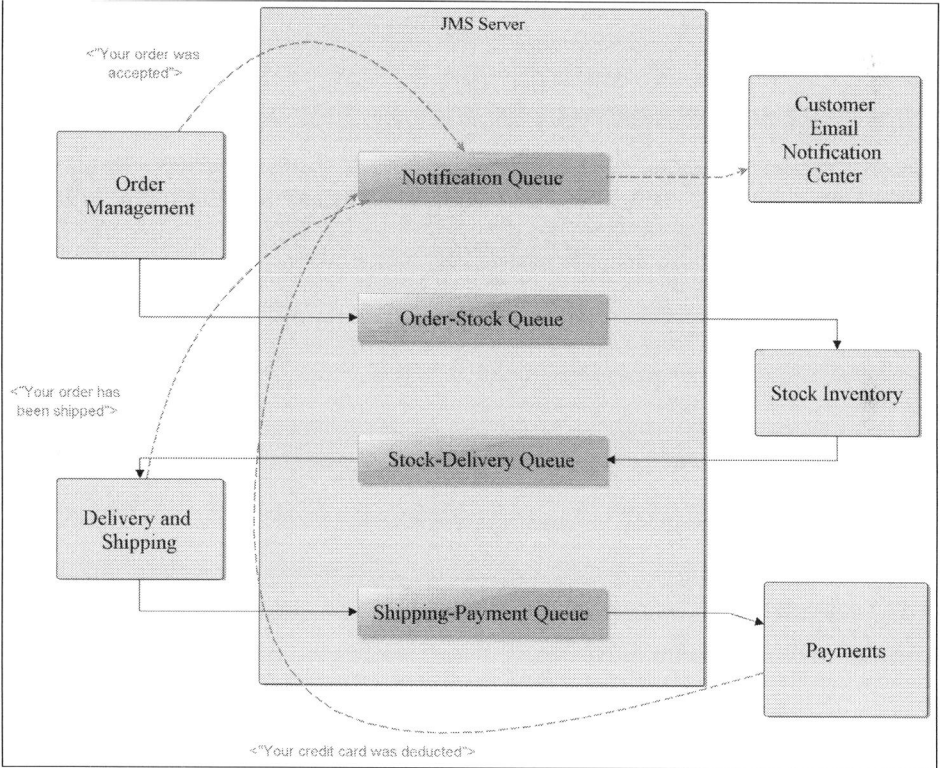

The message queues loosely couple the enterprise components to each other.

Publish-subscribe messaging

In publish-subscribe messaging, a producer sends a message over a topic channel and multiple consumers who have already subscribed to the same channel will receive the same message and therefore process it accordingly. If a consumer is not registered to the channel at the point when the channel is delivering the message, the consumer is not subscribed and will miss the message. Other consumers who are subscribed to the channel will receive the message.

You can think of the pub-sub model as a sort of TV broadcasting, although this similarity is allegoric. The viewer or digital tuner has to be tuned to the TV channel in order to receive the content.

The producer does not have to register with the topic channel in order to send a message, but they do need to know the topic name and how to find the topic channel. Consumers just have to subscribe to the topic channel and they can unsubscribe at any time. The topic channel is also a reliable conduit of messages. Each message supplied to the topic channel will be delivered to registered consumers. If there are no consumers on the topic channel, then the message will be lost at the point of delivery.

The pub-sub messaging model is inherently asynchronous in nature, since it delivers one message to probably hundreds or possibly thousands of consumers. In JMS, it is possible to block and wait on sending a message to a topic channel, but most of time applications do not do this. It is also possible for subscribers to receive messages both asynchronously and synchronously.

Pub-sub model

The pub-sub model makes use of topic channels, where the channel name is the destination address of the message. Multiple recipients can retrieve each message on the channel because the messaging system will handle the responsibility of delivering the message to consumers.

The biggest benefit of the pub-sub model is that the message producer (the publisher) does not need to be aware of the consumers (the subscribers) and therefore the model is amenable to the broadcasting of data. An application that sends financial stock, derivative prices, or market data benefits from the pub-sub model.

Following is an illustration of a pub-sub model for an investment bank. It shows only a very small subset of the physical topic channels for the front-office operations. There are a number of publishers on the left-hand side of the diagram which send XML message data to registered subscribers on the right-hand side.

The USD GBP and the EUR USD publishers are message producers in the Foreign Exchange (FOREX) domain. The USD GBP publisher updates on the movement of the US Dollar and British Pounds currencies and likewise the EUR USD publisher updates on USD Dollar and Euro movements.

External customers who use the bank's online e-commerce trading solution tend to trade only in response to the value of a single currency: "When the British Pound rises to £1.45 against the Dollar, perform this action." A consumer may be interested in Euros and not at all interested in Japanese Yen. Therefore, JMS message consumers are subscribed to a particular currency in order to receive real-time currency updates. (It is up to the applications to feed these updates to the external customer and these components, are not shown in the diagram.)

The Stock Loan and the Government Bond publishers are message producers in the Money Market (MM) domain. The message consumers registered for the Money Market topic will process updates to any external customers.

This pub-sub model is very appropriate for loosely-coupled producers and consumers that require a broadcast-style conduit of communication.

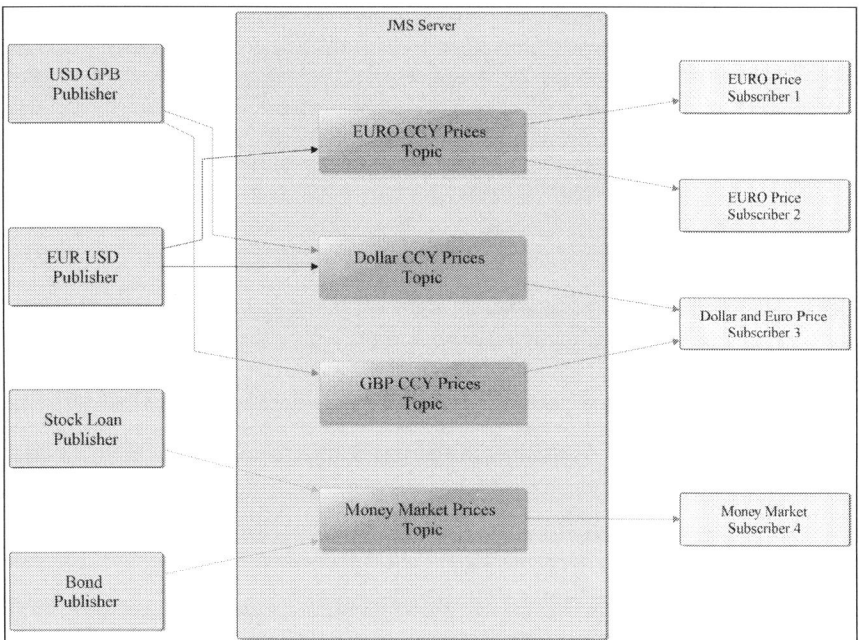

JMS definitions

JMS is a specification API that abstracts out communication through messaging systems into a portable framework. Programming against JMS permits the application to be portable to many messaging systems, proprietary, and open source support. There are several vendors of enterprise messaging systems such as Apache ActiveMQ, IBM WebSphereMQ, JBoss Messaging, Oracle AQ, and Progress Software SonicMQ. JMS allows the developer to connect to different vendor products in a similar fashion to JDBC (Java Database Connectivity).

The JMS specification has some terminology and definitions of its components and describes each component's role and responsibility. The following table outlines the components and responsibilities in a JMS application:

Term	Definition
JMS Provider	Specifies the conduit message system that makes JMS API available. The provider has the responsibility to route and deliver messages
JMS Client	Specifies any Java or Java EE application that makes use of the JMS API
JMS Consumer	Specifies the JMS client that consumes JMS messages
JMS Producer	Specifies the JMS client that produces JMS messages
JMS Message	Specifies the message abstraction that flows through the conduit. A message consists of a header, properties, and payload (also known as the body)

We should point out that JMS is not just a messaging system API for two or more Java or Java EE applications to communicate with. JMS can also allow Java systems to communicate data to other systems which are not written in Java and/or the JVM. There are several JMS providers that have extensive support of alternative operating systems, vertical stacks, and architectures such as Microsoft .Net and other proprietary technologies.

JMS 2.0 introduces a simplified API that makes the developer's programming life far easier in comparison to a traditional API. The classic API, which last updated with JMS 1.1, unified the concepts of point-to-point (queues) and publish-subscribe (topic) into a concise whole.

JMS classic API

The JMS 1.1 API has been referred to as the classic API since Java EE 7 was released. The classic API married together two previously incompatible library framework calls: queues and topics. The standard package for JMS classic is `javax.jms`.

JMS simplified API

The JMS 2.0 API is simplified and offers all of the features of the classic API yet requires fewer Java interfaces. Moreover, JMS 2.0 introduces flexible annotations for maximum developer affordance. The standard package for the JMS simplified API is defined as `javax.jms`, and it contains main interfaces and annotations.

JMS message types

JMS 2.0 supports a set of message types. The most common type that developers will encounter, especially in a professional environment, are text type messages, namely `javax.jms.TextMessage`, since an awful lot of enterprise applications send and receive XML data across disparate systems.

Here is a list of the common JMS message types:

JMS Message Type	Description
ByteMessage	This message type represents a series of bytes
MapMessage	This type represents a set of name and value pairs
ObjectMessage	This type represents a serialized Java object
StreamMessage	This type represents a sequence of primitive data types
TextMessage	This type represents a set of `java.lang.String` objects

A quick JMS 2.0 example

There is an awful lot of theory for messaging systems, especially if you have never encountered such architecture before. In this section, we are going to send a simple text message to a queue using JMS 2.0.

We will start with a stateless EJB session, because we need an endpoint to receive a client request. Here is the code for `PayloadCheck`:

```
package je7hb.jms.essentials;
import javax.annotation.Resource;
import javax.ejb.Stateless;
import javax.inject.Inject;
import javax.jms.JMSConnectionFactory;
import javax.jms.JMSContext;
import javax.jms.Queue;
import java.util.*;
```

```java
@Stateless
public class PayloadCheck {
    @Inject
    @JMSConnectionFactory("jms/demoConnectionFactory")
    JMSContext context;

    @Resource(mappedName = "jms/demoQueue")
    private Queue inboundQueue;

    List<String> messages = new ArrayList<>();

    public void sendPayloadMessage( String payload ) {
        System.out.printf(
           "%s.sendPayloadMessage(%s) Thread: %s\n",
            getClass().getSimpleName(), payload,
           Thread.currentThread());
        context.createProducer().send( inboundQueue, payload);
        messages.add(payload);
    }

    public List<String> getMessages() {
        return messages;
    }
}
```

In later sections of this chapter, we cover and explain the full details of the JMS 2.0 API. All you need to know for now is that the `javax.jms.JMSContext` object is the new way of accessing the JMS provider and the messaging system. The Java EE application server, in this case GlassFish Embedded Container 4, injects the `JMSContext` instance into the EJB `PayloadCheck` with `javax.jms.Queue`. The `sendPayloadMessage()` method stores each successful text message in a list collection which is accessible by the client through the `getMessages()` method.

We need a unit test for this code, so we will rely on the Arquillian Framework to help us to do the verification. The unit test looks like this:

```java
package je7hb.jms.essentials;
import org.jboss.arquillian.container.test.api.Deployment;
import org.jboss.arquillian.junit.Arquillian;
import org.jboss.shrinkwrap.api.ArchivePaths;
import org.jboss.shrinkwrap.api.ShrinkWrap;
import org.jboss.shrinkwrap.api.asset.EmptyAsset;
import org.jboss.shrinkwrap.api.spec.JavaArchive;
```

```
import org.junit.Test;
import org.junit.runner.RunWith;
import javax.ejb.EJB;
import static org.junit.Assert.*;

@RunWith(Arquillian.class)
public class PayloadCheckTest {
    @Deployment
    public static JavaArchive createDeployment() {
        JavaArchive jar = ShrinkWrap.create(JavaArchive.class)
                .addClasses(PayloadCheck.class)
                .addAsManifestResource(
                        EmptyAsset.INSTANCE,
            ArchivePaths.create("beans.xml"));
        return jar;
    }

    @EJB PayloadCheck service;

    @Test
    public void shouldFireMessage() {
        service.sendPayloadMessage("hello");
        service.sendPayloadMessage("world");
        assertEquals("hello", service.getMessages().get(0));
        assertEquals("world", service.getMessages().get(1));
    }
}
```

This simple test verifies the message based purely on the order of the statements in sendPayloadMessage(). If there was an exception raised when sending the text message to the queue, then the payload text will not be recorded, which satisfies the condition of the test.

With Arquillian and embedded GlassFish, we need to configure extra resources. The first is the Arquillian file that directs the framework to load an additional server configuration.

Here is the said file, aquillian.xml, which is found under the src/main/resources folder:

```
<?xml version="1.0" encoding="UTF-8"?>
<arquillian xmlns="http://jboss.org/schema/arquillian"
    xmlns:xsi="http://www.w3.org/2001/XMLSchema-instance"
    xsi:schemaLocation="
```

```xml
                http://jboss.org/schema/arquillian
                http://jboss.org/schema/arquillian/arquillian_1_0.xsd">
    <container qualifier="glassfish-embedded" default="true">
      <configuration>
        <property name="resourcesXml">
          src/test/resources-glassfish-embedded
          /glassfish-resources.xml
        </property>
      </configuration>
    </container>
</arquillian>
```

When the Arquillian file starts up the embedded GlassFish server, we have to configure administrative objects for our unit test. We configure the message queue, the connection factory, and the JNDI names. These administrative objects are configured in the `glass-resources.xml` file, which is found in a separate source folder tree, namely `src/test/resources-glassfish-embedded`.

This is the next resource file:

```xml
<?xml version="1.0" encoding="UTF-8"?>
<!DOCTYPE resources PUBLIC
    "-//GlassFish.org//DTD GlassFish Application Server 3.1
    Resource Definitions//EN"
    "http://glassfish.org/dtds/glassfish-resources_1_5.dtd">
<resources>
    <admin-object-resource enabled="true"
      jndi-name="jms/demoQueue"
      res-type="javax.jms.Queue" res-adapter="jmsra">
      <property name="Name" value="PhysicalQueue"/>
    </admin-object-resource>
    <connector-connection-pool
      name="jms/demoDestinationFactoryPool"
      connection-definition-name=
        "javax.jms.QueueConnectionFactory"
      resource-adapter-name="jmsra"/>
    <connector-resource enabled="true" jndi-name=
      "jms/demoConnectionFactory"
      pool-name="jms/demoDestinationFactoryPool"  />
</resources>
```

Running the full application provides the expected test results: a green bar.

Establishing a JMS connection

In order to send and receive any messages in JMS, an application requires a handle to a JMS provider.

Connecting to a JMS provider

A JMS client connects to a JMS provider through administrative objects. These administrative objects can be injected into the application if the developer uses annotations or they can be retrieved by navigating to the Java Native Directory Interface in a Java EE application server or by directly looking up the name and programming in the JMS API.

Inside a Java EE application server, the connection details of the administrative objects are established through external configuration. The JMS specification does not explicitly define how the administration objects are set up. Java EE application servers allow applications to set up administrative objects through XML files. Most products, including GlassFish, have a separate web-based administration console where operations can set up connection factories and connection pools.. In the Java EE specification, this is the role of the Deployer and Administrator (see *Online Chapter, Moving Java EE.next to the Cloud*).

JMS defines two administrative objects: `javax.jms.ConnectionFactory` and `javax.jms.Destination`.

Connection factories

The connection factory is the provider object that creates a connection to the JMS provider and a destination address in order to send a message. The interface responsible for supplying connections is called `javax.jms.ConnectionFactory`. The connection factory is rather similar to `javax.sql.DataSource` in the JDBC specification. `DataSource` provides a database connection to a relational database. `ConnectionFactory` provides a connection to the messaging system conduit.

Here is the interface definition:

```
package javax.jms;
public interface ConnectionFactory {
    Connection createConnection()
    throws JMSException;

    Connection createConnection(
```

```
        String userName, String password)
    throws JMSException;

    /* Since JMS 2.0 */
    JMSContext createContext();

    JMSContext createContext(
        String userName, String password);

    JMSContext createContext(
        String userName, String password, int sessionMode);

    JMSContext createContext(int sessionMode);
}
```

In the JMS 1.1 standard, the connection factory provides access to the `javax.jms.Connection` object, which is the connection that represents either a queue (P2P) or topic (pub-sub).

Since Java EE 7 and JMS 2.0, connections to the messaging systems are now preferred through the new overloaded methods on `createContext()`, which returns `javax.jms.JMSContext`. The other methods are overloaded variations of them. The `createContext(` method creates or retrieves a default JMS connection for the application server, which is really only useful for testing. The other take a combination of the login credentials and optionally accept a connection mode. See the later section on JMSContexts for the modes.

It is worth noting that `javax.jms.Connection` are now compatible with Java SE 7 try-resource syntax as they extend `java.lang.AutoCloseable`.

Default connection factory

JMS 2.0 defines a default connection factory for Java EE full-provide application servers which your application can use, which means all Java EE 7 applications have definite access to a JMS connection. The object is called JNDI (`java:comp/jmsDefaultConnectionFactory`). Your application can always assume the default connection factory is there and use it. Retrieving the default connection factory is as simple as injecting the `@Inject` annotation on the `JMSContext` object.

This is a code snippet that injects `JMSConnectionFactory` into a bean:

```
@Inject
@JMSConnectionFactory("java:comp/defaultJMSConnectionFactory")
private JMSContext context;
```

Message destinations

The message destination is the abstraction over the conduit that connect the Java application to the messaging system. A message destination has provider address to identify its location in the messaging system. The address allows other endpoint to send message over the channel. A JMS destination is called a queue for point-to-point communications, otherwise it is called topic for the pub-sub model.

In JMS, this representation is the marker interface `javax.jms.Destination`, which happens to be a super interface of `javax.jms.Queue` and `javax.jms.Topic`.

Here is a condensed definition of these interfaces:

```
package javax.jms;

public interface Destination { }

public interface Queue extends Destination {
    String getQueueName() throws JMSException;
    String toString();
}

public interface Topic extends Destination {
    String getTopicName() throws JMSException;
    String toString();
}
```

Message destinations were introduced in JMS 1.1 in order to unify the two messaging models.

JMSContext

`javax.jms.JMSContext` is the main interface in the simplified JMS 2.0 specification. The intention of this new interface was to merge the two different ways of configuring and administrating JMS clients in the previous specifications.

In the earlier specification, there were a lot of different objects involved in order to make a connection to the JMS provider, create a message destination, create a message, and send the message on the connection.

For new applications with JMS 2.0, a developer simply injects `JMSContext` into their code, especially if it runs inside a supporting Java EE 7 application server.

The Java interface `JMSContext` defines a number of important methods:

Method	Description
`createContext( int deliveryMode ): JMSContext`	Creates a new `JMSContext` using the same connection as this one and creates a new JMS session with the requested session mode.
	In a Java EE application server environment, and where `JMSContext` is injected into the application class, this call is prohibited and results in `IllegalStateRuntimeException`.
`createProducer(): JMSProducer`	Creates a new `JMSProducer`, which can be used to configure and send messages.
`getClientID()`	Gets the client identifier for `JMSContext` connection.
`setClientID()`	Sets the client identifier for `JMSContext` connection. Calling this method is prohibited inside a Java EE or EJB application server. If the application invokes this message in such an environment, `javax.jms.InvalidClientIDEXception` results.
`start()`	Starts (or restarts) the delivery of incoming messages by the JMS connection. A call to start on a connection that has already started is ignored.
	In a Java EE application server environment, and where `JMSContext` is injected into the application class, this call is prohibited and results in `IllegalStateRuntimeException`.
`stop()`	Temporarily stops the delivery of incoming messages by the JMS connection.
	In a Java EE application server environment, and where `JMSContext` is injected into the application class, this call is prohibited and results in `IllegalStateRuntimeException`.

Method	Description
`close()`	Closes the `JMSContext` and the underlying producers and consumers. Temporary destinations are also deleted. This method may well block the calling application until any incomplete asynchronous send operations are completed.
`createBytesMessage(): BytesMessage`	Creates a `BytesMessage` object in order to send a message containing a stream of uninterrupted bytes.
`createMapMessage(): MapMessage`	Creates a `MapMessage` object in order to send a message containing name-value pairs.
`createMessage(): Message`	Creates a `Message` object in order to send only header information.
`createObjectMessage(): ObjectMessage`	Creates an `ObjectMessage` in order to send a serializable Java object.
`createStreamMessage(): StreamMessage`	Creates a `StreamMessage` in order to send a message defining a stream of primitive values.
`createTextMessage(): TextMessage`	Creates a `TextMessage` in order to send `java.lang.String` messages.
`createTextMessage(String text): TextMessage`	Creates a `TextMessage` in order to send `java.lang.String` messages.
`getTransacted(): boolean`	Gets the Boolean flag if this `JMSContext` is transacted or not.
`getSessionMode(): int`	Gets the session mode constant for this `JMSContext`.
`commit()`	Commits all messages done in this transaction and releases any locks currently held.
	This call is prohibited for container-managed connections. Doing so will cause `IllegalStateRuntimeException` to be raised.

Method	Description
`rollback()`	Rolls back any messages done in this transaction and releases any locks currently held by this `JMSContext`.
	This call is prohibited for container-managed connections. Doing so will cause `IllegalStateRuntimeException` to be raised.
`recover()`	Stops message delivery in `JMSContext` session and restarts message delivery with the oldest unacknowledged message. The delivery will then continue in serial order.
	This call is prohibited for container-managed connections. Doing so will cause `IllegalStateRuntimeException` to be raised.
`createConsumer( Destination destination ): JMSConsumer`	Creates a `JMSConsumer` for the specified destination using the supplied message selector.
`createDurableConsumer( Topic topic, String topicName ): JMSConsumer`	Creates an unshared durable subscription on the specified topic and creates a consumer in that durable subscription.
`createSharedDurableConsumer( Topic topic, String topicName ): JMSConsumer`	Creates a shared durable subscription on the specified topic and creates a consumer in that durable subscription.
`createSharedDurableConsumer( Topic topic, String topicName ): JMSConsumer`	Creates a shared non-durable subscription on the specified topic and creates a consumer in that non-durable subscription.
`createBrowser(Queue queueName): QueueBrowser`	Creates a `QueueBrowser` object in order to peek at the messages on the specified queue.
`createTemporaryQueue(): QueueBrowser`	Creates a `TemporaryQueue` object that will only live for the lifetime of the JMSContext.
`createTemporaryTopic(): TemporaryTopic`	Creates a `TemporaryTopic` object that will only live for the lifetime of the JMSContext.

Method	Description
`unsubscribe(String topicName)`	Unsubscribes a durable subscription that has been created by a client.
`acknowledge()`	Acknowledges all messages consumed by `JMSContext` session.

The `JMSContext` interface also declares static constants, which are useful for controlling message acknowledgement behavior in the downstream system. These are called **delivery modes**:

Constant Name	Description
AUTO_ACKNOWLEDGE	Specifies the session and automatically acknowledges a client's receipt of a message either when the session has returned from an invocation of a call or when the message listener has been invoked and the handler successfully returns.
	An alias of the `Session.AUTO_KNOWLEDGE`.
CLIENT_ACKNOWLEDGE	Specifies session that the client controls when messages have been acknowledged. This session mode is designed for a message listener that reads lots of messages in a batch mode (unacknowledged) and then later returns the acknowledgement for each processed message.
	An alias of `Session.CLIENT_KNOWLEDGE`.
DUPS_OK_ACKNOWLEDGE	Specifies the session to lazily acknowledge the delivery of messages, which might result in the delivery of duplicate message, especially if the JMS provider fails (crashes or is forcefully shutdown). The consumer must be aware of the possibility of incoming duplicate messages. This mode affords lower overheads by minimizing the requirement for eager automatic acknowledgements.
	An alias of `Session.DUP_OKS_ACKNOWLEDGE`.
SESSION_TRANSACTED	Specifies the session to deliver and consume messages in a local transaction, which will subsequently either be committed or rolled back by the message listener explicitly.
	An alias of `Session.SESSION_TRANSACTED`.

The `JMSContext` is a very useful instance in a server-side application because it allows the developer to rely on annotations. The best way to get a `JMSContext` is to inject it into the application logic. Inside a Java EE environment, there are restrictions on calling certain methods that would interfere with the application server that can cause undefined behavior. An exception is thrown if you attempt to call `commit()`, `rollback()`, or `recover()` on a message destination. If these calls were allowed, then they could be detrimental to the operation of the Java EE server, because suddenly the application could take ownership over internal managed resources when it is not supposed to.

On the client side, the developer must create or retrieve a JMSContext manually. Java EE 7 does not define standalone behavior. Perhaps this is a weakness of the current JMS 2.0 specification. It should be possible to inject a `JMSContext` in a Java SE application by using a standalone CDI container such as JBoss Weld.

JMSContext in a Java EE server

`JMSContext` behaves differently inside an application running on a Java EE server in comparison to a Java SE environment. Inside a Java EE application server or EJB server, the `JMSContext` can be injected into the application. For an application running under the web profile server with a JMS provider extension, the `JMSContext` can also be injected into the application. The benefit of having only one object is obviously beneficial to dependency injection. The application server takes care of creating, opening or closing the context.

Retrieving a JMSContext

There are two ways to retrieve a `JMSContext`:

- A developer can create a `JMSContext` from `ConnectionFactory` by simply calling the `createContext()` method. This allows a Java SE application to only have one object to get a JMS connection. Once the application is finished with the context, simply call `close()`.

- The second way requires a Java EE application server or container, and the developer uses the CDI annotation `@javax.annotation.Inject` to inject the `JMSContext` into the class.

Sending JMS messages

An application sends a message to the JMS provider using a `javax.jms.JMSProducer` producer. This producer can be obtained from a `JMSContext` in the simplified API in JMS 2.0 by calling the `createProducer()` method.

Upgrading message producers from JMS 1.1

In JMS 1.1, creating a `javax.jms.MessageProducer` object sends the messages. Developers who are fortunate enough to experience this API will see code that looks similar to this:

```
// JMS 1.1
Connection conx =
  queueConnectionFactory.createConnection();
Session session = conx.createSession(true,
  Session.AUTO_ACKNOWLEDGE);
MessageProducer producer = session.createProducer()
producer.setDeliverDelay(10*1000)
producer.setPriority(7)
producer.setTimeToLive(1000)
producer.setDeliverMode(DeliveryMode.NON_PERSISTENT)
producer.send(destination, message );
```

The older API only provides bean setter methods in order to configure destination parameters. `JMSProducer` is the preferred way for JMS 2.0 because it always supports the fluent-style of interface; it has method chaining:

```
// JMS 2.0
JMSContext context = /* Injected */
JMSProducer producer = context.createProducer()
producer.setDeliverDelay(10*1000)
  .setTimeToLive(1000)
  .setPriority(7)
  .setDeliverMode(DeliveryMode.NON_PERSISTENT)
  .send(destination, message );
```

The method chaining is clearer, eminently readable, and affords declarative code.

Sending messages synchronously

Synchronous sending occurs when the JMS client sends a message to the channel and the provider does not return the thread of control to the sender until it knows that the consumer endpoint has received and acknowledged that successful consumption of the message. This is an example of block-and-wait.

The `JMSProducer` defines these methods as synchronous operations in the simplified API:

```
send(Destination destination, Message message)
send(Destination destination, String body)
send(Destination destination, Map<String,Object> body)
send(Destination destination, byte[] body)
send(Destination destination, Serializable body)
send(Destination destination, String body)
```

Note that there is no need to create the intermediate `Message` type object. Incidentally, the developer can set custom key value and pair properties on the `JMSProducer` instance using the method `setStringProperty()`.

Sending messages asynchronously

A `JMSProducer` can also send messages asynchronously so the caller does not block-and-wait on the consumer to successfully acknowledge the message on the channel. This is a performance feature that is intended for unmanaged environment Java SE applications rather than inside an application server.

The `JMSProducer` defines a `setAsync()` method in the simplified API and it takes a single argument: an implementation of the Java interface class `javax.jms.CompletionListener`.

The definition of `CompletionListener` is as follows:

```
package javax.jms;
public interface CompletionListener {
  void onCompletion(Message message);
  void onException(Message message, Exception exception);
}
```

A completion listener must be registered prior to calling any of the `send()` overloaded methods on `JMSPublisher`. The JMS provider invokes the callback `onCompletion()` method when the consumer successfully consumes the message. It will invoke the callback method `onException()` instead when a failure occurs delivering the message to the consumer.

> `setAsync()` on a `JMSProducer` may not be called inside a Java EE web or EJB container. Asynchronous sending is designed for standard JMS applications running on Java SE. There is another way, and that is to write a concurrent worker, `java.lang.Runnable` or `java.util.concurrency.Callable`, that creates and sends messages on a destination object, `JMSProducer`. Concurrent tasks are made available in Java EE 7 Concurrency Utilities (JSR 236) through the new service `ManagedExecutorService`. Read more in *Appendix D, Java EE 7 Assorted Topics*.

JMS message headers

Every JMS message has a map collection of header fields which are name and value pairs. The message header is sent to all the JMS clients and they are able to read the complete message with the headers on the consumer side.

The names of the header fields begin with the prefix 'JMS' string; here is a table of the headers and their descriptions:

Header Field	Side	Description
`JMSDestination`	Provider	Contains the destination for the message.
`JMSDeliverMode`	Provider	Specifies the delivery mode when the message was sent.
`JMSMessageID`	Provider	Specifies the value that uniquely identifies each message sent by the JMS provider. The JMS provider always assigns the value and starts with the prefix 'ID:' string
`JMSTimestamp`	Provider	This field contains the time that the message was sent from the JMS client and accepted by the provider.
`JMSCorrelationID`	Provider	This field links one message with another in order to group together messages. This is a field that the client application can customize whilst sending the message. The correlation field typically associates a request message with a reply message.
`JMSReplyTo`	Client	Specifies a `Destination` supplied by a client when the message is sent. The consumer then sends the response to the target channel.

Header Field	Side	Description
JMSRedelivered	Provider	This field informs the consumer that a message was delivered but not acknowledged in the past. It is a strong hint to check for a duplicate message with the same ID in the backend database.
JMSType	Client	Specifies the message type identifier supplied by the client.
JMSExpiration	Provider	Specifies the expiration time whenever a message producer sends a message with which the JMS provider calculates an expiration time by adding the time-to-live values on the context. The value is measured in milliseconds since midnight, 1st January, 1970.
JMSPriority	Client	Specifies the priority of the message. The value of 0 is the lowest priority and the value of 9 is the highest. The range 0-4 gradations are defined as *normal* priority and the range 5-9 gradations are defined as *expedited* in the standard.

Most of these properties are set on the `javax.jms.Message` type, but they can be set on the JMSProducer type directly in a fluent API style.

The standard reserves the JMSX property prefix for JMSdefined properties. These are defined as key and value pairs on the message header and are important for message consumers.

Setting message properties

An application can also set additional properties on JMS messages just before it is sent to the provider. There is a complete set of overloaded `setProperty()` methods for every Java primitive except char. The method `setProperty( String, Object )` allows a Java primitive wrapper to be passed such as `java.lang.Long`. Calling `setProperty` with the same key and a different value overwrites the previous key-value association.

Setting a message delivery delay

In JMS 2.0, it is also possible to set a delivery delay on messages in which the case JMS provider understands that the message must be delayed on the message destination and not delivered until the delay period expires.

An application can call the method `setDeliveryDelay(long)` on the JMSProducer instance, which accepts a single argument: the delay period in milliseconds.

> **Delivery delay of bank trade messages**
>
>
> Why is this feature so useful? Imagine a bank that trades on the stock market in two geographic locations. One location for the bank is in London, Great Britain, and the other in New York, United States. The financial centers are only open for certain trading hours during the day. Let us say that both are open from 08:00 to 16:00. Let's also say we have a trader called Brian in London who agrees a new deal with a counterparty and then creates a new trade at exactly 09:00. This trade is dependent on a derivative data that is derived from information effective in the USA. The full execution of the trade cannot take place until the market in New York opens in four hours time at 01:00 London time because the time zone difference between London and New York is five hours (GMT -5:00). The London trading system can still post a trade message to the downstream system for further execution because it can add a special message property to delay delivery of the message for 4 hours. The downstream will only receive the trade message once the delay expires.

Receiving JMS messages

An application can receive a JMS message by creating a consumer from a destination. In the JMS 2.0 simplified API, an application can create a `javax.jms.JMSConsumer` object from the `JMSContext`. The method `createConsumer()` generates the consumer instance.

Upgrade from JMS 1.1

A JMS 1.1. application explicitly creates a `javax.jms.MessageConsumer` object from a connection factory and session. With this message destination object, it reads the messages from the destination. The traditional code looks similar to this example:

```
// JMS 1.1
Connection conx =
    queueConnectionFactory.createConnection();
Session session = conx.createSession(true,
    Session.AUTO_ACKNOWLEDGE);
MessageConsumer consumer = session.createConsumer(queue)
TextMessage textMessage =
    (TextMessage)messageConsumer.receive(1000);
System.out.printf("Message received was %s\n",
    textMessage.getText() );
```

In JMS 2.0, writing code with `JMSConsumer` is preferred. Here is the rewritten example using this object instance:

```
// JMS 2.0
JMSContext context = /* Injected */
JMSConsumer consumer = context.createConsumer(queue)
String text = consumer.receiveBody( String.class, 1000 );
```

With the `receiveBody()` method on the `JMSConsumer` instance, there is no need to cast the receive message to a `TextMessage` explicitly to get the body of the message, because the call will return the type of object required directly. If there is an error on conversion, then the JMS provider will raise a `javax.jms.JmsRuntimeException` exception.

Receiving messages synchronously

Synchronous reception of messages occurs when the JMS client makes an invocation to read a message on the channel and the JMS provider does not return the thread of control to the sender, until it has a message on the channel that can be retrieved. This is an example of blocking-and-waiting.

Here is a condensed definition of the `JMSConsumer` interface:

```
package javax.jms;

public interface JMSConsumer extends AutoCloseable {
    String getMessageSelector();

    MessageListener getMessageListener()
      throws JMSRuntimeException;

    void setMessageListener(MessageListener listener)
    throws JMSRuntimeException;

    Message receive();
    Message receive(long timeout);
    Message receiveNoWait();

    void close();

  <T> T receiveBody(Class<T> c);
  <T> T receiveBody(Class<T> c, long timeout);
  <T> T receiveBodyNoWait(Class<T> c);
}
```

The methods `receive()`, `receive( long timeout)`, or `receiveNoWait()` allow a client application to request the next message on the channel, which will be an abstract `Message` object. Unfortunately, the developer has to cast the object to the correct type.

The two `receiveBody()` methods return the payload of the message and have better affordance because they allow the JMS provider to cast the object to the request object, which is especially useful if the client is not interested in the header of the JMS message. However, if the application requires the header information such as the correlation ID of the message, these calls are not appropriate. If the message is not a supported type, or the payload of the message is not assignable to the supplied class type argument, then the provider raises a `javax.jms.MessageFormatRuntimeException` exception.

These `receive*()` methods operate synchronously and will block-and-wait until a message is put on the channel if it is empty at the time of the call.

The `close()` method will terminate the delivery of messages to the consumer. The `close()` method is the only method on the consumer which can be invoked from a separate thread, which is useful for managed concurrency services in a Java EE environment. Closing a consumer will block the calling thread if the JMS Consumer is in the middle of at least one `receive()` call.

Receiving messages asynchronously

In order to receive JMS messages asynchronously, the application registers `javax.jms.MessageListener` on the `JMSConsumer` object instance.

The Java interface for the message listener is really straightforward:

```
public interface MessageListener {
  void onMessage(Message message);
}
```

It is considered bad practice for a `MessageListener` to throw a `RuntimeException`. Instead, application code should trap fatal errors and log them somewhere or push these failures to a central monitoring server. During the asynchronous delivery of a message, a `RuntimeException` could cause the JMS provider to continuously redeliver a message forever, especially if the session is set to `AUTO_ACKNOWLEDGE` or `DUPS_OK_ACKNOWLEDGE`.

There is an exception to the rule where the `MessageListener` is part of the session that is set to `TRANSACTED`, so the session will be committed or rolled back. However, even then the application can explicitly perform the duty and also log the failure for the business of maintenance and operational support. Let's change gears and move from publication to consumption of messages. There are two fundamental ways to consume methods: shareable and non-shareable. These two categories can be further divided into durable or non-durable.

Non-shared subscriptions

In the simplified JMS 2.0, API there is no distinction in the way a developer creates a consumer reading from a queue from that of topic destination. The various overloaded methods, `createConsumer()` on `JMSContext`, will create `JMSConsumer` that is not sharable and not durable.

Every call to `createConsumer()` (and in JMS 1.1, `createSubscriber()` on the traditional `javax.jms.TopicSession`) will create a new non-shareable and non-durable subscription without a name. The subscriber will live for the duration of the `JMSConsumer` object.

The `createConsumer()` method always takes a `Destination`, which can be a `Queue` or `Topic`. Remember there is no distinction in the simplified API. The `messageSelector` argument in the overloaded variants specifies a filter for messages in the topic channel. If `messageSelector` is set to null, then all messages are received.

These are the API definitions:

```
JMSConsumer createDurableConsumer(Topic topic,
    String name );
JMSConsumer createDurableConsumer(Topic topic,
String name, String messageSelector,
    boolean noLocal);

JMSConsumer createSharedDurableConsumer(Topic topic,
    String name);
JMSConsumer createSharedDurableConsumer(Topic topic,
    String name, String messageSelector);
```

The third variant of `createConsumer()` accepts a `noLocal` Boolean parameter that specifies that messages published to a topic by their own connection must not be added to the subscription. This flag is designed for JMS consumers that publish new messages to the same connection. Set this flag to `true` if you are executing this behavior.

Once the `JMSConsumer` object is closed, the subscribers are terminated.

Shared subscriptions

JMS 2.0 introduces consumers that can be shared between different Java threads. This feature is particularly aimed at JMS clients running in Java SE environments and fixes a known issue with subscriptions on topic destinations. Messages from a topic are consumed from a subscription, and a subscription receives every message sent to the topic.

The issue with JMS 1.1 was that only one subscription on a topic could have only one consumer at a time. This was a limitation that severely limited the scalability of subscription: an application could not share the subscription topic between two Java threads for processing, or multiple JVM, or even multiple machines.

In JMS 2.0, there is a new type of topic-only subscription called shared subscriptions, and they can be durable or non-durable. Shared-subscriptions can have any number of consumers either in the same JVM or between two or more JVMs or multiple server machines. This makes shared subscriptions eminently scalable for those environments that prefer to only rely on Java SE and a JMS provider.

To create a sharable consumer, there are various `createSharedDestination()` methods on the `JMSContext` class in JMS 2.0.

The shareable consumer API is rather plain:

```
JMSConsumer createSharedConsumer(Topic topic,
  String sharedSubscriptionName);

JMSConsumer createSharedConsumer(Topic topic,
  String sharedSubscriptionName, String messageSelector);
```

Here, the developer must supply a `Topic` destination and, obviously, the common name of the subscription channel between the threads, JVMs, or machines.

Durable topic consumers

The durable consumers on a topic are extremely useful in e-commerce applications where every subscriber reliably receives all the messages in the channel. This translates to not losing a customer's orders in a large warehouse enterprise or a new or amended trade coming into the bank's straight-through-processing system.

The standard defines a durable subscription as the mode of communication where an application needs to receive all the messages published on a topic, including the messages published when there is no consumer associated with it. The JMS provider has the responsibility to retain a record of the durable subscription and to deliver messages from the topic channel to the consumer. The provider ensures messages are saved until they are delivered and acknowledged by a durable consumer. If a JMS message expires, then the provider is allowed to purge the message from the topic or save it somewhere else for operational support, if any.

In the simplified JMS 2.0, API durable consumers can be created with a variety of overloaded methods (`createDurableConsumer()` and `createSharedDurableConsumer()`) on the `JMSContext` instance. Durable consumers can be shared or non-shared on a connection.

The API for creating durable subscriptions looks like this:

```
JMSConsumer createDurableConsumer(Topic topic,
String name );
JMSConsumer createDurableConsumer(Topic topic,
String name, String messageSelector,
boolean noLocal);

JMSConsumer createSharedDurableConsumer(Topic topic,
String name);
JMSConsumer createSharedDurableConsumer(Topic topic,
String name, String messageSelector);
```

The durable consumer requires a subscription channel name in which the application must be specified. The name is an identifier of the client.

The JMS provider persists the durable subscriptions and therefore this fact immediately creates a trade-off between throughput and storage space. Messages will accumulate in the channel until they are deleted because the application calls the `unsubscribe()` method on the `JMSContext`.

So, inside your order processing subscriber for the warehouse enterprise, you are required to unsubscribe for a durable subscription.

Starting and stopping connections

In a Java SE environment, in order to receive messages from the JMS, the actual `JMSContext` must be started. This is of less importance when an application runs inside an EJB container or a server environment.

For a standalone application, it is important to invoke the `JMSContext.start()` method to set off the connection for the publication of messages and also to receive messages.

Conversely, calling the `JMSContext.stop()` methods begins the process of terminating the JMS connection to the provider. This call will block, of course, if there are active threads actually pushing messages or delivery messages in the provider's implementation.

A Java EE application with the inject JMS connection is prohibited from calling these methods. See the section on CDI injection for further information.

Redelivery of messages

Since JMS 2.0, providers are now required to provide a new JMS message header property called `JMSXDeliveryCount`. This value is set to the number of delivery attempts, and it now allows an application to portably know across vendors when a message has been resent.

The delivery count helps in situations where an incoming message such as an XML message has a syntactical or semantic failure which causes the processing to fail. The consumer throws a runtime exception and the stack frame unwinds all the way down to the JMS providers, which then thinks the message has failed to be delivered and therefore connects to the channel again for redelivery. This situation is essentially an infinite loop. Before JMS 2.0, there was no standard means to know how to handle repeated failed messages. With the new mandatory property `JMSXDeliveryCount`, an application can take evasive action.

Given a `Message` instance, call `getIntProperty("JMSXDeliveryCount")` to get the delivery count. A value of two or more means the message has been redelivered to the consumer.

Other JMS-defined properties

Incidentally, there are other optional standard JMS defined properties that can be useful. Here are some of them:

Name	Type	Set By	Description
JMSXUserID	String	Provider on Send	Defines the identity of the user sending the message
JMSXAppID	String	Provider on Send	Defines the application identity sending the message
JMSXDeliveryCount	int	Provider on Receive	The number of message delivery attempts on receiving consumers (mandatory for JMS 2.0 providers)
JMSXRcvTimestamp	Long	Provider on Receive	The receive time that the provider delivers the message to the consumer
JMSXGroupID	String	Client	Defines the identity group that the message belongs to
JMSXGroupSeq	Int	Client	Defines the sequence number for the message that belongs to a group of messages

This concludes the section on publishing messages to JMS and receiving messages. Let us move on to message-driven beans.

Message-driven Beans (MDBs)

A **Message-driven Bean (MDB)** is a stateless, transaction-aware component (service end-point) that consumes JMS messages asynchronously, and they are managed by a Java EE application server and EJB container. MDBs are similar to EJBs because they are complete enterprise beans, similar to stateless session beans. The EJB container is responsible for managing the lifecycle of the endpoint. MDB live inside the EJB container and the container looks after the environment, the security, and the resources, including transactions and concurrency. Most importantly, the container will also handle message acknowledgement and concurrency.

MDBs process messages concurrently and have a thread safety designed by default. There are no remote or local bean interfaces for MDBs, which means the application does not invoke methods on MDB directly, because they respond only to asynchronous messages. MDBs are scalable to hundreds and thousands of asynchronous JMS messages.

Chapter 9

In Java EE 7, a message-driven bean is declared with an annotation: `@javax.ejb.MessageDriven`. This annotation accepts an array of annotations for a configuration called `@javax.ejb.ActivationConfigProperty`.

Here is an example of a MDB:

```java
package je7hb.jms.essentials;
import javax.ejb.*;
import javax.jms.*;

@MessageDriven(
  mappedName = "jms/demoQueue",
  activationConfig = {
    @ActivationConfigProperty(
      propertyName="acknowledgeMode",
      propertyValue = "Auto-acknowledge"
    ),
    @ActivationConfigProperty(
      propertyName="messageSelector",
      propertyValue = "SpecialCode = 'Barbados'"
    ),
  }
)
public class PayloadCheckMDB implements MessageListener {
    @EJB
    private PayloadCheckReceiverBean receiver;

    public void onMessage(Message message) {
        try {
            TextMessage textMsg = (TextMessage)message;
            String text = textMsg.getText();
            receiver.addMessage(text);
        }
        catch (Exception e) {
            e.printStackTrace(System.err);
        }
    }
}
```

The class `PayloadCheckMDB` is annotated with `@MessageDriven` and it extends the `MessageListener` JMS interface. `PayloadCheckReceiverBean`, which is an EJB, is injected into the MDB. We do this because MDBs are asynchronous by default, and therefore we want to avoid recording the state in the message bean.

The `@MessageDriven` annotation accepts a `mappedName` parameter which identifies the connection; the `MessageDestination` that this MDB connects to. The activation configuration key-value pairs define the acknowledgment mode for the JMS session. There is also a `messageSelector` which filters the JMS messages that this MDB will receive.

 Please note the different package name for `@javax.ejb.MessageDriven`, which is a big clue that message-driven beans are truly enterprise beans!

Inside the `onMessage()` method, we retrieve the text of the `Message` instance and save it into the receiver bean.

Here is the code for the receiver bean:

```java
public class PayloadCheckReceiverBean {
    private CopyOnWriteArrayList<String> messages =
        new CopyOnWriteArrayList<>();

    public void addMessage(String text) {
        messages.add(text);
    }

    public List<String> getMessages() {
        return messages;
    }
}
```

The `PayloadCheckReceiverBean` is a singleton and a stateless session EJB which uses a concurrent collection to store messages. It is a singleton because we want to preserve its state for the duration of the unit test that follows.

Chapter 9

To complete the picture, we need a revised version of the earlier JMS sender EJB. Here is the code snippet for that bean:

```
package je7hb.jms.essentials;

/* ... similar to the previous ... */

@Stateless
public class PayloadCheckSenderBean {
    @Inject
    @JMSConnectionFactory("jms/demoConnectionFactory")
    JMSContext context;

    @Resource(mappedName = "jms/demoQueue")
    private Queue inboundQueue;

    List<String> messages = new ArrayList<>();

    public void sendPayloadMessage( String payload ) {
        sendPayloadMessage(payload,null); }

    public void sendPayloadMessage(
        String payload, String code ) {
        JMSProducer producer =
         context.createProducer();
         if (code != null ) {
            producer.setProperty("SpecialCode", code);
        }
        producer.send(inboundQueue, payload);
        messages.add(payload);
    }
    public List<String> getMessages() {
        return messages;
    }
}
```

The other EJB, `PayloadCheckSenderBean`, now has a refactored overloaded method, `sendPayloadMessage()`, which sends a message with a JMS header property or not. Choosing the two argument version of the method adds a property to the outgoing message with the key `SpecialCode`. This is the form for the message selector in the MDB.

[447]

Here is the full unit to exercise `PayloadCheckMDB`:

```java
package je7hb.jms.essentials;

/* ... similar to the previous ... */

@RunWith(Arquillian.class)
public class PayloadCheckMDBTest {

    @Deployment
    public static JavaArchive createDeployment() {
        JavaArchive jar = ShrinkWrap.create(JavaArchive.class)
            .addClasses(
                    PayloadCheckMDB.class,
                    PayloadCheckSenderBean.class,
                    PayloadCheckReceiverBean.class)
            .addAsManifestResource(
                    EmptyAsset.INSTANCE,
            ArchivePaths.create("beans.xml"));
        return jar;
    }

    @EJBPayloadCheckSenderBean sender;
    @EJBPayloadCheckReceiverBean receiver;

    @Test
    public void shouldFireMessageAtMDB() throws Exception {
        sender.sendPayloadMessage("hello");
        sender.sendPayloadMessage("Wanda", "Barbados");
        sender.sendPayloadMessage("world");
        sender.sendPayloadMessage("Fish", "Barbados");
        Thread.sleep(1000);
        List<String> messages = receiver.getMessages();
        assertEquals(2, messages.size());
        assertTrue(messages.contains("Wanda"));
        assertTrue(messages.contains("Fish"));
    }
}
```

In this Arquillian integration test, we inject two EJBs, `PayloadCheckSenderBean` and `PayloadCheckReceiverBean`, into the class. We do this to get around the fact that it is not possible to inject the MDB directly into a test because the CDI (and EJB) container prohibits this dependency on an asynchronous entity.

Inside the test method `shouldFireMessageAtMDB()`, we send four messages to the MDB. Two messages have the special property and the others have not. We deliberately delay for a bit because we are dealing with asynchronous behaviors, network I/O, and an embedded server. The singleton EJB `PayloadCheckReceiverBean` should have two messages in its store. We also use the `assertTrue()` call instead of the `assertEquals()` because we can never be sure of order of the messages because of Java concurrency and multiple threads. The list collection could be `[Wanda,Fish]` or `[Fish,Wanda]`. We only care about the message delivery.

>  **The order of messages**
>
> Messaging systems are more flexible and serve better throughput if they can cope with out-of-order messages. The JMS standard does not guarantee the order of the messages and how they will be delivered. The order of messages is completely at the discretion of the JMS provider implementation. Some providers like IBM MQ Series and Oracle WebLogic JMS have a feature that allows administrators to define the order of the messages. The OpenMQ product inside of the GlassFish server delivers messages in FIFO order, but then again, when it is tied to asynchronous MDBs inside a server with Java threads, your results will vary. Typically, the message payload itself will have an order ID or candidate keys of columns that the application can use to re-order the message itself in a group of messages.

JMS 2.0 adds the standard configuration of JMS connections for MDBs. It is now possible to configure the JNDI name of the message destination through annotations. The developer can also configure the connection factory, client ID, and the name of the durable subscription through annotations.

Activation configuration property

As we have seen, MDBs are asynchronous and are bound to a JMS connection. The connection can be local to the application server, and most implementations are external. In other words, an application can use another message queue implementation, and it will normally be a remote service. MDBs are allowed to be binded to different JMS providers, both local and remote. This is where the activation configuration properties and the corresponding annotation @`ActivationConfigProperty` help out.

Here is a table of the important key names for the `@ActivationConfigProperty` annotation:

Configuration Name	Description
`destinationLookup`	New in JMS 2.0, this property specifies the lookup name for an MDB of `Queue` or `Topic` defined by an administrator that messages will be read from.
	The setting can also be set in an `ejb-jar.xml` file.
`destinationFactoryLookup`	New in JMS 2.0, this property specifies the lookup name for an MDB of `ConnectionFactory` defined by an administrator that messages will be read from.
	The setting can also be set in an `ejb-jar.xml` file.
`acknowledgeMode`	Specifies the session acknowledgement for an MDB. The allowed values are `Auto-acknowledge` and `Dups-ok-acknowledge`. The default is `AUTO_ACKNOWLEDGE`.
`messageSelector`	Specifies the conditional expression that allows an MDB to select specific JMS messages. The default is to allow all messages through for reception.
`destinationType`	Specifies whether the destination is a queue or a topic. The valid values are `javax.jms.Queue` or `javax.jms.Topic`.
`subscriptionDurability`	Specifies if the MDB is part of a durable subscription or not. The valid values are `Durable` or `NonDurable`. The default value is the non-durable variety.
`clientId`	New in JMS 2.0, this optional property sets the client identifier for connecting to the JMS provider.
`subscriptionName`	New in JMS 2.0, this optional property sets the name of the durable or non-durable subscription.

Message selectors

The message selector is an important facility for MDB to receive only messages that are interesting from the JMS queue or topic. Message selectors use `javax.jms.Message` header properties in conditional expressions.

The expressions are based on a subset of the SQL-92 conditional expression syntax that is used in the WHERE clauses of database SQL statements. Hence, they are very familiar to database administrators. Message selectors are allowed to use Boolean expressions, unary operators, and literal values. They can be become quite complex.

Here is an example of a more advanced message selector:

```
@ActivationConfigProperty(
  propertyName="messageSelector",
  propertyValue =
    "(SpecialCode = 'Barbados' AND VerNum > 2)" +
    "OR (WorkRole='Admin')"
),
```

Obviously, a JMS message header would have one or two of these additional properties defined in order for this MDB to receive the data.

JMS exception handling

Since JMS 2.0, many of the methods in the simplified API now prefer to throw types based on `javax.jms.RuntimeException`, which is an unchecked exception. If you have already existing code from the earlier Java EE specification and it is compatible with JMS 1.1, then they will continue to throw the checked exceptions derived from the base class `javax.jms.JMSException`. The following table is an overview of the possible JMS exception types:

JMS Exception	Description
`IllegalStateRuntimeException`	The JMS provider throws an illegal state exception if there is a call that would put the provider in an inconsistent state or is a prohibited operation.
`JMSSecurityRuntimeException`	The JMS provider throws this exception when it rejects the user name / password credential submitted by the JMS client in order to achieve a connection.
`InvalidClientIDRuntimeException`	The provider throws this exception when the client ID is rejected or unrecognized according to the configuration of the administrative objects.
`InvalidSelectorRuntimeException`	The provider throws this exception if it fails to parse and understand a message selector.
`MessageEOFException`	A checked exception that the JMS provider throws when a client attempts to read a `StreamMessage` beyond the end of its input stream.

JMS Exception	Description
MessageFormatRuntimeException	This exception is thrown by the provider when the client attempts to use a data type not support by the message.
MessageNotWritableRuntimeException	The client has attempted to write to a read-only message.
ResourceAllocationRuntimeException	The JMS provider cannot fulfill the request to create a topic subscription or temporary queue due to the lack of operating system or provider-specific resources.
TransactionInProgressRuntimeException	This is caused by a JMS client calling a Session.commit() or JMSContext.commit() when the session is already part of a distributed Java transaction.
TransactionRolledBackRuntimeException	This is caused by a JMS client calling a Session.commit() or JMSContext.commit() when the session has already been set to be rolled back.

Upgrading JMS 1.1 code

There is a lot of code out there in business that simply cannot be rewritten from scratch. Some of it will almost certainly be using JMS 1.1 from the J2EE. If we cannot chuck it away, then how do we upgrade to JMS 2.0?

Establish a JMS 1.1 connection

It is worth learning about the traditional way of building a JMS connection to the provider in order to upgrade legacy code bases to Java EE 7.

In Java EE 5, which was the first enterprise standard to support Java annotations, you might see code that looks like this:

```
// JMS 1.1
import javax.jms.*;
import javax.annotation.*;

public SomeMessagingClient {
  @Resource(mappedName="myQueueConnectionFactoryName")
  ConnectionFactory queueConnectionFactory;

  @Resource(mappedName="myQueue")
```

```
Queue queue;

@Resource(mappedName="myTopicConnectionFactoryName")
ConnectionFactory topicConnectionFactory;

@Resource(mappedName="myTopic")
Topic topic;

/* ... */

public void processWithQueue( String text )
throws Exception {
  Connection conx =
    queueConnectionFactory.createConnection();

  Session session = conx.createSession(true, 0 );
  try {
    TextMessage msg = session.createTextMessage();
    msg.setText( text );
    session.createProducer(queue).send(msg);
  }
  finally {
    conx.close();
  }
}
/* ... */
}
```

In such source code from Java EE 5 and Java EE 6, the annotation `@javax.annotation.Resource` injects the JMS connection factory and the message destination into the application client, assuming the code runs inside an application server. The connection factory is used in the client code to create a connection.

Here is an example of code that sends a message on the preceding queue:

```
public void processWithQueue( String text )
throws Exception {
  Connection conx =
    queueConnectionFactory.createConnection();
  Session session = conx.createSession(true,
      Session.AUTO_ACKNOWLEDGE );
  try {
    TextMessage msg = session.createTextMessage();
```

```
      msg.setText( text );
      session.createProducer(queue).send(msg);
    }
    finally {
      conx.close();
    }
  }
}
```

The preceding code looks very verbose, and you as a developer have to deal with checked exceptions and the possibility of interpreting the outcomes around a JMSException.

The new JMSContext object now provides the same behavior, and therefore the developer can replace @Resource injections with one @Inject and one @JMSContextConnectionFactory annotation:

```
// JMS 2.0
public SomeMessagingClient {
  @Inject
  @JMSContextConnectionFactory(
    "jms/myQueueConnectionFactoryName")
  JMSContext queueContext

  @Resource(mappedName="myQueue")
  Queue queue;

  @Inject
  @JMSContextConnectionFactory(
    "jms/myTopicConnectionFactoryName")
  JMSContext queueContext

  @Resource(mappedName="myTopic")
  Topic topic;

  /* ... */

  public void processWithQueue( String text )
  throws Exception {
    queueContext.createProducer().send(queue, text );
  }

  public void processWithTopic( String text )
  throws Exception {
    topicContext.createProducer().send(topic, text );
  }
    /* ... */
}
```

This previous code is the form of dependency injection that is typical for Java EE 7 applications, especially those that run inside an application server or EJB container. In the next section, we will dig deeper into dependency injection.

JMS and dependency injection

JMS 2.0 is a major improvement because the specification leverages Java annotations. The standard also recognizes the advanced features of the Java EE 7 platform. In particular, JMS is designed to integrate with CDI, EJB, and other new endpoints.

Injecting CDI beans

JMS 2.0 supports context and dependency injection through injection of the `JMSContext`. We have already seen examples. It is also possible to inject the connection factory and then create a context.

Here is a code snippet that demonstrates this technique:

```
class XMLPublisher {
  @Resource(mappedName="xmlQueueConnectionFactory")
  ConnectionFactory queueConnectionFactory;

  @Resource(mappedName="xmlQueue")
  Queue queue;

  private static Logger logger =
    Logger.getLogger(XMLPublisher.class)

  public void sendXML(XMLDocument doc) {
    try (JMSContext context =
      queueConnectionFactory.createContext();) {
      context.send(queue, doc.getText());
    }
    catch( JMSRuntimeException e) {
      logger.error(
        "unable to sent message doc: "+
        doc.getId(), e);
    }
  }
}
```

In the `sendXML()` method of this `XMLPublisher` class, we take full advantage of the recent try-acquire-release statement and the `AutoClosable` type of the `JMSContext` to ensure that we always close the context. We also trap any unchecked exception to record to a log system that exists somewhere in the application.

The CDI container is used to inject into the connection factory object and also the destination with `@Resource`.

Injection of JMSContext resources

The injection of `JMSContext` objects can also be customized more precisely. It is possible to configure the connection factory name, but we can also control the session mode and also the login security credentials.

Here is a code snippet that applies a session mode and login to the connection:

```
@Inject
@JMSConnectionFactory("jms/fastQConnectionFactory")
@JMSSessionMode(JMSContext.DUPS_OK_ACKNOWLEDGE)
@JMSPasswordCredential(userName="admin",password="sinc3r3")
private JMSContext context;
```

The annotation `@javax.jms.JMSSessionMode` specifies the session connection mode for the channel. The default value is `JMSContext.AUTO_ACKNOWLEDGE`, and hence this annotation is only applied to connections that do not acknowledge automatically.

The annotation `@javax.jms.JMSPasswordCredential` specifies user login credentials for a secure connection.

The injected `JMSContext` has a scope when the application runs inside a Java EE application server or EJB container:

- If the injected `JMSContext` instance is a part of a JTA transaction, then the scope will be transactional
- If the injected `JMSContext` instance is not part of a JTA transaction, then the scope is a request

The application server also automatically manages the lifetime of the `JMSContext`; it has the responsibility for closing the context. The server will also inject a shared `JMSContext` instance if it knows that the connection factory, session mode, and also the security credentials are the same.

A Java EE application using an injected `JMSContext` from the CDI container is prohibited from calling certain methods on this object instance. These methods may cause undesired behavior, and they are `start()`, `stop()`, `commit()`, `rollback()`, `recover()`, `acknowledge()`, and `setExceptionListener()`.

Injecting EJB beans

The JMS client has full access to enterprise beans if it is run inside a Java EE application server or EJB container. Many Java EE applications already make use of message-driven beans and call other EJBs.

In the web profile, using JMS and EJB are considered extensions, and therefore your application is more responsible for configuration of the infrastructure. Therefore, from an architectural point-of-view, your application might be more at risk from vendor lock-in, especially if you lean on proprietary and non-open source features. However, usually a very good architect and lead designer can abstract certain features away into a critical corner of the application architecture.

Sometimes you have no choice in this matter because the business wants a specific profile and the Java EE standard does not support the functionality that the requirements need.

Definition of JMS resources in Java EE

In JMS 2.0, supporting providers are allowed to optionally implement the JMS Resource by definition annotations. Much of this work was left over from the aborted attempt to move Java EE 7 to the cloud-computing platform, and these existing annotations remain implemented in the reference implementation GlassFish 4.0.

There are two annotations: `@javax.jms.JMSConnectionFactoryDefinition` and `@JMSDestinationDefinition`. They define inside an application source code the connection factory and message destination respectively.

Here is a code snippet of the two annotations:

```
@JMSConnectionFactoryDefinition(
    name="java:global/jms/demoConnectionFactory",
    interfaceName="javax.jms.ConnectionFactory",
    description="Demo connection factory",
    user="admin",
    password="sinc3r3",
    transaction=true,
    maxPoolSize=25, minPoolSize=1)
```

```
    public class WebEndpoint { /* ... */ }

 @JMSDestinationDefinition(
    name="java:global/jms/demoQueue",
    interfaceName="javax.jms.Queue",
    description="Demo connection factory",
    destinationName="demoQueue" )
    public class DataEndpoint { /* ... */ }
```

The properties `name`, `interfaceName`, `description`, and `destinationName` are relatively comprehensible and are equivalent to the configuration for administrative objects.

Some of the properties are optional or default such as `clientId`, `resourceAdaptor`, `user`, `password`, and `transaction`.

Some of the properties such as `maxPoolSize` and `minPoolSize` are vendor specific.

The original idea for these two annotations was to automatically provision a Java Servlet and an EJB with a connection without requiring information to be set in an XML descriptor file. The provisioning of the resource would have taken place in a PaaS environment.

Incidentally, you can make use of the `@javax.jmx.JMSDestinationDefinitions` for annotating an array of definitions on a Servlet, EJB, or any other Java EE managed object.

Summary

This chapter covered the Java Message System, which sounds like a process, but is actually a long standing API that pre-dates even the first edition of the Java EE platform. Indeed, the history of messaging systems stretches all the way back to the 1960's and batch processing architecture, where messages were sent by database and backend storage.

You were educated on messaging systems, why they exist, and what they were designed to do. We now know that there are essentially two kinds of messaging: point-to-point and publish-and-subscribe.

JMS supports both models. Moreover, in the 2.0 edition of the specification, JMS has a simplified API which lends itself to dependency injection. The `JMSContext` is the entry into JMS. From there, we can find `ConnectionFactory` and `MessageDestination` types, of which there are two implementations: `Queues` and `Topics`.

Chapter 9

A JMS message has two components: the header properties and the payload. The payload is one of these types: `BytesMessage`, `MapMessage`, `ObjectMessage`, `StreamMessage`, or a `TextMessage`. They all can be sent by a `JMSProducer` and received by a `JMSReceiver`.

Messages can be sent both synchronously and asynchronously. Messages can also be received synchronously or asynchronously. However, if your application runs inside an application server or EJB container, there are limitations.

Finally, we arrived at a discussion of message-driven beans, which are managed by the EJB container and come by default with asynchronous invocations, support for container managed transactions, thread-safe concurrency, security, and scalability.

In the next chapter on bean validation, we will look at ways of validating the value objects before they hit your business logic, persistent database, or backing store.

10
Bean Validation

Barbara Liskov and Stephen Zilles (Abstract Data Types, 1974) said, "Some of the operations in the cluster for that "type" are polymorphic; the operations mays be defined over many type domains, subject to the constraint that the types of any given argument set are type-consistent."

In object oriented programming, we are mostly familiar with value objects, which are types that have encapsulation of data and accessibility operators. Value objects generally do not have business rules, or e-commerce entity complex behavior, and thus they are represented as **Plain-Old-Java-Objects** (**POJOs**). The way developers write JavaBeans now means value objects in Java are basic Java Beans.

So why is there all the fuss over these value objects? Values objects are often validated in the application. In our business applications, we developers habitually write lots of boilerplate code that sanity checks the properties of value objects. We check if a particular field or property is null or not null, if the property is the correct type, whether it can be an empty string or not, if the property is a decimal, floating-point or an integer, or even whether a property's value fits in a bounded range of values. To add insult to injury, we then also write more of the same user-defined validation checking code in our web applications and in the presentation tier. Our lack of reuse and regretful duplication of code is complete in this challenge when our value objects are marshaled as persistence capable objects, because we repeat ourselves with the similar validation code before saving or updating it to the database.

Unfortunately this validation code is repeated in different tiers of the application; the code is not universal or shared or specific to the application, and more often than not mistakes will exist in the checking. This leads to inconsistencies of validation within an application. Well, Java EE 7 has a standard solution, which is called **Bean Validation**.

Introduction to Bean Validation

The focus of Bean Validation API 1.1 is *ease-of-use*. The expert group designed the update so that developers can apply a single constraint for multiple layers of their applications. These constraints can be applied at the presentation layer on web frameworks such as JavaServer Faces and Apache WebWork, at the business layer where your logic works, and of course the data storage layer. With Bean Validation, developers need to define the constraints only once, and then inside the application you invoke the validation anywhere you want to check.

For Java EE 7 application servers, Bean Validation can be automatically applied to persistence capable object, which means JPA gets constraint validation for free. For web frameworks running under the Java EE 7 Web Profile, Bean Validation can also be automatically applied to JSF when there is an HTTP request sent to the web layer as the request is mapped to Managed Beans.

The Bean Validation framework is usable outside of Java EE standard as well. The reference implementation to the Bean Validation has integration with other frameworks such as GWT, Wicket, and Tapestry. The Spring Framework, since version 3.1, also has an integration module to the previous Bean Validation implementation, version 1.0.

New features in 1.1

Bean Validation 1.1 specification introduces several new features:

- It provides better integration with CDI, which has a few components to all injections of custom validators into your application.
- It adds new kinds of factories—providers and resolvers—to allow the developer to customize the validation.
- Developers can write constraints on parameters and return values of arbitrary methods and constructors. This feature is called **method validation,** and it permits the declarative validation of methods with pre and post-conditions.
- Constraint validation messages can now be properly internationalized for other languages and locale with string formatting.
- Bean Validation 1.1 now integrates and uses the **EL 3.0**, the standard Expression Language JSR 341 standard.

The expert group has really attempted to make our engineering working lives much better.

> **XSS Cross-Site Scripting**
>
>
>
> **Cross-Site Scripting (XSS)** is the term for client-side hacking of web applications to exploit flaws in the implementation logic where there is lack of validation, weak security, and advantage to be gained, including manipulating system credentials in to order to become an authorized administrator or super user. XSS enables attackers to inject unauthorized observer scripts into the application and thereby gain administrative privileges in web pages viewed by other legitimate users. Fortunately, Java is static compiled, but direct SQL and dynamic languages such as PHP, Ruby and Groovy are prone to scripting attacks, if they are not protected from malicious evolutions.
>
> Bean Validation 1.1 can help with a standard validation on value objects and persistence capable objects. It is worth following the advice of the XSS Prevent Cheat Sheet `https://www.owasp.org/index.php/XSS_(Cross_Site_Scripting)_Prevention_Cheat_Sheet` and also using an additional Java prevention framework such as Coverity Security Library `https://github.com/coverity/coverity-security-library`.

Let's move on to a simple example of Bean Validation.

A quick example

Bean Validation takes advantage of annotations, which specify how to verify the constraints on a value object. The constraints can be found under the Java package name `javax.validation.constraints`.

The reference implementation for Bean Validator 1.1 is the open source framework **Hibernate Validator,** which is the reference implementation of the specification. The website `http://beanvalidation.org` is the standard location for the current and previous specifications.

An example of value object that is annotated with constraints is as follows:

```
public final class Person {
    @NotNull
    private final String firstName;
    @NotNull
    private final String lastName;

    @Min(18) @Max(65)
    private int age;

    public Person(final String firstName,
```

```
            final String lastName, final int age) {
        this.firstName = firstName;
        this.lastName = lastName;
        this.age = age;
    }

    public String getFirstName() {return firstName; }
    public String getLastName() {return lastName; }
        public int getAge() { return age; }
}
```

The `Person` class is an immutable value object. It is thread-safe because the state cannot be altered, `this` reference does not escape the constructor, and all properties are marked as `final` and are fully initialized in the constructor, but that is beside the point.

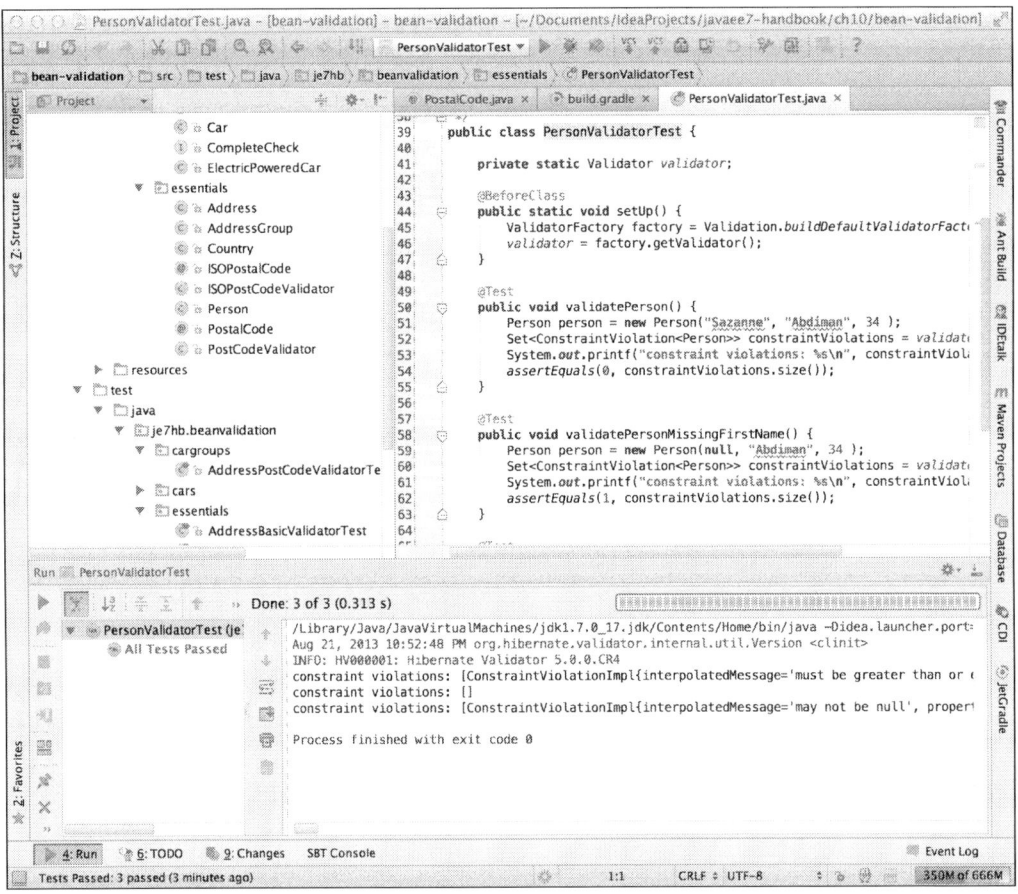

The properties firstName and lastName are marked with the @NotNull, which declares a constraint to the class member to ensure that the value is not null.

The property age is marked with the two annotations @Min and @Max, which declares two constraints for a numeric field with the value. In UK English, this says the person's age must be an adult and not retired (the male pension age is currently still 65 years in Great Britain in 2013).

Let's write a simple unit test to verify these constraints with Hibernate Validator framework:

```
package je7hb.beanvalidation.essentials;
import static org.junit.Assert.*;
import org.junit.*;
import javax.validation.*
import java.util.Set;

public class PersonValidatorTest {
    private static Validator validator;

    @BeforeClass
    public static void setUp() {
        ValidatorFactory factory = Validation.buildDefaultValidatorFactory();
        validator = factory.getValidator();
    }

    @Test
    public void validatePerson() {
        Person person = new Person("Sazanne", "Abdiman", 34 );
        Set<ConstraintViolation<Person>> constraintViolations
          = validator.validate(person);
        assertEquals(0, constraintViolations.size());
    }

    @Test
    public void validatePersonMissingFirstName() {
        Person person = new Person(null, "Abdiman", 34 );
        Set<ConstraintViolation<Person>> constraintViolations
          = validator.validate(person);
        assertEquals(1, constraintViolations.size());
    }
```

Bean Validation

```
    @Test
    public void validatePersonMissingWrongAge() {
        Person person = new Person("Kieran", "Abdiman", 16 );
        Set<ConstraintViolation<Person>> constraintViolations
  = validator.validate(person);
        assertEquals(1, constraintViolations.size());
    }
}
```

This unit test `PersonValidatorTest` verifies the constraints applied to the value object. In the `@BeforeClass` static method `setUp()`, we create a bean validator using a factory. The class `javax.validation.ValidatorFactory` in the API allows an application to retrieve the default validator, which is a type of `javax.validation.Validator`.

Once we have the validator in a static member of the test, we write the test methods. We first create a value object in each test, and then invoke the validator's `validate()` method, which returns a set collection of `javax.validation.ConstraintViolation` objects. We check the size of the set collection to verify the tests. (Obviously for full acceptance criteria and pedantic behavioral-driven Design we would write more tests for full compliance.) If the set collection is empty and the size of violations is zero then the object is valid and has passed the validator.

Constraint declarations

The bean validation specification has built-in constraints that cover the common constraints that a developer will encounter, albeit for basic validation.

Elements of a constraint

An annotated constraint in bean validation is declared through the key annotation `@javax.validation.contraints.Constraint` and three other properties.

Message property

The `message` property specifies the text and/or the Expression Language statement that the validation engine will use or evaluate when the constraint is violated.

```
String message() default  "{je7hb.beanvalidation.essentials.
PostalCode.message}";
```

The annotation property `message` defines a default resource in order to look up the validation error message. For internationalization purposes, validation error messages are read by the class `java.util.ResourceBundle` through language specific property files.

Groups property

The `groups` property specifies the group of violation that this constraint belongs to. This is set by the developer, to control and configure partial validations and groups of validations, applied to value objects.

```
Class<?>[] groups() default {};
```

Groups are defined by Java class references and the default value is an empty array. This annotation property `group` allows validation constraints to be collected together in a named association. In this case, there is no group specified.

Payload property

The `payload` property defines the object instances, which are associated with the constraint. The payload is an advanced concept, which allows the validation client to associate metadata information with the constraint declaration. Payloads are not portable to different validators, usually.

```
Class<? extends Payload>[] payload() default {};
```

The default value is an empty array. The `Payload` instance is an empty marker interface to some custom opaque object instance and thus illustrates perfectly the non-portability of this annotation property.

List of built-in constraints

Let us look now at the default built-in constraints for Bean Validation 1.1:

Constraint name	Description	Allowed types
`@Null`	Specifies the element must be a `null` reference pointer.	Any
`@NotNull`	Specifies the element must not be a `null` reference pointer.	Any
`@AssertTrue`	Specifies the element must be `true`	`Boolean` and `boolean`
`@AssertFalse`	Specifies the element must be `false`	`Boolean` and `boolean`

Bean Validation

Constraint name	Description	Allowed types
@Min	Specifies the element must be a number value that is greater than or equal to the minimum value supplied. Because of floating arithmetic rounding errors `float` and `double` are not supported.	`BigDecimal`, `BigInteger`, `byte`, `short`, `int`, and `long`
@Max	Specifies the element must be a number value that is less than or equal to the minimum value supplied. Because of floating arithmetic rounding errors `float` and `double` are not supported.	`BigDecimal`, `BigInteger`, `byte`, `short`, `int`, and `long`
@DecimalMin	Similar to `@Min` but adds the ability to set the value as String parameter. The number value must be greater than or equal to the supplied value. FP restriction also applies here.	`BigDecimal`, `BigInteger`, `CharSequence`, `byte`, `short`, `int`, and `long`
@DecimalMax	Similar to `@Max` but adds the ability to set the value as String parameter. The number value must be less than or equal to the supplied value. FP restriction also applies here.	`BigDecimal`, `BigInteger`, `CharSequence`, `byte`, `short`, `int`, and `long`
@Size	The element's size must be inside the supplied inclusive boundary limits.	`CharSequence`, `Collection`, `Map` and primitive array
@Digits	The element is a number within an accepted range that defines the maximum digits for the integer portion of the number and the maximum digits for the fraction portion of the number.	`BigDecimal`, `BigInteger`, `CharSequence`, `byte`, `short`, `int`, and `long`
@Past	The element must be dated in the past according to the current time of the Java Virtual Machine.	`java.util.Date` and `java.util.Calendar`
@Future	The element must be dated in the future according to the current time of the Java Virtual Machine.	`java.util.Date` and `java.util.Calendar`
@Pattern	The element must match against a supplied regular expression pattern that conforms to the Java convention.	`CharSequence`

The annotations `@DecimalMin` and `@DecimalMax` both have an inclusive parameter that is by default set to true.

Many constraint annotations now also accept a `CharSequence` instance and therefore an application can also validate on `StringBuilder`.

In the quick example, we already saw some of these constraints `@NotNull`, `@Min` and `@Max` in action. All of the default constraints are runtime annotations. They can be applied to Java constructors, fields, methods, method parameters, and other annotation types.

Hibernate Validator built-in constraints

The reference implementation, Hibernate Validator, also has built-in constraints that are part of the specification 1.1.

Constraint Name	Description	Allowed Types
`@CreditCardNumber`	Specifies the element must be a match for standard credit card account number.	`CharSequence`
`@Email`	Specifies the element must be a valid well-formed email address.	`CharSequence`
`@Length`	Specifies the string length is between a minimum and maximum inclusive.	`CharSequence`
`@NotBlank`	Specifies the string is not blank or `null`.	`CharSequence`
`@NotEmpty`	Specifies the element collection or string is not empty.	`CharSequence`, `Collection`, `Map` and primitive array
`@Range`	Specifies the element must be the range between minimum and maximum inclusive values.	`BigDecimal`, `BigInteger`, `CharSequence`, `byte`, `short`, `int`, and `long`
`@SafeHtml`	Specifies the element text is an HTML without script elements or malicious code.	`CharSequence`
`@URL`	Specifies the element test is a valid well-formed URL.	`CharSequence`

These annotations are found under the Java package `org.hibernate.validator.constraints`.

[469]

Constraint violations

The method `validate()` on the Validator class returns a set collection of `ConstraintViolation` instances. Constraints are designed to be declared just once and allow the client to execute them anywhere in the application code.

The standardized `ConstraintViolation` *looks like this:*

```java
package javax.validation;
import javax.validation.metadata.ConstraintDescriptor;

public interface ConstraintViolation<T> {
  String getMessage();
  String getMessageTemplate();
  T getRootBean();
  Class<T> getRootBeanClass();
  Object getLeafBean();

  // Since 1.1
  Object[] getExecutableParameters();
  // Since 1.1
  Object getExecutableReturnValue();

  Path getPropertyPath();
  Object getInvalidValue();
  ConstraintDescriptor<?> getConstraintDescriptor();

  // Since 1.1
  <U> U unwrap(Class<U> type);
}
```

The violation can be interrogated for the tokenized message `getMessage()` and the raw text `getMessageTemplate()` before post processing for internationalization and formatting. The method `getRootBean()` informs the application which bean is ultimately the container or common master of the violation. The `getLeafBean()` returns the bean that contains the failure.

The application can retrieve the actual value that caused the violation with `getInvalidValue()`. The `getPropertyPath()` method retrieves the node path of the navigation properties to get from the root bean (value object) to the leaf bean (dependent value object). The Path is a Java interface that represents the navigation path from one object to another in an object graph. The data structure is based on the chain of individual node elements.

As Bean Validation 1.1, it is possible to retrieve the execution parameters and return through the calls `getExecutableParameter()` and `getExecutableReturnValue()`. These calls were introduced to support method validation.

There is a special method called `unwrap()` that allows applications to gain access to opaque specific provider data and additional proprietary API. Of course, the use of this means that your resultant code is not portable from, say, Hibernate Validator to another implementation. On the other hand, the specification permits providers to add custom behavior.

Finally, it is possible to retrieve the meta-data around the constraint descriptor associated with this constraint with a call to `getConstraintDescriptor()`. This call is designed to help the developer write custom validator annotations.

Applying constraint definitions

As we have seen, applying built-in constraints to value objects is almost painless. What happens if you want a constraint that is not covered by the built-in types? Bean Validation allows the developer to write custom constraints.

Let's review a value object that has an entity relationship with another one. Here is the code for the `Country` object:

```java
package je7hb.beanvalidation.essentials;
import org.hibernate.validator.constraints.NotEmpty;

public class Country {
    private String isoName;
    @NotEmpty
    public String getISOName() { return isoName; }
    public Country() { }
}
```

This is the `Address` object, the master of the detail:

```java
package je7hb.beanvalidation.essentials;
import javax.validation.Valid;
import javax.validation.constraints.*;

public class Address {
    private String flatNo;
    private String street1;
    private String street2;
```

```
    private String city;
    private String postalCode;
    private Country country;

    @NotNull @Size(max=50)
    public String getStreet1() { return street1; }
    @NotNull @Size(max=50)
    public String getStreet2() { return street2; }

    @PostalCode(
    message="Wrong postal code")
    public String getPostalCode() { return postalCode; }

    @NotNull @Valid
    public Country getString() { return country; }

  // Constructor & setter methods ommitted
}
```

The value object for class `Address` has field members: `flatNo`, `street1`, `street2`, `city`, `postalCode` and `country` in order to represent a person's living or home address. We have applied constraint annotations applied to the getter methods. The `@Size` and `@NotNull` constraints are applied to street1 and street2 respectively, to ensure that the backing store field sizes are checked.

The `getCountry()` method is an example of declaring a delegating constraint on a dependent object. The annotation `@javax.annotation.Valid` cascades the validation checking to the dependent object property on the instance. We can also supply the `@Valid` constraint to method calls to a method parameter or the instance returned from a method call. We shall learn how to apply method validation later in this chapter.

The `@PostalCode` validation and annotation is an example of a custom constraint.

Custom validators

Writing a custom validator is fairly straightforward. The first step is to write an annotation that depends on the `@javax.validation.Constraint`.

Here is the `@PostCode` constraint annotation:

```
package je7hb.beanvalidation.essentials;
import javax.validation.*;
import java.lang.annotation.*;
```

```
import static java.lang.annotation.RetentionPolicy.*;
import static java.lang.annotation.ElementType.*;

@Documented
@Constraint(validatedBy = PostCodeValidator.class)
@Target({
  METHOD, FIELD, ANNOTATION_TYPE, CONSTRUCTOR,
  PARAMETER })
@Retention(RUNTIME)
public @interface PostalCode {
    String message() default
  "{je7hb.beanvalidation.essentials.PostalCode.message}";
    Class<?>[] groups() default {};
    Class<? extends Payload>[] payload() default {};
    String country() default "gb";
}
```

The @Constraint refers to the class that provides the custom validator, in this case PostCodeValidator. The annotation is declared as runtime-type retention with injection points for constructors, fields, methods, parameters, and other constraint annotations. The message declaration refers to a key inside a resource bundle to look up an internationalized text.

Your custom annotation can define extra parameters and in the @PostalCode we define a country parameter to define the locale for validating the postal code.

The custom constraint PostCodeValidator extends a parameterized type interface javax.validation.ConstraintValidator:

```
package je7hb.beanvalidation.essentials;
import javax.validation.*;
import java.util.regex.*;

public class PostCodeValidator
implements ConstraintValidator<PostalCode,String> {
private String country;
    private Pattern pattern =
        Pattern.compile(
"[A-Z][A-Z]\\d{1,2}[ \t]*\\d{1,2}[A-Z][A-Z]");

    @Override
```

Bean Validation

```
      public void initialize(PostalCode postalCode) {
this.country = postalCode.country();}

      @Override
      public boolean isValid(String value,
         ConstraintValidatorContext context) {
        if ( value == null) {
           return true;
        }
        Matcher m = pattern.matcher(value.toUpperCase());
        return m.matches();
      }
}
```

The parameterized interface ConstraintValidator<U extends Annotation, V> defines the logic for a generic type that validates an input generic type V. The generic type must be a Java annotation type A.

There are two methods to implement: initialize() and isValid(). The provider calls the initialize() method with the instance of the annotation. We can access extra annotation parameter values and we save the value as a field in this instance for future use in the next method. Actually, we are not using the extra parameter in the validation in this demonstration.

The provider calls isValid() method with a String value and the javax.validation.ConstraintValidatorContext instance. We always validate null reference pointer values as successful, because we do not want to interfere with @NotNull being applied by the user. The PostCodeValidator class uses a regular pattern to match British postal codes. So we validate the input value against the pattern using a matcher. If the regex matches true, then it must be good.

> **Custom validators and null**
>
> Most custom validations ignore the case, when the element value is a. If the value is null then the validation returns true. If the element value is not null then an attempt is made to validate the element. This is helpful for situations in web application where the user may not yet define the field.

[474]

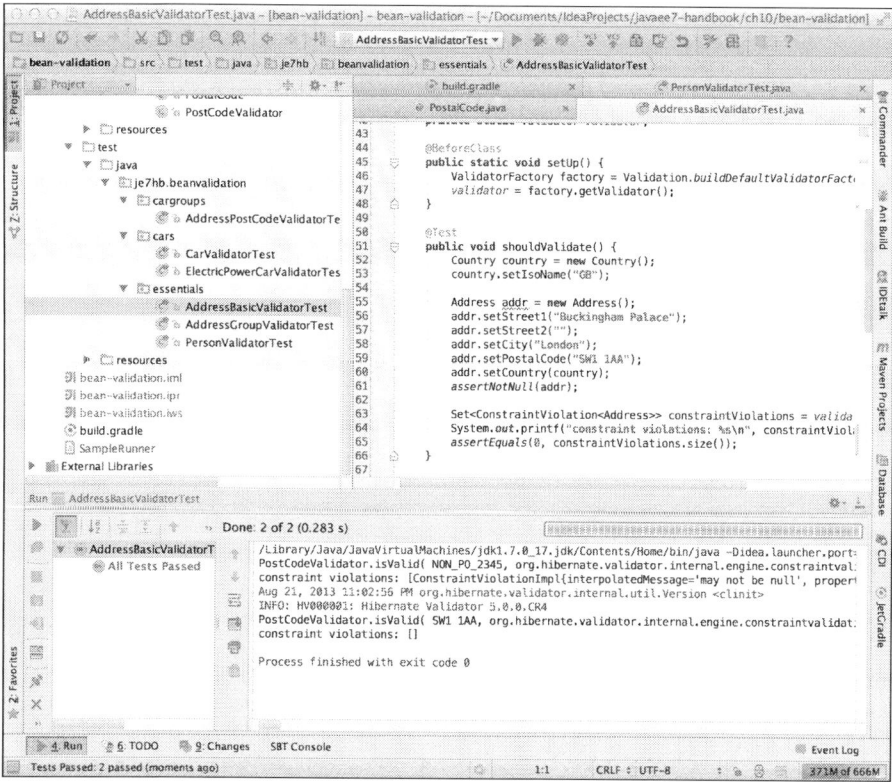

Groups of constraints

We have seen that constraints are grouped together and validated on a value object. The constraints validate on the property or field member of an object instance. Whilst this is good enough for basic properties, we often need flexibility in our applications. Bean Validation, however, provides additional validation for class instances and partial validation for groups of constraints.

Class-level constraints

A constraint can also be applied to the class itself, and then it is called a **class-level** constraint. The class-level constraints permit the ability to inspect more than one single property of the class. Therefore, they provide a means to validate associated fields or properties. In order to apply a class-level constraint annotation, you declare it on the class itself.

We shall write a new class-level constraint to validate only UK post codes for an address value object.

Bean Validation

First we need a different value type, `AddressGroup`:

```java
@ISOPostalCode(message="ISO uk or gb only")
public class AddressGroup {
    private String flatNo;
    private String street1;
    private String street2;
    private String city;
    private String postalCode;
    private Country country;

    @NotNull @Size(max=50)
    public String getStreet1() { return street1; }

    @NotNull @Size(max=50)
    public String getStreet2() { return street2; }

    public String getPostalCode() { return postalCode; }

    @NotNull @Valid
    public Country getCountry() { return country; }

    /* ... */
}
```

This value object makes use of the custom constraint annotation `@ISOPostalCode`. Notice that the property `postCode` no longer has the single property constraint any more.

Let's define our annotation `@ISOPostalCode` now:

```java
@Documented
@Constraint(validatedBy = ISOPostCodeValidator.class)
@Target(TYPE)
@Retention(RUNTIME)
public @interface ISOPostalCode {
    String message() default
"{je7hb.beanvalidation.essentials.ISOPostalCode.message}";
    Class<?>[] groups() default {};
    Class<? extends Payload>[] payload() default {};
}
```

We also restrict the use of this annotation to only classes with the `@Target(TYPE)` definition. This is a design choice, naturally. The annotation refers to the class type that performs the checking: `ISOPostCodeValidator`.

This is the code for the validator:

```
package je7hb.beanvalidation.essentials;
import javax.validation.*;
import java.util.regex.*;

public class ISOPostCodeValidator
implements ConstraintValidator<ISOPostalCode,AddressGroup> {
    private Pattern pattern =
        Pattern.compile(
"[A-Z][A-Z]\\d{1,2}[ \t]*\\d{1,2}[A-Z][A-Z]");

    @Override
    public void initialize(ISOPostalCode annotation) { }

    @Override
    public boolean isValid(AddressGroup value,
            ConstraintValidatorContext context) {
        if (value == null) { return true; }
        String isoName = "";
        if ( value.getCountry() != null ) {
           isoName =
             value.getCountry().getISOName().toUpperCase();
        }
        if ( isoName.equals("UK") || isoName.equals("GB")) {
           Matcher m = pattern.matcher(
             value.getPostalCode());
           return m.matches();
        }
        else return false;
    }
}
```

The class `ISOPostCodeValidator` is a type of constraint parameterized with the type `ConstraintValidator<ISOPostalCode,AddressGroup>`. In short, this constraint validates two dependent properties: the post code and the IOS country name.

The method `isValid()` already accepts an `AddressGroup` instance. We verify that the correct international country has been set, and retrieve the ISO name from the dependent `Country` instance and its `country` property. If the ISO name is appropriately valid then we can apply the regular expression and attempt to validate the `postcode` property. If the ISO name is set neither to UK or GB, then the class-level constraint fails validation.

Bean validation can also validate groups of constraints and we will look into this feature next.

Bean Validation

Partial validation

Constraints belong to a default group interface `javax.validation.groups.Default`, when the developer does supply `groups` annotation parameter. The type `Default` is actually an empty Java interface. Hence the Bean Validation provider will invoke the constraints attached to all constructors, fields, properties, and methods for a value object. Applications can create partial validation rules by creating separate empty Java interfaces, which denote custom groups.

Suppose we want to validate a car value object from the automotive industry with different validators: one to completely verify the properties and the other to just check some of the details.

We can write a new `Car` entity like the following:

```java
package je7hb.beanvalidation.cars;
import javax.validation.constraints.*;

public class Car {
    @NotNull(groups=BasicCheck.class)
    private final String carMaker;

    @Min(value=2, groups={BasicCheck.class,
            CompleteCheck.class})
    private int seats;

    @Size(min=4, max=8, groups=BasicCheck.class)
    private String licensePlate;

    @Min(value=500, groups={BasicCheck.class,
            CompleteCheck.class})
    private int engineSize;

    public Car(String carMaker, int seats,
    String licensePlate) {
        this(carMaker, seats, licensePlate, 0 );
    }

    public Car(final String carMaker,
    final int seats,
    final String licensePlate,
    final int engineSize) {
        this.carMaker = carMaker;
```

```
            this.seats = seats;
            this.licensePlate = licensePlate;
            this.engineSize = engineSize;
        }

    /* ... */
}
```

The only addition to value type Car is the group parameter on the constraint annotations, which specifies the interface to associate each constraint with a group. The actual parameter is a variable-length argument and therefore a constraint can be associated with multiple groups.

The Java interfaces representing the groups are extremely simple:

```
public interface BasicCheck { }
public interface CompleteCheck { }
```

So a unit to verify these checks to Car instances supplies the references to the group classes for the validation. Here is the unit test code snippet:

```
package je7hb.beanvalidation.cars;

/* ... omitted imports ... */
public class CarValidatorTest {
    private static Validator validator;

    @BeforeClass
    public static void setUp() { /* ... */ }

    @Test
    public void shouldBasicValidateCar() {
        Car car = new Car("Austin Martin", 0, "AM12457", 0 );
        Set<ConstraintViolation<Car>> constraintViolations
          = validator.validate(car, BasicCheck.class );
        assertEquals(0, constraintViolations.size());
    }

    @Test
    public void shouldCompletelyValidateCar() {
        Car car = new Car("Bentley", 4, "BY4823", 2560 );
```

```
        Set<ConstraintViolation<Car>> constraintViolations
    = validator.validate(car, BasicCheck.class,
        CompleteCheck.class);
        assertEquals(0, constraintViolations.size());
    }

    @Test
    public void shouldNotCompletelyValidateCar() {
        Car car = new Car("Sedaca", 0, "XYZ1234", 0 );
        Set<ConstraintViolation<Car>> constraintViolations
    = validator.validate(car, BasicCheck.class,
        CompleteCheck.class );
        assertEquals(2, constraintViolations.size());
    }
}
```

The differences between the unit test methods `shouldBasicValidateCar()` and `shouldCompletelyValidateCar()` for the test `CarValidatorTest` are the group interface classes `BasicCheck` and `Complete` respectively. We only partially populate properties of the `Car` instance inside `shouldBasicValidateCar()`. We also call the validator's `validate()` method with the group interfaces, which is also a variable-length argument.

The method `shouldNotCompletelyValidateCar()` verifies the constraints with the group `CompleteCheck`, which should fail the validation because the `Car` instance is not correctly constructed. A car cannot have zero seats nor can it have zero engine size.

Constraint inheritance

Another way of achieving partial constraints is to organize value objects in object class hierarchies. If we have different extension types of `Car` such as `ElectricPoweredCar` or `HybridPoweredCar` then each sub-type could have more additional constraints. The specification mandates that the provider executes all constraint annotations on implemented interfaces and the parent class.

Here is an example of inheritance of constraints with an electric powered vehicle.

```
    public class ElectricPoweredCar extends Car {
        @DecimalMin(value="25.0",
        groups={BasicCheck.class, CompleteCheck.class})
        private final double powerKiloWatts;
        @DecimalMin(value="100.0",
```

```
        groups={BasicCheck.class, CompleteCheck.class})
        private final double rangeInMiles;

        public ElectricPoweredCar(
                String carMaker, int seats, String licensePlate,
                int engineSize, double powerKiloWatts,
                double rangeInMiles) {
            super(carMaker, seats, licensePlate, engineSize);
            this.powerKiloWatts = powerKiloWatts;
            this.rangeInMiles = rangeInMiles;
        }
    /* ... */
}
```

Group constraints can also inherit from other groups. An example of hierarchy of Java interfaces is as follows:

```
interface BasicCheck extends Default { }
interface CompleteCheck { }
interface PayableCheck extends CompleteCheck, BasicCheck { }
```

The `PayableCheck` inherits both from the `Basic` and `Complete` constraints, but notice that the basic constraints are subtypes of `Default`. This means that the Bean Validator provider will run `BasicCheck` group constraints at the same time and level as the default group. The `CompleteCheck` group constraint will be explicit and specific to those constraints. The Bean Validator provider will run all of the constraints against `PayableCheck` group constraint if individual constraints are associated with it.

Ordering groups of constraints

Constraints can be ordered in groups so that the application can control how value objects are validated. The Bean Validation provider is at liberty to evaluate constraints in any order that it pleases, regardless of which groups they belong to. In order to enforce control, the specification supplies the `@javax.validation.GroupSequence` annotation. The `@GroupSequenceannotation` defines the order of groups and informs the Bean Validation provider how to apply the constraints on a given group.

Let us look at an example of group sequence on another version of the address value object:

```
package je7hb.beanvalidation.cargroups;
import je7hb.beanvalidation.essentials.PostalCode;
```

```java
import javax.validation.GroupSequence;
import javax.validation.constraints.*;
import javax.validation.groups.Default;

@PostalCodeSensitiveChecker(groups =
Address.AreaSensitive.class)
public class Address {
    @NotNull @Size(max = 50) private String street1;
    @Size(max = 50) private String street2;
    @NotNull @PostalCode private String postCode;
    @NotNull @Size(max = 30) private String city;

    public interface AreaSensitive {}

    @GroupSequence({AreaSensitive.class, Default.class})
    public interface Complete {}

    /* ... getters and setters ... */
}
```

The `Address` class defines two empty interfaces `AreaSensitive` and `Complete`. There is also a class-level constraint validator `@PostalCodeSensitiveChecker`, which verifies that the postal code property matches a specific location.

The group sequence on the nested interface `Complete` changes the order of validation to evaluate the `AreaSensitive` group before the `Default` group.

It is possible to refine the validation with the following unit test:

```java
@Test
public void shouldValidateWithSpecificAreaOnly() {
Address addr = new Address();
addr.setPostCode("SW1 AA");
Set<ConstraintViolation<Address>> constraintViolations
= validator.validate(addr,
Address.AreaSensitive.class );
  assertEquals(0, constraintViolations.size());
}
```

The test method `shouldValidateWithSpecificAreaOnly()` evaluates against only the sensitive area by passing the interface group constraint class `AreaSensitive`. We pass the group constraint class to the validator's `validate()` method. We can evaluate the value object against the complete checker:

```
@Test
public void shouldValidateWithComplete() {
    Address addr = new Address();
    addr.setStreet1("1 Granger Avenue");
    addr.setCity("London");
    addr.setPostCode("SW1 3KG");
    Set<ConstraintViolation<Address>> constraintViolations
       = validator.validate(addr, Address.Complete.class );
    assertEquals(0, constraintViolations.size());
}
```

The annotation `@PostalCodeSensitiveChecker` only permits postcodes starting with SW1. The Bean Validator provider, first, invokes constraints for the `Complete` group, which are then applied, and then it invokes the `Default` constraints. The provider will stop the evaluation chain of groups on the first constraint of a group that fails. This algorithm helps us to order a sequence of group validations based on how expensive the constraint verification is to run. We can, therefore, inform the Bean Validation provider to evaluate cheap constraint checks before the expensive ones like those that would make an imaginary relational database query.

Let's move on to how Bean Validation can help us check inputs and outputs of business service layer interfaces.

Method-level constraints

It is standard industry practice for good architects to design enterprise applications in sets of tiers with many modules containing public interfaces around opaque implementations. These interfaces are often critical to servicing requests from a client endpoint such as dependent EJB call, web service, or web request. Bean Validation 1.1 allows us to write constraints around these endpoints with a new feature called Method-level constraints.

Method-level validation can only be applied to non-static methods and also constructors. The provider will ignore method-level constraints on static methods.

Method-level constraints require interception technology through the integration with CDI, Spring Framework, or Guice. It works for constructors as well as methods and the validation is implemented as a crosscutting concern.

Bean Validation

Bean Validation 1.1 is available for both Java EE 7 Full and Web profile application servers. For earlier Java EE editions, in particular the Web profiles Java EE 5 and 6, the administrator must configure the validator to a CDI container in a proprietary configuration. Note that GlassFish 4 contains the reference implementation Hibernate Validator 5.

Let us start with a stateless session EJB that will stand in a business service that we want to constrain. It is a payment service that takes an account and returns a ticket acknowledging payment and a new account value.

Here is the definition of the `PaymentServiceImpl`:

```java
package je7hb.beanvalidation.payments;
import javax.ejb.Stateless;
import javax.validation.Valid;
import javax.validation.constraints.*;
import java.math.BigDecimal;
import java.util.Date;

@Stateless
public class PaymentServiceImpl  {
    @NotNull
    @SecureReceipt @Valid
    public Receipt payEntity(
      @NotNull @Valid Account account,
      @NotNull @Size(min = 5, max = 32) String counterparty,
      @NotNull @DecimalMin("0.0") BigDecimal amount)
    {
        String msg;
        if ( counterparty.contains("Bridgetown"))
            msg = "SEC123";
        else
            msg = "Boo! Hoo!";
        Account acct2 = new Account(
                account.getAccount(),
                account.getAmount().subtract(amount));
        return new Receipt(msg,counterparty,acct2,
                new Date());
    }
}
```

The method `payEntity()` has constraints applied on the arguments for the account, the counterparty, and the monetary value. It also has a custom constraint `@SecureReceipt` applied on the return value and also a `@NotNull` constraint. The Bean Validation provider through the interception technology is able to check the input arguments and also the return value. The `@Valid` constraint informs the Bean Validation provider to recursively apply the constraints to the dependent object. So in this example, we check the input `Account` value object and also the returned `Receipt` object instance.

The code snippet for `SecureReceipt` annotation looks like this:

```
@Documented
@Constraint(validatedBy = SecureReceiptValidator.class)
@Target({ METHOD })
@Retention(RetentionPolicy.RUNTIME)
public @interface SecureReceipt {
    String message() default
"{je7hb.beanvalidation.payment.SecureReceipt.message}";
    Class<?>[] groups() default {};
    Class<? extends Payload>[] payload() default {};
}
```

The class-level constraint implementation `SecureReceiptValidator` object looks like this:

```
public class SecureReceiptValidator
    implements ConstraintValidator<SecureReceipt,Receipt> {
    @Override
    public void initialize(SecureReceipt annotation) { }

    @Override
    public boolean isValid(Receipt value,
                           ConstraintValidatorContext context) {
if ( value == null) return true;
        return value.getMessage().trim().startsWith("SEC");
    }
L}
```

The `isValid()` method in `SecureReceiptValidator` verifies the return object `SecureType` and has a message that starts with a string `SEC`. This is a perfect example of how an application can ensure that a business layer has not been compromised and actually provides the correct result to a web client—a RESTful client endpoint or an EJB endpoint.

See the book's source code for the Arquillian unit test class and the value objects `Account` and `Receipt`.

Method validation rules

- Given a method M that is a member of class type T and is passed a value object A, its preconditions may not be strengthened in subtypes of T and A.
- Given a method M, which is a member of class type T and returns a value object R, its post-conditions may not be weakened in subtypes of T and R.

These rules are imposed by the Bean Validation specification in order to preserve the **Barbara Liskov Substitution Principle**, which governs the behavior of subtyping. An object is open for extension but closed for modification, and as such if there is a value type of A that extends S then I can replace it with another type B that extends S.

Integration with Java EE

Bean Validation has an abstract configuration component called a **Service Provider Interface** (**SPI**), which allows it to integrate with Spring Framework and Guice. Any custom constraint validator implementation can inject any dependency. Any dependency injection container that integrates with Bean Validation framework has the responsibility to instantiate a `ValidatorFactory` instance.

Bean Validation delegates the management of the lifecycle to the various supported containers, including CDI. Any type of **MessageInterpolator**, **TraversableResolver**, **ConstraintValidatorFactory** instances are also managed from a dependency injection framework.

In environments where there is no default integration or a standalone Java SE runtime, the application is required to configure `ValidatorFactory` and a custom `ConstraintValidatorFactory` instance. The application may choose to use a dependency injection framework such as JBoss Weld, Guice, or the Spring Framework.

Bean Validation 1.1 integrates with the JPA 2.0 or better and developers get this support for free as it is defined by the Java EE 7 specification. Again there is a choice if the integration is part of CDI container and it is provided as an entity injection mechanism that is hidden from the application or part of the JPA provider itself before objects are flushed to the database through the persistence session.

Default access to validator and validator factory

In Java EE 7, the Bean Validator must make available the JNDI paths: `java:comp/ValidatorFactory` for the default `ValidatorFactory`, and `java:comp/Validator` for the `Validator` instance.

Similar to JNDI injection, any CDI container operating under Java EE 7 must allow injection of the default `ValidatorFactory` instance. So the following code snippet is completely legal in both the Full and Web profiles:

```
@Inject private ValidatorFactory validatorFactory;
@Inject private Validator validator;
```

Java EE 7, however, does cater for alternative Bean Validation providers with the `@Qualifier` annotation assuming that there is an instance of a factory located somewhere else in the system. The developer would ensure there is an obvious `@Producer` CDI managed bean in their application.

JAX-RS 2.0 integration

Bean Validation 1.1 has integration with JAX-RS 2.0 in the Java EE 7 specification. It also integrates with Java Server Faces. Incidentally, JAX-RS support is a special application of Method-level constraint validation. A provider method-level constraint intercepts JAX-RS request and responses.

The Bean Validator specification has some rules on this standard implementation and how it responds to validation failures. The following are the rules:

- Violations on constraints on parameters to a RESTful endpoint generate a HTTP error response code in the 400 – 499 range
- Violations on constraints on the return value to a RESTful endpoint generate a HTTP error response code in the 500 – 599 range

The following is an example of JAX-RS planning resource from *Chapter 8, RESTful Services JAX-RS 2.0*, with constraints applied to the request and response:

```
@Path("plans")
public PlanningResource {
    @Path("{id}")
    @GET
    @Produces(MediaType.APPLICATION_JSON)
    @NotNull
```

```
        public Response getPlanList(
            @PathParam("id")
            @Size( min=8, max=12)
            @SecureIdChecker  String id ) {
            List<Plan> plans = findPlanCollectionById(id);
            Collections.sort( plans
                new AscendingDateOrderComparator() );
            GenericEntity entity =
                new GenericEntity<List<Plan>>(plans);
            return Response.ok(entity).build();
        }
    }
```

This concludes the chapter on Bean Validation. For more details, please inspect this handbook's source code and read the specification for clarity.

Summary

Bean Validation is a crucial part of the Java EE 7 platform. It does small things and it does them very well as we learnt in this chapter. Bean Validation allows the developer to extend the Java type system in a programmatic fashion through *design-by-contract* at runtime albeit not at static compilation time. Bean Validation is governed by constraints, which are defined by annotations.

A constraint has an interpreted message property, a group set, and a payload. Constraints can be grouped together in order to perform full or partial validation or specific order evaluation.

In order to execute value object checking with annotated constraints, the application must gain access to the Bean Validation `ValidatorFactory` instance and then obtain a `Validator` instance. The advantage of this model means evaluation of constraints is mostly in the control of incumbent applications.

The specification has a set of standard constraints such as `@NotNull`, `@Max` and `@DecimalMin`. The reference implementation Hibernate Validator has the standard set of constraints from the specification, and it supplies additional useful constraints such as `@NotEmpty`, `@Range`, and `@Email`.

Groups of constraints can be ordered. A class-level constraint allows checking of interdependent properties in a value object. Method-level constraint in conjunction with a suitable interception technology allows non-static methods to be evaluated for correctness through their method parameters and associated return values.

Finally, Bean Validation has considerable integration features for CDI, JPA, and JAX-RS technologies and even other containers outside of the Java EE 7 environment.

In the next chapter, we will advance much further into Java Persistence.

11
Advanced Topics in Persistence

E. F. Codd, 1970 said, "Future users of large databanks must be protected from having to know how the data is organized in the machine (the internal representation)". In this chapter, we will look at the advanced topics for Java Persistence that builds on the knowledge we cemented in *Chapter 4, Essential Java Persistence* and *Chapter 5, Object-Relational Mapping with JPA*.

Persistence of map collections

The ability to manage persistence capable objects with `java.util.Map` type collections has been around since JPA 2.0, so this is not strictly a Java EE 7 feature. Map collections are extremely useful for Java applications, where data can be accessed in data types that are organized into key-and-value pairs. This structure of data is redundant from the point of view of a relational database of joined tables. Therefore, the key of a map with a target object is not persisted.

The MapKey relationship

The annotation `@javax.persistence.MapKey` associates an owning entity with the target entity when data type of the collection is a type of `java.util.Map`. The key into the map collection is the target primary key of the target entity or the persistent field or property that uniquely identifies the target entity as the value.

Advanced Topics in Persistence

There is only one attribute for `@MapKey`:

Attribute	Type	Description	Default Value
Name	String	This optional attribute specifies the property in the source entity that serves as a key.	N/A – the provider to use the primary key of the associated entity

Let's look an example of map collection associations that relates a table of recording artists to their albums.

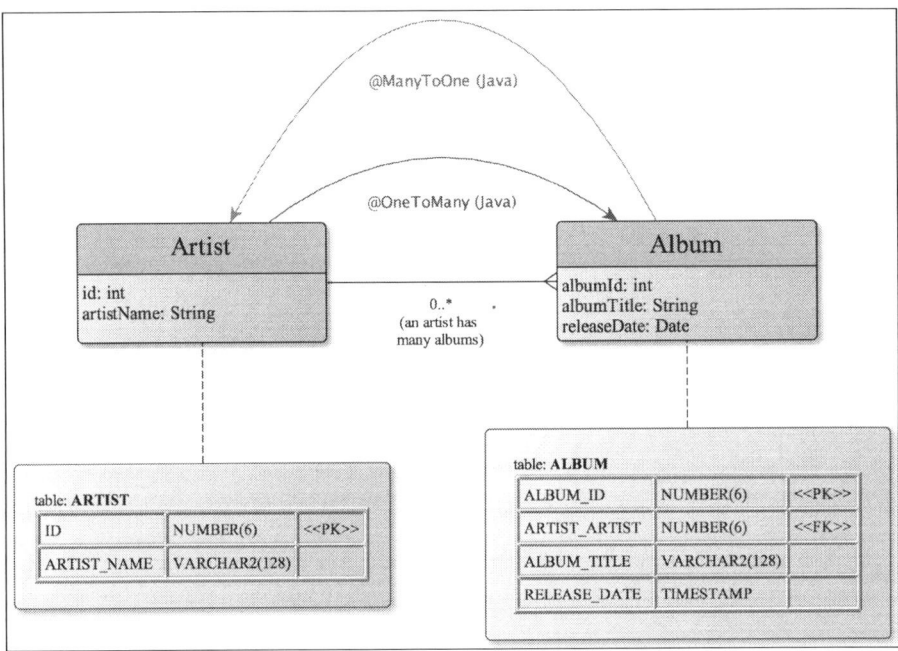

This is the code for `Artist`, which is cut down to save space.

```
packageje7hb.jpa.advanced.maps;
/* ... omitted ... */

@Entity
public class Artist {
    @Id @Column(name="ARTIST_ID")
privateintartistId;

    @NotEmpty
```

```
@Column(nullable = false, name="ARTIST_NAME")
private String artistName;

@OneToMany(mappedBy="artist", cascade = CascadeType.ALL)
@MapKey()
private Map<Integer,Album> albums = new HashMap<>();

public Artist() { }

   /* ... */
}
```

The relationship between an `Artist` and their `Album` instances is one-to-many, usually. The obvious exception to this rule is the compilation album, but this is neither here nor there. Therefore we annotate the bi-directional relationship accordingly with `@OneToMany`. The `@MapKey` annotation associates a map collection relationship and by default it configures the key of the collection as the primary key of the target entity, which in this case is the `Album` entity.

Here is the target entity, `Album`:

```
packageje7hb.jpa.advanced.maps;
/* ... omitted ... */

@Entity
public class Album {
    @Id @Column(name="ALBUM_ID")
privateintalbumId;

@Column(nullable = false, name = "ALBUM_TITLE")
    @NotEmpty
private String title;

@ManyToOne(cascade = CascadeType.ALL)
@JoinColumn(name="ALBUM_ARTIST")
private Artist artist;

@Column(nullable = false, name="RELEASE_DATE")
    @Past @Temporal(TemporalType.DATE)
private Date date;

   /* ... omitted ... */
}
```

Advanced Topics in Persistence

For the `Album` entity, the `@ManyToOne` reverses the owning association back to the Artist entity. This is already familiar to you from *Chapter 5, Object-Relational Mapping with JPA* on entity relationships. We have sprinkled a few of the Bean Validation annotations such as `@Past` and `@NotEmpty` in the entities.

Let's look at the integration test for these persistence entities.

```
@RunWith(Arquillian.class)
public class MapCollectionPersistenceTest {
    @Deployment
public static JavaArchivecreateDeployment() {
        /* ... omitted ... */
    }

    @PersistenceContextEntityManagerem;
    @Resource UserTransactionutx;

    @Test
public void shouldSaveArtistWithAlbum() throws Exception {
        Artist artist1 = new Artist(1002, "Joni Mitchell");
        Album album = new Album();
album.setAlbumId(8002);
album.setArtist(artist1);
album.setTitle("Blue");
album.setDate( new DateTime(1971, 6, 22,
            0, 0, 0).toDate() );
artist1.getAlbums().put( album.getAlbumId(), album );

utx.begin();
em.persist(artist1);
utx.commit();

        Artist artist2 = em.find(Artist.class, 1002);
assertEquals(artist1.getArtistName(),
artist2.getArtistName());
assertEqualMaps(artist1.getAlbums(),
artist2.getAlbums() );
    }

static<K,V> void assertEqualMaps(Map<K,V>m1, Map<K,V>m2)
    {      /* ... */  }
}
```

The test method `shouldSaveArtistWithAlbum()` exercises two entities, `Artist` and `Album`. As with all entity relationships on the Java side of JPA, the developer is responsible to ensure association is completely defined between the owner and target entities from both directions.

The static method `assertEqualsMap()` is a custom assertion method that verifies two map collections are the same.

JPA provider creates or expects a database table called `ARTIST` and `ALBUM`. There is an extra column called `ALBUM_ARTIST` that associates the target entity to the source. It is instructive to examine the console debug output for this unit test:

```
[EL Fine]: sql: -- INSERT INTO ARTIST (ARTIST_ID, ARTIST_NAME) VALUES (?, ?)
  bind => [1002, Joni Mitchell]
[EL Fine]: sql: -- INSERT INTO ALBUM (ALBUM_ID, RELEASE_DATE, ALBUM_TITLE, ALBUM_ARTIST) VALUES (?, ?, ?, ?)
  bind => [8002, 1971-06-22, Blue, 1002]
```

The MapKey join column relationship

So far we saw an association with a map collection using a primary key of the target entity. It is possible to go further with a different key for associated entities such that the JPA provider creates or relies upon a database join table. It is also possible to extend a basic join table with additional properties, such that it has the appearance of a fully independent entity bean.

The annotation `@MapKeyColumn` specifies the mapping for the key column of a map whose key is a basic JPA type. The annotation `@MapKeyClass` specifies the type of a map key for association, which can be a basic type, an embedded class or another entity.

Applying a `@OneToMany` annotation with `@MapKeyColumn` on a field or property informs the JPA provider to create a join table between source and target entities. The developer can configure the name, null-ability, and cascade operations of the join table with `@JoinColumn` and `@JoinColumns` annotations.

The annotation `@MapKeyJoinColumn` specifies the column mapping of the entity that is used as the key. The key join column for the map can be another reference database table, part of a join table, or field referenced in the map collection table.

Advanced Topics in Persistence

Developers can create quite sophisticated associations to two or more database tables with the @MapKeyJoinColumn annotation. We will look at an example of code that associates the recording artist to live events and a type of event. An artist is usually involved in a tour, and for the active lifetime of the artist, they will have several tours, and each tour is a type. A tour can be a global( )one, spanning multiple cities on many continents, or it can be exclusive to a set town, television production, a collaborative group effort, or sometimes charitable to a good cause.

How can we represent this business requirement in JPA using map collections?

Let's start with a new version of the Artist entity:

```
@Entity
public class Artist {
    @Id @Column(name="ARTIST_ID") private long id;
@Column(nullable=false, name="ARTIST_NAME")
private String name;

@OneToMany(mappedBy="artist",cascade = CascadeType.ALL)
@MapKeyJoinColumn(name="EVENT_TYPE_ID")
private Map<EventType, LiveEvent> events
        = new HashMap<>();
public Artist() {}   /*...*/
}
```

The biggest change is the parameterized type for the map collection, which is Map<EventType, LiveEvent>, where we apply the @MapKeyJoinColumn. The key column is a part of an entity, EventType, and has the database column name EVENT_TYPE_ID.

Here is the persistence entity EventType; it only has two properties, the primary key and the name:

```
@Entity @Table(name="EVENT_TYPE")
public class EventType {
    @Id @Column(name="EVENT_TYPE_ID") private long id;
    @Basic @Column(name="EVENT_TYPE_NAME")
private String type;
publicEventType() {}      /*...*/
}
```

Because we overrode the default column name in JPA for the primary key to EVENT_TYPE_ID, we must also configure the @MapKeyJoinColumn with the same target database column name.

Finally, we have the entity for storing data about events called `LiveEvent`:

```
@Entity @Table(name="LIVE_EVENT")
public class LiveEvent {
    @Id @Column(name="LIVE_EVENT_ID") private long id;
@Column(nullable=false, name="ARTIST_NAME")
private String name;
@OneToOne(cascade = CascadeType.ALL)
privateEventTypeeventType;

@ManyToOne(cascade = CascadeType.ALL)
private Artist artist;

publicLiveEvent() {}         /*...*/
}
```

We declare a `@OneToOne` unidirectional association for the join table between the entities: `LiveEvent` and `EventType`. If we preferred to share event types among live events, we could change to the association to `@OneToMany`. We declare a bidirectional reverse association `@ManyToOne` from `LiveEvent` to `Artist`.

Running the actual unit test from the book's source code creates three database tables: `ARTIST`, `EVENT_TYPE` and `LIVE_EVENT`. The JPA provider adds an additional column, `EVENTTYPE_EVENT_TYPE_ID`, to the `LIVE_EVENT` table.

Again, it is helpful to examine the JPA console output:

```
[EL Fine]: sql: -- INSERT INTO ARTIST (ARTIST_ID, ARTIST_NAME) VALUES
(?, ?)
   bind => [1002, Lady Gaga]
[EL Fine]: sql: -- INSERT INTO EVENT_TYPE (EVENT_TYPE_ID,
EVENT_TYPE_NAME) VALUES (?, ?)
   bind => [808, WORLD TOUR]
[EL Fine]: sql: -- INSERT INTO LIVE_EVENT (LIVE_EVENT_ID, ARTIST_NAME,
ARTIST_ARTIST_ID, EVENTTYPE_EVENT_TYPE_ID) VALUES (?, ?, ?, ?)
   bind => [97502, The Monster Ball Tour, 1002, 808]
[EL Fine]: -- UPDATE LIVE_EVENT SET EVENT_TYPE_ID= ? WHERE
   (LIVE_EVENT_ID= ?)
   bind => [808, 97502]
```

Let's now move on to stored procedures.

Calling stored procedures

Many relational databases have a concept of executable SQL routines, which is a function or procedure that is called from SQL. These functions or procedures are stored sets of predefined SQL statements that are written to perform an action in the database, and they are typically stored and accessed by the database server. Executable SQL routines support parameters, which can be of three types: inbound, outbound, and a reference cursor to a result set.

Relational database providers supply a degree of executable SQL routine in their products. **Stored procedures** is the common name for SQL invoked routines that accept zero or more inbound parameters and return zero or more result sets, or set values on outbound parameters. SQL-invoked routines that just perform immutable calculations which do not modify the database and return a single value or a table are known as **user-defined functions**.

Many businesses have written stored procedures to encapsulate complex business logic that runs directly on the database. They see a huge advantage in using a specific SQL provider's database feature to provide security and audits, or the interception of access of critical information in order to enrich or restrict views of data.

Businesses also write custom stored procedures to compute complex queries and values close to the database data. Stored procedures generally reduce the traffic between the application and database server, because instead of sending multiple raw SQL statements that have to be deciphered and compiled into statements, the application merely sends the invoked procedure's name, executes the procedure, and retrieves the result. Stored procedures and functions are transparent and reusable across applications.

The downsides to stored procedures are that they are not easily debugged from the application and they also incur a high load cost on top of the database. The maintenance of business logic written stored procedures over the long term becomes increasingly complex and that is yet another criticism. Because stored procedures are not usually portable between database products, businesses find themselves locked into mission critical operational rules deep inside a particular vendor's product.

Stored procedure query

JPA 2.1 now provides a standard method of calling stored procedures from the `EntityManager` instance, which is `createStoredProcedureQuery()`. This method accepts a single `String` that represents the name of the stored procedure inside the database. The call returns a `javax.persistence.StoredProcedureQuery` instance.

The most important methods of `StoredProcedureQuery` are outlined in the following table:

Method	Description
`StoreProcedureQueryregisterStoreProcedureParameter( String paramName, Class<?> type, ParameterMode mode )`	Sets the parameter name and type for the stored procedure with the mode parameter type.
`StoreProcedureQuerysetParameter ( String paramName, Object value )`	Associates the named parameter for the stored procedure with a value.
`boolean execute()`	Executes the stored procedure that should return one or more result sets.
`intexecuteUpdate()`	Executes the stored procedure that should only perform an update of rows.
`List getResultSet()`	Retrieves the current result set.
`Object getSingleResult()`	Retrieves a value from the current result set, which has only one row and one value.
`Boolean hasMoreResults()`	Returns true if there is another result set to retrieve from the stored procedure.
`intgetUpdateCount()`	Returns the rows affected count from the last execution of a stored procedure.

`StoredProcedureQuery` readily supports named parameters for those database servers that support this feature. There are also integer positional parameter variants of the `setParameter()` and `registerStoreParameter()` calls. For time specific properties with `java.util.Date`, the developer must use the overloaded methods that accept a `TemporalType`.

Advanced Topics in Persistence

The `javax.persistence.ParameterMode` is a Java enumerated type, which has the following values: `IN`, `OUT`, `INOUT`, and `REF_CURSOR`. A stored procedure can be both an input and output parameter, and `INOUT` caters to those parameters. Some database servers such as Oracle DB return reference cursors instead of the result set directly. The `REF_CURSOR` implies that the result set is retrieved from the `Cursor` type.

MySQL remote server example

MySQL is a popular open source database server that supports stored procedures.

Here is a simple stored procedure definition, which creates the procedure called `READ_TAX_SP`:

```
CREATE PROCEDURE READ_TAX_SP (IN param1INT)
  BEGIN
    SELECT * FROM TAX_CODE WHERE TAX_CODE_ID = param1;
  END
```

The procedure has one inbound parameter `param1` and returns only one dynamic result set. In MySQL and many other databases, a stored procedure can return more than one result set or none at all. This procedure, `READ_TAX_SP`, makes a simple query in a database table, `TAX_CODE`, which retrieves the tax code and tax name.

Here is the definition of the `TAX_CODE` database table:

```
CREATE TABLE TAX_CODE( TAX_CODE_IDBIGINT,
    NAME VARCHAR(16), PRIMARY KEY(TAX_CODE_ID));
INSERT INTO TAX_CODE VALUES ( 101, 'FULL_TIME');
INSERT INTO TAX_CODE VALUES ( 102, 'CHARITY');
INSERT INTO TAX_CODE VALUES ( 103, 'TEMPORARY');
INSERT INTO TAX_CODE VALUES ( 104, 'EMPLOYED');
INSERT INTO TAX_CODE VALUES ( 105, 'EMPLOYED');
```

We create the database table and pre-fill it with sample data. The semicolon character at the end of each line separates different SQL statements in the script.

Dynamic result set retrieval

So how do we invoke this method in JPA 2.1? We simply acquire an `EntityManager` instance and make the necessary calls. Here is a sample of an Arquillian integration test that performs this query.

```
package je7hb.jpa.advanced.storedproc1;
/* ... omitted imports ... */
@RunWith(Arquillian.class)
@CreateSchema({"scripts/create-schema.sql"})
public class StoredProcedureJPATest {
    @Deployment
    public static JavaArchivecreateDeployment() {
        JavaArchive jar = ShrinkWrap.create(JavaArchive.class)
            .addClasses(Utils.class)
            .addAsResource(
               "test-persistence.xml",
               "META-INF/persistence.xml")
            .addAsManifestResource(
            EmptyAsset.INSTANCE,
               ArchivePaths.create("beans.xml"));
               return jar;
    }

    @PersistenceContextEntityManager em;
    @Resource UserTransaction utx;

    @Test
    public void shouldInvokeStoredProcedure()
    throws Exception {
        StoredProcedureQuery query =
          em.createStoredProcedureQuery("READ_TAX_SP")
            .registerStoredProcedureParameter(
              "TAX_CODE_ID", Integer.class, ParameterMode.IN)
            .setParameter("TAX_CODE_ID", 101);
        boolean status = query.execute();
        List rs=  query.getResultList();
        System.out.printf("**** rs=%s\n", rs );
        assetNotNull(rs);
        Object row[] = (Object[])rs.get(0);
        for (int col=0; col<row.length; ++col ) {
            System.out.printf("row[%d]=%s\n", col, row[col]);
        }
    }
}
```

Advanced Topics in Persistence

The annotation `@CreateSchema` applied to the class `StoredProcedureJPATest`. It actually is part of the Arquillian Persistence extension and it executes a SQL script before the tests are run. In this case, we execute the database creation script, which also includes the necessary `DROP TABLE IF EXISTS` and `DROP PROCEDURE IF EXISTS` statements.

In the method `shouldInvokeStoredProcedure()`, we create `StoredProcedureQuery` from the entity manager given the stored procedure to execute. The JPA provider does not know how to invoke the procedure automatically, therefore, we must register the parameter name, type, and parameter mode type. Developers should also note the method chaining ability of `StoredProcedureQuery` during configuration of the stored procedure parameters.

A screenshot of the program's output running against GlassFish 4 managed server, is as follows:

```
[#|2013-08-22T20:16:35.898+0100|INFO|glassfish 4.0||_ThreadID=31;_ThreadName=Thr
ead-7;_TimeMillis=1377198995898;_LevelValue=800;|
  [EL Fine]: sql: Connection(2091673474)---CREATE PROCEDURE EMP_READ_BY_REGION_SP
( IN region INT ) BEGIN SELECT e.EMPLOYEE_ID, e.FIRST_NAME, e.LAST_NAME, r.NAME
FROM EMPLOYEE e, REGION r WHERE e.REGION_ID = r.REGION_ID; END|#]

[#|2013-08-22T20:16:35.899+0100|INFO|glassfish 4.0||_ThreadID=31;_ThreadName=Thr
ead-7;_TimeMillis=1377198995899;_LevelValue=800;|
  - 0|#]

[#|2013-08-22T20:16:35.920+0100|INFO|glassfish 4.0||_ThreadID=31;_ThreadName=Thr
ead-7;_TimeMillis=1377198995920;_LevelValue=800;|
  [EL Fine]: sql: Connection(1226273685)---{ CALL READ_TAX_SP(?) }
    bind => [101]|#]

[#|2013-08-22T20:16:35.923+0100|INFO|glassfish 4.0||_ThreadID=31;_ThreadName=Thr
ead-7;_TimeMillis=1377198995923;_LevelValue=800;|
  ****************** status=true|#]

[#|2013-08-22T20:16:35.928+0100|INFO|glassfish 4.0||_ThreadID=31;_ThreadName=Thr
ead-7;_TimeMillis=1377198995928;_LevelValue=800;|
  ****************** rs=[[Ljava.lang.Object;@3c25f639]|#]

[#|2013-08-22T20:16:35.928+0100|INFO|glassfish 4.0||_ThreadID=31;_ThreadName=Thr
ead-7;_TimeMillis=1377198995928;_LevelValue=800;|
  ****************** row=101|#]

[#|2013-08-22T20:16:35.928+0100|INFO|glassfish 4.0||_ThreadID=31;_ThreadName=Thr
ead-7;_TimeMillis=1377198995928;_LevelValue=800;|
  **** row[0]=101|#]

[#|2013-08-22T20:16:35.928+0100|INFO|glassfish 4.0||_ThreadID=31;_ThreadName=Thr
```

Also note that we then register a parameter by a specific name, and then we also use that same name to set the inbound value (and also the output bound value; see the next section). In setting the parameter name, we do not have to match the parameter inside the stored procedure, because we are building the metadata dynamically, outside of the database in Java.

Calling the `getResultList()` method on the query instance retrieves the first result set in this query. We expect only one of them. The raw list collection is actually a collection of primitive object arrays. We should see one row with an object array of an `Integer` and `String` instance to represent the primary key and the name from the `TAX_CODE` table.

The unit test in this project, `StoredProcedureJPATest`, runs the Arquillian container framework as a remote GlassFish server instance. In other words, GlassFish and the MySQL servers must already be configured and running on your development in order for the test to succeed.

Retrieving outbound parameter values

As described earlier, stored procedure parameters can also be outbound or input and output bound. Retrieving the values of outbound parameters is the reverse of setting the input parameters, as long as the parameters mode is registered.

Let's create a more complicated stored procedure that gives us an output bound parameter. This procedure is called COMPOUND_INTEREST_SP and it calculates the compound interest rate formula:

```
CREATE PROCEDURE COMPOUND_INTEREST_SP(
    IN P FLOAT, IN r FLOAT, IN n FLOAT,
    IN t FLOAT, OUT A FLOAT )
  BEGIN
    DECLARE X INT;
    DECLARE nt, power, total FLOAT;
    SET nt = n * t;
    SET X = nt;
    SET total = 1;
    SET power = 1 + R / N;
    WHILE  X> 0 DO
        SET total = total * power;
        SET X = X - 1;
    END WHILE;
    SET A = P * total;
  END
```

This MySQL specific procedure accepts several parameters: four are inbound and the last one is outbound and serves the return value. P is the initial amount, also known as the principal value, r is the annual nominal interest rate, n is the number of times the interest is compounded per year, and t is the number of years of the loan. The specifics of the rate calculation can be found at http://en.wikipedia.org/wiki/Compound_interest. Here is a new unit test class to verify the operation of calling the stored procedure:

```java
package je7hb.jpa.advanced.storedproc1;
/* ... omitted imports ... */

@RunWith(Arquillian.class)
@CreateSchema({"scripts/create-schema.sql"})
public class CompoundInterestRateStoredProcJPATest {
    // omitted code similar to the previous

    @Test
    public void shouldInvokeStoredProcedureWithOutbound()
    throws Exception {
        StoredProcedureQuery query =
            em.createStoredProcedureQuery(
                "COMPOUND_INTEREST_SP")
              .registerStoredProcedureParameter(
                "P", Float.class, ParameterMode.IN)
              .registerStoredProcedureParameter(
                "r", Float.class, ParameterMode.IN)
              .registerStoredProcedureParameter(
                "n", Integer.class, ParameterMode.IN)
              .registerStoredProcedureParameter(
                "t", Integer.class, ParameterMode.IN)
              .registerStoredProcedureParameter(
                "A", Float.class, ParameterMode.OUT)
              .setParameter("P", new Float(1500))
              .setParameter("r", new Float(0.043))
              .setParameter("n", new Integer(4))
              .setParameter("t", new Integer(6));
        boolean status = query.execute();
        assertFalse(query.hasMoreResults());
        Double A = ( Double)
            query.getOutputParameterValue("A");
        assertEquals( 1938.84, A, 0.005 );
    }
}
```

The big difference in `CompoundInterestRateStoredProcJPATest` is the registration of the second parameter as a parameter, `A`, with `ParameterMode.OUT`. After creating the `StoreProcedureQuery` instance and configuring it using the method chaining style, we just invoke `executeUpdate()` as we are not expecting any dynamic result sets. Retrieving the output of the stored procedure is simply calling `getOutputParameterValue()` and casting to the return value at the correct time.

Creating dynamic queries with a stored procedure in JPA 2.1 is relatively easy; we can also take advantage of the new features with service endpoints such as session EJBs. We shall look into this in more detail in the next section.

Stored procedure query annotations

JPA 2.1 introduces named stored procedure queries that can be attached to entity objects and mapped super classes, which allows developers to retrieve entities remove it in a standard way. The annotation `@javax.persistence.NamedStoredProcedureQuery` is the basis for sophisticated mapping of a procedure to an entity, which is rather flexible and supportive of legacy databases.

Here is a table of the key attributes of `@NamedStoredProcedureQuery`:

Attribute name	Type	Description	Default
name	String	Specifies the name of the stored procedure query in Java	Required
procedureName	String	Specifies the name of the stored procedure in the relational database	Required
procedures	StoredProcedure-Parameter[]	Defines an array list of stored procedure parameters	Empty array
resultClasses	Class[]	Specifies an array list of entity types that the dynamic result sets will map to	Empty array
resultSetMappings	String[]	Informs the JPA to map the result sets' metadata to `@SQLResultSetMapping`	Empty array
hints	QueryHint[]	A set of vendor-specific, non-portable settings	Empty array

Let's look at an example of using this annotation in an application that could use a stored procedure to retrieve employee records by some specific region. We shall assume that the database table is owned and administered by another department and we do not have access to the tables in our team. However, the administrators kindly gave us a schema.

Advanced Topics in Persistence

From the schema, here are the database table definitions:

```
CREATE TABLE EMPLOYEE ( EMPLOYEE_IDBIGINT,
FIRST_NAMEVARCHAR(32), LAST_NAMEVARCHAR(32),
REGION_IDBIGINT, PRIMARY KEY(EMPLOYEE_ID) );
CREATE TABLE REGION ( REGION_IDBIGINT, NAME VARCHAR(16),
   PRIMARY KEY(REGION_ID));
```

The employee entity is linked to the region entity by a foreign key; each employee has a region. Remember, the administrators have locked direct access to these tables.

The details of the stored procedure are as follows:

```
CREATE PROCEDURE EMP_READ_BY_REGION_SP( IN region INT )
  BEGIN
    SELECT e.EMPLOYEE_ID, e.FIRST_NAME, e.LAST_NAME, r.NAME
      FROM EMPLOYEE e, REGION r
      WHERE e.REGION_ID = r.REGION_ID;
  END
```

The procedure `EMP_READ_BY_REGION_SP` is open and accessible to the internal staff. It retrieves all the employees that match the supplied region ID.

This example is highly contrived, but this could be a situation that you, the developer, might face in your business tomorrow. So how do we retrieve the employees from the stored procedure using JPA?

We define the `Employee` entity in Java with the following properties:

```
package je7hb.jpa.advanced.storedproc1;
/* ... omitted imports ... */

@NamedStoredProcedureQuery(
    name = "Employee.findByRegion",
    procedureName = "EMP_READ_BY_REGION_SP",
    resultClasses = Employee.class,
    parameters = {
        @StoredProcedureParameter(
            mode=IN, name="REGION_ID",
            type=Integer.class)
    }
)
@Entity
@Table(name="EMPLOYEE")
@SecondaryTable(
    name="REGION",
```

```
        pkJoinColumns = {
            @PrimaryKeyJoinColumn(name = "REGION_ID") }
    )
    public class Employee {
        @Id @Column(name="EMPLOYEE_ID")
        String id;
        @Column(name="FIRST_NAME")
        String firstName;
        @Column(name="LAST_NAME")
        String lastName;
        @Column(name="NAME",table="REGION")
        String region;

        public Employee() { }
        // omitted getters, setters and toString()
    }
```

We annotate the entity with `@NamedStoredProcedureQuery` and specify the name `Region.findByRegion`, the stored procedure name `EMP_READ_BY_REGION_SP`, and the parameters. Of particular note is the `resultClasses` attribute that is set to the `Employee` entity class, and it informs the JPA provider to map result() sets to this object instance.

The entity `Employee` is annotated with `@Table` to specify the database table explicitly. We declare the relationship between the employee and the region with the annotation `@SecondaryTable`, which defines the target table and its primary key column. To complete the mapping, we annotate the `region` field with the secondary table, `REGION`. JPA, surprisingly, will process this relationship with only the `Employee` class to hand.

It is important to note( ) that we disable automatic generation of the database tables for this entity. Here is Arquillian `EmployeeEntityStoredProcTest` to verify the operation of calling the stored procedure:

```
    package je7hb.jpa.advanced.storedproc1;
    /* ... omitted imports ... */

    @RunWith(Arquillian.class)
    @CreateSchema({"scripts/create-schema.sql"})
    public class EmployeeEntityStoredProcTest
        // ... similar to previous

        @Test
        public void shouldComputeCompoundInterestRate()
        throws Exception {
```

```
            StoredProcedureQuery query =
                em.createNamedStoredProcedureQuery(
                    "Employee.findByRegion")
                .setParameter("REGION_ID", 83001);
        query.execute();
        List list = query.getResultList();
        assertNotNull(list);
        List<Employee> employees = (List<Employee>)list;
        assertTrue(employees.size() > 0 );
    }
}
```

This test demonstrates calling the named stored procedure query with parameters. The JPA provider does the work of invoking the database procedure and converting the result set to a list collection of `Employee` instances.

Now, let's move on to criteria query features in JPA 2.1.

Understanding the criteria API

The Java Persistence Criteria API allows the developer to create dynamic JPQL queries in the Java programming language. In JPA 2.1, it is now possible to execute bulk criteria statements. The Criteria query API defines an abstract expression tree that is generally optimal and compatible with the JPA provider to turn it into a database query or execution update statement: data manipulation language. The abstract expression tree is designed to be similar to the JPQL in terms of semantics and operation. We can think of the Criteria API as a facility to build a meta-model of statements that consist of entities, mapped super classes, and embedded classes inside a persistence unit.

Criteria queries

Criteria queries rely on an annotation processor to generate the metadata for persistence-capable objects. It is possible to build the meta-model manually for relatively simple classes.

The `javax.persistence.criteria` package contains the main elements of the Criteria API including `CriteriaBuilder`, `CriteriaQuery`, `Expression`, `From`, `Root`, and `Join`.

The package `javax.persistence.metamodel` contains interfaces and one annotation that defines a meta-model for a persistence capable object. You will find interfaces such as `Attribute`, `BasicType`, and `EntityType`, and there is one annotation, `StaticMetamodel`. Most of the time you will use the JPA provider's annotation processor to build these meta-models. It is rare to write meta-models by hand.

Let's revisit another version of the `Employee` entity class. Here is the definition for it:

```
@Entity
public class Employee {
    @Id @Column(name = "EMP_ID") private int id;
    @Column(name = "FIRST_NAME") private String firstName;
    @Column(name = "LAST_NAME")  private String lastName;
    privateBigDecimal salary;
    @Column(name = "DAILY_RATE")
    privateBigDecimaldailyRate;

    @ManyToOne(cascade = CascadeType.ALL)
    @JoinColumn(name = "TAX_CODE_ID")
    privateTaxCodetaxCode;

    @ManyToOne(cascade = CascadeType.ALL)
    @JoinColumn(name = "REGION_ID")
    private Region region;
    // ... omitted
}
```

We added the following fields: the daily pay rate for contractors, and the annual salary for an employee, director, or other staff member.

The `TaxCode` and `Region` entities are very straightforward entities with just a primary key column with a nomination: `TAX_CODE_ID` or `REGION_ID` with `NAME`. A tax code has many employees and zero or more employees share a region too.

If we wanted to find all of the employees who earned greater than or equal to a certain high salary, we could write the following JPQL:

```
SELECT e FROM Employee e WHERE e.salary>= 50000
```

Advanced Topics in Persistence

On the other hand we can write a criteria API statement to build the query dynamically in Java. Here is a code snippet of a test that highlights the task:

```java
@RunWith(Arquillian.class)
public class EmployeeCriteriaQueryTest {
    /* ... omitted imports ... */
    @PersistenceContext em;

    @Test
    public void shouldExecuteCriteriaQuery() {
        CriteriaBuilder builder = em.getCriteriaBuilder();
        CriteriaQuery<Employee> c =
            builder.createQuery(Employee.class);
        Root<Employee> p = c.from(Employee.class);
        Predicate condition = builder.ge(
            p.get(Employee_.salary), new BigDecimal("50000"));
        c.where(condition);
        TypedQuery<Employee> q = em.createQuery(c);
        List<Employee> result = q.getResultList();
        assertEquals(NUM_DIRECTORS, result.size());
    }
}
```

First, we retrieve a `CriteriaBuilder` from the entity manger. Next, we build a parameterized `CriteriaQuery` instance, which is the entry point in the meta-model of the query. Every criteria query requires a root object instance that represents the result set class, which is the meaning of `from()` call on the builder. At this juncture, we have semantically built the equivalent of the JPQL statement `SELECT e FROM Employee e`.

We then create a `Predicate` object to serve as a condition to the `CriteriaQuery` instance. The predicate is built from `javax.persistence.Path` references to either a single attribute or another compound path. These Path references are associated with a literal value, the `BigDecimal`, or combined together in either a unary or binary expression operation. See the `CriteriaBuilder.ge()` method, which is the *greater than* or *equal to* operator. Remember, we build the expression equivalent in Java.

It certainly helps to see the manually built static meta-model class `Employee_`. Yes, that is the class name with the appended underscore character.

```java
@StaticMetamodel(Employee.class)
public class Employee_ {
    static SingularAttribute<Employee, Integer> employeeId;
    static SingularAttribute<Employee, String>  firstName;
    static SingularAttribute<Employee, String>  lastName;
```

```
    static SingularAttribute<Employee, BigDecimal> salary;
    static SingularAttribute<Employee, BigDecimal> dailyRate;
    static SingularAttribute<Employee, TaxCode> taxCode;
    static SingularAttribute<Employee, Region>  region;
}
```

We annotate the `Employee_` entity with `@StaticMetamodel` in order to define the static meta-model for the corresponding `Employee` entity. We do this for the benefit of Criteria API queries. The doubly parameterized type `SingularAttribute` represents a single value field or properties of the entity, mapped super-class, or embedded class `javax.persistence.metamodel` package. The attribute is a `Path` element.

There are other classes (`CollectionAttribute`, `ListAttribute`, `SetAttribute`, and `MapAttribute` and associated Java collection instances) that stand for one-to-many and many-to-many relationships on fields and properties. These attributes are types of `PluralAttribute` also in the same package. It is now clear how an annotation processor handles most of this boiler code for us with tens and perhaps hundreds of Java Persistence entities!

The biggest benefit of the Criteria API is that we can dynamically build our filters in Java programming depending on the user input. We can add additional predicates or remove them. We can combine them in additional ways. JPA thus allows the application developer to write dynamic search operations in the natural language of the user. These operators hide the technical detail of piecing together a set of functions.

This final piece of code depicts the combinatorial search for the optional the first and last names.

```
public void advancedSearch(
        String firstName, String lastName )
{
    CriteriaBuilder builder = em.getCriteriaBuilder();
    CriteriaQuery<Employee> c =
        builder.createQuery(Employee.class);
    Root<Employee> p = c.from(Employee.class);
    List<Predicate> predicates = new ArrayList<>();
    if ( firstName != null ) {
        predicates.add(
          builder.like(p.get(Employee_.firstName),
                    firstName));
    }
    if ( lastName != null ) {
```

```
            predicates.add(
                builder.like(p.get(Employee_.lastName),
                        lastName));
        }
        c.where(predicates.toArray(new Predicate[]{}));
        TypedQuery<Employee> q = em.createQuery(c);
        List<Employee> result = q.getResultList();
            // Do some real work here!
}
```

In the `advancedSearch()` method, we create a list collection of predicate elements. Depending on the count of method parameters, it accept 0, 1, or 2 predicates that are the equivalent of `WHERE firstNameLIKE :f` or `WHERE lastNAME LIKE :n`. We bind these sub filters together with the `where()` method on the `CriteriaQuery` method, which effectively performs the same as the `AND` operator.

We've covered JPA 2.0, so and now we shall look at the new bulk update and delete features in JPA 2.1.

CriteriaUpdate

JPA now supports bulk updates in the Criteria API. There is a new interface, `CriteriaUpdate`, that is obtainable from the entity manager. This interface has a number of overloaded `set()` methods, which accept the `SingularAttribute` or `Path` instance. In other words, `CriteriaUpdate` is almost the same as a `CriteriaQuery`, but with the ability to update the entity, mapped supper-classes, or embedded classes; and it does so through the static meta-model.

With our employee record examples, suppose we want to change all the tax codes for all staff that earn greater than or equal to 50,000 dollars per year; we can write this JPQL statement:

```
UPDATE Employee e
   SET e.taxCode = TaxCode( 504, 'Director' )
   WHERE e.salary>= 50000
```

With the new `CriteriaUpdate` instance, we can write a unit test with a method that performs the equivalent operation. Here is the test code:

```
public class EmployeeCriteriaUpdateTest
extends AbstractEmployeeCriteriaTest {
    /* ... */

    @Test
    public void shouldExecuteCriteriaUpdate() throws Exception {
```

```java
            CriteriaBuilder builder = em.getCriteriaBuilder();
            CriteriaUpdate<Employee> c =
                builder.createCriteriaUpdate(Employee.class);
            Root<Employee> p = c.from(Employee.class);
            Predicate condition = builder.ge(
                p.get(Employee_.salary), new BigDecimal("50000"));
            c.where(condition);
            TaxCode taxCode = new TaxCode(504, "Director");
            c.set(p.get(Employee_.taxCode), taxCode);
            utx.begin();
            Query query = em.createQuery(c);
            int rowsAffected = query.executeUpdate();
            assertTrue(rowsAffected> 0 );
            utx.commit();
    }
}
```

Let's examine the Arquillian test `EmployeeCriteriaDeleteTest` in detail. In the method `shouldExecuteCriteriaUpdate()`, we build the expression graph as before with Predicate and then configure the filter of `CriteriaUpdate` by calling the `where()` method with the Predicate instance. We then configure the meta-model with the update expressions by invoking the `CriteriaUpdate set()` method. There can be more than one update expression and therefore we can change multiple properties in the entity at a single time.

As with all JPA updates that change the persistence unit, we retrieve the server `UserTransaction` instance and join an existing transaction boundary or start one. We create a JPA query from the `CriteriaUpdate` instance and then execute it. The affected row's return value tells us if the JPA update was successful or not; at least one row should have been updated for this test.

CriteriaDelete

Similarly to update entities in bulk, there are times when an application wants to remove a collection of entities that fulfill a set of conditions. This is the purpose of the **CriteriaDelete** interface, which is a new interface in JPA 2.1.

Incidentally, both `CriteriaUpdate` and `CriteriaDelegate` interfaces are direct subclasses of a new JPA 2.1 interface, `CommonAbstractCriteria`. Incidentally, the `CriteriaQuery` and `Subquery` interfaces have a common parent interface `AbstractQuery`.

Advanced Topics in Persistence

Now let's suppose we want to remove all staff from the employee records, who earn 50,000 dollars per year or more. We can write a JPQL statement as follows:

```
DELETE FROM Employee e
   WHERE e.salary>= 50000
   AND e.taxCode = TaxCode( 504, 'Director' )
```

The `CriteriaDelete` interface only allows the target entity to be configured with `from()` methods and defines a set of Predicate instances with overloaded `where()` methods.

The equivalent code in Java to remove the entities is illustrated in the Arquillian test, `EmployeeCriteriaDeleteTest`. Here is the code:

```
@RunWith(Arquillian.class)
public class EmployeeCriteriaDeleteTest
extends AbstractEmployeeCriteriaTest {
    /* ... */

    @Test
    public void shouldExecuteCriteriaDelete()
    throws Exception {
        assertNotNull(em);
        CriteriaBuilder builder = em.getCriteriaBuilder();
        CriteriaDelete<Employee> c =
        builder.createCriteriaDelete(Employee.class);
        Root<Employee> p = c.from(Employee.class);
        Predicate condition1 = builder.ge(
            p.get(Employee_.salary),
            new BigDecimal("50000"));
        Predicate condition2 = builder.equal(
            p.get(Employee_.taxCode),
            new TaxCode(504, "Director"));
        c.where(condition1, condition2);
        utx.begin();
        Query query = em.createQuery(c);
        int rowsAffected = query.executeUpdate();
        assertTrue(rowsAffected> 0);
        utx.commit();
    }
}
```

As usual we obtain a `CriteriaBuilder` instance from the entity manager, but this time we ask for a `CriteriaDelete` instance. We define the target entity by calling `from()`. We create two conditions and apply these `Predicate` instances to the `CriteriaDelete` instance. The `where()` method accepts a variable length number of arguments, which is the AND operation in JPQL. This completes building the abstract expression tree for the delete statement.

Since removal of entities effectively changes rows inside target database, we must begin a transaction boundary before we execute the query using the entity manager. Once again, we read the update count from the `executeUpdate()` call. There should be at least one affected row in the test.

The Criteria API is a very useful part of Java Persistence for building dynamic queries, and now it is possible write bulk updates and removals too.

Entity graphs

JPA fundamentally permits field and properties for persistence capable objects, mapped superclasses and embedded classes, to be retrieved as `FetchType.EAGER` or `FetchType.LAZY`. Just for the purposes of revision we shall note that `FetchType.LAZY` is the default for `@OneToMany` and `@ManyToMany` associations; `FetchType.EAGER` is the default for `@OneToOne` and `@ManyToOne` associations.

An entity graph is a template that is defined in the form of metadata or an object created by the dynamic Entity Graph API, which captures the path and boundaries for a query or operation. Another way of stating the definition is that an entity graph is an application configurable fetch plan that instructs the JPA provider on how to retrieve entities from the database server.

In computer science terms, a graph is a collection of nodes connected by edges. Nodes are JPA entities and edges are the relationships between entities. A **sub graph** is a smaller representation of connected nodes derived from a graph. A sub graph is a set of nodes and partial edges taken from the master graph.

JPA 2.1 introduces the notion of an entity graphs object, which can be an annotation or programmatically created. Entity graphs can only be applied to a JPA query or entity manager `find()` operations.

Advanced Topics in Persistence

There are three low-level classes to be aware of: `EntityGraph`, `AttributeNode`, and `Subgraph`, which are found in the package `javax.persistence`.

Interface	Description
`Subgraph<T>`	Represents a sub graph of entities that are managed by association. A sub-graph can contain further attributes and sub-graphs.
`EntityGraph<T>`	Holds the meta model of the fetch plan for an entity and the attributes that will be retrieved eagerly, which can include sub-graphs of further dependent entities.
`AttributeNode<T>`	Represents the attribute of the entity graph, which may also hold the map collection of sub-graph of entities.

An entity graph, however, can be defined with annotations: `@NamedEntityGraph`, `@NamedAttributeNode`, and `@NamedSubgraph`. These correspond to the Java interfaces.

The following diagram illustrates the relationship between a graph and a subgraph:

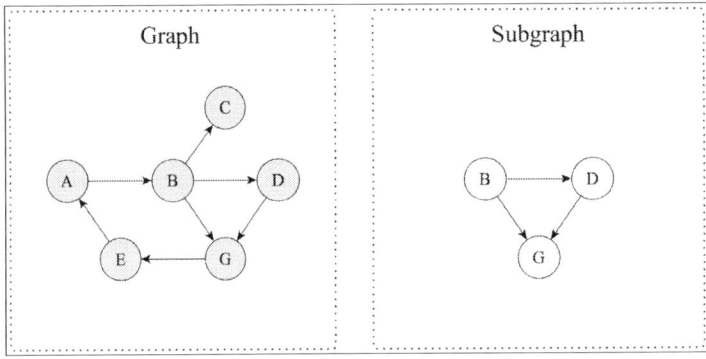

A graph and a related sub-graph

Here are the key attributes for `@NamedEntityGraph`:

Attribute name	Type	Description	Default
`name`	String	Specifies the name of the entity graph	Empty
`attributeNodes`	`NamedAttributeNode []`	Specifies an optional list of attributes that will be eagerly fetched as part of this plan	Empty

Attribute name	Type	Description	Default
includeAllAttributes	boolean	If true then includes all of the attributes of the entity class without explicitly listing them	false
subgraphs	NamedSubgraph[]	A list of sub-graphs included in this fetch plan	Empty

Here are the key attributes for `@NamedEntityGraph`:

Attribute name	Type	Description	Default
value	String	Specifies the name of the attribute that is eagerly fetched	Required
subgraph	String	A reference to another managed type (sub-graph) which has its own fetch plan definition	Empty
keySubgraph	String	For sub-graphs that reference an association java.util.Map type, this attribute configures the key into a collection	Empty

Here are the key attributes for `@NamedSubgraph`:

Attribute name	Type	Description	Default
name	String	Specifies the name of the sub-graph	Required
type	Class	The sub-graph type	void.class
attributeNodes	NamedAttributeNode[]	Attributes of the sub-graph	Empty

Advanced Topics in Persistence

Worked example of a fetch plan

We shall revisit the recording music business as our domain. The important entities, as we have already seen, are the artist, concert event, and album. Suppose we throw another domain object such as *legally binding contracts* into this mix. If every entity was fetched eagerly then we could face the possibility of retrieving row upon row from joined database tables in our little database. This would probably not be great for efficiency in our web application, so I think that calls for a fetch plan!

Let's present our dependent entities first starting with the refactoring of the artist's music event:

```
@Entity
@Table(name = "CONCERT_EVENT")
public class ConcertEvent {
    @Id @Column(name="CONCERT_EVENT_ID")
    protected long id;
    @Column(nullable=false, name="ARTIST_NAME")
    protected String name;
    @OneToOne(cascade = CascadeType.ALL)
    protectedEventTypeeventType;

    @ManyToOne(cascade = CascadeType.ALL)
    protected Artist artist;

    @OneToMany(cascade=CascadeType.ALL,
          fetch = FetchType.LAZY )
    protected List<Contract> contracts = new ArrayList<>();

    public ConcertEvent() {} /* ... */
}
```

The `ConcertEvent` entity is the top class in a hierarchy of different recording events including theatre, revenue, and charity. This entity has a primary key `id` and a basic `name` field. It has a many-to-one relationship to the `artist`. We add a new relation; a concert can have many legal `contracts`. We explicitly hint to the JPA Provider to retrieve contracts lazily with `FetchType.LAZY`.

For now, we only require one subclass of the concert event, namely:

```
@Entity
@Table(name="LIVE_EVENT")
@Inheritance
public class LiveEvent extends ConcertEvent{
```

```
    @Size(min=3) protected String stadium;
    @Min(10) protected int capacity;

    publicLiveEvent() {} /* ... */
}
```

The `LiveEvent` entity is a direct sub class of `ConcertEvent`; note that we are using the default mode of `InheritanceType.SINGLE_TABLE`. A live event, we assume, takes place at a `stadium` and has a maximum `capacity`. Essentially, we refactored this previous version of the `LiveEvent` entity by pulling up the members into the new super class. It doesn't matter about the accuracy and precision of the domain model.

Let's define the `Contract` entity to associate with `ConcertEvent`:

```
@Entity
public class Contract {
    @Id @Column(name="CONTRACT_ID")
    private long id;
    private String title;
    @Lob private String document;

    @ManyToOne(cascade = CascadeType.ALL)
    @JoinColumn(nullable = false)
    privateConcertEventconcertEvent;

    public Contract() {}  /* ... */
}
```

The field `document` is annotated with `@Lob` to denote it as capable of storing long-binary objects. Since `document` is a `String`, then the database type is a CLOB for storing character data.

We will create two fetch plans for retrieving the `Artist` and its dependent entities. There are two situations; sometimes it is useful to retrieve just the essential basic properties of artist with the event dependency and sometimes it is useful to retrieve the `Artist` and `ConcertEvent` entities.

Here is a definition of `Artist` with the entity graph as annotations:

```
    @NamedEntityGraphs(value = {
    @NamedEntityGraph(
        name="Artist.NoConcerts",
        attributeNodes={
            @NamedAttributeNode("name") }
    ),
```

```
        @NamedEntityGraph(
            name="Artist.WithConcerts",
            attributeNodes={
                @NamedAttributeNode("name"),
                @NamedAttributeNode("events") }
        ),
    })
    @Entity
    public class Artist {
        @Id @Column(name="ARTIST_ID")
        private long id;
        @Column(nullable=false, name="ARTIST_NAME")
        private String name;
        @OneToMany(mappedBy="artist",cascade = CascadeType.ALL)
        @MapKeyJoinColumn(name="EVENT_TYPE_ID")
        private Map<EventType, ConcertEvent> events = new HashMap<>();

        public Artist() {}   /* ... */
    }
```

The entity `Artist` is annotated with `@NamedEntityGraphs`. We declare two `@NamedEntityGraph` annotations in an array. Each entity graph represents a fetch plan for the JPA provider and must have a unique name across the persistence unit. The fetch plan is attached to the entity that is being annotated and its dependent object if a sub-graph is used. Each entity graph has an option set of `@NamedAttributeNode` that identifies the field or properties of the entity that should be eagerly loaded by the JPA provider.

In summary, the named entity graph `Artist.NoConcert` loads the artist without retrieving the concert information. or in other words, the map collection of `ConcertEvent` elements is lazily loaded. The named entity graph `Artist.WithConcerts` informs the JPA provider to load the `Artist` and the collection of `ConvertEvent` entities.

Fetch plans, therefore, allow the application to control the performance of querying deeply dependent objects. Loading the concert data eagerly also entails loading the sub types, which could also have other eagerly loaded dependent entities. However, because the `Contract` association is `FetchType.LAZY` then it is not loaded by the first query with the `Artist.WithConcerts` fetch plan. Here I am using a fetch plan and entity graph synonymously.

Chapter 11

As usual, let's look at an Arquillian test that demonstrates the entity graph feature. Here is the cut-down code for the class `ArtistEntityGraphRetrievalTest`:

```java
@RunWith(Arquillian.class)
public class ArtistEntityGraphRetrievalTest {
    // ... code omitted
    @PersistenceContextEntityManager em;
    @Resource UserTransaction utx;

    @Test @InSequence(1)
    public void shouldSaveArtistWithAlbum() throws Exception{
    StringBuilder text = new StringBuilder();
    for ( int j=0; j<256; ++j) {
        text.append((char)(65 + Math.random() * 26)); }
        Contract contract =
            new Contract( 5150, "M and Ms", text.toString());
        EventType eventType =
            New EventType(808, "WORLD TOUR");
        Artist artist = new Artist(1002, "Lady Gaga" );
        LiveEvent event = new LiveEvent(97502,
            "The Monster Ball Tour",
            eventType, artist, "Tokyo Dome", 55000 );
        event.getContracts().add(contract);
        contract.setConcertEvent(event);
        artist.getEvents().put( eventType, event );

        utx.begin();
        em.persist(artist);
        utx.commit();

        Artist art2 = em.find(Artist.class, artist.getId());
        Utils.assertEqualMaps(
        art2.getEvents(), art2.getEvents());
    }

    // ...
}
```

[521]

We create sample data with a recording artist and the dependent entities in the first test method, `shouldSaveArtistWithAlbum()`. We take full advantage of Arquillian's ability to execute test methods in a defined order with the annotation `@InSequence`, which takes a single value to indicate the execution order; higher numbers are lower priority. It allows us to write a test method that executes before the others for the purpose of populating the database. This test, of course, runs against a real database. I used MySQL.

We construct the `Construct` entity with a document that contains 256 random characters. Imagine if this entity had a large dataset; retrieving every document for each row in the database, indeed, would be suboptimal-I think you get the picture. The remaining part of set up, builds the entities and connects them together. We must ensure the relationships are correctly defined on the Java side for bidirectional associations so that correspond to the entity relationships between the physical database tables (or views).

Let's verify the operation of the first fetch graph with a test method:

```java
private Artist getArtistWithEntityGraph( String entityGraph) {
  EntityGraph artistGraph = em.getEntityGraph(entityGraph);
  return (Artist) em.createQuery("Select a from Artist a")
      .setHint("javax.persistence.fetchgraph", artistGraph)
      .getResultList()
      .get(0);
}

@Test  @InSequence(2)
public void shouldLoadArtistWithoutConcerts() throws Exception{
  Artist artist = getArtistWithEntityGraph(
      "Artist.NoConcerts");
  PersistenceUnitUtil util =
      em.getEntityManagerFactory()
          .getPersistenceUnitUtil();
  assertTrue(util.isLoaded(artist, "id"));
  assertTrue(util.isLoaded(artist, "name"));
  assertFalse(util.isLoaded(artist, "events"));
}
```

The method `getArtistWithEntityGraph()` is a helper function to set the fetch plan for the current entity manager. We ask the entity manager for a named `EntityGraph` instance. At the same time, when we make a JPA query, we set a hint on the `Query` instance with the `javax.persistence.fetchgraph` key special and the `EntityGraph` value. The method chaining on the query makes this ever so convenient; we execute it and retrieve a single result, which is the artist from the earlier test method `shouldSaveArtistWithAlbum()`.

The test method `shouldLoadArtistWithoutConcerts()` is also annotated with `@InSequence` with a higher value. We make use of the refactored method `getArtistWithEntityGraph()` in order to retrieve the `Artist` entity with a known fetch plan. We retrieve the internal fetch plan of the entity manager from the factory instance. There is a special utility class `PersistenceUnitUtil`, which has some useful methods. The `isLoaded()` method checks if the entity has an attribute fetched by the persistence context. The attribute is available to the application for use, if this method returns `true`.

The entity graph `Artist.NoConcerts` applied to a query hints to the JPA provider to load the artist and retrieve the `id` and `name`, but the `events` collection is not fetched. This is the purpose of the test.

Let's look at the third test `shouldLoadArtistWithConcerts()`, which should be straightforward to understand now:

```
@Test  @InSequence(3)
public void shouldLoadArtistWithConcerts() throws Exception{
  PersistenceUnitUtil util =
      em.getEntityManagerFactory().getPersistenceUnitUtil();
  Artist artist =
      getArtistWithEntityGraph("Artist.WithConcerts");
  assertTrue(util.isLoaded(artist, "id"));
  assertTrue(util.isLoaded(artist, "name"));
  assertTrue(util.isLoaded(artist, "events"));
}
```

Advanced Topics in Persistence

The only difference between this test and the last one is the named entity graph and the assertion. We shall do something very useful with sub-graphs or dependent collection entities associated with the root entity.

```
[#|2013-08-23T10:07:34.352+0100|INFO|glassfish 4.0|javax.enterprise.web|_ThreadI
D=43;_ThreadName=admin-listener(3);_TimeMillis=1377248854352;_LevelValue=800;_Me
ssageID=AS-WEB-GLUE-00172;|
  Loading application [test] at [/test]|#]

[#|2013-08-23T10:07:34.452+0100|INFO|glassfish 4.0|org.jvnet.mimepull.WeakDataFi
le|_ThreadID=43;_ThreadName=admin-listener(3);_TimeMillis=1377248854452;_LevelVa
lue=800;|
  File /var/folders/kr/vj5fd5s91g76_t348ndnbtxr0000gn/T/MIME2269256818293192356.
tmp was not deleted|#]

[#|2013-08-23T10:07:35.152+0100|INFO|glassfish 4.0||_ThreadID=31;_ThreadName=Thr
ead-7;_TimeMillis=1377248855152;_LevelValue=800;|
  [EL Fine]: sql: Connection(1540186660)--INSERT INTO ARTIST (ARTIST_ID, ARTIST_
NAME) VALUES (?, ?)
        bind => [1002, Lady Gaga]|#]

[#|2013-08-23T10:07:35.154+0100|INFO|glassfish 4.0||_ThreadID=31;_ThreadName=Thr
ead-7;_TimeMillis=1377248855154;_LevelValue=800;|
  [EL Fine]: sql: Connection(1540186660)--INSERT INTO EVENT_TYPE (EVENT_TYPE_ID,
 EVENT_TYPE_NAME) VALUES (?, ?)
        bind => [808, WORLD TOUR]|#]

[#|2013-08-23T10:07:35.156+0100|INFO|glassfish 4.0||_ThreadID=31;_ThreadName=Thr
ead-7;_TimeMillis=1377248855156;_LevelValue=800;|
  [EL Fine]: sql: Connection(1540186660)--INSERT INTO CONCERT_EVENT (CONCERT_EVE
NT_ID, ARTIST_NAME, ARTIST_ARTIST_ID, EVENTTYPE_EVENT_TYPE_ID, DTYPE) VALUES (?,
 ?, ?, ?, ?)
        bind => [97502, The Monster Ball Tour, 1002, 808, LiveEvent]|#]

[#|2013-08-23T10:07:35.157+0100|INFO|glassfish 4.0||_ThreadID=31;_ThreadName=Thr
ead-7;_TimeMillis=1377248855157;_LevelValue=800;|
```

The output of running entity graph Arquillian test

Let's expand our set of fetch plans, which are annotated to the `Artist` entity, by one more method, `@NamedEntityGraph`.

```
@NamedEntityGraphs(value = {
    /* ... see previous ... */ ,
    @NamedEntityGraph(
        name="Artist.WithConcertsAndContracts",
        attributeNodes={
            @NamedAttributeNode("name"),
            @NamedAttributeNode(
                value = "events",
                subgraph = "specialEvents"),
        },
```

```
        subgraphs = {
            @NamedSubgraph(
                name="specialEvents",
                attributeNodes={
                    @NamedAttributeNode("name"),
                    @NamedAttributeNode("contracts"),
                }
            ),
        }
    ),
})
```

Here in this entity graph, named `Artist.WithConcertsAndContracts`, we want to eagerly retrieve the concert events and also the contracts. If you remember, the contracts field was annotated as `FetchType.LAZY`, so we strongly hint the JPA provider to override the default fetch plan to this association between a `ConcertType` and `Contract` entities. In the fetch plan for the `Artist` entity, we associate a named sub-graph called `specialEvents` with the named attribute node, `events`. This ensures that the JPA provider eagerly fetches the `ConcertType` map collection.

We define a `@NameSubgraph` called `specialEvents`, which configures the eager loading of node attributes in the `ConcertType` entity. The named sub-graph eagerly retrieves the `name` field and the `contracts` association.

Let's prove this fetch plan with a final Arquillian unit test.

```
@Test   @InSequence(5)
public void shouldLoadArtistWithLiveConcertsAndContracts()
   throws Exception{
   PersistenceUnitUtil util =
      em.getEntityManagerFactory().getPersistenceUnitUtil();
   Artist artist = getArtistWithEntityGraph(
      "Artist.WithConcertsAndContracts");
   ConcertEvent event = artist.getEvents()
      .values().iterator().next();
   assertTrue(util.isLoaded(event, "id"));
   assertTrue(util.isLoaded(event, "name"));
   assertTrue(util.isLoaded(event, "eventType"));
   assertTrue(util.isLoaded(event, "contracts"));
}
```

In the test method `shouldLoadArtistWithLiveConcertsAndContracts()`, we retrieve the recording artist with the entity graph `Artist.WithConcertsAndContracts`. This time around, we retrieve the first concert event from the collection, because we know it should be there. With the `ConcertEvent` instance, we test that specific named attributes have been loaded. We expect the contracts map collection to have been fetched.

>  **Entity graph attribute versus the default fetch plan**
>
> Does the entity or sub graph attribute override an explicitly coded lazy attribute? Yes, mappings for attributes of the related entity can be overridden through a sub-graph. If the attribute node is not supplied in the entity graph, then the default or explicit setting for that attribute takes effect.

Fetch graphs are useful for merging an entity in the detached state with an incoming persistence context. This concludes the subsection on the entity graphs.

Miscellaneous features

JPA 2.1 and Java EE 7 are such huge topics that it is impossible to give full credence to every item in the specification, however here are some miscellaneous features, which I think are well worth the pursuit. Let's start with custom JPQL functions.

Custom JPQL functions

Business applications that use a relational database have custom predefined SQL functions, which are beyond the JPA standard. In JPA 2.1, the query language has been extended to support invoking these custom functions, albeit your application is locked to a database vendor's server and schema.

```
SELECT a FROM Artist a, Lawyer m
WHERE FUNCTION("ContractSignedOff", a.events, m.id )
```

Here is the JPQL example for the custom SQL function `ContractSignedOff`, which is predefined, say in MySQL, and returns a result set of the `Artist` entities.

Down-casting entities

This feature concerns inheritance hierarchies. If the JPA provider is asked to retrieve a list of entities that are typed by a superclass U, then JPA will retrieve all entities that are subclasses of U including any that match the type U. These are the twin benefits of object class hierarchies and polymorphic queries. This is a very useful feature of object-relational mapping, except for situations where you want to filter conspicuously on attributes for certain sub-class entities.

> Polymorphism is the ability, in a computer programming language, to create a variable, function, or type that has more than one form.

JPA 2.1 allows filtering on a specific subclass and the specific properties of the subentity by downcasting to the subentity type. There is a new function in JPQL called TREAT() that takes a class type.

Here is an example with the recording artist entities:

```
SELECT a.name, e.id, e.name
   FROM Artist a, ConcertEvent e
     JOIN TREAT(e AS LiveEvent) k
  WHERE k.capacity>= 10000 AND e.artist = a
```

The downcast allows us to access the subclass state of the ConcertEvent entity in the FROM and WHERE clauses. The query searches for recording artists associated with live concert events LiveEvent, which have a venue capacity greater than or equal to 10000 people.

We can filter or restrict based on multiple classes in the hierarchy. Here is an example based on the business marketing user story from *Chapter 5, Object Relational Mapping with JPA*:

```
SELECT m FROM Marketing m

WHERE
   (TREAT(m AS DirectMarketing).customerOrientation
     = "Television Adverts" ) OR
   (TREAT(m AS AgencyMarketing).agencyBudget > 250000 )
```

This example retrieves data filter explicitly to the different sub-entity types of the Marketing entity.

Synchronization of persistence contexts

Applications written for JPA 2.1 can now create persistence contexts that are not synchronized with an active JTA transaction. In the earlier specifications, the entity managers and the persistence context were always automatically synchronized with the transaction. After a transaction was committed, the persistence context would write the affected entities to the database during the flush operation.

Sometimes in applications there were areas and situations where a JTA transaction is neither required nor necessary. This would be the case in a web application with a business function with a lot of operations going and where we want to delay the final commit until we are ready. We have multiple transactions going in parallel elsewhere, but this particular operation is unaffected until it joins the current transaction.

The annotation `@PersistenceContext` has a new attribute called `synchronization`. Setting its value to `SynchronizationType.UNSYNCHRONIZED` gives us an unsynchronized persistence context. The context will share the active JTA transaction, but it will not be synchronized to it. The changes are only applied when there is a call to `EntityManager.joinTransaction()`.

> **Unsynchronized persistence context limits**
>
>
>
> There are limitations to unsynchronized persistence contexts. It is definitely possible to invoke the usual entity manager calls `persist()`, `merge()`, `refresh()`, and `remove()` calls in the thread context, but other calls that depend on a current transaction will fail immediately. The key to the unsynchronized persistence context is that an application can make changes to the entities however it wants; all you do is call `joinTransaction()`. By the way, a `rollback()` method causes all the entities associated with the persistence context to be detached.

Entity listeners with CDI

Entity listeners are POJO associated with JPA entity that allows JPA provider lifecycle events to be monitored on the target entity bean. Entity listeners have been around since JPA 1.0. The annotation `@EntityListeners` registered a variable argument set of POJOs against an entity. Life cycle events can be detected by adding an annotation to the method in the listener. These life cycle annotations are `@PrePersist`, `@PostPersist`, `@PreUpdate`, `@PostUpdate`, `@PreRemove`, and `@PostRemove`.

In JPA 2.1, entity listeners are now compatible with Context Dependency and Injection for the first time. So if your listeners also use CDI to inject other dependent objects, then you are in business, as this example of logging services depicts:

```java
public class EmployeeWatchDataLogger {
  @Inject CloudServiceBean logger;

  @PrePersist
    public void prePersist(Object object) {
        logger.log("prePersist", object);
    }

    @PostPersist
    public void postPersist(Object object){
        logger.log("postPersist", object);
    }

    @PostLoad void onPostLoad() { /* ... */ }
    @PreUpdate void onPreUpdate() { /* ... */ }
    @PostUpdate void onPostUpdate() { /* ... */ }
    @PreRemove void onPreRemove() { /* ... */ }
    @PostRemove void onPostRemove() { /* ... */ }

  // JPA 2.1
    @PostConstruct
    public void postConstruct(){
        logger.connect();
    }

    @PreDestroy
    public void preDestroy(){
        logger.disconnect();
    }
}
```

The entity listener `EmployeeWatchDataLogger` can be associated with the appropriate entity `Employee`. Here is the code for that:

```java
@Entity
@EntityListeners(value={EmployeeWatchDataLogger.class})
public class Employee {  /* ... */ }
```

Advanced Topics in Persistence

Native query constructor mapping

There is another new annotation called `@ConstructorResult` in JPA 2.1 that maps results to detached entities or non-entities. We can define a native query, which performs a SQL statement and specifies an additional argument of the SQL Result Set Mapping that is able to transform the result set into an object.

Let's suppose we want to find the association between employees and departments. Here is the code snippet that creates a native SQL to retrieve those results:

```
Query q = em.createNativeQuery(
"SELECT e.id, e.lastName, e.firstName, d.name as dept" +
"FROM Employee e, Department d " +
"WHERE e.department = d",
  "EmployeeDeptProjection");
```

In order to be of use, we define a named `@SQLResultSetMapping` as `EmployeeDeptProjection`, which instructs the JPA provider to make association between to relevant detached entity or non-entity.

```
@SqlResultSetMapping(
name="EmpoyeeDeptProjection",
    classes={
     @ConstructorResult(
     targetClass=EmployeeDepartProjection.class,
        columns={
         @ColumnResult(name="id"),
         @ColumnResult(name="lastName"),
         @ColumnResult(name="firstName"),
         @ColumnResult(name="dept")
         }
     )
    }
  )
class EmployeeDepartProjection {
  public void EmployeeDepartProjection( String id,
    String lm, String fm, String d) { /*... */ }
  /* ... */
}
```

JPA 2.1 provides a new `@ConstructorResult` annotation, which defines the target class for the entity and constructor argument. The `@ColumnResult` annotations map the result set columns to the constructor arguments, which must be in the order that they are specified in the Java code. The target class for `@ConstructorResult` for this example is a non-entity, but it can be an entity class too, in which the JPA provider creates a detached instance.

It is interesting to note that `@SQLResultSetMapping` accepts classes of `@ConstructorResult`. Also `SQLResultSetMapping` references can also be utilized in JPA stored procedure queries.

This is as far as we will go with JPA advanced topics for this book. Let's conclude what we have learnt in this chapter.

Summary

In this chapter, we covered the advanced areas of JPA, which are usually a necessity in professional software development. Certainly, there are many institutions that rely on stored procedures, and so we learnt how JPA 2.1 could invoke those predefined functions and retrieve a result set as an entity or non-entity. We saw how to supply `Parameter.Mode` for those procedure parameters, which have input and output modes: `IN`, `OUT`, `INOUT`, or `REF_CURSOR`.

We can now write entity associations that are a type of `java.util.Map`. The annotation that helps us is `@MapKey`. There are variants such as `@MayKeyColumn` and `@MapKeyJoinColumn` that gives us, the application developer, more control of object-relational mapping.

We journeyed onwards to Criteria API and bulk updates and deletes. This is a new feature of JPA 2.1. On this path of performance efficiency, we saw how entity graphs allow us to control entities and how their dependent sub-graphs of entities can be fetched. Finally, we reviewed miscellaneous updates to the specification including the downcasting of super entities to sub-entities in inheritance relationships.

The final chapter of this book will look to the future: Java EE 8 and cloud computing. I encourage you to go online, download the *Online Chapter, Moving Java EE.next to the Cloud* from the link `http://www.packtpub.com/sites/default/files/downloads/7942EN_Chapter_12_Moving_Java_EE_next_to_the_cloud.pdf`.

A
Java EE 7 Platform

This appendix covers the Java EE 7 platform, which was released to the world on Wednesday, June 12, 2013. In *Chapter 1, Java EE 7 HTML5 Productivity*, you will find an introduction to the overall architecture.

Platform containers

Fundamentally, the Java EE 7 platform contains three containers: **Enterprise Java Beans (EJB)** in *Chapter 3, Enterprise Java Beans*, **Context and Dependency Injection (CDI)** in *Chapter 2, Context and Dependency Injection* and **Servlet** in *Chapter 6, Java Servlets and Asynchronous Request-Response*.

The EJB container manages endpoints, EJBs, which by default support transactions, concurrency, and remoting. EJBs do not have a contextual scope. Stateful EJBs share a one-to-one relationship with the EJB client. Stateless EJBs may be shared by magnitude orders of clients simultaneously in a pool of instances.

The CDI container manages the POJOs with a contextual scope; these managed beans have a scoped life cycle and may or may not be communication service endpoints. CDI managed beans can be conversational. They can be made transactional with the JTA 1.2 `@Transactional` annotation. They can also have concurrency and asynchronous behavior through careful application of the Concurrency Utilities API.

The Servlet container manages the lifecycle of specific types of beans: `Servlet`, `ServletFilter`, `ContextListener`, `HttpSessionListener`, and other web container listeners. The servlet container is also responsible for dynamic content such as JSP, JSF, and other types of templates.

Dependency Injection (**DI**) is type safe, because the information is available on the Java interface or object is available to the Java compiler. DI is available across the Java EE 7 containers. In fact, all specifications are explicitly updated to rely on annotations and dependency injection, and a developer should rely on **Configuration over Configuration** as the preferred method to build applications.

Resource Injection (**RI**) is not type safe because databases, messaging endpoints, and managed executors are injected by name. In Java EE 7, these resources must be administratively created. Because the type information is unavailable, there is no way for the Java compiler to create and verify references by name through annotations (or XML descriptors).

Let's summarize this advice on dependency injection:

- Use `@Inject` annotation to inject local session beans and beans with contextual scope from the CDI container.
- Use `@EJB` annotation for injecting references to remote session EJBs.

Global JNDI naming

Sometimes there really is no other choice but to rely on **Java Naming and Directory Interface** (**JNDI**) to access a resource, bean, or connector through dependency lookup. The Java EE 7 container generates a global JNDI name for enterprise endpoints such as stateless and singleton session beans. The standard enforces the following scheme:

```
java:global[/<app-name>]/<module-name>/<bean-name>#<fully-qualified-interface-name>
```

We can, therefore, reliably access every deployed session bean portably across application servers.

Packaging

Java EE 7 application servers expect user software to be packed into a JAR, WAR, EAR, or RAR file. These are all fundamentally ZIP archives.

Java Archive (**JAR**) files contain EJB modules and CDI Managed Beans with optional class path resources. The JAR file is the standard packaging of Java classes. EJB modules may optionally have an associated XML deployment descriptor (`/META-INF/ejb-jar.xml`).

Appendix A

Web Archive (WAR) files contain web applications. A WAR file contains special markup language HTML files, dynamic content files in the JSP or JSF form or other presentation templates, a web XML deployment descriptor (/WEB-INF/web.xml), Java classes with optional resources. The web deployment descriptor configures the context root of the application, servlets, filters, listeners, and resources such as JMS destinations, managed executors, and database connections. Library archive files are stored in the specific folder (WEB-INF/lib). Compiled Java classes have their own reserved folder (/WEB-INF/classes).

Resource Adapter Archive (RAR) files are descriptors of XML files, Java classes, and other objects specifically aimed for Java EE Connector Architecture applications. A RAR file has a XML deployment descriptor (/META-INF/ra.xml).

Here is an example of a RAR file for JCA that stores data to the container's file system:

```xml
<?xml version="1.0" encoding="UTF-8"?>
<connector xmlns="http://java.sun.com/xml/ns/connector
    xmlns:xsi="http://www.w3.org/2001/XMLSchema-instance"
    xsi:schemaLocation="http://java.sun.com/xml/ns/j2ee
    http://java.sun.com/xml/ns/j2ee/connector_1_6.xsd"
    version="1.6">
    <display-name>File System Adapter</display-name>
    <vendor-name>JBoss</vendor-name>
    <eis-type>FileSystem</eis-type>
    <resourceadapter-version>1.0</resourceadapter-version>
    <resourceadapter>
        <resourceadapter-class>
            je7hb.jca.basic.DummyResourceAdapter
        </resourceadapter-class>
        <outbound-resourceadapter>
            <connection-definition>
                <managedconnectionfactory-class>
                je7hb.jca.basic.FSManagedConnectionFactory
                </managedconnectionfactory-class>
                <config-property>
                    <config-property-name>
                    FSRootFolder
                    </config-property-name>
                    <config-property-type>
                    java.lang.String
                    </config-property-type>
```

```xml
                    <config-property-value>
                    /tmp/fstore
                    </config-property-value>
                </config-property>
                <connectionfactory-interface>
                je7hb.jca.basic.FolderContextFactory
                </connectionfactory-interface>
                <connectionfactory-impl-class>
                je7hb.jca.basic.FolderContextFactoryImpl
                </connectionfactory-impl-class>
                <connection-interface>
                javax.naming.directory.DirContext
                </connection-interface>
                <connection-impl-class>
                je7hb.jca.basic.FSDirContext
                </connection-impl-class>
            </connection-definition>
            <transaction-support>NoTransaction
            </transaction-support>
        </outbound-resourceadapter>
    </resourceadapter>
```

Enterprise Archive (EAR) files contain one or more Java EE components, which can be EJB or Web modules. They can also contain RAR modules. An EAR file typically also has an associated XML deployment descriptor (/META-INF/application.xml).

Here is an example of an EAR file:

```xml
<?xml version="1.0" encoding="UTF-8"?>
<application xmlns="http://java.sun.com/xml/ns/javaee"
    xmlns:xsi="http://www.w3.org/2001/XMLSchema-instance"
    xsi:schemaLocation="http://java.sun.com/xml/ns/javaee
        http://java.sun.com/xml/ns/javaee/application_6.xsd"
        version="7" >
    <application-name>post-trade-services</application-name>
    <initialize-in-order>true</initialize-in-order>
    <module>
      <web>
        <web-uri>ptsp-portal-web-2.1.0.war</web-uri>
        <context-root>ptsp-portal</context-root>
      </web>
    </module>
     <module>
       <ejb>ptsp-core-2.1.0.jar</ejb>
       <ejb>ptsp-services-2.1.4.jar</ejb>
```

```xml
      <ejb>ptsp-container-2.3.7.jar</ejb>
      <ejb>ptsp-valuations-2.1.2.jar</ejb>
   </module>
   <library-directory>lib</library-directory>
</application>
```

Bean XML configuration location

The file `beans.xml` configures CDI. An empty file is required in Java EE 6 in order to trigger the CDI container to start scanning and processing annotations. In Java EE 7, CDI is on by default and you no longer need this explicit file, if you don't want it. However, we recommend its usefulness for portability with older Java EE 6 and third-party frameworks.

Developers should understand where to save the `beans.xml` file:

- Locate the file `beans.xml` in the `/META-INF` folder for EJB module, a library jar, EJB jar, an application client jar, or RAR archive.
- Locate the file `beans.xml` in the `/WEB-INF/classes` folder for a web application archive.
- Locate the file `beans.xml` on the JVM's class path if there is no obvious file named `beans.xml` in the META-INF directory of any component. (Unsurprisingly, we strongly recommend against choosing this option in a Java EE application! For Java SE, though, this is perfectly fine.)

Persistence XML configuration location

The file `persistence.xml` defines the persistence unit for a Java EE application to connect to a relational database. Normally, you find one file, which contains one or two connectors to databases. Sometimes, however, there may be two or three different `persistent.xml` files aimed at tackling complicated requirements in a business enterprise with several persistence database choices (separate trade, order management, and audit databases spring to our minds).

It is important for developers, to know exactly where to place the `persistent.xml` file:

- Locate the `persistence.xml` in the `/META-INF/` folder for an EJB jar, a library jar or RAR file.
- Locate the `persistence.xml` in the `/WEB-INF/classes/META-INF` folder for a web application.

Upgrading to Java EE 7 from J2EE versions

Java EE 7 is now an immense step up in productivity from the J2EE 1.4 specification, yet there are many businesses out there still reliant on source code with legacy practices. Java EE 7 strongly leans on the annotations, therefore we recommend your business upgrades their Java SE environment to at least JDK 7. In February 2013, Oracle Java SE 6 declared End-of-Life of public releases (`http://www.oracle.com/technetwork/java/eol-135779.html`).

The serious actual effort of upgrading J2EE to Java EE is proportional to the number of lines in your application, whether it is based at all Java SE 5 or better, using generics, enumerations, and annotations. It depends on the interaction complexity in your existing software. The task can be straightforward, lasting several careful, agile development iterations, but it equally can be very tough to upgrade your software. Upgrading from J2EE in the future is set to get even harder, especially when the next standard, which is aimed at *Moving to the Cloud*, comes aboard. Our advice is simply to upgrade sooner rather than later.

Here are a few tips to help the architectural team along with this upgrade:

- **Please test and test continuously**: Write lots of full encompassing unit and integration test suites, if you do not have them. Ensure your application is running against a continuous integration server like **Jenkins**, **Hudson**, or Atlassian's **Bamboo**.

- **Prefer annotations to XML configuration**: Refactor your old stateless and stateful session EJB to annotated `@java.ejb.Stateless` and `@java.ejb.Stateful`. Replace singleton beans that utilize proprietary application server APIs with the standard `@java.ejb.Singleton` beans.

- **Prefer DI**: Use the full power of strongly typed dependency injection. Prefer to inject dependencies in EJB with CDI `@javax.annotation.Inject` and replace those older JNDI lookup service codes. Prefer Resource Injection for database connections, JMS destinations, and concurrency executors with `@Resource` injection.

- **Simplify transaction declarations**: Replace and remove declarations for container manager transactions, because they are implied in EJBs.

- **Remove older EJB Remote and Home Java interfaces**: Do this because they are no longer required in Java EE 7. We assume that you have tests!

- **Take care of J2EE Entity Beans**: Examine cases where J2EE entity beans are being used very carefully. Refactor them into JPA entity beans in the Entity Control Boundary (see *Chapter 1, Java EE 7 HTML5 Productivity*) pattern. Move the business logic surrounding the older entity beans into the appropriate architectural layers.
- **Clean up XML deployment descriptors**: Prefer the recent Java EE ease-of-development feature: **Convention-Over-Configuration**. Delete extraneous and unnecessary XML configuration where appropriate.
- **Upgrade messaging**: Upgrade your Message Driven Beans with annotations to use JMS 2.0. Many enterprises send messages asynchronously; upgrade those senders to annotations around JMS 2.0.
- **Review the upgrade**: Review the lifecycle of endpoints, consider the impact of management for session beans, remoting, transaction handling, concurrency, and state management.
- **Prefer Java EE 7 asynchronous feature**: Upgrade the application parts that rely on proprietary application server's asynchronous and concurrency features; see if you can replace them with the Java EE 7 platform standard. Pour over the **Concurrency Utilities** and `@Asynchronous` methods in EJB.

These tips should help you get over the curve to a fully working, tested, and ingrained Java EE 7 application. Only then should your architects decide on approaching new features: CDI, JAX-RS, and WebSocket.

> **Golden rule of performance and migration**: Test before, test afterwards, and measure the difference between the results.

Legacy application programming interfaces

CORBA and Object Request Broker is a technology designed in the late 1990s into the millennium, which provided inter process communication over distributed systems. This standard of communication is still maintained by the Object Management Group. IIOP systems can be implemented in any language such as Java, C++, or C#. RMI is the Java implementation over this protocol.

The full specification of Java EE 7 permits the removal requirement for supporting EJB. **CMP (Container Managed Persistence)**, **BMP (Bean Managed Persistence)**, JAX-RPC, deployment API instead are made optional. Support, therefore, for CORBA, is now optional for application server products.

The following table lists the other older technologies that are supported or are optional in the Java EE 7 standard:

Name	Description
RMI-IIOP	Remote Method Invocation over Internet Inter-ORB protocol is a framework designed to support interaction of abstract protocols of object request brokers, specifically with legal CORBA services.
Java IDL	Java Interface Definition Language is a component service and tooling that permits Java EE application components to invoke CORBA objects. The functionality is closely associated with RMI-IIOP. Java applications, therefore, can act as bonafide clients of CORBA services. Only legacy Java EE application may require this service.
JAF	JavaBean Activation Framework is an extension support framework. It is designed to allow developers to write code that handles data in different MIME types. JAF is extensively used by the JavaMail API
JAAS	Java Authentication and Authorization Service is part of the Java SE; some Java EE 7 application server products may elect to use it as a security feature.
JAXP	Java API for XML Parsing, a framework for using SAX and DOM XML parsers in Java.
STAX	Streaming API for XML, a framework for processing and parsing XML documents using a stream pipeline of input to output, which can be very efficient for large data sets.

GlassFish 4 reference implementation

GlassFish 4 is the reference implementation of the Java EE 7 specification and as such has fully working implementations of the individual standards. It contains an EJB and Servlet container. GlassFish utilizes the JBoss Weld container for CDI bean types. At the time of writing, the newly revamped website `http://glassfish.java.net/` contains many resources for Java EE 7 developers including documentation, PDF files, videos from the Developer Days conferences, and mailing list links.

In the next section we will set up the GlassFish for MySQL on a local workstation.

Installing basic GlassFish

Download the latest version from the website as a ZIP archive. Unzip into a folder of your choice. You will see the following structure, depending on your Windows or Mac or UNIX preference:

```
drwxr-xr-x   8 tomanderson   wheel   272 31 May 02:47 bin/
drwxr-xr-x  11 tomanderson   wheel   374 31 May 02:47 glassfish/
drwxr-xr-x   9 tomanderson   wheel   306 31 May 03:38 javadb/
drwxr-xr-x   5 tomanderson   wheel   170 31 May 03:39 mq/
drwxr-xr-x   4 tomanderson   wheel   136 31 May 03:38 pkg/
```

The `bin` folder contains the important utility command `asadmin` (or `asadmin.bat`). You can start GlassFish by executing the following command:

```
asadmin start-domain --verbose
```

This launches GlassFish with a default server in a non-clustered environment with an initial domain (`glassfish/domains/domain1`). Domains are a way to cluster servers in a managed configuration and further information about them can be found in the GlassFish resources, outside of this book. The `--verbose` argument is useful for watching debuggable output from the standard output.

You can stop the server at any time with `Control-C` shortcut in the terminal window. A more elegant approach would be to stop the server from another terminal window. Here is the syntax of this:

```
asadmin stop-domain
```

Stop and start the server and with your favorite web browser surf to your machine's `http://localhost:8080/`, which is the default port number for GlassFish. There is an administration console that allows configuration at `http://localhost:4848/`. The default username is admin and there is no default password.

It is possible to secure the server by changing the default password with the following administration command. Here it is:

```
asadmin change-admin-password
```

Enter the default password, which is empty, and type the brand new one. For secure access outside of the local machine, you will also need to allow secure administration. Here is that command:

```
asadmin enable-secure-admin
```

Configuring MySQL database access

Installing MySQL access in GlassFish first requires the JDBC driver `mysql-connector-java-5.1.25-bin.jar` being copied to the `glassfish/lib` folder. Restart the GlassFish server.

Afterwards, configure MySQL access through the administration console. The next part assumes that you have already created a database schema in MySQL, set up the login user, and applied privileges.

In the administration console, locate the JDBC resource on the left hand side pane of the display page by navigating to **Resources | JDBC | JDBC Connection Pool**. Create a brand new connection pool.

Enter the **Pool Name** as `ArquillianPool` (this field is required). Set the **Resource Type** to `javax.sql.DataSource`, which is the non-distributed transactional local resource. Set the **Database Driver Vendor** to `MySQL`. Click on the **Next** button to continue to the next screen.

Apply the following setting in the **Additional Properties** page:

```
DatabaseName = arquillian
Password = arquillian
URL = jdbc:mysql://localhost:3306/Arquillian
User = arquillian
```

There are about 177 different database properties for MySQL driver, so take your time to get the details correct.

Locate the JDBC resource on the left hand side pane of the display page: **Resources | JDBC | JDBC Resource**. Create a brand new resource. Set the **Name** as the JNDI lookup destination: `jdbc/arquillian`. This name is very important because it must be the same as the Resource Injection reference in your code: `@Resource("/jdbc/Arquillian")`.

Appendix A

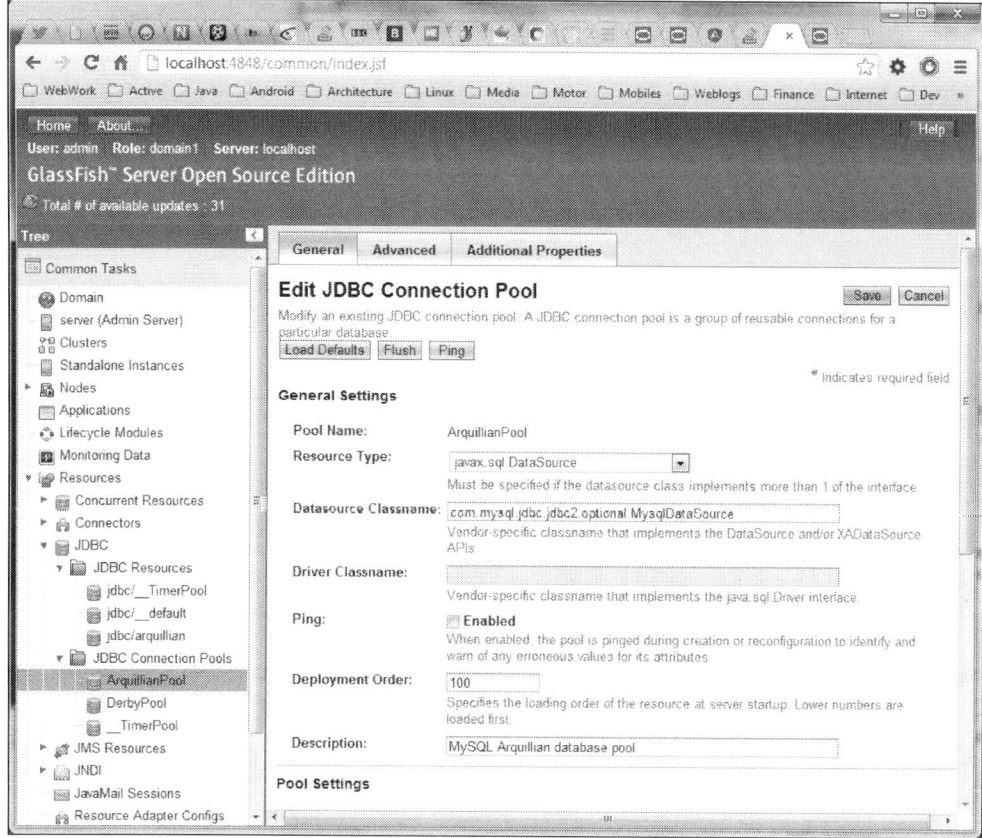

From the drop-down list for **Pool Name**, associate the resource with the JDBC Connection Pool: `ArquillianPool`. Test your connection in the administration console; it should be valid, and therefore usable.

Configuring command line

The same tasks can be completed at the command line using the administration utility. It is also applicable to a shell script for automation. Here is the equivalent command to create the JDBC Connection pool:

```
asadmin create-jdbc-connection-pool\
  --datasourceclassname \
```

Java EE 7 Platform

```
com.mysql.jdbc.jdbc2.optional.MysqlConnectionPoolDataSource \
--restype javax.sql.DataSource \
--property User=arquillian:\
Password=arquillian:\
URL=jdbc:mysql://localhost:3306/arquillian
ArquillianPool
```

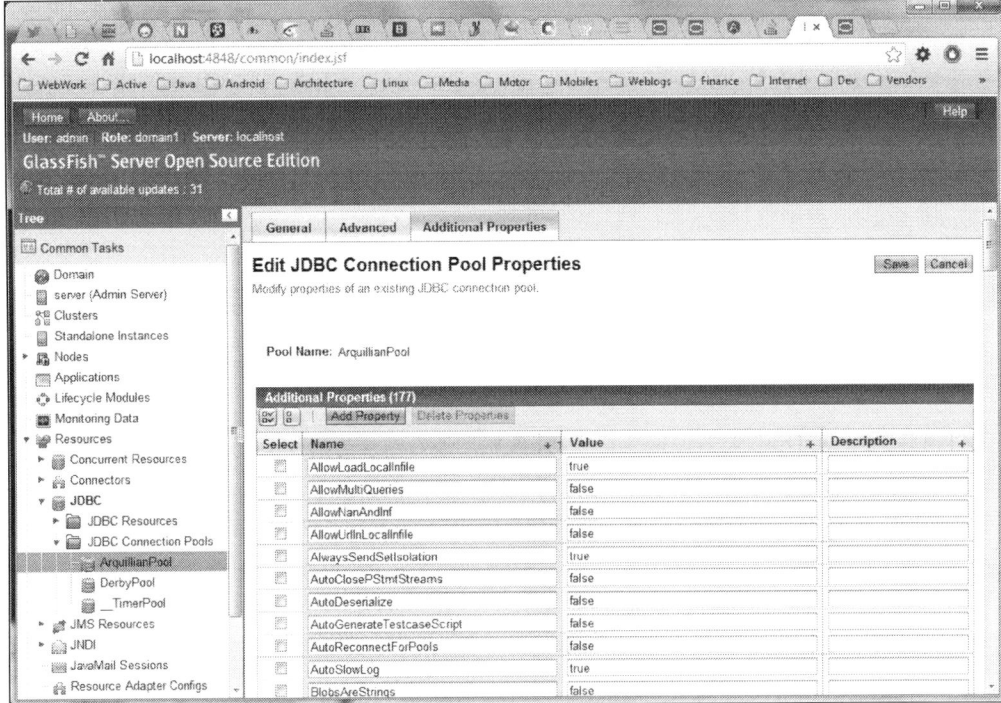

Here is the equivalent command line to create the JDBC Resource:

```
asadmin create-jdbc-resource \
  --connectionpoolid ArquillianPool \
  jdbc/arquillian
```

Default resources

In line with the Java EE 7 specification, GlassFish defines a couple of default resources. For database connectivity, there is a default Apache Derby database under the JNDI name `jdbc/__default`. Developers can simply access this as a `@PersistenceContext` for a JPA entity manager or a `@DataSource` JDBC reference in the code.

There is also a JMS 2.0 default connection factory under the JNDI name `jms/__defaultConnectionFactory`. Applications can pull in this resource with a simple `@JMSContext` annotation.

In should be noted that these default resources are simply for basic enterprise applications, tutorials, and examples. They should not ever be used in a production environment. No doubt serious enterprise applications will require more substantial configurations beyond these couple of default resources.

B
Java EE 7 Persistence

This appendix covers miscellaneous topics on Java Persistence.

Persistence unit

The `persistence.xml` file is a simple XML deployment descriptor file that defines a persistence unit. This file configures the name of the `EntityManager` service, which manages a set of entity instances. The XML configuration also defines how each `EntityManager` connects to the database. A persistence unit may declare one or more uniquely named `EntityManager` instances.

The root element of the `persistence.xml` file is the `persistence` XML element and it contains a set of `persistence-unit` XML complex elements.

Here is a simple declaration of `persistence.xml` for JPA 2.1:

```xml
<persistence version=""2.1""
  xmlns=""http://xmlns.jcp.org/xml/ns/persistence""
  xmlns:xsi=""http://www.w3.org/2001/XMLSchema-instance""
  xsi:schemaLocation=""http://xmlns.jcp.org/xml/ns/persistence
  http://www.oracle.com/webfolder/technetwork/
    jsc/xml/ns/persistence/persistence_2_1.xsd"">

    <persistence-unit name=""trading""
    transaction-type=""JTA"">
        <jta-data-source>jdbc/trading</jta-data-source>
    </persistence-unit>
    <persistence-unit name=""audit""
    transaction-type=""JTA"">
        <jta-data-source>jdbc/audit</jta-data-source>
    </persistence-unit>
</persistence>
```

Java EE 7 Persistence

The `transaction-type` XML element for a persistence unit can be either `JTA` or `RESOURCE_LOCAL`. Specifying the values, `JTA` indicates that the entity manager partakes in distributed transactions, whereas `RESOURCE_LOCAL` indicates that the database transactions are just local to the particular application running in that Java EE application server on this JVM.

The element `jta-data-source` defines a JTA data source configured in the application server. The element `non-data-source` defines a non-JTA data source.

The element `provider` defines a particular persistence provider. Of course, the necessary configuration must be applied to the application server, or it should be supplied already by the product.

Here is an example of a persistence unit with both JPA properties and vendor properties:

```
<persistence version=""2.1"" ...>
  <persistence-unit name=""ratings""
    transaction-type=""JTA"">
  <provider>org.hibernate.ejb.HibernatePersistence
  </provider>
    <non-jta-data-source>jdbc/rating</non-jta-data-source>
    <properties>
    <property name=""javax.persistence.schema-generation.
      database.action"" value=""create""/>
    <property name=""javax.persistence.schema-generation.
      scripts.action"" value=""drop-and-create""/>
    <property name=""javax.persistence.schema-generation.
      scripts.create-target"" value=""/tmp/create-sql.ddl""/>
    <property name=""javax.persistence.schema-generation.
      scripts.drop-target"" value=""/tests/drop-sql.ddl""/>
    <property name=""hibernate.flushMode""
      value=""FLUSH_AUTO"" />
    <property name=""hibernate.hbm2ddl.auto""
      value=""none"" />
    </properties>
  </persistence-unit>
</persistence>
```

The `<properties>` element is a container of `<property>` elements that configure a name and value pair. In the preceding example, the standard properties are prefixed with `javax.persistence`. The persistence provider is set to Hibernate JPA and there are a couple of properties defined that are only relevant to that ORM solution, namely `hibernate.flushmode` and `hibernate.hbm2ddl.auto`.

Appendix B

XML schema documents for Java EE 7

Oracle has reorganized the location of XML Schema Definitions for Java EE 7. All of the schemas are in present in the link `http://xmlns.jcp.org/xml/ns/javaee` and effectively they are under the auspices of the Java Community Process. For XML validation of resources like `persistence.xml`, you can find more information on exact XSD locations at `http://www.oracle.com/webfolder/technetwork/jsc/xml/ns/javaee/index.html`.

Properties

JPA 2.1 specification defines a set of standard properties that allows the application to optionally generate schemas or execute scripts in connection to the data source. The `<properties>` element in the `persistence.xml` file specifies both standard and vendor specific properties.

Here is a table of the JPA 2.1 properties; the property must be prefixed with `javax.persistence` to complete the correct name:

Property Name	Description
`schema-generation.create-script-source`	Specifies the name of a pre-packaged application script or a file that creates tables, views, or user SQL functions.
`schema-generation.drop-script-source`	Specifies the name of a pre-packaged application script or a file that drops tables, views, or user SQL functions.
`schema-generation.sql-load-script-source`	Specifies the name of a pre-packaged application script or a file that loads data into database tables.
`schema-generation.database.action`	Informs the persistence provider how to generate the schema for the persistence unit. The valid values are `none`, `create`, `drop-and-create`, and `drop`.
`schema-generation.scripts.action`	Informs the persistence provider how to generate scripts with **Database Definition Language** (**DDL**) for the persistence unit. The valid values are `none`, `create`, `drop-and-create`, and `drop`.
`schema-generation.create-source`	Informs the persistence provider about the ordering of processing during the startup of the persistence unit regarding object-relational mapping metadata, DDL script, or both. The valid values are `metadata`, `script`, `metadata-then-script`, or `script-then-metadata`.

Property Name	Description
schema-generation.drop-source	Informs the persistence provider about the ordering of processing during the shutdown of the persistence unit regarding object-relational mapping metadata, DDL script, or both. The valid values are metadata, script, metadata-then-script, or script-then-metadata.
jdbc.driver	Fully qualified name of the driver class (Java SE only).
jdbc.url	Driver specific URL (Java SE only).
jdbc.user	Database connection username (Java SE only).
jdbc.password	Database connection password (Java SE only).
lock.timeout	Specifies a hint for pessimistic lock timeout in milliseconds.
query.timeout	Specifies a hint for query timeout in milliseconds.
validation.group.pre-persist	Defines groups of entities that are targeted for validation upon the pre-persist event.
validation.group.pre-update	Defines groups of entities that are targeted for validation upon the pre-update event.
validation.group.pre-remove	Defines groups of entities that are targeted for validation upon the pre-remove event.

XML representation of object-relational mapping

As an alternative to annotations on entities, JPA supports object-relational mapping from an XML. The file is called orm.xml that is located in the /META-INF folder of the persistence unit. Developers can also explicitly name the XML mapping file using the mapping-file element. The XML representation can be useful for third-party library entities that predate annotation capabilities in Java SE 5 and where the business has no control of the source code access.

Here is a persistence unit that illustrates the concept:

```
<persistence version=""2.1"" ... >
    <persistence-unit name=""legacyTrading""
    transaction-type=""JTA"">
        <jta-data-source>jdbc/legacyDB</jta-data-source>
    <mapping-file>my-orm.xml</mapping-file>
    <jar-file>LegacyTradeEntities.jar</jar-file>
    <class>com.fxtradelib.Trade.class</class>
    <class>com.fxtradelib.Order.class</class>
    <class>com.txtradelib.Counterpart.class</class>
```

```
        </persistence-unit>
</persistence>
```

The `jar-file` element indicates that the persistence provider also searches the additional JAR file for managed persistence entities. The `class` element explicitly identifies provider Java types that are entity classes, embeddable classes, and mapped super classes.

JPA miscellaneous features

This section covers some advanced JPA 2.1 mapping features.

Converters

JPA 2.1 defines converters for translating data values from Java to database specific values. Converters make it easy to write Java interpreters for special monetary values, enumerated text values, and Boolean values. It is very common in business to have different designations for Boolean in a production database. Some tables may have text columns, say T, F or Y, N and others have integers 0 and 1.

Here is a converter that translates trade data in a database in order to determine if the bank is buying or selling to and from a counterparty.

```
enum Direction { BUY, SELL }

@Converter
public class TradeDirectionConverter
    implements AttributeConverter<Direction,String>
{
    @Override
    public String convertToDatabaseColumn(Direction attribute) {
        switch (attribute) {
            case BUY: return ""P"";
            default: return ""S"";
        }
    }

    @Override
    public Direction convertToEntityAttribute(String dbData) {
        dbData = dbData.trim().toLowerCase();
        if ( dbData.equals(""P""))
            return Direction.BUY;
        else
            return Direction.SELL;
    }
}
```

The convertor class `TradeDirectionConverter` extends the `AttributeConverter` Java generic interface, new in JPA 2.1. The developer simply implements two methods `convertToEntityAttribute()` and `convertToDatabaseColumn()` as the conversion process is bidirectional.

We can apply this converter to the entities with the `Direction` type. Here is an example of the converter in a foreign-exchange bank trade entity.

```
@Entity @Table(name = ""FXTRADE"")
public class ForexTrade {
    /* ... */
    @Convert(converter=TradeDirectionConverter.class)
    Direction direction;
    /* ... */
}
```

We explicitly declare the convertor with the `@Convert` annotation that references the conversion class.

JPA 2.1 also allows converters to be applied globally across the entire domain. To allow this, the converter must be annotated as `@Converter(autoApply = true)`. Global convertors do not require an entity to be explicitly annotated with `@Convert` on the field or properties. These definitions, therefore, can be removed for global converters.

> A word of caution about JPA conversions: be careful with your JPQL statements such that they reflect the Java side of the conversion. Take care with native SQL query statements and mixing Java queries so that they reflect the end result of data that is actually stored inside the database.

Native constructor results

It is possible to build a projection, which is a partial view of an entity having a narrower collection of columns, with a JPQL statement using the syntax: `SELECT NEW`. Unfortunately, in the previous specification, it was not possible to write native SQL using JPA to build entities and non-entities.

Here is a JPQL query to view a financial banking trade as a non-entity:

```
SELECT NEW TradeView(t.id, t.book, t.tradeDate,
   t.settlementDate, t.amount, t.ccy )
FROM Counterparty c JOIN c.trades t
WHERE t.amount >= 250000 AND
   t.book = ""Exchange West"" AND t.ccy = ""USD""
```

In JPA 2.1 the new annotation `@ConstructorResult` is designed for native SQL queries to build an entity or non-entity. The `@ConstructorResult` is combined with the `@ColumnResult` to build a dynamic constructor argument list by type.

Here is an example of a native SQL query that creates a bond trade:

```
@NamedNativeQuery(
  name=""BondTradeView.findByAccountId"",
  query=""SELECT B.TRADE_ID, B.NOTIONAL, A.ACC_NAME, ""+
    ""A.CPTY_NAME FROM TRADE B, ACCOUNT A ""+
    ""WHERE B.TYPE=''BOND'' ""+
    ""AND B.ACC_ID = A.ACC_ID AND A.ACC = :ID "",
  resultSetMapping=""bondtradeview""
)
@SqlResultSetMapping(name=""bondtradeview"",
  classes={
    @ConstructorResult(targetClass=BondTradeView.class, columns={
        @ColumnResult(name=""TRADE_ID"", type=Integer.class),
        @ColumnResult(name=""NOTIONAL"", type=BigDecimal.class),
        @ColumnResult(name=""ACC_NAME"", type=String.class),
        @ColumnResult(name=""CPTY_NAME"", type=String.class)
    })
  }
)
public class BondTradeView {
  /* ... */
}
```

In order to use `@ConstructorResult` correctly, we must apply it to a SQL result set mapping and also the named native query.

Transactions and concurrency

Persistence units encapsulate the object-relational mapping to the database. This section is about how they encounter transactions, concurrency, and multiple requests.

Entity managers

Here are some helpful rules about `javax.ejb.EntityManager`:

- Prefer to inject `EntityManager` as a dependency in a Java EE application. Therefore, the application server takes care of its lifecycle and the responsibility to close the persistence unit. Use `@PersistenceContext`.
- Do not cache or store in between requests: The `EntityManager` instance is not thread-safe.
- The `EntityManager` instance manually retrieved from `EntityManagerFactory` must be closed in a retrieval method request for that particular state lest it goes out of scope, escapes, and potentially becomes a memory leak.
- An `EntityManager` that represents a JTA data source must be associated with a transaction by calling the `joinTransaction()` method. This is particularly true in a Java EE 6 web container.
- Obtain `UserTransaction` through dependency injection and remember to call `begin()` and `end()` to demarcate the transaction boundaries. The only exceptions to this rule are persistence units that are explicitly bound with `Synchronization.UNSYNCHRONIZED`.
- Do use `EntityManagerFactory` to look up the persistence context in a Java SE application. The factory, definitely, is thread-safe.
- Do close the `EntityManager` instance with a final clause in Java SE application. Sadly the interface cannot yet be made both `AutoClosable` with Java SE 7 and also retrospectively compatible with Java SE 5 or 6.

Transactions, entity managers, and session EJBs

Inside a Java EE environment, `EntityManager` is configured with a transaction by default. It can either be `PersistenceContextType.TRANSACTION` or `PersistenceContextType.EXTENDED`. The extended variety can only be injected into stateful session EJBs.

Transactions are demarcated on session EJB methods, which by default are set for `TransactionAttribute.REQUIRED`. Developers can explicitly annotate methods with `TranactionAttribute.SUPPORTS` or `TranactionAttribute.MANDATORY`, but this is normally unnecessary. In a Java EE application, a transaction-able method in a session EJB will be associated with the `EntityManager` object instance by default.

During operations in TRANSACTION mode, the application server will take responsibility for transactions in this scenario. The entities attached to the persistence unit are alive for the entire duration of the transaction. Once the method ends normally (or abnormally) the transaction is completed. The entities are detached from the persistence unit. When the entities are detached, then any changes to them are not synchronized to a database.

Transactions associated with entity managers can survive through nested invocations of other reference EJB calls, assuming that they permit and support transactions. This is called Transaction Propagation. All JPA entities remain intact and attached to the current entity manager.

Here is the table that summarizes the different cases of EntityManager for manual operation, in a stateless and stateful session bean.

Modus Operandi	Manual Creation	Stateless Session Bean	Stateful Session Bean
EntityManager	Thread-unsafe	Thread-unsafe	Thread-unsafe
EntityManagerFactory	Thread-safe	N/A	N/A
Responsibility for releasing	Developer must close in a final block	N/A	N/A
Multiple thread capabilities (concurrency access)	Developer takes responsibility	EJB container and application server take control	EJB container is in control
UserTransaction association	Developer must demarcate manually and also use @Inject UserTransaction	Automatic with dependency injection (DI)	Automatic with dependency injection (DI)
What happens to EntityManager after the end of the current transaction call?	Developer must guarantee EntityManager is closed	Automatically call close() after the end of transaction method call	Automatic closure for TRANSACTION mode or continuation of lifetime EXTENDED transaction mode
Lifetime of entities in the current EntityManager	Developer decides when to commit() or rollback()	Entities are detached after the transaction method call completes	Remain attached to the manager until the EJB is removed by caller

Modus Operandi	Manual Creation	Stateless Session Bean	Stateful Session Bean
Cascade of transaction through EJB reference (Transaction propagation)	N/A	Yes (with internal cache of entities)	Yes (with client specific cache of entities)
Domain objects or detached entities serialized from an EJB client	Entities must be manually merged with `EntityManager`	Entities must be manually merged with `EntityManager`	For EXTENDED transaction mode, entities are never detached

The abbreviation N/A stands for Not Applicable.

`EntityManager` has methods that require an active transaction: `persist()`, `merge()`, `remove()`, `refresh()`, and `flush()`. If there is no associated current transaction then these methods will raise a `TransactionRequiredException`.

Stateful session beans

Stateful session beans are a special case of `EntityManager` when they are used in the extended persistence unit situation `PersistenceContextType.EXTENDED`. Entities remain attached and synchronized with the entity manager during interactions between the caller and the EJB.

In a web application this 1:1 relationship requires some thought and logic as the long-lived entities will stick around in a client specific cache of instances. In a long conversation, this behavior may be problematic, because the managed entities are not visible out of the transaction. The changes to the database are buffered inside the entity manager. In order to get the changes reflected in the database, it may be necessary to invoke the `EntityManager.flush()` method at certain intervals. Of course, this will affect the ability to roll back to the beginning of the conversation and could be the bane of Java database development: lost updates seen by another user.

Because of the client specific cache of stateful session bean, we strongly recommend avoiding concurrency access with the same caller.

The managed entities will be attached until the caller invokes the stateful session bean's removal operation, which causes its dissociation from the caller and only then will the entity manager synchronize instance with the database and then detach the entities.

Concurrency access locks

JPA supports both optimistic and pessimistic locking facilities. By default, JPA updates rows in a database table using optimistic locking.

Optimistic locking

Optimistic locking is a lenient strategy for dealing with concurrency access to shared entities held by `EntityManager`. With this strategy, which tends to scale better than pessimistic locking, the application can retrieve the data, make some changes to it, and write it to the database. Data version validation is performed during the write phase to the database.

To provide optimistic locking of entity in JPA, annotate a field or property with the `@Version` constraint. Preferably use an integer field. Here is an example:

```
@Entity
@Inheritance
@DiscriminatorColumn(name=""TRADE_TYPE"")
@Table(name=""TRADE"")
public abstract class Trade {
  @Id private long id;
  @Version private long version;
    // ...
}
```

The persistence provider performs optimistic locking by comparing the value of the `@Version` field in the entity instance with the `VERSION` column from the database. Initially the provider reads the entity from the database and has a record of the current version. Therefore, the provider knows that another concurrent operation has successfully updated the entity when the values are different. If there is a difference in value during the write phase, `EntityManager` will raise an `OptimisticLockException`.

Adding this annotation on an integer value allows the provider to make a faster check on an entity's version without having to check every single field or property for equivalence. The persistence provider updates the `@Version` field or property automatically. User code should not interfere with this arrangement.

Pessimistic locking

Sometimes there is a strong business requirement for strict locking of database rows. JPA has support for pessimistic locking. An entity can be locked with a call to the `EntityManager.lock()`, `refresh()`, or `find()` methods. There are different types of locks available through the enumeration `LockModeType` including the default optimistic. The enumerations are: NONE, OPTIMISTIC, OPTIMISTIC_FORCE_INCREMENT, PESSIMISTIC_FORCE_INCREMENT, PESSIMISTIC_READ, PESSIMISTIC_WRITE, READ, WRITE, and OPTIMISTIC_FORCE_INCREMENT.

The underlying database itself must support pessimistic locking. In order to achieve pessimistic locking, the JPA providers take advantage of the database server features, such as database row locks and sometimes extended native SQL language statements: SELECT ... FOR UPDATE.

Each of the `LockModeType` enumerations has a trade-off. It is interesting that there are two types of pessimistic modes: reading and writing. Locking an entity with a pessimistic query could lead to performance bottlenecks as it prevents other concurrency operations from reading the particular row from the database.

Here is an example of a pessimistic write operation for a trade confirmation operation:

```
@Stateless
public class TradeConfirmService {
  //...
  void confirmTrade( String tradeIdRef, String ref ) {
    Query query = entityManager.createNamedQuery(
        ""Trade.findTradeByIdRef""
        .setParameter(""id"", tradeIdRef );
    List<Trade> trades = query.getResultList();
    Trade trade = trades.get(0);
    em.refresh( trade, PESSIMISTIC_WRITE );
    trade.setConfirmFlag(true);
    trade.setTraderConfirmRef(ref);
    em.flush(); // optional
  }
}
```

A trade is retrieved optimistically using a named query. It is pessimistically locked for the write operation with the `refresh()` call on the entity manager. New values are set on the trade instance and `EntityManager` is flushed to update the database.

C
Java EE 7 Transactions

This appendix covers miscellaneous topics on Java EE 7 transactions.

Transactions

Java EE 7 supports transactions, which are a group of important operations, commands, or behaviors that are executed as a unit of work. A true transaction must follow the ACID principles: Atomic, Consistent, Isolated, and Durable. In Java EE 7, behaviors involved in a transaction may be synchronous or asynchronous, and they involve persisting entities to a database with JPA, sending or receiving messages using JMS, sending content over the network, invoking EJBs, and can even include other external systems.

These are the ACID principles of transactions:

Term	Description
Atomicity	Atomicity declares a unit of work in a transaction with a set of sequential or parallel operations. It stipulates that either all operations are successfully performed or none of them. A transaction can commit or roll back. (do all or nothing)
Consistency	Consistency states that at the conclusion of the transaction, the data is left in an expected and required state. The database is not broken or invalidated with false constraints or half-baked information. (integrity of data and system)
Isolation	Isolation states that changes in the processing of the current transaction are not visible to the outside environment, processes, or another concurrent transaction running. (lack of interference)
Durable	A transaction is durable when it completes through a commit action that makes the change completely visible to other applications and the outside world. (physical write of data to storage)

Java EE 7 meets the requirements for ACID transactions. Enterprise Java Beans are transactional by default. CDI managed beans can be uplifted into ACID transactions with the application of the annotation `@javax.transaction.Transactional`.

Java Transaction API

Java Transaction API (JTA) is the cornerstone of all Java EE transactions. JTA looks after local and distributed transactions. Non-JTA transactions are a matter for standalone Java SE applications. The popular confusion abounds when developers are configuring persistence unit facilities for the first time (the `persistence.xml` files). The XML element `jta-data-source` is used in Java EE and `non-jta-data-source` for Java SE.

Two-phase commit transactions

Relational databases generally have an internal component called a **Two-Phase Commit Transaction Manager** (2PC) to ensure ACID principles. The two-phase commit is a protocol, which is based on resource managers, veto authorities, and acknowledgements, and takes place at the end of a transaction. The JTA specification refers to a **XA (Extended Architecture)** transaction manager and its participant resources.

The first phase in 2PC is called the prepare command. It consists of a transaction manager communicating with resources through the protocol with the notification that a commit is about to be issued. A resource has a chance to declare whether it can fulfill committing the transaction or not. If it can, the resource prepares the work to save the data and acknowledges with a prepared response, otherwise it vetoes the protocol, which effectively rolls the entire transaction back.

The second phase in 2PC only proceeds once all resources have given their unanimous consent. The transaction manager then sends a commit command to the resources. Each resource applies the changes to the database. This is usually a short error-free operation and afterwards the resource acknowledges with a final commit-done command to the transaction manager.

Appendix C

Heuristic failures

Sometimes issues will occur in 2PC transactions, and usually they occur in the second phase of commit. One or more resources will actually fail to save the data changes to the database leaving it in an inconsistent state. Heuristic failures are the result of network outages, power failures, hardware failures such as disk I/O error, or other extremes that sometimes go wrong in any data center anywhere in the world. The JTA manager will raise an unwelcome `javax.transaction.HeuristicMixedException`. At the worst case scenario, you might even achieve a `HeuristicRolledBackException`. Heuristics are not recovered automatically and sadly they necessitate a replay of a database server's transaction log if and when these vendor features are enabled on production! The following diagram gives an example of the sequence of actions taking place in the transaction activity:

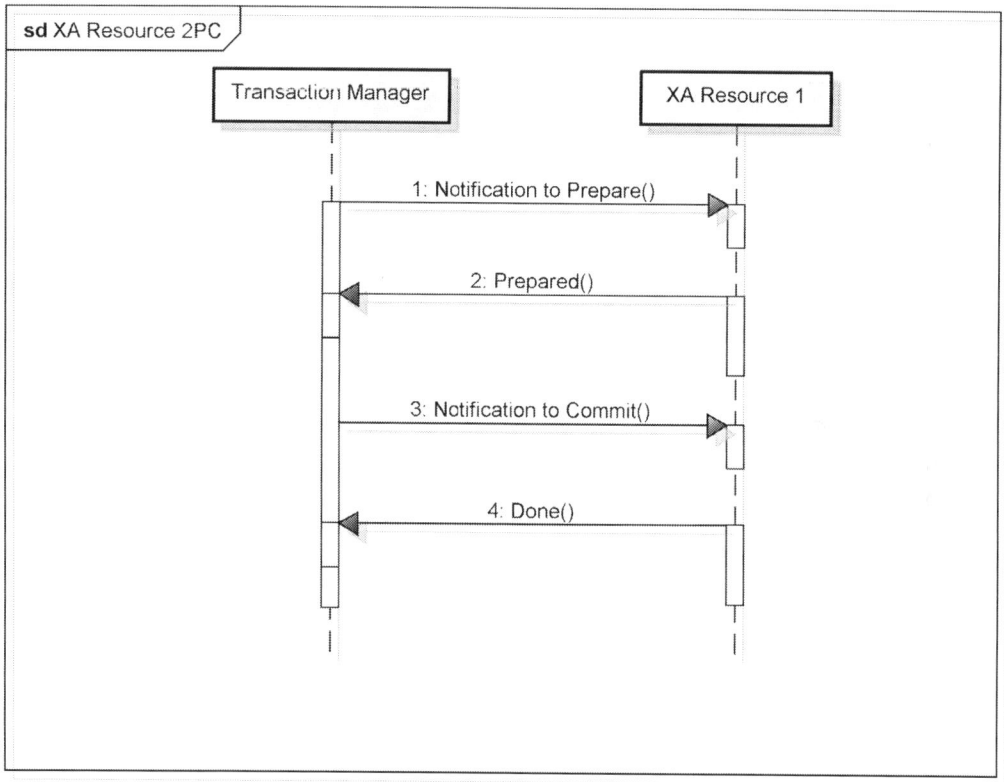

Local transactions

A transaction is deemed **local** when it is working with resources, which are co-located within a running JVM and the application server. A local transaction involves no distributed resources.

A local transaction can be either non-XA or XA transaction on the Java EE 7 platform. A non-XA local transaction takes place with standard JDBC or JPA environment without involvement of a 2PC XA transaction manager. A XA local transaction is one that takes place within the remit of a 2PC XA transaction manager.

Some application servers such as JBoss WildFly are able to optimize a single non-XA local transaction so that they participate in a set of XA resources in a 2PC transaction. The optimization is called last non-XA resource commit.

Distributed transactions

A transaction is deemed distributed when it is executed across different JVMs and operating system process boundaries, and across the network. Because of the JTA specification, the EJB and CDI containers can participate in distributed transaction with other containers and third-party XA resources like database servers. A distributed transaction can span a cluster of application servers running on JVMs that may or may not be on the same machine or co-located across hardware racks in a remote data center.

Transaction services

JTA provides transaction support to EJB and now in Java EE 7 to CDI managed beans annotated with `@Transactional`. The EJB specification provides declarative services to session and singleton beans. In the EJB container, the transactions are either **Container-Managed Transactions (CMT)** or **Bean-Managed Transactions (BMT)**.

Container-Managed Transactions (CMT)

Container-Managed Transactions are normally annotated on EJBs with the declaration `@javax.ejb.TransactionAttribute`. This annotation can be applied to the type or to individual methods. It accepts a `@javax.ejb.TransactionAttributeType` enumeration value.

For CDI managed beans the JTA 1.2 specification provides a brand new annotation `@javax.transactional.Transactional`, to elevate ordinary POJOs into the transactional instances. The annotation accepts a nested enumerated class `@javax.transactional.Transactional.TxType` as a value.

Appendix C

Transaction demarcation in the older J2EE specification was outlined in an XML deployment descriptor (`/META-INF/ejb-jar.xml`) as part of the EJB module. It is still possible to override annotated EJBs with customized transaction service and using XML.

We now outline the CMT services available in Java EE 7 in the following table:

TransactionAttribute or TxType	Description
REQUIRED	The container or interceptor creates a new transaction upon entering the target method, if there is no existing transaction already. Upon completion of the target method, it commits the transaction. This is the default transaction attribute value.
REQUIRES_NEW	The container or interceptor always creates a new transaction before entering the target method. Upon completion it commits the transaction.
MANDATORY	The container or interceptor expects an existing transaction to be already in effect before entering the method. If this is not the case, the EJB container raises an exception `EJBTransactionRequired` or CDI interceptor throws a `TransactionalException` exception with nested `TransactionRequiredException`.
SUPPORTS	The container or interceptor effectively performs no special operations because the target method is invariant to the existence of a current transaction. If a transaction exists, then the target method is invoked in a transactional scope. Otherwise it is invoked without a transaction context. On return from the target method, any preceding transaction context will remain in effect.
NOT_SUPPORTED	The container or interceptor disassociates any transaction context, if it exists, before calling the target method. Upon return from the target method, any proceeding transaction context is re-associated with the thread context, which preserves consistency to those operations.
NEVER	The container or interceptor will only execute the target if there is no associated and existing transaction context. If there is a transaction context, then the EJB container will raise `EJBException` or the CDI interceptor throws a `TransactionalException` with nested `InvalidTransactionException`.

CDI managed beans that take part in CMT rely on the existence of a dedicated interceptor that lies behind the scenes handling the transactional services and communicates with JTA and **Java Transaction Services (JTS)**. This implementation-defined interceptor is provided by Java EE 7 product.

Container-managed `EntityManager` instances must be JTA types so that they can join transactions.

Bean-Managed Transactions (BMT)

Bean-managed transactions are types of transactions where the application EJB or CDI managed bean takes control of transaction management itself. First of all, `UserTransaction` is injected into the bean or it is retrieved by dependency lookup through JNDI.

For EJB that are using legacy J2EE constraint that you are upgrading to Java EE 7, it may help to inject `javax.ejb.EJBContext` as a resource. Working with the BMT is a matter of working with the `UserTransaction` object. Ensure that you demarcate the transaction boundaries accordingly with the `begin()` call. At the end of the transaction, either you call `commit()` for normal termination or call `rollback()` for abnormal circumstances.

Here is a stateless session bean that demonstrates how to apply the transaction services:

```
@Stateless
@TransactionManagement(TransactionManagementType.BEAN)
public class InvoiceServiceBMT {
  @Resource EJBContext context;

  public Invoice saveInvoice( Invoice invoice )
  throws Exception {
     UserTransaction tx = context.getUserTransaction();
    try {
      tx.begin();
      em.persist(invoice);
      tx.commit();
    } catch (Exception e) {
      tx.rollback();
    }
    return invoice;
  }
  /* ... */
}
```

To achieve BMT, we declare the EJB `InvoiceServiceBMT` with the `@TransactionManagement` annotation with the value `BEAN` to override the default value `CONTAINER`. Inside the method, we explicitly create a new transaction context and execute the necessary business logic.

We can also achieve a halfway house solution, where the EJB is still known to the container, but it creates its own transaction context. Here is an alternative implementation:

```
@Stateless
@TransactionAttribute(TransactionAttributeType.SUPPORTS)
public class InvoiceServiceBMTAlt {
  @Resource EJBContext context;

  public Invoice saveInvoice( Invoice invoice )
  throws Exception { /* same impl */ }
  /* ... */
}
```

We set transaction context to `SUPPORTS`, because it is immaterial whether this `InvoiceServiceBMTAlt` has an existing transaction context or not before the `saveInvoice()` target method is called. Inside the method, we create a new transaction context. So effectively this BMT bean is creating its own `REQUIRES_NEW` feature.

The same technique can be achieved with CDI managed beans by injecting the `@UserTransaction` object instance. CDI managed beans, by default, do not take part in EJB transactions, and therefore `@TransactionManagement` does not apply to them.

Bean-managed `EntityManager` instances must be either JTA or non-JTA types. If they are of the latter type then they cannot participate in JTA transactions.

Isolation levels

Isolation levels are an important part of transaction management, because they allows administrators to configure interference between concurrency operations in the enterprise application. Transaction isolation affects the overall consistency. There are different levels of isolation, namely: dirty reads, non-repeatable reads, phantom reads, and serializable. To understand these levels, one needs at least two concurrent transactions: TX1 and TX2.

A dirty read occurs when a transaction TX1 reads uncommitted changes made by another concurrency transaction TX2. The situation is especially unpalatable when TX2 roll backs it transaction, which means that TX1 reads something it shouldn't have.

A non-repeatable read occurs when a transaction TX1 reads shared data, at least twice, in order of sequence for time intervals: t1 and t3. Where t1 happens before t2, which happens before t3. The other concurrent transaction TX2 meanwhile updates shared data at time interval t2 and then commits, thereby invalidating TX1 second read at time interval t3.

A phantom read occurs when a transaction TX1 reads shared data at least twice in order of sequence time intervals t1 and t3 just like an unrepeatable read. Except this time, the number of rows read by TX at t1 is [A1] and at t3 they are [A1, A2]. Meanwhile, the other concurrent transaction TX2 inserts a new row of data [A2] at time interval t2 and commits, which causes the ghostly apparition: a phantom record.

When two transactions like TX1 and TX2 are sequentially processed, one after the other, such that there is no such of interference, their concurrency operations are then serializable.

JDBC provides four transaction isolation levels: Read Uncommited, Read Committed, Repeatable Read, and Serializable. Depending on the level chosen they will eliminate the issues around dirty reads, non-repeatable reads, and phantom reads.

Appendix C

The following diagram describes the various isolation levels:

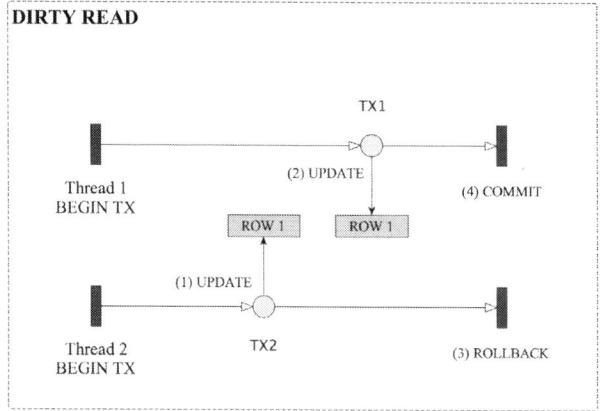

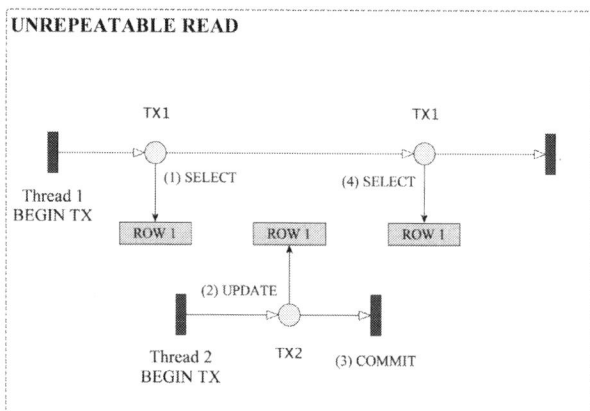

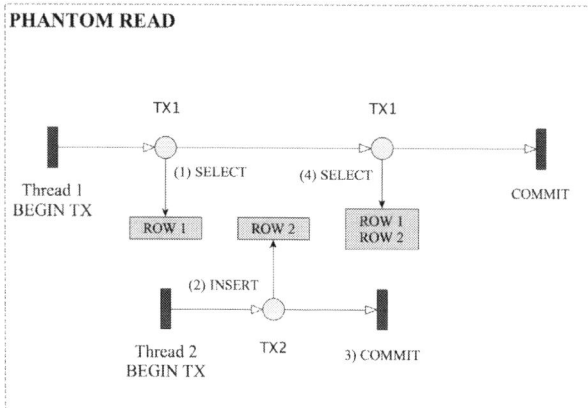

JDBC allows a Java application to query the isolation level of the database through the `java.sql.Connection` and the `getTransactionIsolation()` method. An application can also call `setTransactionIsolation()` to set up a new isolation, say from `TRANSACTION_READ_COMMITTED` to `TRANSACTION_SERIALIZABLE` as long as the database server and the JDBC driver can support it.

For a Java SE application this is acceptable, however, for Java EE application the data sources and entity manager configurations are generally shared across EJB and web modules. Changing the resource dependencies programmatically can lead to trouble for shared applications and modules. Java EE 7 products typically furnish an administration console, which allow a data source's isolation levels to be configured at deployment.

Here is a summary of the isolation levels and their impact on consistency:

Isolation Level	Dirty Reads	Non-Repeatable Reads	Phantom Reads
READ_UNCOMMITED	Can occur	Can occur	Can occur
READ_COMMITED	Prevented	Can occur	Can occur
REPEATABLE_READ	Prevented	Prevented	Can occur
SERIALIZABLE	Prevented	Prevented	Prevented

Generally, for Java EE 7 applications that inject `EntityManagers` and `DataSource` instance, it may be unwise to configure isolation level programmatically.

Nevertheless, there are some techniques to show and here is one that unwraps the JDBC connection behind `EntityManager`:

```
@Stateless
public class ReceiptGenerator {
  @PersistenceContext("mastersAtWorkDB")
  EntityManager em;

  public void generateReceipt() {
    em.flush();
    Connection conx = em.unwrap(Connection.class);
    int savedLevel = conx.getTransactionLevel();
    conx.setTransactionLevel(
      Connection.TRANSACTION_SERIALIZABLE);
    doMoreWork();
    em.flush();
    conx.setTransactionLevel(savedLevel);
    /* ... */
  }
  /* ... */
}
```

The entity manager's unwrap method allows the application to gain access to the vendor provider classes for the JPA implementation. In the example, we only want access to the JDBC connection. Given vendor provider like Hibernate JPA, we could reveal EntityManager and retrieve Hibernate's session object instance using the unwrap facility. There are inherent dangers to changing isolation levels in mid flow with concurrency transaction operations, because we are reliant on the JPA provider's synchronization pending instances to the database at the time of the flush() calls.

In summary, JPA in the form of Java EE 7 does not support custom isolation levels. However, different vendors of JPA providers and Java EE 7 products do provide extensions, which may be configured through an additional XML deployment descriptor and annotations. The buck stops with the underlying database server and isolation levels that they actually do support. For example, if you use Oracle and attempt to configure REPEATABLE_READ, it will downgrade the isolation level to READ_COMMITTED instead (http://docs.oracle.com/cd/B12037_01/server.101/b10743/consist.htm#i5702).

JNDI lookup

Developers can always perform a dependency lookup of the current transaction context. The UserTransaction instance inside a Java EE application is as follows:

```
InitialContext jndiContext = new InitialContext();
UserTransaction tx = jndiContext.lookup(
  "java:comp/UserTransaction")
```

The preceding example of code is found commonly in legacy J2EE applications based on JDK 1.4 and predates Java annotations.

This concludes the section on Java EE 7 transactions.

D
Java EE 7 Assorted Topics

This appendix elucidates briefly the key features of the concurrency utilities and the JSON-P APIs.

Concurrency utilities

JSR 236, the concurrency utilities API, is a new edition to the Java EE 7 platform that provides asynchronous processing to applications using container-managed threads. In Java EE standards prior to 7, it was expressly forbidden or undefined for service endpoints, like servlets or EJBs, to spawn their own threads, because those Java threads were outside the control of the container. Although it was not portable, many applications broke this rule and found ways for the application to manage threads for the lifecycle of its deployment, sometimes using vendor specific APIs.

In Java EE 7, concurrency utilities provide managed versions of the Java SE concurrency facilities. The new concurrency utilities facilities live inside the Java package `javax.enterprise.concurrent`. The following table describes the interfaces:

Interface Name	Description
`ManagedExecutorService`	A container-managed implementation of the Java SE `ExecutorService`. This type of executor asynchronously invokes tasks that are submitted to it by the application.
`ManagedScheduled-ExecutorService`	A container-managed implementation of the Java SE `ScheduledExecutorService`. This type of executor invokes submitted tasks at a set future time and tasks can be invoked periodically.

Interface Name	Description
ContextService	This provider component allows an application to create contextual tasks. A context here means an application context containing concurrent encapsulation of the Java EE environment including transactions.
ManagedThreadFactory	A container-managed implementation of the Java SE ThreadFactory. A thread factory is a facility for Java threads mostly from a pool.

Environment reference

In *Chapter 1, Java EE 7 HTML 5 Productivity*, we briefly showed some code for `ManagedExecutorService`. It was injected into the component with the following code:

```
@Resource(name="concurrent/LongRunningTasksExecutor")
ManagedExecutorService executor;
```

The application server does not automatically provision the `ManagedExecutorService` instances. Unfortunately, they must be configured in an XML deployment descriptor. Here is a `web.xml` file that illustrates the additional configuration:

```xml
<?xml version="1.0" encoding="UTF-8"?>
<web-app ...>
    <display-name>Xen Tracker</display-name>
  <!-- ... -->
    <resource-env-ref>
        <description>
            A Executor for RESTful operations.
        </description>
        <resource-env-ref-name>
            concurrent/LongRunningTasksExecutor
        </resource-env-ref-name>
        <resource-env-ref-type>
            javax.enterprise.concurrent.ManagedExecutorService
        </resource-env-ref-type>
    </resource-env-ref>
</web-app>
```

A similar configuration is required for the other two types: `ManagedThreadFactory` and `ManagerScheduledExectorService`. All Java EE 7 products are required to supply a default `ManagedThreadFactory` under the JNDI lookup name `java:comp/DefaultManagedThreadFactory`. The `resource-env-ref-name` reference specifies the reference name of the environment resource and the `resource-env-ref-type` reference specifies the Java data type of the resource.

Application container context

The application server is responsible for transferring a context, an application container context, to the non-container thread of context. This allows the application thread to interact with the application server in a responsible way. However, the container must manage the application thread from its internal thread pool: it is the most important stipulation. In particular, the application server does the following:

- Saves the existing context of the current application thread
- Identifies the correct application container context
- Applies the identified application container context to the application thread and then allows the task to proceed
- After the task completes it restores the previous context to the thread

The application server will apply an application container context to the following tasks: `java.lang.Runnable` and `java.util.concurrent.Callable`. This procedure is known as applying contextual services to tasks.

The concurrency utilities specification describes optional contextual support for the following classes: `ManagedTaskListener` and `Trigger`.

Contextual tasks

A contextual task is essentially the bundling of a concurrent task (runnable and callable) with the application context container. A task becomes a contextual task whenever it is submitted to a managed execution service or thread factory.

In order to access additional information, a contextual task can optionally implement the Java interface `javax.enterprise.concurrency.ManagedTask`. The task can invoke `getExecutionProperties()`, which returns a map of properties. The execution properties permit the task to set an identity with the property name `IDENTITY_NAME`.

The task can communicate hints back to the container. For example, property `LONGRUNNING_HINT` (or `javax.enterprise.concurrent.LONGRUNNING_HINT` can be set to `true` or `false`, which informs the container that this task is going to be long running or not. The other execution property `TRANSACTION` may be set to `SUSPEND` or `USE_TRANSACTION_OF_EXECUTION_THREAD` in order to communicate a hint about the transaction context in the contextual task.

In 2005 whilst working for an investment banking client in the city of London, I developed an asynchronous task with a proprietary J2EE asynchronous API. It was part of the CommonJ IBM/BEA specification. The project was to read client valuation data from an external system by FTP, parse these valuation files into domain object, and store them inside the bank's client trading portal. Given that we now have Java EE 7 technology, how would I have refactored my 2005 code into modern use?

Here is my initial stab at the code:

```java
public class ClientValuationsProcessTask
implements Callable<ClientValuation>, ManagedTask {
    Map<String,String> properties = new HashMap<>();
    TaskListener listener = new TaskListener();

    public ClientValuationProcessTask(
        String fileId) {
        properties = new HashMap<>();
        properties.put(ManagedTask.IDENTITY_NAME,
            "ClientValuationsProcessTask_"+fileId);
        properties.put(ManagedTask.LONGRUNNING_HINT,"true");
    }

    public ClientValuation call() {
        // Parse the XML file referenced from id
        // Create a value object
        ClientValuation valuation = foo();
        return valuation;
    }

    public Map<String, String> getExecutionProperties() {
        return properties;
    }

    public ManagedTaskListener getManagedTaskListener() {
        return listener;
    }

    class TaskListener implements ManagedTaskListener { ... }
}
```

Because I can work with Java SE 7 now rather than J2EE 1.4, the first refactoring is to use `Callable` to return the domain object, `ClientValuation`. This allows another contextual task to reclaim the domain object in reduce operation (or fold) the results. I could have several `ClientValuationProcessTask` instances all running concurrently in a map operation. Furthermore, I can hint to the application server that, actually, my `ClientValuationProcessTask` is going to take a long time, since this task will parse a XML file and create some value object, by supplying `LONGRUNNING_HINT` key setting the value to `true`.

`ManagedTask` must also implement the `getManagedTaskListener()` call, which can return a `null` or an instance `ManagedTaskListener`. The `ManagedTaskListener` allows the task to listen to life cycle events about the associated contextual task.

Here is the exposition of the `TaskListener` inner class:

```java
class TaskListener implements ManagedTaskListener {
    public void taskSubmitted( Future<?> future,
        ManagedExecutorService executor, Object task) {
        /* ... */ }

    public void taskAborted(Future<?> future,
        ManagedExecutorService executor, Object task,
        Throwable exception) {
        /* ... */ }

    public void taskDone(Future<?> future,
        ManagedExecutorService executor, Object task,
        Throwable exception) {
        /* ... */ }

    public void taskStarting(Future<?> future,
        ManagedExecutorService executor, Object task) {
        /* ... */ }
}
```

The `ManagedTaskListener` provides a way to take some action when the contextual task is aborted. For example, the `ManagedExecutorService` is about to shut down when the `Future` is cancelled from the user side.

`ContextService` is a way for a Java EE application to create contextual tasks without using the standard `ManagedExecutor` facilities. This is an advanced facility for developers and designers who know concurrency programming very well. Teams who provide libraries in enterprise integration and workflow management and open source frameworks should get involved here and take advantage of porting their products over to standard Java EE 7.

Here is some sample code of a singleton EJB that encapsulates `ExecutorService` with `ContextService`:

```
@Singleton
ClientValuationTaskManager {
  @Resource(name="concurrent/ThreadFactory")
  ThreadFactory threadFactory;
  @Resource(name="concurrent/ContextService")
  ContextService contextService;

  ExecutorService executor;

  @PostConstruct
  public void setup() {
    executor =
      Executors.newThreadPool(10, threadFactory);
  }

  public Future submitTask(
    ClientValuationProcessTask callable ) {
    Runnable proxyRunnber =
      contextService.createContextualProxy(
        callable, Callable.class);
    Future future = executor.submit(proxyRunner);
    return future;
  }

  /* ... */
}
```

This completes the short discussion on concurrency utilities.

JSON-P

JSR-353 **JSON Processing (JSON-P)** is the major addition to the Java EE 7 specification, because today's online businesses and institutions rely on this protocol for multiple channel architecture. It has the ability to service many media types such as web, e-mail, voice, data communication, and others, with a single source of business truth: the data service interface. Moreover, these services tend to be RESTful architectural endpoints rather than the Web-Services SOAP variety that drove the industry a decade earlier (circa 2003).

JSON-P is actually made up of two parts: a memory efficient streaming and an object model API.

Streaming

The streaming part of the JSON-P API is very useful for picking out bits and pieces of JSON from a large document without consuming a vast amount of memory. This is quite a boon if your application handles multitude RESTful over HTTP requests and the volume and size is big. The parsing side with streaming, then, is good.

Of course, applications also want to send JSON documents out to the clients and the output world. For those circumstances where the applications are volume broadcasting JSON documents to a swarm of waiting consumers, then a memory efficient way of sending data is also rather useful for server-side endpoints that must handle scale and unpredictability. The following screenshot shows the streaming part of the JSON-P API:

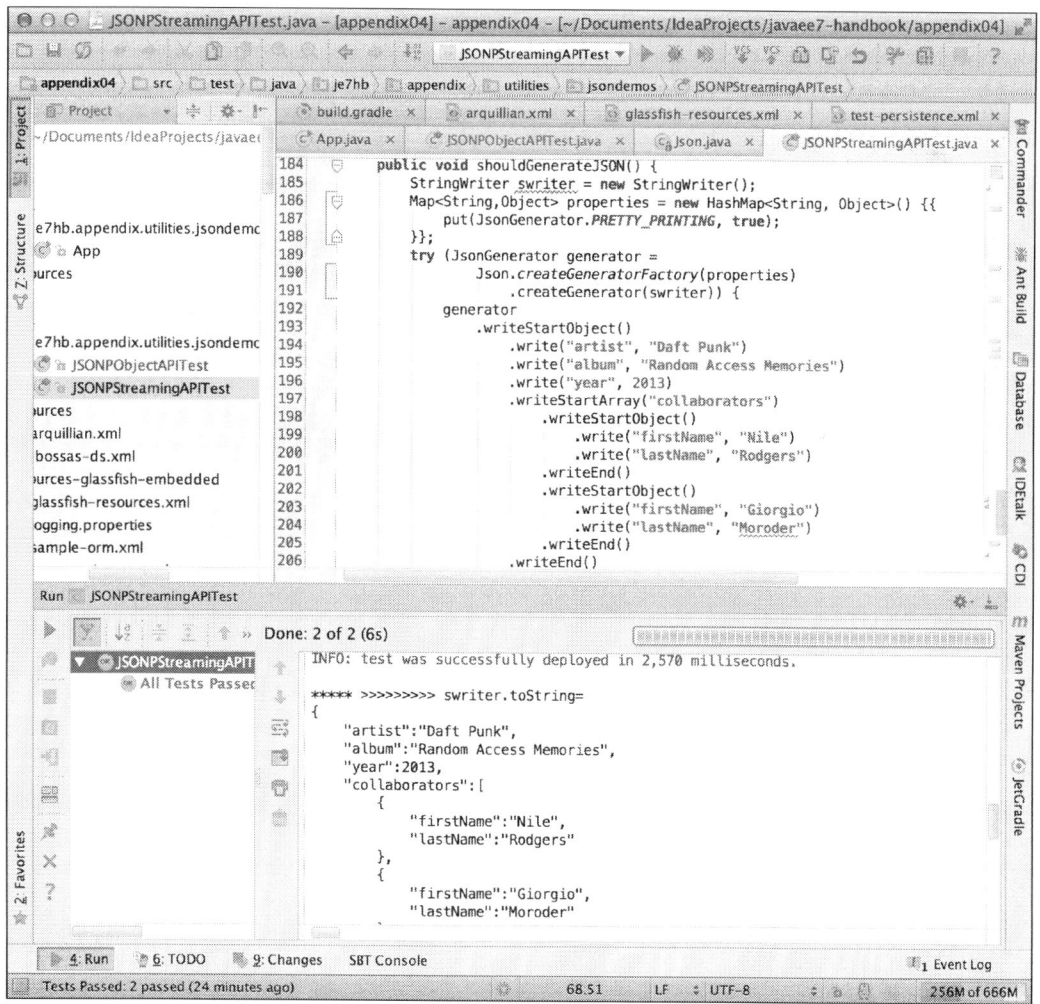

Parsing JSON with Streaming API

Parsing JSON begins with the Java package `javax.json.stream` and the classes `JsonParser` and `JsonParserFactory`. The utility class `javax.json.Json` has a few methods to create a `JsonParser` from a `java.io.InputStream` or `java.io.Reader`. The parser reads JSON as a stream and returns a set of read-only events. This manner is very memory efficient for consuming JSON, because the data structures are only briefly kept during the parsing phrase. The feel of the API is similar to JAXP (Java for XML Processing).

Here is an Arquillian integration test that demonstrates parsing from JSON documented on the Wikipedia on JSON page:

```java
@RunWith(Arquillian.class)
public class JSONPStreamingAPITest {
    @Deployment
    public static JavaArchive createDeployment() { /*...*/ }

    static String TEST_JSON =
        "{\n" +
        "    \"firstName\": \"John\",\n" +
        "    \"lastName\": \"Smith\",\n" +
        "    \"age\": 25,\n" +
        "    \"address\": {\n" +
        "        \"streetAddress\": \"21 2nd Street\",\n" +
        "        \"city\": \"New York\",\n" +
        "        \"state\": \"NY\",\n" +
        "        \"postalCode\": 10021\n" +
        "    }\n" +
        "}"
        ;

    @Test
    public void shouldParseJSONSchema() {
        StringReader sreader = new StringReader(TEST_JSON);
        JsonParser parser = Json.createParser(sreader);
        JsonParser.Event event = parser.next();
        assertEquals(START_OBJECT, event);
        while (parser.hasNext()) {
            event = parser.next();
            if ( event == KEY_NAME) {
                switch (parser.getString()) {
                    case "firstName":
                        parser.next();
                        assertThat( parser.getString(), is("John"));
```

```
              break;
          case "lastName":
            parser.next();
            assertThat( parser.getString(), is("Smith"));
              break;
          case "age":
            parser.next();
            assertThat( parser.getInt(), is(25));
              break;
        }
      }
    }
  }
}
```

In order to determine the location of the parser as it processes each part of the JSON stream, we must inspect JsonParser.Event, which is actually an enumeration. This enum has the following values: START_ARRAY, END_ARRAY, START_OBJECT, END_OBJECT, VALUE_FALSE, VALUE_NULL, VALUE_TRUE, KEY_NAME, VALUE_STRING, and VALUE_NUMBER. Each value represents the parser's marker.

Generating JSON with Streaming API

The JSON-P can also generate JSON in memory efficient fashion. Java interfaces are JsonGenerator and JsonGeneratorFactory, and they are also part of the package javax.json.stream.

Writing JSON output with the Streaming API is much easier than the parsing. Developers should reach for one of the Json.createGenerator() methods that accepts either a java.io.OutputStream or a java.io.Writer.

Here is a unit test method to demonstrate writing JSON using streaming mode:

```
@Test
public void shouldGenerateJSON() {
    StringWriter swriter = new StringWriter();
    try (JsonGenerator generator =
             Json.createGenerator(swriter)) {
        generator
          .writeStartObject()
            .write("artist", "Daft Punk")
            .write("album", "Random Access Memories")
            .write("year", 2013)
            .writeStartArray("collaborators")
              .writeStartObject()
```

```
                    .write("firstName", "Nile")
                    .write("lastName", "Rodgers")
                .writeEnd()
                .writeStartObject()
                    .write("firstName", "Giorgio")
                    .write("lastName", "Moroder")
                .writeEnd()
            .writeEnd()
        .writeEnd();
    }

    String expected = "{\"artist\":\"Daft Punk\"," +
    "\"album\":\"Random Access Memories\",\"year\":2013,\"" +
    "collaborators\":[{\"firstName\":\"Nile\"," +
    "\"lastName\":\"Rodgers\"},{\"firstName\":" +
    "\"Giorgio\",\"lastName\":\"Moroder\"}]}";
    assertThat(swriter.toString().length(), is(not(0)));
    assertThat(swriter.toString(), is(expected));
}
```

The key methods on the `JsonGenerator` are `writeStartObject()`, `writeStartArray()`, and the overloaded variations of `write()`. Each JSON object or array must be terminated with a `writeEnd()` call. Of course the API ensures that the JSON schema is followed exactly.

Object model

The JSON-P has a second form that reads and writes JSON documents wholly in memory. The larger your JSON document, the greater the amount of memory that is consumed.

Parsing JSON with the object model

Parsing JSON from a string representation is relatively straightforward. Your application requires a `javax.json.JsonReader` instance, which can be created from the `Json` static utility class. From there, it is just a case of building a JSON schema as an internal tree data structure.

The object model is very convenient to build structures. It can also be useful to aggregate responses together from separate JSON documents into another larger structure. When Java SE 8 arrives with the Lambdas then we could see certain applications take advantage of parallel JSON document generation with the fork-join model.

Appendix D

This is a unit test that illustrates how to parse JSON with the Object Model:

```java
@RunWith(Arquillian.class)
public class JSONPObjectAPITest {
    @Deployment
    public static JavaArchive createDeployment() { /*...*/ }

    static String TEST_JSON =
        "{\n" +
        "    \"firstName\": \"John\",\n" +
        "    \"lastName\": \"Smith\",\n" +
        "    \"age\": 25,\n" +
        /*... */ + "}"
        ;

    @Test
    public void shouldParseJSONSchema() {
        StringReader sreader = new StringReader(TEST_JSON);
        JsonReader reader = Json.createReader(sreader);
        JsonObject obj = reader.readObject();
        assertThat( obj.getString("firstName"), is("John"));
        assertThat( obj.getString("lastName"), is("Smith"));
        assertThat( obj.getInt("age"), is(25));
        JsonObject address = obj.getJsonObject("address");
        assertNotNull(address);
        assertThat( address.getString("streetAddress"),
                is("21 2nd Street"));
        assertThat( address.getString("city"), is("New York"));
        assertThat( address.getString("state"), is("NY"));
        assertThat( address.getInt("postalCode"), is(10021));
    }

}
```

The `JsonReader` has two principal methods: `readObject()`, which you call when the application expects a JSON object, and the alternative `readArray()`, which handles JSON arrays. Assuming there are no exceptions and the input JSON is expected, then your application reads the attribute key and values. `JsonObject` has several methods such as `getString()`, `getInt()`, and `getBoolean()` and there are default value variants of these methods too. `JsonArray` has more or less the same methods except they take an index argument for convenience.

Incidentally, `JsonObject` is a type of `Map<String,JsonValue>` and that means we can query the existence of JSONP attribute keys. The super class of `JsonObject` and `JsonArray` is the `JsonValue` and their direct ancestor type is a `JsonStructure`.

Generating JSON with the object model

Generating JSON with the object model API is a piece of cake too. It closely resembles the Streaming API in concept. The key types are `javax.json.JsonWriter`, `JsonBuilderFactory,` and `JsonObjectBuilder`.

Here is a final unit test that demonstrates writing JSON with the object model:

```
@Test
public void shouldWriteJSON() {
    JsonBuilderFactory factory = Json.createBuilderFactory(null);
    JsonObjectBuilder builder = factory.createObjectBuilder();
    JsonObject obj =

    builder.add("artist", "Daft Punk")
        .add("album", "Random Access Memories")
        .add("year", 2013)
        .add("collaborators",
            factory.createArrayBuilder()
            .add( factory.createObjectBuilder()
                .add("firstName", "Nile")
                .add("lastName", "Rodgers")
                .build())
            .add( factory.createObjectBuilder()
                .add("firstName", "Giorgio")
                .add("lastName", "Moroder")
                .build())
            .build()
        )
        .build();

    StringWriter swriter = new StringWriter();
    try (JsonWriter writer =
            Json.createWriter(swriter)) {
        writer.writeObject(obj);
    }
    String expected = "{\"artist\":\"Daft Punk\"," +
    "\"album\":\"Random Access Memories\",\"year\":2013,\"" +
    "collaborators\":[{\"firstName\":\"Nile\"," +
    "\"lastName\":\"Rodgers\"},{\"firstName\":" +
    "\"Giorgio\",\"lastName\":\"Moroder\"}]}";
    assertThat(swriter.toString(), is(expected));
}
```

First, we create a `JsonBuilderFactory` from the `Json` static utility class. We can optionally pass in a property map. For example, if we wanted to print the JSON output prettily, we could pass in a map collection to control the configuration like this:

```
JsonBuilderFactory factory = Json.createBuilderFactory(
    new HashMap<String, Object>() {{
        put(JsonGenerator.PRETTY_PRINTING, true);
    }});
```

We create a `JsonObjectBuilder` instance from the factory. The `JsonObjectBuilder` follows the builder pattern style. For each JSON object created as an intermediate instance, it has to be completed with the call to `build()`, which changes the internal mode of instance to be read-only, thereby freezing the state of `JsonValue`. Each attribute is added to the JSON object and arrays are added by creating another JSON instance, either a `JsonArray` or a `JsonObject`, which are created from the factory.

The `javax.json.JsonWriter` is the type responsible for writing the JSON internal instances into either a `java.io.OutputStream` or `java.io.Writer`.

In short, the static utility class `Json` is the main entry point to JSON-P. Beneath the infrastructure lies another type `javax.json.spi.JsonProvider` that controls the implementation loaded at a runtime. At the time of writing, only GlassFish has a JSON-P provider, but because the `JsonProvider` follows the `java.util.ServiceLoader` mechanism, this means that an alternative one can be defined at deployment. If the application supplies a `META-INF/services/javax.json.spi.JsonProvider` file with a single line that states the fully qualified class name of the new provider, then it will be used instead. Bean validation follows the same mechanism.

Recommended reading

So now I assume that you have read this book. I hope you enjoyed it and explored Java EE 7. Where to go next? This is my recommended reading list.

- *Arquillian Testing Guide* by *John D Ament, Packt Publishing*, 2013: This is a nice book that goes far more into the details of the open source tool Arquillian, which I used throughout the development of code and also write about in my book. It covers Arquillian Extensions such as Persistence and Transactions. I recommend *Ament's* book particularly if you want to pursue the topic further.

- *Gradle Effective Implementation Guide* by *Hubert Klein Ikkink, Packt Publishing*: Gradle has made sufficient advances in the Java world and wider community, in particular Google's Android platform is standardizing on this build framework and tool. I recommend *Ikkink's* book for learning Gradle; it was one of the first books that I read that covered areas such as WAR, EAR, and configuration very well.

- *Real World Java EE Patterns - Rethinking Best Practices* by *Adam Bien*, who is a fellow Java Champion, *Adam Bien Press*, 2012: This is a great book for advanced J2EE and intermediate Java EE developers who face the prospect of upgrading legacy systems and want a refresher in the more recent way of developing Java Enterprise applications.

- *Responsive Web Design with HTML 5* and *CSS 3* by *Ben Fria, Packt Publishing*, 2012: I recommend this book for those Java developers who need to brush up on the latest adaptive and response web design, especially for those people who work extensively with content management, creative, and adaptive teams. This book is a companion to the Java development on the server side and is more about the User Interface Engineering.

Index

Symbols

2PC
  about 560
  heuristic failures 561
. AddPackage() 147
@ApplicationPath annotation 353
@ApplicationScoped 271
@AroundInvoke method 83
@AssertFalse constraint 467
@AssertTrue constraint 467
@Basic Annotation 136
@BeforeClass static method 466
@ClientEndpoint 336
@Column annotation 23, 137-140
@ColumnResult 553
@Constraint 473
@ConstructorResult 553
@Convert annotation 552
@CreditCardNumber constraint 469
@DecimalMax constraint 468
@DecimalMin constraint 468
@Digits constraint 468
@EJB annotation 534
@Email constraint 469
@Encrypt annotation 409
@Entity annotation 131, 135, 136
<filter> element 283
<filter-mapping> element 282
@FormParm annotation 364
@Future constraint 468
@GeneratedValue annotation 134, 201
@GeneratedValue Annotation 135
@GET annotation 355
@GroupSequence annotation 481
@Id annotation 23, 25, 135

@Inject annotation 534
@ISOPostalCode 476
@javax.ejb.Asynchronous annotation 123
@javax.ejb.LocalBean 121
@javax.ejb.Stateless annotation 99
@javax.enterprise.inject.Any 49
@javax.enterprise.inject.Default 49
@javax.enterprise.inject.Named 49
@javax.enterprise.inject.New 49
@javax.entity.Basic annotation 136
@javax.entity.Column annotation 138
@javax.persistence.Entity 130
@javax.persistence.GeneratedType, values
  AUTO value 199
  IDENTITY value 199
  SEQUENCE value 199
  TABLE value 199
@javax.persistence.GeneratedValue 199
@javax.persistence.SequenceGenerator 202
@javax.servlet.WebServlet 314
@javax.transactional.Transactional.TxType 562
@javax.validation.GroupSequence annotation 481
@javax.websocket.ClientEndpoint annotation 336
@javax.websocket.OnMessage annotation 316
@javax.websocket.server.ServerEndpoint annotation 315
@JMSContextConnectionFactory annotation 454
@JoinColumn annotation, attributes
  columnDefinition attribute 207
  foreignKey attribute 207
  insertable attribute 207

name attribute 206
nullable attribute 207
referencedColumn-Name attribute 206
table attribute 207
unique attribute 207
updatable attribute 207
@Length constraint 469
<load-on-startup> element 275
@ManyToMany annotation
  mapping with 184, 185
@ManyToMany annotation, attributes
  cascade attribute 221
  fetch attribute 221
  mappedBy attribute 221
  targetEntity attribute 221
@ManyToOne annotation
  mapping with 183, 184
@ManyToOne annotation, attributes
  cascade attribute 218
  fetch attribute 218
  optional attribute 218
  targetEntity attribute 218
<mapping-file> XML element 187
@Max constraint 468
@MessageDriven 445
@Min constraint 468
@NameBinding annotation 411
@NamedStoredProcedureQuery
  attributes 505
@NotBlank constraint 469
@NotEmpty constraint 469
@NotNull annotation 23
@NotNull constraint 467
@Null constraint 467
@OnClose 320
@OnError 320
@OneToMany annotation
  about 24
  mapping with 182, 183
@OneToMany annotation, attributes
  fetch attribute 211
  mappedBy attribute 211
  orphanRemoval attribute 211
  targetEntity attribute 211
@OneToOne annotation
  about 205
  mapping with 180, 181

@OnMessage 316, 320
@OnOpen 320
@Past constraint 468
@PathParam annotation 33, 364
@Pattern constraint 468
@PersistenceContext annotation 186
@PostActivate() method 118
@PostalCodeSensitiveChecker annotation
  483
@PostalCode validation 472
@PostCode constraint 472
@PostConstruct annotation 57, 398
@PreDestroy annotation 57, 116, 398
@PrePassivate method 118
@Produces annotation 355
<properties> element 548
@PUT annotation 364
@Range constraint 469
@SafeHtml constraint 469
@ServerEndpoint annotation 314, 315
<servlet> element 275
<servlet-mapping> element 275
@Size constraint 468
@Table annotation 136, 165
@TableGenerator annotation 201, 202
@Transactional annotation 533
@TransactionManagement annotation 565
@Transient Annotation 135
@URL constraint 469
@UserTransaction object instance 565
@Valid constraint 485
--verbose argument 541
@Version field 557
@WebServlet annotation
  attributes 260

A

AbstractQuery class 514
ACID (Atomicity, Consistency, Isolation,
  and Durability) 159
ACID principles, transactions
  atomicity 559
  consistency 559
  durable 559
  isolation 559

activation configuration properties, MDB
  about 449
  acknowledgeMode 450
  clientId 450
  destinationFactoryLookup 450
  destinationLookup 450
  destinationType 450
  messageSelector 450
  subscriptionDurability 450
  subscriptionName 450
addChatUser() method 331
addMessageHandler(MessageHandler handler) method 321
Address class 482
addUser() method 363
advanced CDI
  alternatives 74-76
  lifecycle component example 72-74
advancedSearch() method 512
AESCipherInterceptor class 407, 409
afterAllTests() method 366
ALL operation 197
annotation, stored procedure query 505-508
API 12
API, Enterprise Full Profile
  EJB 20
  JavaMail 20
  JAX-RS 20
  JAX-WS 20
  JDBC 20
  JMS 20
  JNDI 20
  JPA 20
  JTA 20
  Managed Beans 20
API, Java EE 7 15, 17
API, Web Profile
  Bean Validation 1.1 19
  Context and Dependency Injection 1.1 18
  Enterprise Java Bean Lite 3.2 18
  Java Persistence 2.1 18
  Java Server Faces 2.2 18
  Java Servlet API 3.1 18
  Java Transaction API 1.2 18
  JAX-RS 2.0 19
  JSON-P 1.0 19
  Web Socket 1.0 18

Application Client container 12
application container context 284, 573
appStartUp() method 112
arbitrary objects
  injecting, Producers used 69-71
architectural style, REST
  about 348
  for collections of entities 349
  for single entities 350, 351
architecture, Java EE 7
  application Client container 12
  EJB container 12
  Java Applets container 12
  web container 12
aroundReadFrom() method 407
aroundWriteTo() method 407
Arquillian
  about 76, 356
  disposable methods 79-81
  features 76, 77
  setup 77, 78
Arquillian configuration
  for embedded GlassFish server 150, 151
  integration test, running 152
asJsonObject() method 386
Aspect Oriented Programming (AOP) 407
assertEqualsMap() method 495
assertEquals() method 449
assertTrue() method 449
asText() method 342
AsyncContext class 294
asynchronous context 284
asynchronous invocation 123, 124, 393, 395
Asynchronous JavaScript and XML Request and Response (AJAX) 310
Asynchronous Java Servlets 289
asynchronous JAX-RS server side endpoints 396-398
asynchronous method invocation 98
asynchronous reader
  example 291-294
asynchronous writer 298
AsyncInvoker class 389
async() method 393
AsyncReadListener 295
AsyncResponse object 35
asyncSupport attribute 294

AsyncWriterServlet 300, 304
atomicity 559
AttributeNode interface 516
AUTO value 199

B

Barbara Liskov Substitution Principle 486
base table, hierarchy
  about 231
  benefits 234
  drawback 234
  user story, example 231-234
basic injection
  about 45
  constructor injection 46, 47
  field injection 45
  setter injection 46
Batch Processing API 13
Bean-Managed Transactions. See BMT
Bean scopes, CDI
  Application 55
  Conversation 56
  Dependent 56
  Request 55
  Session 55
beans.xml file 537
Bean type 44
Bean Validation
  about 15, 461, 462
  Bean Validation 1.1 462
  example 463-466
Bean Validation 1.1
  about 19
  features 462
Bean XML configuration
  location 537
beforeAllTests() method 366
begin() call 564
Behavioral-Driven Design pattern 368
binary format 319
binary object (BLOB) mapping 137
bin folder 541
BMP (Bean Managed Persistence) 539
BMT 562-565
boolean execute() method 499
Boolean hasMoreResults() method 499

boundary layer 37
built-in constraints
  @AssertFalse 467
  @AssertTrue 467
  @DecimalMax 468
  @DecimalMin 468
  @Digits 468
  @Future 468
  @Max 468
  @Min 468
  @NotNull 467
  @Null 467
  @Past 468
  @Pattern 468
  @Size 468
built-In qualifiers
  @javax.enterprise.inject.Any 49
  @javax.enterprise.inject.Default 49
  @javax.enterprise.inject.Named 49
  @javax.enterprise.inject.New 49
business interfaces
  local access 120
  no interface, views 121, 122
  remote access 120
  types, summarizing 121
business logic, XenTracker application 25, 27

C

CarProductResource class 373
CarProduct Servlet 270
cascade attribute 205, 218, 221
Cascade.REMOVE operations 198
cascades
  ALL operation 197
  DETACH operation 197
  MERGE operation 197
  onto dependent entities 196
  operations 196, 197
  operations, enumerations 197
  orphans in relationships, removing 197, 198
  PERSIST operation 197
  REFRESH operation 197
  REMOVE operation 197
Cascading Style Sheets. See CSS

CDI
  @PostConstruct annotation 57
  @PreDestroy annotation 57
  about 14, 41, 533
  basic injection 45
  Bean names 53
  beans 42
  beans, attributes 43
  Bean scopes 55
  bean types 42
  bean types, as Java types 43, 44
  built-in contextual container scopes 42
  classpath scanning 49
  container 533
  crosscutting concerns 82
  initializing 56
  new instances, generating 52
  presentation views 53
  qualifiers 47
CDI Beans
  CDI application, configuring 59
  injecting 455
  programmatic lookup 58, 59
CDI classpath scanning 49
CDI container
  and EJB container 124
  Servlets, aligning to 305, 306
ChatCommand 342
ChatCommand.convert() method 343
ChatCommandDecoder 343
ChatCommandEncoder 342
ChatRoom class 331
ChatServerEndpoint class 326
check() method 84, 88, 107
class-level constraint 475, 476
ClientBuilder class 389
Client class 389
ClientEchoEndpoint 335
ClientRequestContext class 390
ClientRequestFilter class 390
ClientResponseContext class 390
ClientResponseFilter class 390
client side filters
  about 401
  ClientRequestFilter 401
  ClientResponseFilter 401
Client Web Socket Endpoint 312

close(CloseReason reason) method 323
close() method 31, 323
CloseReason parameter 337
CMP (Container Managed Persistence) 539
CMT 562
CMT services
  MANDATORY 563
  NEVER 563
  NOT_SUPPORTED 563
  REQUIRED 563
  REQUIRES_NEW 563
  SUPPORTS 563
columnDefinition attribute 207
COMET 289, 311
commit() 564
Common Object Request Broker Architecture. *See* CORBA
completed() method 395
component, XenTrack application
  boundary layer 37
  control layer 37
  entity layer 37
composite primary keys
  @EmbeddableAnnotation, using 171-173
  @EmbeddedId Annotation, using 173-175
  @IdClass annotation 169-171
  about 169
ConcertEvent entity 518-520
ConcertType entity 525
concurrency access locks 557
concurrency utilities
  about 571
  application container context 573
  ContextService interface 572
  contextual tasks 573
  environment reference 572
  ManagedExecutorService interface 571
  ManagedScheduled-ExecutorService interface 571
  ManagedThreadFactory interface 572
Concurrency Utilities 14
ConductorBean 119
Configuration over Configuration 534
configurator attribute 315, 336
connection factory, JMS
  about 425
  default connection factory 426

consistency 559
constraint
  built-In constraints 467, 468
  class-level constraint 475, 477
  definitions, applying 471, 472
  elements 466
  groups 475
  groups, ordering 481-483
  Hibernate validator, built-In constraints 469
  inheritance 480, 481
  inheritance, example 480, 481
  method-level constraints 483-485
  violations 470, 471
constraint, elements
  groups property 467
  message property 466
  payload property 467
ConstraintValidatorFactory 486
ConstraintViolation 470
Construct entity 522
constructor injection 46, 47
container-less Java web application 263-268
Container-Managed Transactions. *See* CMT
ContainerRequestFilter 399
ContainerResponseFilter 399
containers
  alignment to 305
containsKey() method 34
context 39
Context and Dependency Injection. *See* CDI
Context and Dependency Injection 1.1 18
context listener 283
ContextService interface 572, 575
contextual tasks 573-576
control layer 37
converters 551
convert() method 342
convertToDatabaseColumn() method 552
convertToEntityAttribute() method 552
CORBA 96
Coverity Security Library
  URL 463
createConsumer() method 437
createContext() method 432
createProducer() method 433
createProject() method 33

CreditProcessor.check() method 86
Criteria API
  about 508
  benefits 511
  Criteria delete 513, 515
  Criteria queries 508-512
  Criteria update 512, 513
CriteriaBuilder.ge() method 510
Criteria delete 513, 515
Criteria queries 508-512
CriteriaQuery method 512
Criteria update 512, 513
crosscutting concerns, CDI
  interceptors 82, 83, 86
Cross-Site Scripting. *See* XSS
CSS 10
custom JPQL function 526
custom validator
  and null 474
  writing 472-474

D

database sequence types 198
Decoder.BinaryStream 344
decoders attribute 315, 336
Decoder.TextStream 344
decorators 87, 89, 90
DELETE method 255
deleteUser() method 364
delivery modes, JMSContext
  about 431
  AUTO_ACKNOWLEDGE 431
  CLIENT_ACKNOWLEDGE 431
  DUPS_OK_ACKNOWLEDGE 431
  SESSION_TRANSACTED 431
DeltaSpike CDI container tests
  using 64-68
Dependency Injection (DI) 40, 98, 534
deployment, EJB 98
deployWithRename() method 266
description attribute 282
destroy() method 252, 253
DETACH operation 197
Developer productivity theme
  about 13
  specification 13

Developer productivity theme, specification
  Batch Processing API 13
  Concurrency Utilities 14
  JSON-P 14
  WebSocket 14
dispatcherTypes attribute 281
displayName attribute 282
distributed transactions 562
doFilter() method 283
doGet() method 259, 270
doListen() method 315
domain 40
doSend() function 318
down-casting entities 527
dumpCart() method 110
durable 559
durable consumers, JMS messages 441
dynamic binding, JAX-RS
  filters, with interceptors 411
dynamic queries, JPQL 176
dynamic result set
  retrieving 501-503

E

eagerly binding
  and lazily binding, trade-off 193-195
EAGER value 192
EchoWebSocketServer class 314
**eclipselink.create-ddl-jdbc-file-name
    property 149**
**eclipselink.ddl-generation.output-mode
    property 149**
eclipselink.ddl-generation property 149
**eclipselink.drop-ddl-jdbc-file-name
    property 149**
eclipselink.jdbc.driver property 149
eclipselink.jdbc.password property 150
eclipselink.jdbc.url property 149
eclipselink.jdbc.user property 150
eclipselink.logging.level.sql property 149
eclipselink.logging.parameters property 149
EIA 15, 413
EJB
  about 12, 20, 95, 533
  criticism 96
  entity bean type 97

  features 98
  lightweight scope 125, 126
  message bean type 97
  protocols 96
  references 122, 123
  session bean type 97
  simplification 97
  types 97
EJB beans
  injecting 457
EJB container
  about 12, 533
  and CDI container 124
ejbCreate() method 116
EJBs. *See* **EJB**
EL 3.0 462
EL name 44
EmbeddedAsyncReaderRunner class 297
EmbeddedAsyncWriterRunner 304
EmbeddedRunner
  code 264, 266
Employee entity class 509
encapsulation 40
encodeCommonReply() method 329
encodeMessageReply() method 329
Encoder.BinaryStream 344
Encoder.TextStream 344
Endpoint 309
EndpointConfig 343
Enterprise Archive (EAR) file 536
Enterprise Full Profile
  about 19, 20
  API 20
Enterprise Information Architecture. *See*
    EIA
Enterprise Java Bean Lite 3.2 18
Enterprise Java Beans. *See* **EJB**
entities, XenTracker application 22-25
  Project entity 22-25
  Task entity 22-25
entity 130
entity bean
  about 130, 131, 165
  example 131
  finesse, adding 191
entity bean, definition
  @Basic Annotation 136, 137

@Column Annotation 137, 138
@Entity Annotation 136
@Table Annotation 136
about 135
entity bean, example
  Plain Old Java Object 131, 132
  simple entity bean 133, 134
entity bean, lifecycle
  about 153
  entity state, detached 153
  entity state, managed 153
  entity state, new 153
  entity state, removed 154
entity bean, relationships
  @ManyToMany annotation, mapping with 184, 185
  @ManyToOne annotation, mapping with 183
  @OneToMany annotation, mapping with 182, 183
  @OneToOne annotation, mapping with 180, 181
entity beans, annotating
  about 139
  with instance variables 139, 140
  with property accessors 140, 142
entity bean, test
  Arquillian configuration, for embedded GlassFish server 150, 151
  Gradle build file 143, 144
  integration test 146, 147
  persistence context XML configuration 148-150
  running 143
  stateful session bean 144, 145
entity bean type 97
Entity class 390
Entity Control Boundary (ECB) design pattern 36, 37
entity graph
  about 515-517
  example 518-526
EntityGraph interface 516
entity inheritance hierarchy, mapping
  about 225, 226
  base table, hierarchy 231
  single database table, hierarchy 226

  table-per-class, hierarchy 235
entity layer 37
entity listeners 529
EntityManager
  about 154, 554
  cases 555
  methods 556
  persistence context 154
  retrieving, by factory 162, 164
  retrieving, by injection 162
  retrieving, by JNDI lookup 164, 165
  transactional support 160
  UserTransaction association 555
EntityManagerFactory 554
EntityManager.flush() method 556
EntityManager instance 554
EntityManager.lock() method 558
EntityManager methods, persistence context
  about 154, 156
  entity bean instances, detaching 159
  entity bean instances, refreshing 158
  existing instances, persisting 157, 158
  new instances, persisting 156, 157
  pending instances, flushing to database 159
EntityManager.persist() method 156
EntityManager.refresh() method 158
EntityManager.remove() method 157
entity managers 554
entity persistence, troubleshooting
  entity relationship 241, 243
  fetch, performance 241
  lazily binding 241
  object corruption 244
  orphan, removal 243
  queries 243
entity relationships
  about 204
  many-to-many mapping 220
  many-to-one mapping 217-219
  one-to-many mapping 211, 212
  one-to-one Mapping 204, 206
equals() method 327
error-handler pages
  configuring 278
example, JMS 414
example, MDB 444
executeUpdate() method 515

Expression Language (EL) 14, 43
Extended Architecture. *See* XA

F

FacilitatorBean 119
FactoryFinder class 390
factory production 50-52
failed() method 395
fetch attribute 205, 211, 218, 221
fetching 192
FetchType.EAGER 192
FetchType.LAZY 192, 194
field binding
  about 192
  eagerly binding 192
  lazily binding 192
field injection 45
filter() method 401
filterName attribute 281
filters, JAX-RS. *See* JAX-RS filters
findAllProjects() method 27
find() method 558
find() operation 515
findProjectById() method 27
findTaskById() method 27
finesse
  adding, to entity beans 191
fire() method 91
foreignKey attribute 207
form parameters
  extracting 373
from() method 514
full duplex 309
Full Profile. *See* Enterprise Full Profile

G

GeneratedType.IDENTITY enumeration
    203, 204
GeneratedType.SEQUENCE enumeration
    202, 203
GeneratedType.TABLE enumeration
    200, 201
generic entities
    383
getArtistWithEntityGraph() method 522,
    523

getAsyncRemote() method 323
getBasicRemote() method 323
getBoolean() method 34
getClasses() method 353
getConstraintDescriptor() 471
getContainer() method 321
getCountry() method 472
getExecutableParameter() 471
getExecutableReturnValue() 471
getExecutionProperties() 573
getId() method 323
getInvalidValue() method 470
getInvoices() method 195
getLeafBean() method 470
getList() resource method 397
getManagedTaskListener() call 575
getMaxBinaryMessage-BufferSize() method
    323
getMaxIdleTime() method 322
getMaxTextMessage-BufferSize() method
    323
getMessageHandlers() method 322
getMessage() method 470
getMessageTemplate() method 470
get() method 58
GET method 31, 254
getNegotiated-Extensions() method 322
getNegotiated-Subprotocol() method 322
getNextAgentName() method 100
getNumber() method 34
getOpenSessions() method 324
getOrderItems() method 107
getOutputParameterValue() method 504
getParameter() method 268
getPathParameters() method 324
getProduct() method 386
getProducts() method 387
getProjectList() method 34, 35
getProperties() method 353
getPropertyPath() method 470
getProtocolVersion() method 322
getQueryString() method 324
getRequestParameter-Map() method 323
getRequestURI() method 323
getResultList() method 503
getRootBean() method 470
getServletConfig() method 253

getServletInfo() method 253
getSingletons() method 353
getString() method 34
getTransactionIsolation() method 568
getUnavailableSeconds() 254
getUser() method 363
getUserPrincipal() method 324
getUserProperties() method 324
GlassFish
 command line configuration 543, 544
 default resources 545
 installation 541
 MySQL database access, configuring 542, 543
GlassFish 4
 about 540
 reference implementation 540
Gradle
 standalone project, building 63
Gradle build file
 for entity bean test 143, 144
Gradle build project 262, 263
groups annotation parameter 478
groups property 467

H

half-duplex 309
handleTransaction method 83
hashCode() method 327
header fields, JMS message
 JMSCorrelationID 435
 JMSDeliverMode 435
 JMSDestination 435
 JMSExpiration 436
 JMSMessageID 435
 JMSPriority 436
 JMSRedelivered 436
 JMSReplyTo 435
 JMSTimestamp 435
 JMSType 436
headers 269
HEAD method 255
HeuristicRolledBackException 561
hibernate.flushmode 548
hibernate.hbm2ddl.auto 548
Hibernate validator

@CreditCardNumber constraint 469
@Email constraint 469
@Length constraint 469
@NotBlank constraint 469
@NotEmpty constraint 469
@Range constraint 469
@SafeHtml constraint 469
@URL constraint 469
 about 463
 built-In constraints 469
hints attribute 505
HouseholdCredit class 70
HTML 10
HTML5 10, 11, 311
HTML5WebSocket 309
HTTP 310
HttpServlet class
 methods 254
HttpServletRequest instance 268
HttpServletRequest interface 269
HttpServletResponse instance 268, 273
HTTP Servlets
 about 254, 255
 container-less Java web application 263, 266, 267
 deployment model 255-257
 Gradle build project 262, 263
 simple Servlet 258, 259
 URL path mapping 260, 261
HttpSession instance 271
Hypermedia 345
Hypermedia as the Engine of Application State (HATEOS) 385
Hypermedia linking
 performing 385-388
Hyper-Text Markup Language. *See* HTML
Hypertext Transfer Protocol. *See* HTTP

I

IDENTITY value 199
IIOP 96
Implementation 44
initialize() method 106, 474
init() method 251, 266
initParams attribute 281
init(ServletConfig config) method 253

insertable attribute 207
instance variables
  used, for annotating entity beans 139, 140
  versus property accessors 142
Integrated Developer Environment (IDE) 63
interceptors 14, 44, 82, 83
Internet Inter-ORB Protocol. *See* **IIOP**
intexecuteUpdate() method 499
intgetUpdateCount() method 499
InvocationCallback class 390
Invocation class 390
isFinished() method 292
isLoaded() method 523
isolation 559
isolation levels
  about 565-569
  READ_COMMITED 568
  READ_UNCOMMITED 568
  REPEATABLE_READ 568
  SERIALIZABLE 568
isOpen() method 322
ISOPostCodeValidator class 477
isSecure() method 322
isValid() method 474, 485

J

J2EE versions
  Java EE 7, upgrading to 538, 539
JAAS 540
JAF 540
Java API for XML Parsing. *See* **JAXP**
Java Applets container 12
Java Archive (JAR) files 12, 255, 534
Java Authentication and Authorization Service. *See* **JAAS**
JavaBean Activation Framework. *See* **JAF**
Java Community Process
  about 12
  URL 12
Java Community Process (JCP) 18
Java Connector API (JCA) 15
Java Cryptography Extension (JCE) API 409
Java EE
  Full Profile edition, API 15
  integration with 486
  platform 15, 17
  profile 18
Java EE 7
  about 9
  API 12, 15, 17
  architectural interfaces 9
  architecture 12
  Developer productivity theme 13
  persistence unit 547
  refinements 14
  standard platform component 12
  transactions 559
  upgrading to, from J2EE versions 538, 539
  XenTracker application 21
  XML schema documents 549
Java EE 7 Platform Edition 12
Java for RESTful Services (JAX-RS) 15
Java IDL 540
Java interface 40
Java Interface Definition Language. *See* **Java IDL**
java.lang.String 319
JavaMail 20
Java Management Extensions (JMX) 25
Java Message Service. *See* **JMS**
Java Naming and Directory Interface (JNDI)
  naming 534
java.nio.ByteBuffer 319
Java Persistence 17
Java Persistence 2.1 18
Java Persistence API. *See* **JPA**
Java Persistence API (JPA 2.1) 14
Java Persistence Query Language. *See* **JPQL**
JavaScript Schema Object Notation (JSON) 19
Java SE 6
  URL 538
Java SE edition 14
Java Server Faces 2.2 18
Java Servlet API 3.1 18
Java Servlets
  about 248
  destruction 252
  initialization 251
  lifecycle 250
  loading 250
  mapping 274, 275
  request and response 252, 254

Java Servlets 3.1 14
Java Servlet specification
  features 306
  single thread model 308
  URL path mapping, rules for 307
Java Specification Request (JSR) 12
Java Transaction API *See* JTA
Java Transaction API 1.2 18
Java Virtual Machine. *See* JVM
Java Web Socket
  about 341
  invoking 316
Java WebSocket API
  @ClientEndpoint 336
  about 319, 335, 340
Java WebSocket chat server
  about 324
  asynchronous operations 334
  server side 325-331
  web client 331-334
Java Web Sockets
  server-side 314, 315
javax.enterprise.concurrency.ManagedTask 573
javax.io.Serializable marker interface 131
javax.json.JsonReader instance 580
javax.json.JsonWriter 583
javax.json.spi.JsonProvider 583
javax.persistence.CascadeType 196
javax.persistence.jdbc.driver property 189
javax.persistence.jtaDataSource property 189
javax.persistence.nonJtaDataSource property 189
javax.persistence.password property 189
javax.persistence.transactionType property 189
javax.persistence.url property 189
javax.persistence.user property 189
javax.servlet.Filter interface 280
javax.servlet.ServletConfig object 251, 253
javax.transaction.HeuristicMixedException 561
javax.websocket.Endpoint 340
javax.websocket.server.ServerEndpoint annotation 314
javax.websocket.Session interface 321

javax.ws.js.client package
  AsyncInvoker class 389
  Client 389
  ClientBuilder class 389
  Entity class 389
  SyncInvoker class 389
  WebTarget class 389
JAXP 540
JAX-RPC 539
JAX-RS 20
JAX-RS 2.0
  about 19, 31
  features 347
  integration 487
JAX-RS annotations
  @Context 370
  @CookieParam 370
  @DefaultValue 370
  @FormParam 370
  @HeaderParam 370
  @MatrixParam 370
  @PathParam 370
  @QueryParam 370
  default values, using 372
  form parameters, extracting 373, 374
  matrix parameters, extracting 371, 372
  query parameters, extracting 370, 371
JAX-RS client API
  about 389
  asynchronous invocation 393, 395
  synchronous invocation 389, 391, 392
JAX-RS common server annotation
  @Consumes 358
  @DELETE 358
  @GET 358
  @HEAD 358
  @Path 358
  @PathParam 358
  @POST 358
  @Produces 358
  @Provider 358
  @PUT 358
  @QueryParam 358
  @TRACE 358
  about 358
JAX-RS filters
  about 399

binding, with interceptors 409, 411
ClientRequestFilter 399
ClientResponseFilter 399
client side filters 401-405
dynamic binding 411, 412
server side filters 399-401
JAX-RS generic response
 generating 377
 generic entities 383
 Hypermedia linking 385, 386
 Response builder 377-379
 Response status 380, 383
 return types 384
JAX-RS interceptors
 about 405
 ReaderInterceptor 405
 WriterInterceptor 405
JAX-RS providers 399
JAX-RS resources
 defining 359-364
 mapping 354
 testing 365-367
JAX-RS server-side endpoints
 about 357
 field and bean properties 374
 JAX-RS annotations 370
 JAX-RS common server annotation 358
 JAX-RS resources, defining 359-364
 JAX-RS resources, testing 365-368
 Path URI variables 368, 369
JAX-RS subresources
 about 375
 resolution, by subresource location 375, 376
 resolution, by subresource method 376
JAX-WS 20
JDBC 20
JDBC Connection pool 543
jdbc.driver property 550
jdbc.password property 550
jdbc.url property 550
jdbc.user property 550
Jetty Server 17
JMS
 about 20, 413, 414
 example 414-416
 JMS Client 420
 JMS Consumer 420
 JMS Message 420
 JMS Producer 420
 JMS Provider 420
 messaging systems 416
JMS 1.1 API 420
JMS 1.1 code
 upgrading 452
JMS 1.1 connection
 establishing 452-455
JMS 2.0 API 421
JMS 2.0 example 421-424
JMS-CDI integration
 about 455
 CDI beans, injecting 455, 456
 EJB beans, injecting 457
 JMSContext resources, injecting 456
 JMS resources, defining in Java EE 457, 458
JMS Classic API 420
JMS Client 420
JMS connection
 connection factories 425, 426
 default connection factory 426
 establishing 425
 JMSContext 427
 JMSContext, retrieving 432
 JMS provider, connecting to 425
 message destinations 427
JMS Consumer 420
JMSContext
 about 427, 432
 delivery modes 431
 in Java EE server 432
 methods 428
 retrieving 432
 static constants 431
JMSContext resources
 injecting 456
JMSContext.start() method 443
JMSContext.stop() method 443
JMS defined properties
 JMSXAppID 444
 JMSXDeliveryCount 444
 JMSXGroupID 444
 JMSXGroupSeq 444
 JMSXRcvTimestamp 444
 JMSXUserID 444
JMS definitions 420

JMS exception handing
  about 451
  IllegalStateRuntimeException 451
  InvalidClientIDRuntimeException 451
  InvalidSelectorRuntimeException 451
  JMSSecurityRuntimeException 451
  MessageEOFException 451
  MessageFormatRuntimeException 452
  MessageNotWritableRuntime 452
  ResourceAllocationRuntime-Exception 452
  TransactionInProgressRuntime-Exception 452
  TransactionRolledBackRuntime-Exception 452

JMS Message 420

JMS messages, receiving
  connections, starting 443
  connections, stopping 443
  durable consumers 441, 442
  JMS defined properties 444
  messages, receiving asynchronously 439
  messages, receiving synchronously 438, 439
  message, upgrading from JMS 1.1 437, 438
  non-shared subscriptions 440
  redelivery 443
  shared subscriptions 441

JMS messages, sending
  headers 435
  message delivery delay, setting 436
  message producers, upgrading from JMS 1.1 433
  message properties, setting 436
  messages, sending asynchronously 434
  messages, sending synchronously 434

JMS message types
  about 421
  ByteMessage 421
  MapMessage 421
  ObjectMessage 421
  StreamMessage 421
  TextMessage 421

JMS Producer 420

JMS provider
  about 420
  connecting to 425

JMS simplified API 421

JNDI
  about 20
  lookup 569

job scheduling 98

joinTransaction() function 528

JPA
  about 20, 129, 191
  converters 551, 552
  Criteria API 508
  features 551
  map collection 491
  native constructor, results 552, 553

JPA 2.1
  miscellaneous features 526

JPA 2.1 properties
  jdbc.driver 550
  jdbc.password 550
  jdbc.url 550
  jdbc.user 550
  lock.timeout 550
  query.timeout 550
  schema-generation.create-script-source 549
  schema-generation.create-source 549
  schema-generation. database.action 549
  schema-generation.drop-script-source 549
  schema-generation.drop-source 550
  schema-generation. scripts.action 549
  schema-generation.sql-load-script-source 549
  validation.group.pre-persist 550
  validation.group.pre-remove 550
  validation.group.pre-update 550

JPQL
  about 26, 136, 175
  dynamic queries 176
  named queries 177, 178
  positional query arguments 179, 180
  query parameters 178, 179

JSON
  generating, with object model 582, 583
  generating, with streaming API 579, 580
  parsing, with object model 580, 581
  parsing, with streaming API 578, 579

Json.createGenerator() method 579

JsonGenerator 579

JsonGeneratorFactory class 31, 579

JsonObject 581

JsonObjectBuilder instance 583
JSON-P
  about 14, 576
  JSON, generating with object model 582, 583
  JSON, generating with streaming API 579, 580
  JSON, parsing with object model 580, 581
  JSON, parsing with streaming API 578, 579
  object model 580
  streaming 577
JSON-P 1.0 19
JsonParser.Event 579
JSON Processing. *See* JSON-P
JsonReader 581
JsonValue 581
JTA 14, 20, 148, 560
jta-data-source element 548
JVM 95, 248

K

keyStore() method 390

L

largeIcon attribute 282
lazily binding
  about 192, 193
  and eagerly binding, trade-off 193-195
link() method 385
links() method 385
List getResultSet() method 499
list() method 267
listUsers() method 363
LiveEvent entity 519
local access, business interfaces 120
Local invocation 98
local transactions 562
locking
  optimistic locking 557
  pessimistic locking 558
LockModeType enumeration 558
lock.timeout property 550
Long Polling 311
LONGRUNNING_HINT property 574

M

makeGetRequest() method 366
Managed Beans 20
ManagedExecutorService 575
ManagedExecutorService instance 572
ManagedExecutorService interface 571
ManagedScheduled-ExecutorService interface 571
ManagedTaskListener 575
ManagedThreadFactory 573
ManagedThreadFactory interface 572
ManagerScheduledExectorService 573
MANDATORY 563
many-to-many mapping
  about 220
  bidirectional 221-223
  unidirectional 224, 225
many-to-one mapping
  about 217
  bidirectional 220
  with join column 218, 219
map collection
  about 491
  map key join column relationship 495-497
  map key relationship 491-495
map key join column relationship 495-497
map key relationship 491-495
mappedBy attribute 205, 211, 221
mapped superclass 238, 240
matrix parameters
  about 371
  extracting 371
maxMessageSize attribute 316
MDB
  about 444
  activation configuration property 449
  example 445-449
  message selector 450
  messages, processing 444
merge() function 528
MERGE operation 197
message bean type 97
message destinations, JMS 427
Message-Driven Bean. *See* MDB
Message Driven Beans. *See* MDB
MessageHandler 341

MessageInterpolator 486
Message Oriented Middleware 413
message property 466
messageReceived() method 335
message selector, MDB 450
messaging systems
  about 416
  point-to-point messaging 416
  publish-subscribe messaging 418
method-level constraints 483, 485
method overloading 40
methods, JMSContext
  acknowledge() 431
  close() 429
  commit() 429
  createBrowser(): QueueBrowser 430
  createBytesMessage(): BytesMessage 429
  createConsumer(): JMSConsumer 430
  createContext() 428
  createDurableConsumer(): JMSConsumer 430
  createMapMessage(): MapMessage 429
  createMessage(): Message 429
  createObjectMessage(): ObjectMessage 429
  createProducer(): JMSProducer 428
  createSharedDurableConsumer(): JMSConsumer 430
  createStreamMessage(): StreamMessage 429
  createTemporaryQueue(): QueueBrowser 430
  createTemporaryTopic(): TemporaryTopic 430
  createTextMessage(): TextMessage 429
  getClientID() 428
  getSessionMode(): int 429
  getTransacted(): boolean 429
  recover() 430
  rollback() 430
  setClientID() 428
  start() 428
  stop() 428
  unsubscribe(String topicName) 431
method validation 462
method validation rules 486
MIME types
  configuring 277

miscellaneous features
  about 526
  custom JPQL function 526
  down-casting entities 527
  entity listeners 528, 529
  native query constructor, mapping 530, 531
  persistence context, synchronizing 528
Multipurpose Internet Mail Extensions. *See* MIME types
MySQL database access
  configuring 542, 543
MySQL remote server 500

N

name attribute 206, 505
named queries, JPQL 177, 178
naming directory 98
native format 319
native query constructor
  mapping 530, 531
NEVER 563
newBuilder() method 390
New Input Output (NIO) 14, 289
newInstance() method 116
non-XA local transaction 562
NOT_SUPPORTED 563
nullable attribute 207

O

Object getSingleResult() method 499
Object Management Group. *See* OMG
object model
  JSON, creating with 582, 583
  JSON, parsing with 580, 581
object-relational mapping files 187, 188
Object/Relational Mapping (ORM) 129
Observer Design Pattern (ODP) 90
ODP 90
OMG 96
onAllDataRead method 292
onAllDataRead() method 295, 298
onDataAvailable method 292
onError method 292, 299
onError() method 302
one-to-many mapping
  about 211

bidirectional 214, 215
  using, as explicit join table 216, 217
  with join column 213, 214
one-to-one mapping
  about 204
  cascade attribute 205
  fetch attribute 205
  foreign keys, composite 209, 210
  mappedBy attribute 205
  optional attribute 205
  orphanRemoval attribute 205
  one-to-one bidirectional entities, persisting to 209
  one-to-one-entities, bidirectional 208, 209
  one-to-one unidirectional entities, persisting to 208
onException() method 434
onMessage() function 334
onMessage() method 446
onOpen() function 318
onOpen() method 341
onWritePossible method 299
onWritePossible() method 302
OpenJPA 130
openWebSocket() function 333, 334
OptimisticLockException 557
optimistic locking 557
optional attribute 205, 218
OPTIONS method 255
orm.xml file 550
orphanRemoval attribute 198, 205, 211
orphans
  in relationships, removing 197, 198
outbound parameter values
  retrieving 503, 504

P

P2P model
  about 417
  e-Commerce typical application 417
PaaS (Platform as a Service) 17
Path URI variables 368, 369
payEntity() method 485
PayloadCheckMDB 448
Payload instance 467
payload property 467

Persistence Capable Objects (PCO) 129
persistence context
  about 186
  synchronizing 528
PersistenceContext 145
PersistenceContextType.EXTENDED 556
persistence context XML configuration
  for entity bean test 148-150
persistence unit
  about 547
  example 548
  object-relational mapping, XML representation 550
  standard property configuration 189
  XML schema documents, for Java EE 7 549
persistence unit configuration
  structure 186, 187
Persistence XML configuration
  location 537
persistent.xml file 537
persist() function 528
PERSIST operation 197
pessimistic locking 558
Ping and Pong format 320
Plain Old Java Object. *See* POJO
Plain-Old-Java-Objects. *See* POJOs
PlanningResource class
  about 383
  getPlanList() method 383
platform, Java EE 15, 17
point-to-point messaging 416
POJO 14, 99
POJOs 131, 132, 191, 461
polymorphism 40
pong format 320
POST method 31, 254
PostTradeProcessor class 122
procedureName attribute 505
procedures attribute 505
processRequest() method 294, 300
Producers
  used, for arbitrary objects injecting 69
ProductListing Servlet 276
profile, Java EE
  Enterprise Full Profile 18-20
  Web Profile 18, 19
Project entity 22-25

ProjectRESTServerEndpoint 32
properties object 112
property accessors
  used, for annotating entity beans 140, 141
  versus instance variables 142
publish-subscribe messaging 418
Pub-Sub model
  about 418
  investment bank example 418, 419
PUT method 254

Q

qualifiers
  about 44, 47, 48
  built-in qualifiers 49
query parameters
  extracting 370
query parameters, JPQL
  about 178, 179
  positional query arguments 179, 180
query.timeout property 550

R

READ_COMMITED 568
readEntity() method 392
ReadListener 291
readObject() method 581
READ_UNCOMMITED 568
receiveBody() method 438
receiveMessage() method 327
referencedColumn-Name attribute 206
refresh() call 558
refresh() function 528
refresh() method 558
REFRESH operation 197
release() method 110
rel() method 388
remote access, business interfaces 120
RemoteEndpoint.Async 339
RemoteEndpoint.Basic 339
Remote invocation 98
Remote Method Invocation. *See* RMI
Remote Method Invocation over Internet
    Inter-ORB protocol. *See* RMI-IIOP
removeChatUser() method 331
remove() function 528

removeMessageHandler(MessageHandler
    handler) method 322
REMOVE operation 197
removeOrderItem() method 107
removeProject() method 27
REPEATABLE_READ 568, 569
ReportHeader servlet 269
Representational State Transfer. *See* REST
request attributes 269, 270
request context 284
Request For Comments (RFC) 248
request() method 393
request parameters 268
request-response 248
REQUIRED 563
REQUIRES_NEW 563
resetValues() method 57
Resource Adapter Archive (RAR) file 535
Resource Injection (RI) 534
RESOURCE_LOCAL 149, 548
response
  redirecting 272
Response class
  build() method 378
  entity() method 378
  ok() method 378
  type() method 379
ResponseProcessingException class 390
REST
  about 96, 345
  architectural style 348
REST constraints
  cache 346
  client/server 346
  code-on-demand 347
  layered style 347
  stateless 346
  uniform interface 346
RESTful endpoint 31-36
resultClasses attribute 505
resultSetMappings attribute 505
retrieve() method 410
retrieveProjectAndTasks() method 30, 31
return types 384
RMI 96
RMI-IIOP 96, 540
rollback() function 528, 564

S

saveInvoice() target method 565
saveProject() method 27
schema-generation.create-script-source property 549
schema-generation.create-source property 549
schema-generation. database.action property 549
schema-generation.drop-script-source property 549
schema-generation.drop-source property 550
schema-generation. scripts.action property 549
schema-generation.sql-load-script-source property 549
Scope 44
SecureReceipt annotation
  code snippet 485
SecureReceiptValidator object 485
security 98
sendPayloadMessage() method 447
sendXML() method 456
SensitiveResource class 410
SEQUENCE value 199
SEQ_VALUE 202
SERIALIZABLE 568
server side filters
  about 399
  ContainerRequestFilter 399
  ContainerResponseFilter 399
Server Web Socket Endpoint 312
service endpoint, XenTrack application
  about 27
  RESTful endpoint 31-36
  WebSocket endpoint 28-31
service() method 252
Service Oriented Architecture. *See* SOA
Service Provider Interface (SPI) 486
service(ServletRequest request, ServletResponse response) method 253
Servlet
  aligning, to CDI container 305, 306
  context attributes 271, 272
servlet container 533

ServletContext 271
ServletContextDemo 272
ServletException exception 253, 254
Servlet filters
  about 280, 281
  annotation attributes 281
  XML configuration 282, 283
ServletInputStream.isReady() method 292
ServletInputStream method 292
servlet mapping
  JAX-RS resources, mapping 354
  performing 351, 352, 353
  Test-Driven Development, with JAX-RS 354, 355, 357
servletNames attribute 281
ServletRequest 252
session attributes 271
session beans
  about 99
  lifecycle 115
  singleton session beans 111-114
  stateful session beans 103-110
  stateless session beans 99-102
session bean type 97
session context 284
session timeout
  configuring 276, 277
setAsync() method 434
setMaxBinaryMessage-BufferSize(int length) method 323
setMaxIdleTime(long millisecond) method 322
setMaxTextMessage-BufferSize(int length) method 323
set() method 512
setStringProperty() method 434
setter injection 46
setTransactionIsolation() method 568
ShoppingCartBean bean 106
shouldAddOneUser() method 366
shouldAddTwoUsers() method 368
shouldAmendOneUser() method 367
shouldAssembleAndRetrieveBookList() method 357
shouldBasicValidateCar() method 480
shouldCompletelyValidateCar() method 480

shouldExecuteCriteriaUpdate() method 513
shouldFireMessageAtMDB() method 449
shouldInvokeStoredProcedure() method 502
shouldLoadArtistWithoutConcerts() method 523
shouldRetrieveDifferentAgents() method 102
shouldRetrieveHyperbooks() method 389
shouldSaveArtistWithAlbum() method 522
ShrinkWrap 356
ShrinkWrap archives 76
SimpleLoggingFilter 281
SimpleServlet subclasses 259
single database table, hierarchy
  single table strategy, benefits 230
  single table strategy, drawbacks 231
  user story, example 227-230
SingleThreadModel 308
singleton session beans
  about 111-114
  lifecycle 118, 119
smallIcon attribute 282
SOA 96
software engineering
  context 39
  dependency 40
  dependency injection 40
  domain 40
  encapsulation 40
  Java interface 40
  method overloading 40
  polymorphism 40
SpyThriller bean 132
SpyThriller class 131
SSLContext() method 390
Standalone CDI application 60-62
standalone project
  building, Gradle used 63
standard platform component 12
Stateful EJBs 533
stateful session beans
  about 103-110, 556
  lifecycle 116-118
Stateless EJBs 533
stateless session beans
  about 99-102

concurrency and stateless session EJB 102, 103
  lifecycle 115
STAX 540
stereotypes 93
stored procedure query
  about 499, 500
  annotation 505-508
  methods 499
stored procedures
  about 498
  calling 498
  dynamic result set, retrieving 501-503
  MySQL remote server 500
  outbound parameter values, retrieving 503, 504
  stored procedure query 499, 500
  stored procedure query, annotation 505-508
StoreProcedureQueryregisterStoreProcedureParameter() method 499
StoreProcedureQuerysetParameter() method 499
streaming API
  JSON-P 577
  JSON, generating with 579, 580
  JSON, parsing with 578, 579
Streaming API for XML. See STAX
StreamingPriceWebSocketServer 338
String.split() function 334
sub graph 515
Subgraph interface 516
subProtocols attribute 315, 336
SUPPORTS 563
synchronous invocation 389
synchronous reader
  example 290, 291
SyncInvoker class 390
System.exit 297

T

table attribute 207
table-per-class, hierarchy
  about 235
  benefits 237
  drawbacks 238
  user story, example 235-237

TABLE value 199
targetEntity attribute 205, 211, 218, 221
Task entity 24, 25
tearDown() method 68
testWebSocket() function 318
TRACE method 255
TradeDirectionConverter class 552
Train entity class 140
TranactionAttribute.MANDATORY 554
TransactionalCreditProcessor class 84
transactional support
  about 160
  application managed transactions 160, 161
TransactionAttribute.REQUIRED 554
transactions
  about 98, 554, 559
  distributed transactions 562
  local transactions 562
  non-XA local transaction 562
transaction, services 562
transaction-type XML element 548
TraversableResolver 486
Two-Phase Commit Transaction Manager.
    See 2PC
Tyrus 319

U

UnavailableException class 254
UnavailableException exception 253
Uniform Resource Identifiers (URI) 345
Uniform Resource Locator (URL) 349
Uniform Resource Name (URN) 349
unique attribute 207
unsubscribe() method 442
unsynchronized persistence context
  limitations 528
unwrap() method 471
updatable attribute 207
updateProject() method 27
URL path mapping
  about 260, 261
  rules for 307
URL patterns
  mapping 307
urlPatterns attribute 281
user-defined function 498

User Experience (UX) 310
UserTransaction instance 569

V

validate() method 480
validation.group.pre-persist property 550
validation.group.pre-remove property 550
validation.group.pre-update property 550
validator
  default access 487
validator factory
  default access 487
value attribute 281, 315
ViewDealer Servlet 270

W

W3C
  about 10
  URL 10
Web Archive (WAR) 255
Web Archive (WAR) file 535
web client 331, 334
web container 12, 248
web deployment descriptor
  about 273
  and annotations 279
  error-handler pages, configuring 278
  Java Servlets, mapping 274-276
  MIME types, configuring 277
  session timeout, configuring 276
  welcome page, configuring 278
WebFilter attributes 281
web fragments
  about 286
  multiple web fragments 287-289
WebGL 11
Web Hypertext Application Technology
    Working Group. *See* WHATWG
WebMethodUtils utility class 366
Web Profile
  about 17-19
  API 18
Web service invocation 98
WebSocket
  about 14, 311
  examples 319

on server side 320
Web Socket 1.0 18
WebSocket API. *See* **Java WebSocket API**
Web Socket Connection 312
WebSocket endpoint
 about 28-31, 312
 URL 29
WebSocket Endpoint annotations
 lifecycle 320
Web Socket Peer 312
Web Socket protocol 313
Web Socket Sessions 312, 321, 324
WebTarget class 390
Weld 60
WHATWG
 about 10
 URL 10, 310
WHERE clause 176
where() method 512, 513, 515
Whole interface 341
World-Wide Web Consortium. *See* **W3C**
World Wide Web (WWW) 10
writeEnd() method 31
writeStartArray() method 31, 580
writeStartObject() method 31, 580

X

XA 560
XenTrack application
 component 36
 Entity Control Boundary (ECB) design
  pattern 36, 37
 service endpoint 27
XenTracker application
 about 21
 business logic 25, 27
 entities 22-25
XSD locations
 URL 549
XSS 463
XSS Prevent Cheat Sheet
 URL 463

Thank you for buying
Java EE 7 Developer Handbook

About Packt Publishing

Packt, pronounced 'packed', published its first book "Mastering phpMyAdmin for Effective MySQL Management" in April 2004 and subsequently continued to specialize in publishing highly focused books on specific technologies and solutions.

Our books and publications share the experiences of your fellow IT professionals in adapting and customizing today's systems, applications, and frameworks. Our solution based books give you the knowledge and power to customize the software and technologies you're using to get the job done. Packt books are more specific and less general than the IT books you have seen in the past. Our unique business model allows us to bring you more focused information, giving you more of what you need to know, and less of what you don't.

Packt is a modern, yet unique publishing company, which focuses on producing quality, cutting-edge books for communities of developers, administrators, and newbies alike. For more information, please visit our website: www.packtpub.com.

About Packt Enterprise

In 2010, Packt launched two new brands, Packt Enterprise and Packt Open Source, in order to continue its focus on specialization. This book is part of the Packt Enterprise brand, home to books published on enterprise software – software created by major vendors, including (but not limited to) IBM, Microsoft and Oracle, often for use in other corporations. Its titles will offer information relevant to a range of users of this software, including administrators, developers, architects, and end users.

Writing for Packt

We welcome all inquiries from people who are interested in authoring. Book proposals should be sent to author@packtpub.com. If your book idea is still at an early stage and you would like to discuss it first before writing a formal book proposal, contact us; one of our commissioning editors will get in touch with you.

We're not just looking for published authors; if you have strong technical skills but no writing experience, our experienced editors can help you develop a writing career, or simply get some additional reward for your expertise.

Java EE 6 with GlassFish 3 Application Server

ISBN: 978-1-84951-036-3   Paperback: 488 pages

A practical guide to install and configure the GlassFish 3 Application Server and develop Java 6 applications to be deployed to this server

1. Install and configure the GlassFish 3 Application Server and develop Java EE 6 applications to be deployed to this server

2. Specialize in all major Java EE 6 APIs, including new additions to the specification such as CDI and JAX-RS

3. Use GlassFish v3 application server and gain enterprise reliability and performance with less complexity

Java EE 6 Cookbook for Securing, Tuning, and Extending Enterprise Applications

ISBN: 978-1-84968-316-6   Paperback: 356 pages

Packed with comprehensive recipes to secure, tune, and extend your Java EE applications

1. Secure your Java applications using Java EE built-in features as well as the well-known Spring Security framework

2. Utilize related recipes for testing various Java EE technologies including JPA, EJB, JSF, and Web services

3. Explore various ways to extend a Java EE environment with the use of additional dynamic languages as well as frameworks

Please check www.PacktPub.com for information on our titles

Java EE 6 Development with NetBeans 7

ISBN: 978-1-84951-270-1   Paperback: 392 pages

Develop professional enterprise Java EE applications quickly and easily with this popular IDE

1. Use features of the popular NetBeans IDE to accelerate development of Java EE applications

2. Develop JavaServer Pages (JSPs) to display both static and dynamic content in a web browser

3. Covers the latest versions of major Java EE APIs such as JSF 2.0, EJB 3.1, and JPA 2.0, and new additions to Java EE such as CDI and JAX-RS

Java EE Development with Eclipse

ISBN: 978-1-78216-096-0   Paperback: 426 pages

Develop Java EE applications with Eclipse and commonly used technologies and frameworks

1. Each chapter includes an end-to-end sample application

2. Develop applications with some of the commonly used technologies using the project facets in Eclipse 3.7.

3. Clear explanations enriched with the necessary screenshots

Please check **www.PacktPub.com** for information on our titles

Made in the USA
Lexington, KY
12 April 2014